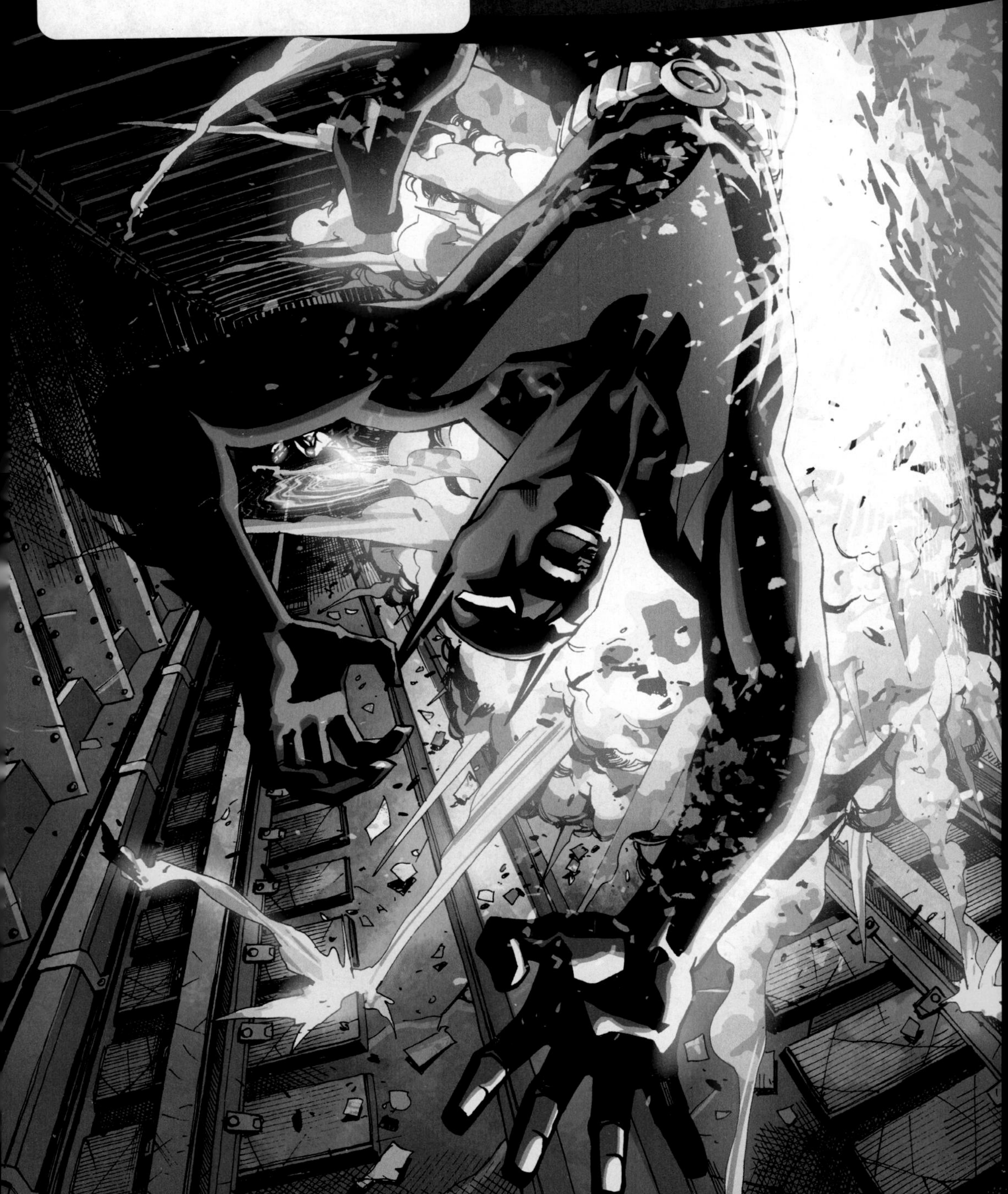

BATMAN BEYOND

VOL.3 THE LONG PAYBACK

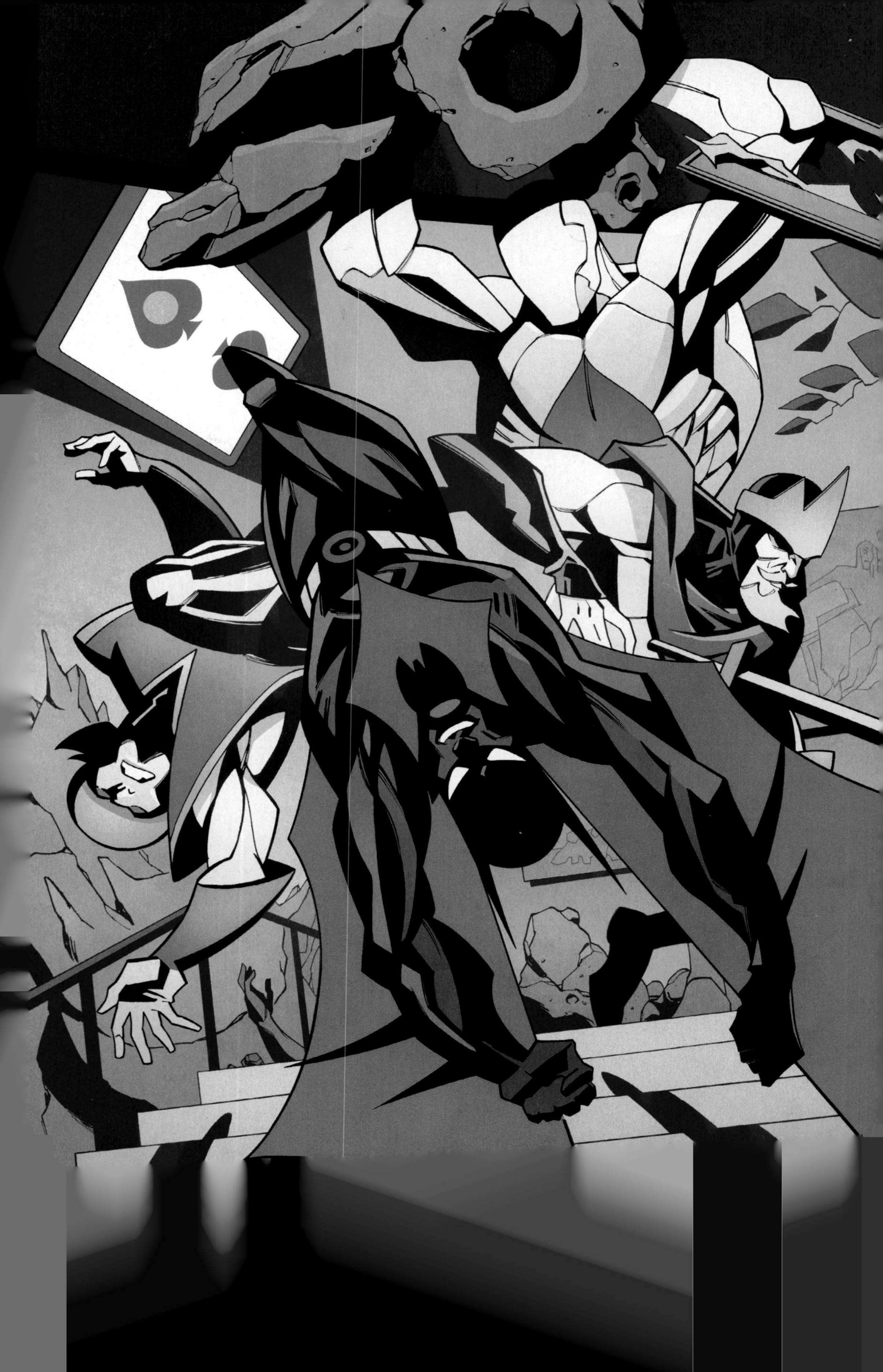

BATMAN BEYOND

VOL.3 THE LONG PAYBACK

DAN JURGENS * **BERNARD CHANG**
writers

PHIL HESTER * **BERNARD CHANG**
pencils

ANDE PARKS * **BERNARD CHANG**
inks

MICHAEL SPICER * **MARCELO MAIOLO**
colorists

TRAVIS LANHAM
letterer

BERNARD CHANG & MARCELO MAIOLO
collection cover artists

BATMAN created by **BOB KANE** with **BILL FINGER**

ROB LEVIN JIM CHADWICK Editors - Original Series
JEB WOODARD Group Editor - Collected Editions * **ALEX GALER** Editor - Collected Edition
STEVE COOK Design Director - Books * **SHANNON STEWART** Publication Design

BOB HARRAS Senior VP - Editor-in-Chief, DC Comics * **PAT McCALLUM** Executive Editor, DC Comics

DIANE NELSON President * **DAN DiDIO** Publisher * **JIM LEE** Publisher * **GEOFF JOHNS** President & Chief Creative Officer
AMIT DESAI Executive VP - Business & Marketing Strategy, Direct to Consumer & Global Franchise Management
SAM ADES Senior VP & General Manager, Digital Services * **BOBBIE CHASE** VP & Executive Editor, Young Reader & Talent Development
MARK CHIARELLO Senior VP - Art, Design & Collected Editions * **JOHN CUNNINGHAM** Senior VP - Sales & Trade Marketing
ANNE DePIES Senior VP - Business Strategy, Finance & Administration * **DON FALLETTI** VP - Manufacturing Operations
LAWRENCE GANEM VP - Editorial Administration & Talent Relations * **ALISON GILL** Senior VP - Manufacturing & Operations
HANK KANALZ Senior VP - Editorial Strategy & Administration * **JAY KOGAN** VP - Legal Affairs * **JACK MAHAN** VP - Business Affairs
NICK J. NAPOLITANO VP - Manufacturing Administration * **EDDIE SCANNELL** VP - Consumer Marketing
COURTNEY SIMMONS Senior VP - Publicity & Communications * **JIM (SKI) SOKOLOWSKI** VP - Comic Book Specialty Sales & Trade Marketing
NANCY SPEARS VP - Mass, Book, Digital Sales & Trade Marketing * **MICHELE R. WELLS** VP - Content Strategy

BATMAN BEYOND VOLUME 3: THE LONG PAYBACK

Published by DC Comics. Compilation and all new material Copyright © 2018 DC Comics. All Rights Reserved.
Originally published in single magazine form in BATMAN BEYOND 13-19. Copyright © 2017, 2018 DC Comics. All Rights Reserved.
All characters, their distinctive likenesses and related elements featured in this publication are trademarks of DC Comics.
The stories, characters and incidents featured in this publication are entirely fictional.
DC Comics does not read or accept unsolicited submissions of ideas, stories or artwork.

DC Comics, 2900 West Alameda Ave., Burbank, CA 91505
Printed by LSC Communications, Kendallville, IN, USA. 7/6/18. First Printing.
ISBN: 978-1-4012-8036-9

Library of Congress Cataloging-in-Publication Data is available.

PEFC Certified

Printed on paper from
sustainably managed
forests, controlled
sources

PEFC/29-31-337   www.pefc.org

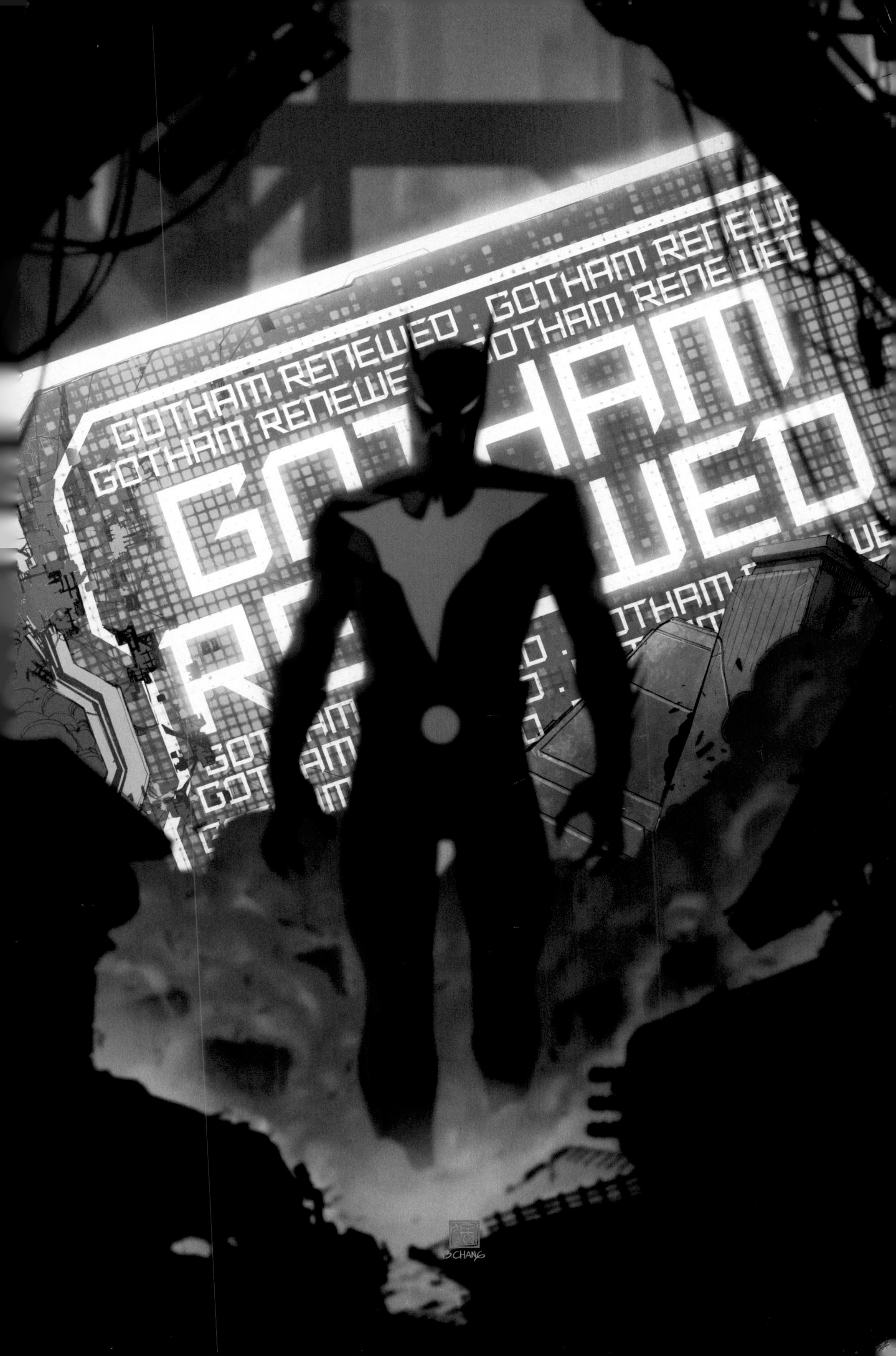
GOTHAM RENEWED : GOTHAM RENEWED
GOTHAM RENEWED : GOTHAM RENEWED
B CHANG

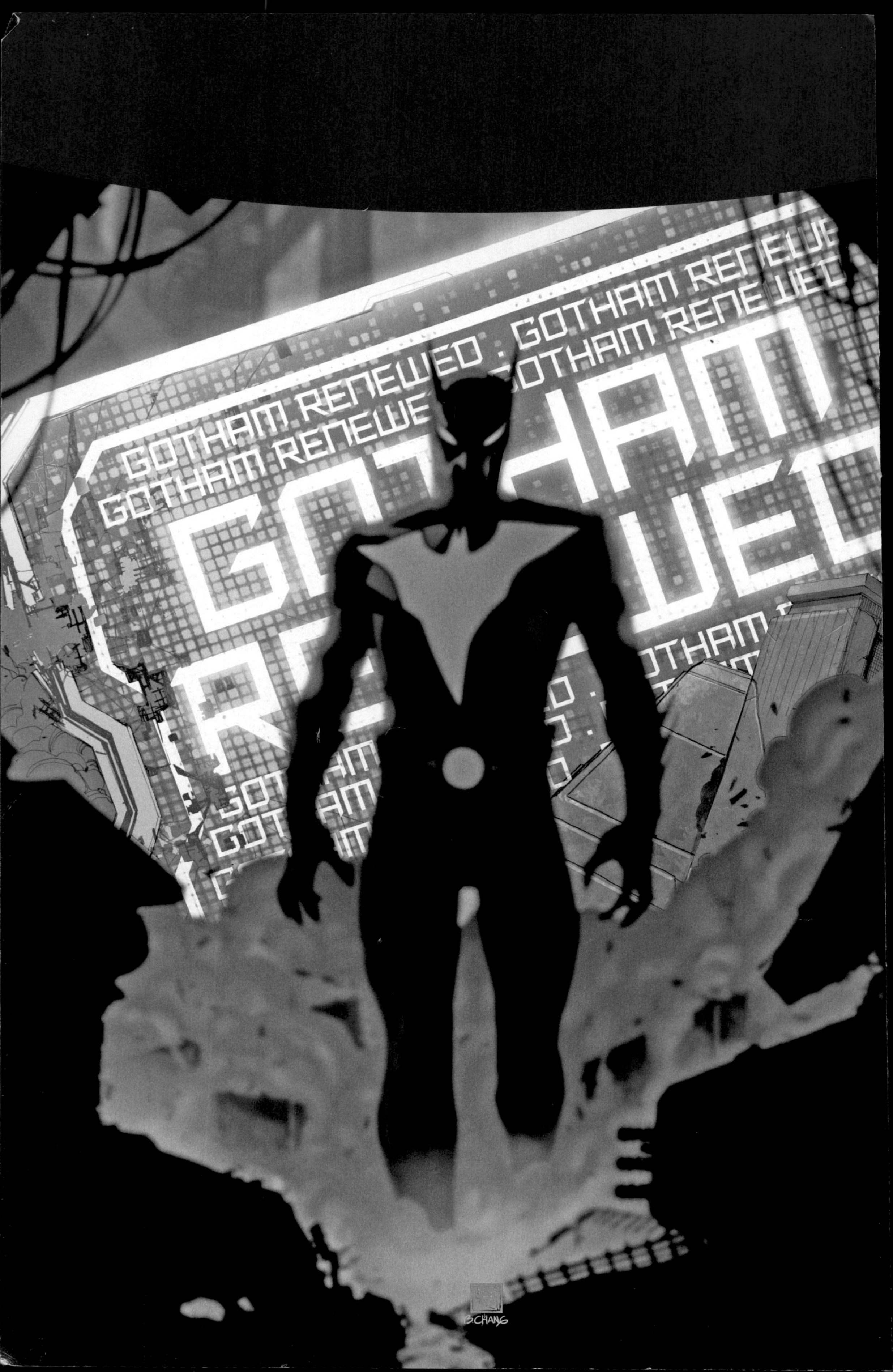
GOTHAM RENEWED : GOTHAM
GOTHAM
B CHANG

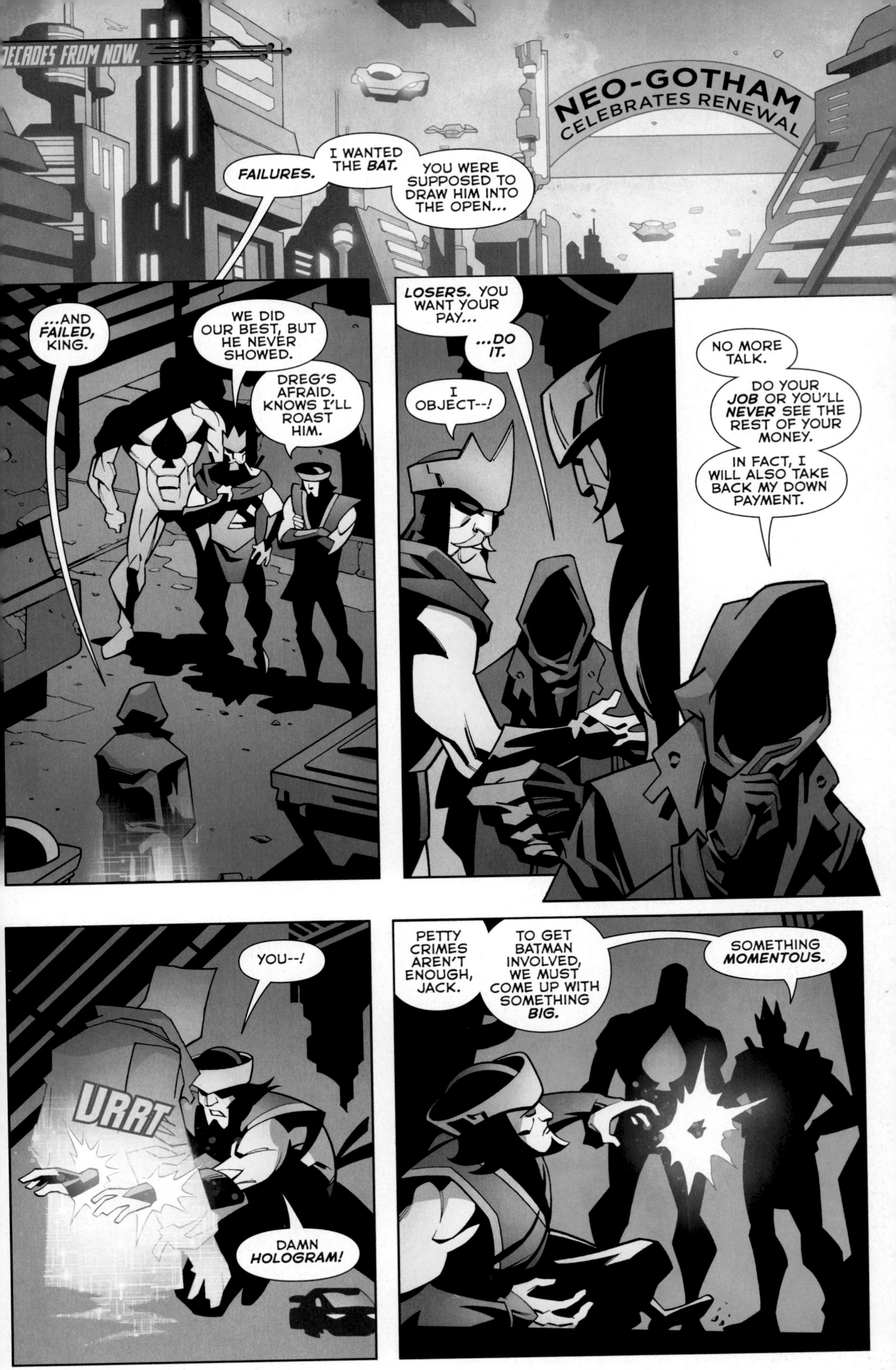
DECADES FROM NOW.
NEO-GOTHAM CELEBRATES RENEWAL
FAILURES.
I WANTED THE BAT.
YOU WERE SUPPOSED TO DRAW HIM INTO THE OPEN...
...AND FAILED, KING.
WE DID OUR BEST, BUT HE NEVER SHOWED.
DREG'S AFRAID. KNOWS I'LL ROAST HIM.
LOSERS. YOU WANT YOUR PAY...
...DO IT.
I OBJECT--!
NO MORE TALK.
DO YOUR JOB OR YOU'LL NEVER SEE THE REST OF YOUR MONEY.
IN FACT, I WILL ALSO TAKE BACK MY DOWN PAYMENT.
YOU--!
URRT
DAMN HOLOGRAM!
PETTY CRIMES AREN'T ENOUGH, JACK.
TO GET BATMAN INVOLVED, WE MUST COME UP WITH SOMETHING BIG.
SOMETHING MOMENTOUS.

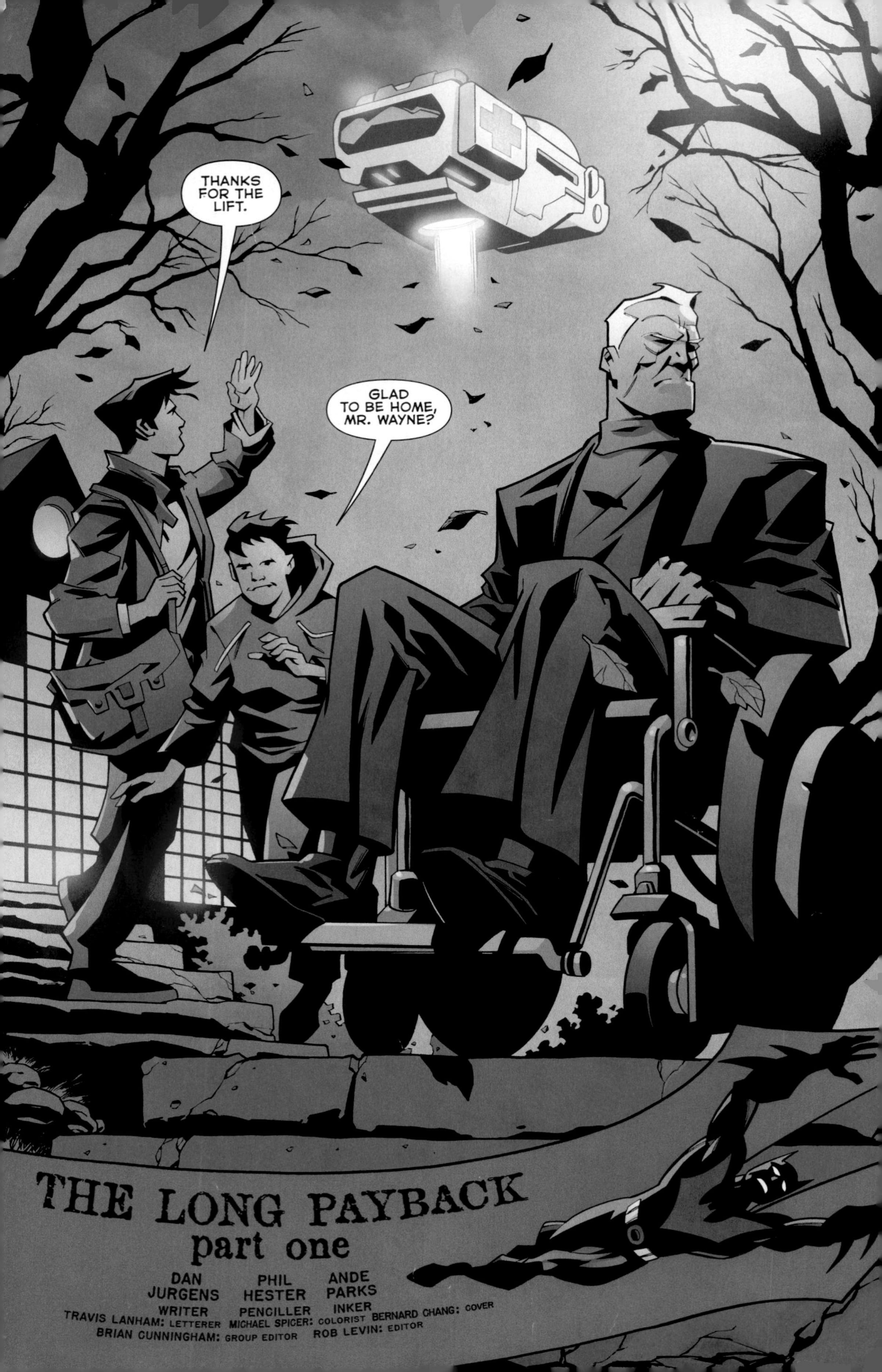
THANKS FOR THE LIFT.
GLAD TO BE HOME, MR. WAYNE?
THE LONG PAYBACK
part one
DAN JURGENS WRITER
PHIL HESTER PENCILLER
ANDE PARKS INKER
TRAVIS LANHAM: LETTERER
MICHAEL SPICER: COLORIST
BERNARD CHANG: COVER
BRIAN CUNNINGHAM: GROUP EDITOR
ROB LEVIN: EDITOR

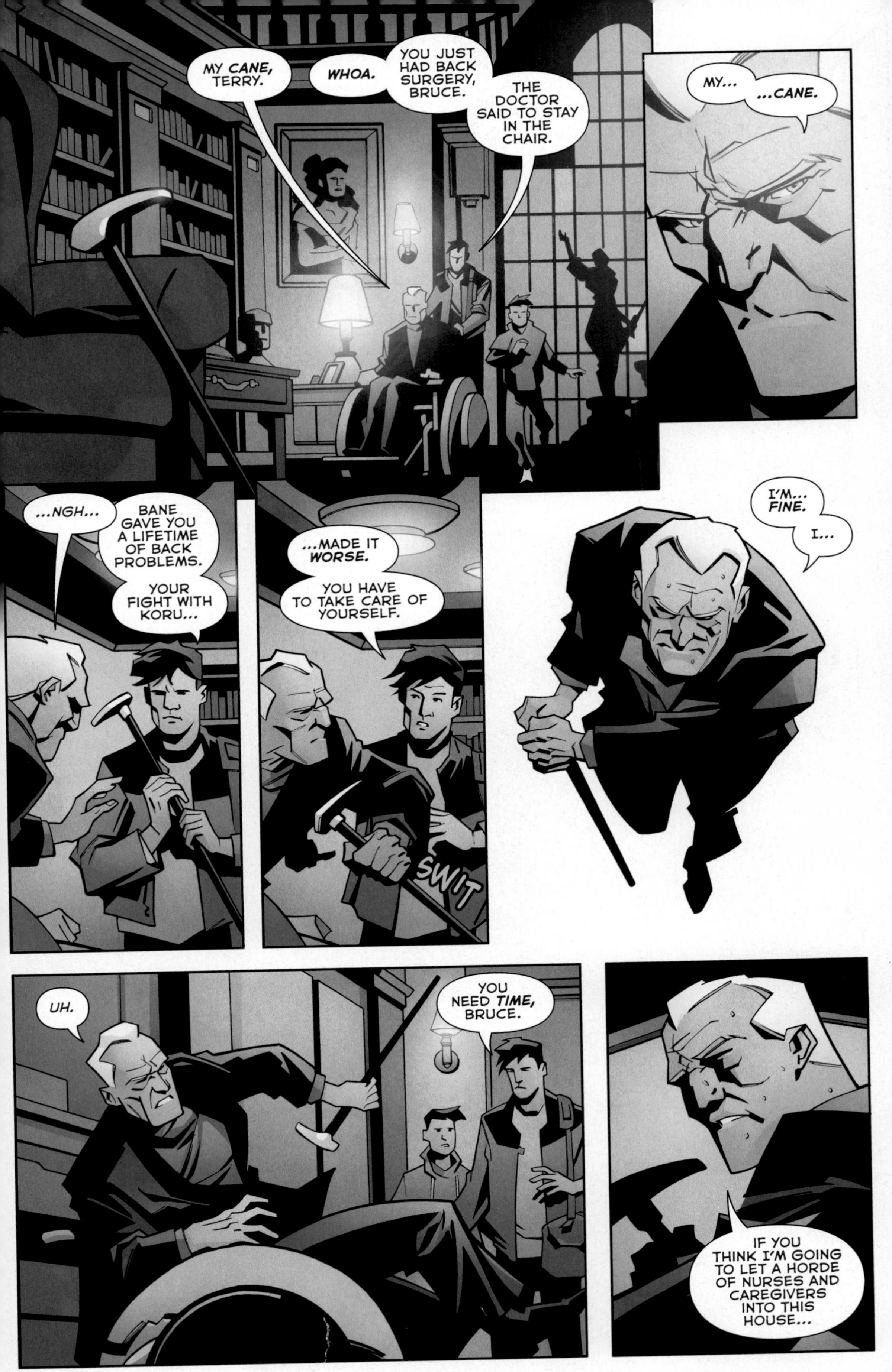
MY CANE, TERRY.
WHOA.
YOU JUST HAD BACK SURGERY, BRUCE.
THE DOCTOR SAID TO STAY IN THE CHAIR.
MY...
...CANE.
...NGH...
BANE GAVE YOU A LIFETIME OF BACK PROBLEMS.
YOUR FIGHT WITH KORU...
...MADE IT WORSE.
YOU HAVE TO TAKE CARE OF YOURSELF.
SWIT
I'M... FINE.
I...
UH.
YOU NEED TIME, BRUCE.
IF YOU THINK I'M GOING TO LET A HORDE OF NURSES AND CAREGIVERS INTO THIS HOUSE...

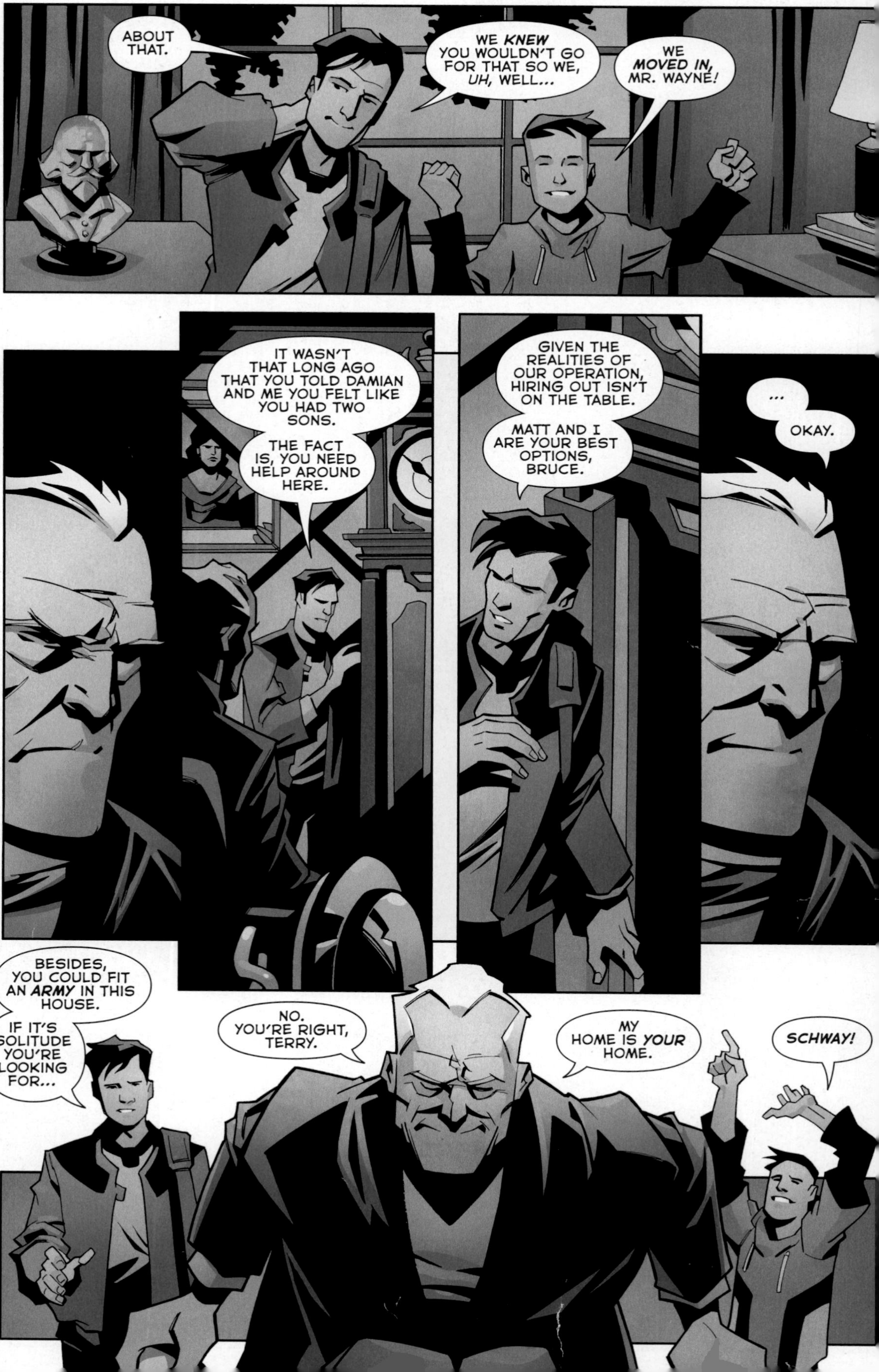
ABOUT THAT.
WE *KNEW* YOU WOULDN'T GO FOR THAT SO WE, *UH,* WELL...
WE *MOVED IN,* MR. WAYNE!
IT WASN'T THAT LONG AGO THAT YOU TOLD DAMIAN AND ME YOU FELT LIKE YOU HAD TWO SONS.
THE FACT IS, YOU NEED HELP AROUND HERE.
GIVEN THE REALITIES OF OUR OPERATION, HIRING OUT ISN'T ON THE TABLE.
MATT AND I ARE YOUR BEST OPTIONS, BRUCE.
...
OKAY.
BESIDES, YOU COULD FIT AN *ARMY* IN THIS HOUSE.
IF IT'S SOLITUDE YOU'RE LOOKING FOR...
NO. YOU'RE RIGHT, TERRY.
MY HOME IS *YOUR* HOME.
SCHWAY!

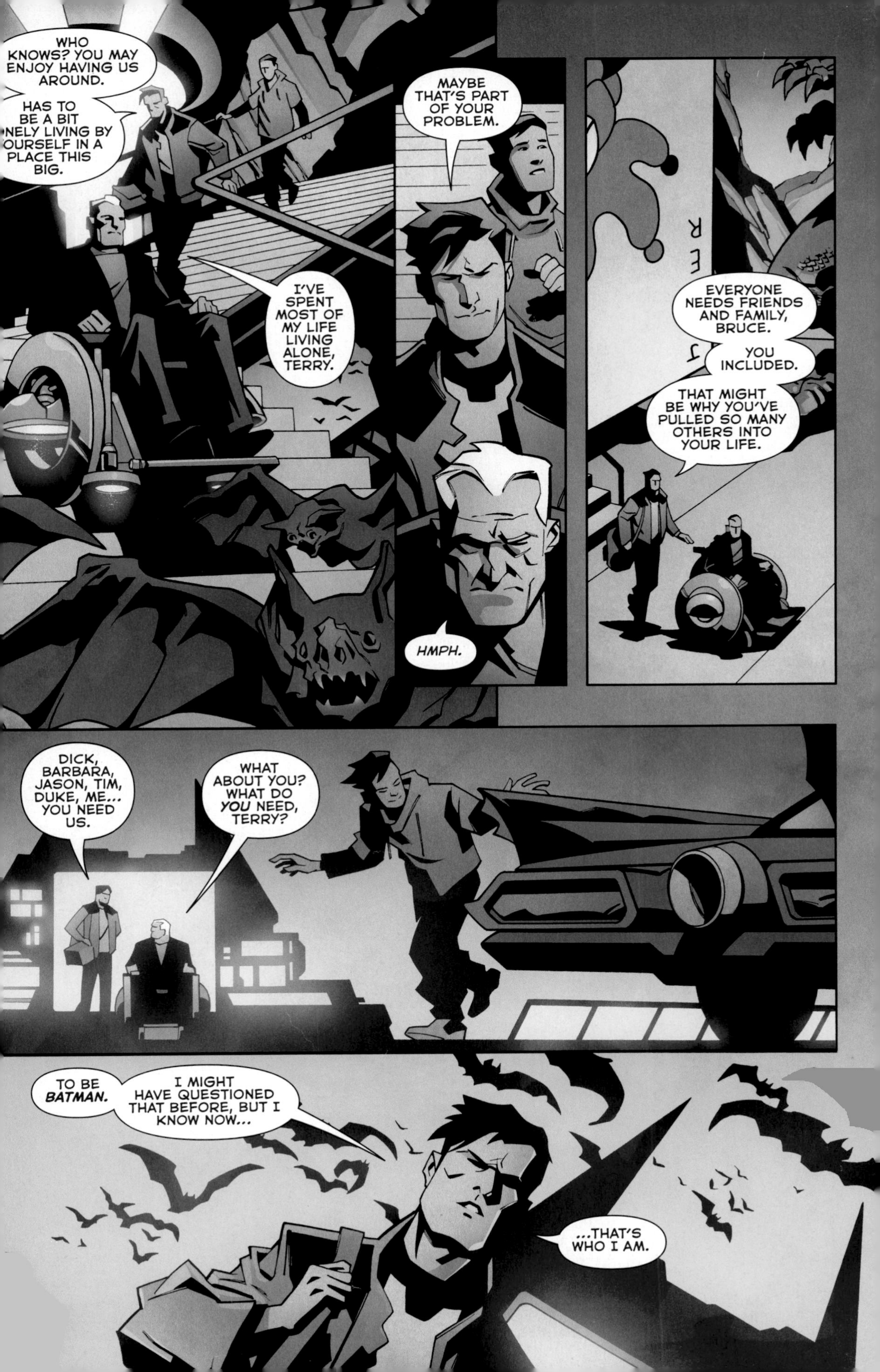
WHO KNOWS? YOU MAY ENJOY HAVING US AROUND.
HAS TO BE A BIT ONELY LIVING BY YOURSELF IN A PLACE THIS BIG.
I'VE SPENT MOST OF MY LIFE LIVING ALONE, TERRY.
MAYBE THAT'S PART OF YOUR PROBLEM.
HMPH.
EVERYONE NEEDS FRIENDS AND FAMILY, BRUCE.
YOU INCLUDED.
THAT MIGHT BE WHY YOU'VE PULLED SO MANY OTHERS INTO YOUR LIFE.
DICK, BARBARA, JASON, TIM, DUKE, ME... YOU NEED US.
WHAT ABOUT YOU? WHAT DO *YOU* NEED, TERRY?
TO BE ***BATMAN.***
I MIGHT HAVE QUESTIONED THAT BEFORE, BUT I KNOW NOW...
...THAT'S WHO I AM.

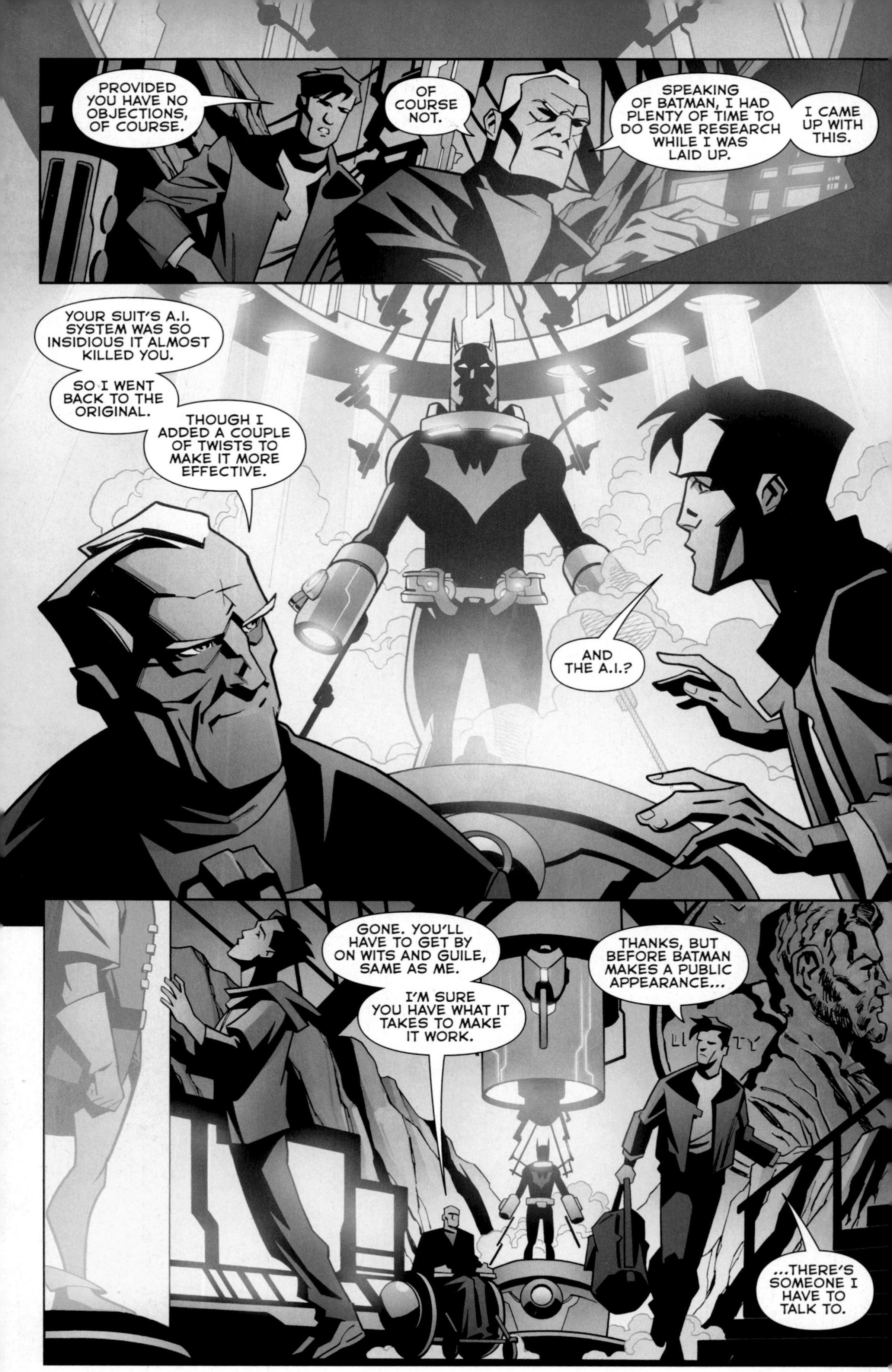
PROVIDED YOU HAVE NO OBJECTIONS, OF COURSE.
OF COURSE NOT.
SPEAKING OF BATMAN, I HAD PLENTY OF TIME TO DO SOME RESEARCH WHILE I WAS LAID UP.
I CAME UP WITH THIS.
YOUR SUIT'S A.I. SYSTEM WAS SO INSIDIOUS IT ALMOST KILLED YOU.
SO I WENT BACK TO THE ORIGINAL.
THOUGH I ADDED A COUPLE OF TWISTS TO MAKE IT MORE EFFECTIVE.
AND THE A.I.?
GONE. YOU'LL HAVE TO GET BY ON WITS AND GUILE, SAME AS ME.
I'M SURE YOU HAVE WHAT IT TAKES TO MAKE IT WORK.
THANKS, BUT BEFORE BATMAN MAKES A PUBLIC APPEARANCE...
...THERE'S SOMEONE I HAVE TO TALK TO.

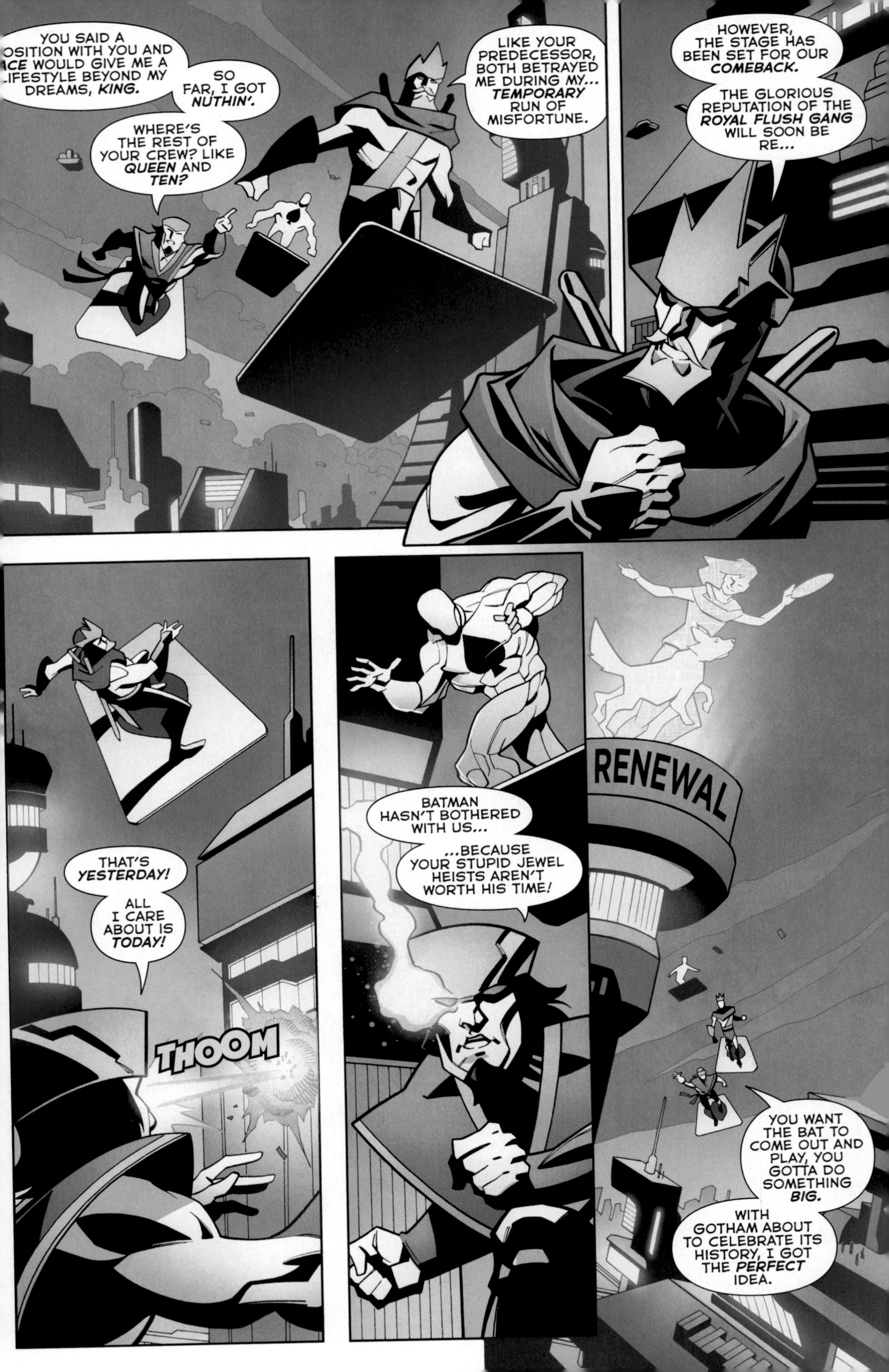

YOU SAID A POSITION WITH YOU AND ACE WOULD GIVE ME A LIFESTYLE BEYOND MY DREAMS, KING.
SO FAR, I GOT NUTHIN'.
WHERE'S THE REST OF YOUR CREW? LIKE QUEEN AND TEN?
LIKE YOUR PREDECESSOR, BOTH BETRAYED ME DURING MY... TEMPORARY RUN OF MISFORTUNE.
HOWEVER, THE STAGE HAS BEEN SET FOR OUR COMEBACK.
THE GLORIOUS REPUTATION OF THE ROYAL FLUSH GANG WILL SOON BE RE...
THAT'S YESTERDAY!
ALL I CARE ABOUT IS TODAY!
THOOM
BATMAN HASN'T BOTHERED WITH US...
...BECAUSE YOUR STUPID JEWEL HEISTS AREN'T WORTH HIS TIME!
RENEWAL
YOU WANT THE BAT TO COME OUT AND PLAY, YOU GOTTA DO SOMETHING BIG.
WITH GOTHAM ABOUT TO CELEBRATE ITS HISTORY, I GOT THE PERFECT IDEA.

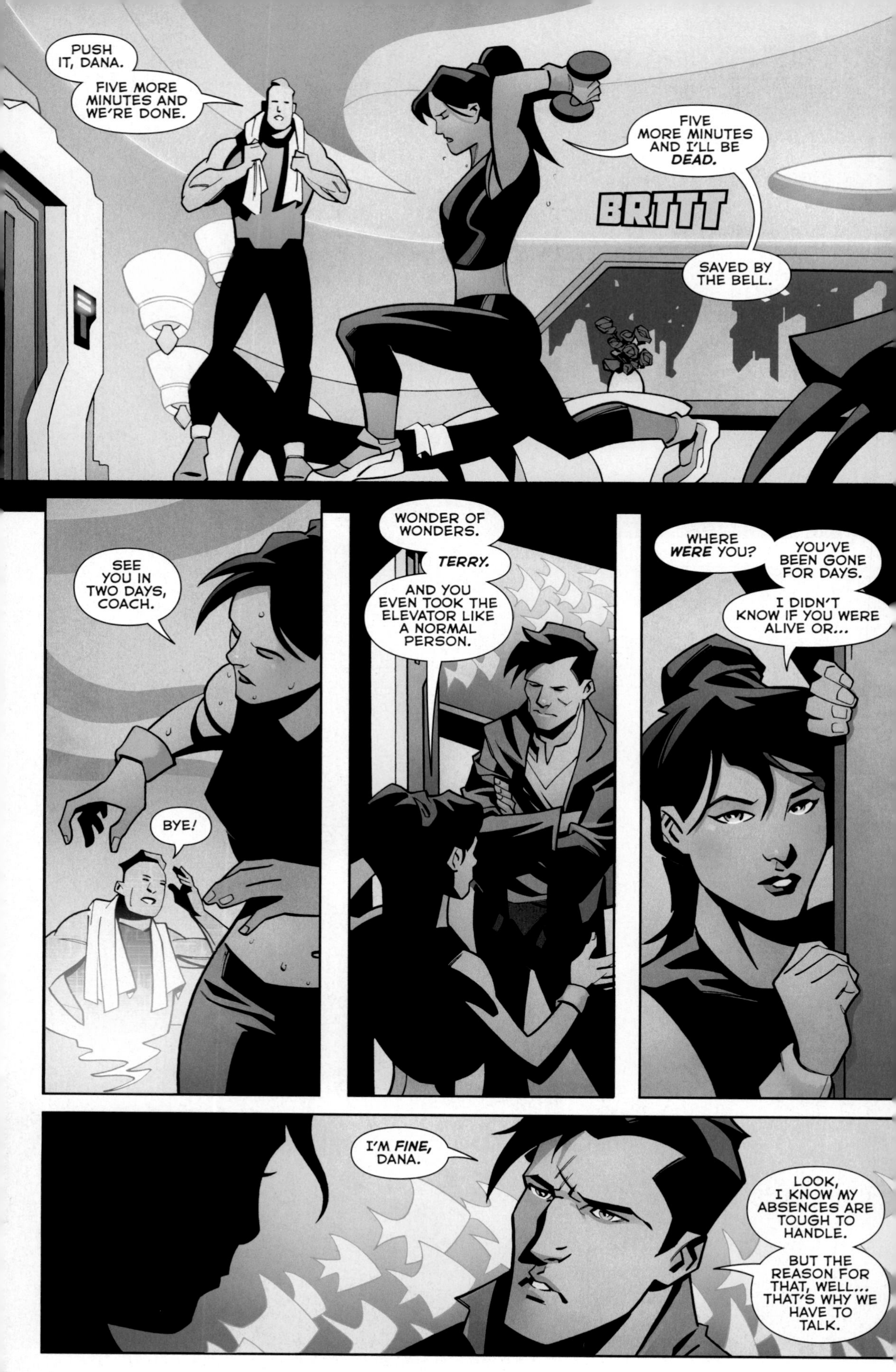
PUSH IT, DANA.
FIVE MORE MINUTES AND WE'RE DONE.
FIVE MORE MINUTES AND I'LL BE *DEAD.*
BRTTT
SAVED BY THE BELL.
SEE YOU IN TWO DAYS, COACH.
BYE!
WONDER OF WONDERS.
TERRY.
AND YOU EVEN TOOK THE ELEVATOR LIKE A NORMAL PERSON.
WHERE *WERE* YOU?
YOU'VE BEEN GONE FOR DAYS.
I DIDN'T KNOW IF YOU WERE ALIVE OR...
I'M *FINE,* DANA.
LOOK, I KNOW MY ABSENCES ARE TOUGH TO HANDLE.
BUT THE REASON FOR THAT, WELL... THAT'S WHY WE HAVE TO TALK.

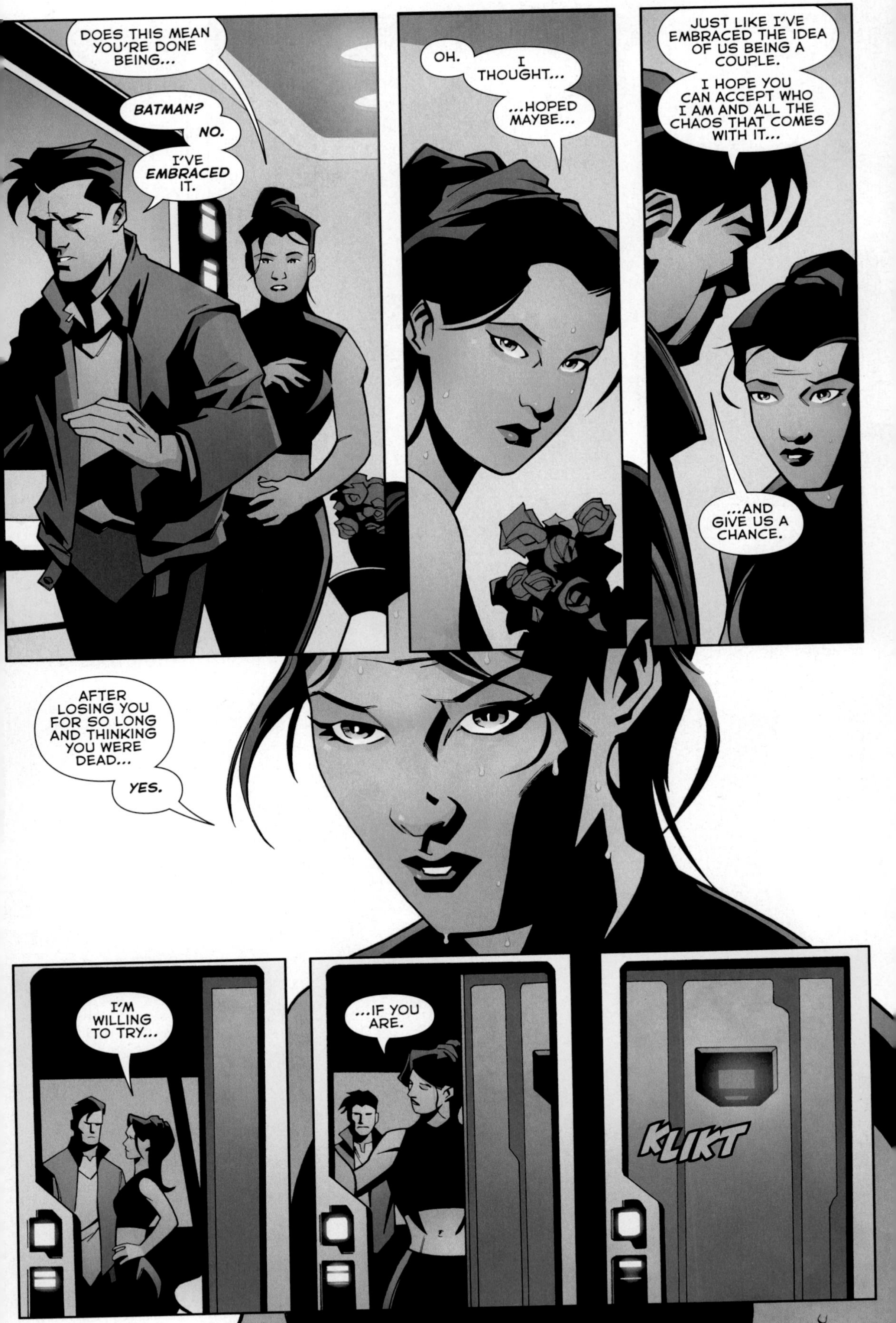
DOES THIS MEAN YOU'RE DONE BEING...
BATMAN?
NO.
I'VE EMBRACED IT.
OH.
I THOUGHT...
...HOPED MAYBE...
JUST LIKE I'VE EMBRACED THE IDEA OF US BEING A COUPLE.
I HOPE YOU CAN ACCEPT WHO I AM AND ALL THE CHAOS THAT COMES WITH IT...
...AND GIVE US A CHANCE.
AFTER LOSING YOU FOR SO LONG AND THINKING YOU WERE DEAD...
YES.
I'M WILLING TO TRY...
...IF YOU ARE.
KLIKT

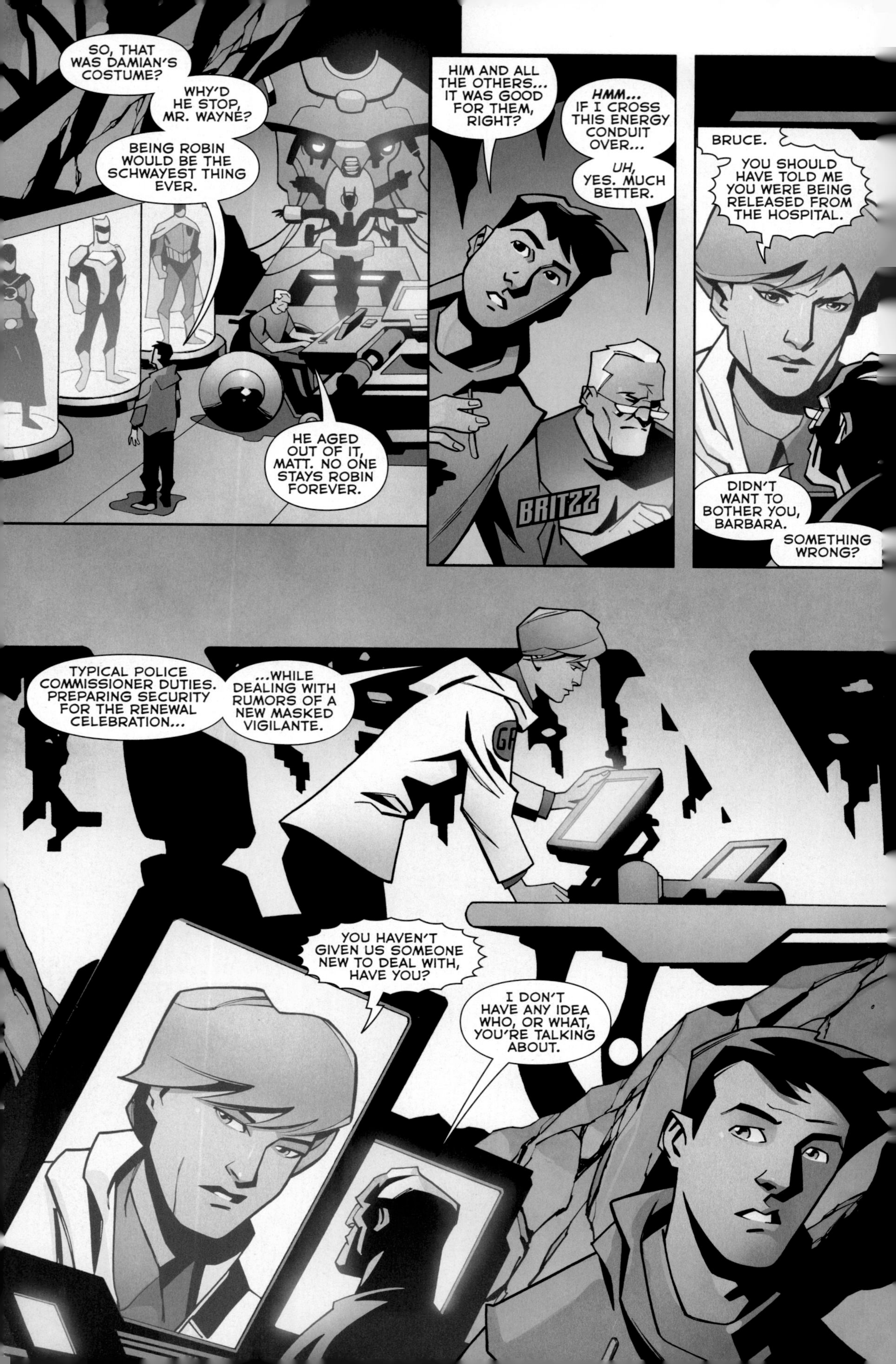

SO, THAT WAS DAMIAN'S COSTUME?
WHY'D HE STOP, MR. WAYNE?
BEING ROBIN WOULD BE THE SCHWAYEST THING EVER.
HE AGED OUT OF IT, MATT. NO ONE STAYS ROBIN FOREVER.
HIM AND ALL THE OTHERS... IT WAS GOOD FOR THEM, RIGHT?
HMM... IF I CROSS THIS ENERGY CONDUIT OVER...
UH, YES. MUCH BETTER.
BRITZZ
BRUCE.
YOU SHOULD HAVE TOLD ME YOU WERE BEING RELEASED FROM THE HOSPITAL.
DIDN'T WANT TO BOTHER YOU, BARBARA.
SOMETHING WRONG?
TYPICAL POLICE COMMISSIONER DUTIES. PREPARING SECURITY FOR THE RENEWAL CELEBRATION...
...WHILE DEALING WITH RUMORS OF A NEW MASKED VIGILANTE.
YOU HAVEN'T GIVEN US SOMEONE NEW TO DEAL WITH, HAVE YOU?
I DON'T HAVE ANY IDEA WHO, OR WHAT, YOU'RE TALKING ABOUT.

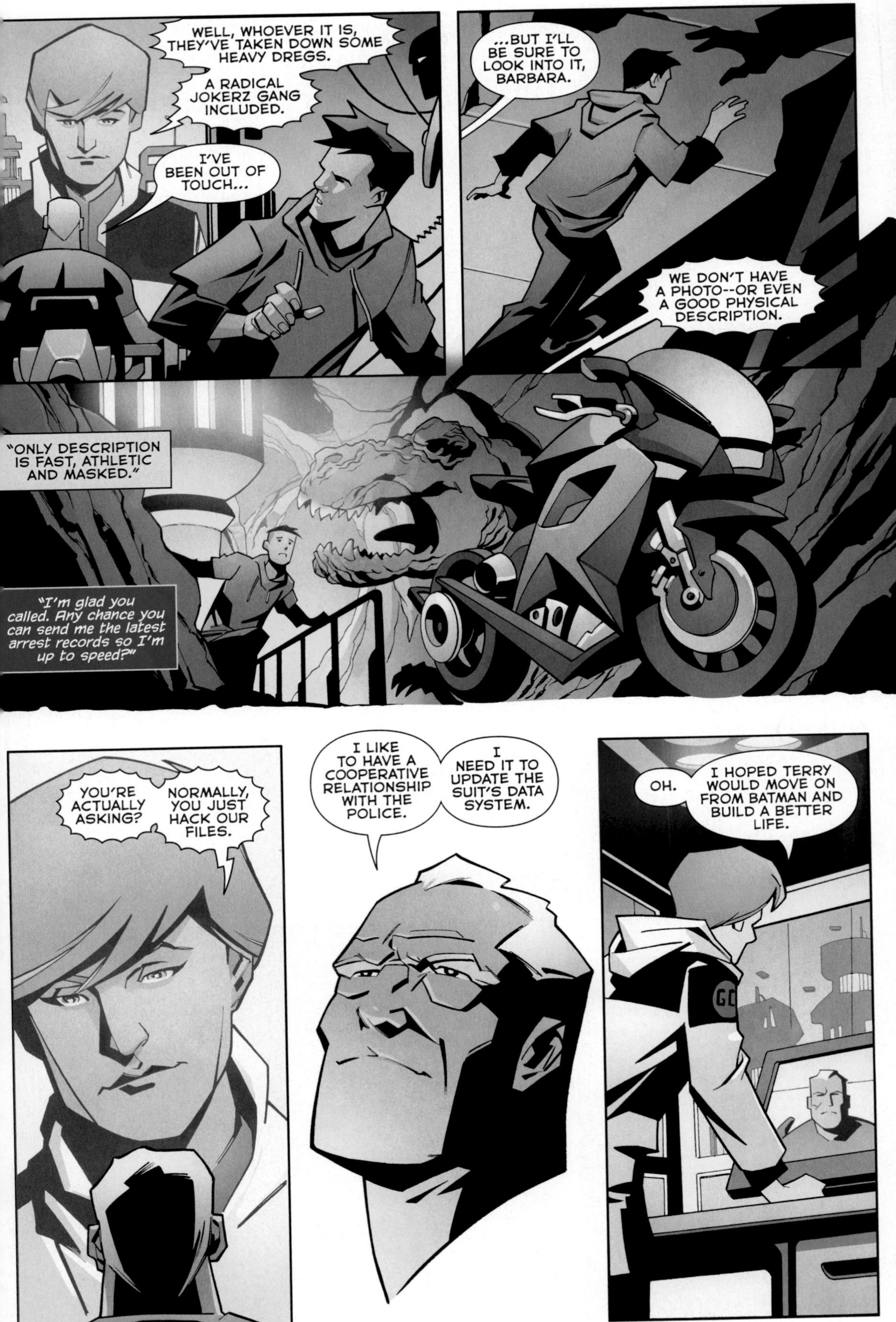
WELL, WHOEVER IT IS, THEY'VE TAKEN DOWN SOME HEAVY DREGS.
A RADICAL JOKERZ GANG INCLUDED.
I'VE BEEN OUT OF TOUCH...
...BUT I'LL BE SURE TO LOOK INTO IT, BARBARA.
WE DON'T HAVE A PHOTO--OR EVEN A GOOD PHYSICAL DESCRIPTION.
"ONLY DESCRIPTION IS FAST, ATHLETIC AND MASKED."
"I'm glad you called. Any chance you can send me the latest arrest records so I'm up to speed?"
YOU'RE ACTUALLY ASKING?
NORMALLY, YOU JUST HACK OUR FILES.
I LIKE TO HAVE A COOPERATIVE RELATIONSHIP WITH THE POLICE.
I NEED IT TO UPDATE THE SUIT'S DATA SYSTEM.
OH.
I HOPED TERRY WOULD MOVE ON FROM BATMAN AND BUILD A BETTER LIFE.
GC

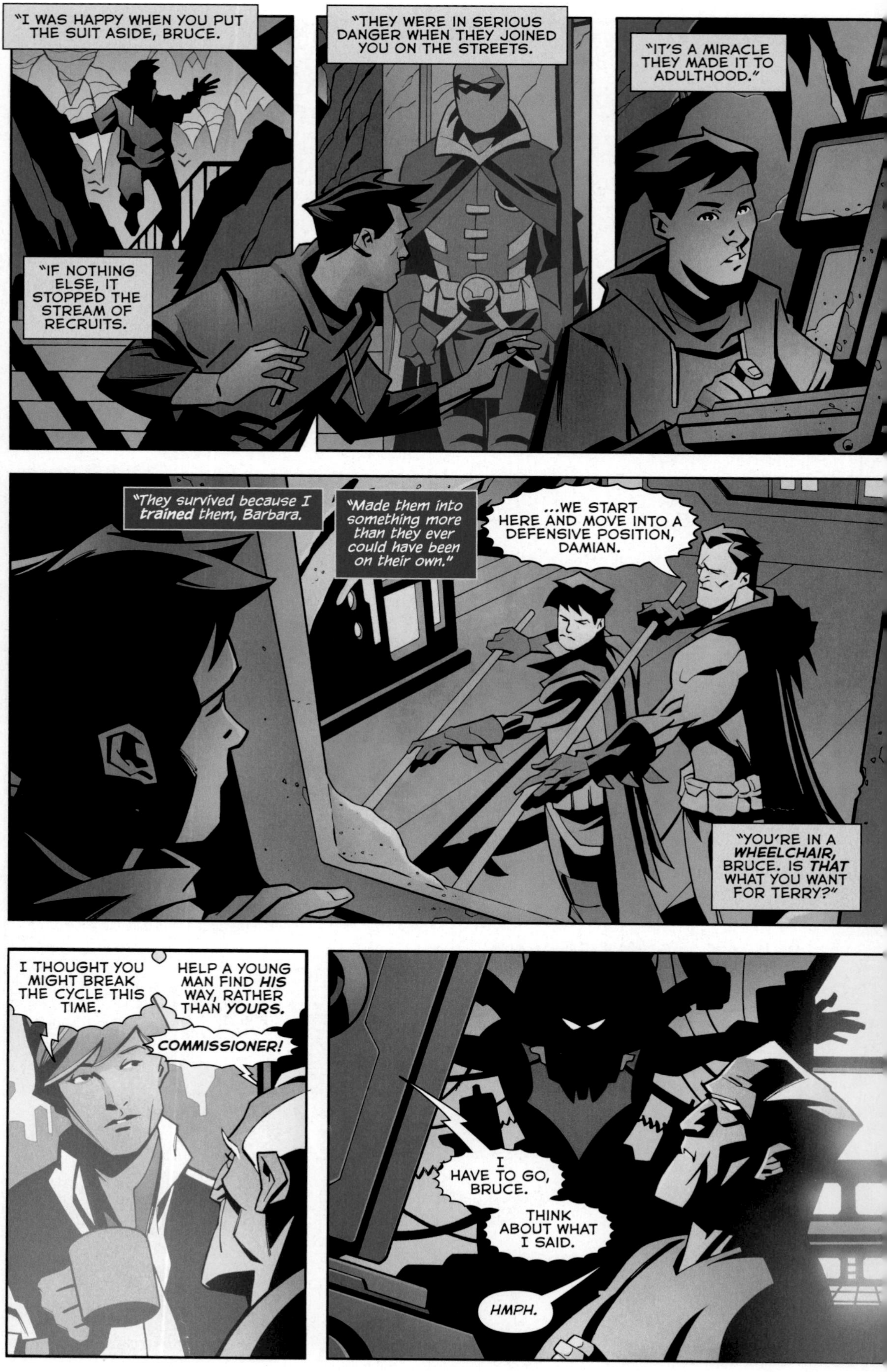
"I WAS HAPPY WHEN YOU PUT THE SUIT ASIDE, BRUCE.
"IF NOTHING ELSE, IT STOPPED THE STREAM OF RECRUITS.
"THEY WERE IN SERIOUS DANGER WHEN THEY JOINED YOU ON THE STREETS.
"IT'S A MIRACLE THEY MADE IT TO ADULTHOOD."
"They survived because I *trained* them, Barbara.
"Made them into something more than they ever could have been on their own."
...WE START HERE AND MOVE INTO A DEFENSIVE POSITION, DAMIAN.
"YOU'RE IN A *WHEELCHAIR,* BRUCE. IS *THAT* WHAT YOU WANT FOR TERRY?"
I THOUGHT YOU MIGHT BREAK THE CYCLE THIS TIME.
HELP A YOUNG MAN FIND *HIS* WAY, RATHER THAN *YOURS.*
COMMISSIONER!
I HAVE TO GO, BRUCE.
THINK ABOUT WHAT I SAID.
HMPH.

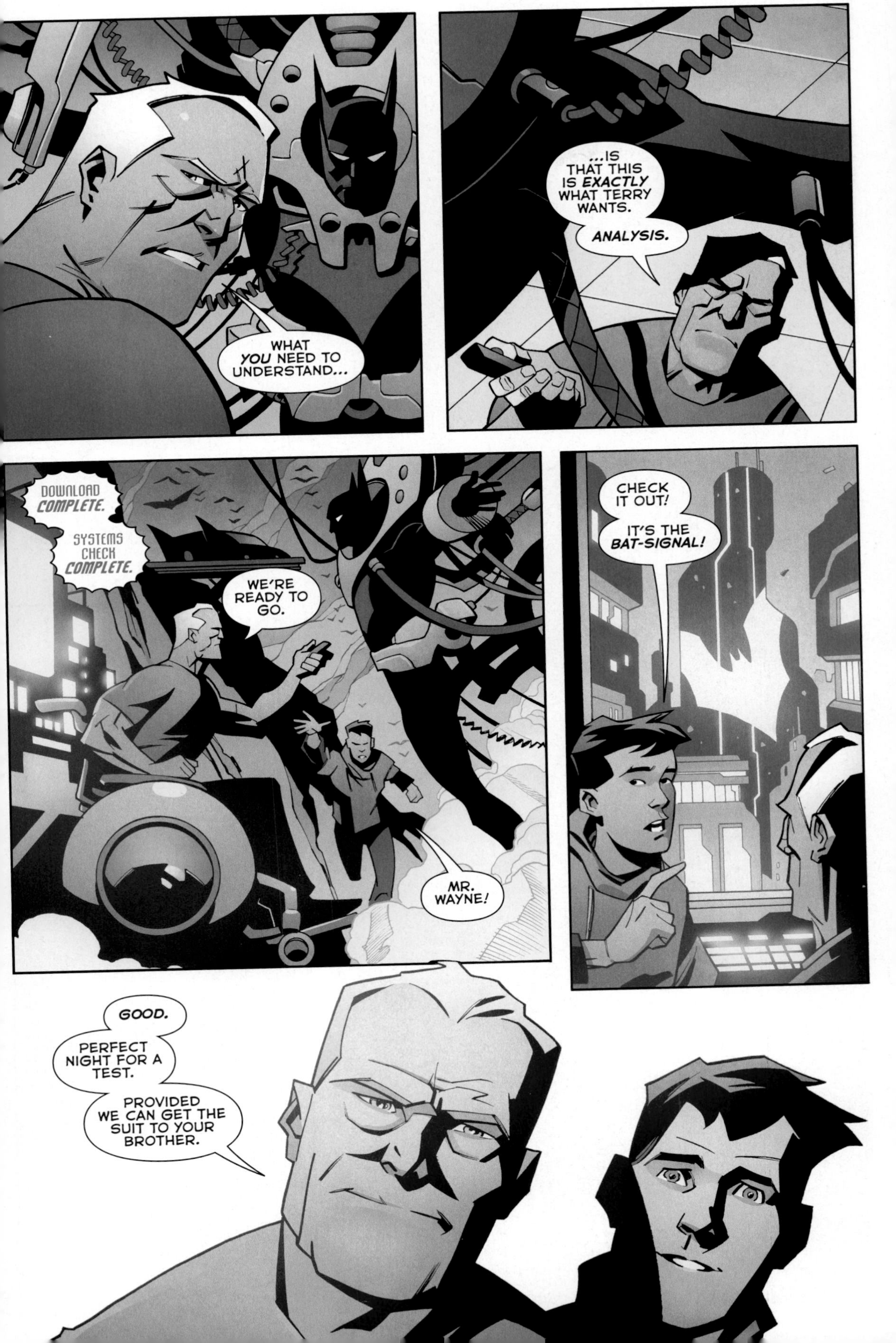
WHAT YOU NEED TO UNDERSTAND...
...IS THAT THIS IS EXACTLY WHAT TERRY WANTS.
ANALYSIS.
DOWNLOAD COMPLETE.
SYSTEMS CHECK COMPLETE.
WE'RE READY TO GO.
MR. WAYNE!
CHECK IT OUT!
IT'S THE BAT-SIGNAL!
GOOD.
PERFECT NIGHT FOR A TEST.
PROVIDED WE CAN GET THE SUIT TO YOUR BROTHER.

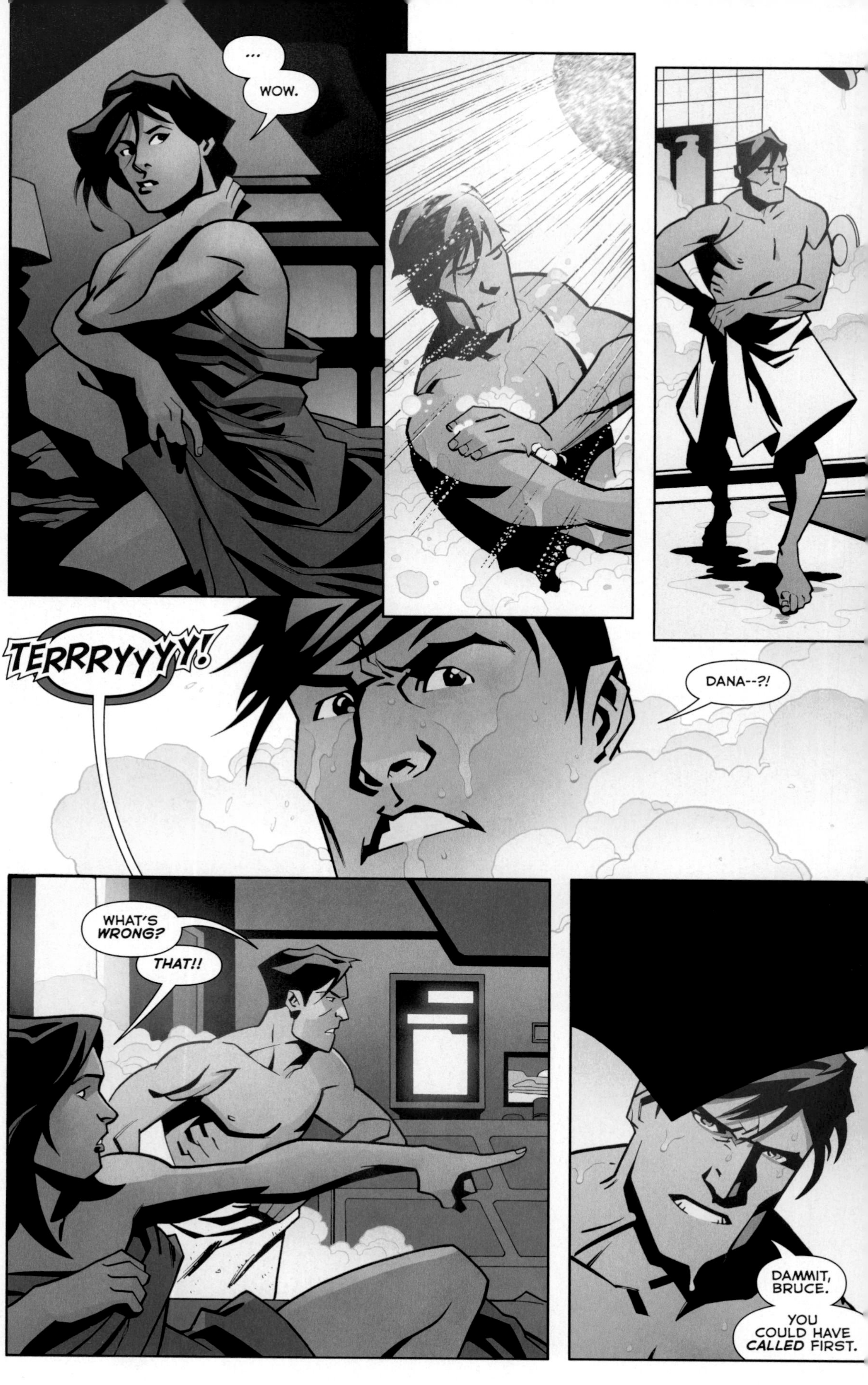
...
WOW.
TERRRYYYYY!
DANA--?!
WHAT'S WRONG?
THAT!!
DAMMIT, BRUCE.
YOU COULD HAVE CALLED FIRST.

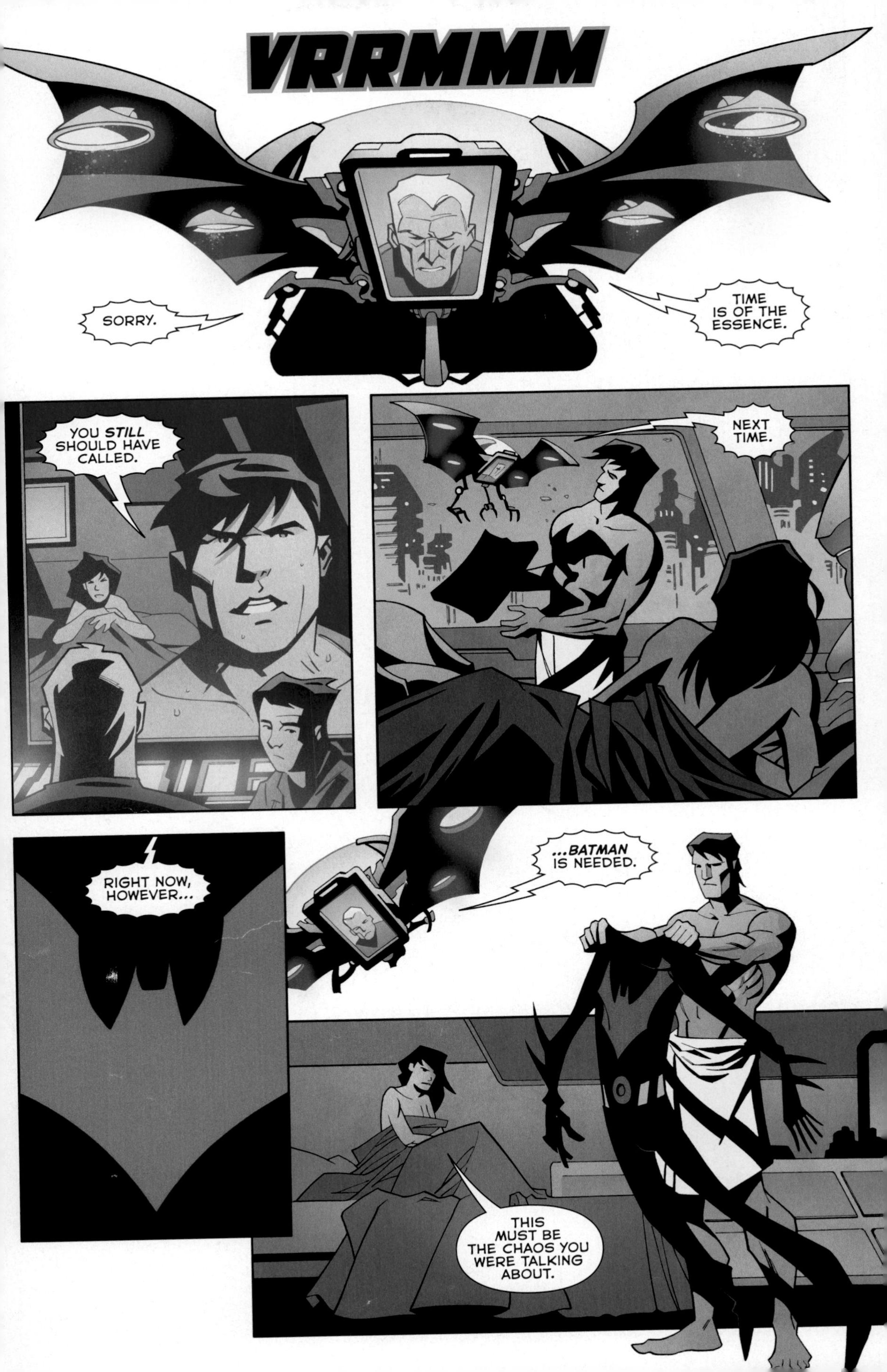
VRRMMM
SORRY.
TIME IS OF THE ESSENCE.
YOU STILL SHOULD HAVE CALLED.
NEXT TIME.
RIGHT NOW, HOWEVER...
...BATMAN IS NEEDED.
THIS MUST BE THE CHAOS YOU WERE TALKING ABOUT.

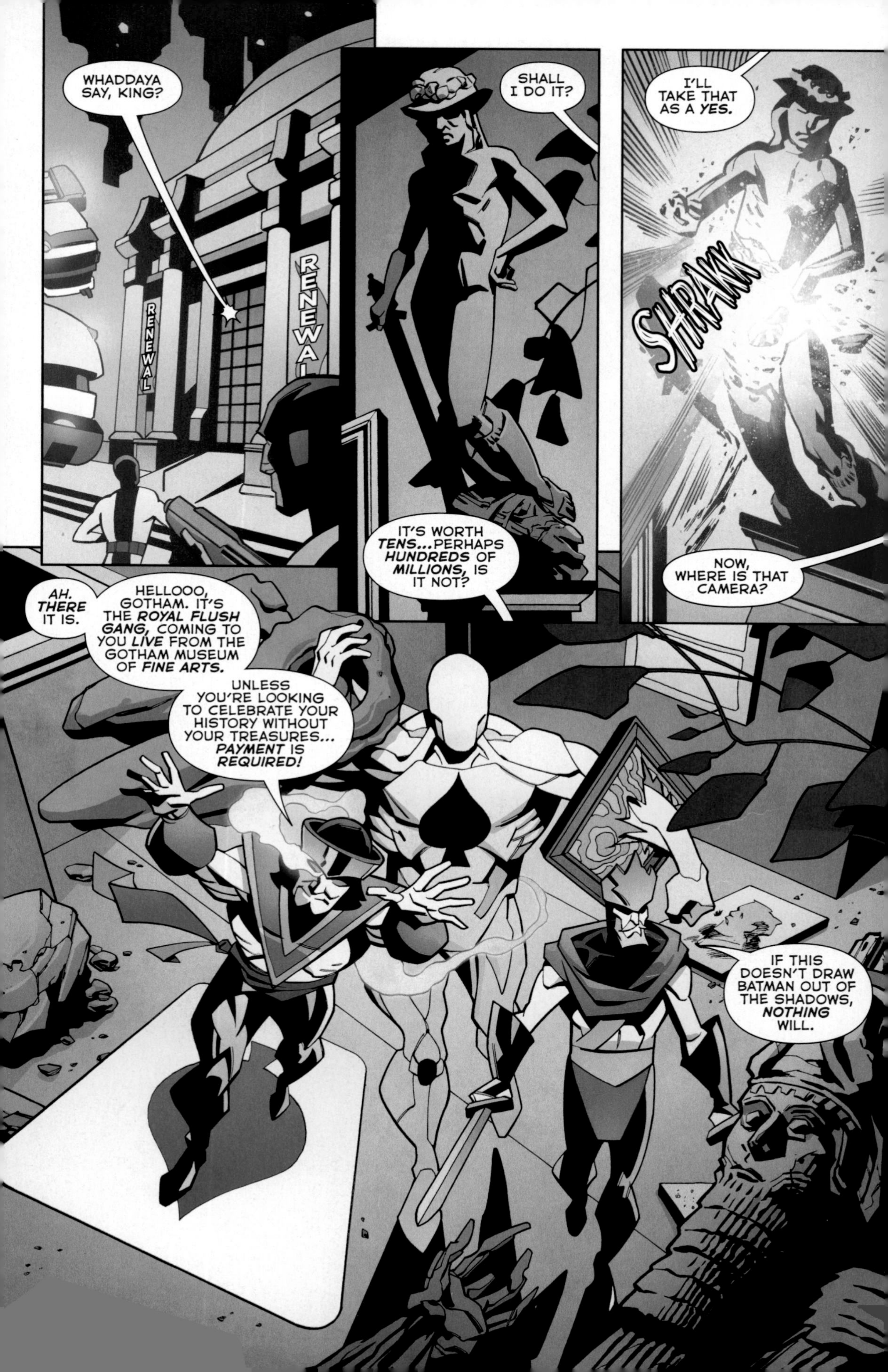
WHADDAYA SAY, KING?
RENEWAL
RENEWAL
SHALL I DO IT?
I'LL TAKE THAT AS A YES.
SHRAKK
IT'S WORTH TENS...PERHAPS HUNDREDS OF MILLIONS, IS IT NOT?
NOW, WHERE IS THAT CAMERA?
AH. THERE IT IS.
HELLOOO, GOTHAM. IT'S THE ROYAL FLUSH GANG, COMING TO YOU LIVE FROM THE GOTHAM MUSEUM OF FINE ARTS.
UNLESS YOU'RE LOOKING TO CELEBRATE YOUR HISTORY WITHOUT YOUR TREASURES... PAYMENT IS REQUIRED!
IF THIS DOESN'T DRAW BATMAN OUT OF THE SHADOWS, NOTHING WILL.

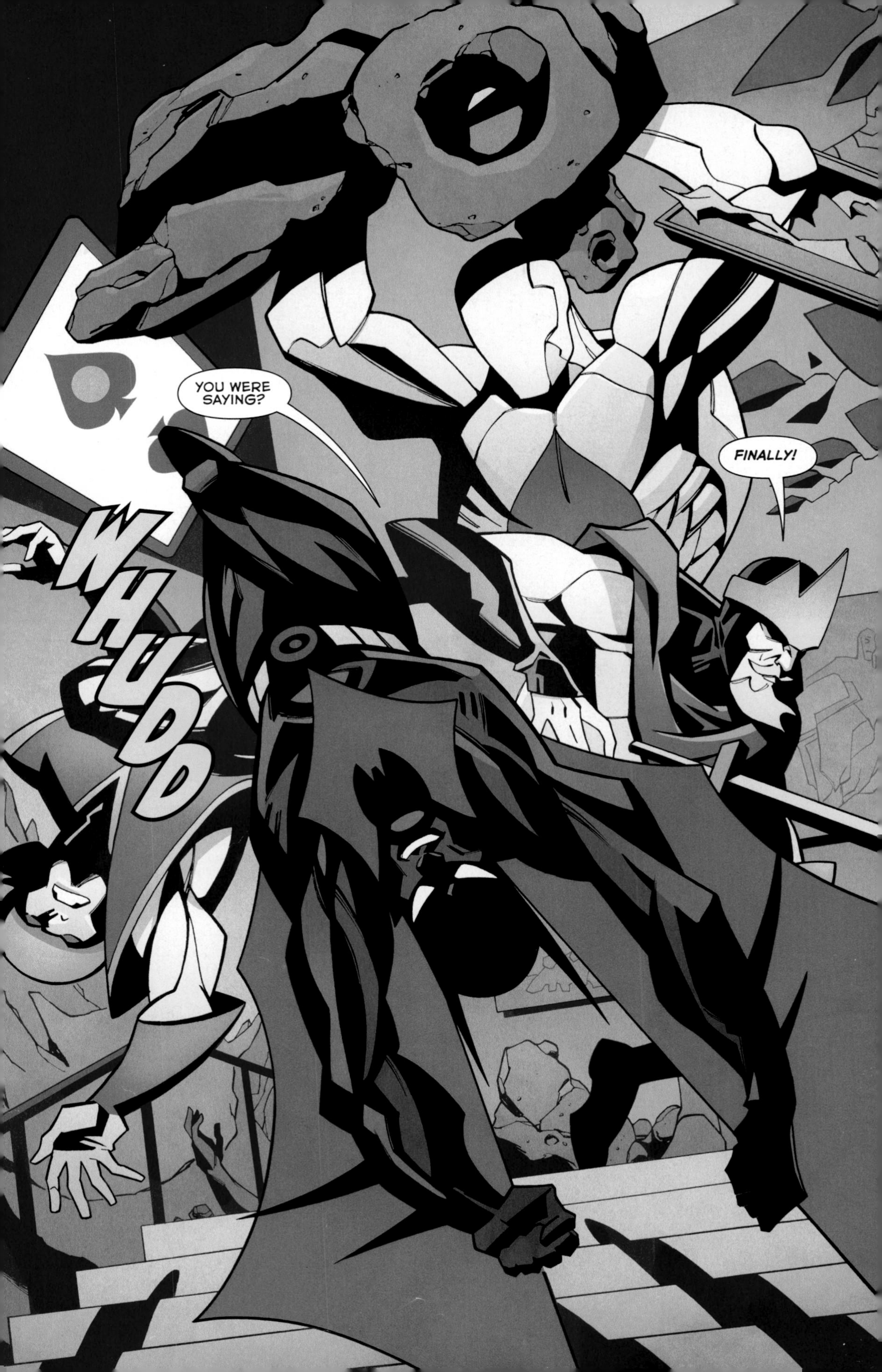
YOU WERE SAYING?
FINALLY!
WHUDD

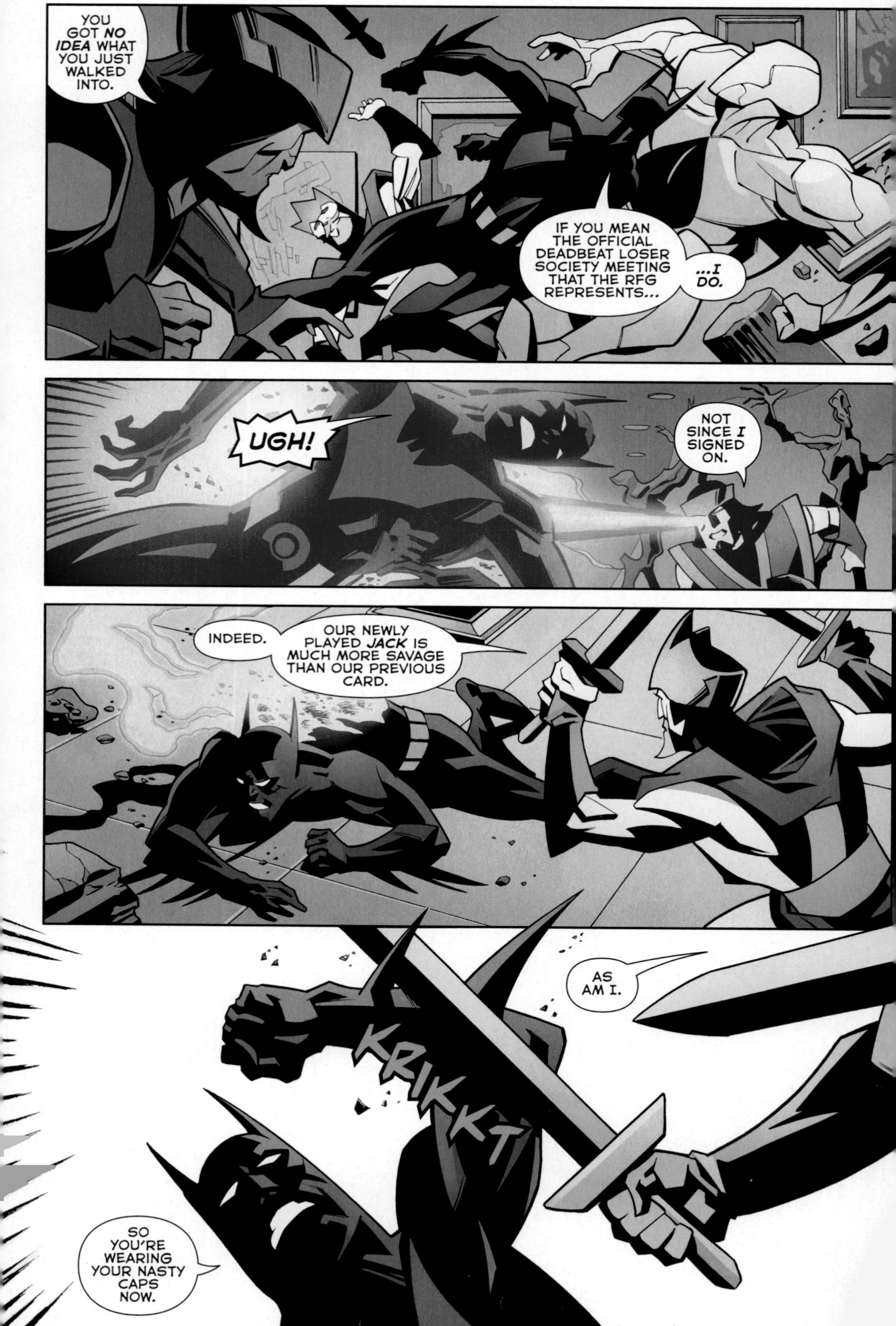
YOU GOT NO IDEA WHAT YOU JUST WALKED INTO.
IF YOU MEAN THE OFFICIAL DEADBEAT LOSER SOCIETY MEETING THAT THE RFG REPRESENTS...
...I DO.
UGH!
NOT SINCE I SIGNED ON.
INDEED.
OUR NEWLY PLAYED JACK IS MUCH MORE SAVAGE THAN OUR PREVIOUS CARD.
AS AM I.
KRIKKKT
SO YOU'RE WEARING YOUR NASTY CAPS NOW.

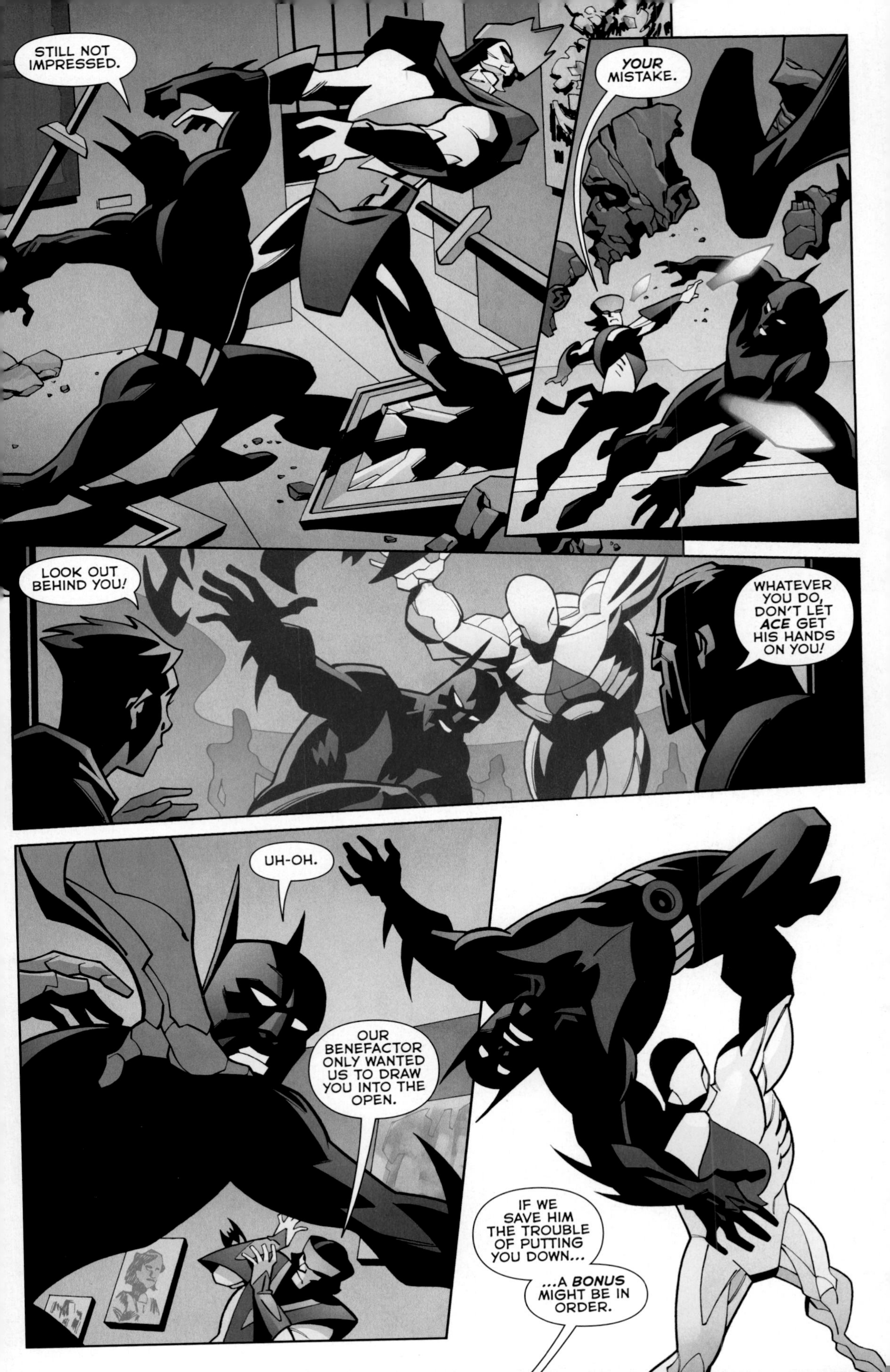
STILL NOT IMPRESSED.
YOUR MISTAKE.
LOOK OUT BEHIND YOU!
WHATEVER YOU DO, DON'T LET ACE GET HIS HANDS ON YOU!
UH-OH.
OUR BENEFACTOR ONLY WANTED US TO DRAW YOU INTO THE OPEN.
IF WE SAVE HIM THE TROUBLE OF PUTTING YOU DOWN...
...A BONUS MIGHT BE IN ORDER.

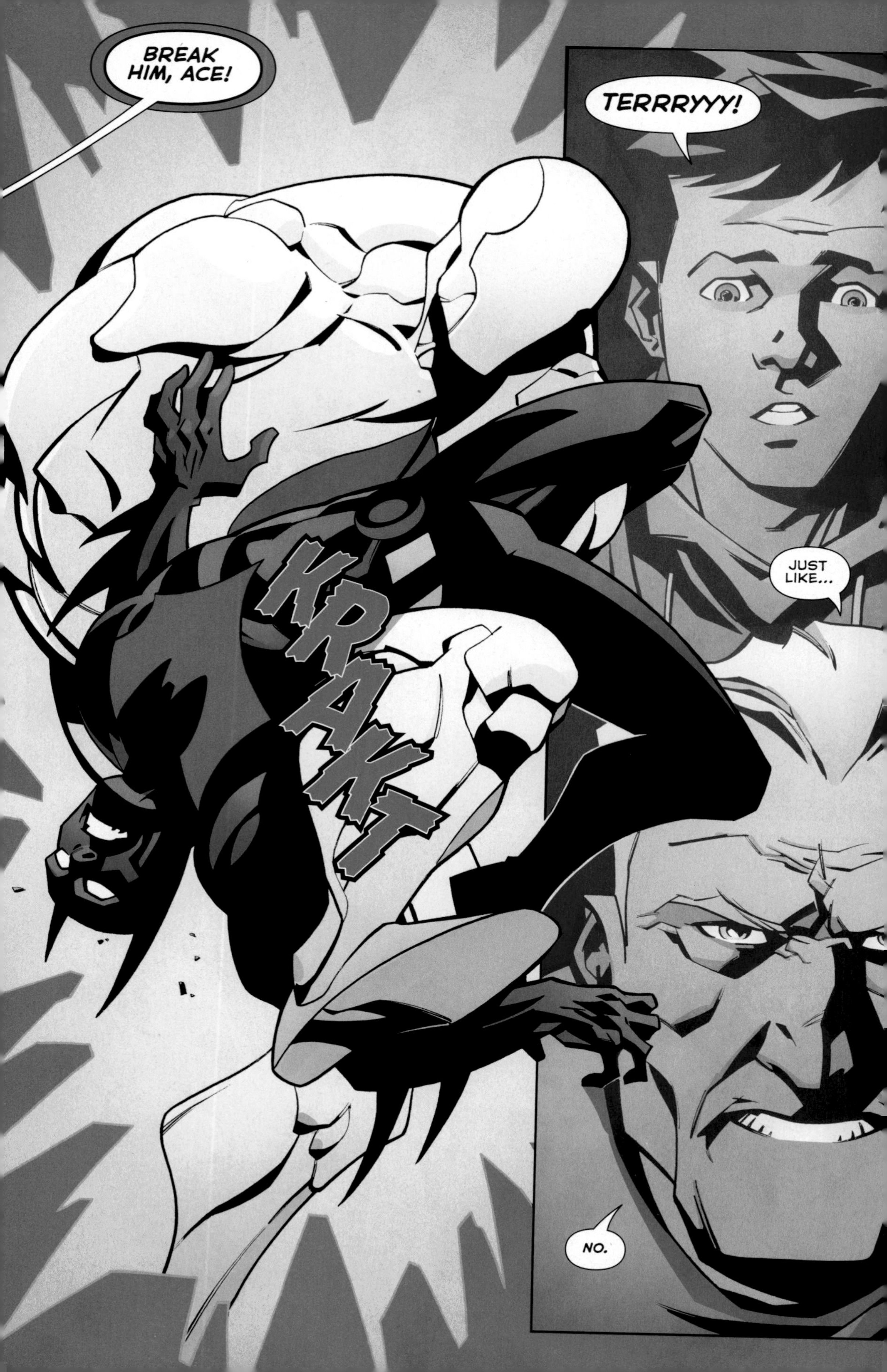
BREAK HIM, ACE!
TERRRYYY!
KRAKT
JUST LIKE...
NO.

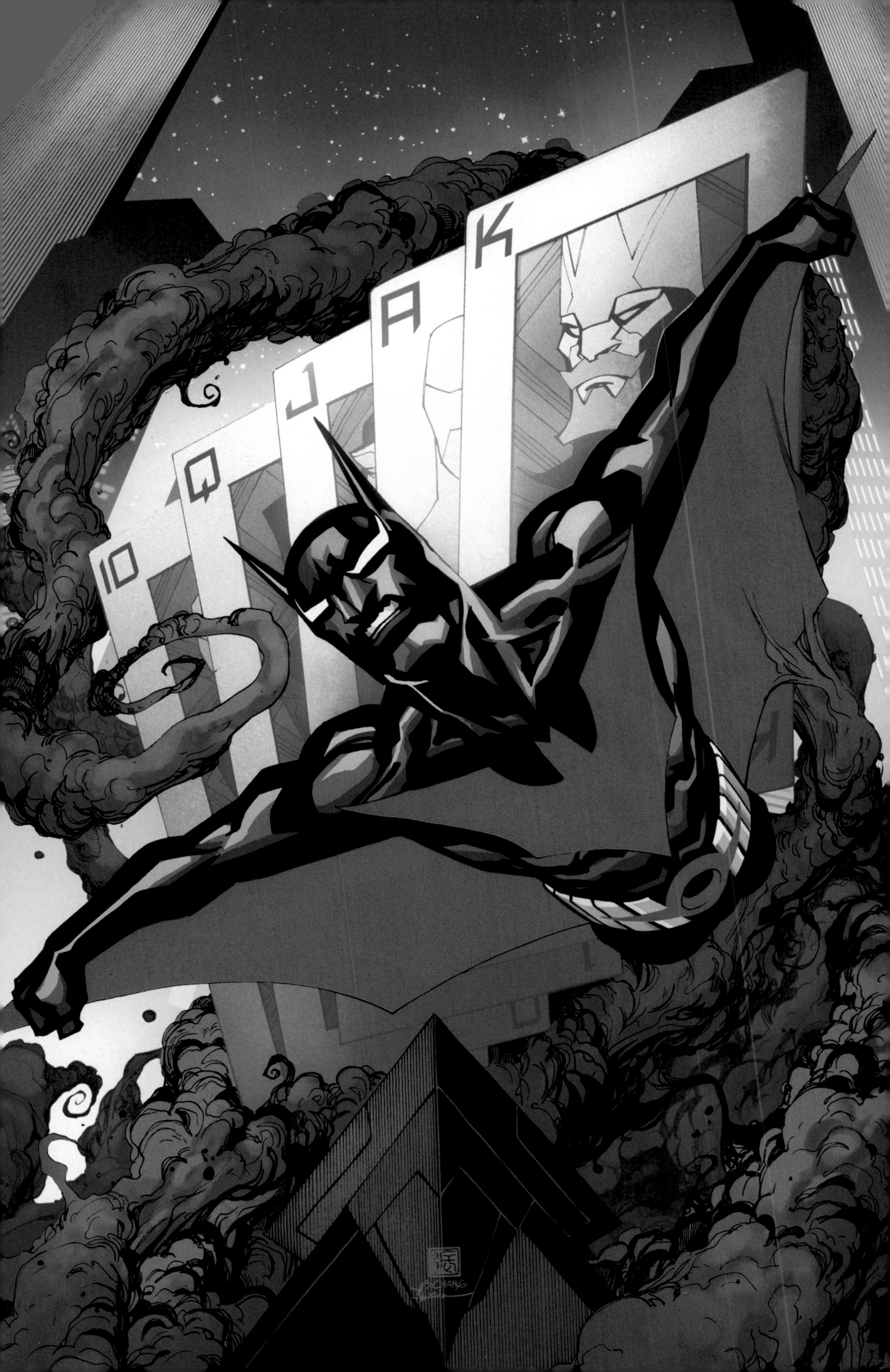

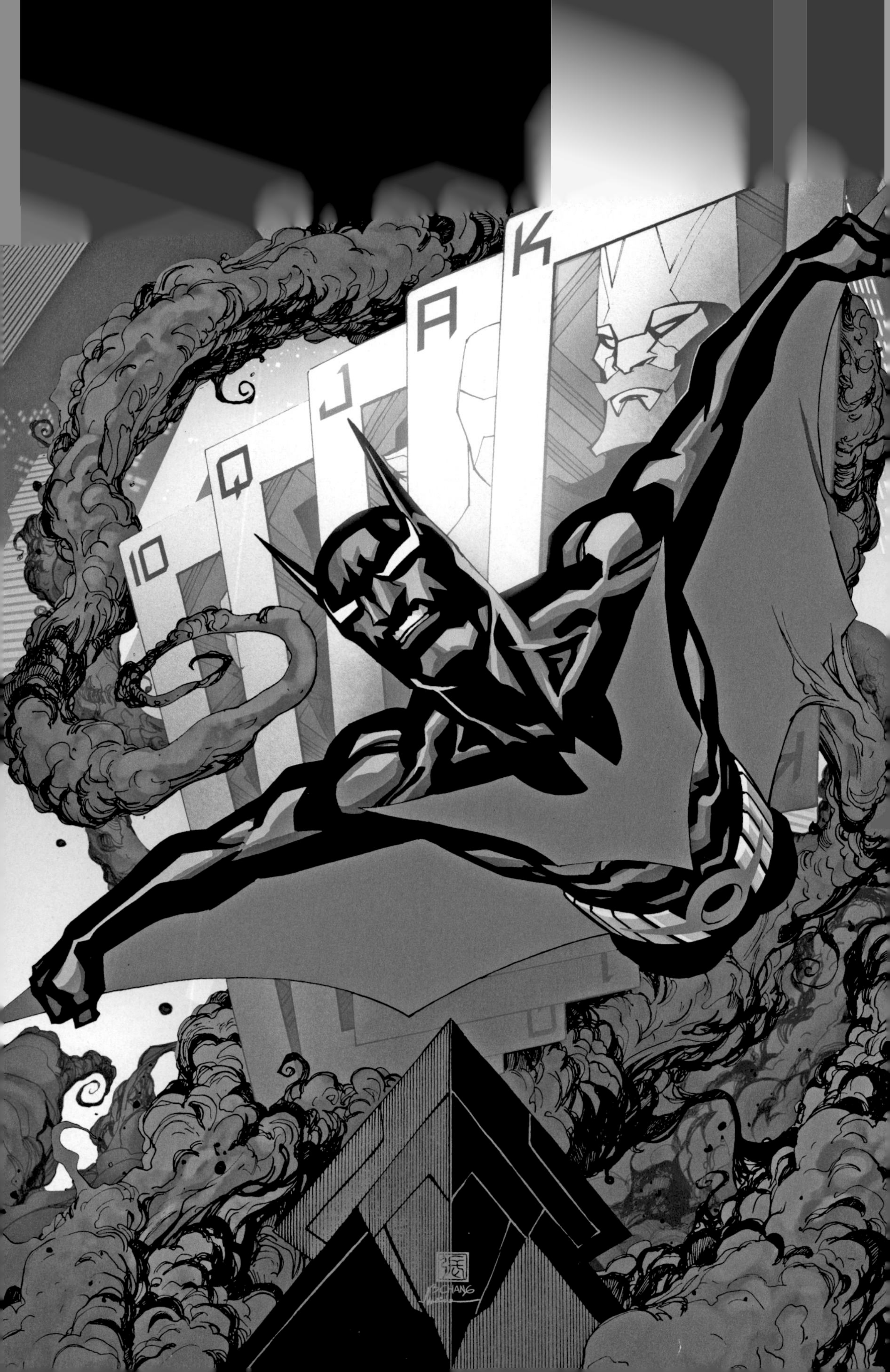
10
Q
J
A
K

"I TRULY HOPED THAT YOU WOULD STEER TERRY *AWAY* FROM THE BUSINESS, BRUCE.

"MORE HAN ANYONE, YOU KNOW THE *COST*."

I do, Barbara.

I've lived with it all my life.

Were I a praying man...

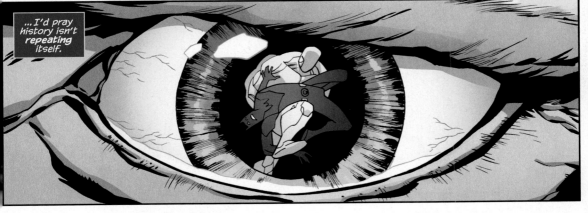

...I'd pray history isn't *repeating* itself.

But I'm not a praying man.

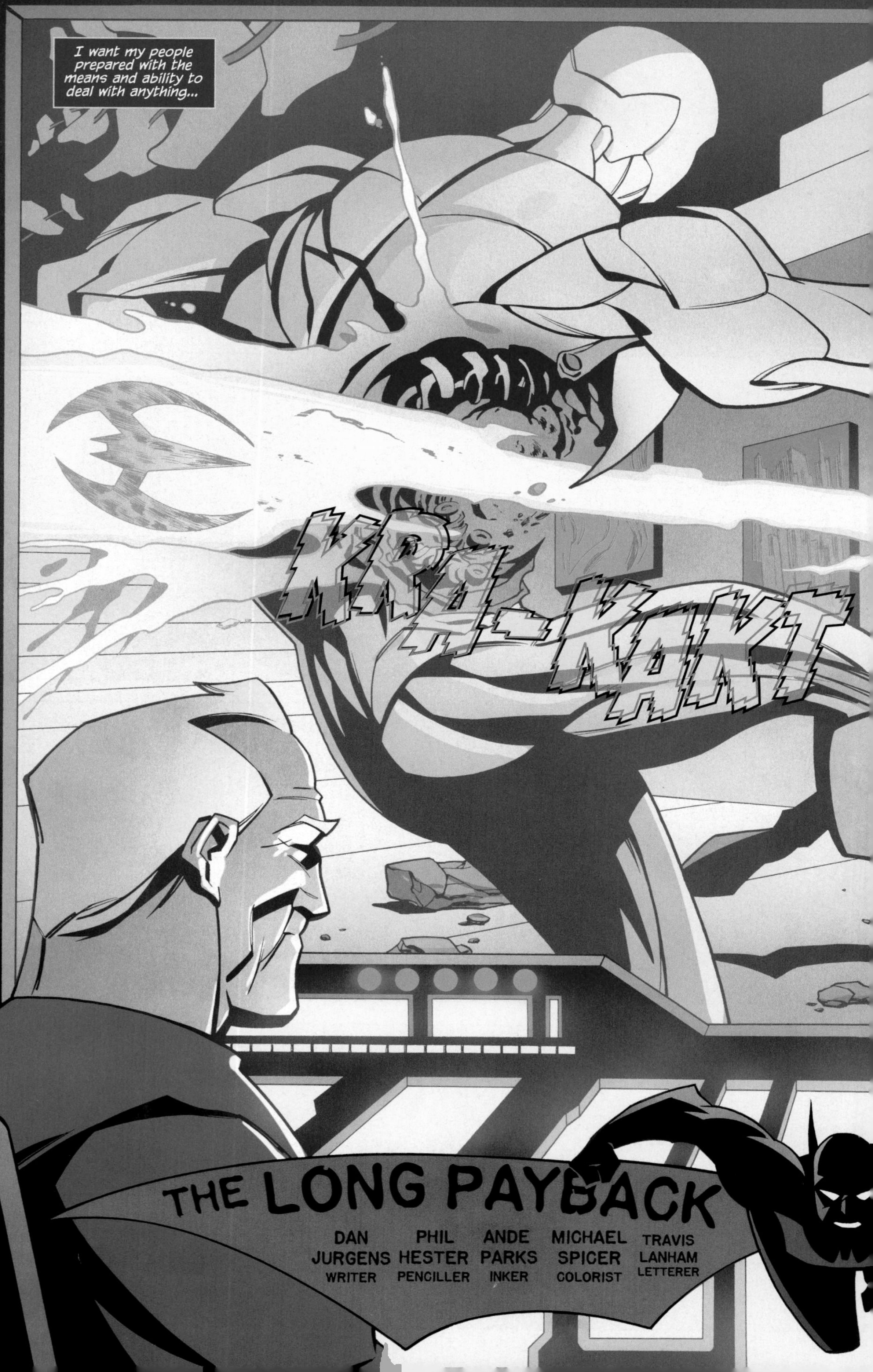
I want my people prepared with the means and ability to deal with anything...
KRA-KAKT
THE LONG PAYBACK
DAN JURGENS WRITER
PHIL HESTER PENCILLER
ANDE PARKS INKER
MICHAEL SPICER COLORIST
TRAVIS LANHAM LETTERER

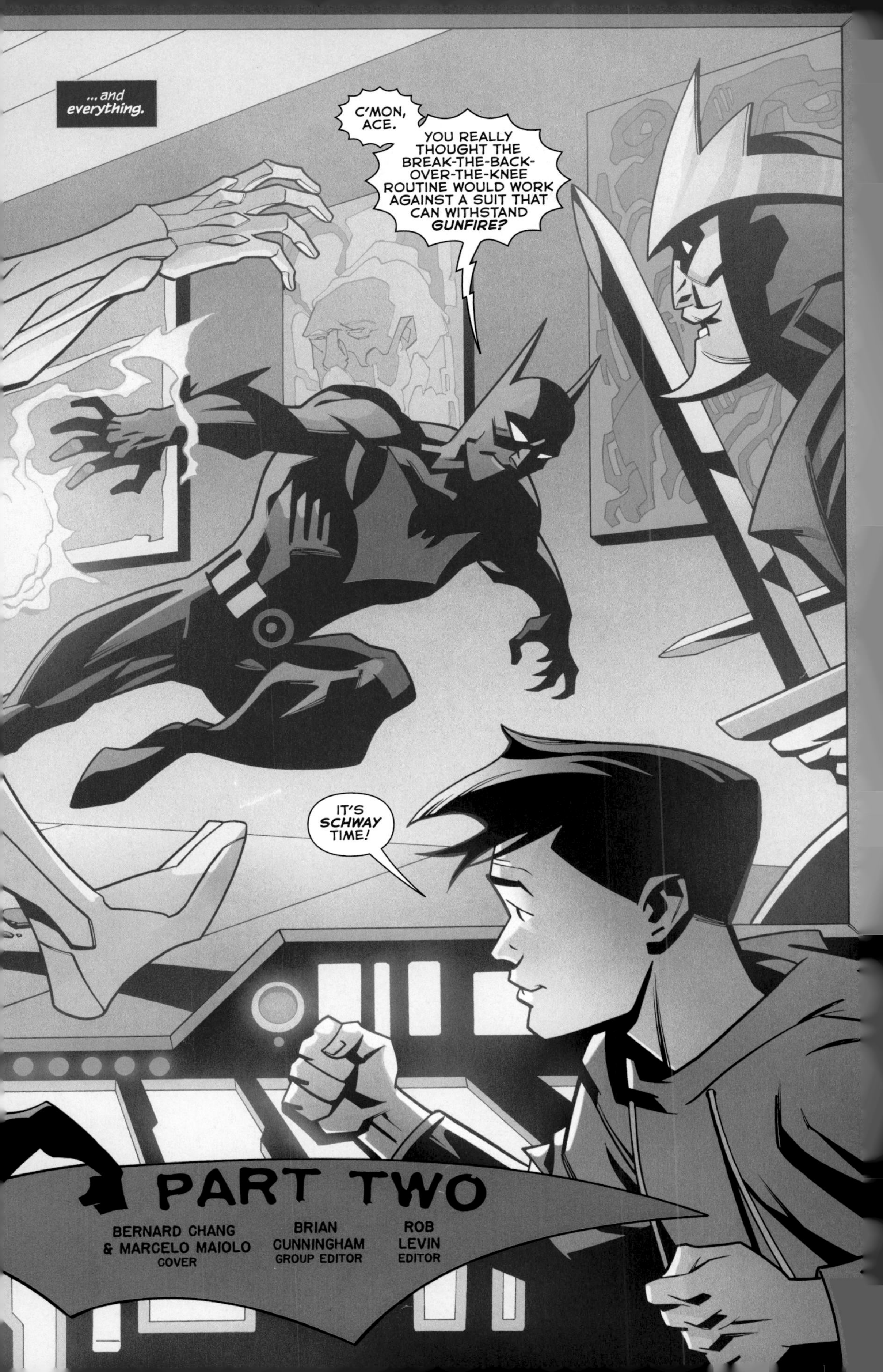
...and everything.
C'MON, ACE.
YOU REALLY THOUGHT THE BREAK-THE-BACK-OVER-THE-KNEE ROUTINE WOULD WORK AGAINST A SUIT THAT CAN WITHSTAND GUNFIRE?
IT'S SCHWAY TIME!
PART TWO
BERNARD CHANG & MARCELO MAIOLO COVER
BRIAN CUNNINGHAM GROUP EDITOR
ROB LEVIN EDITOR

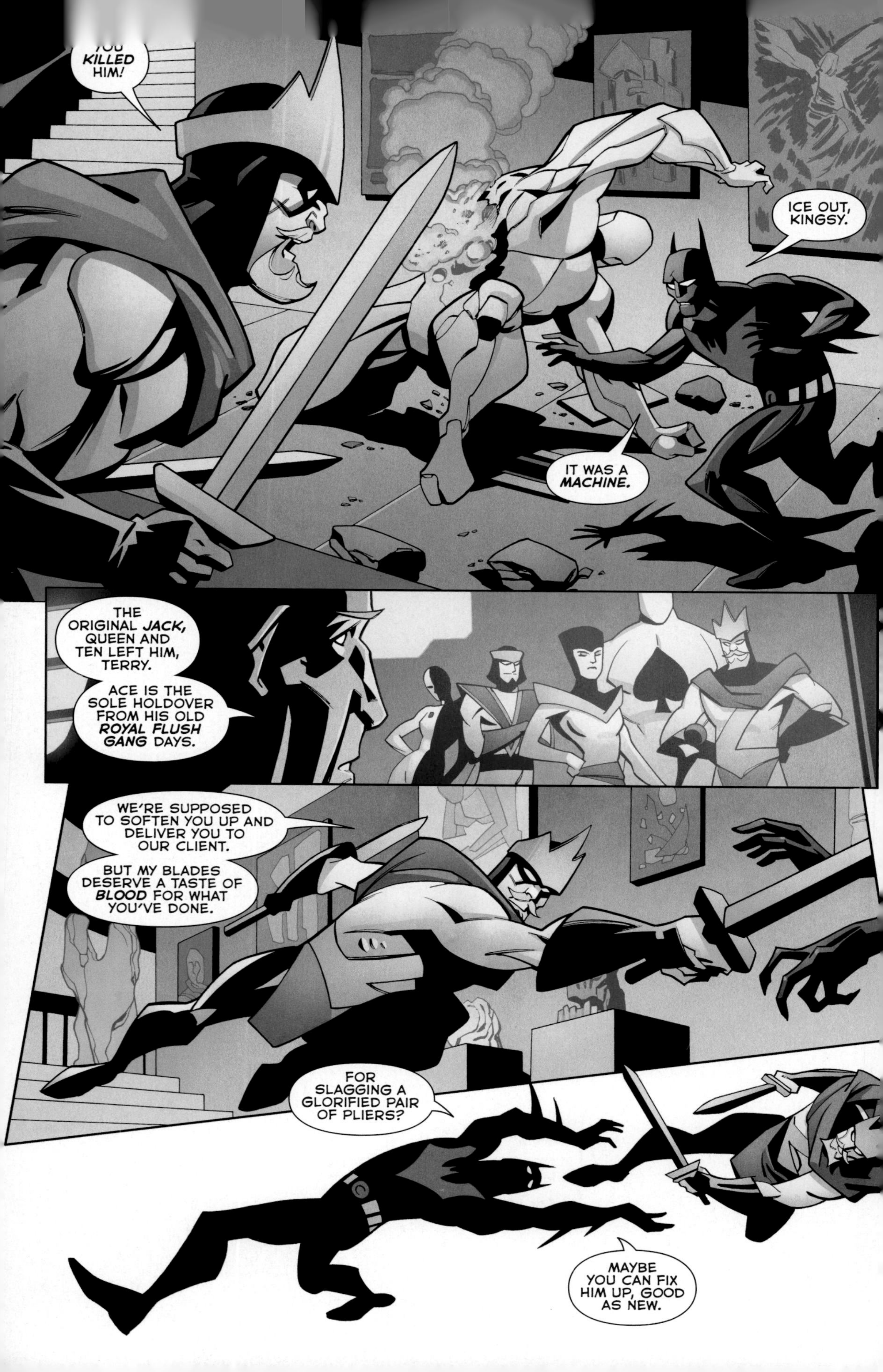
YOU KILLED HIM!
ICE OUT, KINGSY.
IT WAS A MACHINE.
THE ORIGINAL JACK, QUEEN AND TEN LEFT HIM, TERRY.
ACE IS THE SOLE HOLDOVER FROM HIS OLD ROYAL FLUSH GANG DAYS.
WE'RE SUPPOSED TO SOFTEN YOU UP AND DELIVER YOU TO OUR CLIENT.
BUT MY BLADES DESERVE A TASTE OF BLOOD FOR WHAT YOU'VE DONE.
FOR SLAGGING A GLORIFIED PAIR OF PLIERS?
MAYBE YOU CAN FIX HIM UP, GOOD AS NEW.

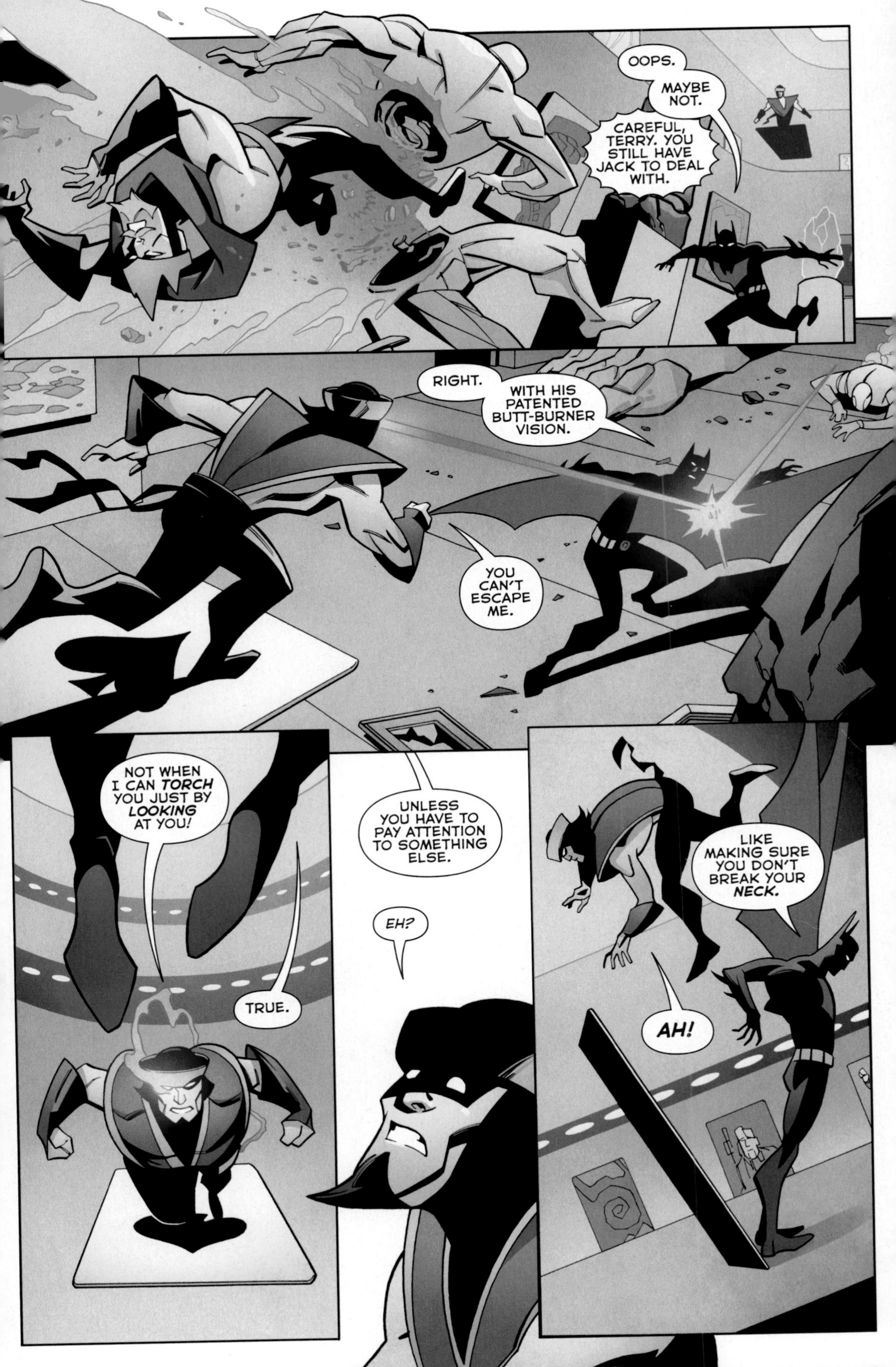
OOPS.
MAYBE NOT.
CAREFUL, TERRY. YOU STILL HAVE JACK TO DEAL WITH.
RIGHT.
WITH HIS PATENTED BUTT-BURNER VISION.
YOU CAN'T ESCAPE ME.
NOT WHEN I CAN TORCH YOU JUST BY LOOKING AT YOU!
TRUE.
UNLESS YOU HAVE TO PAY ATTENTION TO SOMETHING ELSE.
EH?
LIKE MAKING SURE YOU DON'T BREAK YOUR NECK.
AH!

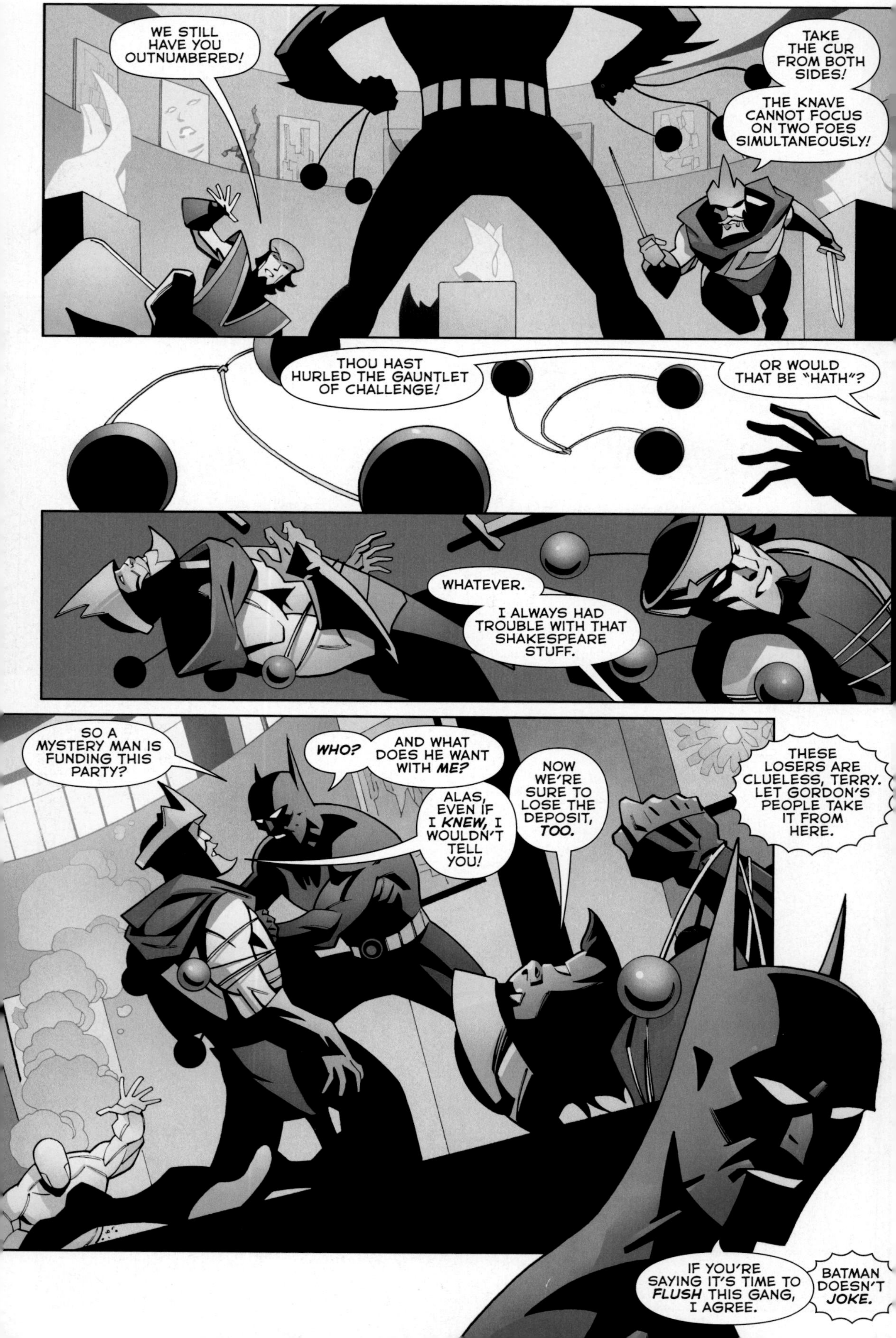
WE STILL HAVE YOU OUTNUMBERED!
TAKE THE CUR FROM BOTH SIDES!
THE KNAVE CANNOT FOCUS ON TWO FOES SIMULTANEOUSLY!
THOU HAST HURLED THE GAUNTLET OF CHALLENGE!
OR WOULD THAT BE "HATH"?
WHATEVER.
I ALWAYS HAD TROUBLE WITH THAT SHAKESPEARE STUFF.
SO A MYSTERY MAN IS FUNDING THIS PARTY?
WHO? AND WHAT DOES HE WANT WITH ME?
ALAS, EVEN IF I KNEW, I WOULDN'T TELL YOU!
NOW WE'RE SURE TO LOSE THE DEPOSIT, TOO.
THESE LOSERS ARE CLUELESS, TERRY. LET GORDON'S PEOPLE TAKE IT FROM HERE.
IF YOU'RE SAYING IT'S TIME TO FLUSH THIS GANG, I AGREE.
BATMAN DOESN'T JOKE.

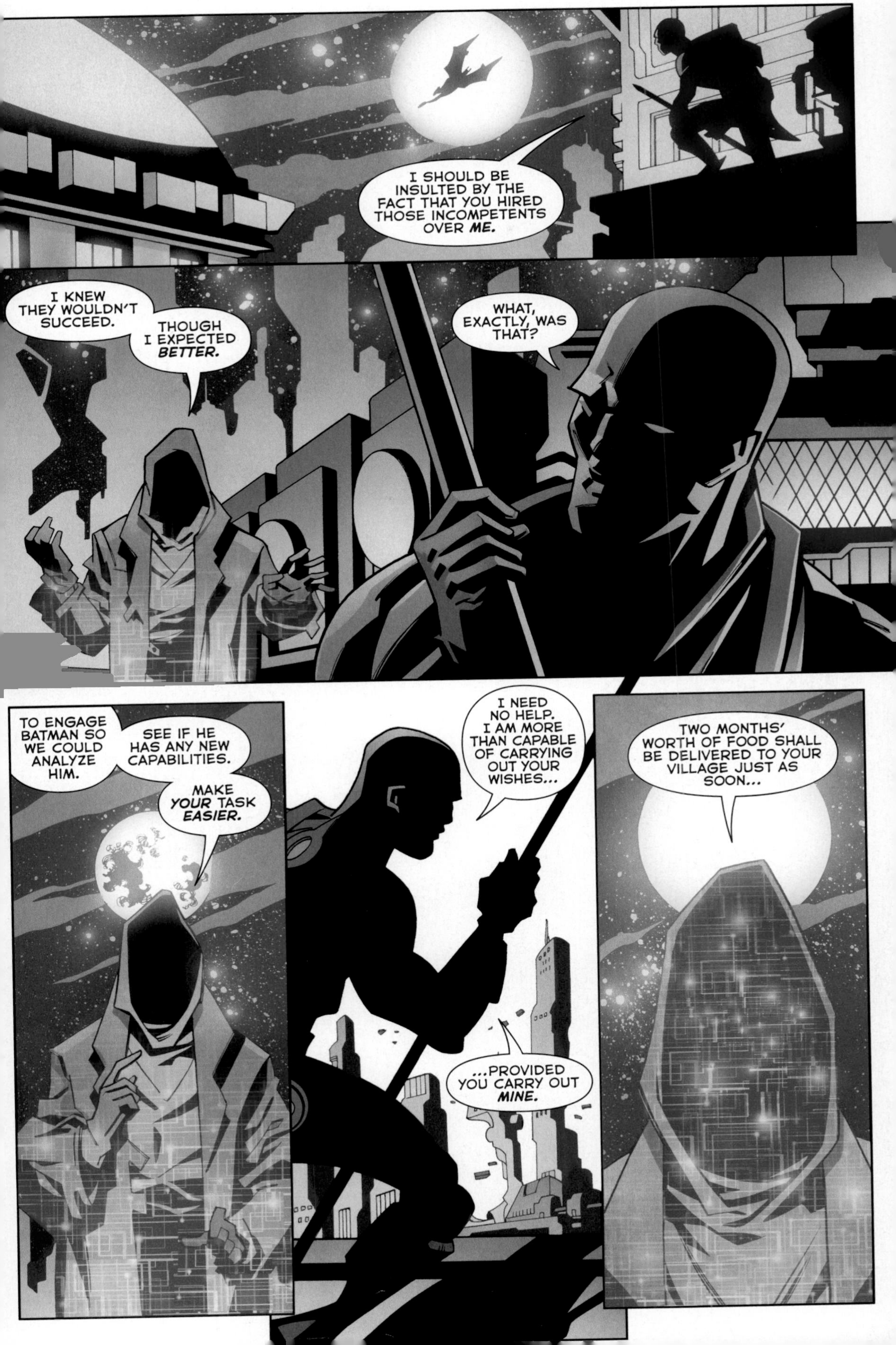
I SHOULD BE INSULTED BY THE FACT THAT YOU HIRED THOSE INCOMPETENTS OVER *ME.*
I KNEW THEY WOULDN'T SUCCEED.
THOUGH I EXPECTED *BETTER.*
WHAT, EXACTLY, WAS THAT?
TO ENGAGE BATMAN SO WE COULD ANALYZE HIM.
SEE IF HE HAS ANY NEW CAPABILITIES.
MAKE *YOUR* TASK *EASIER.*
I NEED NO HELP. I AM MORE THAN CAPABLE OF CARRYING OUT YOUR WISHES...
...PROVIDED YOU CARRY OUT *MINE.*
TWO MONTHS' WORTH OF FOOD SHALL BE DELIVERED TO YOUR VILLAGE JUST AS SOON...

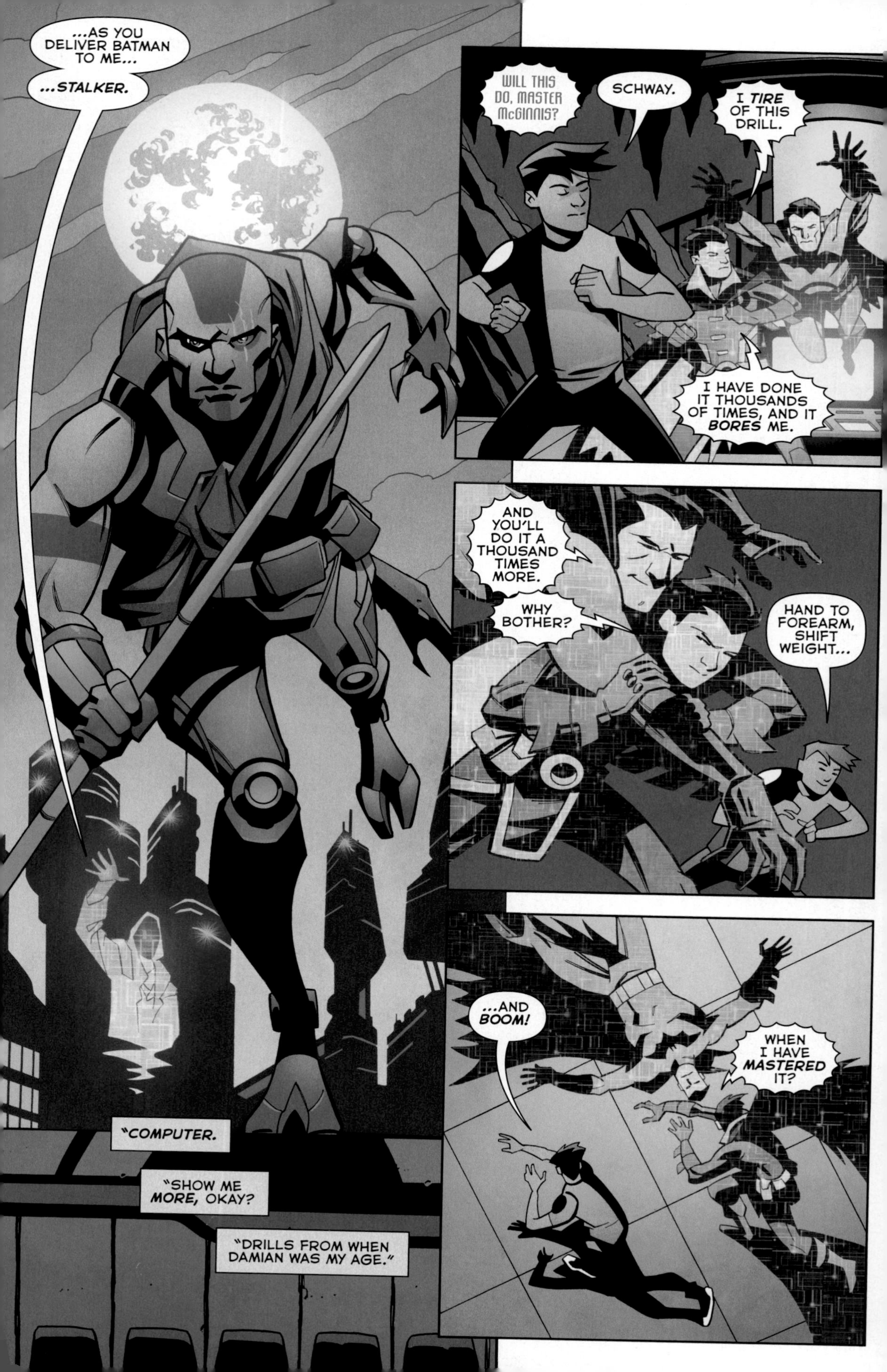
...AS YOU DELIVER BATMAN TO ME...
...STALKER.
WILL THIS DO, MASTER McGINNIS?
SCHWAY.
I TIRE OF THIS DRILL.
I HAVE DONE IT THOUSANDS OF TIMES, AND IT BORES ME.
AND YOU'LL DO IT A THOUSAND TIMES MORE.
WHY BOTHER?
HAND TO FOREARM, SHIFT WEIGHT...
...AND BOOM!
WHEN I HAVE MASTERED IT?
"COMPUTER.
"SHOW ME MORE, OKAY?
"DRILLS FROM WHEN DAMIAN WAS MY AGE."

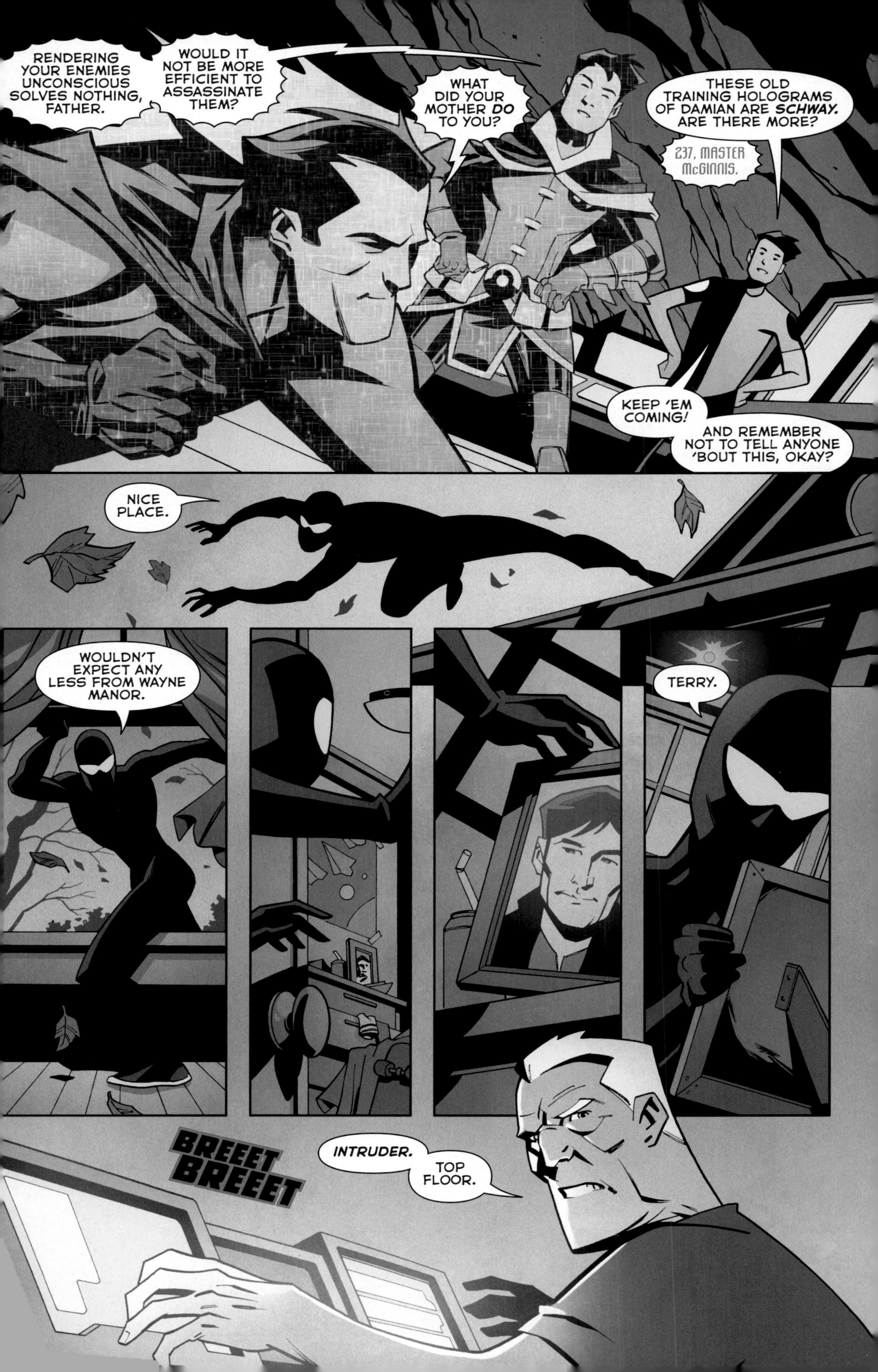
RENDERING YOUR ENEMIES UNCONSCIOUS SOLVES NOTHING, FATHER.
WOULD IT NOT BE MORE EFFICIENT TO ASSASSINATE THEM?
WHAT DID YOUR MOTHER *DO* TO YOU?
THESE OLD TRAINING HOLOGRAMS OF DAMIAN ARE *SCHWAY.* ARE THERE MORE?
237, MASTER McGINNIS.
KEEP 'EM COMING!
AND REMEMBER NOT TO TELL ANYONE 'BOUT THIS, OKAY?
NICE PLACE.
WOULDN'T EXPECT ANY LESS FROM WAYNE MANOR.
TERRY.
BREEET BREEET
INTRUDER.
TOP FLOOR.

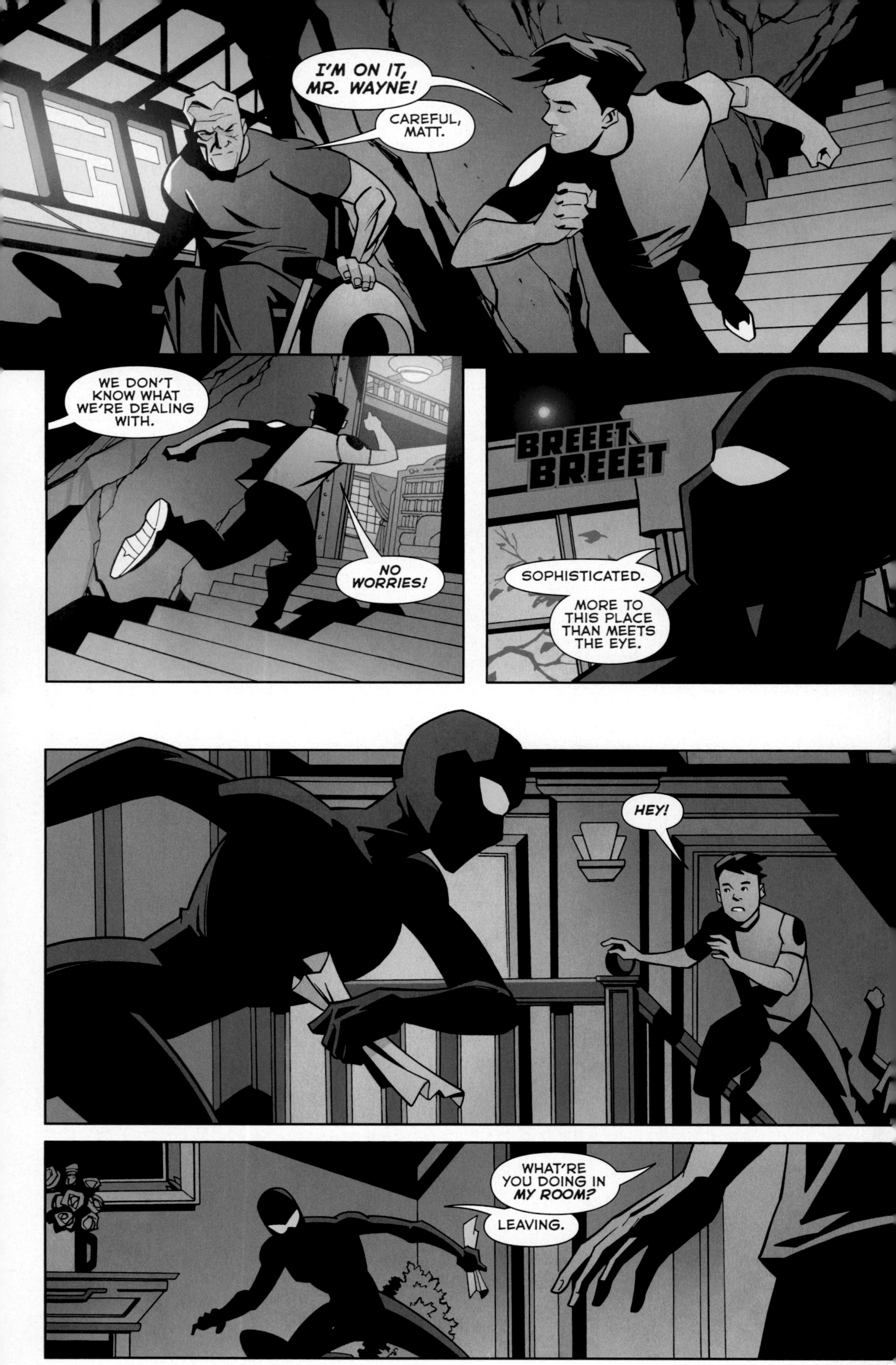
I'M ON IT, MR. WAYNE!
CAREFUL, MATT.
WE DON'T KNOW WHAT WE'RE DEALING WITH.
NO WORRIES!
BREEET BREEET
SOPHISTICATED.
MORE TO THIS PLACE THAN MEETS THE EYE.
HEY!
WHAT'RE YOU DOING IN MY ROOM?
LEAVING.

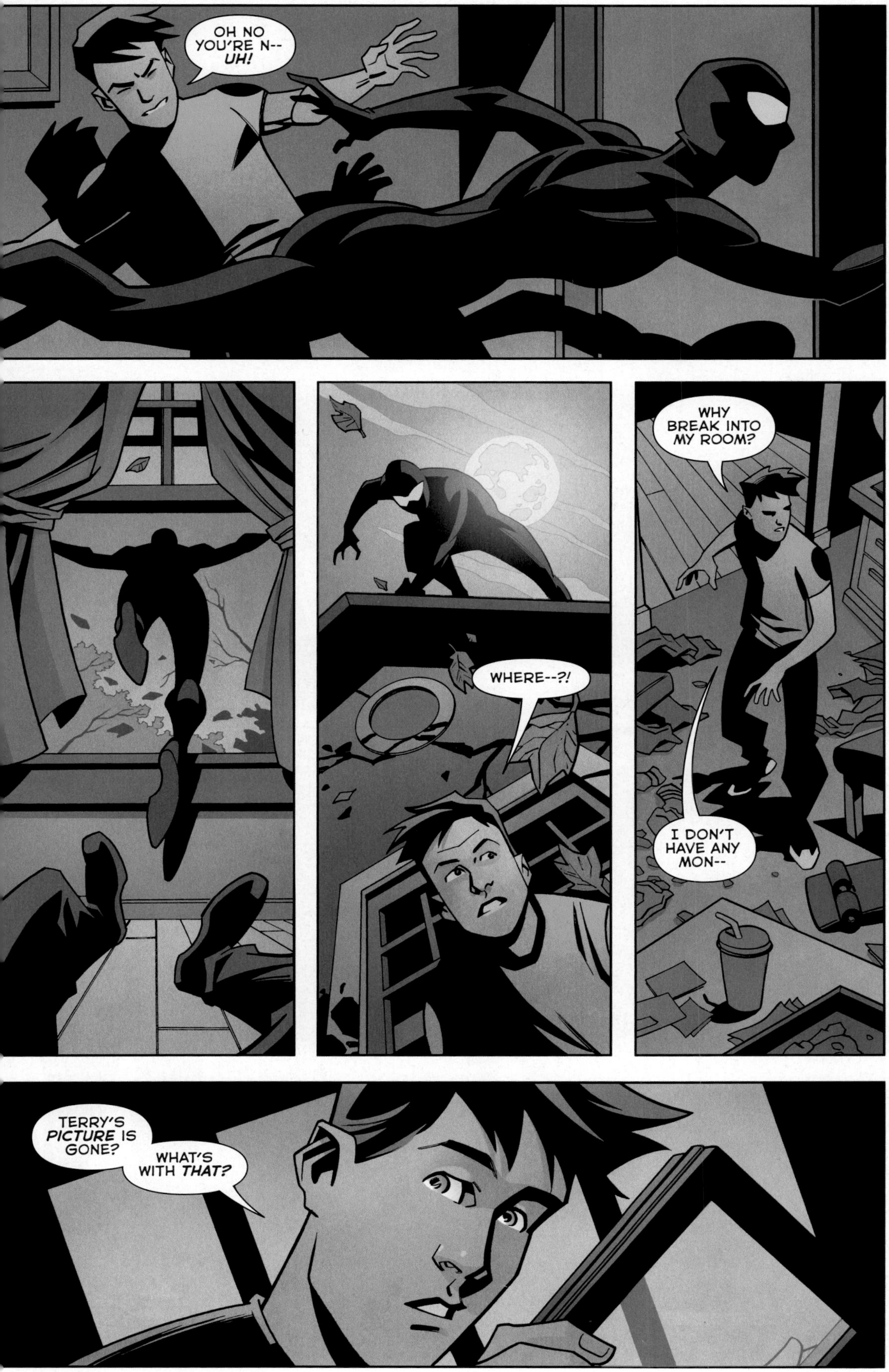
OH NO YOU'RE N-- UH!
WHY BREAK INTO MY ROOM?
WHERE--?!
I DON'T HAVE ANY MON--
TERRY'S PICTURE IS GONE?
WHAT'S WITH THAT?

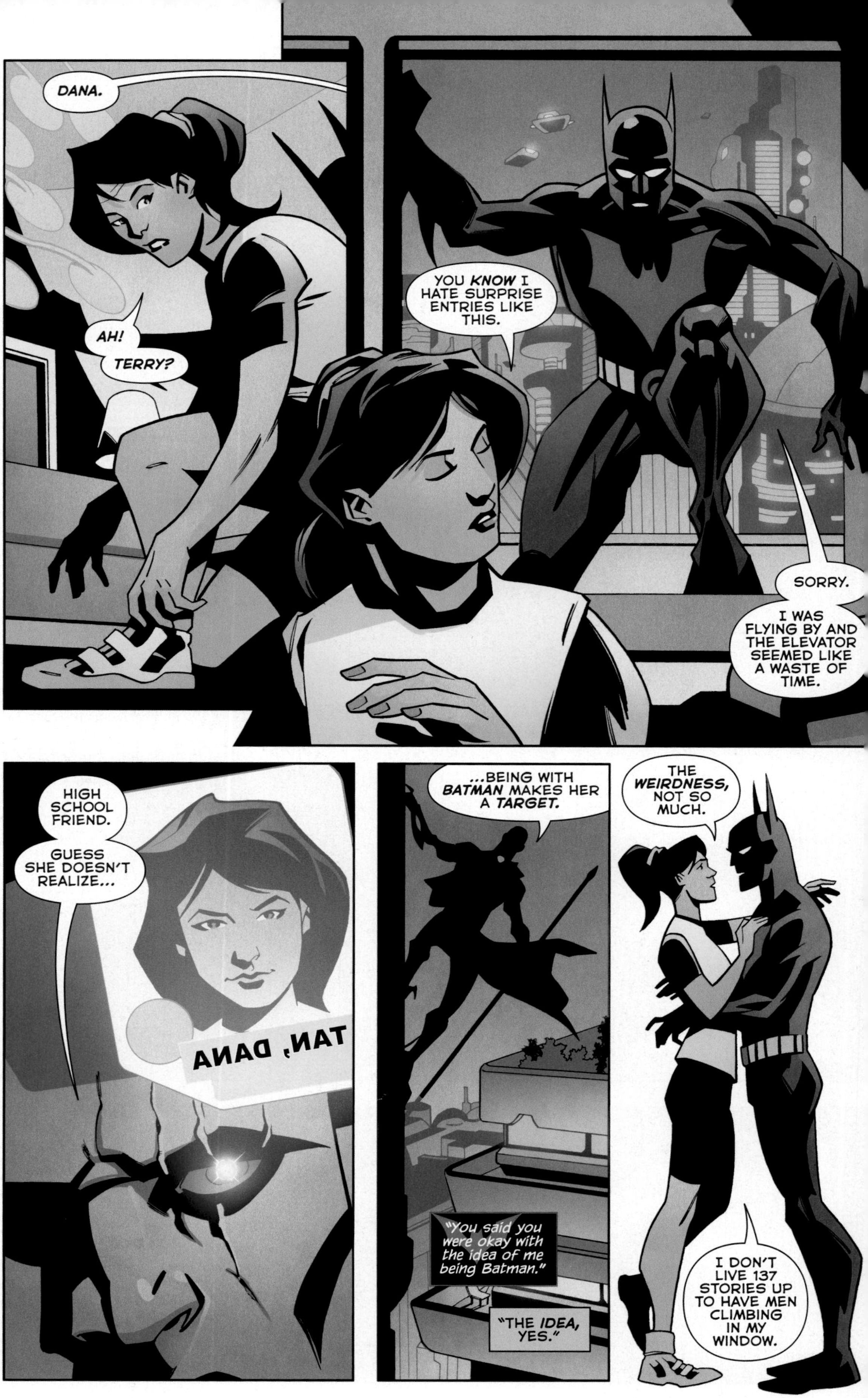
DANA.
AH!
TERRY?
YOU *KNOW* I HATE SURPRISE ENTRIES LIKE THIS.
SORRY.
I WAS FLYING BY AND THE ELEVATOR SEEMED LIKE A WASTE OF TIME.
HIGH SCHOOL FRIEND.
GUESS SHE DOESN'T REALIZE...
TAN, DANA
...BEING WITH *BATMAN* MAKES HER A *TARGET.*
"You said you were okay with the idea of me being Batman."
"THE *IDEA,* YES."
THE *WEIRDNESS,* NOT SO MUCH.
I DON'T LIVE 137 STORIES UP TO HAVE MEN CLIMBING IN MY WINDOW.

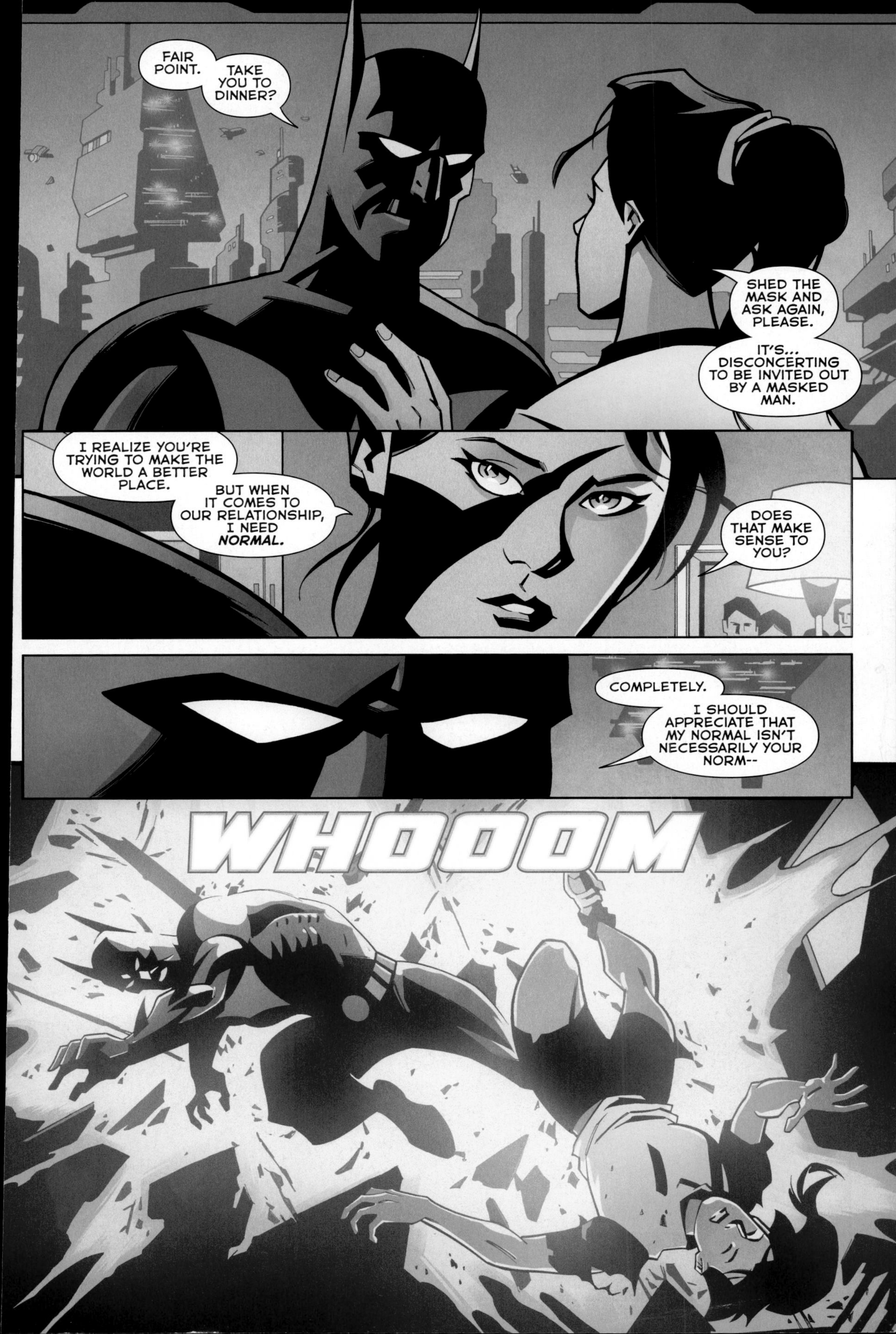
FAIR POINT.
TAKE YOU TO DINNER?
SHED THE MASK AND ASK AGAIN, PLEASE.
IT'S... DISCONCERTING TO BE INVITED OUT BY A MASKED MAN.
I REALIZE YOU'RE TRYING TO MAKE THE WORLD A BETTER PLACE.
BUT WHEN IT COMES TO OUR RELATIONSHIP, I NEED *NORMAL.*
DOES THAT MAKE SENSE TO YOU?
COMPLETELY.
I SHOULD APPRECIATE THAT MY NORMAL ISN'T NECESSARILY YOUR NORM--
WHOOOM

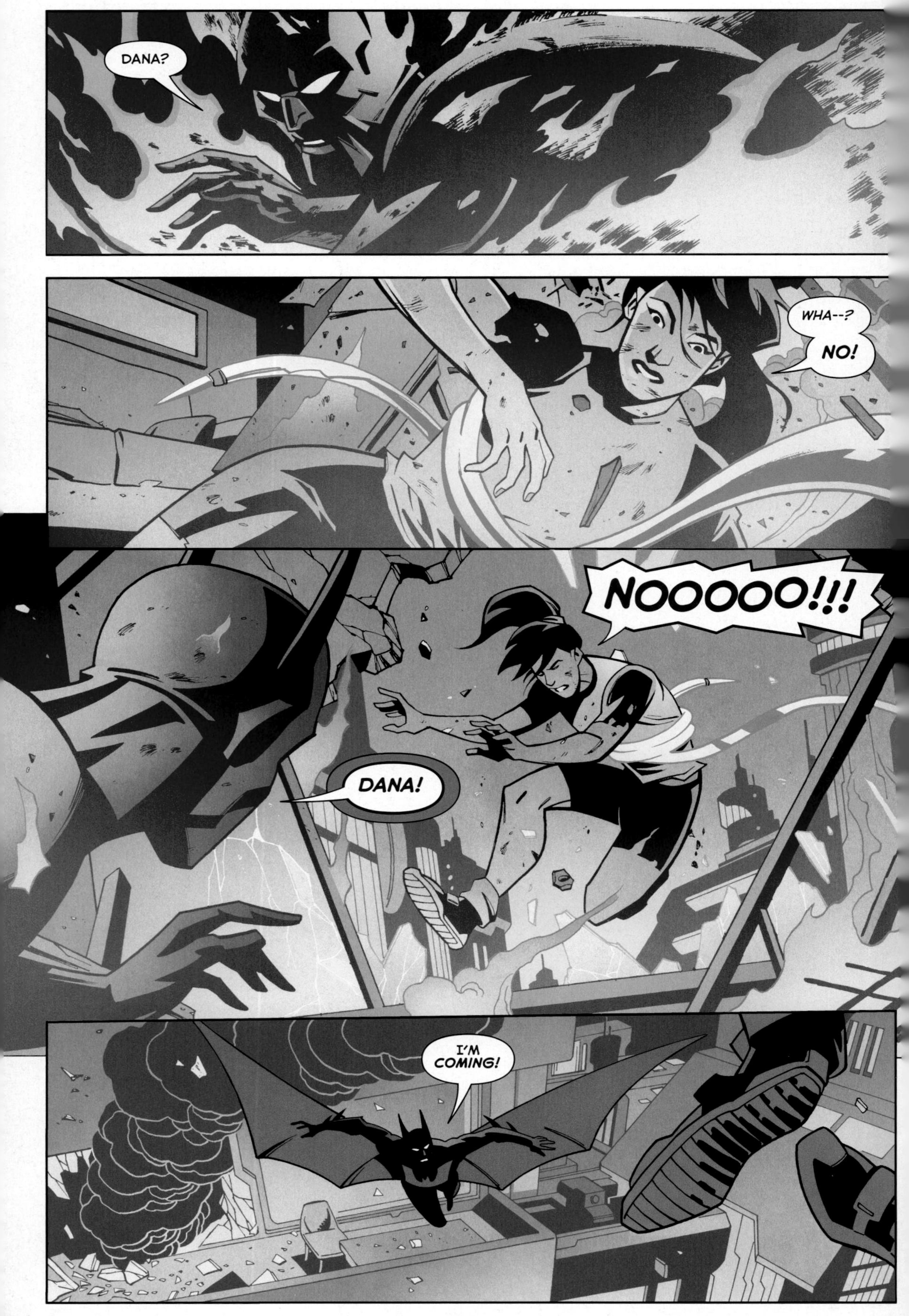
DANA?
WHA--?
NO!
NOOOOO!!!
DANA!
I'M COMING!

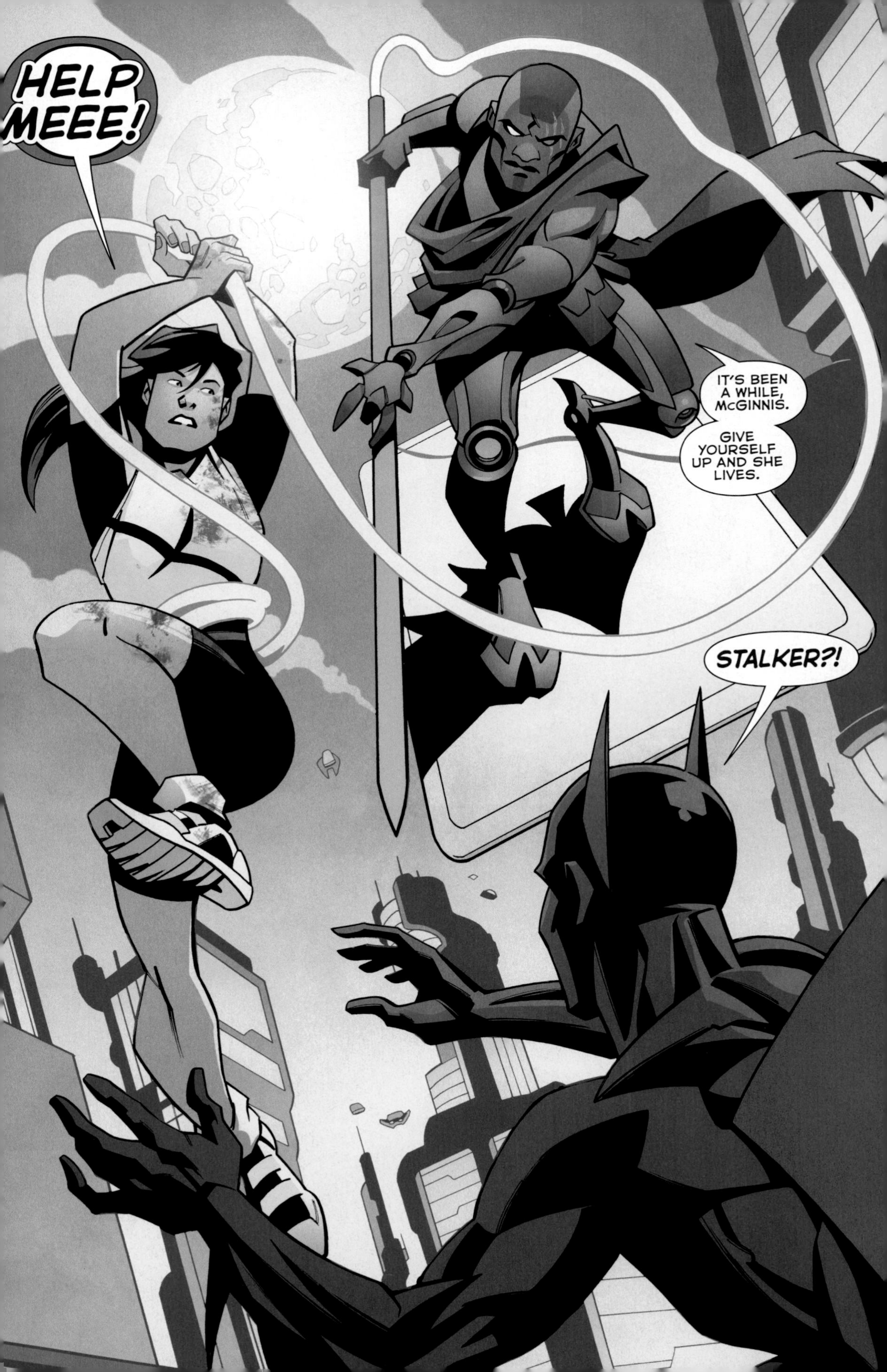
HELP MEEE!
IT'S BEEN A WHILE, McGINNIS.
GIVE YOURSELF UP AND SHE LIVES.
STALKER?!

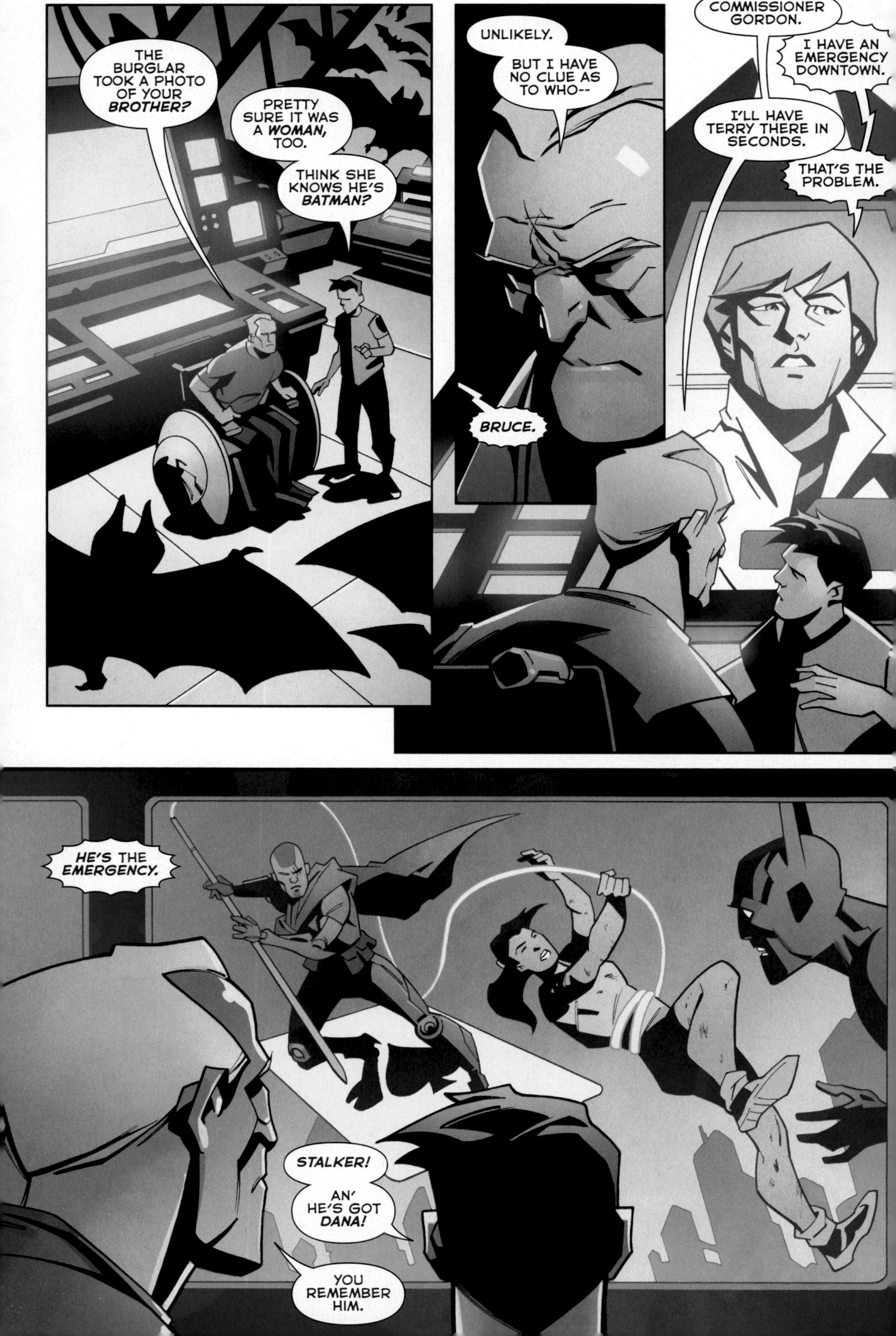
THE BURGLAR TOOK A PHOTO OF YOUR BROTHER?
PRETTY SURE IT WAS A WOMAN, TOO.
THINK SHE KNOWS HE'S BATMAN?
UNLIKELY.
BUT I HAVE NO CLUE AS TO WHO--
BRUCE.
COMMISSIONER GORDON.
I HAVE AN EMERGENCY DOWNTOWN.
I'LL HAVE TERRY THERE IN SECONDS.
THAT'S THE PROBLEM.
HE'S THE EMERGENCY.
STALKER!
AN' HE'S GOT DANA!
YOU REMEMBER HIM.

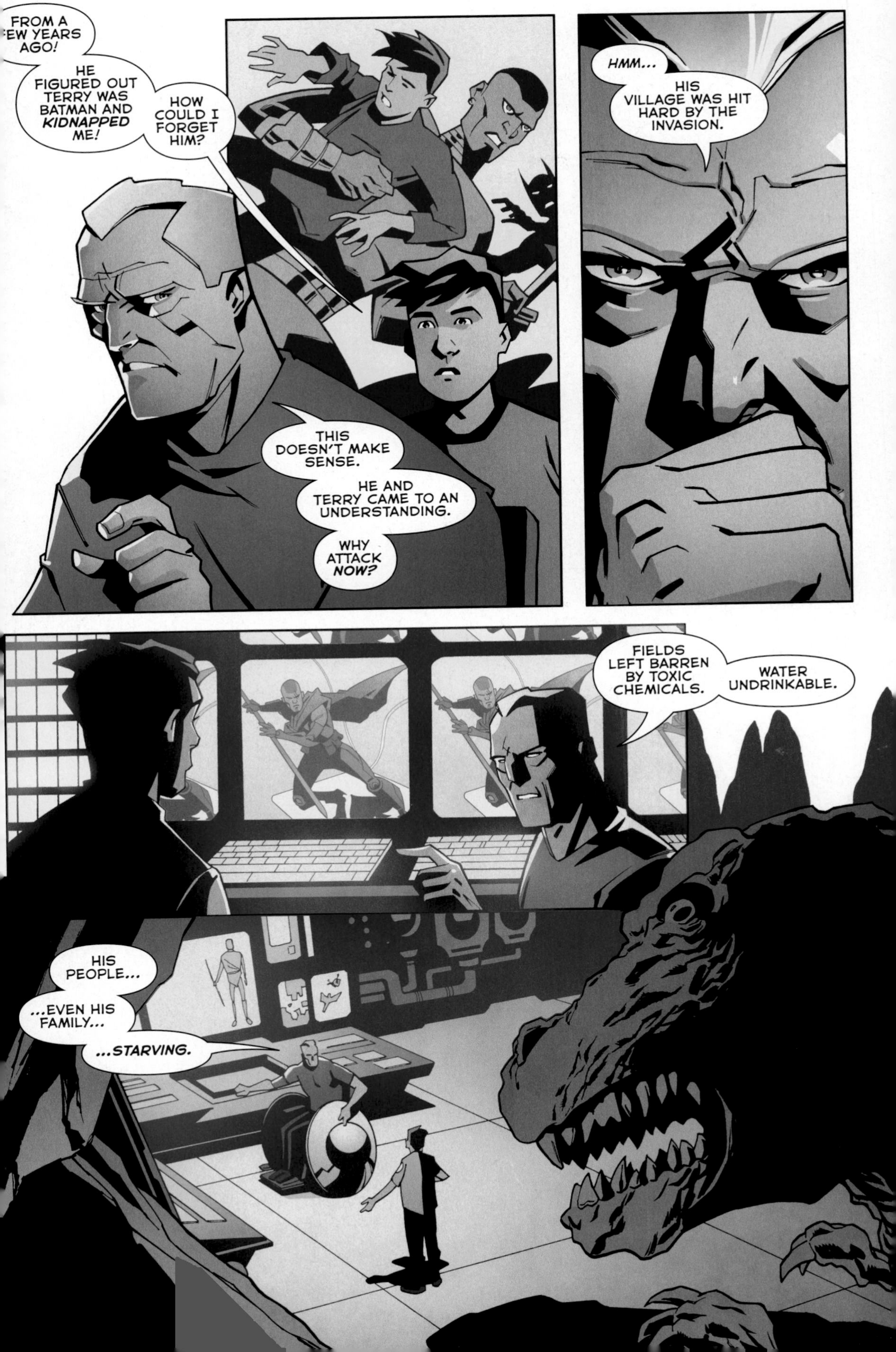

FROM A FEW YEARS AGO!
HE FIGURED OUT TERRY WAS BATMAN AND KIDNAPPED ME!
HOW COULD I FORGET HIM?
THIS DOESN'T MAKE SENSE.
HE AND TERRY CAME TO AN UNDERSTANDING.
WHY ATTACK NOW?
HMM...
HIS VILLAGE WAS HIT HARD BY THE INVASION.
FIELDS LEFT BARREN BY TOXIC CHEMICALS.
WATER UNDRINKABLE.
HIS PEOPLE...
...EVEN HIS FAMILY...
...STARVING.

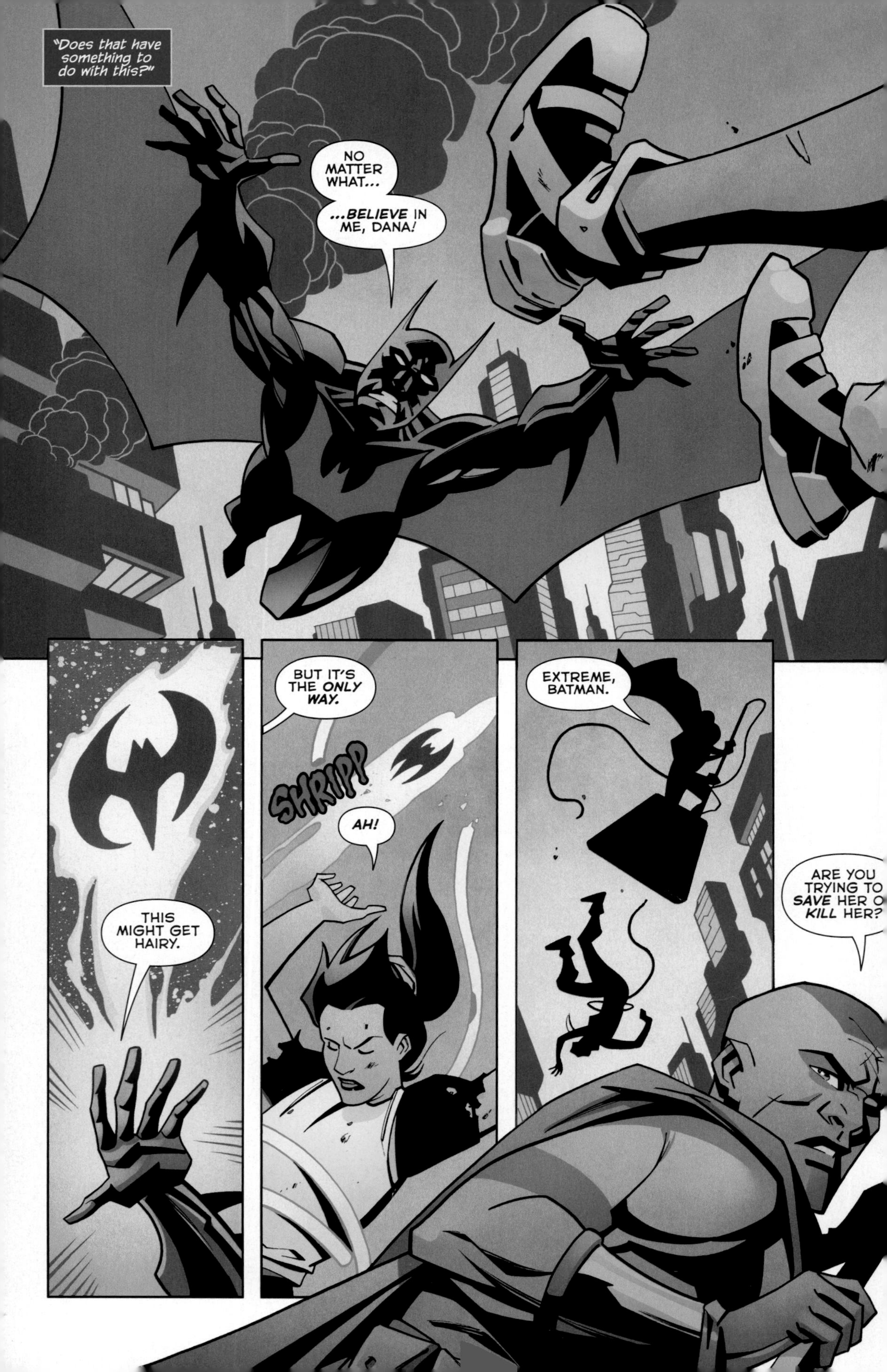
"Does that have something to do with this?"
NO MATTER WHAT...
...BELIEVE IN ME, DANA!
THIS MIGHT GET HAIRY.
BUT IT'S THE ONLY WAY.
SHRIPP
AH!
EXTREME, BATMAN.
ARE YOU TRYING TO SAVE HER O KILL HER?

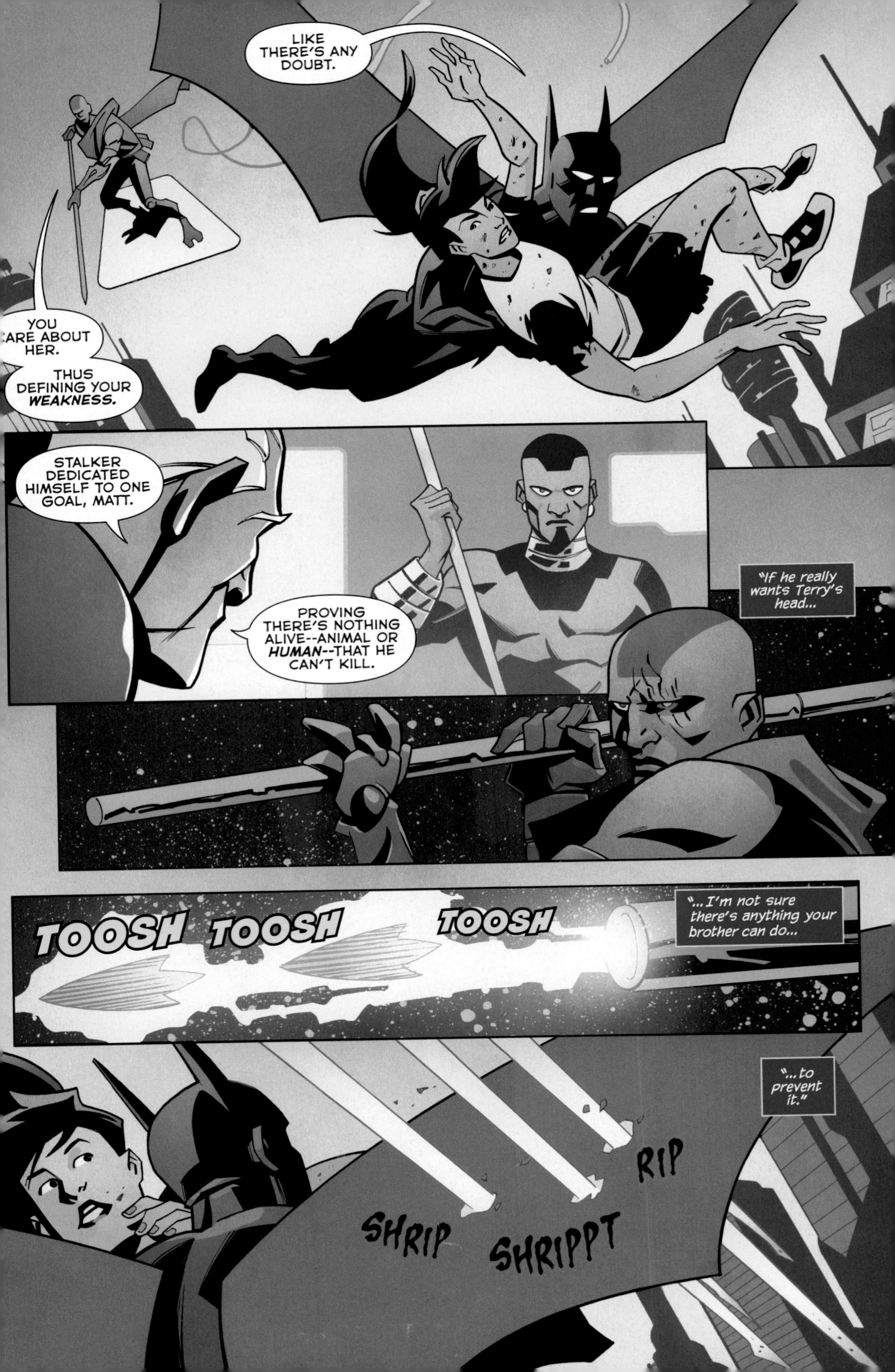
LIKE THERE'S ANY DOUBT.
YOU CARE ABOUT HER.
THUS DEFINING YOUR *WEAKNESS.*
STALKER DEDICATED HIMSELF TO ONE GOAL, MATT.
PROVING THERE'S NOTHING ALIVE--ANIMAL OR *HUMAN*--THAT HE CAN'T KILL.
"If he really wants Terry's head...
TOOSH TOOSH TOOSH
"...I'm not sure there's anything your brother can do...
"...to prevent it."
RIP
SHRIP
SHRIPPT

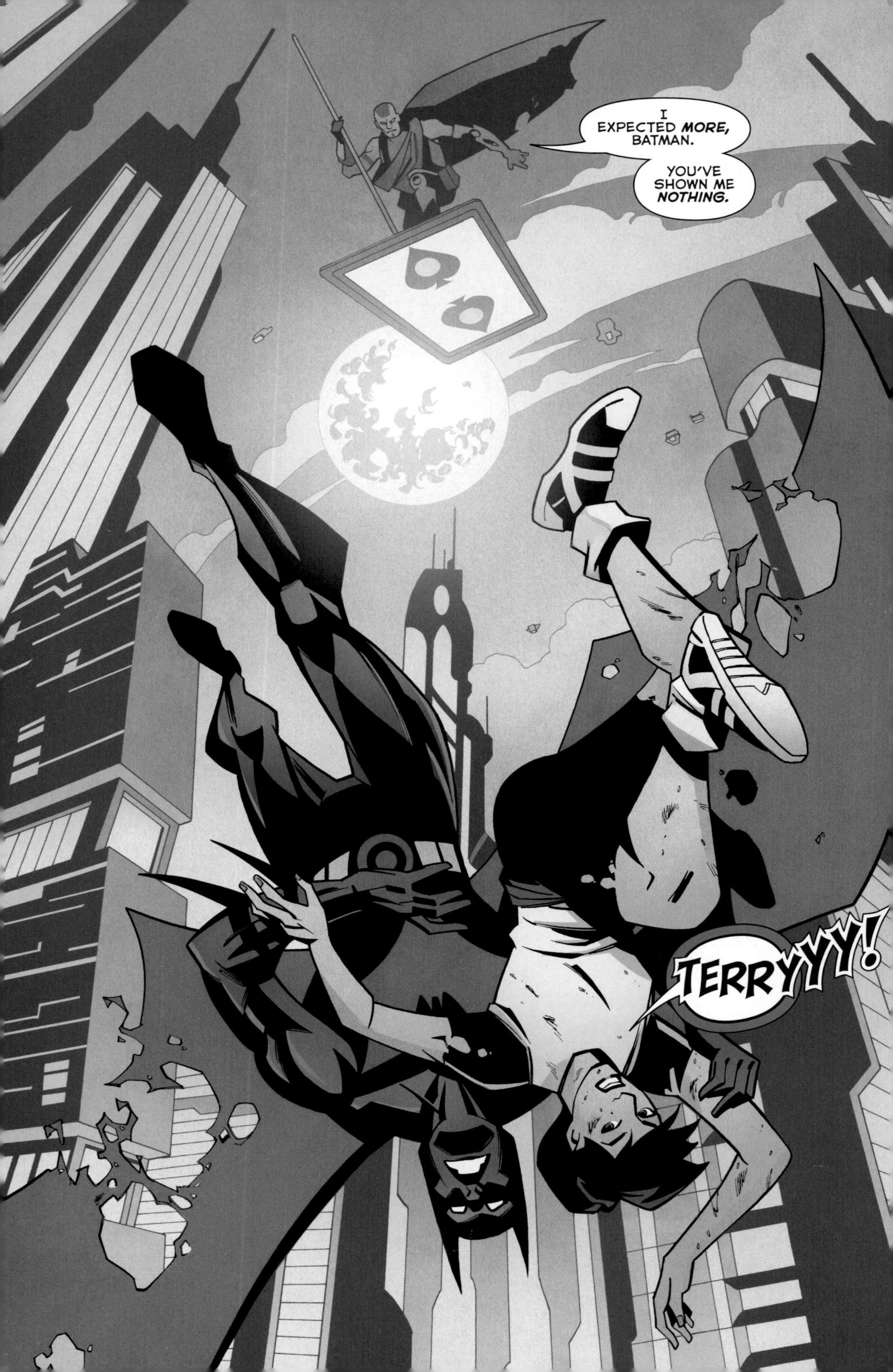
I EXPECTED MORE, BATMAN.
YOU'VE SHOWN ME NOTHING.
TERRYYY!

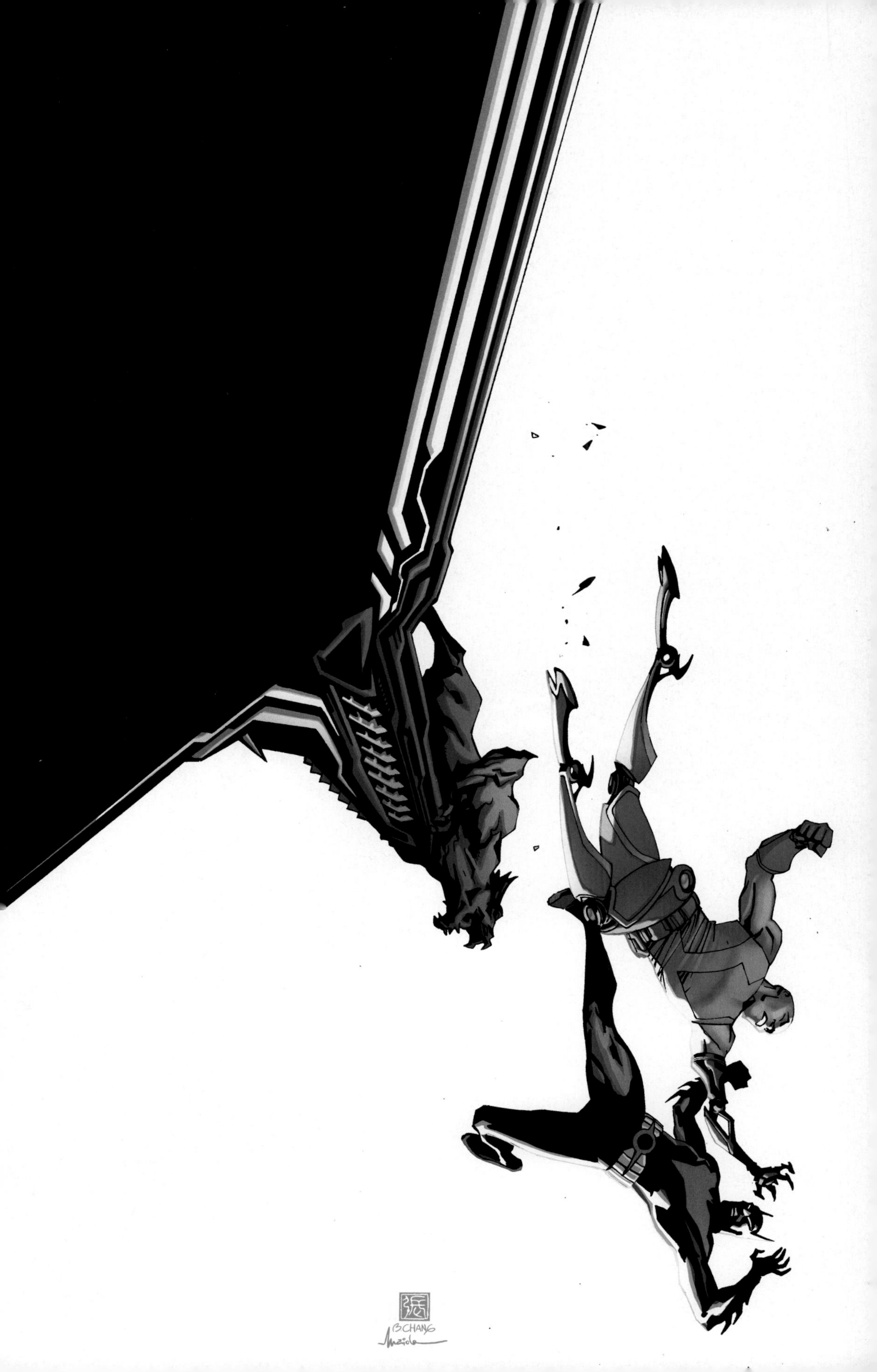

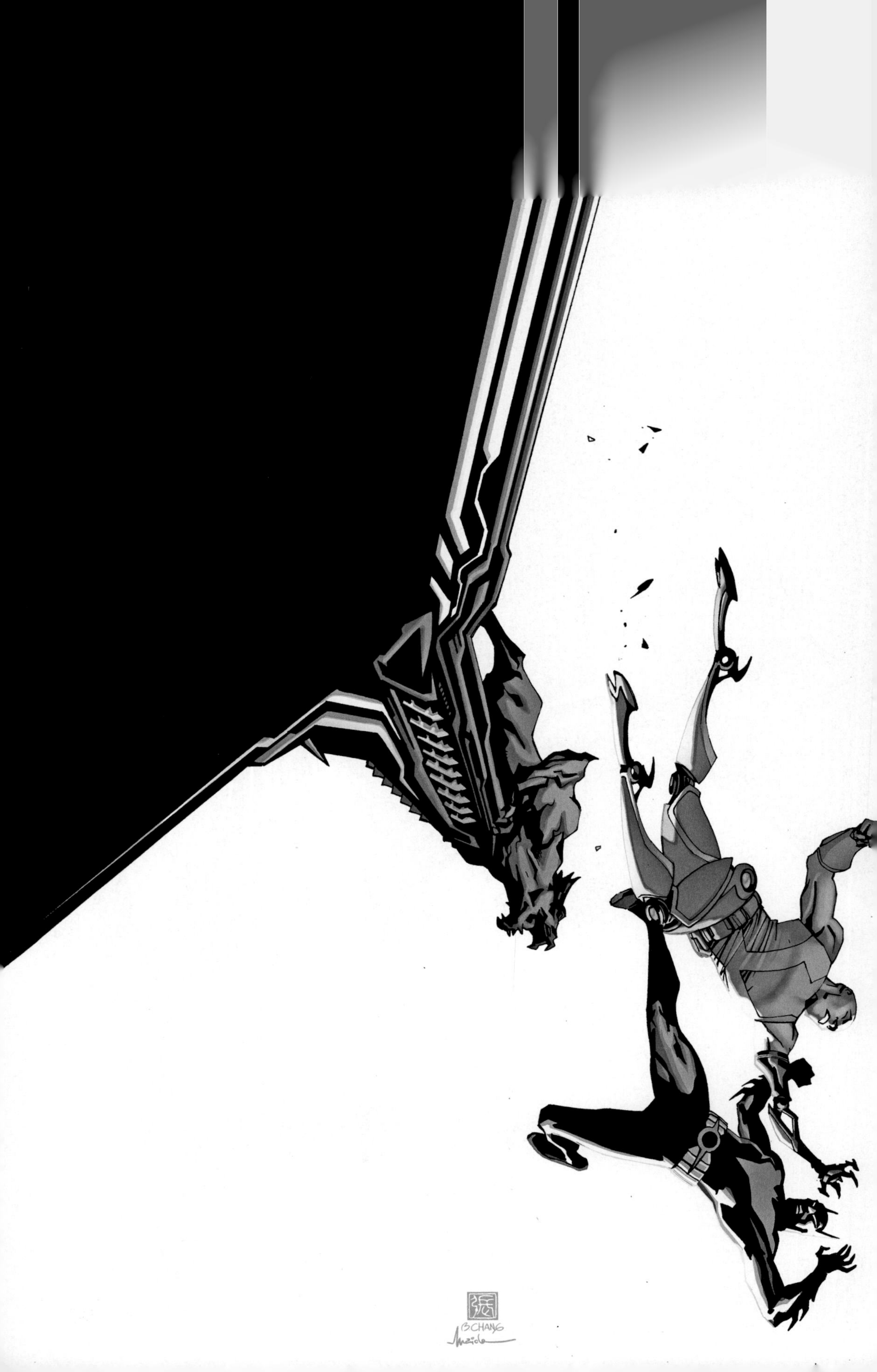
B CHANG

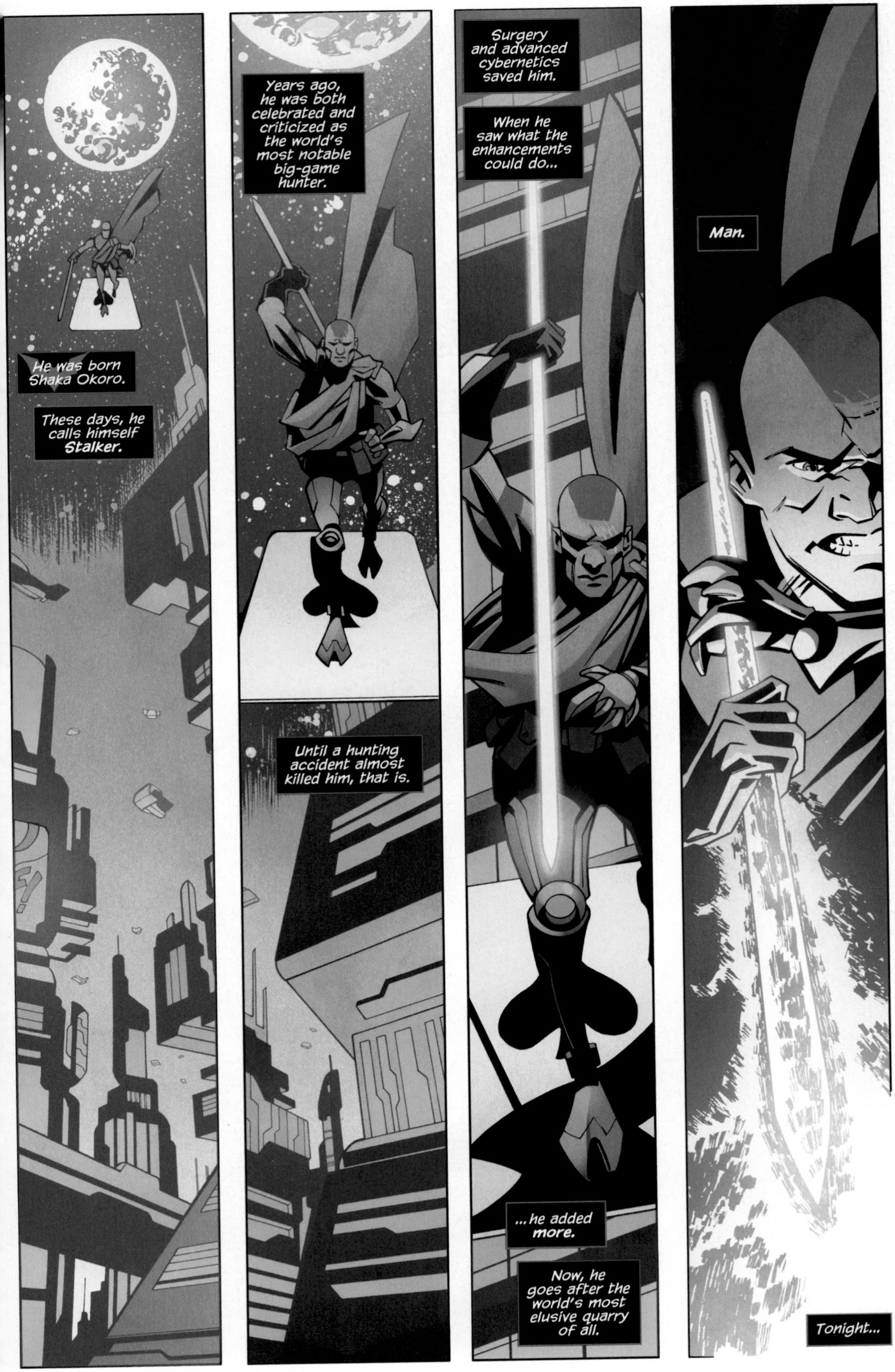
He was born Shaka Okoro.
These days, he calls himself Stalker.
Years ago, he was both celebrated and criticized as the world's most notable big-game hunter.
Until a hunting accident almost killed him, that is.
Surgery and advanced cybernetics saved him.
When he saw what the enhancements could do...
...he added more.
Now, he goes after the world's most elusive quarry of all.
Man.
Tonight...

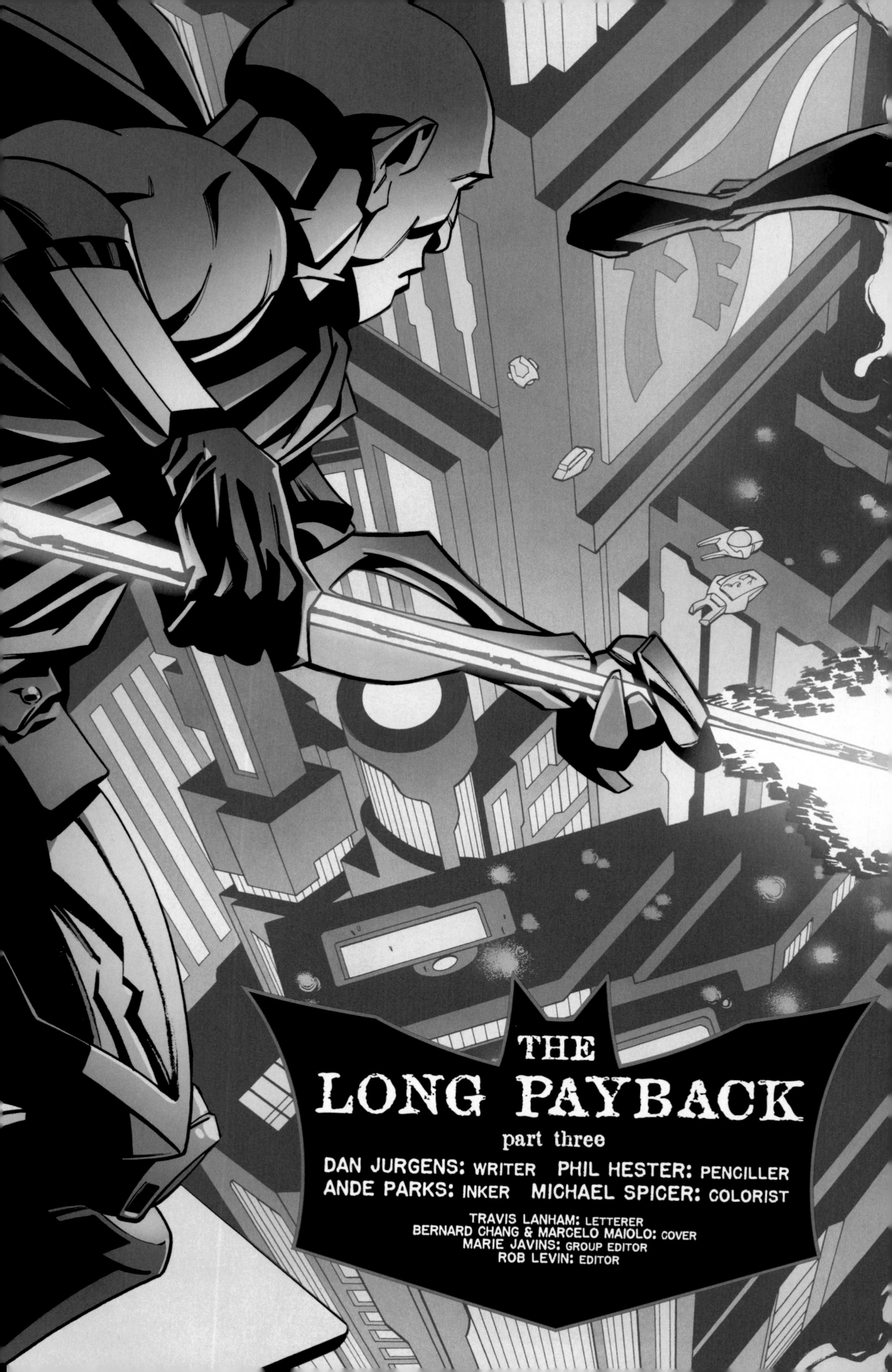
THE
LONG PAYBACK
part three
DAN JURGENS: WRITER PHIL HESTER: PENCILLER
ANDE PARKS: INKER MICHAEL SPICER: COLORIST
TRAVIS LANHAM: LETTERER
BERNARD CHANG & MARCELO MAIOLO: COVER
MARIE JAVINS: GROUP EDITOR
ROB LEVIN: EDITOR

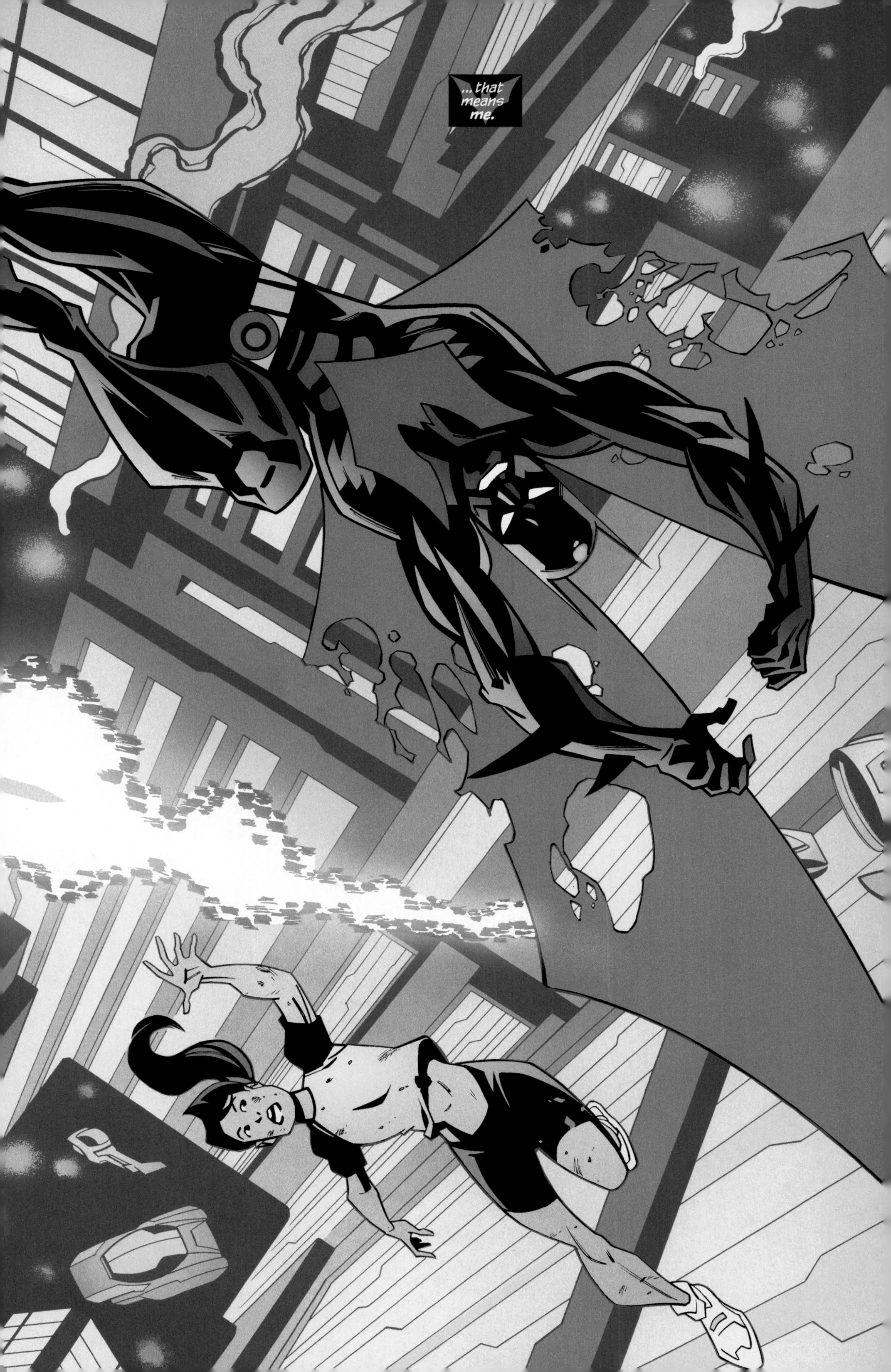
...that means me.

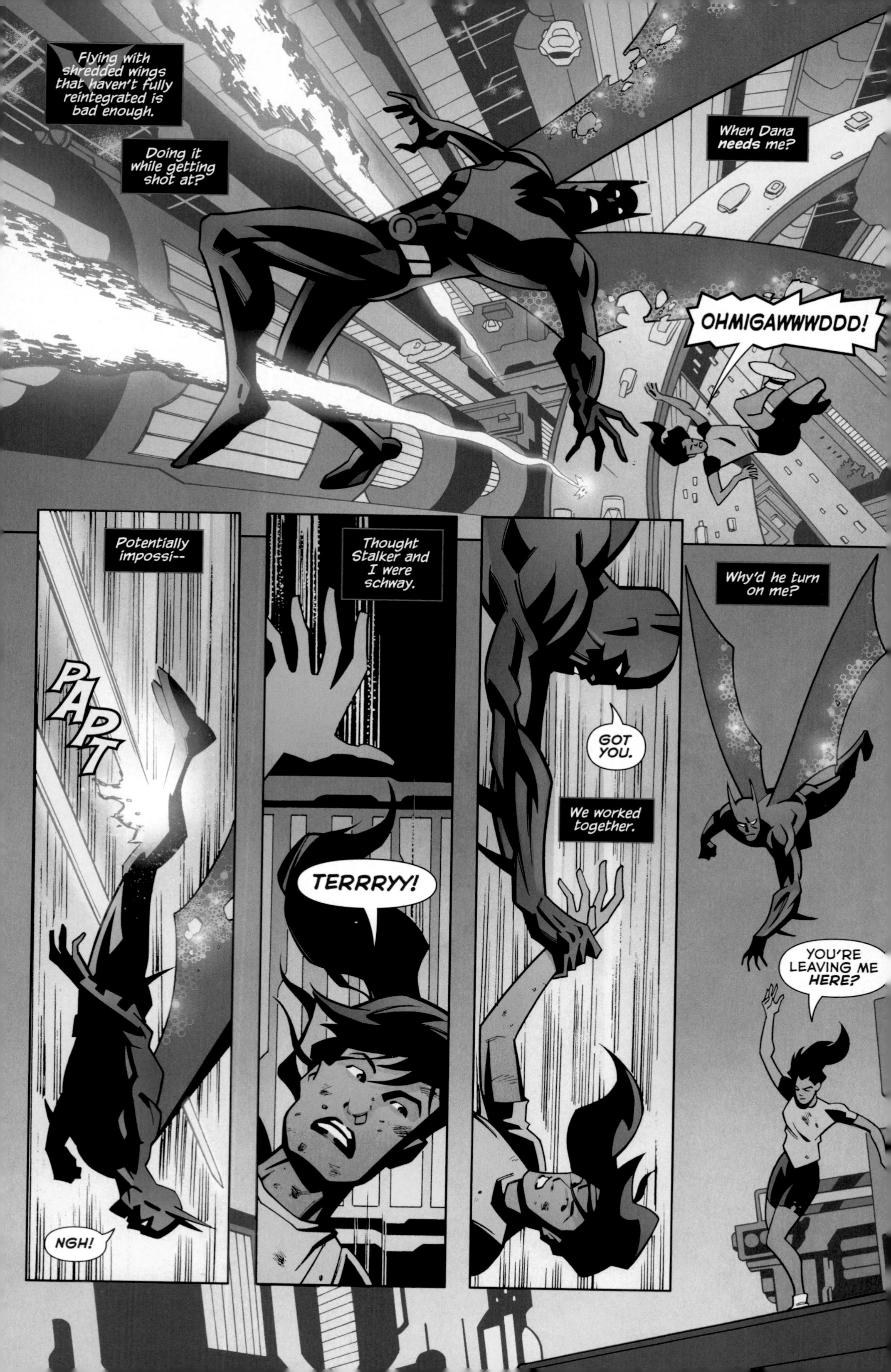

Flying with shredded wings that haven't fully reintegrated is bad enough.
Doing it while getting shot at?
When Dana needs me?
OHMIGAWWWDDD!
Potentially impossi--
PAPT
NGH!
Thought Stalker and I were schway.
TERRRYY!
GOT YOU.
We worked together.
Why'd he turn on me?
YOU'RE LEAVING ME HERE?

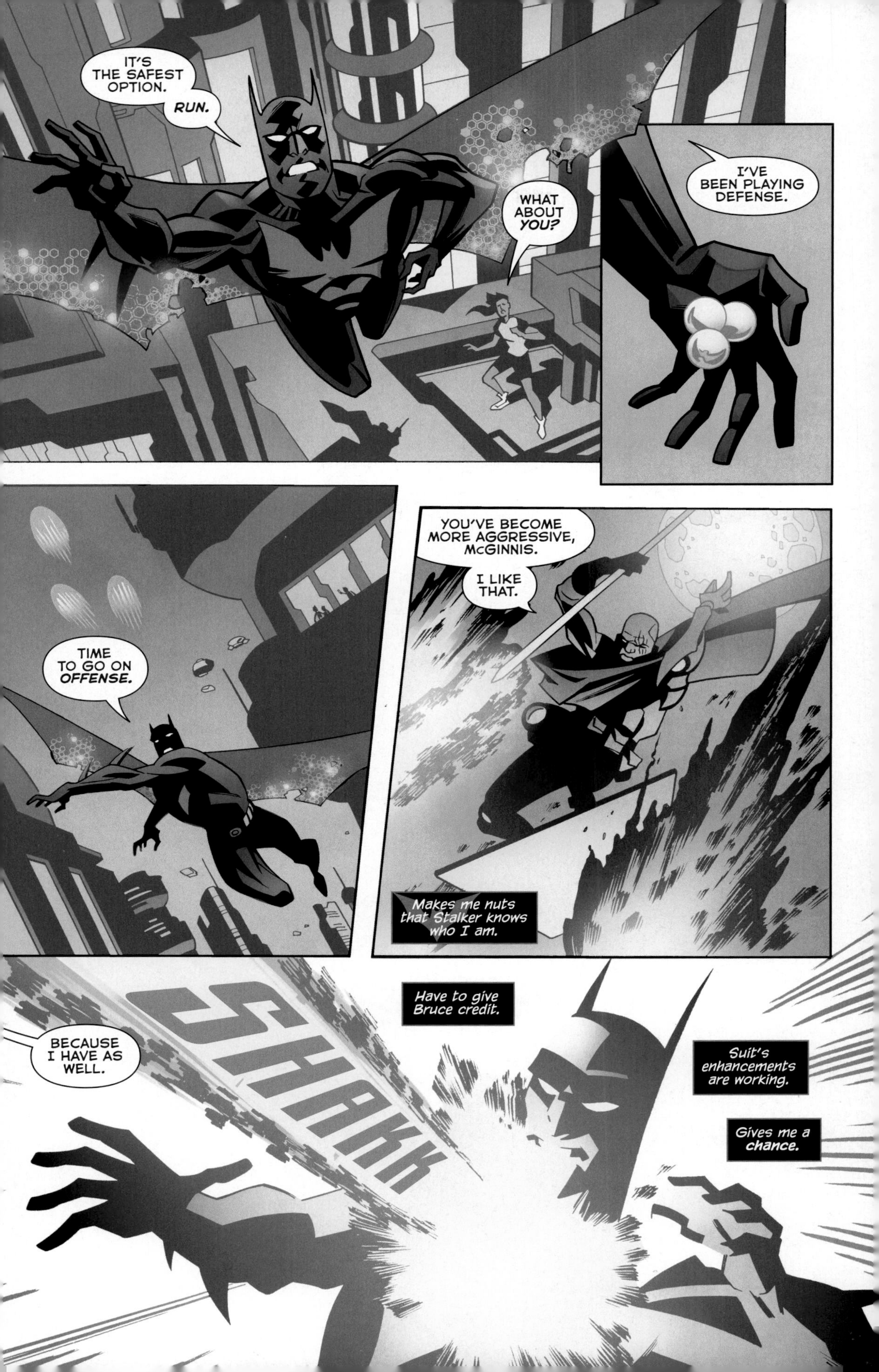
IT'S THE SAFEST OPTION.
RUN.
WHAT ABOUT YOU?
I'VE BEEN PLAYING DEFENSE.
TIME TO GO ON OFFENSE.
YOU'VE BECOME MORE AGGRESSIVE, McGINNIS.
I LIKE THAT.
Makes me nuts that Stalker knows who I am.
SHAKK
Have to give Bruce credit.
BECAUSE I HAVE AS WELL.
Suit's enhancements are working.
Gives me a chance.

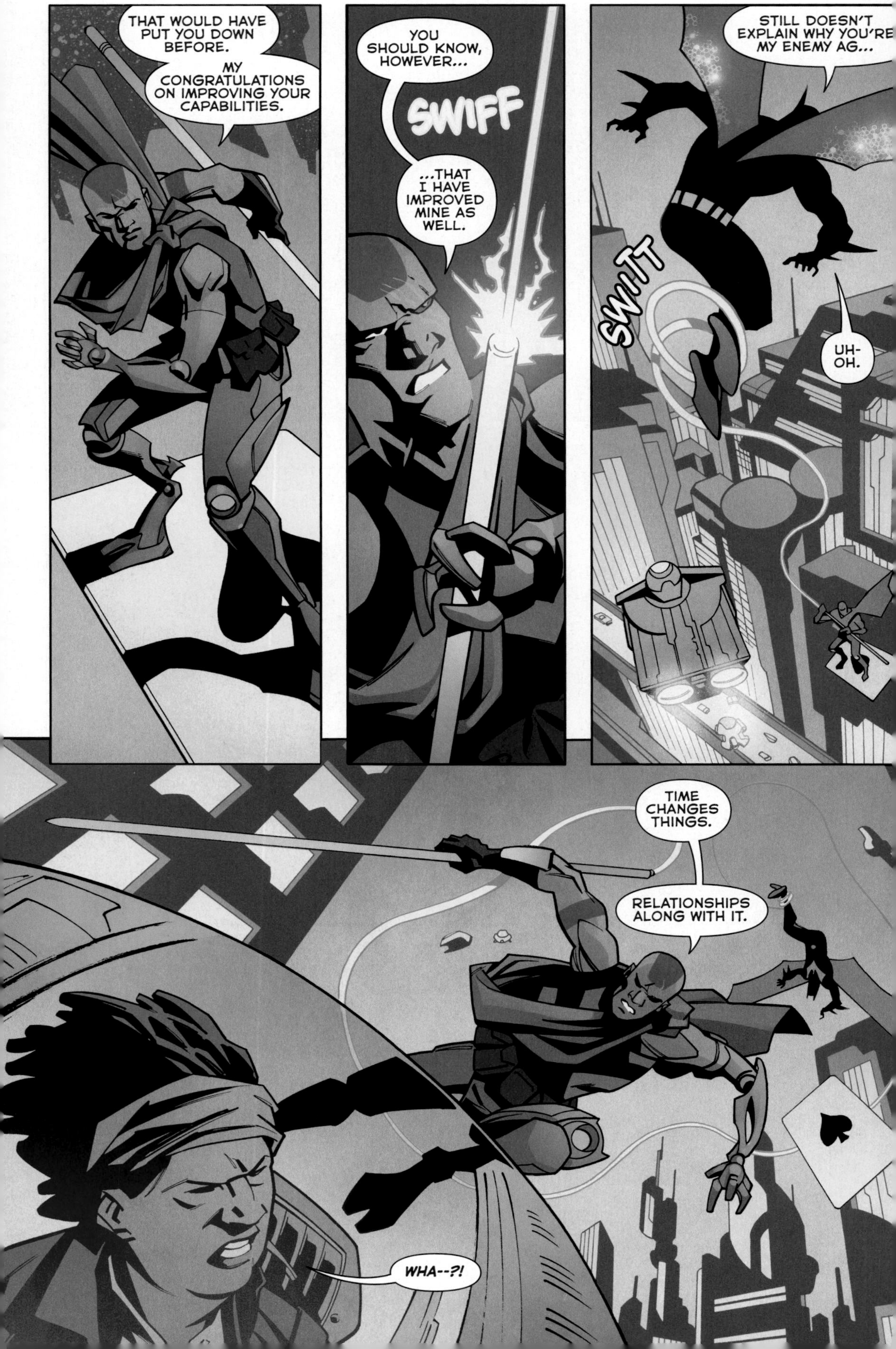
THAT WOULD HAVE PUT YOU DOWN BEFORE.
MY CONGRATULATIONS ON IMPROVING YOUR CAPABILITIES.
YOU SHOULD KNOW, HOWEVER...
SWIFF
...THAT I HAVE IMPROVED MINE AS WELL.
STILL DOESN'T EXPLAIN WHY YOU'RE MY ENEMY AG...
SWITT
UH-OH.
TIME CHANGES THINGS.
RELATIONSHIPS ALONG WITH IT.
WHA--?!

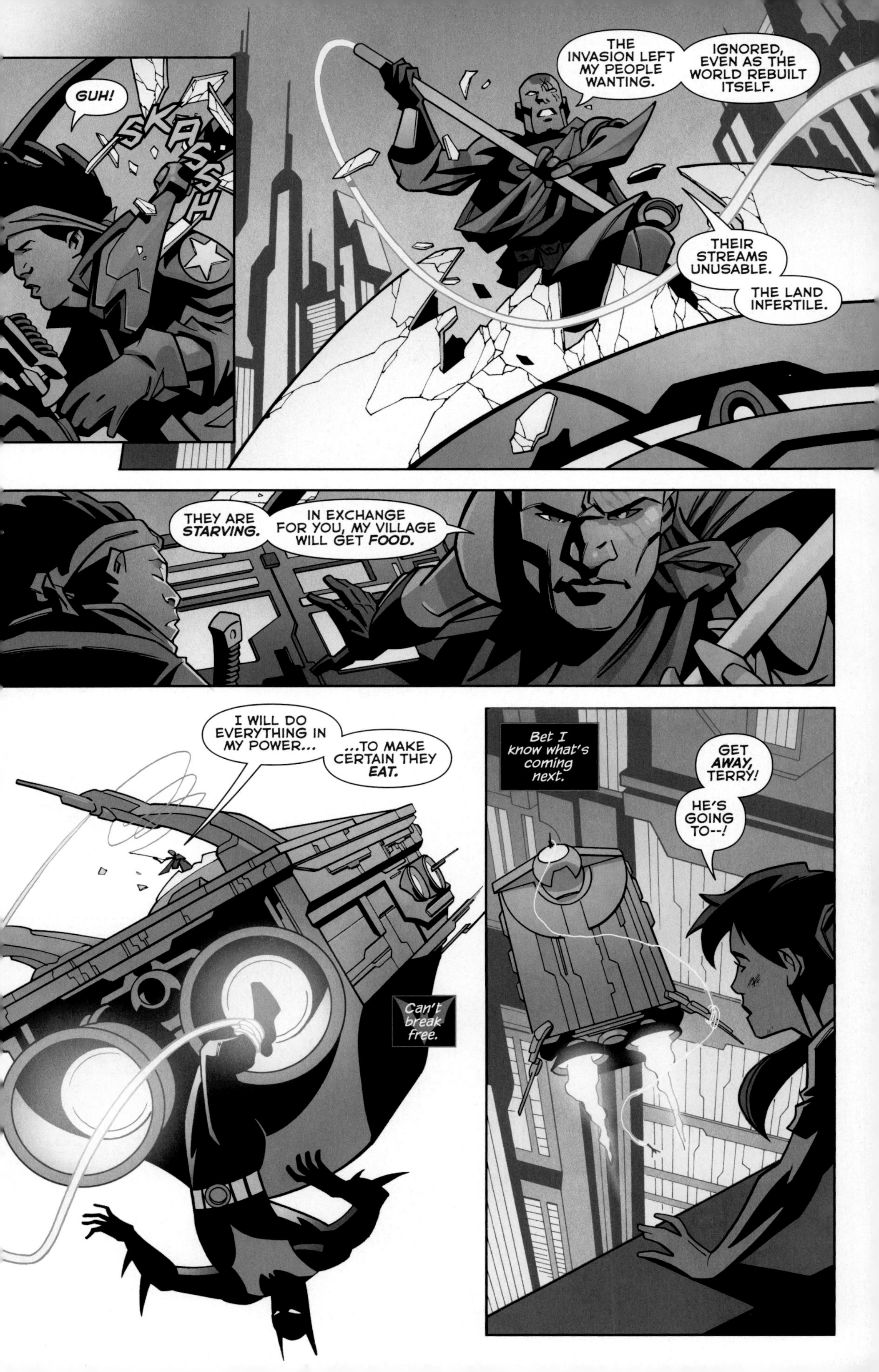
GUH!
SKASSH
THE INVASION LEFT MY PEOPLE WANTING.
IGNORED, EVEN AS THE WORLD REBUILT ITSELF.
THEIR STREAMS UNUSABLE.
THE LAND INFERTILE.
THEY ARE STARVING.
IN EXCHANGE FOR YOU, MY VILLAGE WILL GET FOOD.
I WILL DO EVERYTHING IN MY POWER...
...TO MAKE CERTAIN THEY EAT.
Can't break free.
Bet I know what's coming next.
GET AWAY, TERRY!
HE'S GOING TO--!

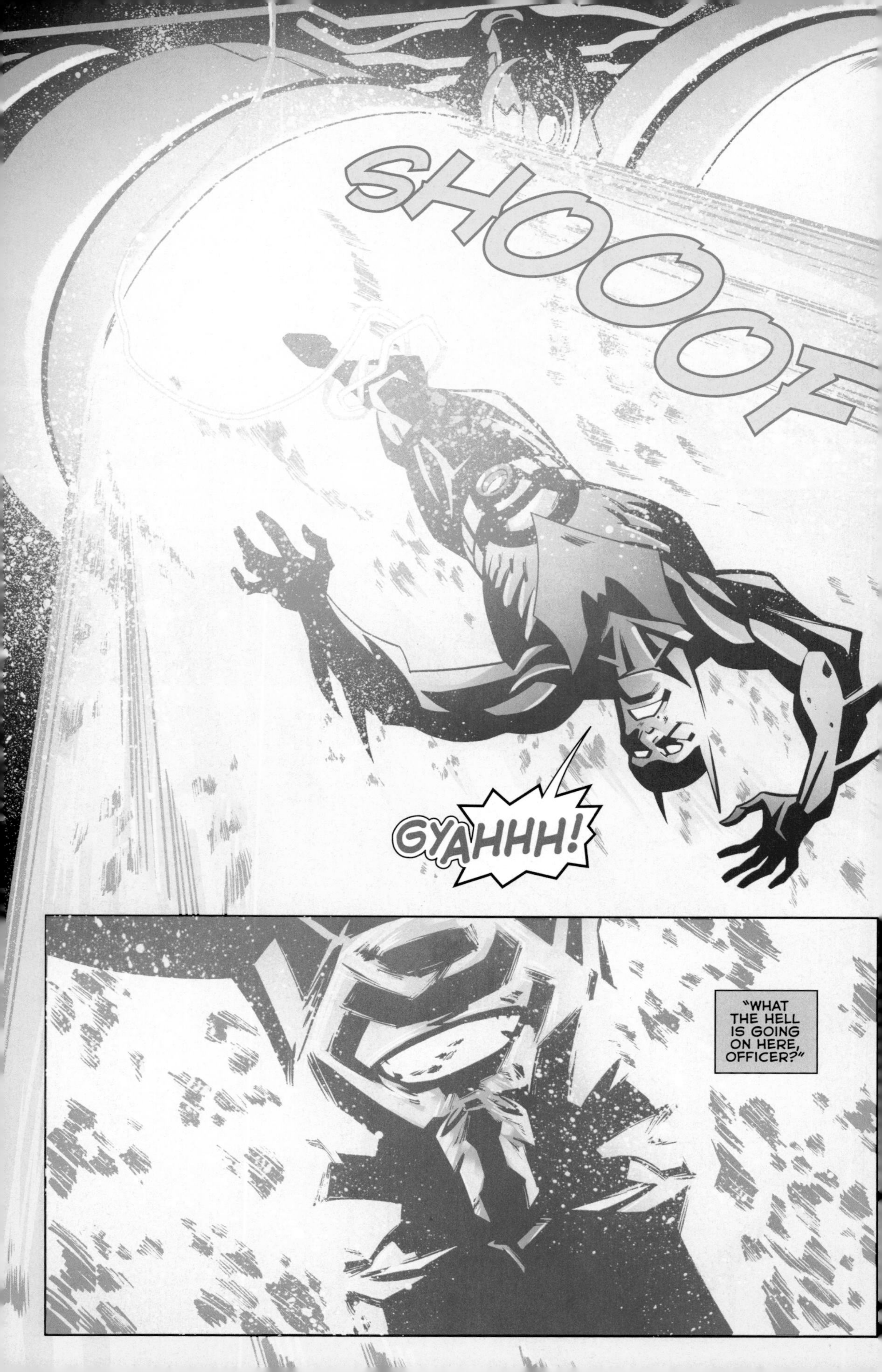
SHOOOF
GYAHHH!
"WHAT THE HELL IS GOING ON HERE, OFFICER?"

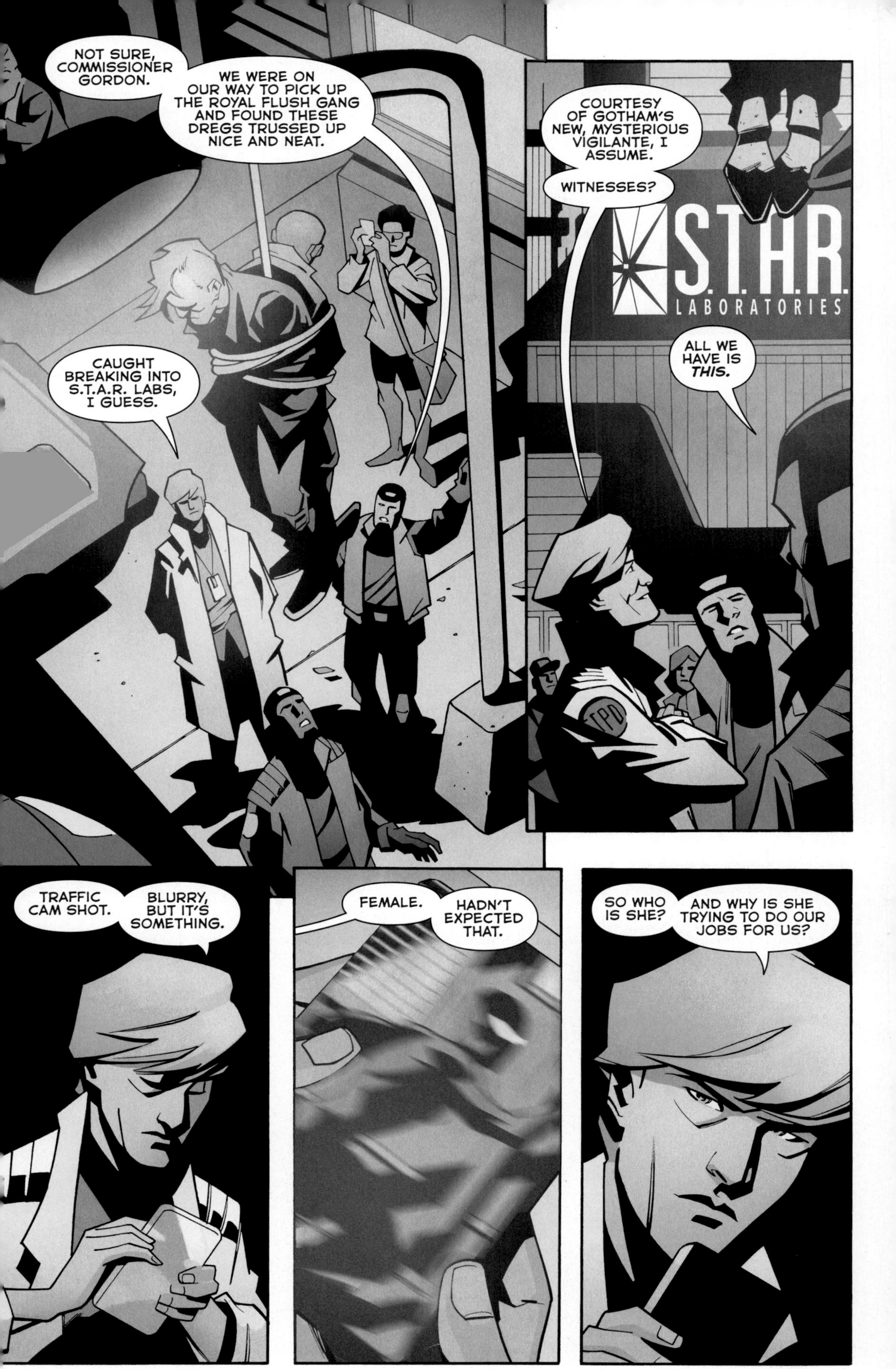
NOT SURE, COMMISSIONER GORDON.
WE WERE ON OUR WAY TO PICK UP THE ROYAL FLUSH GANG AND FOUND THESE DREGS TRUSSED UP NICE AND NEAT.
CAUGHT BREAKING INTO S.T.A.R. LABS, I GUESS.
COURTESY OF GOTHAM'S NEW, MYSTERIOUS VIGILANTE, I ASSUME.
WITNESSES?
S.T.A.R. LABORATORIES
ALL WE HAVE IS *THIS.*
TRAFFIC CAM SHOT.
BLURRY, BUT IT'S SOMETHING.
FEMALE.
HADN'T EXPECTED THAT.
SO WHO IS SHE?
AND WHY IS SHE TRYING TO DO OUR JOBS FOR US?

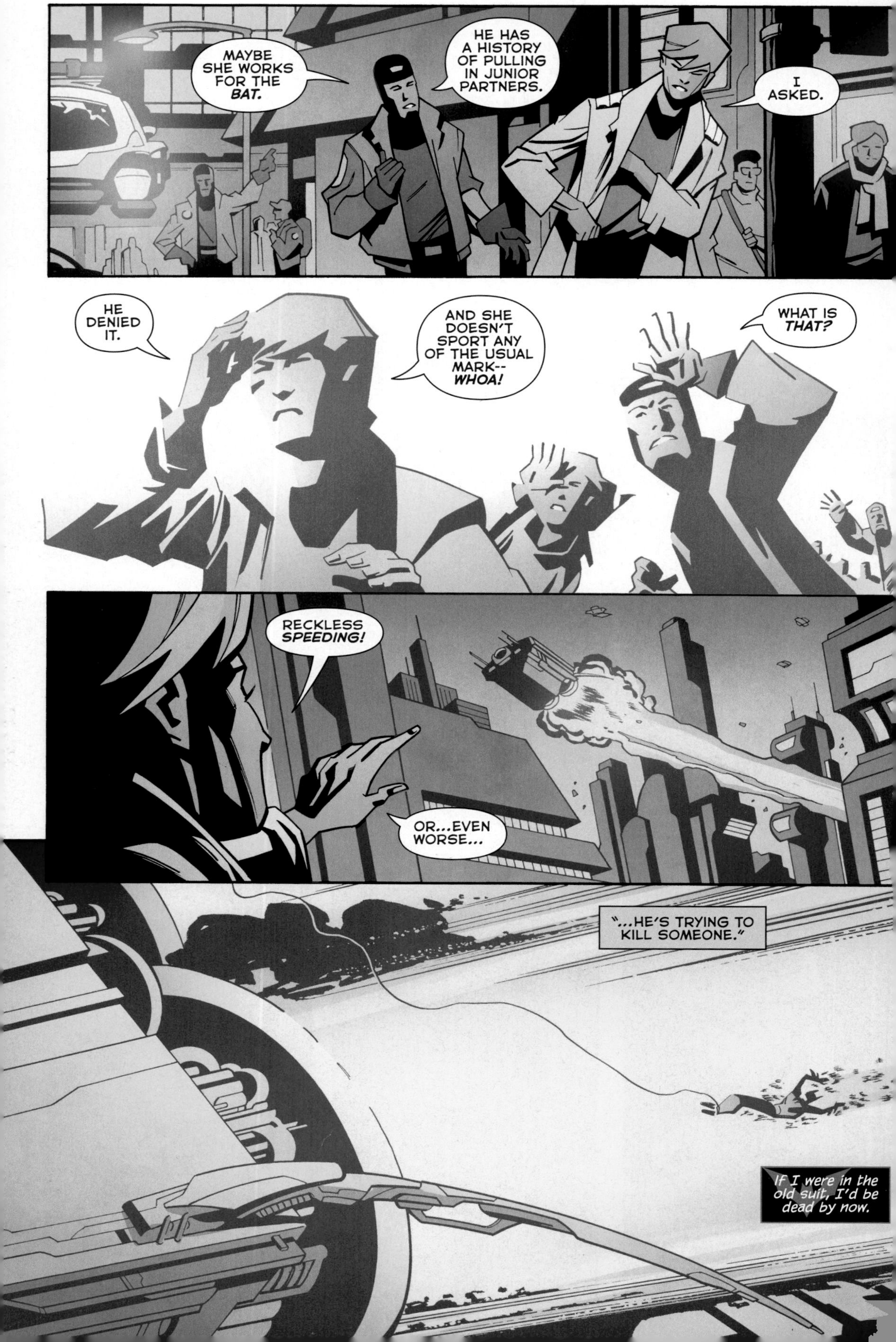
MAYBE SHE WORKS FOR THE *BAT.*
HE HAS A HISTORY OF PULLING IN JUNIOR PARTNERS.
I ASKED.
HE DENIED IT.
AND SHE DOESN'T SPORT ANY OF THE USUAL MARK-- *WHOA!*
WHAT IS *THAT?*
RECKLESS *SPEEDING!*
OR...EVEN WORSE...
"...HE'S TRYING TO KILL SOMEONE."
If I were in the old suit, I'd be dead by now.

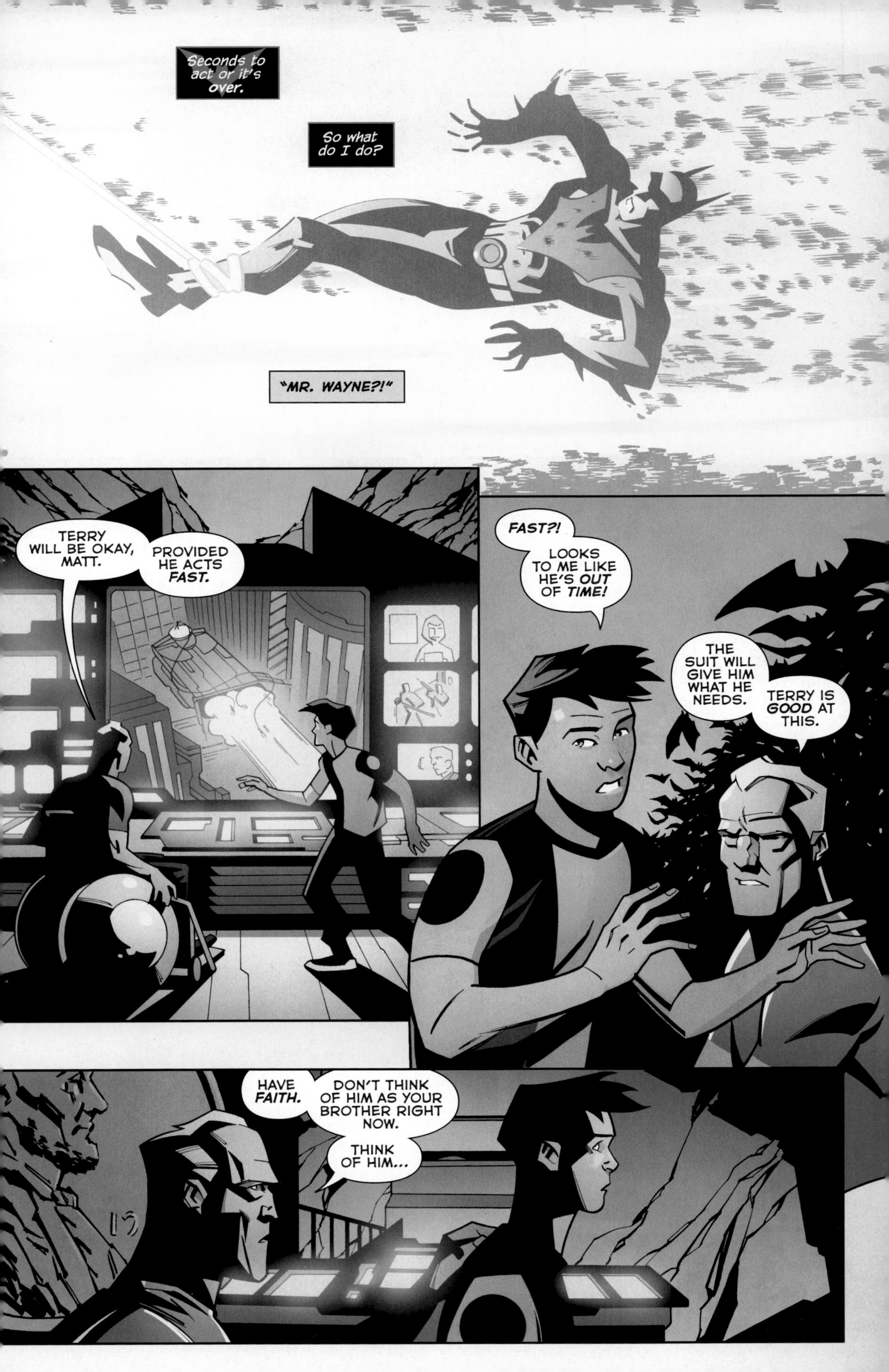

Seconds to act or it's over.
So what do I do?
"MR. WAYNE?!"
TERRY WILL BE OKAY, MATT.
PROVIDED HE ACTS FAST.
FAST?!
LOOKS TO ME LIKE HE'S OUT OF TIME!
THE SUIT WILL GIVE HIM WHAT HE NEEDS.
TERRY IS GOOD AT THIS.
HAVE FAITH.
DON'T THINK OF HIM AS YOUR BROTHER RIGHT NOW.
THINK OF HIM...

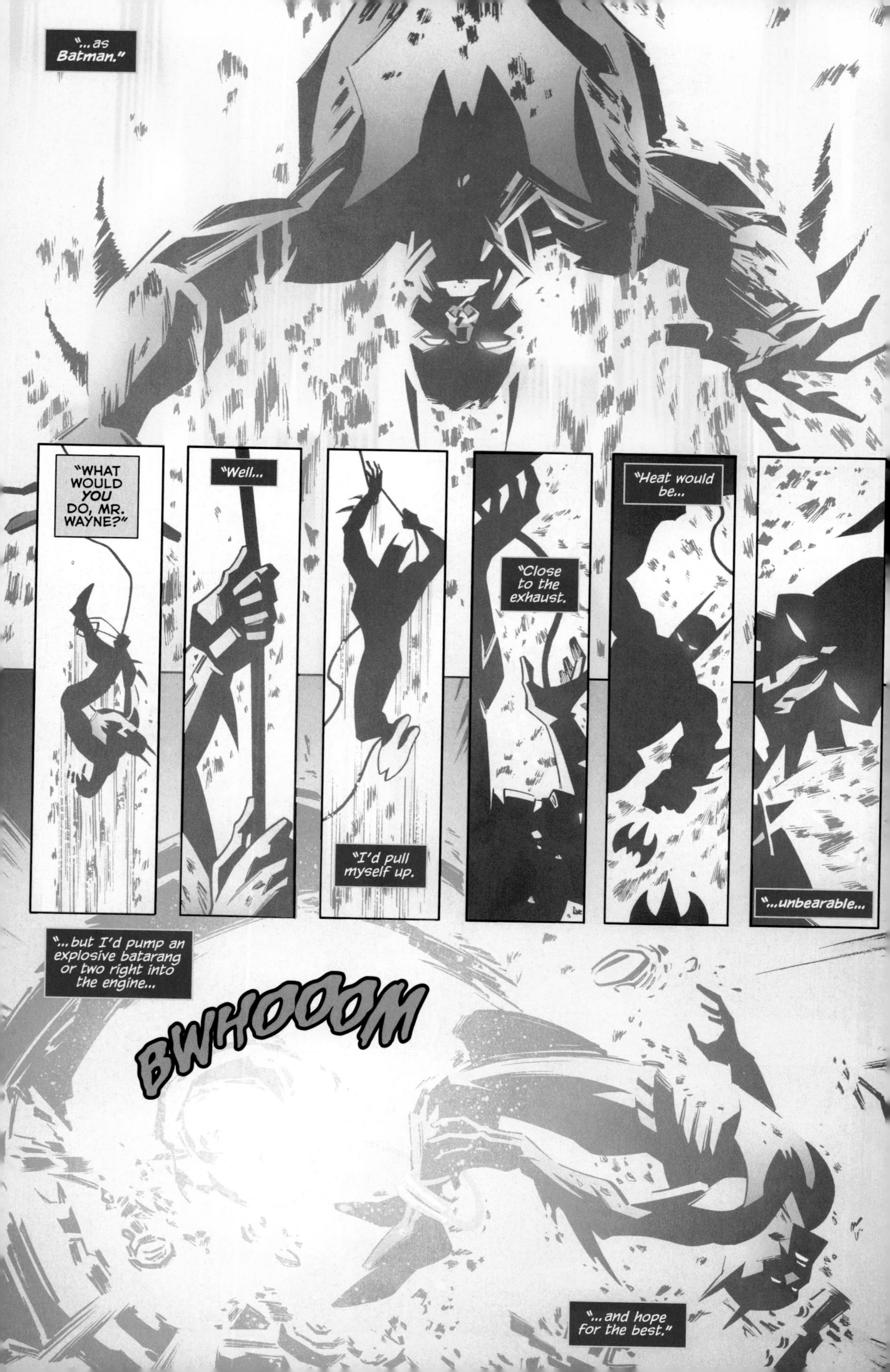
"...as Batman."
"WHAT WOULD YOU DO, MR. WAYNE?"
"Well...
"I'd pull myself up.
"Close to the exhaust.
"Heat would be...
"...unbearable...
"...but I'd pump an explosive batarang or two right into the engine...
BWHOOOOM
"...and hope for the best."

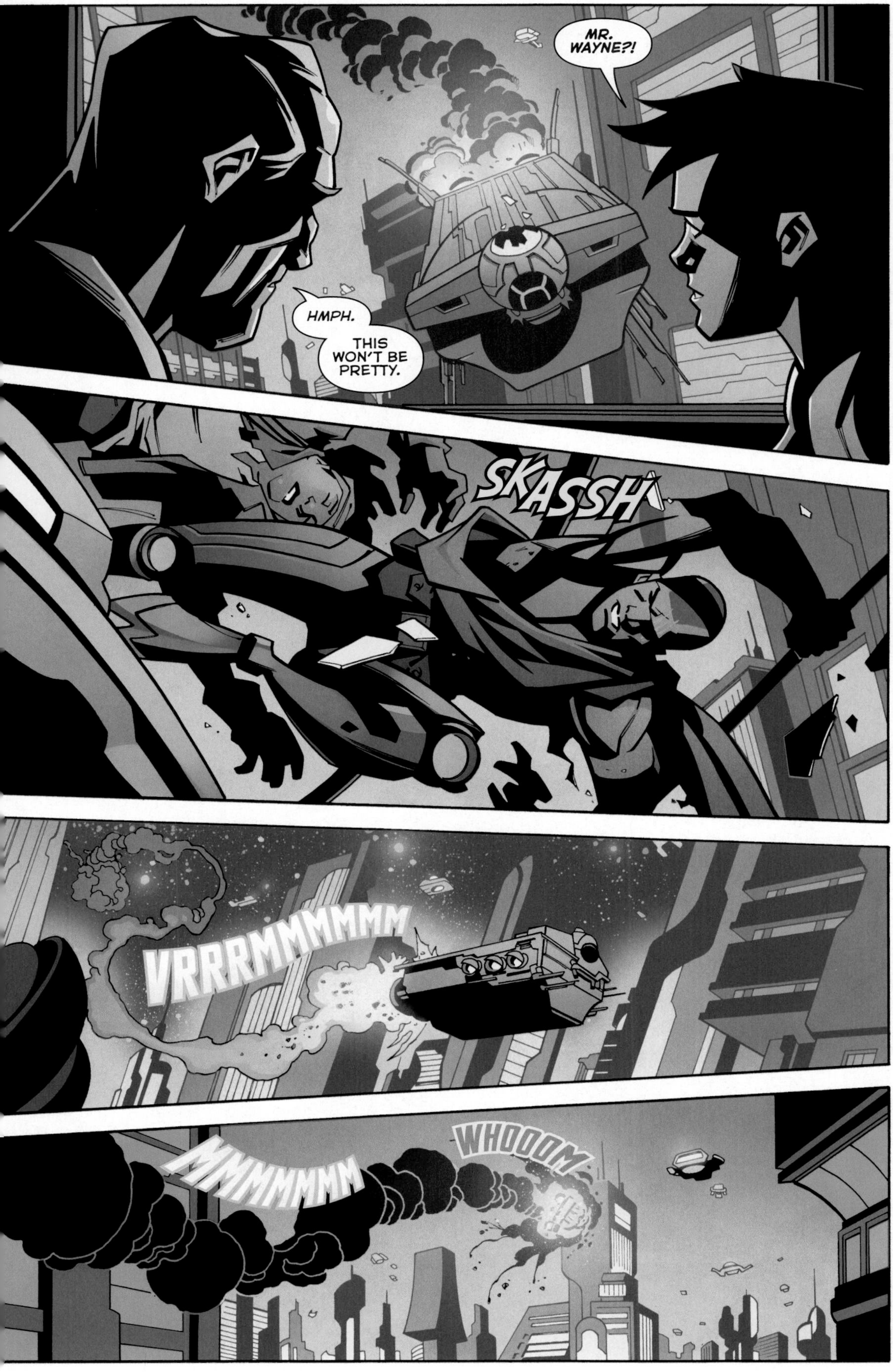

MR. WAYNE?!
HMPH.
THIS WON'T BE PRETTY.
SKASSH
VRRRMMMMMM
MMMMMMM
WHOOOM

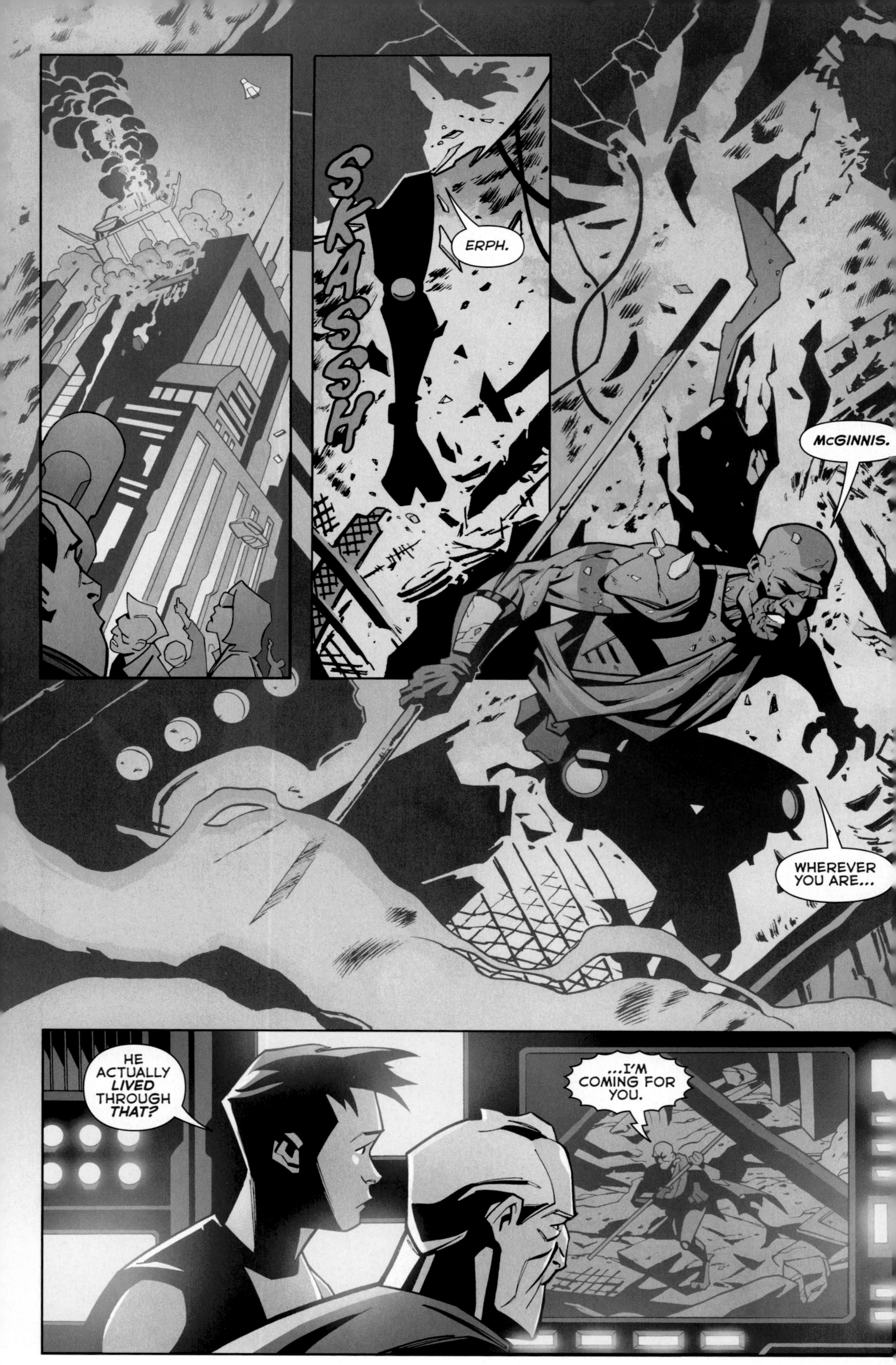
SKASSH
ERPH.
McGINNIS.
WHEREVER YOU ARE...
HE ACTUALLY *LIVED* THROUGH *THAT?*
...I'M COMING FOR YOU.

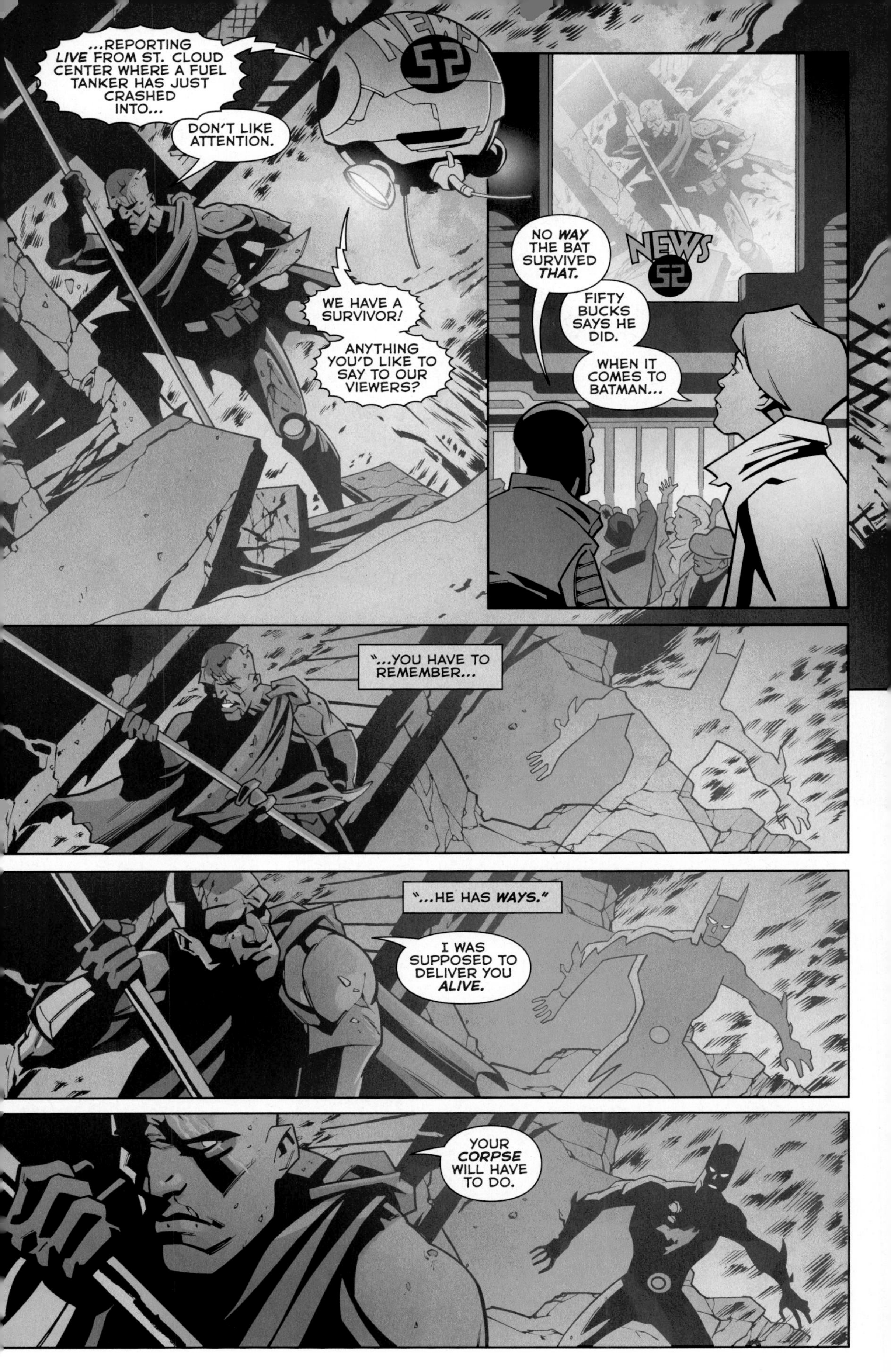
...REPORTING LIVE FROM ST. CLOUD CENTER WHERE A FUEL TANKER HAS JUST CRASHED INTO...
DON'T LIKE ATTENTION.
WE HAVE A SURVIVOR!
ANYTHING YOU'D LIKE TO SAY TO OUR VIEWERS?
NEWS 52
NO WAY THE BAT SURVIVED THAT.
FIFTY BUCKS SAYS HE DID.
WHEN IT COMES TO BATMAN...
"...YOU HAVE TO REMEMBER...
"...HE HAS WAYS."
I WAS SUPPOSED TO DELIVER YOU ALIVE.
YOUR CORPSE WILL HAVE TO DO.

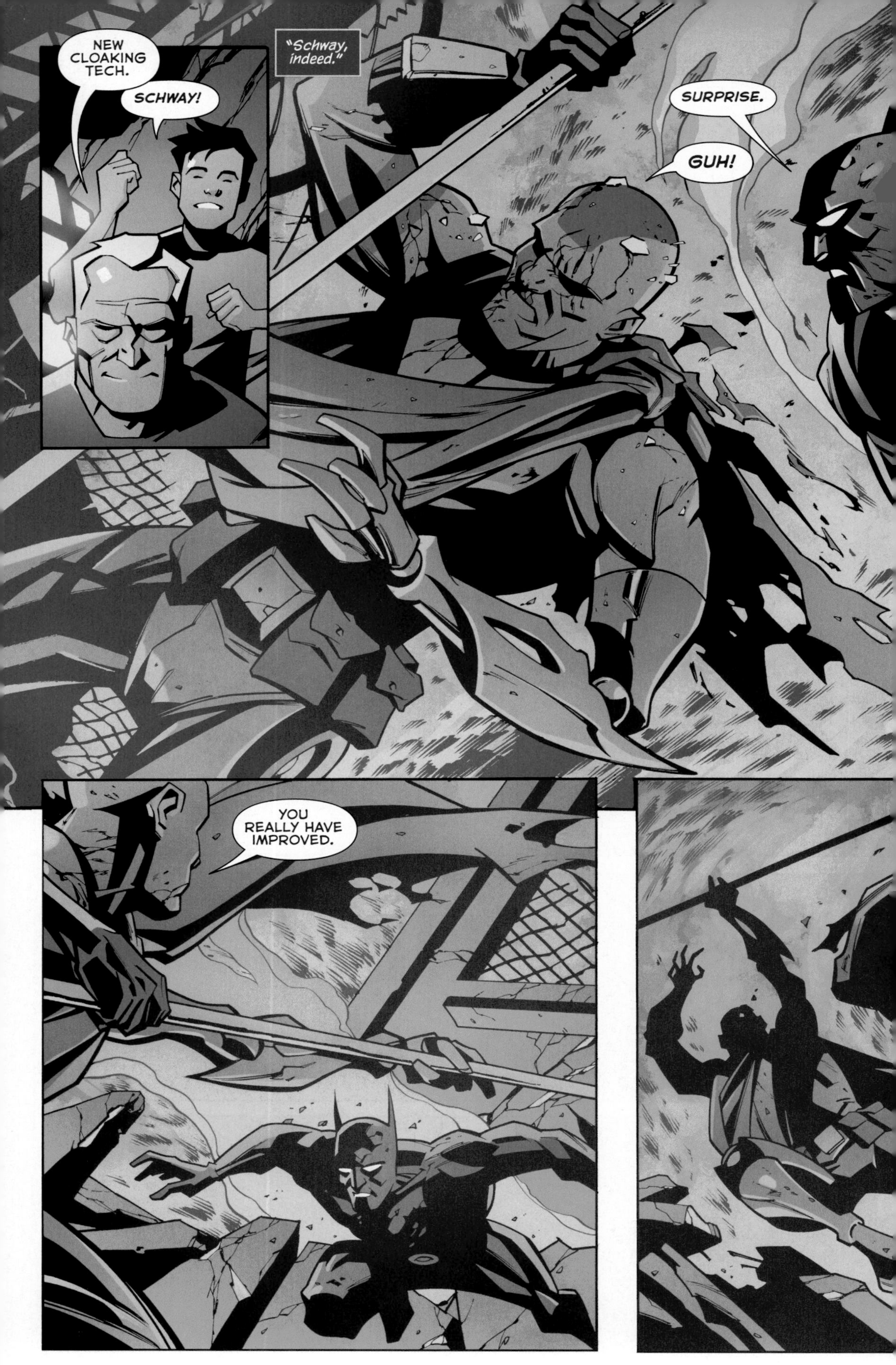
NEW CLOAKING TECH.
SCHWAY!
"Schway, indeed."
SURPRISE.
GUH!
YOU REALLY HAVE IMPROVED.

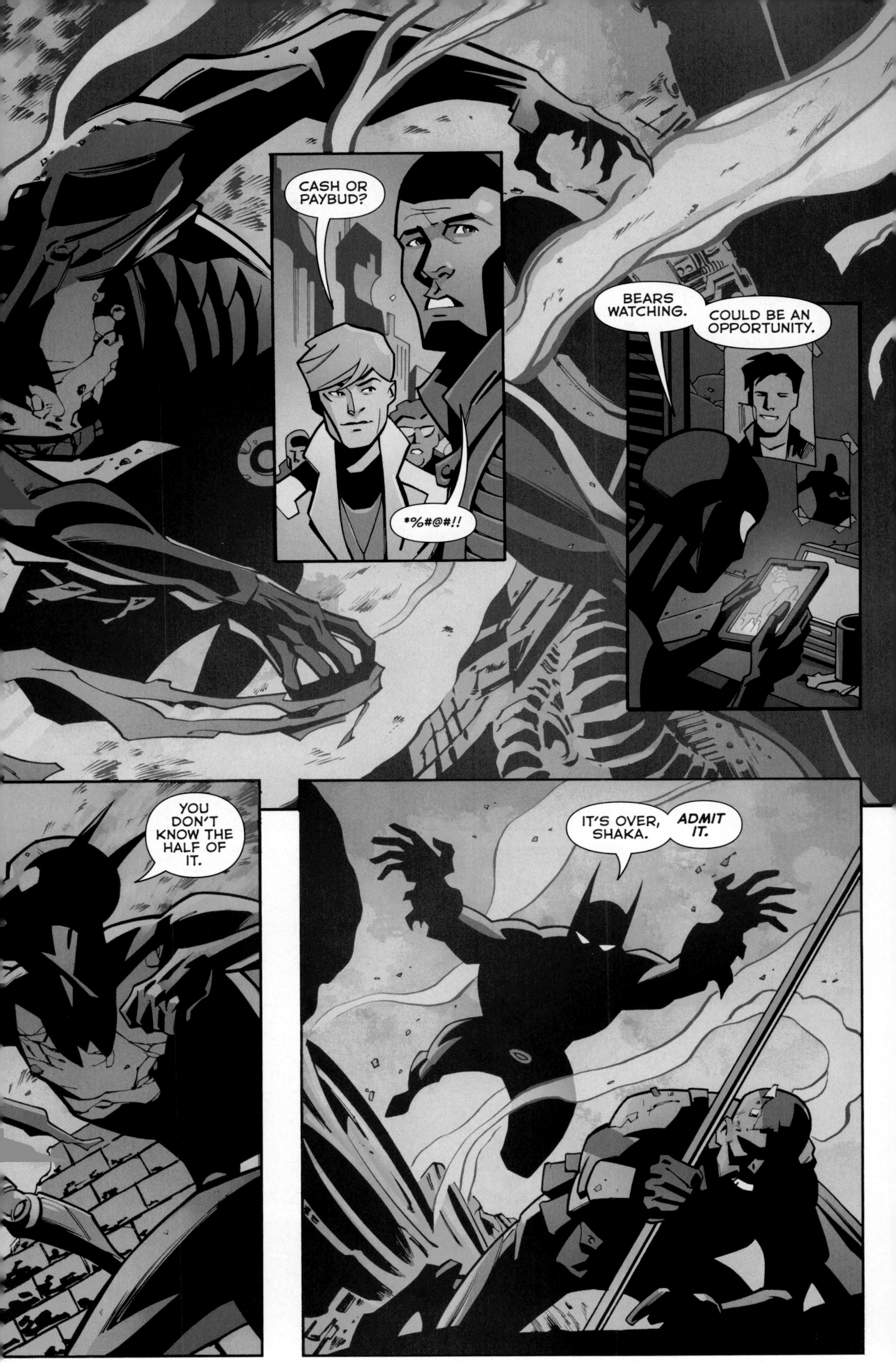
CASH OR PAYBUD?
*%#@#!!
BEARS WATCHING.
COULD BE AN OPPORTUNITY.
YOU DON'T KNOW THE HALF OF IT.
IT'S OVER, SHAKA.
ADMIT IT.

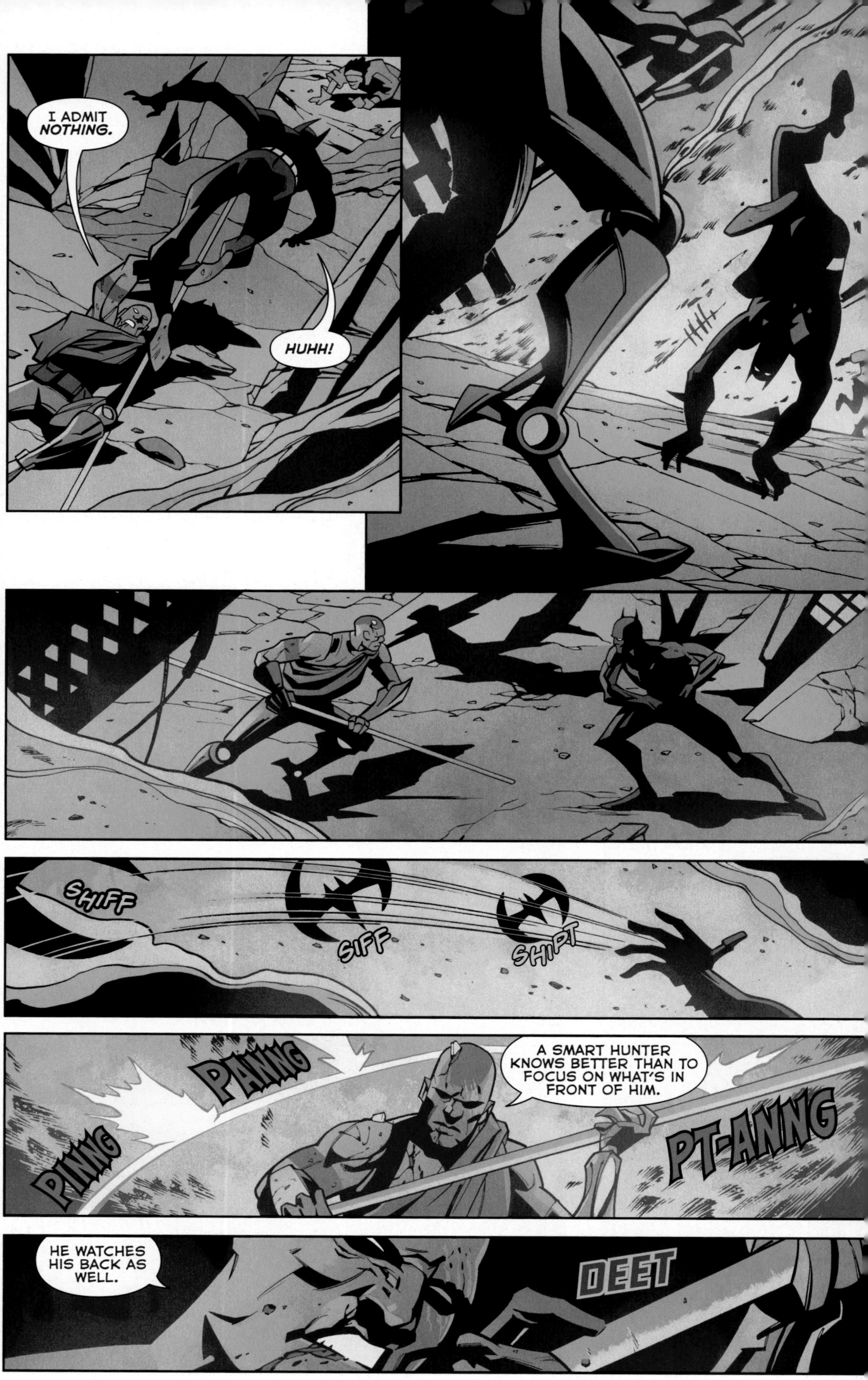
I ADMIT NOTHING.
HUHH!
SHIFF
SIFF
SHIPT
PANNG
A SMART HUNTER KNOWS BETTER THAN TO FOCUS ON WHAT'S IN FRONT OF HIM.
PINNG
PT-ANNG
HE WATCHES HIS BACK AS WELL.
DEET

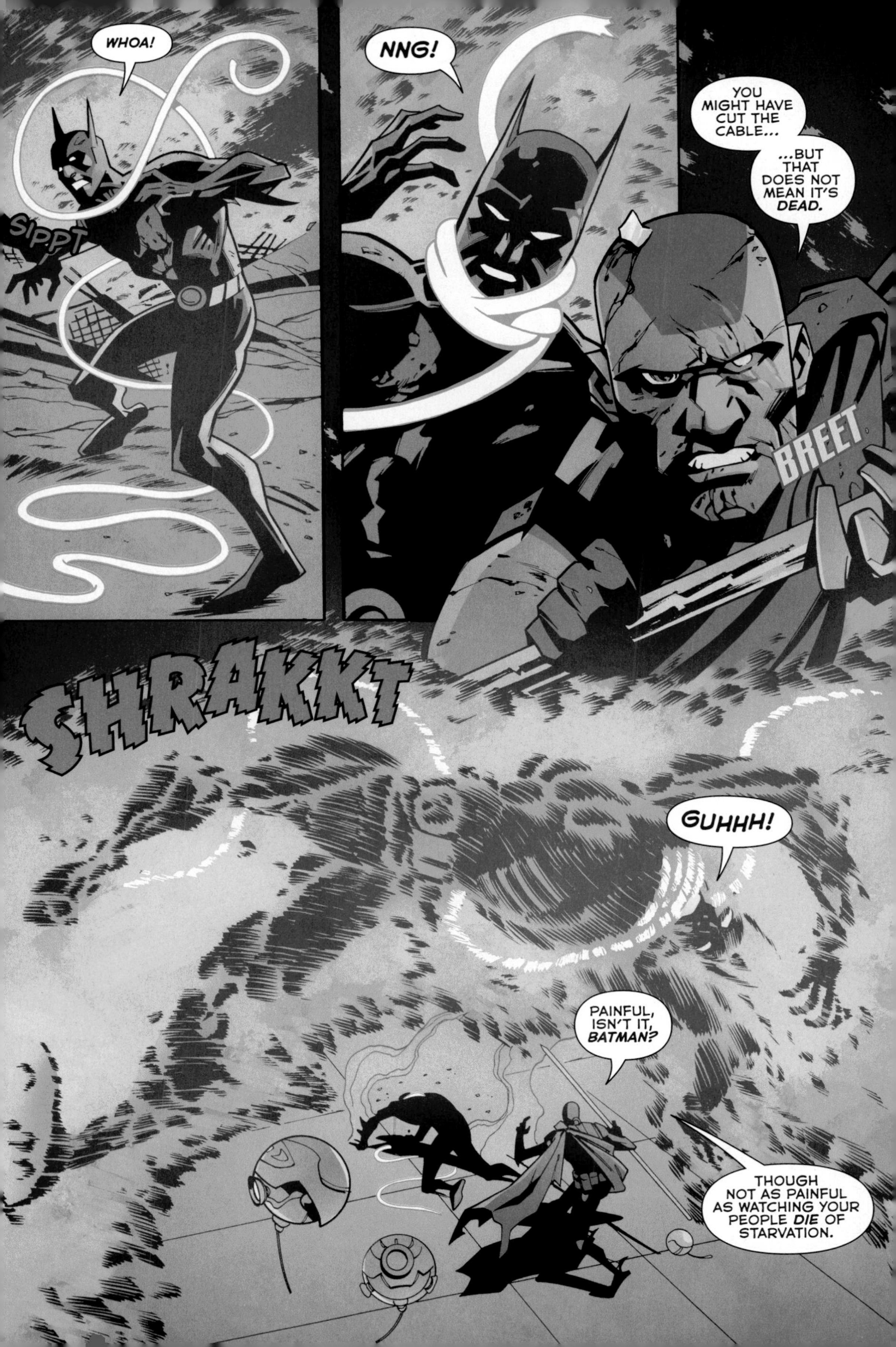
WHOA!
SIPPT
NNG!
YOU MIGHT HAVE CUT THE CABLE...
...BUT THAT DOES NOT MEAN IT'S DEAD.
BREET
SHRAKKT
GUHHH!
PAINFUL, ISN'T IT, BATMAN?
THOUGH NOT AS PAINFUL AS WATCHING YOUR PEOPLE DIE OF STARVATION.

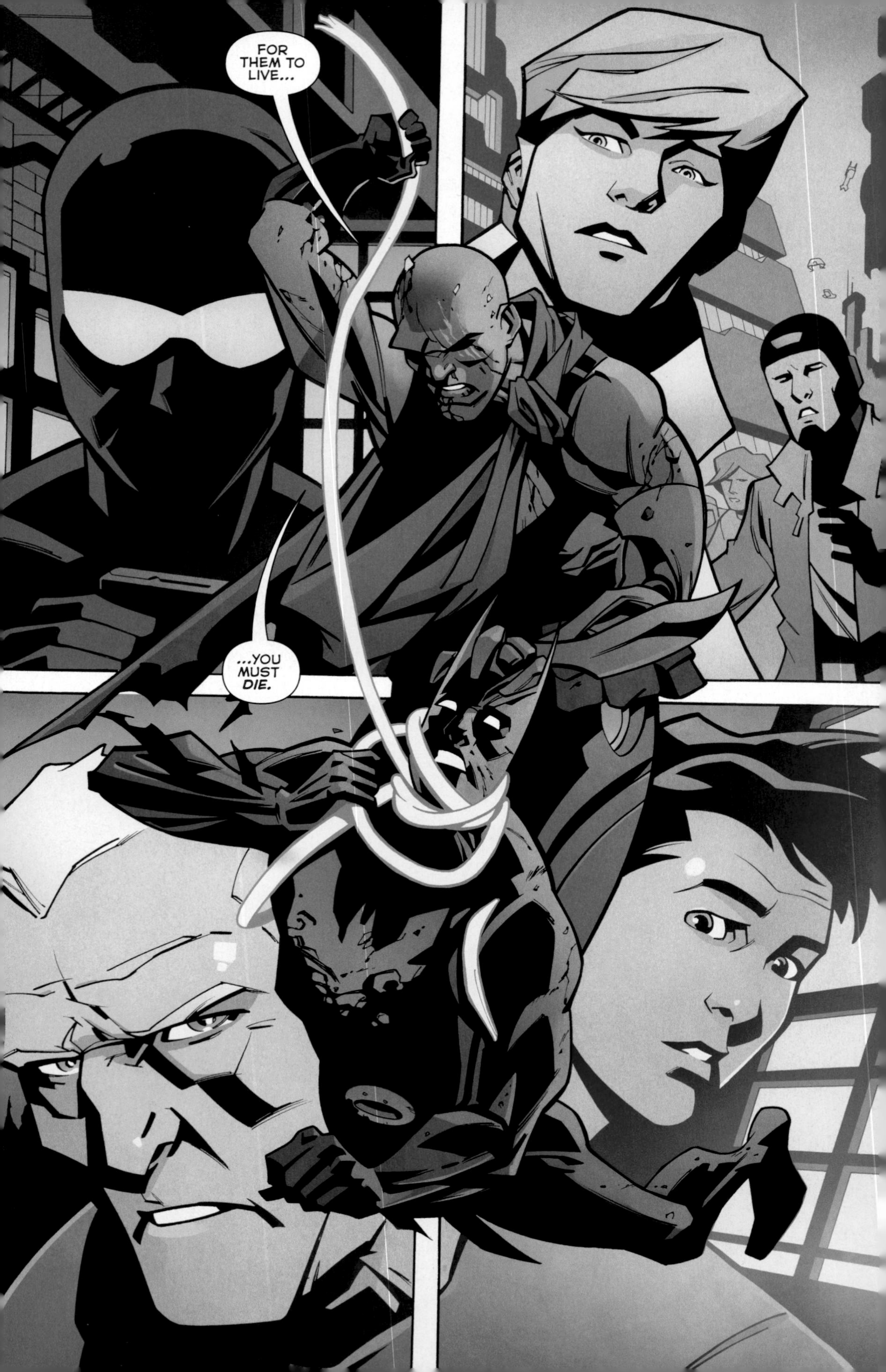
FOR THEM TO LIVE...
...YOU MUST DIE.

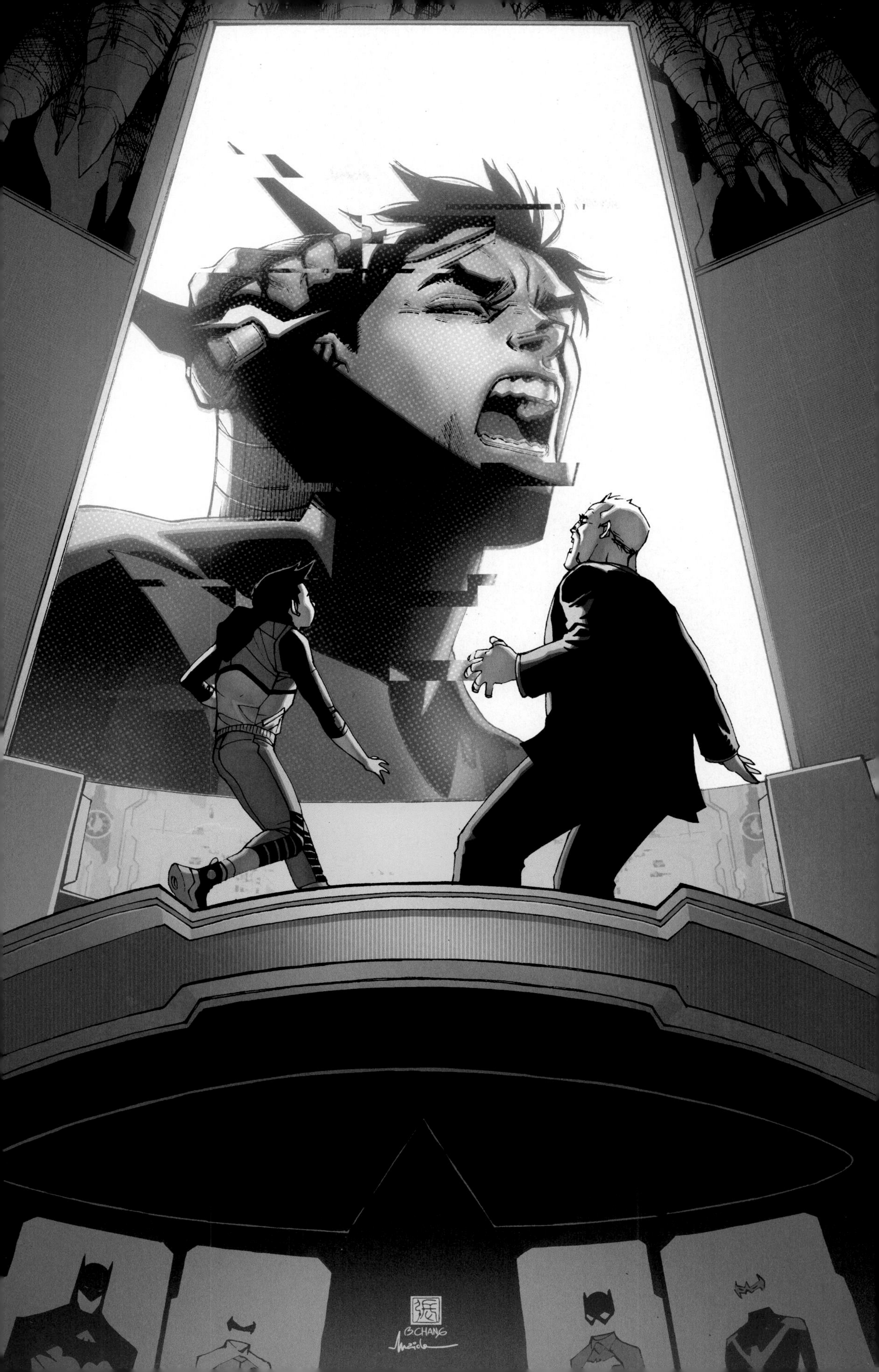
B CHANG

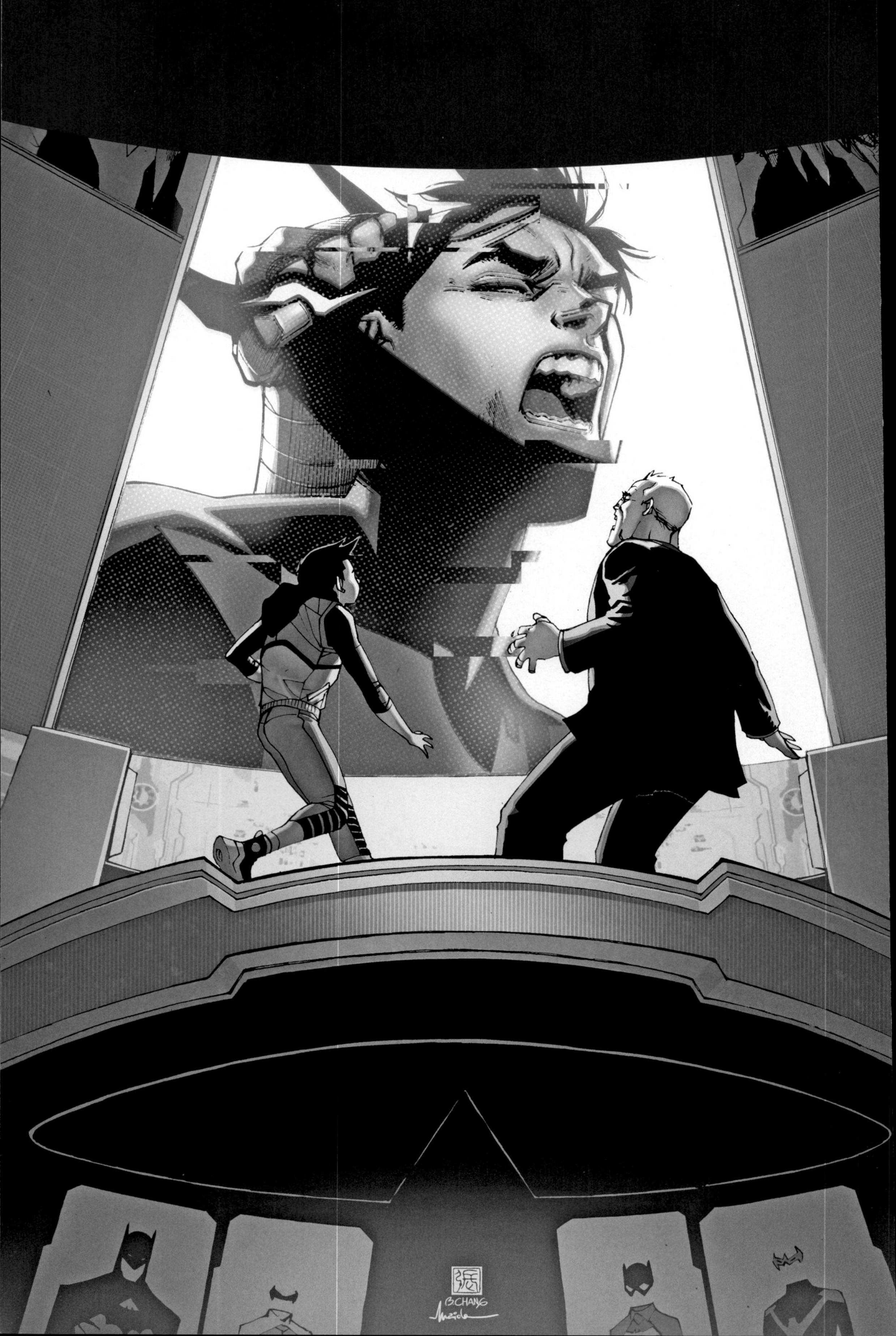
B CHANG

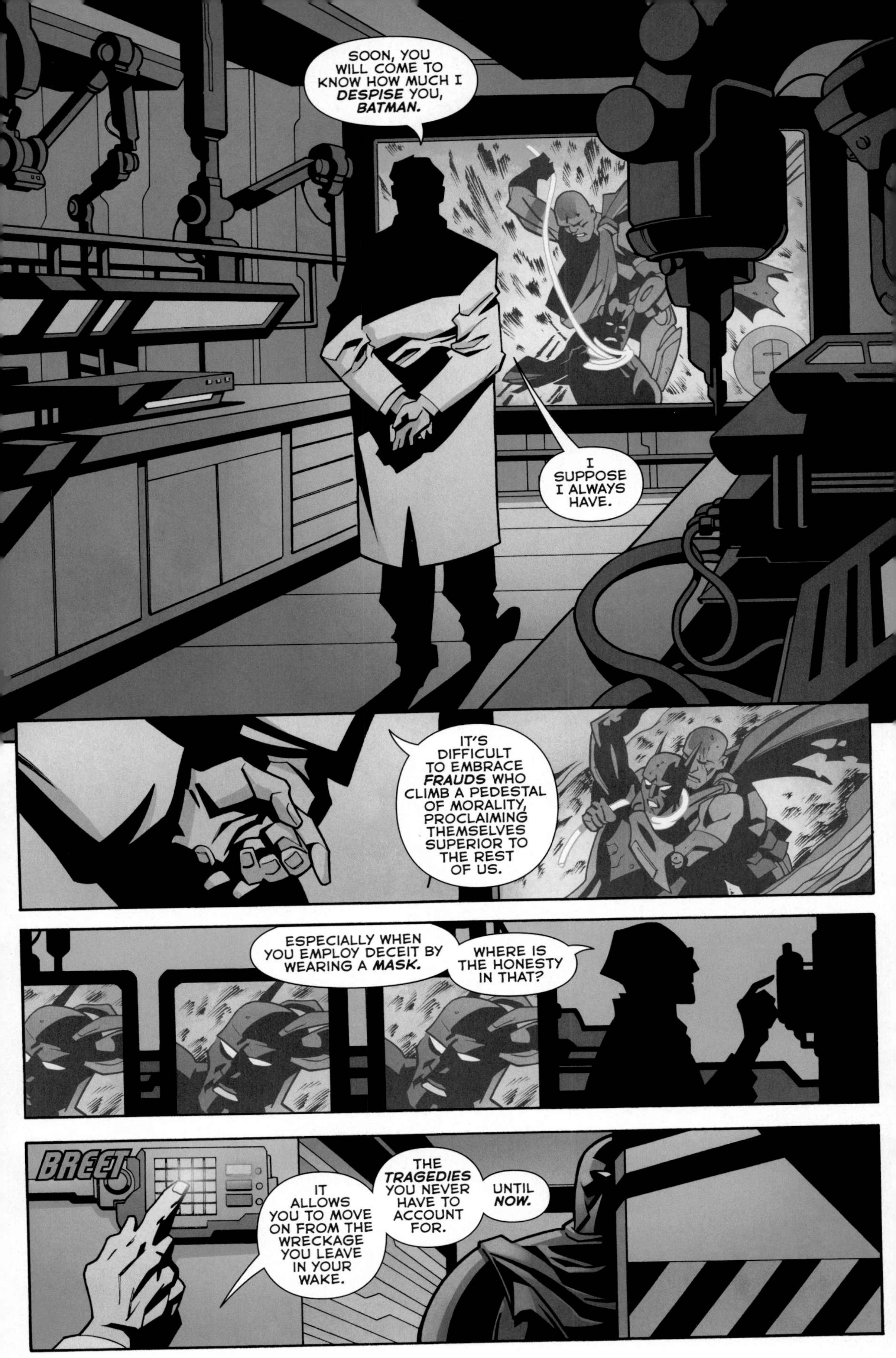
SOON, YOU WILL COME TO KNOW HOW MUCH I DESPISE YOU, BATMAN.
I SUPPOSE I ALWAYS HAVE.
IT'S DIFFICULT TO EMBRACE FRAUDS WHO CLIMB A PEDESTAL OF MORALITY, PROCLAIMING THEMSELVES SUPERIOR TO THE REST OF US.
ESPECIALLY WHEN YOU EMPLOY DECEIT BY WEARING A MASK.
WHERE IS THE HONESTY IN THAT?
BREET
IT ALLOWS YOU TO MOVE ON FROM THE WRECKAGE YOU LEAVE IN YOUR WAKE.
THE TRAGEDIES YOU NEVER HAVE TO ACCOUNT FOR.
UNTIL NOW.

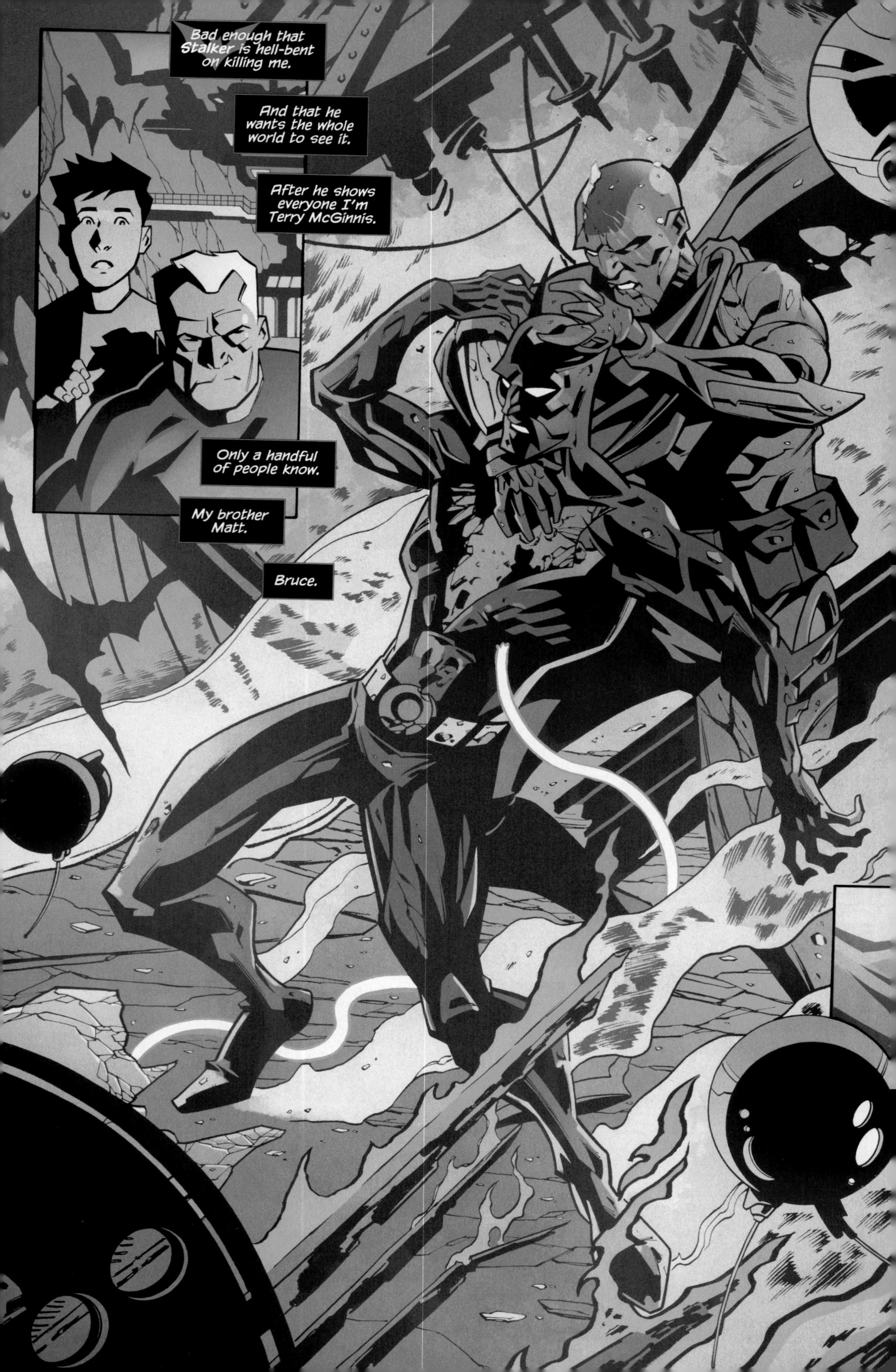
Bad enough that Stalker is hell-bent on killing me.
And that he wants the whole world to see it.
After he shows everyone I'm Terry McGinnis.
Only a handful of people know.
My brother Matt.
Bruce.

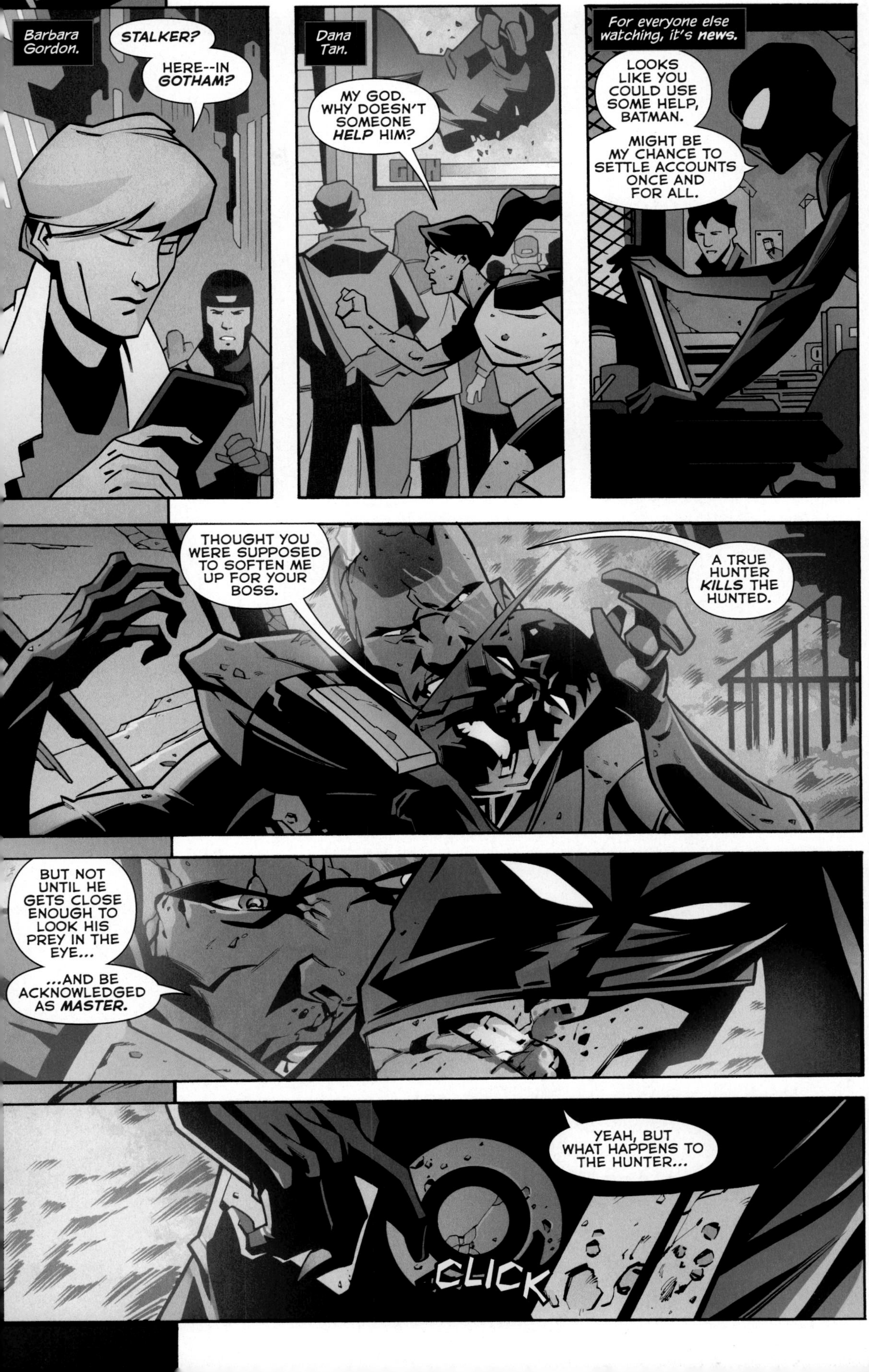
Barbara Gordon.
STALKER?
HERE--IN GOTHAM?
Dana Tan.
MY GOD. WHY DOESN'T SOMEONE HELP HIM?
For everyone else watching, it's news.
LOOKS LIKE YOU COULD USE SOME HELP, BATMAN.
MIGHT BE MY CHANCE TO SETTLE ACCOUNTS ONCE AND FOR ALL.
THOUGHT YOU WERE SUPPOSED TO SOFTEN ME UP FOR YOUR BOSS.
A TRUE HUNTER KILLS THE HUNTED.
BUT NOT UNTIL HE GETS CLOSE ENOUGH TO LOOK HIS PREY IN THE EYE...
...AND BE ACKNOWLEDGED AS MASTER.
YEAH, BUT WHAT HAPPENS TO THE HUNTER...
CLICK

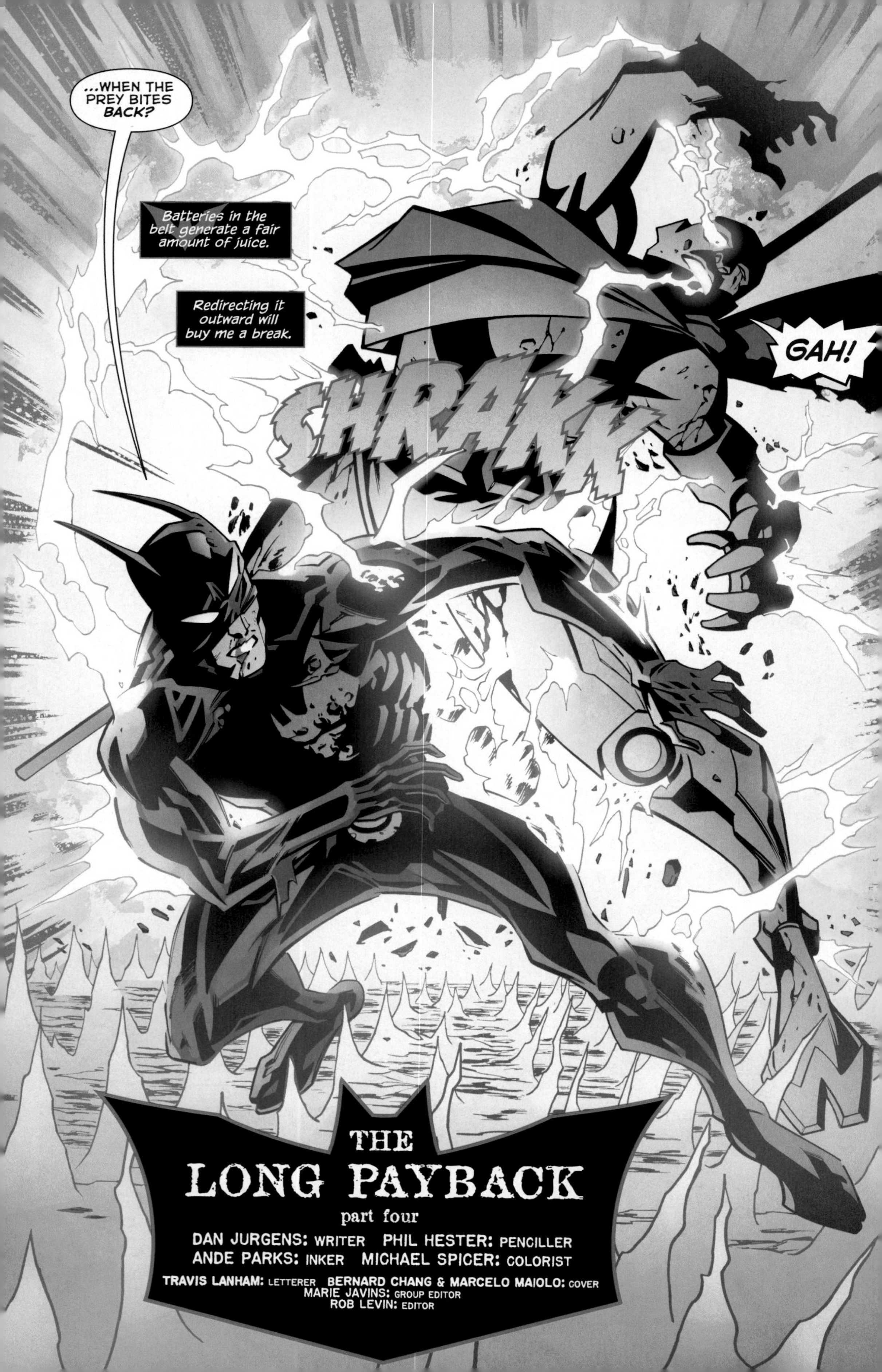

...WHEN THE PREY BITES BACK?
Batteries in the belt generate a fair amount of juice.
Redirecting it outward will buy me a break.
CHRAKK
GAH!
THE LONG PAYBACK
part four
DAN JURGENS: WRITER PHIL HESTER: PENCILLER
ANDE PARKS: INKER MICHAEL SPICER: COLORIST
TRAVIS LANHAM: LETTERER BERNARD CHANG & MARCELO MAIOLO: COVER
MARIE JAVINS: GROUP EDITOR
ROB LEVIN: EDITOR

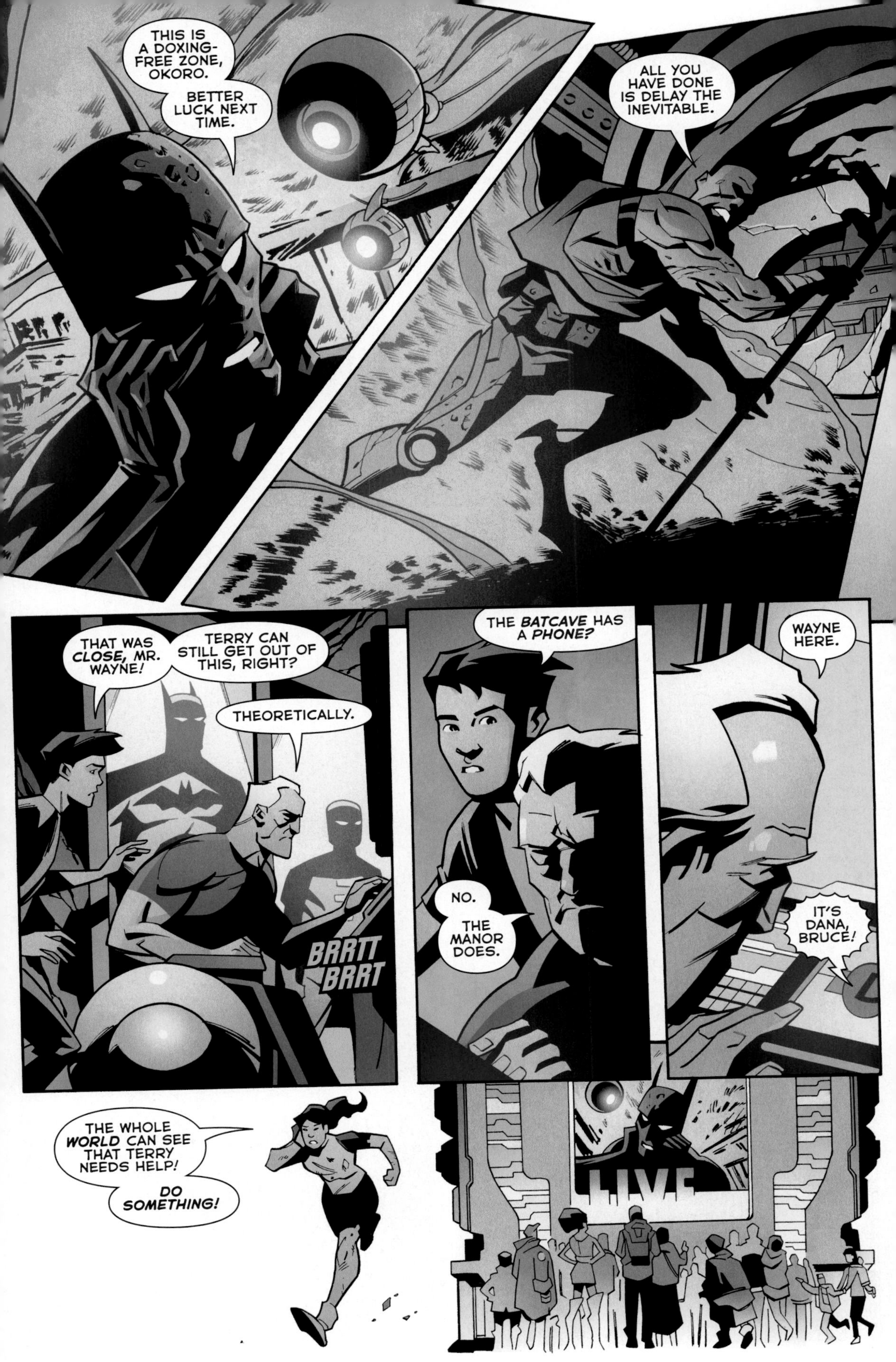
THIS IS A DOXING-FREE ZONE, OKORO.
BETTER LUCK NEXT TIME.
ALL YOU HAVE DONE IS DELAY THE INEVITABLE.
THAT WAS *CLOSE,* MR. WAYNE!
TERRY CAN STILL GET OUT OF THIS, RIGHT?
THEORETICALLY.
BRRTT BRRT
THE *BATCAVE* HAS A *PHONE?*
NO.
THE MANOR DOES.
WAYNE HERE.
IT'S DANA, BRUCE!
THE WHOLE *WORLD* CAN SEE THAT TERRY NEEDS HELP!
DO SOMETHING!
LIVE

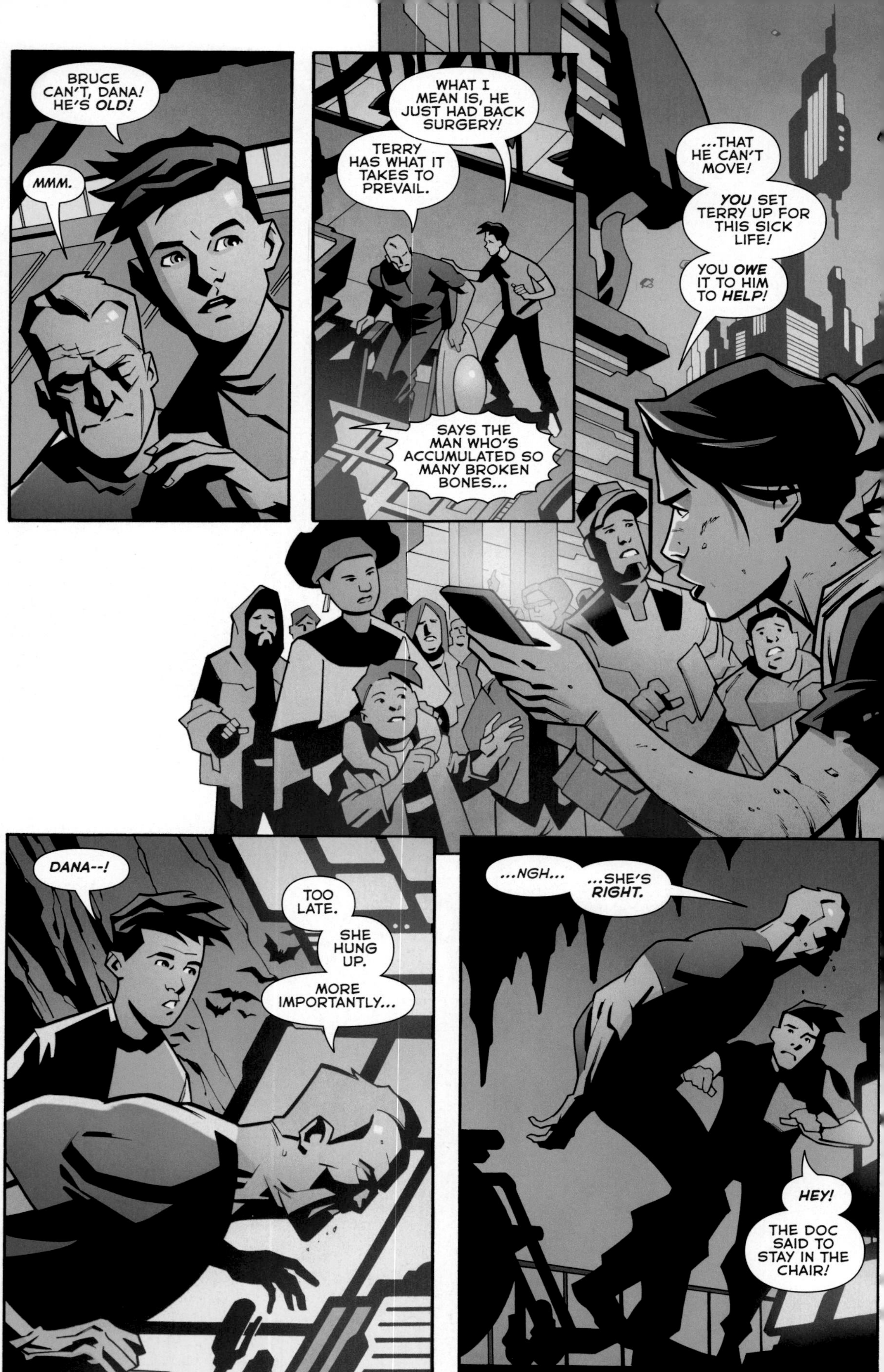
BRUCE CAN'T, DANA! HE'S OLD!
MMM.
WHAT I MEAN IS, HE JUST HAD BACK SURGERY!
TERRY HAS WHAT IT TAKES TO PREVAIL.
SAYS THE MAN WHO'S ACCUMULATED SO MANY BROKEN BONES...
...THAT HE CAN'T MOVE!
YOU SET TERRY UP FOR THIS SICK LIFE!
YOU OWE IT TO HIM TO HELP!
DANA--!
TOO LATE.
SHE HUNG UP.
MORE IMPORTANTLY...
...NGH...
...SHE'S RIGHT.
HEY!
THE DOC SAID TO STAY IN THE CHAIR!

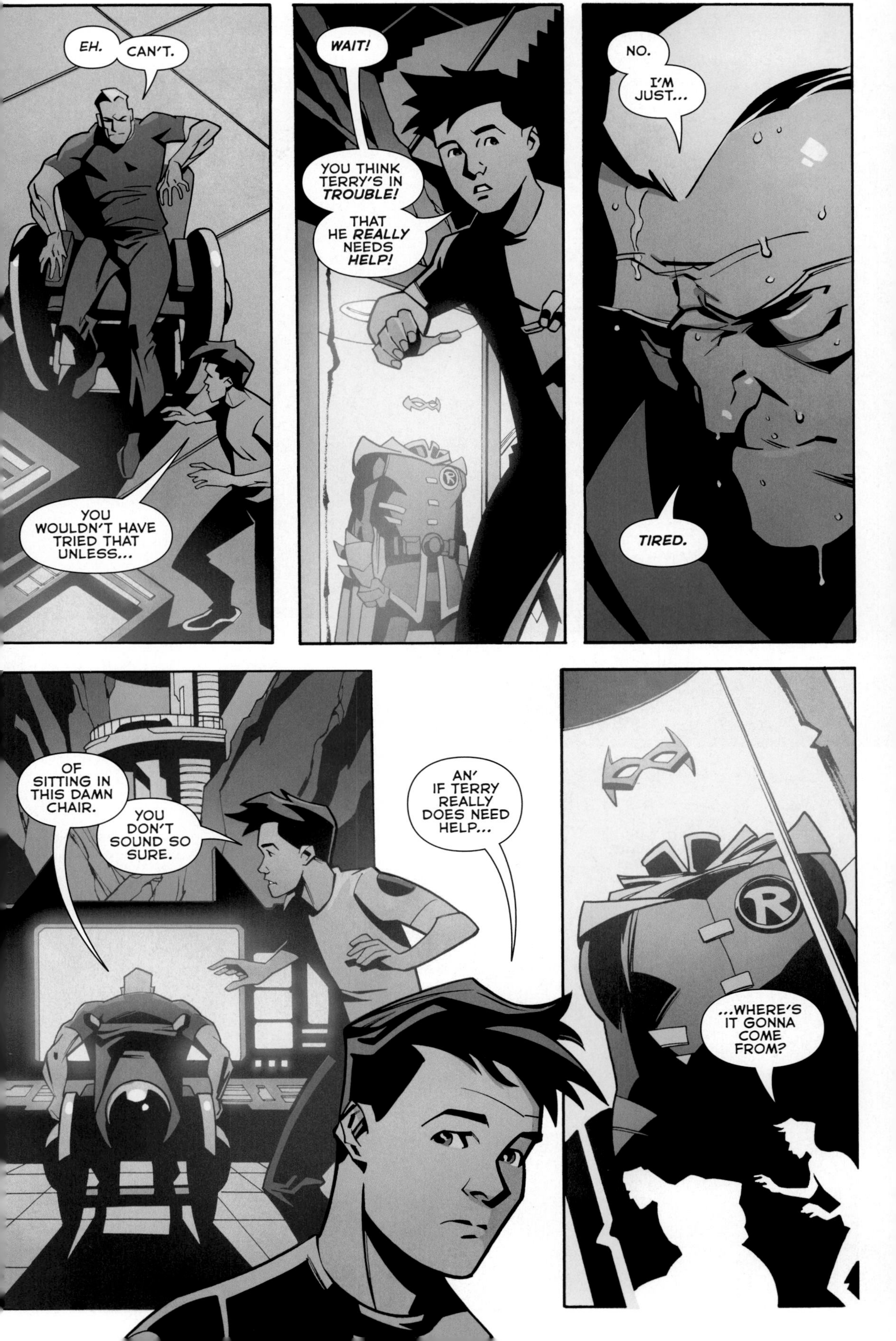
EH.
CAN'T.
YOU WOULDN'T HAVE TRIED THAT UNLESS...
WAIT!
YOU THINK TERRY'S IN TROUBLE!
THAT HE REALLY NEEDS HELP!
NO.
I'M JUST...
TIRED.
OF SITTING IN THIS DAMN CHAIR.
YOU DON'T SOUND SO SURE.
AN' IF TERRY REALLY DOES NEED HELP...
...WHERE'S IT GONNA COME FROM?

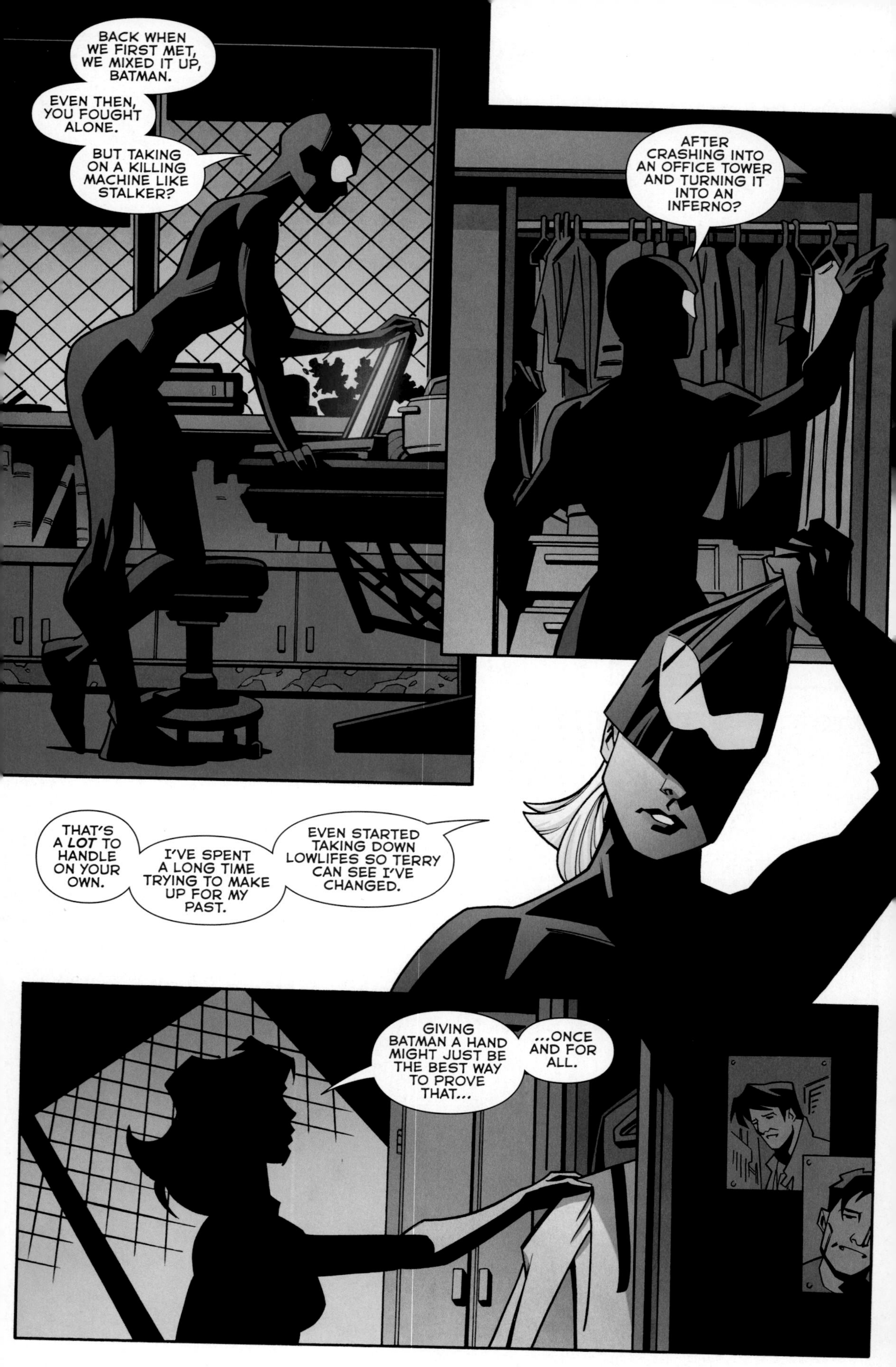
BACK WHEN WE FIRST MET, WE MIXED IT UP, BATMAN.
EVEN THEN, YOU FOUGHT ALONE.
BUT TAKING ON A KILLING MACHINE LIKE STALKER?
AFTER CRASHING INTO AN OFFICE TOWER AND TURNING IT INTO AN INFERNO?
THAT'S A *LOT* TO HANDLE ON YOUR OWN.
I'VE SPENT A LONG TIME TRYING TO MAKE UP FOR MY PAST.
EVEN STARTED TAKING DOWN LOWLIFES SO TERRY CAN SEE I'VE CHANGED.
GIVING BATMAN A HAND MIGHT JUST BE THE BEST WAY TO PROVE THAT...
...ONCE AND FOR ALL.

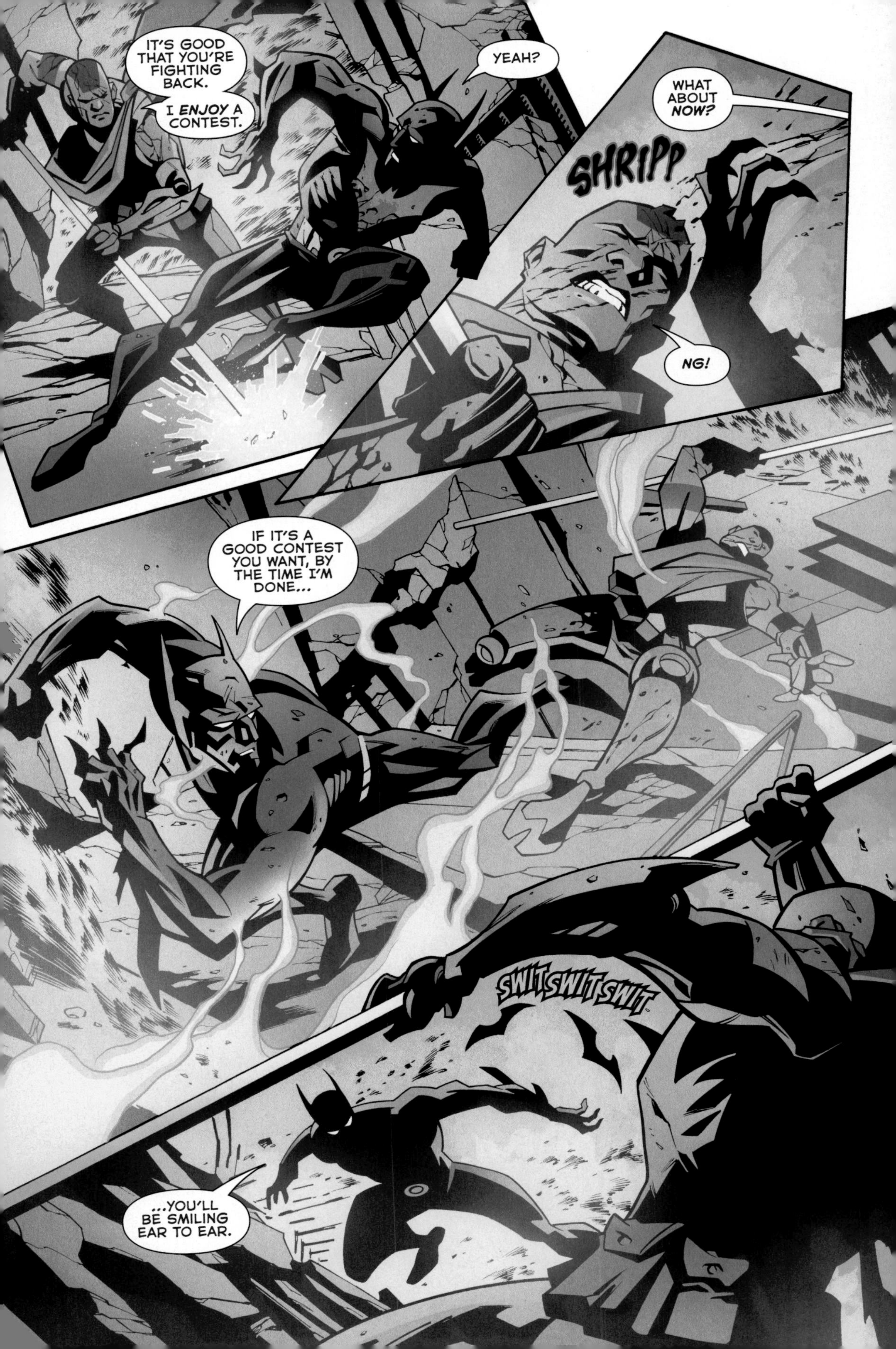
IT'S GOOD THAT YOU'RE FIGHTING BACK.
I *ENJOY* A CONTEST.
YEAH?
WHAT ABOUT *NOW?*
SHRIPP
NG!
IF IT'S A GOOD CONTEST YOU WANT, BY THE TIME I'M DONE...
SWIT SWIT SWIT
...YOU'LL BE SMILING EAR TO EAR.

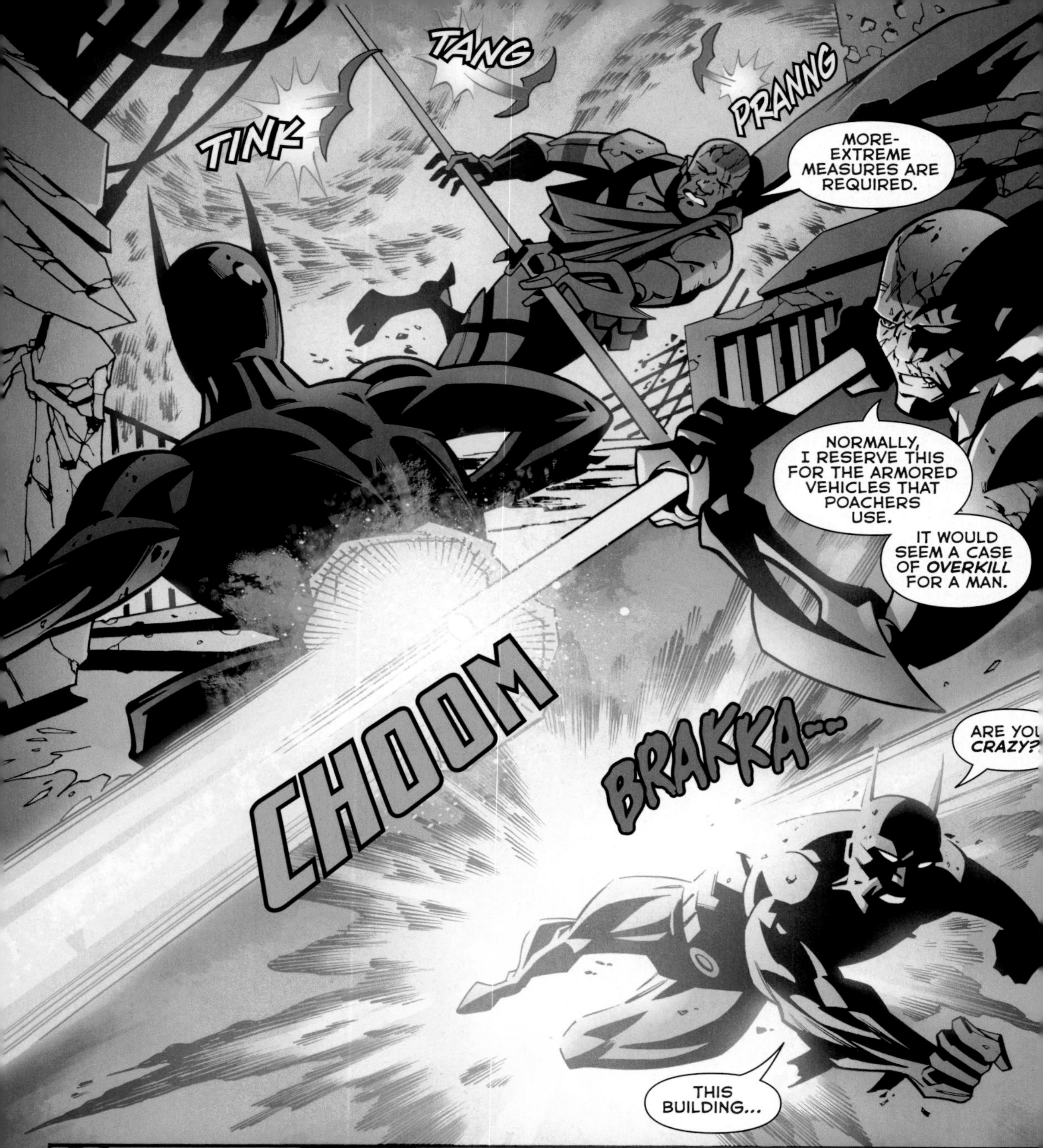
TINK
TANG
PRANNG
MORE-EXTREME MEASURES ARE REQUIRED.
NORMALLY, I RESERVE THIS FOR THE ARMORED VEHICLES THAT POACHERS USE.
IT WOULD SEEM A CASE OF *OVERKILL* FOR A MAN.
CHOOM
BRAKKA--
THIS BUILDING...
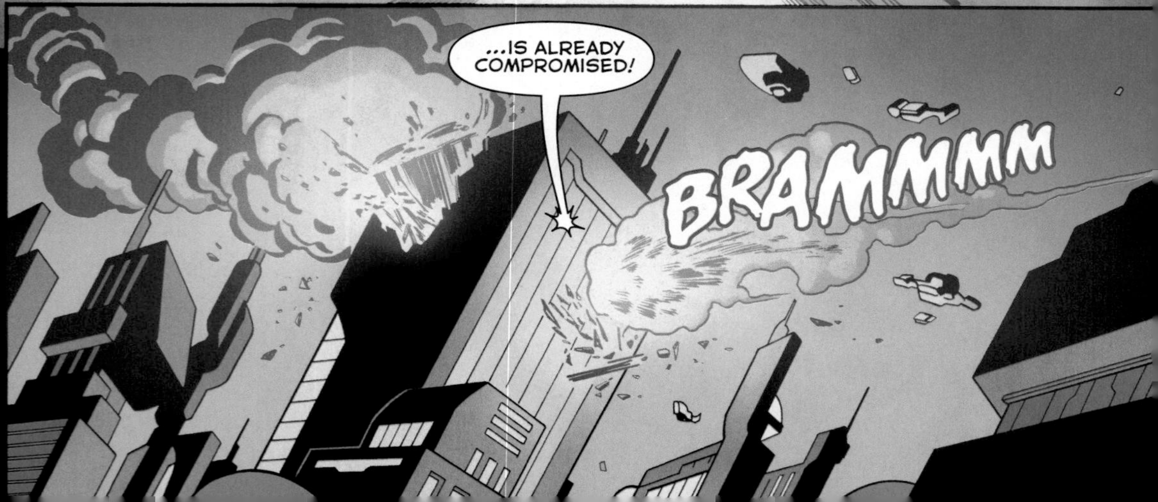
...IS ALREADY COMPROMISED!
BRAMMMM

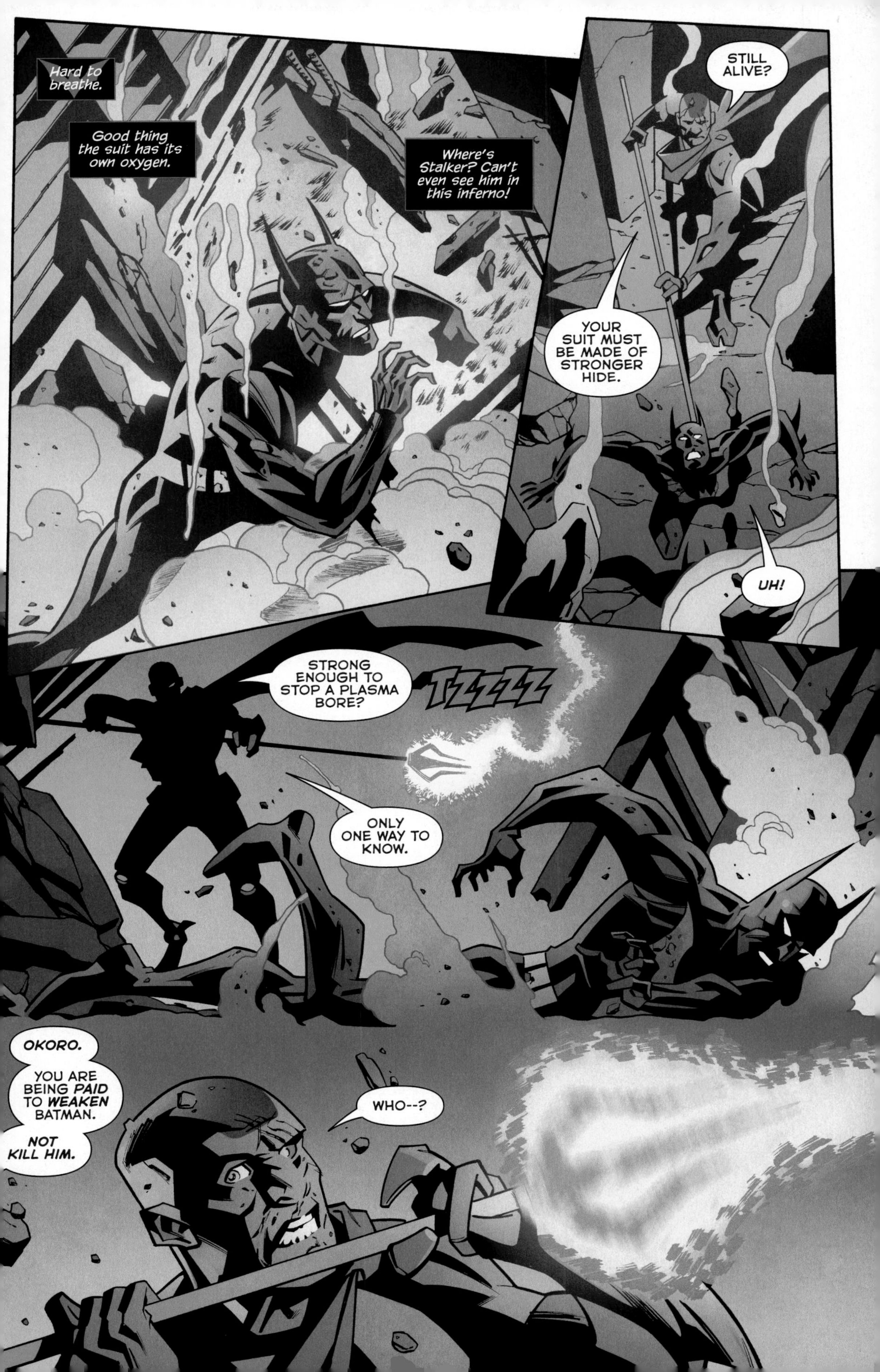
Hard to breathe.
Good thing the suit has its own oxygen.
Where's Stalker? Can't even see him in this inferno!
STILL ALIVE?
YOUR SUIT MUST BE MADE OF STRONGER HIDE.
UH!
STRONG ENOUGH TO STOP A PLASMA BORE?
TZZZZ
ONLY ONE WAY TO KNOW.
OKORO.
YOU ARE BEING *PAID* TO *WEAKEN* BATMAN.
NOT KILL HIM.
WHO--?

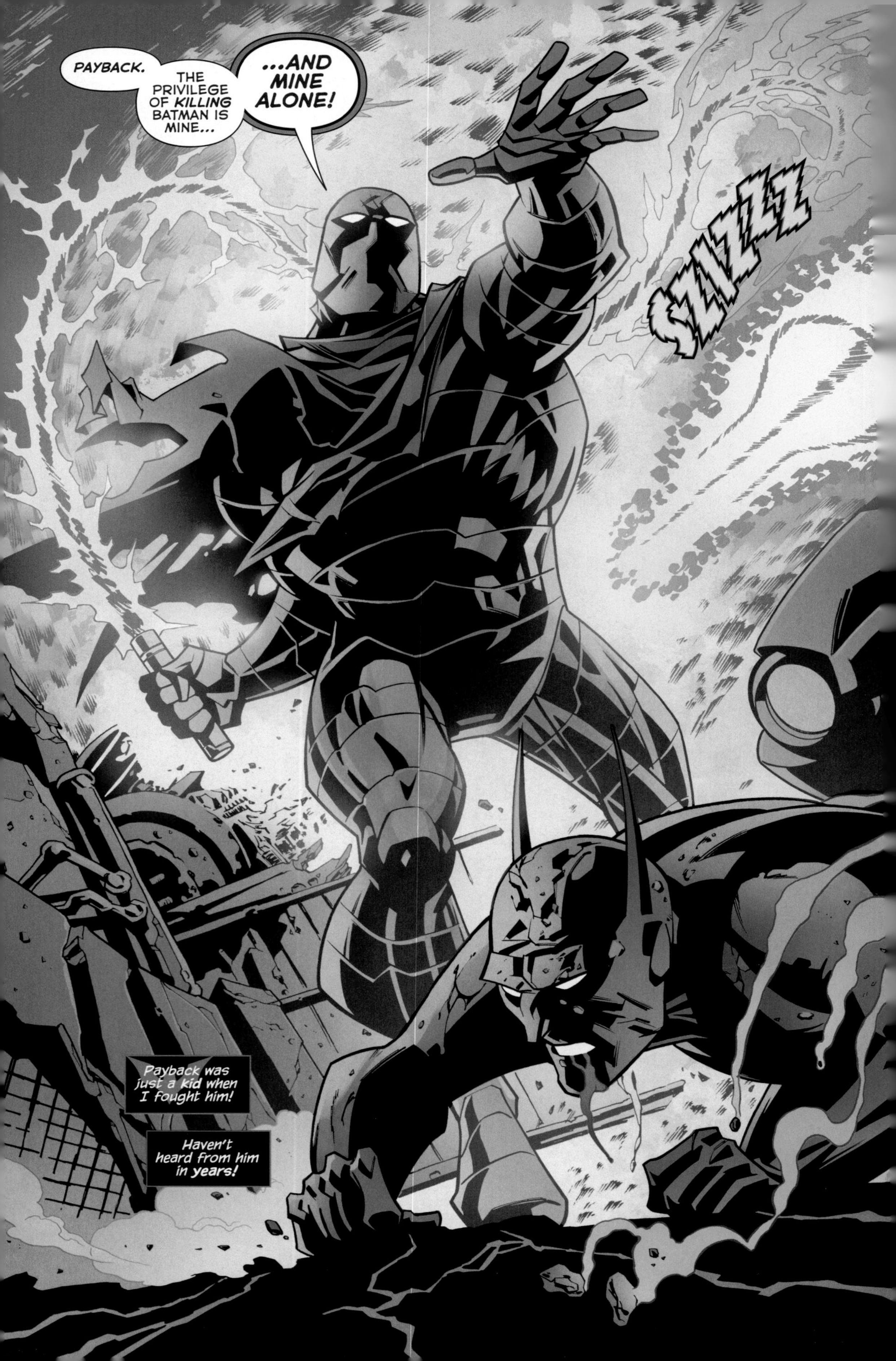

PAYBACK.
THE PRIVILEGE OF KILLING BATMAN IS MINE...
...AND MINE ALONE!
SZZZZZZ
Payback was just a kid when I fought him!
Haven't heard from him in years!

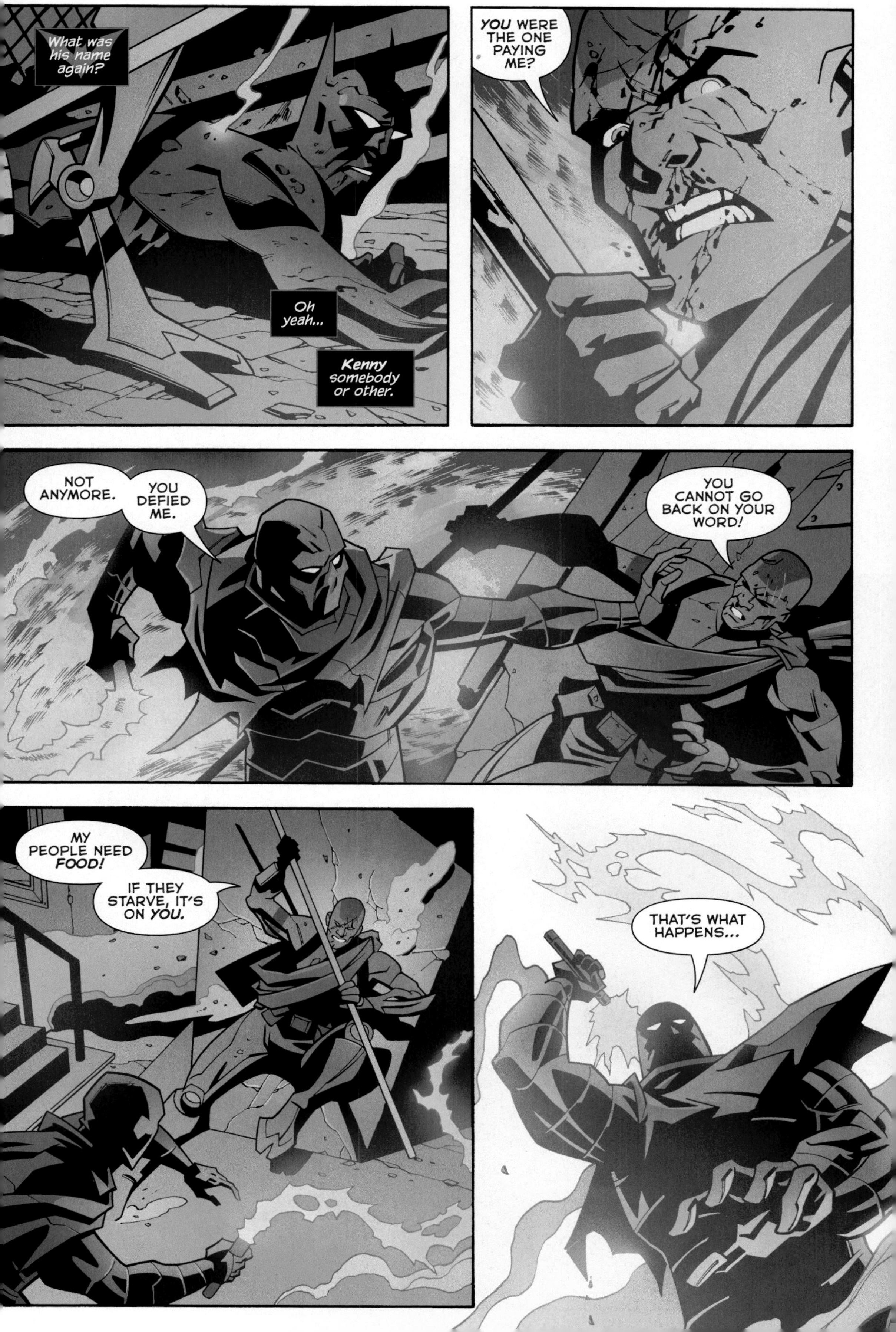
What was his name again?
Oh yeah...
Kenny somebody or other.
YOU WERE THE ONE PAYING ME?
NOT ANYMORE.
YOU DEFIED ME.
YOU CANNOT GO BACK ON YOUR WORD!
MY PEOPLE NEED FOOD!
IF THEY STARVE, IT'S ON YOU.
THAT'S WHAT HAPPENS...

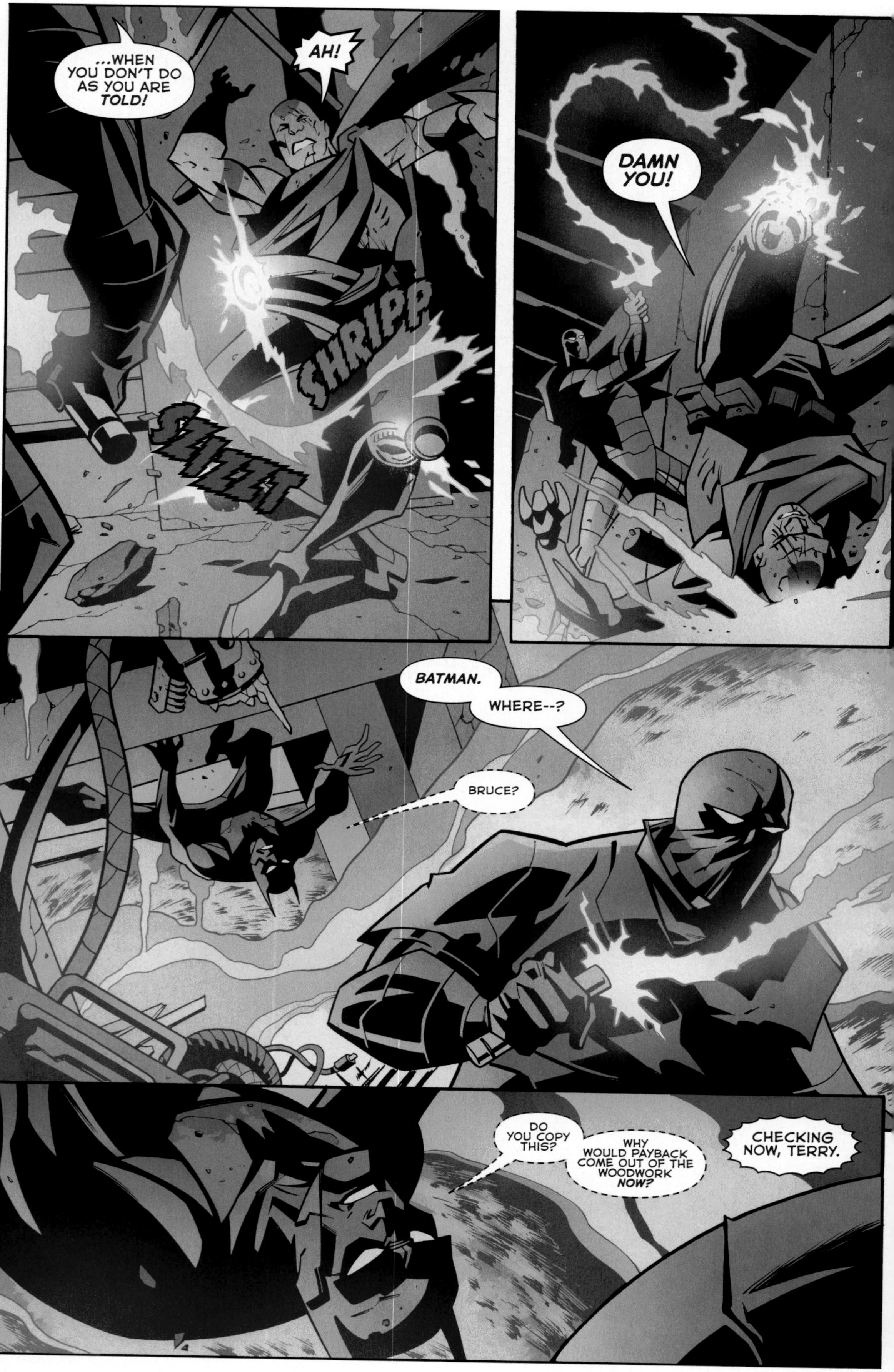
...WHEN YOU DON'T DO AS YOU ARE TOLD!
AH!
SHRIPP
SZZZZZT
DAMN YOU!
BATMAN.
WHERE--?
BRUCE?
DO YOU COPY THIS?
WHY WOULD PAYBACK COME OUT OF THE WOODWORK NOW?
CHECKING NOW, TERRY.

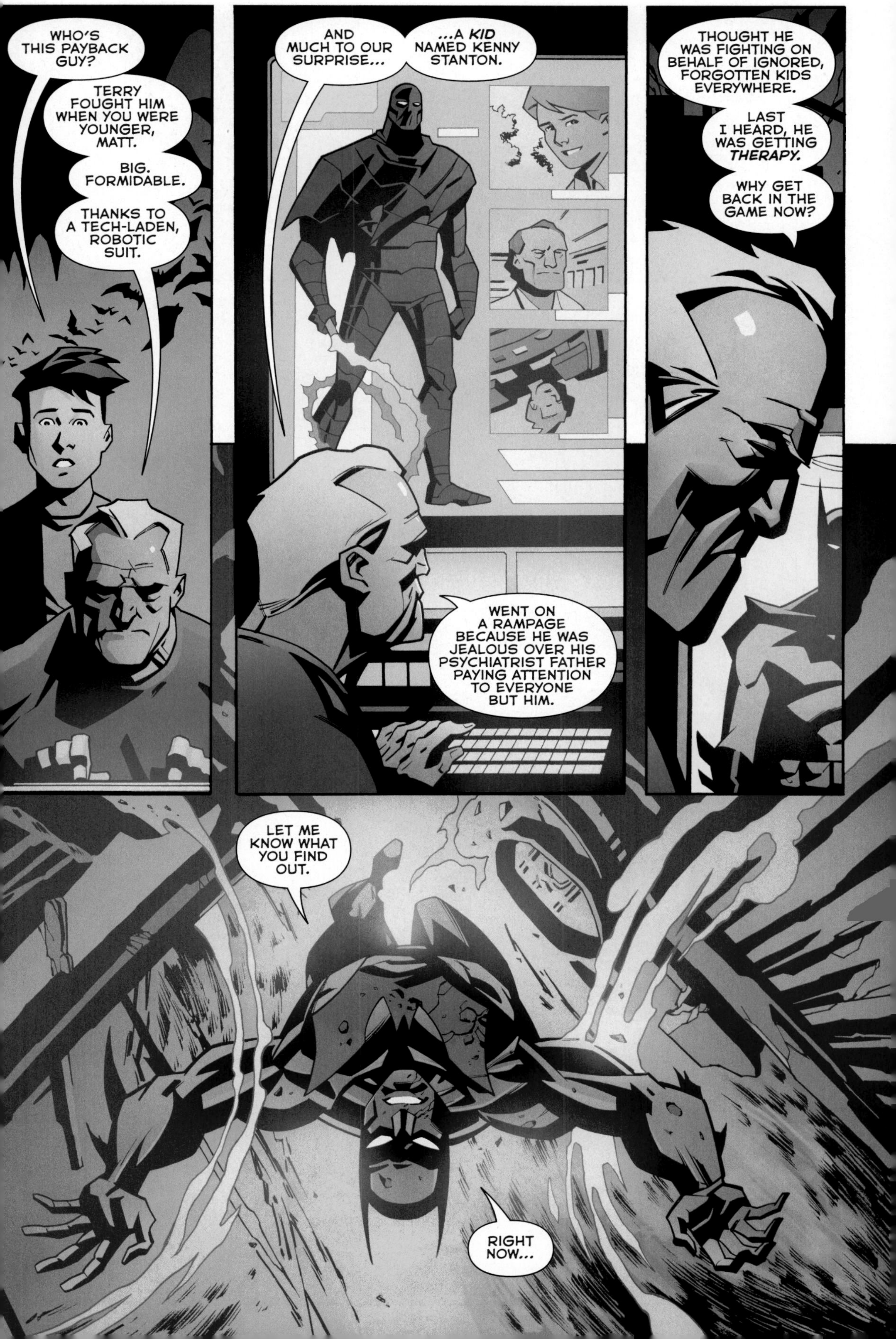

WHO'S THIS PAYBACK GUY?
TERRY FOUGHT HIM WHEN YOU WERE YOUNGER, MATT.
BIG. FORMIDABLE.
THANKS TO A TECH-LADEN, ROBOTIC SUIT.
AND MUCH TO OUR SURPRISE...
...A *KID* NAMED KENNY STANTON.
WENT ON A RAMPAGE BECAUSE HE WAS JEALOUS OVER HIS PSYCHIATRIST FATHER PAYING ATTENTION TO EVERYONE BUT HIM.
THOUGHT HE WAS FIGHTING ON BEHALF OF IGNORED, FORGOTTEN KIDS EVERYWHERE.
LAST I HEARD, HE WAS GETTING *THERAPY.*
WHY GET BACK IN THE GAME NOW?
LET ME KNOW WHAT YOU FIND OUT.
RIGHT NOW...

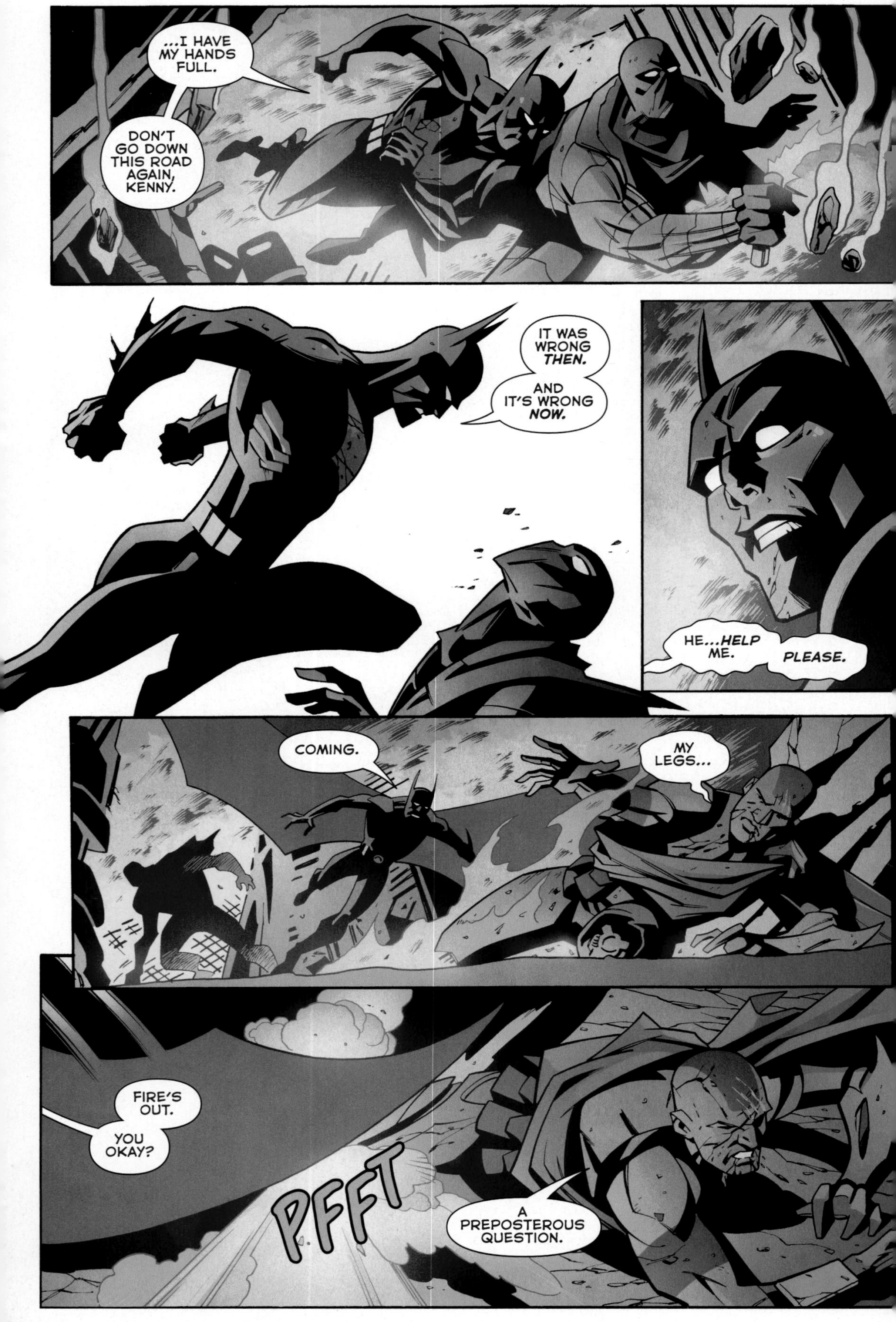
...I HAVE MY HANDS FULL.
DON'T GO DOWN THIS ROAD AGAIN, KENNY.
IT WAS WRONG *THEN.*
AND IT'S WRONG *NOW.*
HE...*HELP* ME.
PLEASE.
COMING.
MY LEGS...
FIRE'S OUT.
YOU OKAY?
PFFT
A PREPOSTEROUS QUESTION.

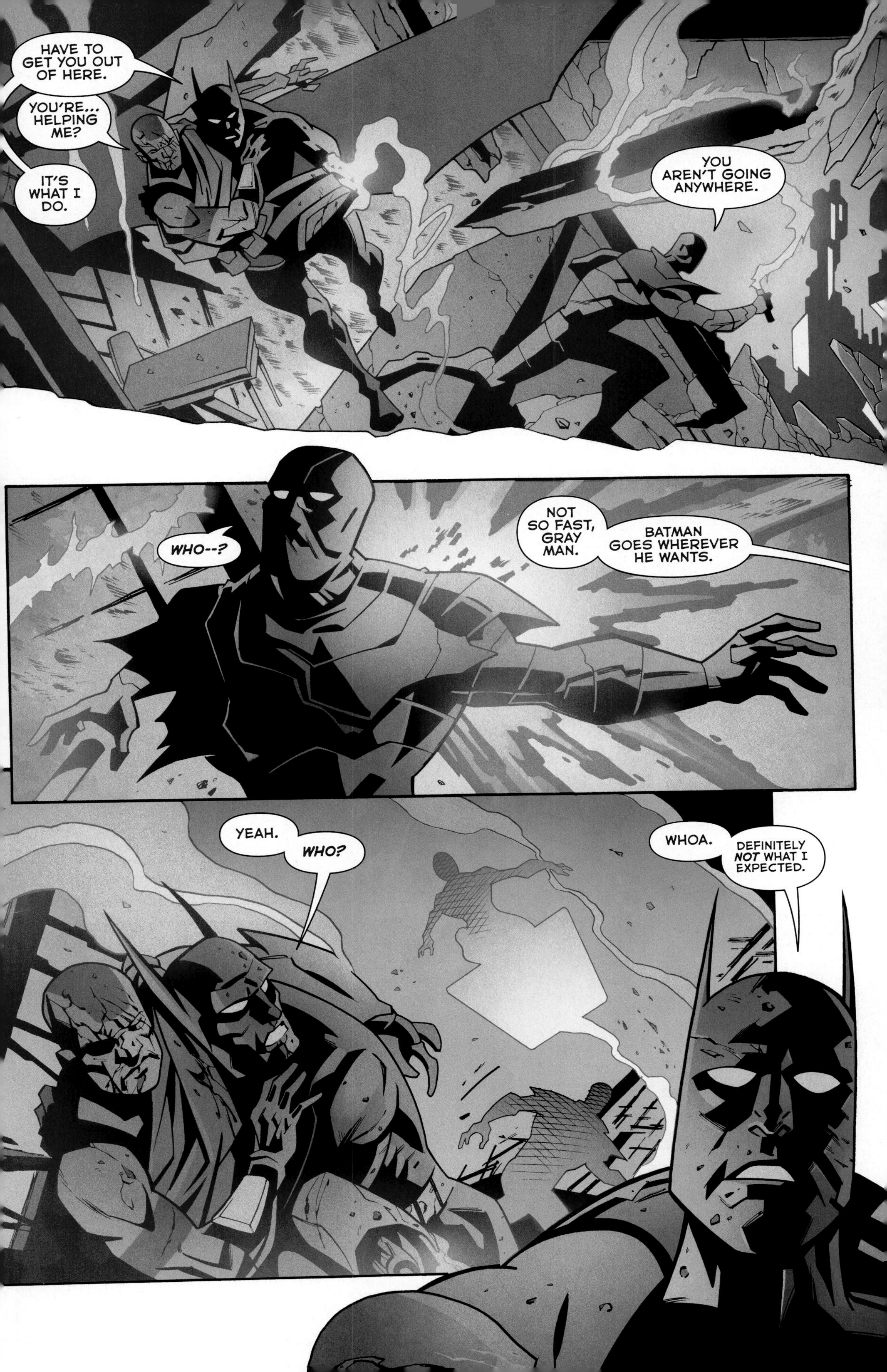
HAVE TO GET YOU OUT OF HERE.
YOU'RE... HELPING ME?
IT'S WHAT I DO.
YOU AREN'T GOING ANYWHERE.
WHO--?
NOT SO FAST, GRAY MAN.
BATMAN GOES WHEREVER HE WANTS.
YEAH.
WHO?
WHOA.
DEFINITELY NOT WHAT I EXPECTED.

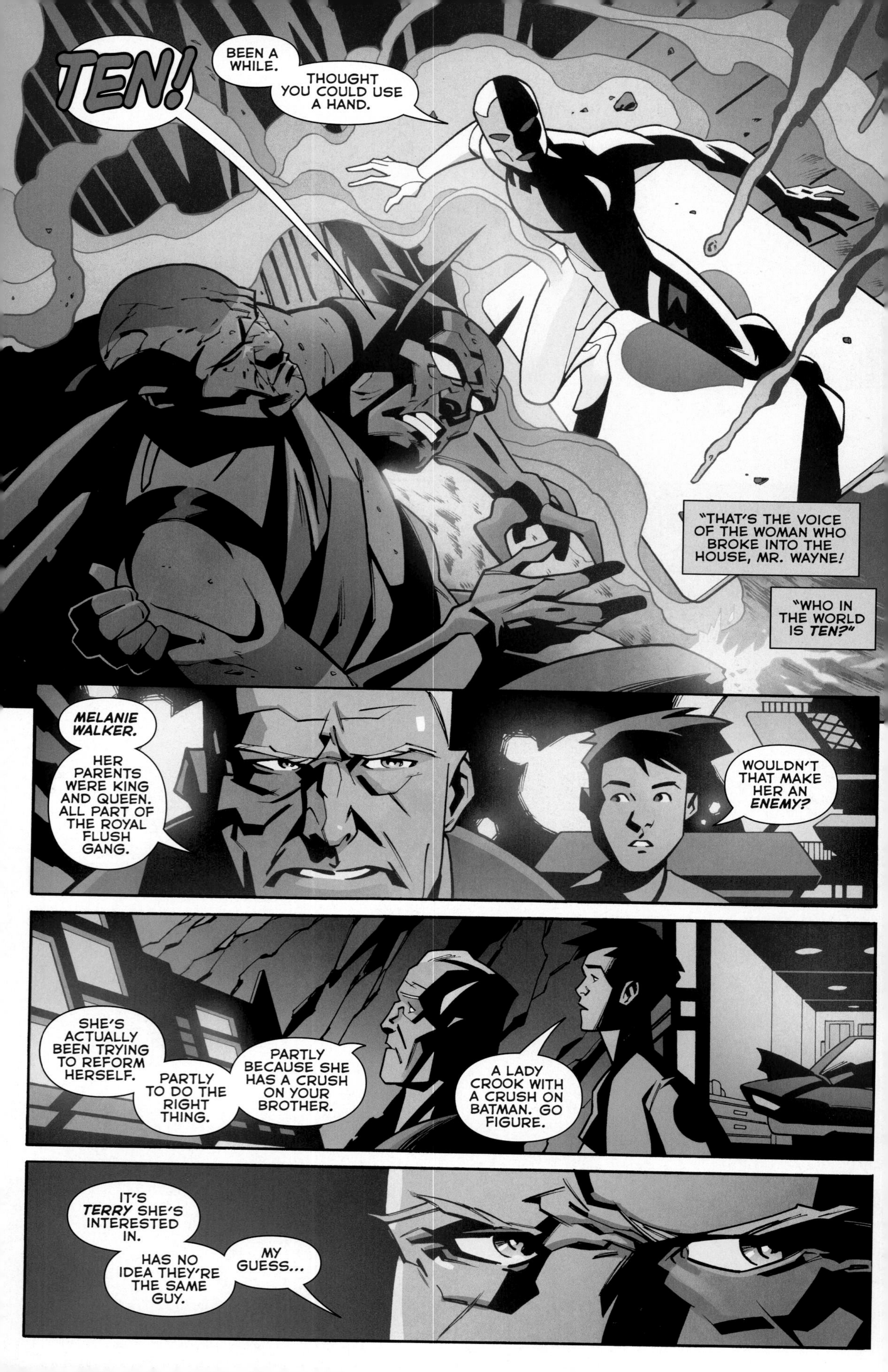
TEN!
BEEN A WHILE.
THOUGHT YOU COULD USE A HAND.
"THAT'S THE VOICE OF THE WOMAN WHO BROKE INTO THE HOUSE, MR. WAYNE!
"WHO IN THE WORLD IS TEN?"
MELANIE WALKER.
HER PARENTS WERE KING AND QUEEN. ALL PART OF THE ROYAL FLUSH GANG.
WOULDN'T THAT MAKE HER AN ENEMY?
SHE'S ACTUALLY BEEN TRYING TO REFORM HERSELF.
PARTLY TO DO THE RIGHT THING.
PARTLY BECAUSE SHE HAS A CRUSH ON YOUR BROTHER.
A LADY CROOK WITH A CRUSH ON BATMAN. GO FIGURE.
IT'S TERRY SHE'S INTERESTED IN.
HAS NO IDEA THEY'RE THE SAME GUY.
MY GUESS...

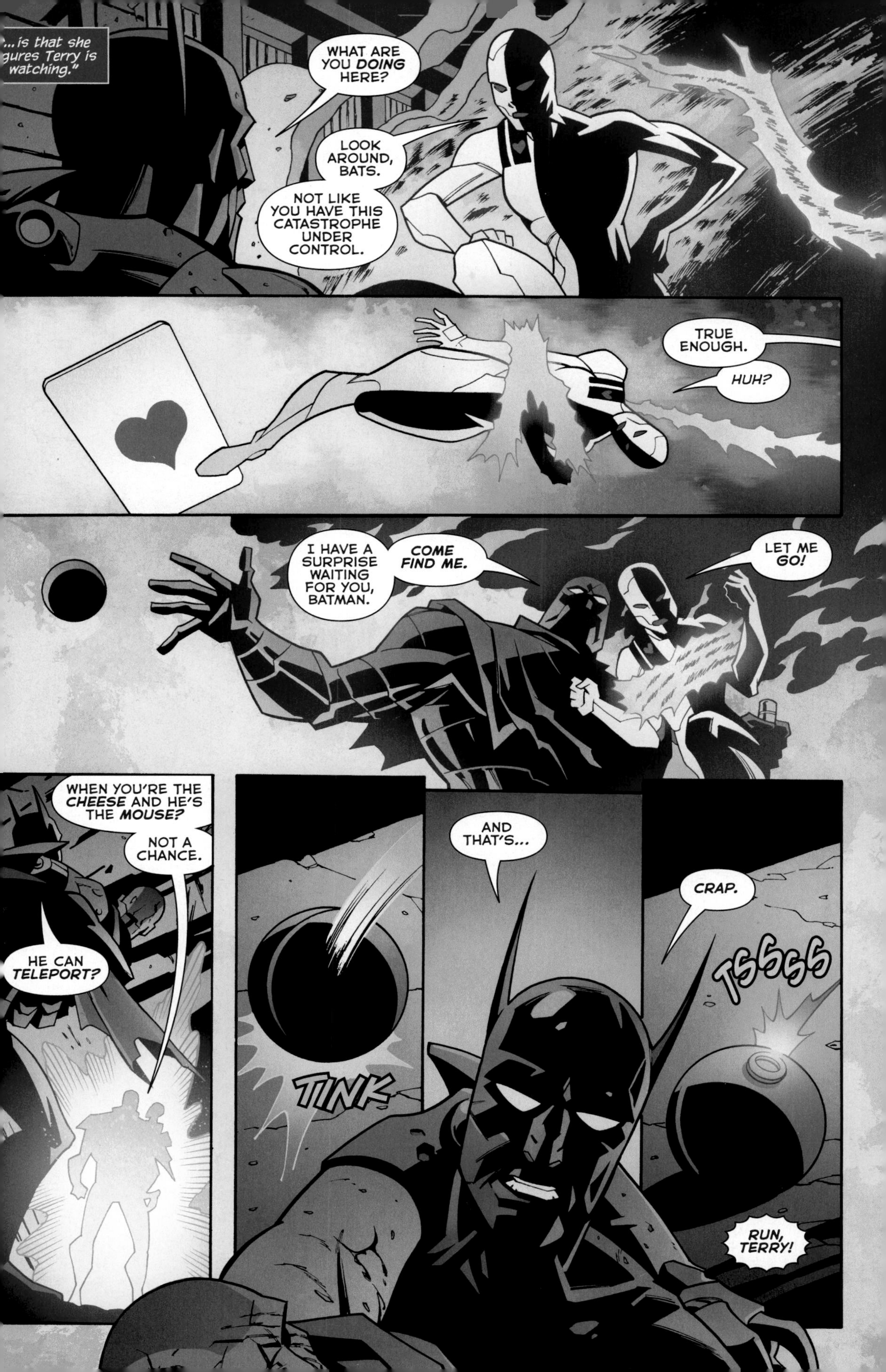

"...is that she figures Terry is watching."
WHAT ARE YOU DOING HERE?
LOOK AROUND, BATS.
NOT LIKE YOU HAVE THIS CATASTROPHE UNDER CONTROL.
TRUE ENOUGH.
HUH?
I HAVE A SURPRISE WAITING FOR YOU, BATMAN.
COME FIND ME.
LET ME GO!
WHEN YOU'RE THE CHEESE AND HE'S THE MOUSE?
NOT A CHANCE.
HE CAN TELEPORT?
AND THAT'S...
TINK
CRAP.
TSSSS
RUN, TERRY!

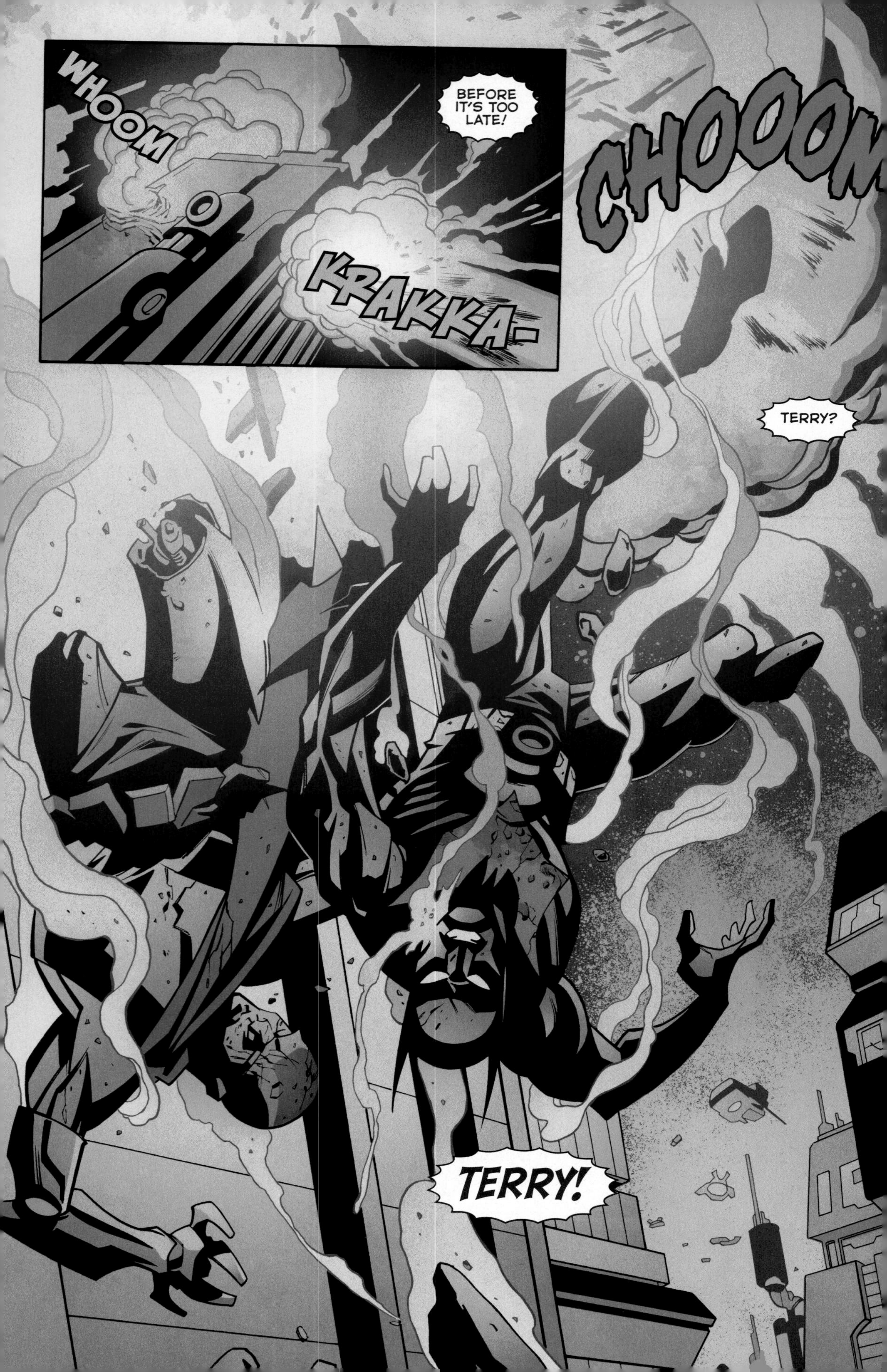

WHOOM
BEFORE IT'S TOO LATE!
KRAKKA-
CHOOOOM
TERRY?
TERRY!

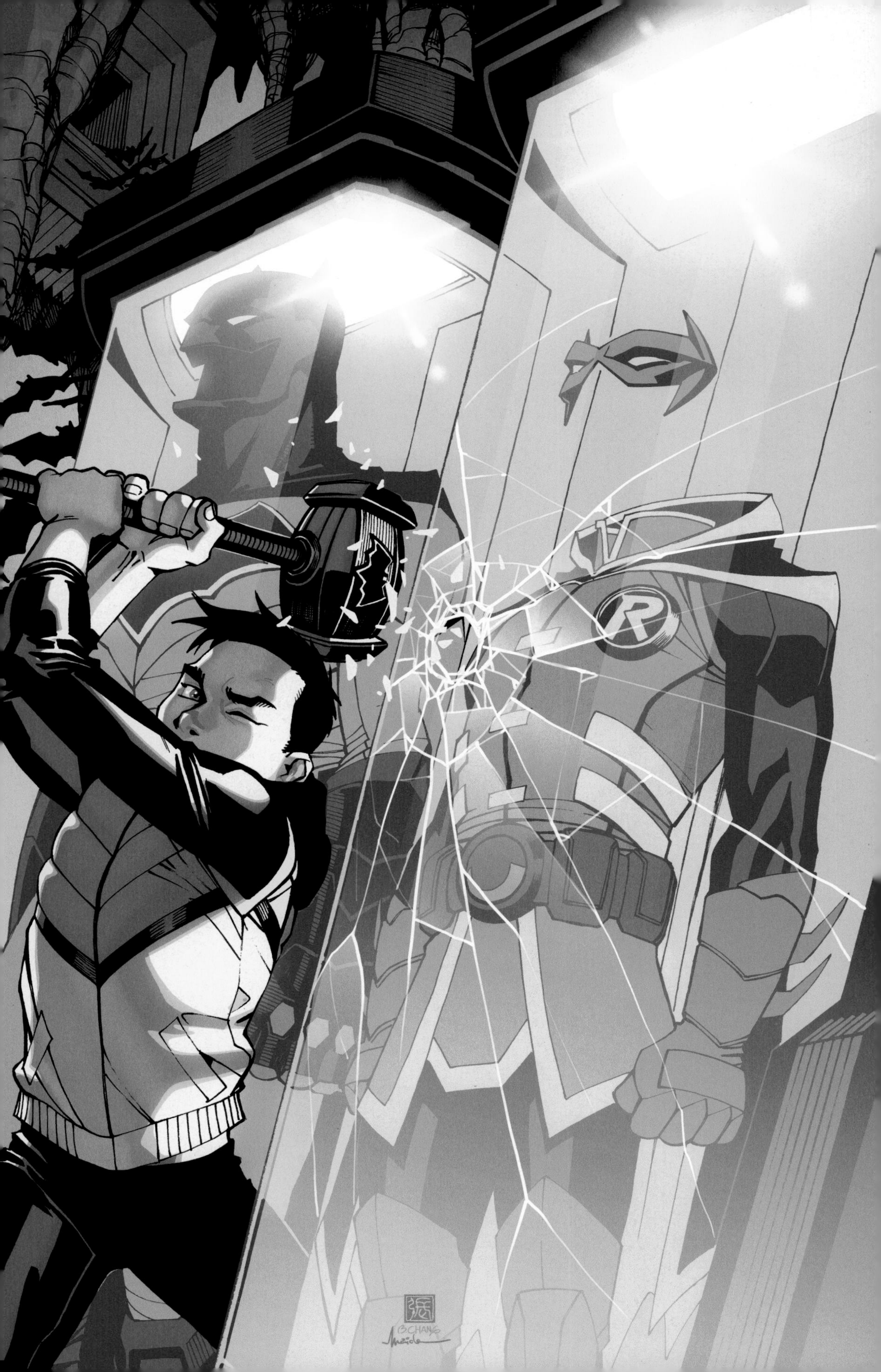
B.CHANG

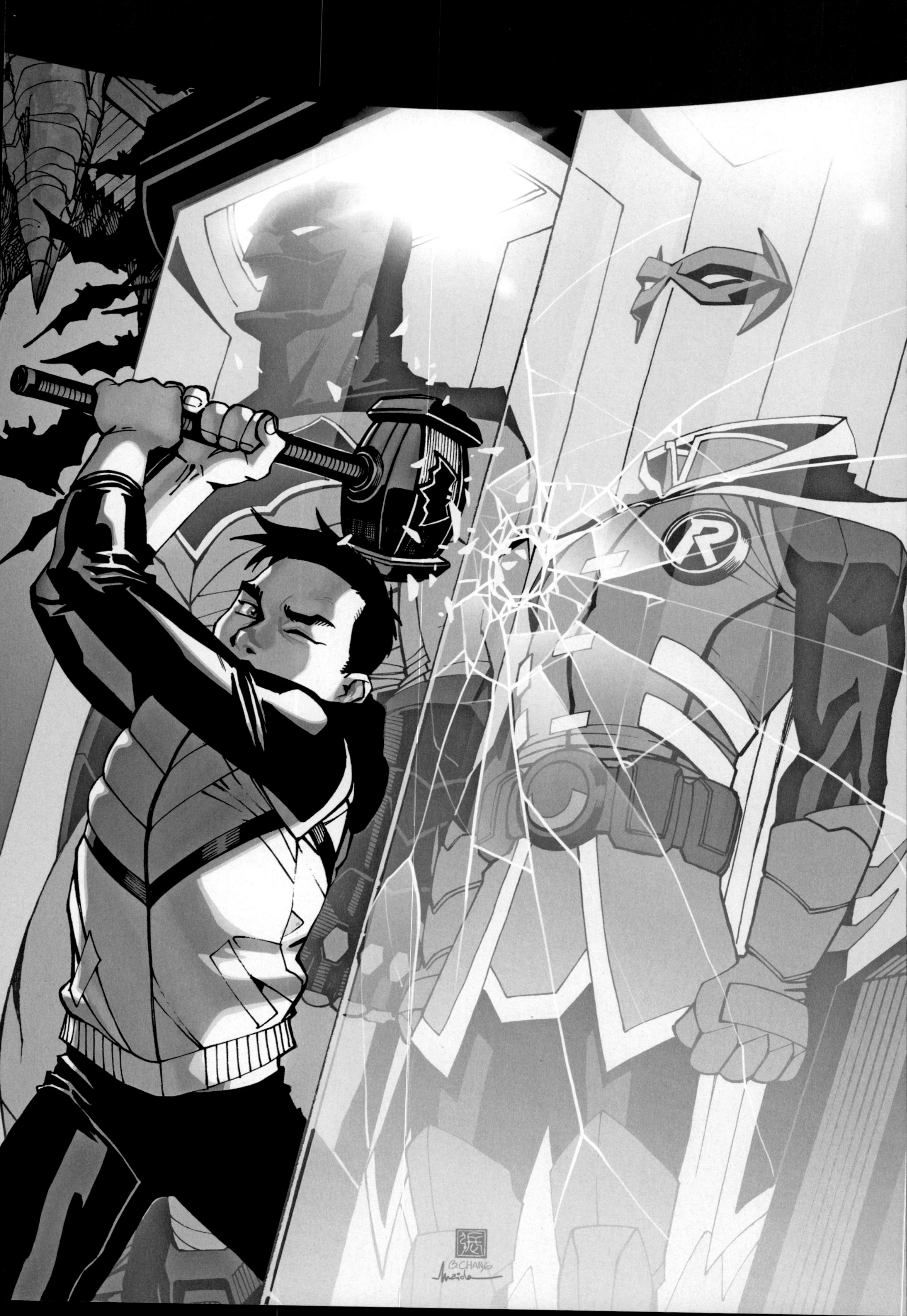
B.CHANG

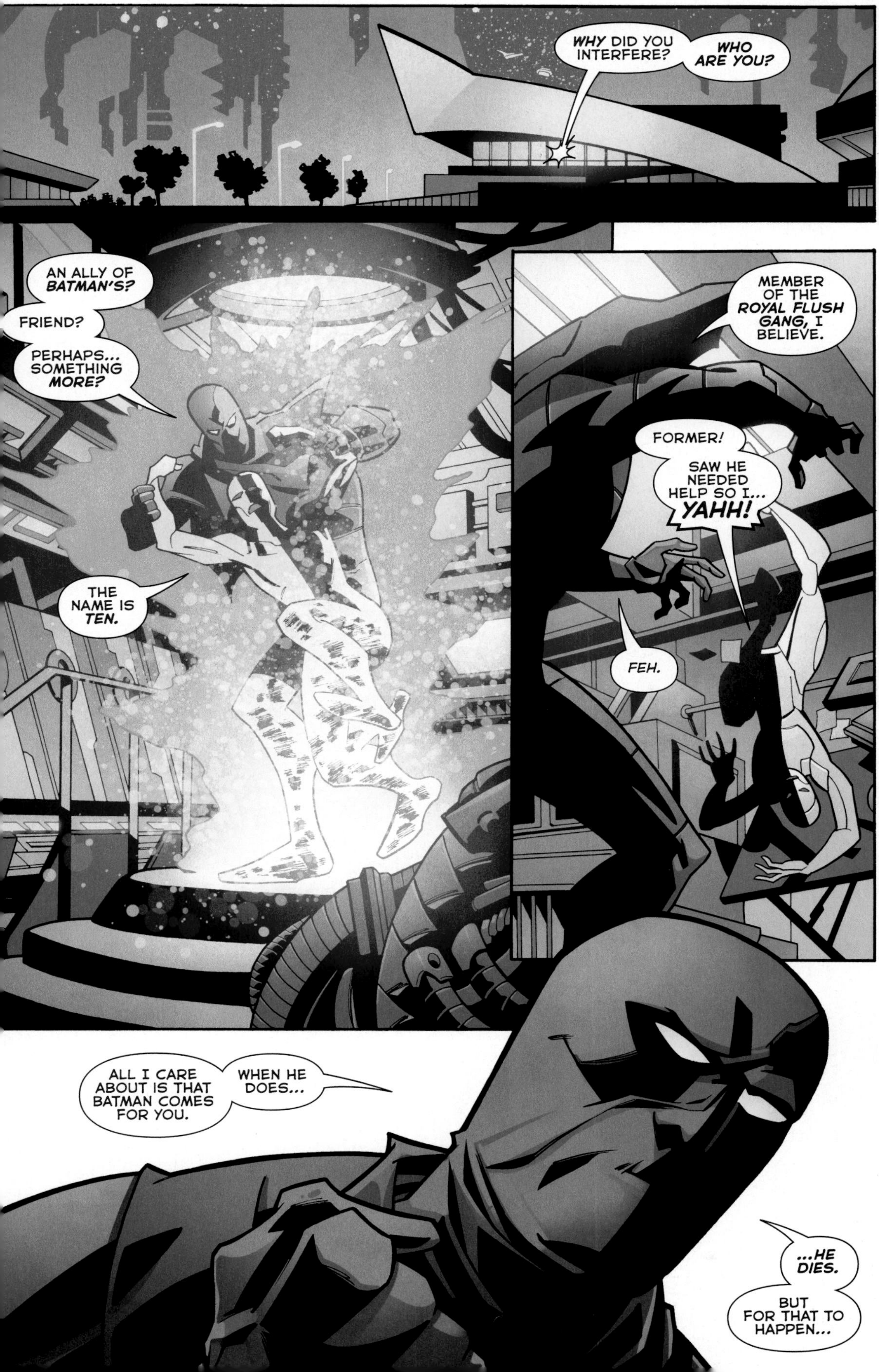
WHY DID YOU INTERFERE?
WHO ARE YOU?
AN ALLY OF BATMAN'S?
FRIEND?
PERHAPS... SOMETHING MORE?
MEMBER OF THE ROYAL FLUSH GANG, I BELIEVE.
FORMER!
SAW HE NEEDED HELP SO I... YAHH!
THE NAME IS TEN.
FEH.
ALL I CARE ABOUT IS THAT BATMAN COMES FOR YOU.
WHEN HE DOES...
...HE DIES.
BUT FOR THAT TO HAPPEN...

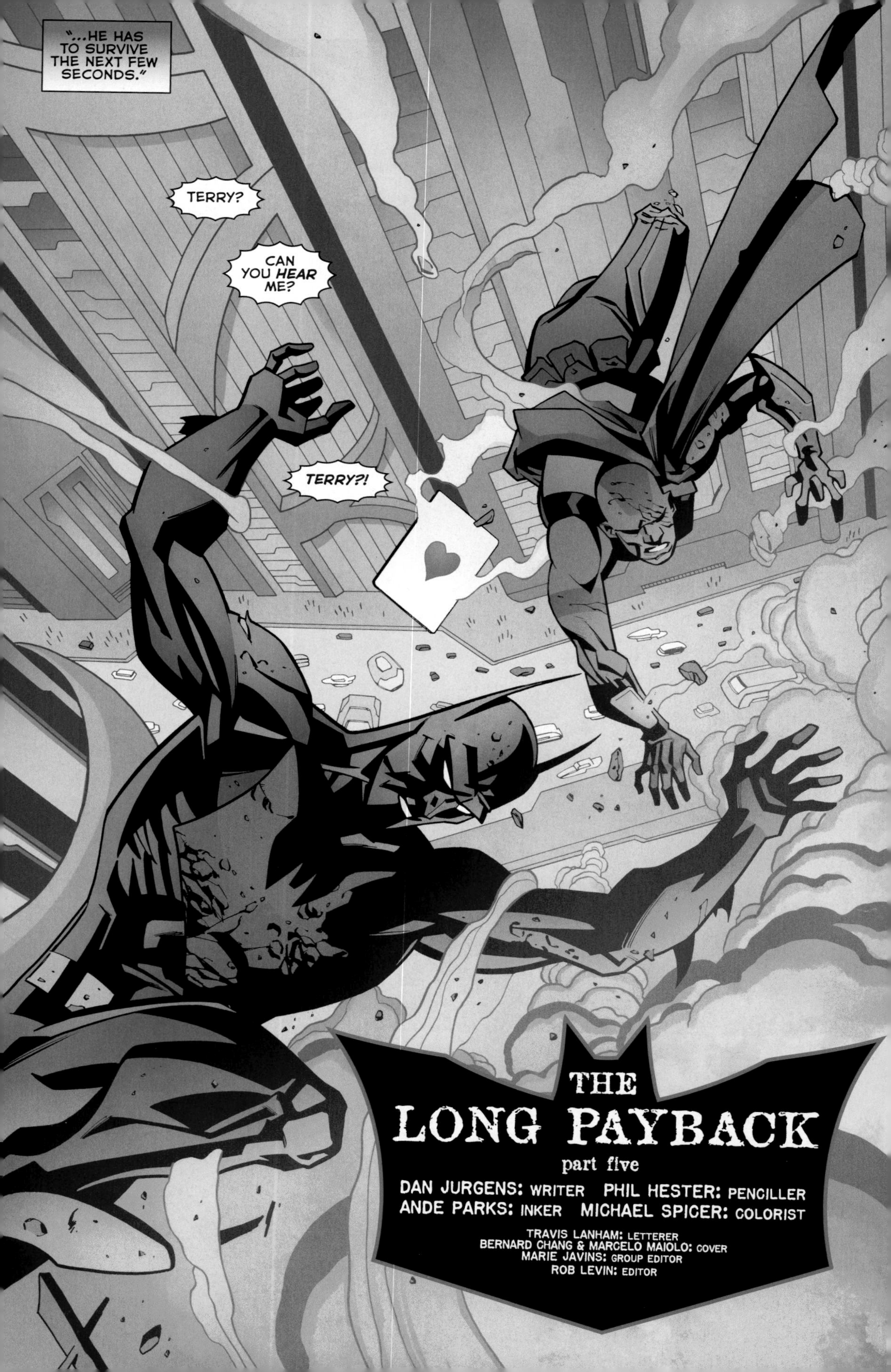
"...HE HAS TO SURVIVE THE NEXT FEW SECONDS."
TERRY?
CAN YOU HEAR ME?
TERRY?!
THE LONG PAYBACK
part five
DAN JURGENS: WRITER PHIL HESTER: PENCILLER
ANDE PARKS: INKER MICHAEL SPICER: COLORIST
TRAVIS LANHAM: LETTERER
BERNARD CHANG & MARCELO MAIOLO: COVER
MARIE JAVINS: GROUP EDITOR
ROB LEVIN: EDITOR

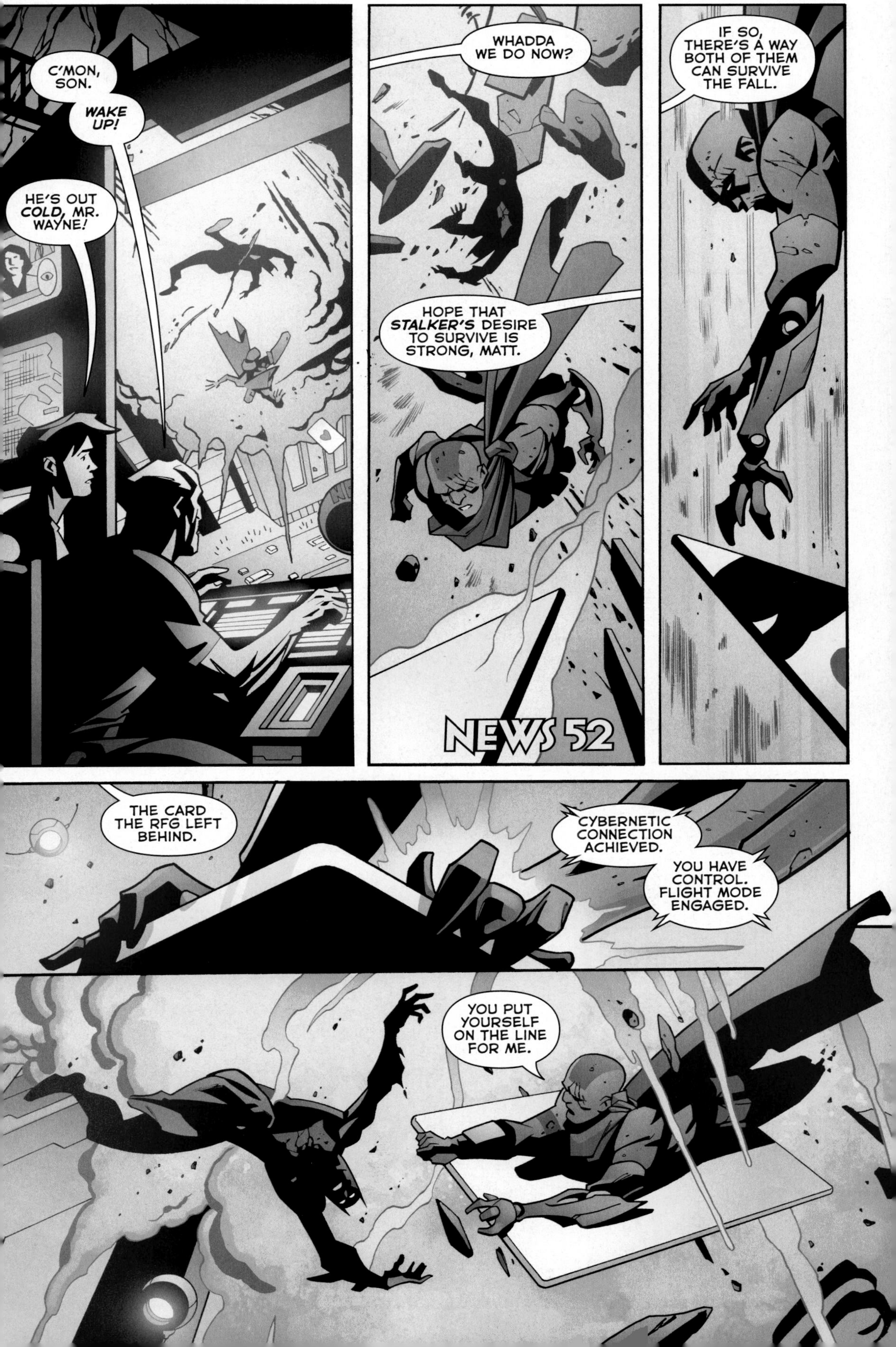
C'MON, SON.
WAKE UP!
HE'S OUT COLD, MR. WAYNE!
WHADDA WE DO NOW?
HOPE THAT STALKER'S DESIRE TO SURVIVE IS STRONG, MATT.
NEWS 52
IF SO, THERE'S A WAY BOTH OF THEM CAN SURVIVE THE FALL.
THE CARD THE RFG LEFT BEHIND.
CYBERNETIC CONNECTION ACHIEVED.
YOU HAVE CONTROL. FLIGHT MODE ENGAGED.
YOU PUT YOURSELF ON THE LINE FOR ME.

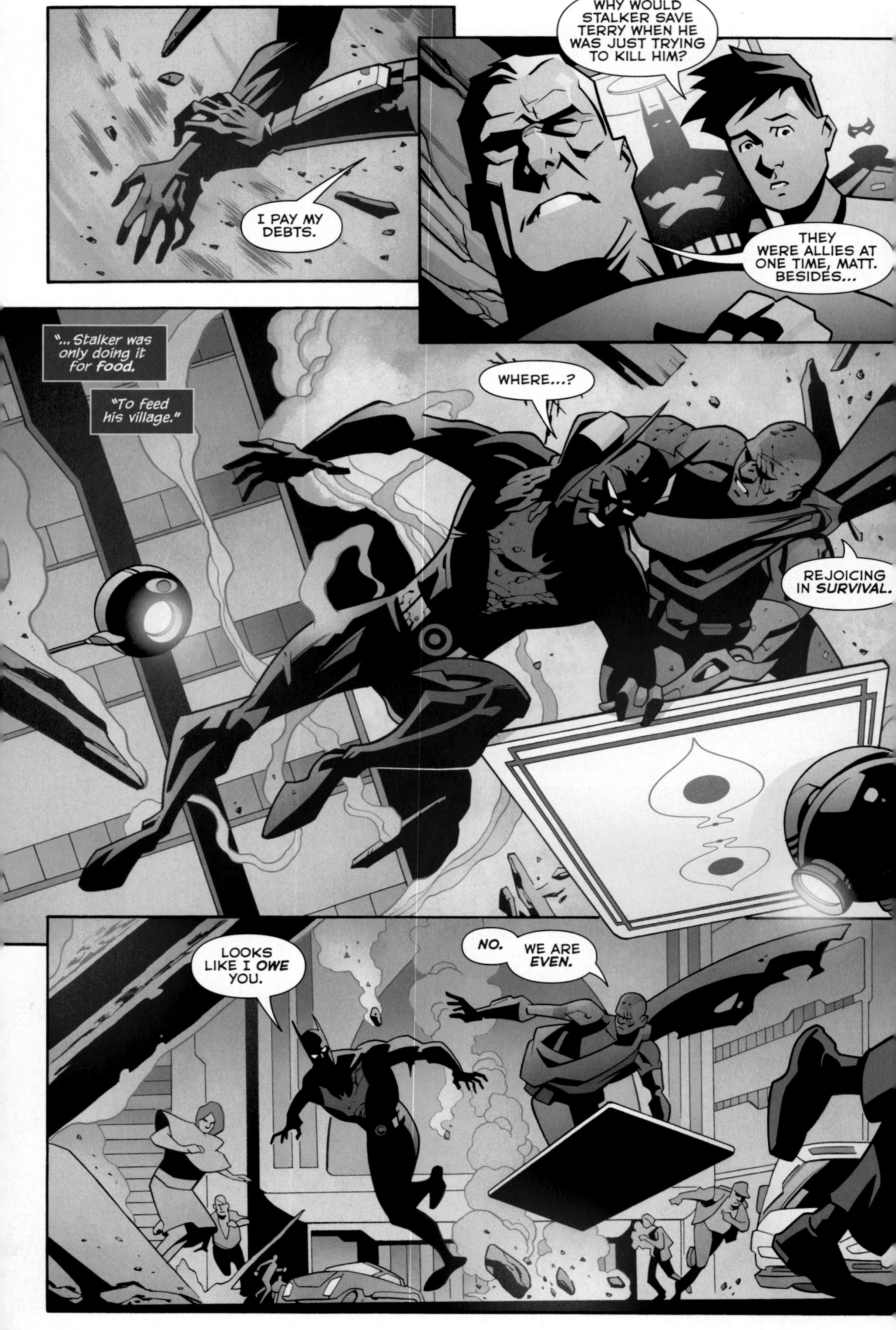
I PAY MY DEBTS.
WHY WOULD STALKER SAVE TERRY WHEN HE WAS JUST TRYING TO KILL HIM?
THEY WERE ALLIES AT ONE TIME, MATT. BESIDES...
"...Stalker was only doing it for food.
"To feed his village."
WHERE...?
REJOICING IN SURVIVAL.
LOOKS LIKE I OWE YOU.
NO. WE ARE EVEN.

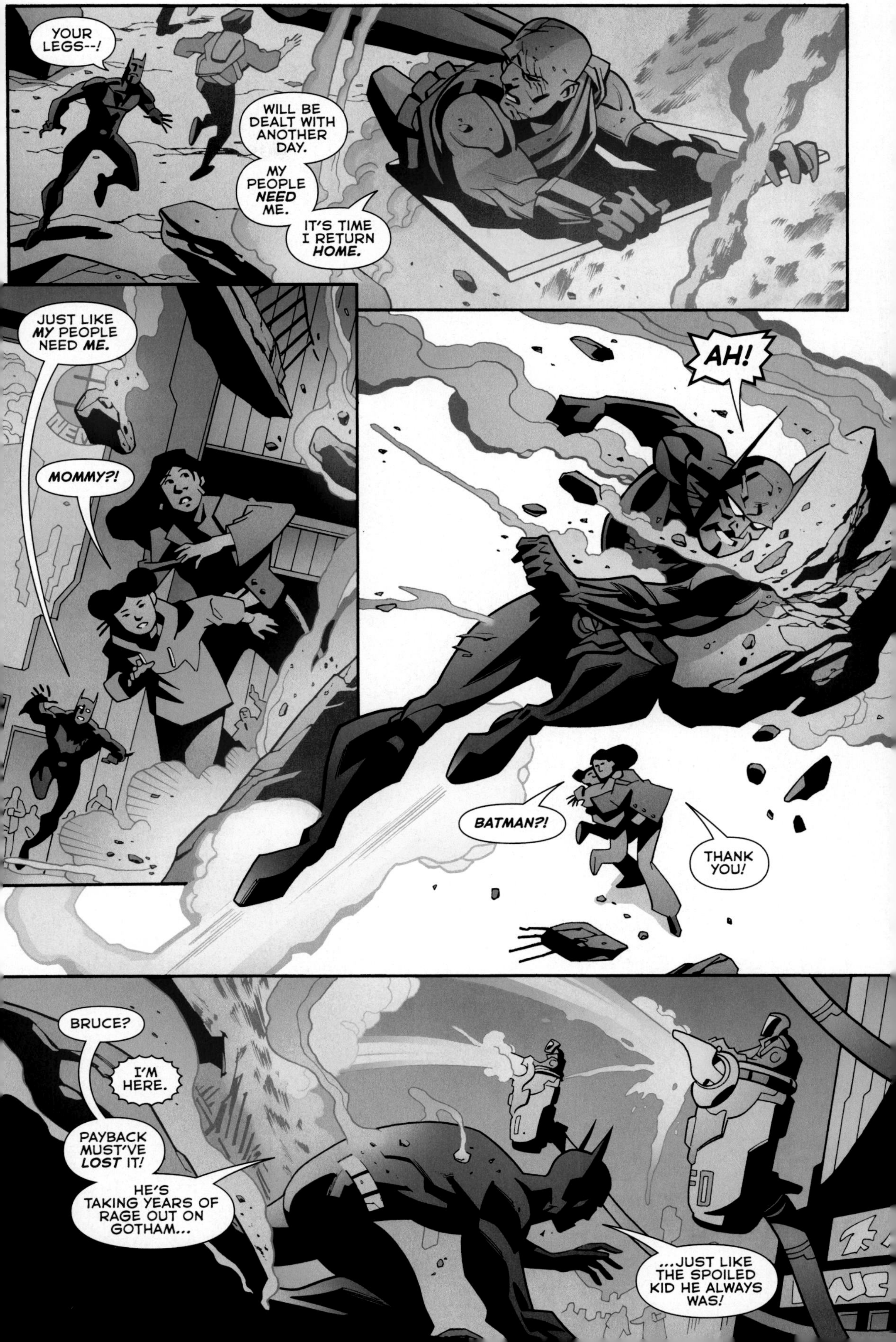

YOUR LEGS--!
WILL BE DEALT WITH ANOTHER DAY.
MY PEOPLE NEED ME.
IT'S TIME I RETURN HOME.
JUST LIKE MY PEOPLE NEED ME.
MOMMY?!
AH!
BATMAN?!
THANK YOU!
BRUCE?
I'M HERE.
PAYBACK MUST'VE LOST IT!
HE'S TAKING YEARS OF RAGE OUT ON GOTHAM...
...JUST LIKE THE SPOILED KID HE ALWAYS WAS!

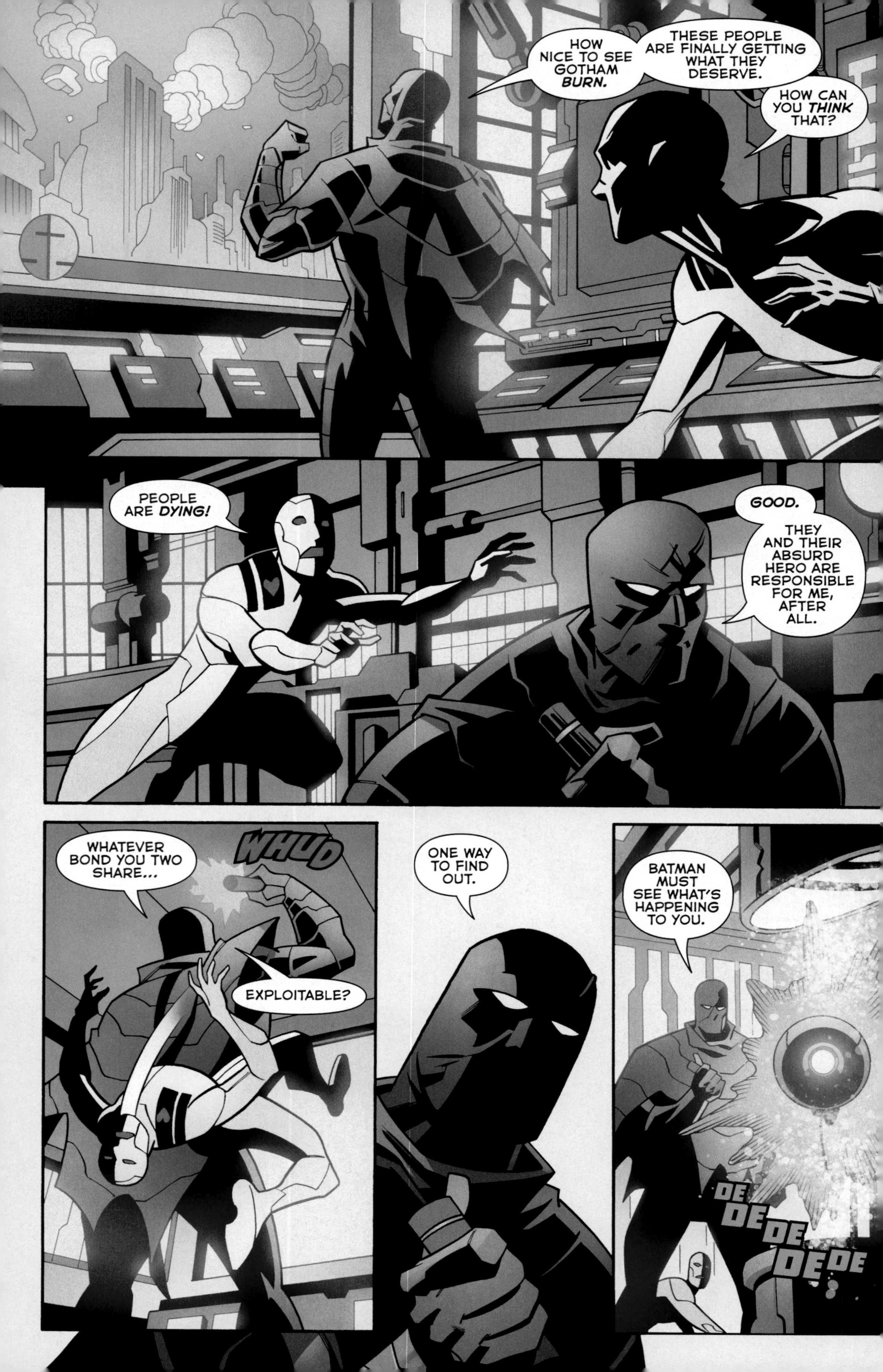
HOW NICE TO SEE GOTHAM BURN.
THESE PEOPLE ARE FINALLY GETTING WHAT THEY DESERVE.
HOW CAN YOU THINK THAT?
PEOPLE ARE DYING!
GOOD.
THEY AND THEIR ABSURD HERO ARE RESPONSIBLE FOR ME, AFTER ALL.
WHATEVER BOND YOU TWO SHARE...
WHUD
EXPLOITABLE?
ONE WAY TO FIND OUT.
BATMAN MUST SEE WHAT'S HAPPENING TO YOU.
DE DE DE DE DE DE

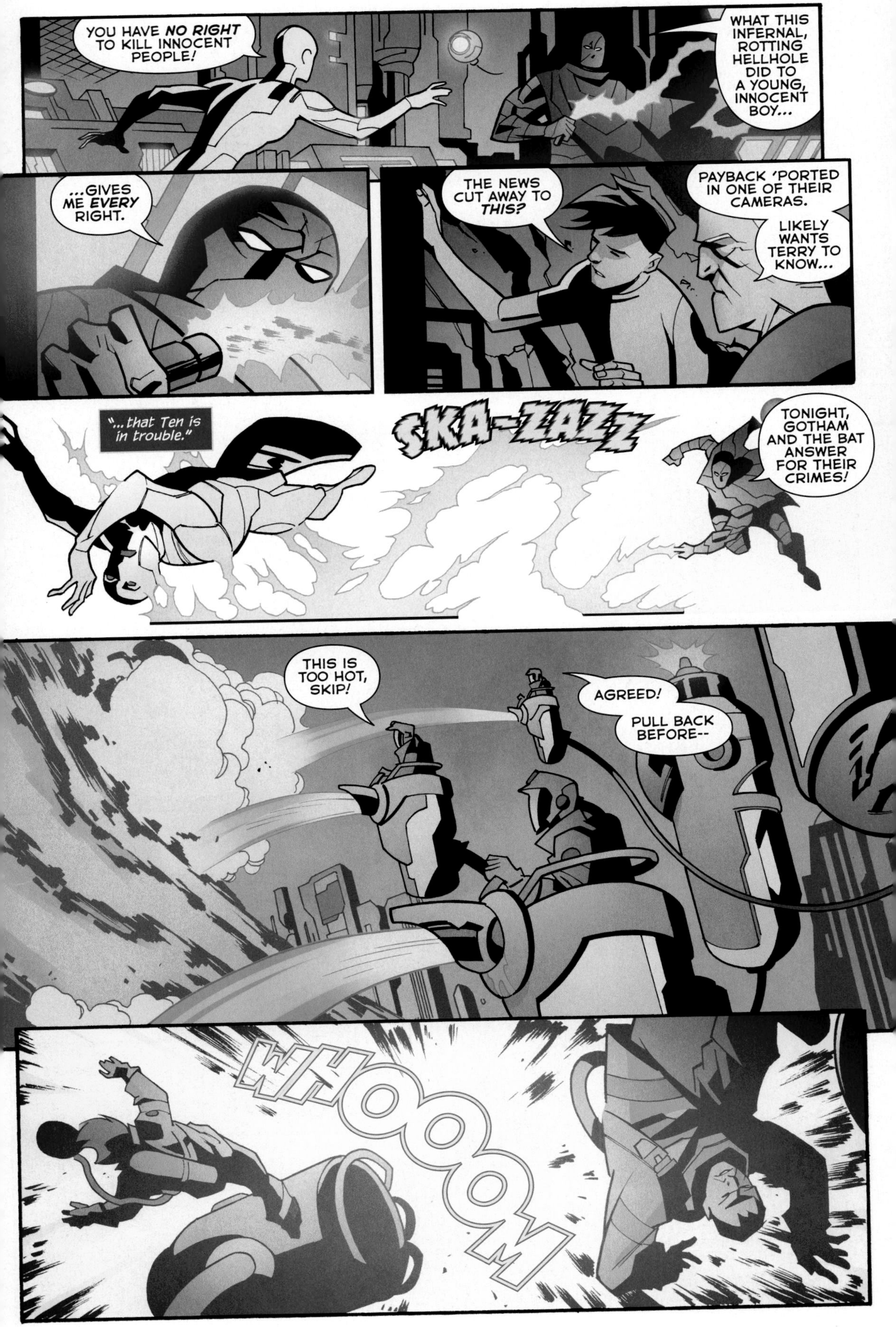
YOU HAVE NO RIGHT TO KILL INNOCENT PEOPLE!
WHAT THIS INFERNAL, ROTTING HELLHOLE DID TO A YOUNG, INNOCENT BOY...
...GIVES ME EVERY RIGHT.
THE NEWS CUT AWAY TO THIS?
PAYBACK 'PORTED IN ONE OF THEIR CAMERAS.
LIKELY WANTS TERRY TO KNOW...
"...that Ten is in trouble."
SKA-ZAZZ
TONIGHT, GOTHAM AND THE BAT ANSWER FOR THEIR CRIMES!
THIS IS TOO HOT, SKIP!
AGREED!
PULL BACK BEFORE--
WHOOOOM

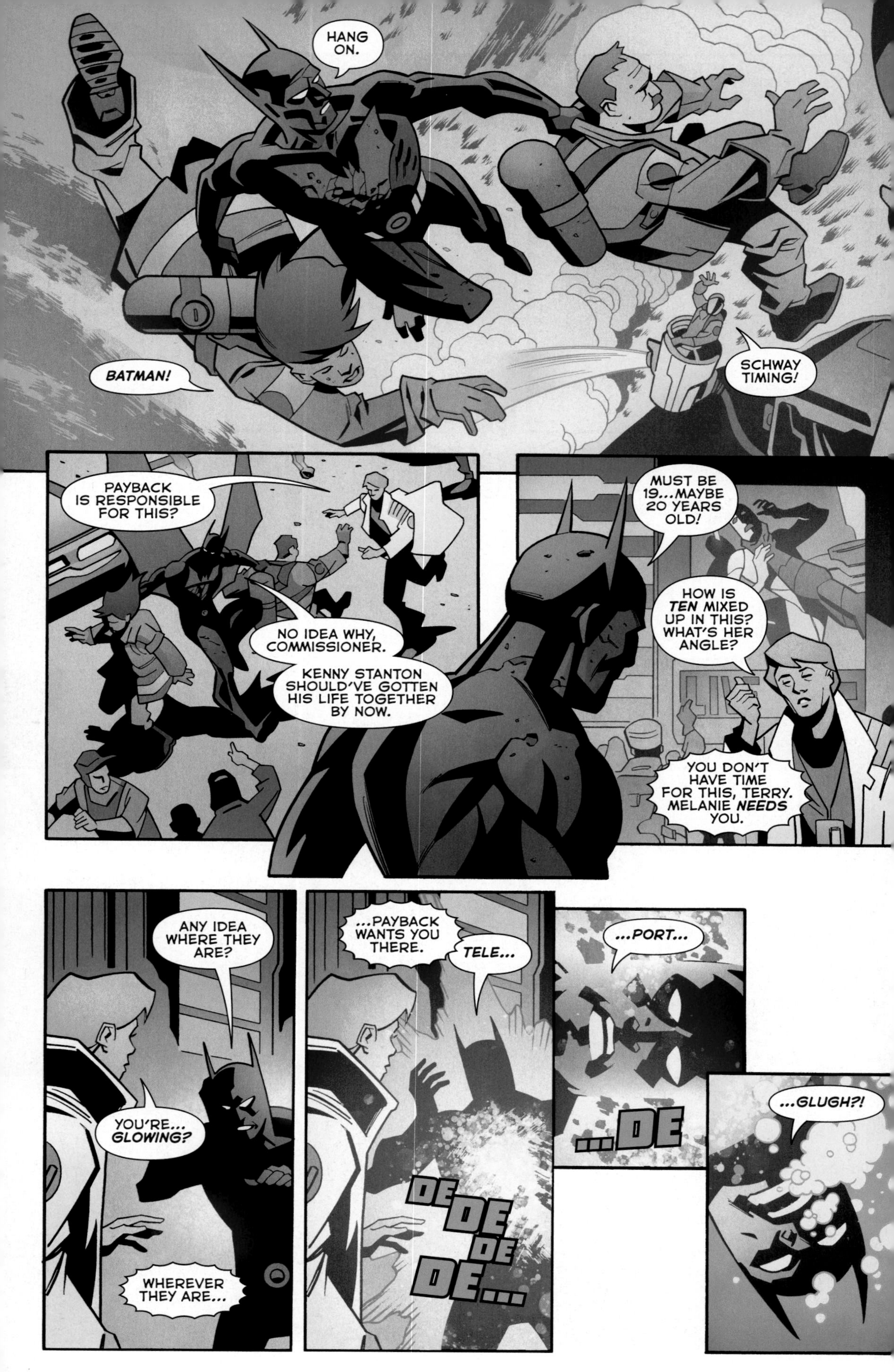
HANG ON.
BATMAN!
SCHWAY TIMING!
PAYBACK IS RESPONSIBLE FOR THIS?
NO IDEA WHY, COMMISSIONER.
KENNY STANTON SHOULD'VE GOTTEN HIS LIFE TOGETHER BY NOW.
MUST BE 19...MAYBE 20 YEARS OLD!
HOW IS TEN MIXED UP IN THIS? WHAT'S HER ANGLE?
YOU DON'T HAVE TIME FOR THIS, TERRY. MELANIE NEEDS YOU.
ANY IDEA WHERE THEY ARE?
YOU'RE... GLOWING?
WHEREVER THEY ARE...
...PAYBACK WANTS YOU THERE.
TELE...
DE DE DE DE...
...PORT...
...DE
...GLUGH?!

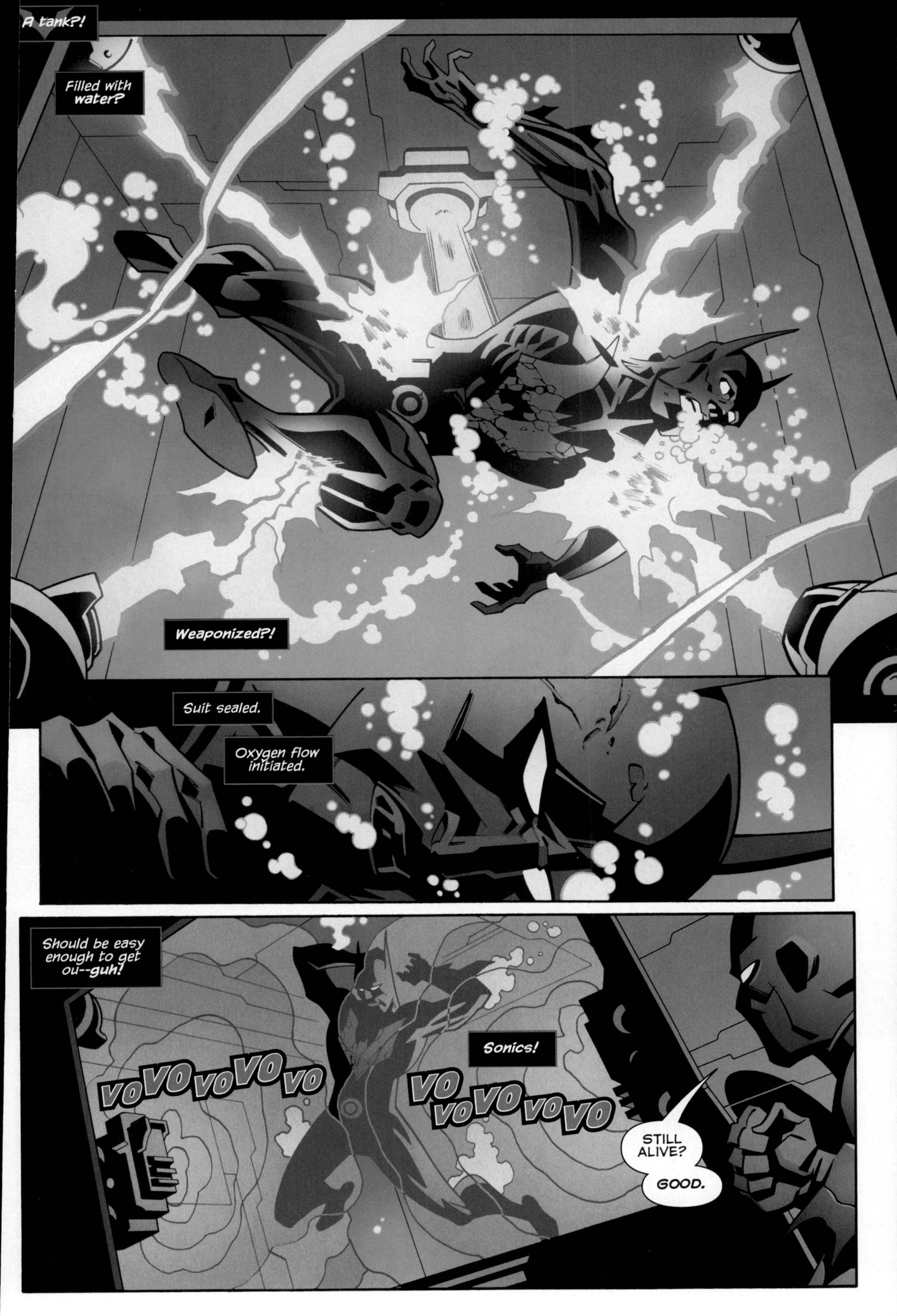
A tank?!
Filled with water?
Weaponized?!
Suit sealed.
Oxygen flow initiated.
Should be easy enough to get ou--guh!
Sonics!
VOVOVOVOVOVO
VO VOVOVOVOVO
STILL ALIVE?
GOOD.

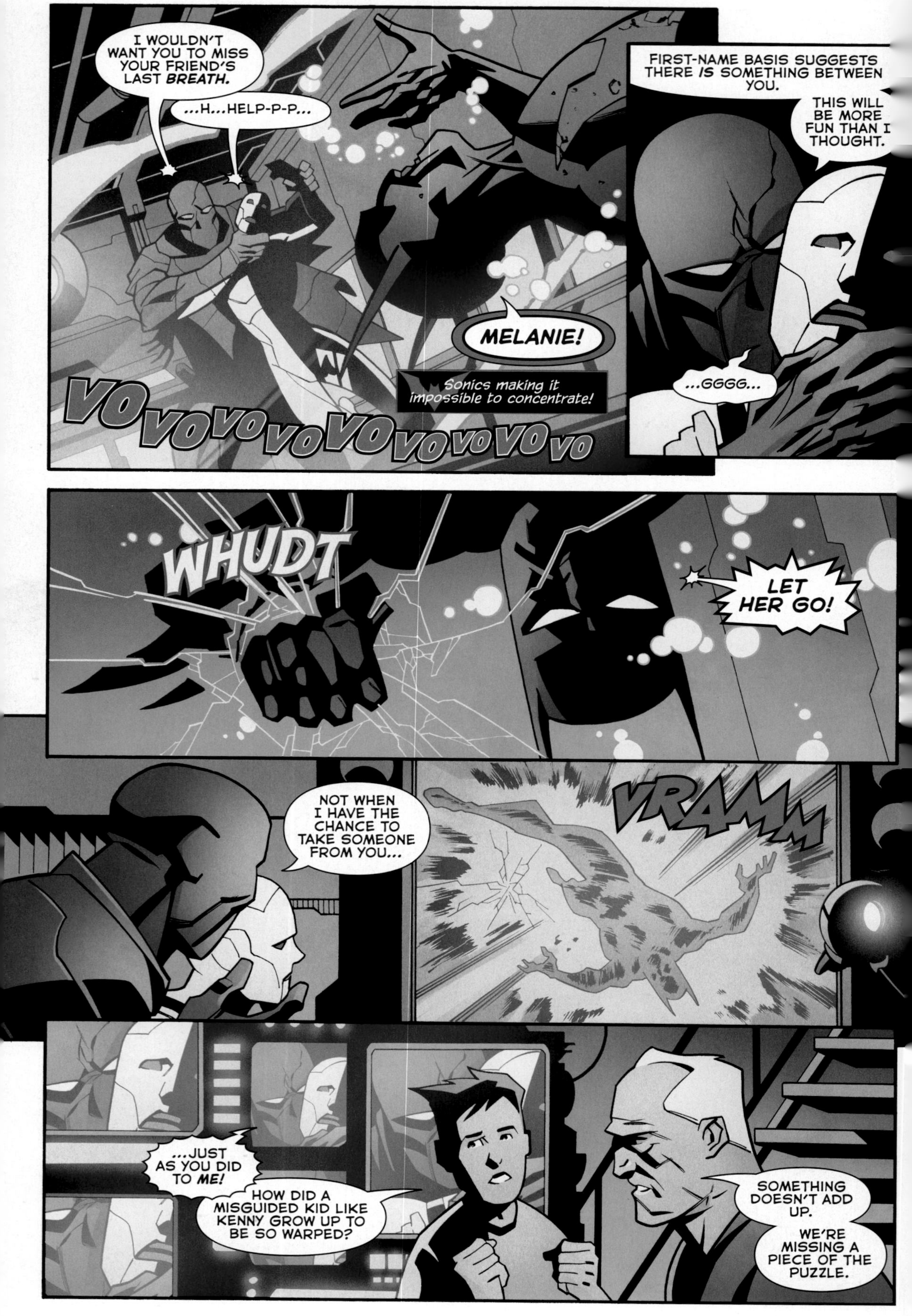
I WOULDN'T WANT YOU TO MISS YOUR FRIEND'S LAST BREATH.
...H...HELP-P-P...
MELANIE!
Sonics making it impossible to concentrate!
VOVOVOVOVOVOVOVOVOVOVO
FIRST-NAME BASIS SUGGESTS THERE IS SOMETHING BETWEEN YOU.
THIS WILL BE MORE FUN THAN I THOUGHT.
...GGGG...
WHUDT
LET HER GO!
NOT WHEN I HAVE THE CHANCE TO TAKE SOMEONE FROM YOU...
VRAMM
...JUST AS YOU DID TO ME!
HOW DID A MISGUIDED KID LIKE KENNY GROW UP TO BE SO WARPED?
SOMETHING DOESN'T ADD UP.
WE'RE MISSING A PIECE OF THE PUZZLE.

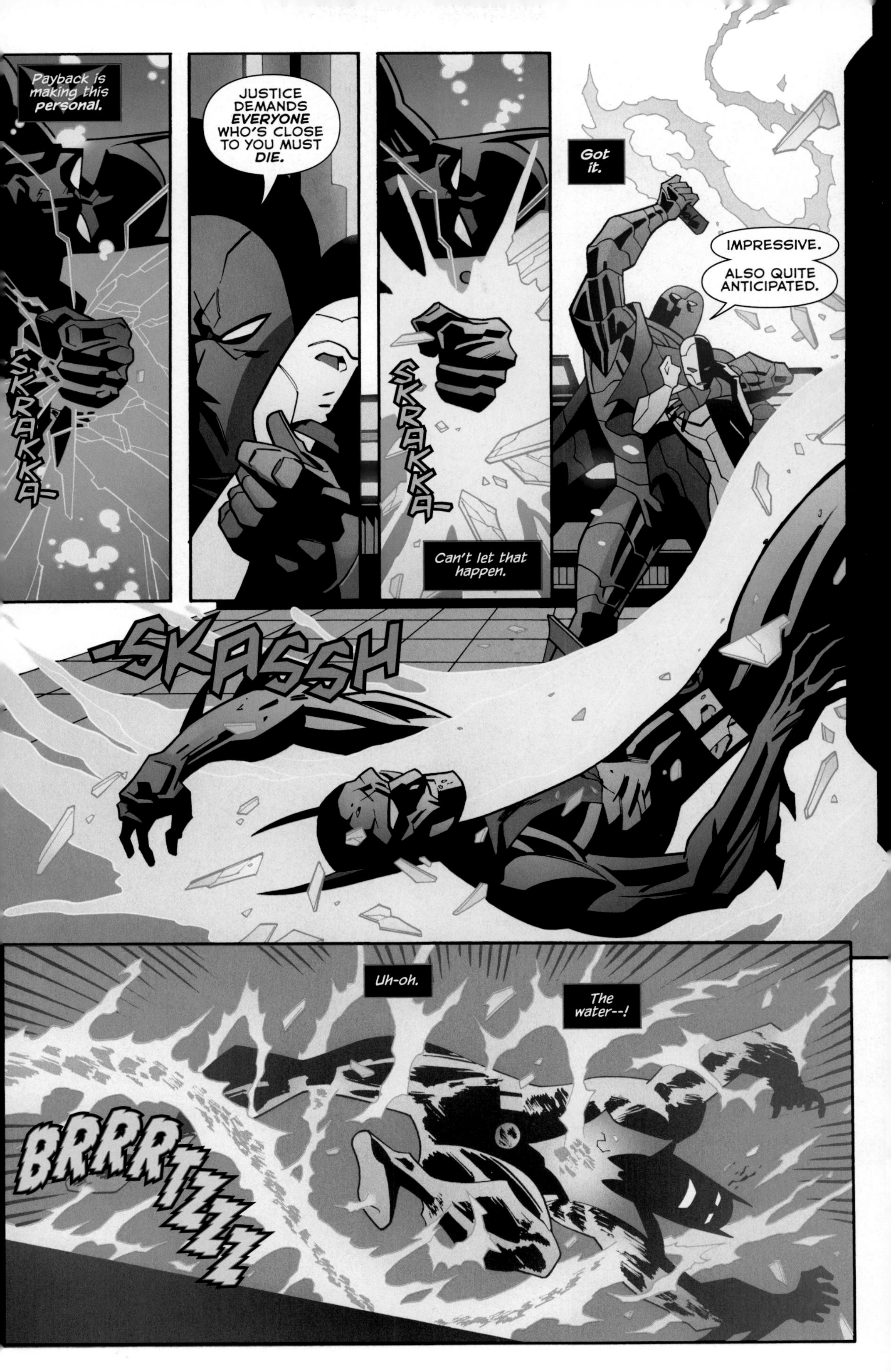

Payback is making this personal.
JUSTICE DEMANDS EVERYONE WHO'S CLOSE TO YOU MUST DIE.
SKRAKKA
SKRAKKA
Can't let that happen.
Got it.
IMPRESSIVE.
ALSO QUITE ANTICIPATED.
SKASSH
Uh-oh.
The water--!
BRRRTZZZ

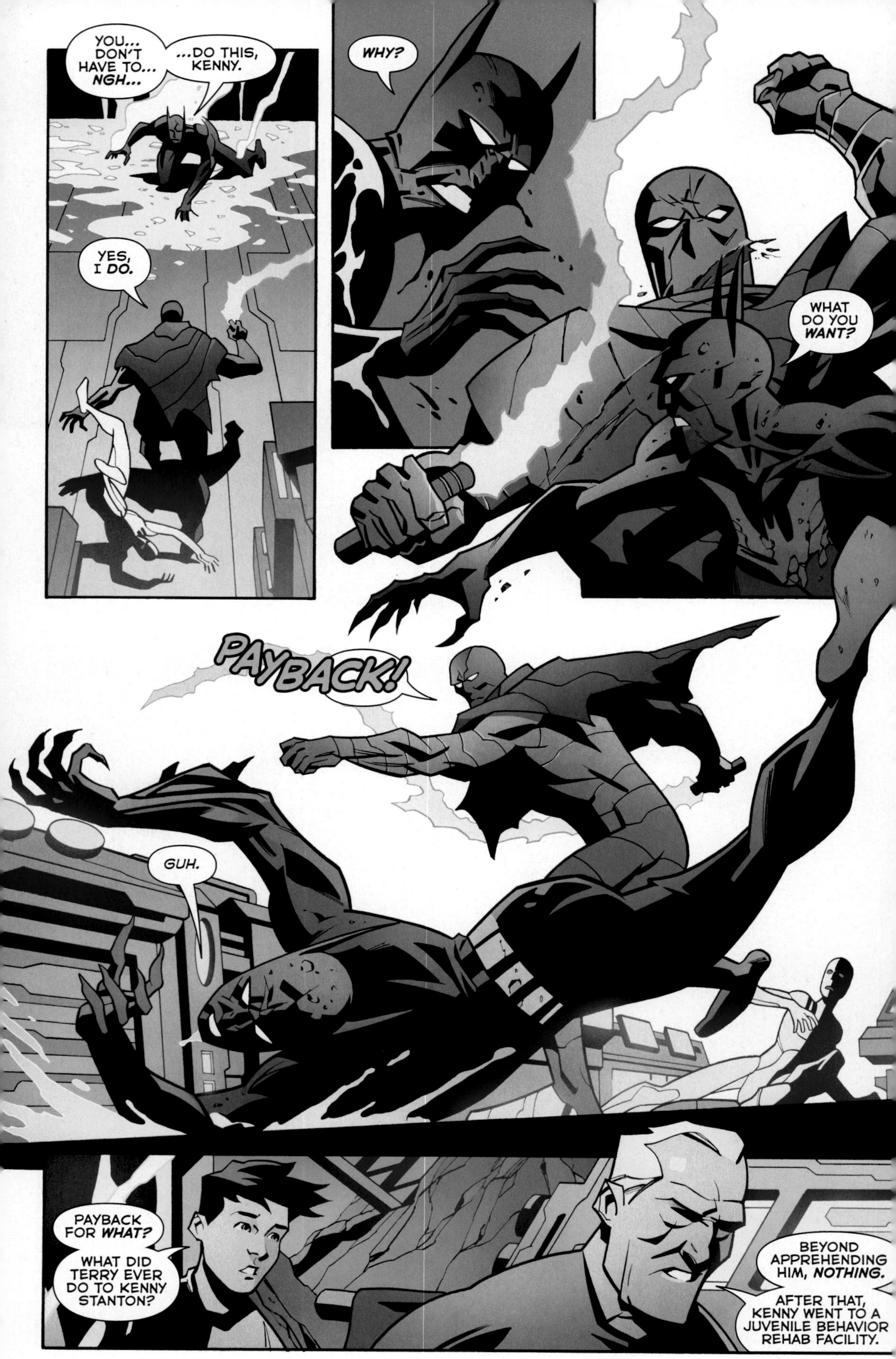

YOU... DON'T HAVE TO... NGH...
...DO THIS, KENNY.
YES, I DO.
WHY?
WHAT DO YOU WANT?
PAYBACK!
GUH.
PAYBACK FOR WHAT?
WHAT DID TERRY EVER DO TO KENNY STANTON?
BEYOND APPREHENDING HIM, NOTHING.
AFTER THAT, KENNY WENT TO A JUVENILE BEHAVIOR REHAB FACILITY.

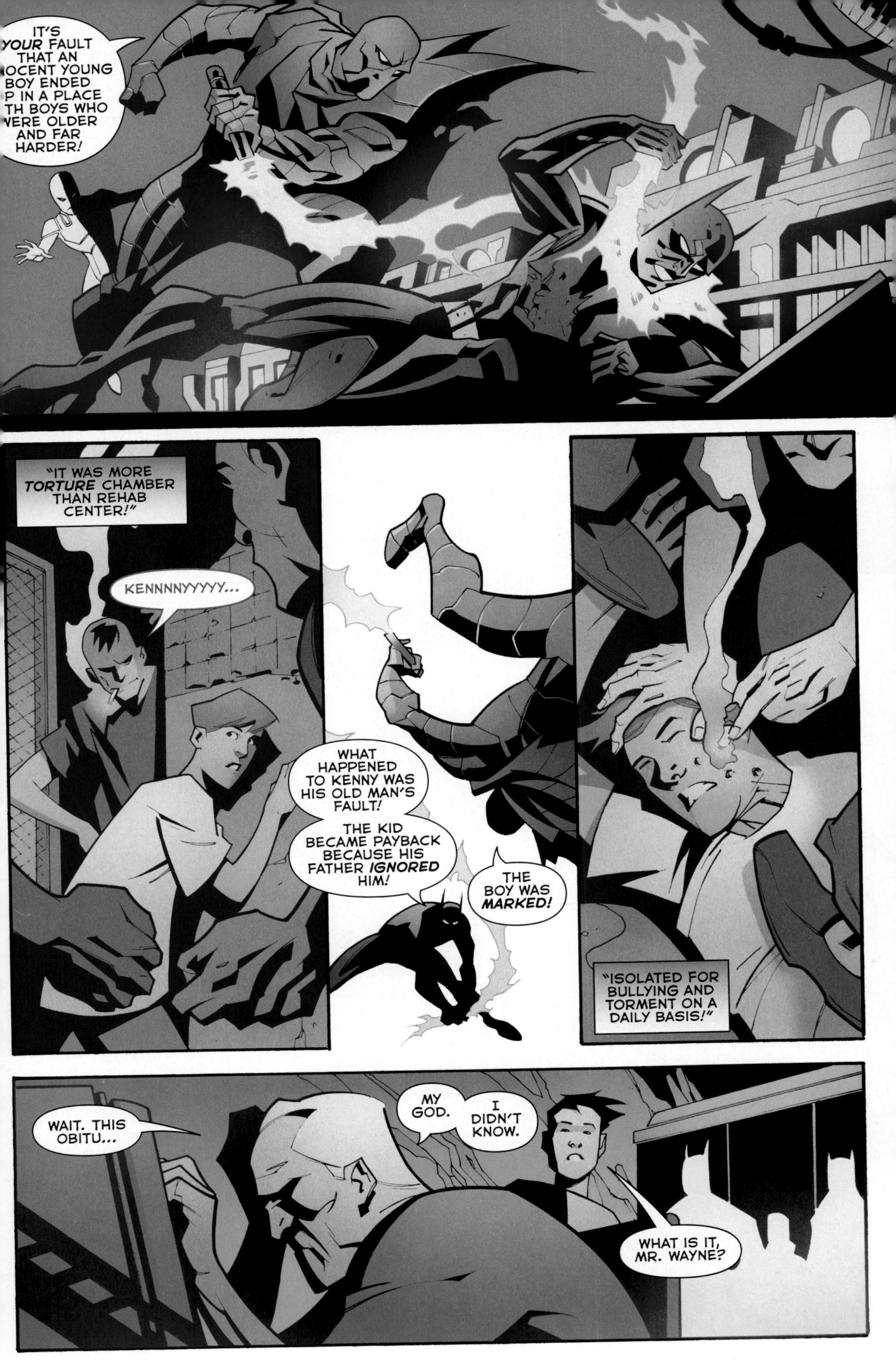
IT'S YOUR FAULT THAT AN NOCENT YOUNG BOY ENDED P IN A PLACE TH BOYS WHO VERE OLDER AND FAR HARDER!
"IT WAS MORE TORTURE CHAMBER THAN REHAB CENTER!"
KENNNNYYYYY...
WHAT HAPPENED TO KENNY WAS HIS OLD MAN'S FAULT!
THE KID BECAME PAYBACK BECAUSE HIS FATHER IGNORED HIM!
THE BOY WAS MARKED!
"ISOLATED FOR BULLYING AND TORMENT ON A DAILY BASIS!"
WAIT. THIS OBITU...
MY GOD.
I DIDN'T KNOW.
WHAT IS IT, MR. WAYNE?

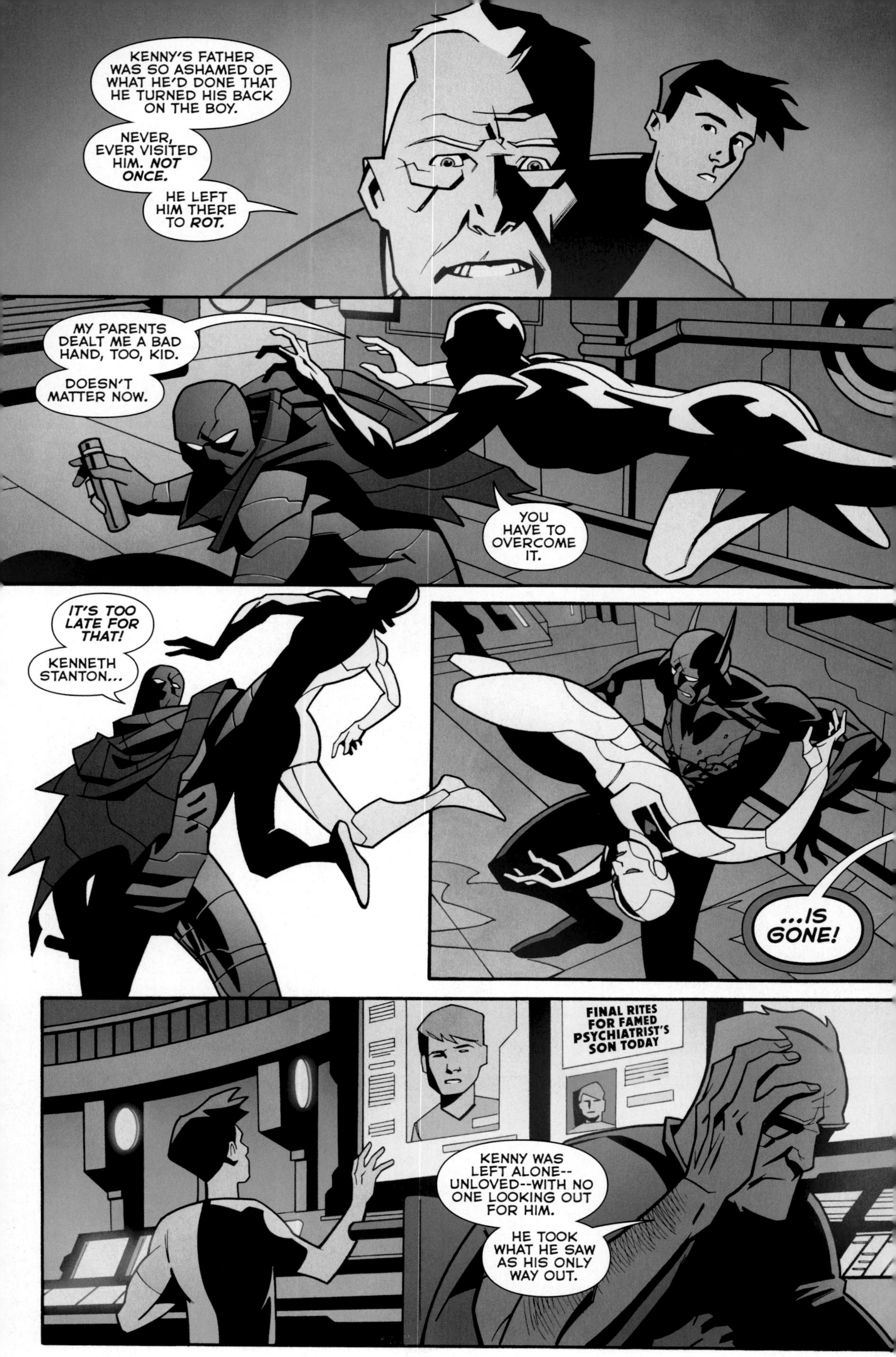
KENNY'S FATHER WAS SO ASHAMED OF WHAT HE'D DONE THAT HE TURNED HIS BACK ON THE BOY.
NEVER, EVER VISITED HIM. NOT ONCE.
HE LEFT HIM THERE TO ROT.
MY PARENTS DEALT ME A BAD HAND, TOO, KID.
DOESN'T MATTER NOW.
YOU HAVE TO OVERCOME IT.
IT'S TOO LATE FOR THAT!
KENNETH STANTON...
...IS GONE!
FINAL RITES FOR FAMED PSYCHIATRIST'S SON TODAY
KENNY WAS LEFT ALONE--UNLOVED--WITH NO ONE LOOKING OUT FOR HIM.
HE TOOK WHAT HE SAW AS HIS ONLY WAY OUT.

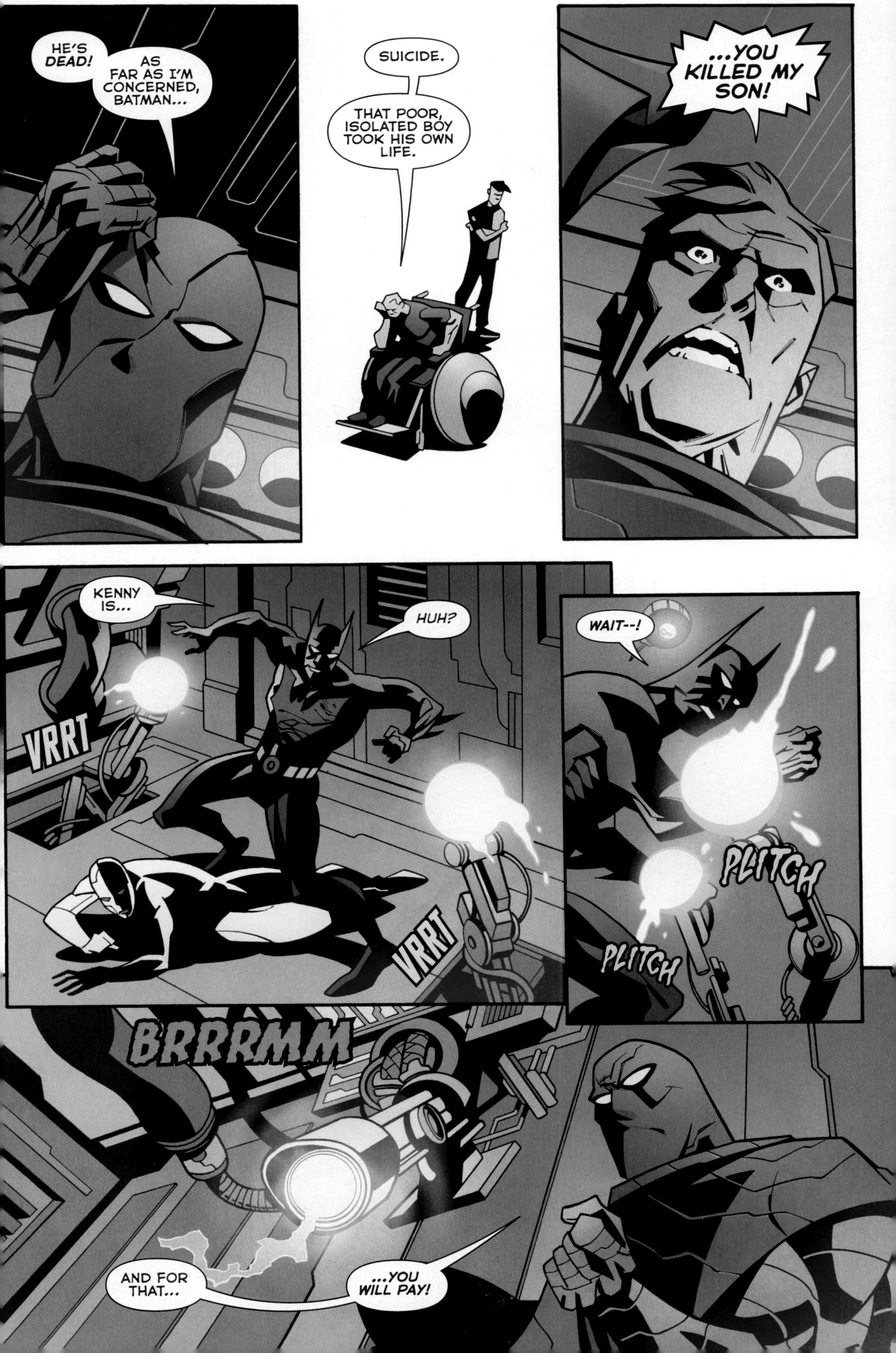
HE'S DEAD!
AS FAR AS I'M CONCERNED, BATMAN...
SUICIDE.
THAT POOR, ISOLATED BOY TOOK HIS OWN LIFE.
...YOU KILLED MY SON!
KENNY IS...
HUH?
VRRT
VRRT
WAIT--!
PLITCH
PLITCH
BRRRRMM
AND FOR THAT...
...YOU WILL PAY!

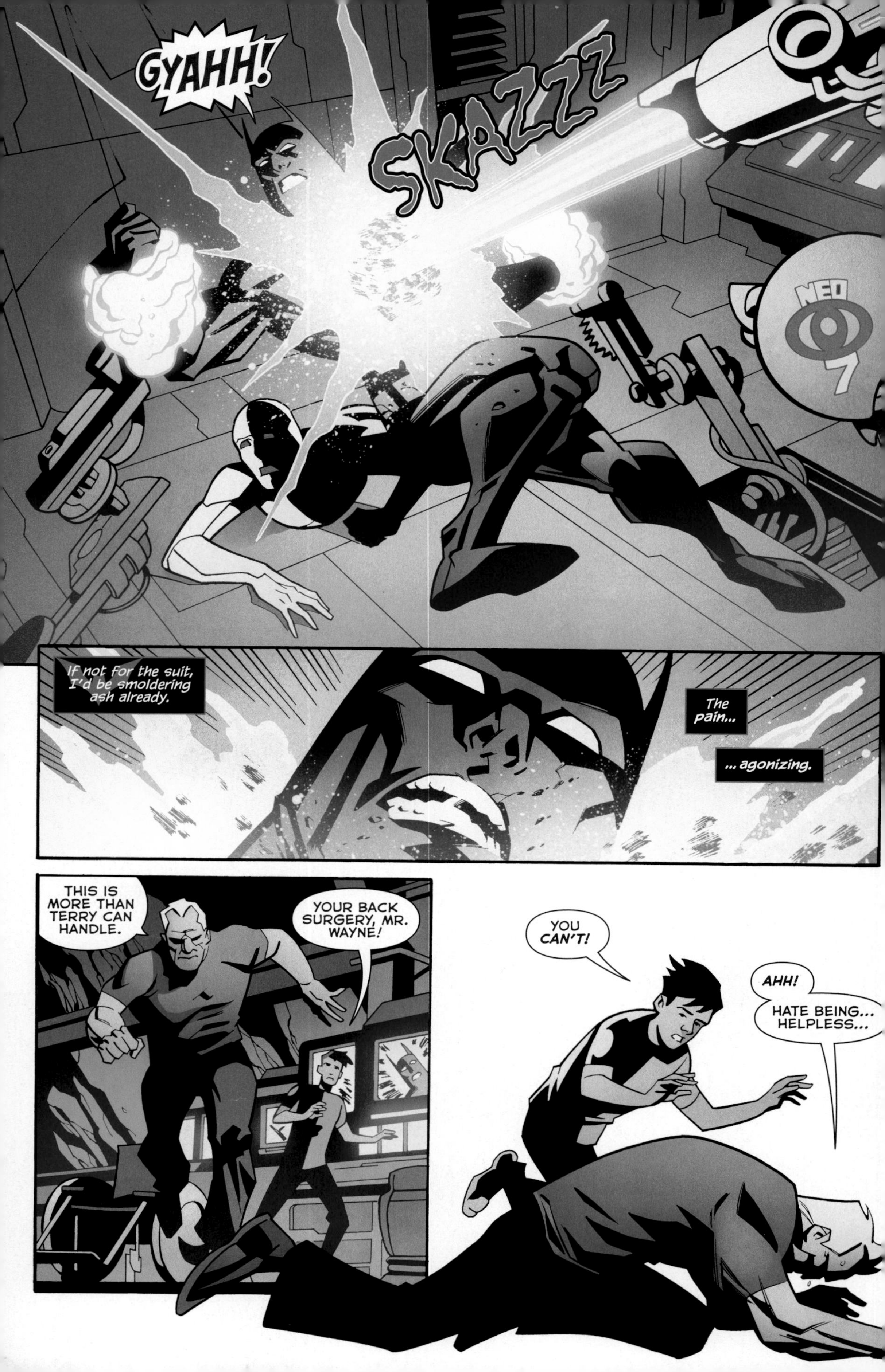
GYAHH!
SKAZZZ
NEO 7
If not for the suit, I'd be smoldering ash already.
The pain...
...agonizing.
THIS IS MORE THAN TERRY CAN HANDLE.
YOUR BACK SURGERY, MR. WAYNE!
YOU CAN'T!
AHH!
HATE BEING... HELPLESS...

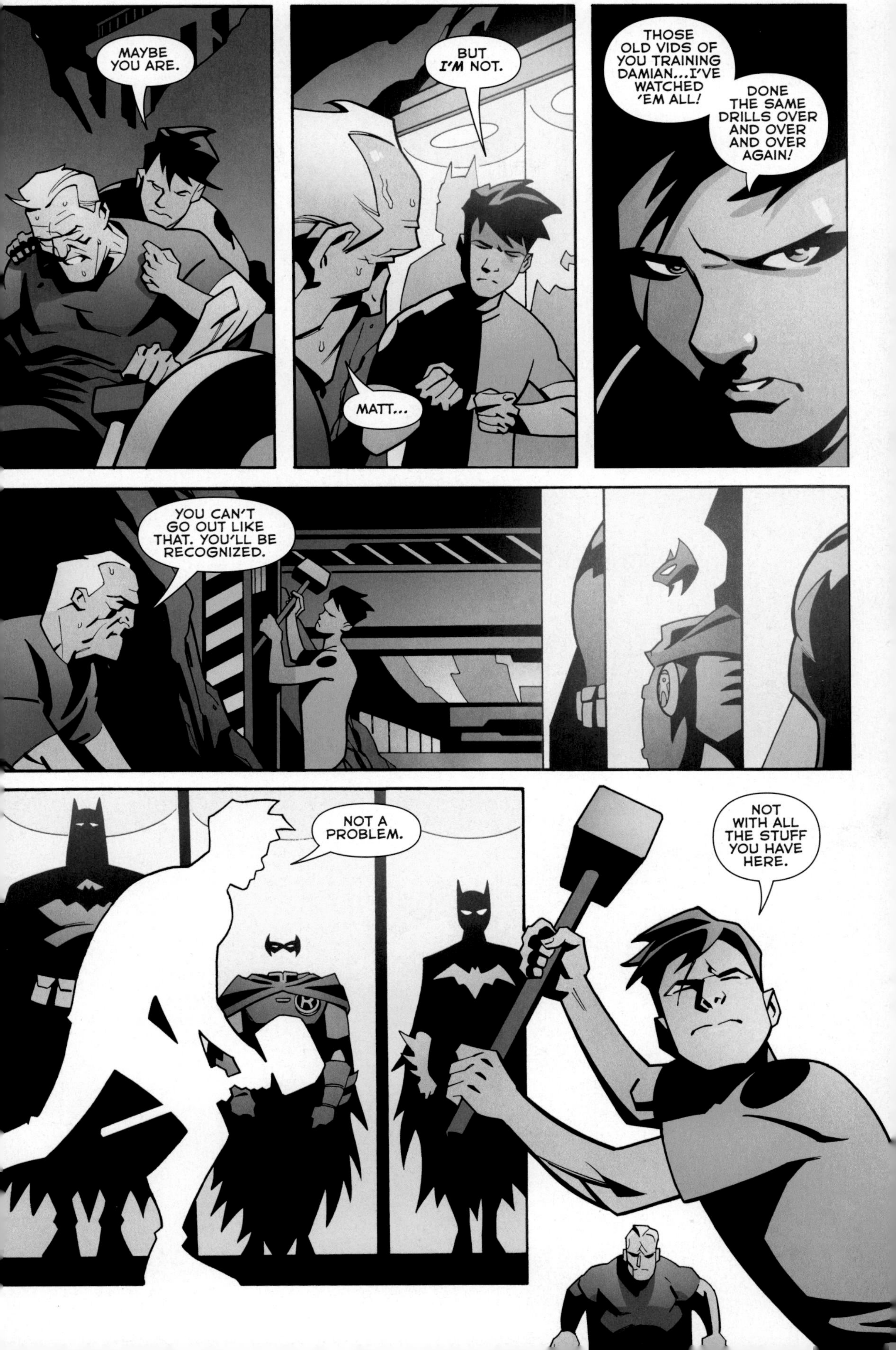
MAYBE YOU ARE.
BUT I'M NOT.
MATT...
THOSE OLD VIDS OF YOU TRAINING DAMIAN...I'VE WATCHED 'EM ALL!
DONE THE SAME DRILLS OVER AND OVER AND OVER AGAIN!
YOU CAN'T GO OUT LIKE THAT. YOU'LL BE RECOGNIZED.
NOT A PROBLEM.
NOT WITH ALL THE STUFF YOU HAVE HERE.

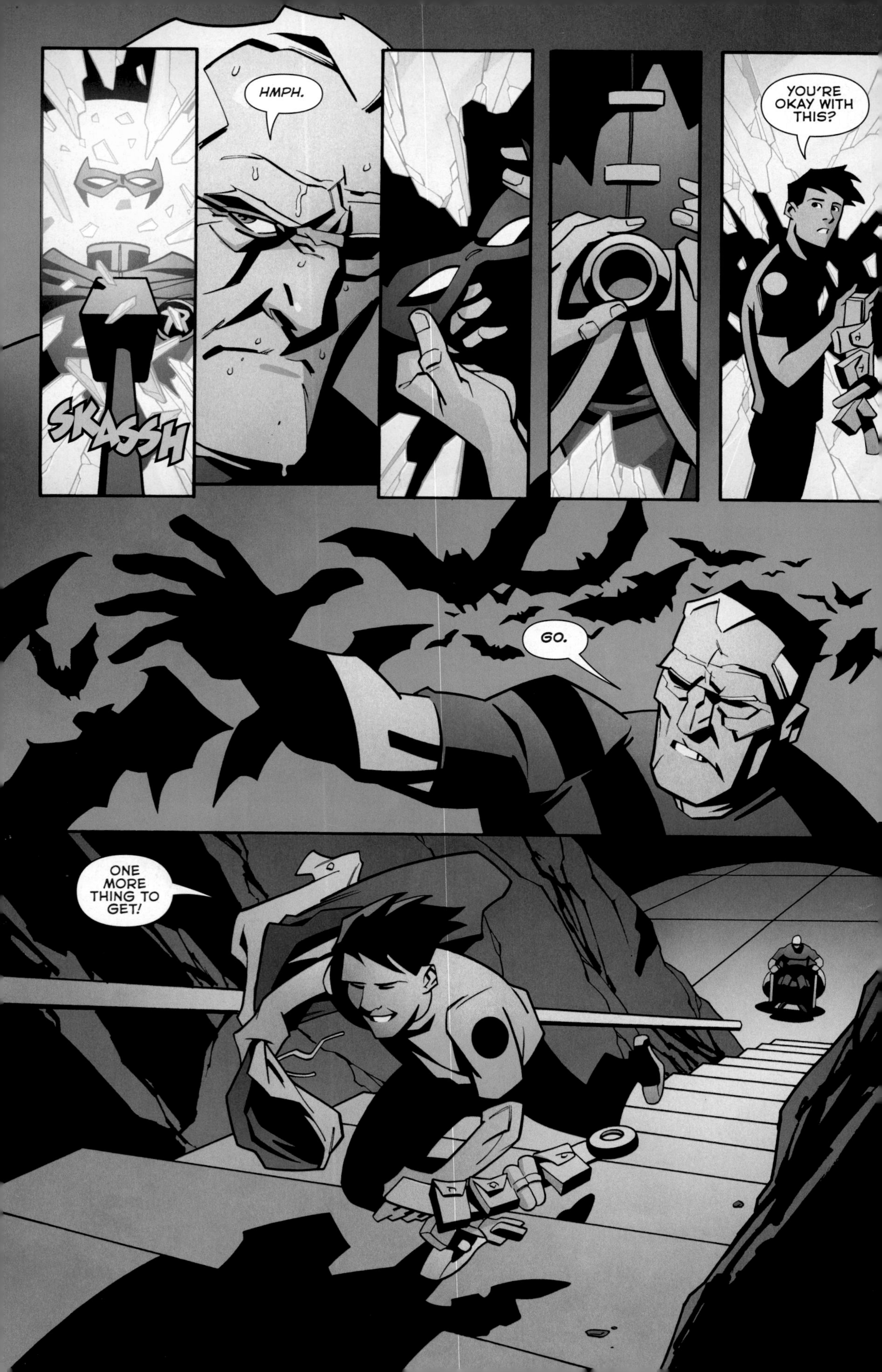
SKASSH
HMPH.
YOU'RE OKAY WITH THIS?
GO.
ONE MORE THING TO GET!

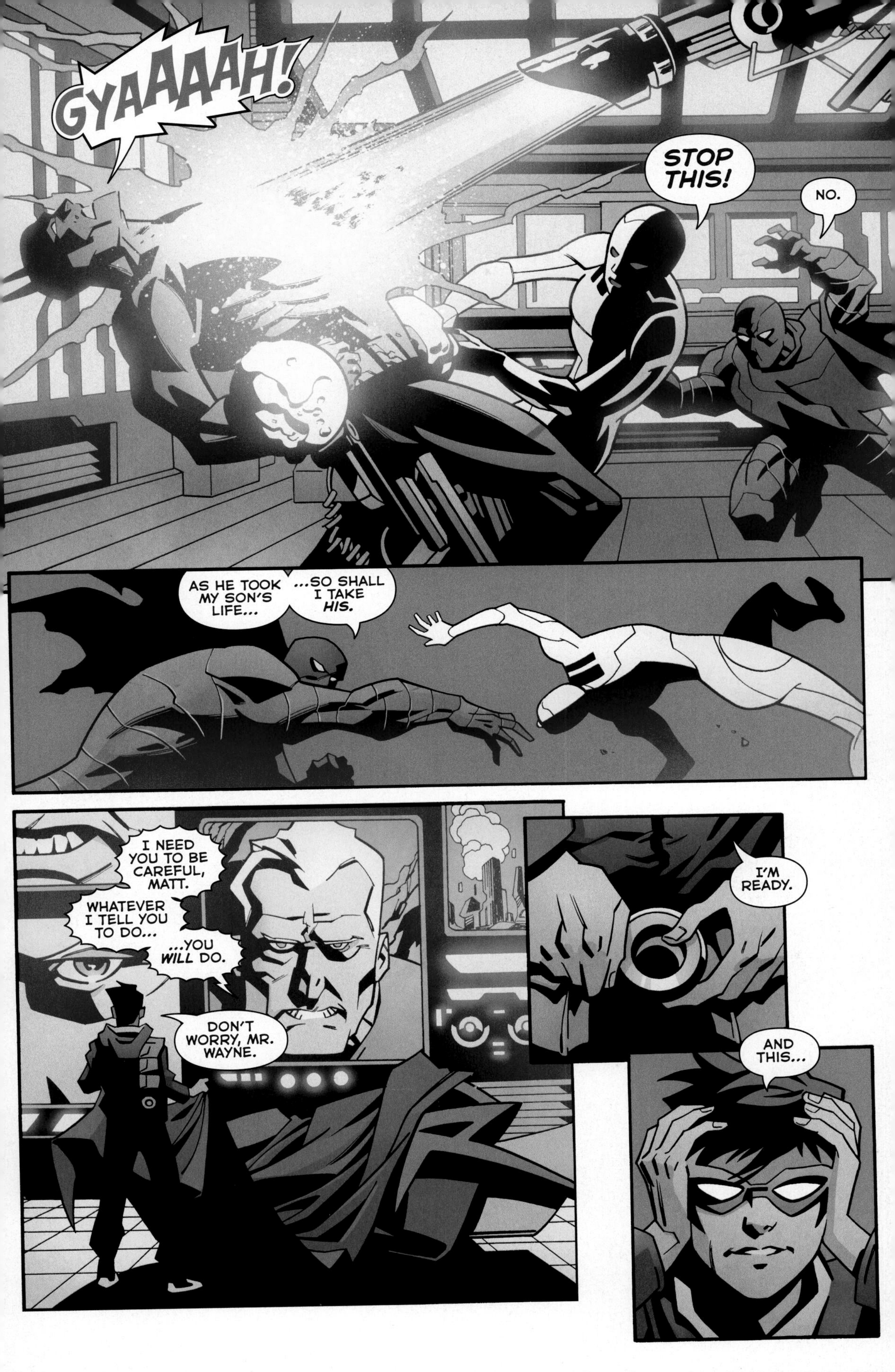
GYAAAAH!
STOP THIS!
NO.
AS HE TOOK MY SON'S LIFE...
...SO SHALL I TAKE HIS.
I NEED YOU TO BE CAREFUL, MATT.
WHATEVER I TELL YOU TO DO...
...YOU WILL DO.
DON'T WORRY, MR. WAYNE.
I'M READY.
AND THIS...

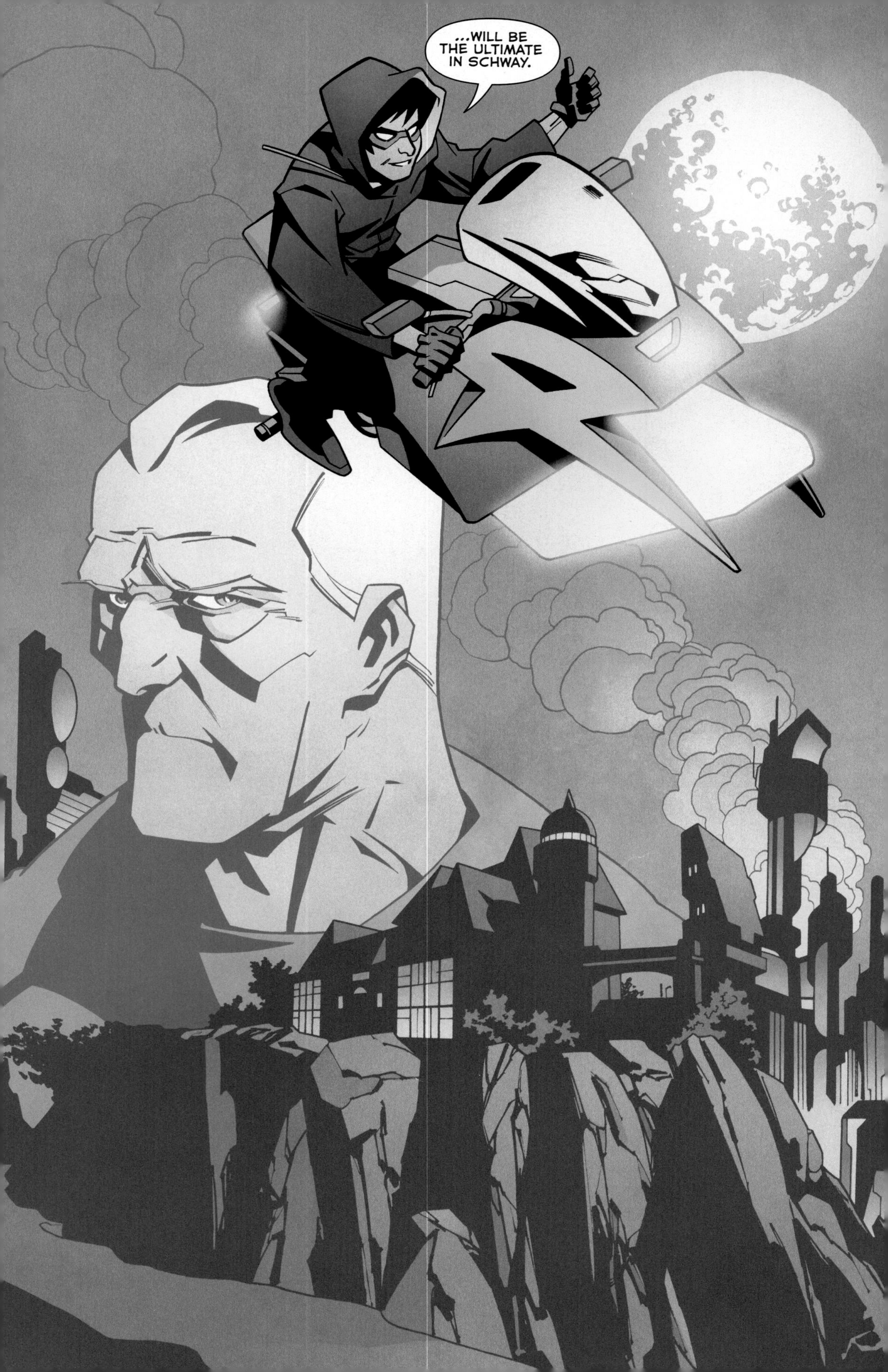
...WILL BE THE ULTIMATE IN SCHWAY.

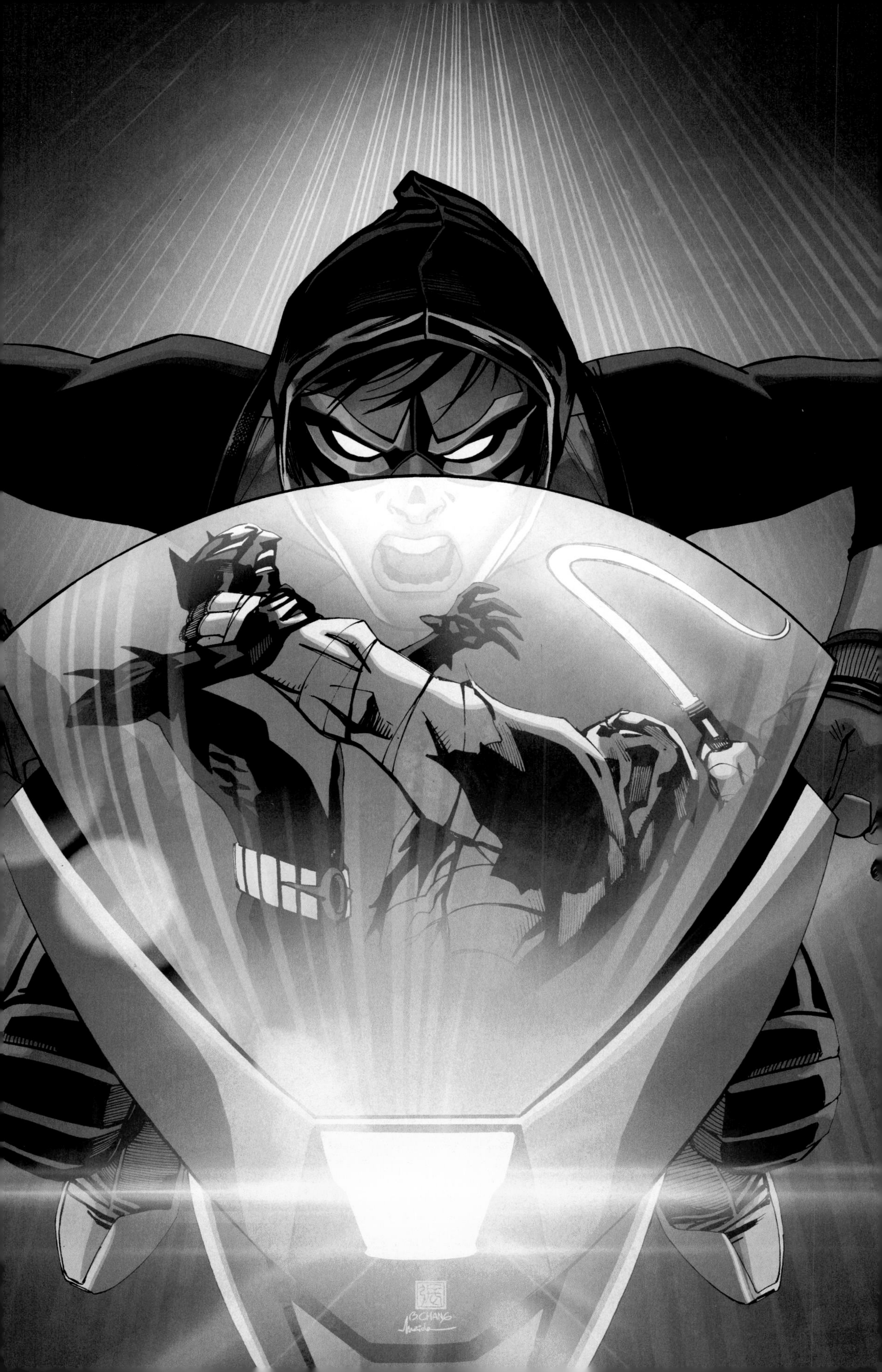
BCHANG

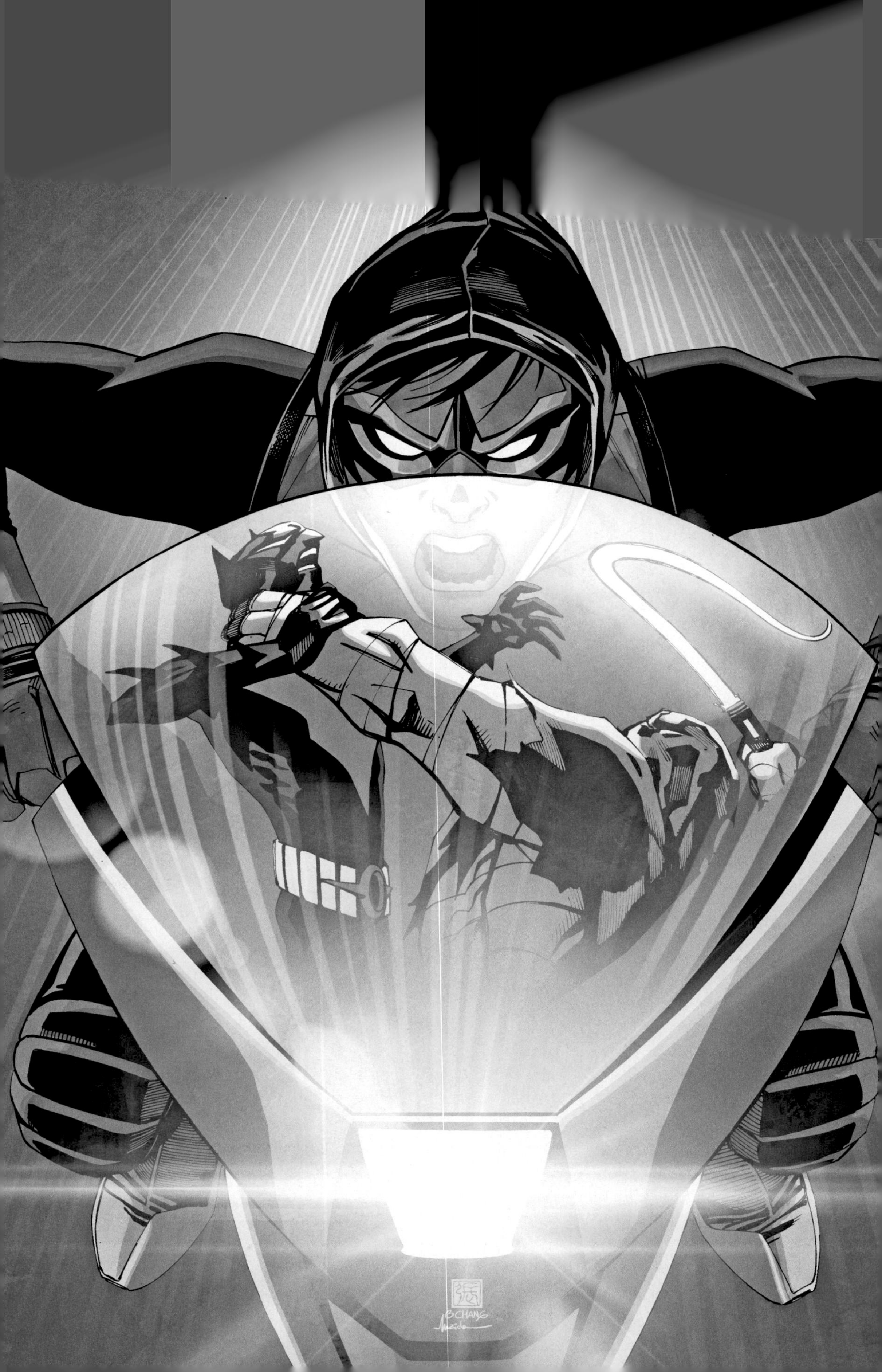
B CHANG

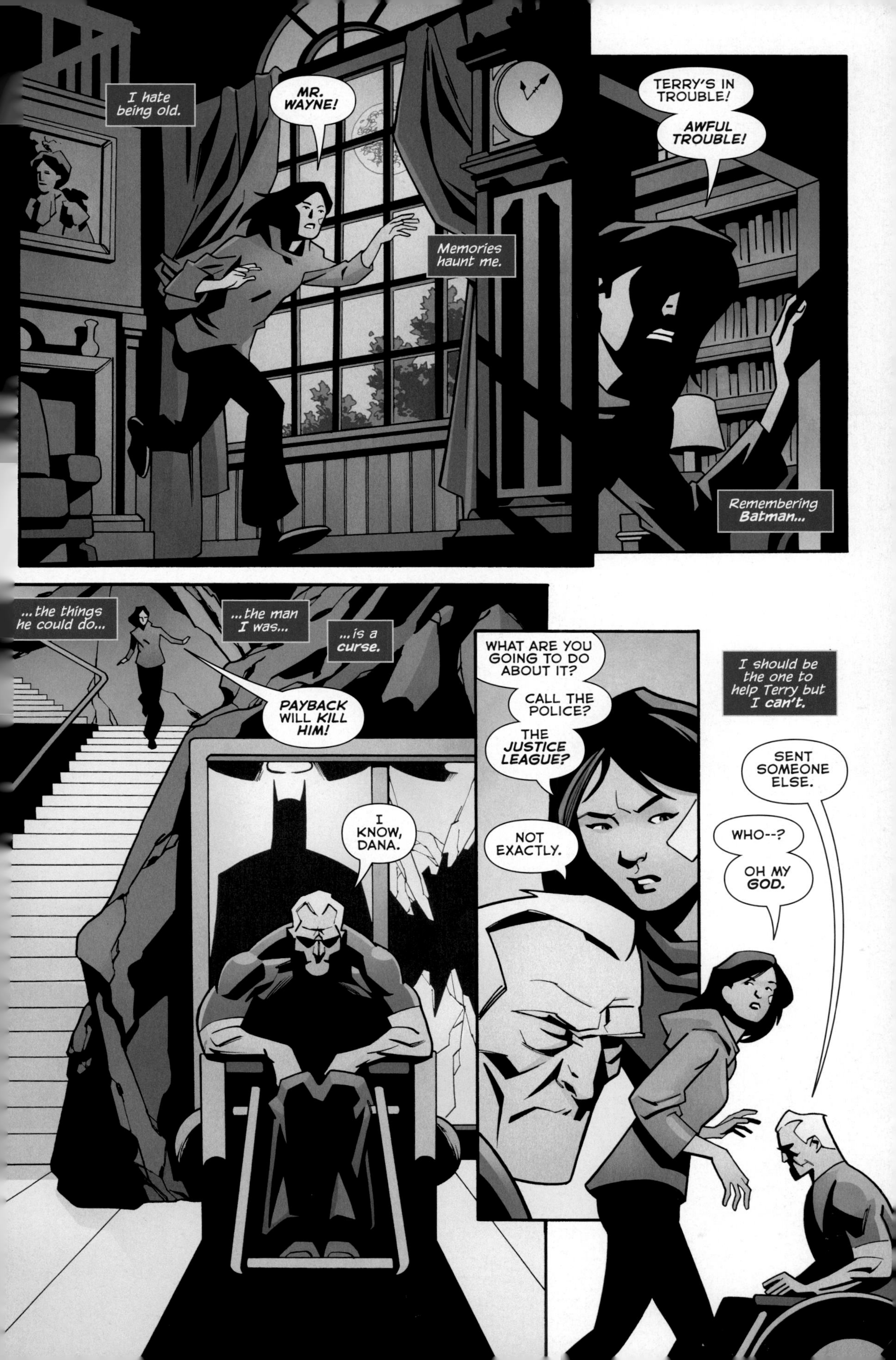
I hate being old.
MR. WAYNE!
Memories haunt me.
TERRY'S IN TROUBLE!
AWFUL TROUBLE!
Remembering Batman...
...the things he could do...
...the man I was...
...is a curse.
PAYBACK WILL KILL HIM!
I KNOW, DANA.
WHAT ARE YOU GOING TO DO ABOUT IT?
CALL THE POLICE?
THE JUSTICE LEAGUE?
NOT EXACTLY.
I should be the one to help Terry but I can't.
SENT SOMEONE ELSE.
WHO--?
OH MY GOD.

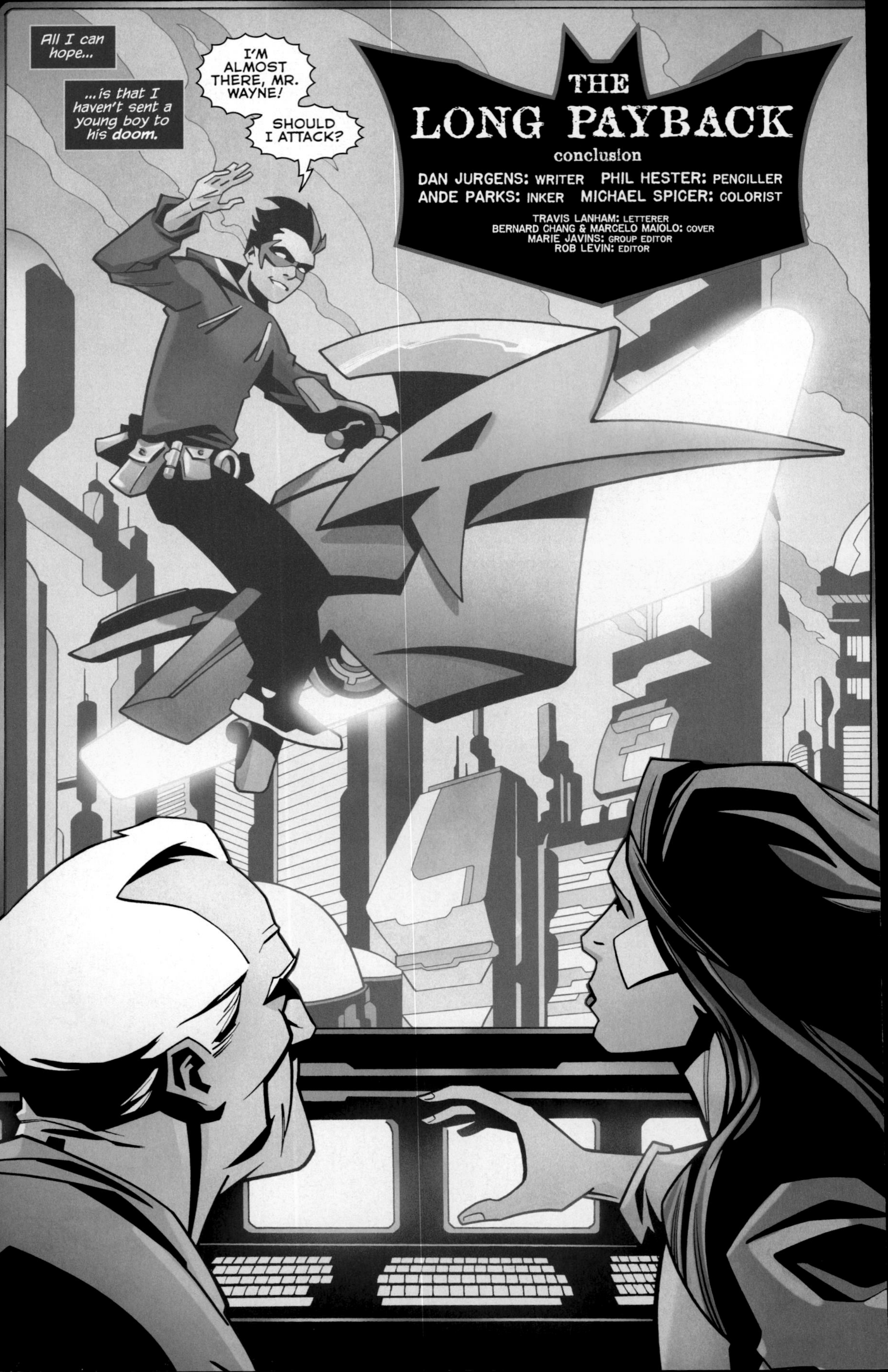
All I can hope...
...is that I haven't sent a young boy to his **doom.**
I'M ALMOST THERE, MR. WAYNE!
SHOULD I ATTACK?
THE LONG PAYBACK
conclusion
DAN JURGENS: WRITER PHIL HESTER: PENCILLER
ANDE PARKS: INKER MICHAEL SPICER: COLORIST
TRAVIS LANHAM: LETTERER
BERNARD CHANG & MARCELO MAIOLO: COVER
MARIE JAVINS: GROUP EDITOR
ROB LEVIN: EDITOR

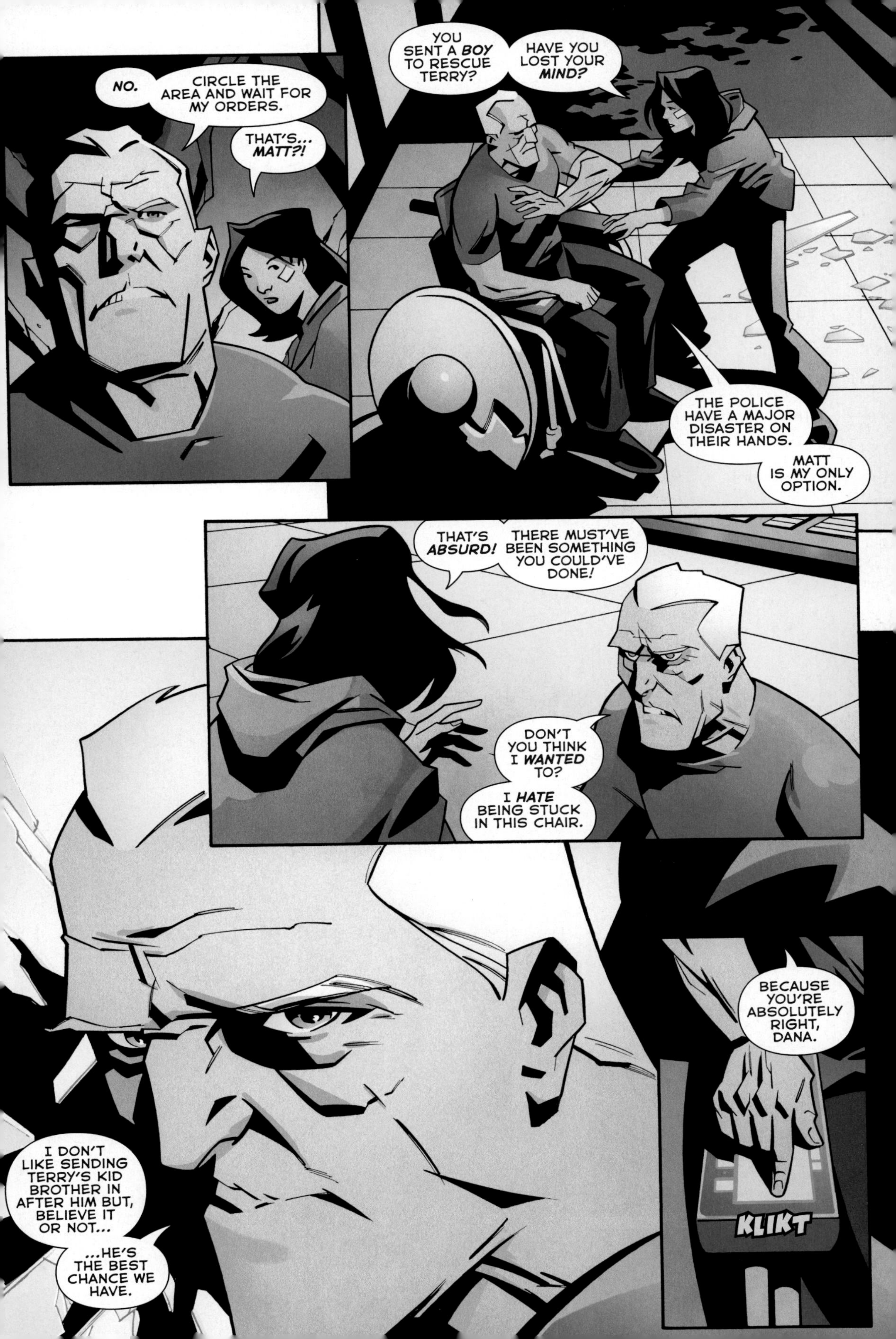

NO.
CIRCLE THE AREA AND WAIT FOR MY ORDERS.
THAT'S... MATT?!
YOU SENT A BOY TO RESCUE TERRY?
HAVE YOU LOST YOUR MIND?
THE POLICE HAVE A MAJOR DISASTER ON THEIR HANDS.
MATT IS MY ONLY OPTION.
THAT'S ABSURD!
THERE MUST'VE BEEN SOMETHING YOU COULD'VE DONE!
DON'T YOU THINK I WANTED TO?
I HATE BEING STUCK IN THIS CHAIR.
I DON'T LIKE SENDING TERRY'S KID BROTHER IN AFTER HIM BUT, BELIEVE IT OR NOT...
...HE'S THE BEST CHANCE WE HAVE.
BECAUSE YOU'RE ABSOLUTELY RIGHT, DANA.
KLIKT

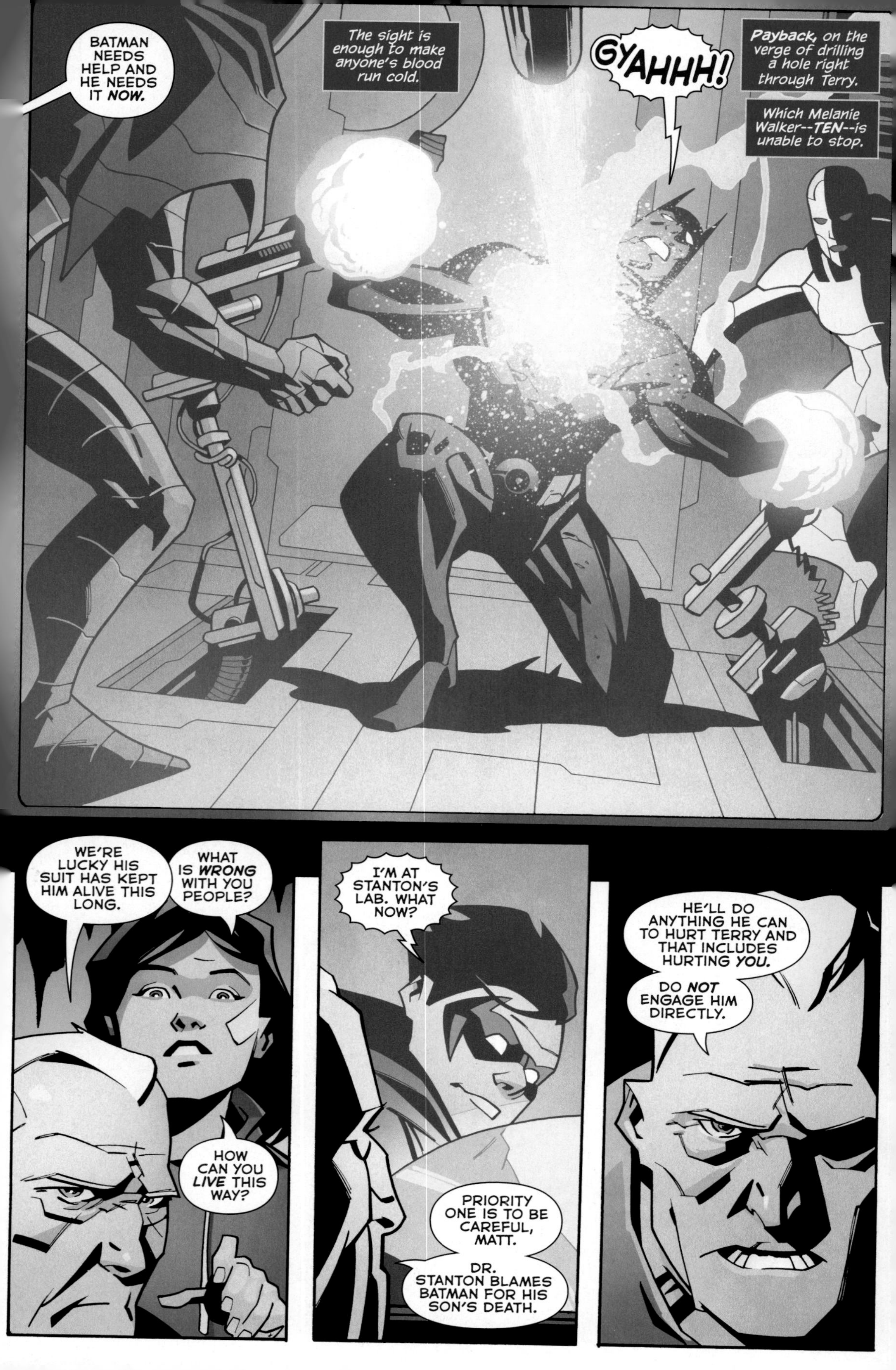
BATMAN NEEDS HELP AND HE NEEDS IT NOW.
The sight is enough to make anyone's blood run cold.
GYAHHH!
Payback, on the verge of drilling a hole right through Terry.
Which Melanie Walker--TEN--is unable to stop.
WE'RE LUCKY HIS SUIT HAS KEPT HIM ALIVE THIS LONG.
WHAT IS WRONG WITH YOU PEOPLE?
HOW CAN YOU LIVE THIS WAY?
I'M AT STANTON'S LAB. WHAT NOW?
PRIORITY ONE IS TO BE CAREFUL, MATT.
DR. STANTON BLAMES BATMAN FOR HIS SON'S DEATH.
HE'LL DO ANYTHING HE CAN TO HURT TERRY AND THAT INCLUDES HURTING YOU.
DO NOT ENGAGE HIM DIRECTLY.

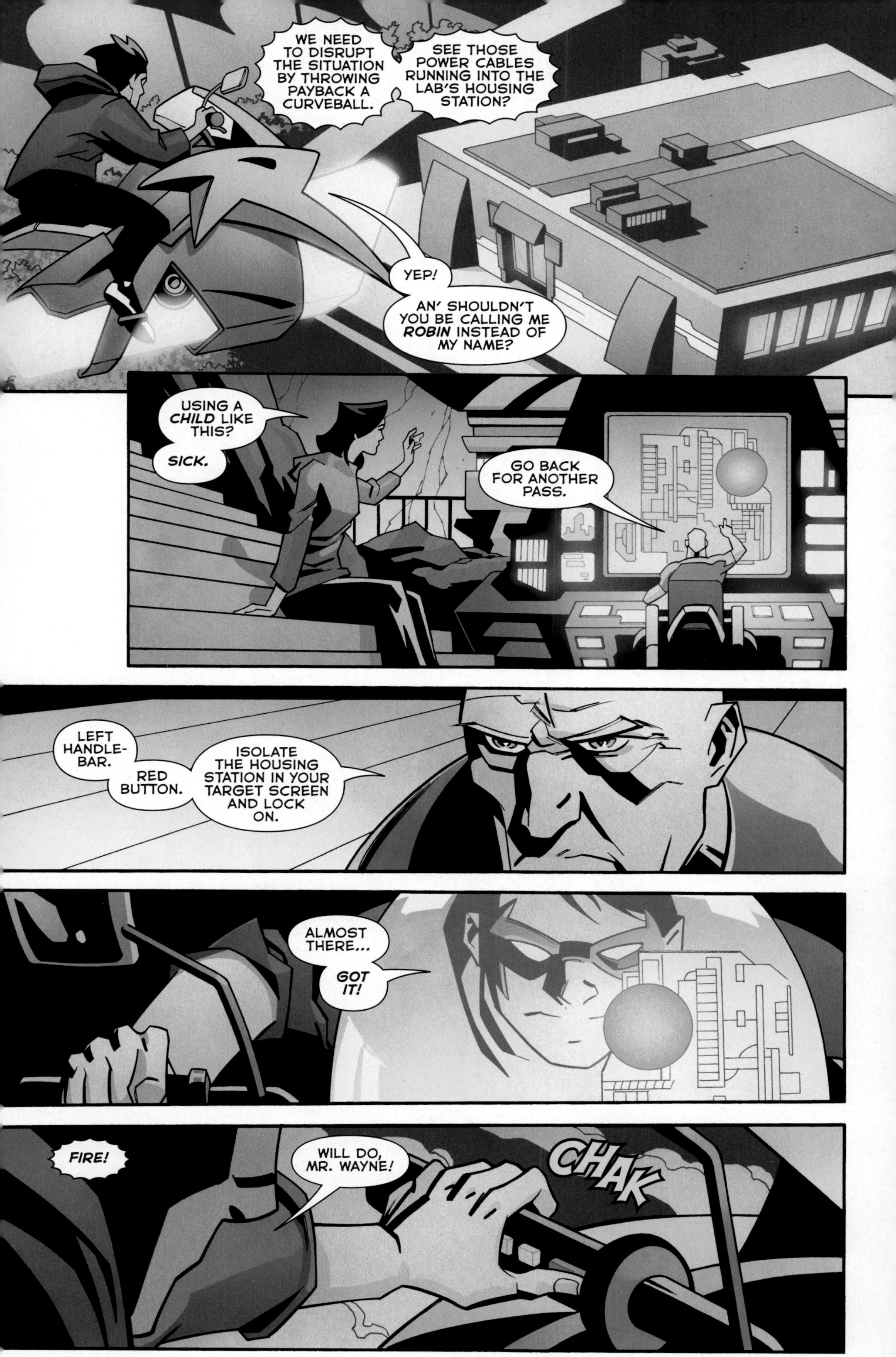
WE NEED TO DISRUPT THE SITUATION BY THROWING PAYBACK A CURVEBALL.
SEE THOSE POWER CABLES RUNNING INTO THE LAB'S HOUSING STATION?
YEP!
AN' SHOULDN'T YOU BE CALLING ME ROBIN INSTEAD OF MY NAME?
USING A CHILD LIKE THIS?
SICK.
GO BACK FOR ANOTHER PASS.
LEFT HANDLE-BAR.
RED BUTTON.
ISOLATE THE HOUSING STATION IN YOUR TARGET SCREEN AND LOCK ON.
ALMOST THERE...
GOT IT!
FIRE!
WILL DO, MR. WAYNE!
CHAK

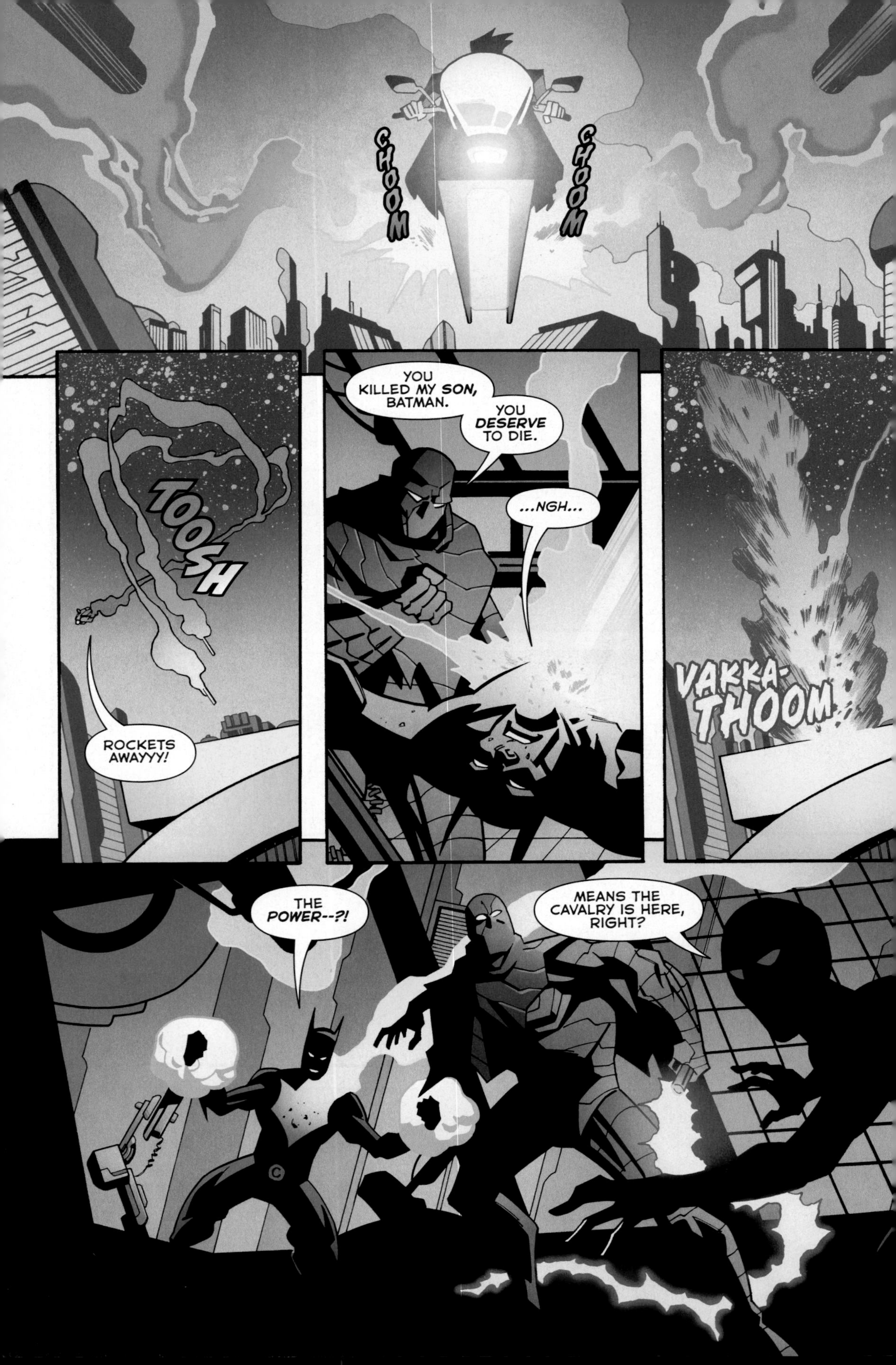
CHOOM
CHOOM
TOOSH
ROCKETS AWAYYY!
YOU KILLED MY SON, BATMAN.
YOU DESERVE TO DIE.
...NGH...
VAKKA-THOOM
THE POWER--?!
MEANS THE CAVALRY IS HERE, RIGHT?

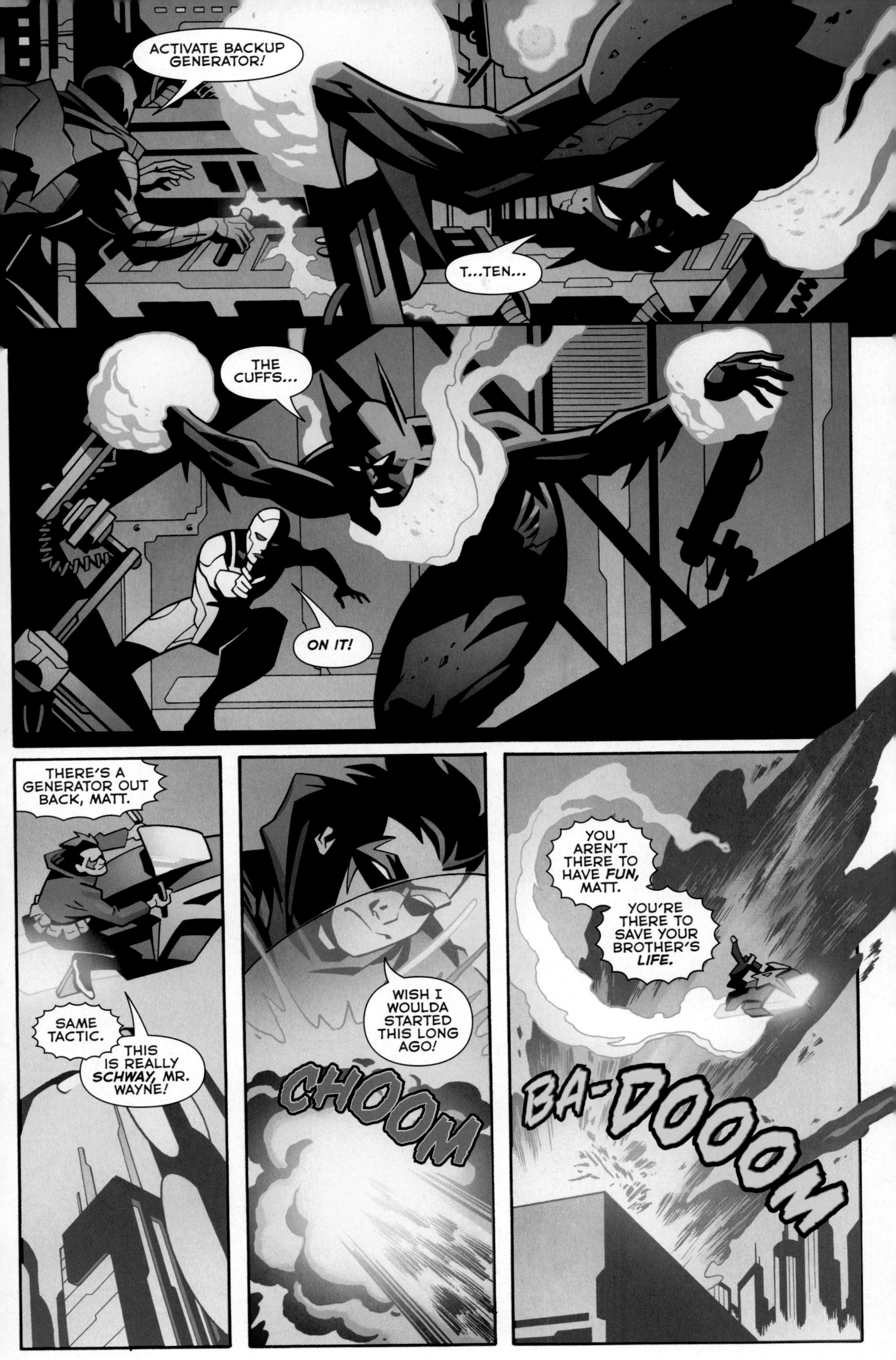
ACTIVATE BACKUP GENERATOR!
T...TEN...
THE CUFFS...
ON IT!
THERE'S A GENERATOR OUT BACK, MATT.
SAME TACTIC.
THIS IS REALLY SCHWAY, MR. WAYNE!
WISH I WOULDA STARTED THIS LONG AGO!
CHOOM
YOU AREN'T THERE TO HAVE FUN, MATT.
YOU'RE THERE TO SAVE YOUR BROTHER'S LIFE.
BA-DOOOM

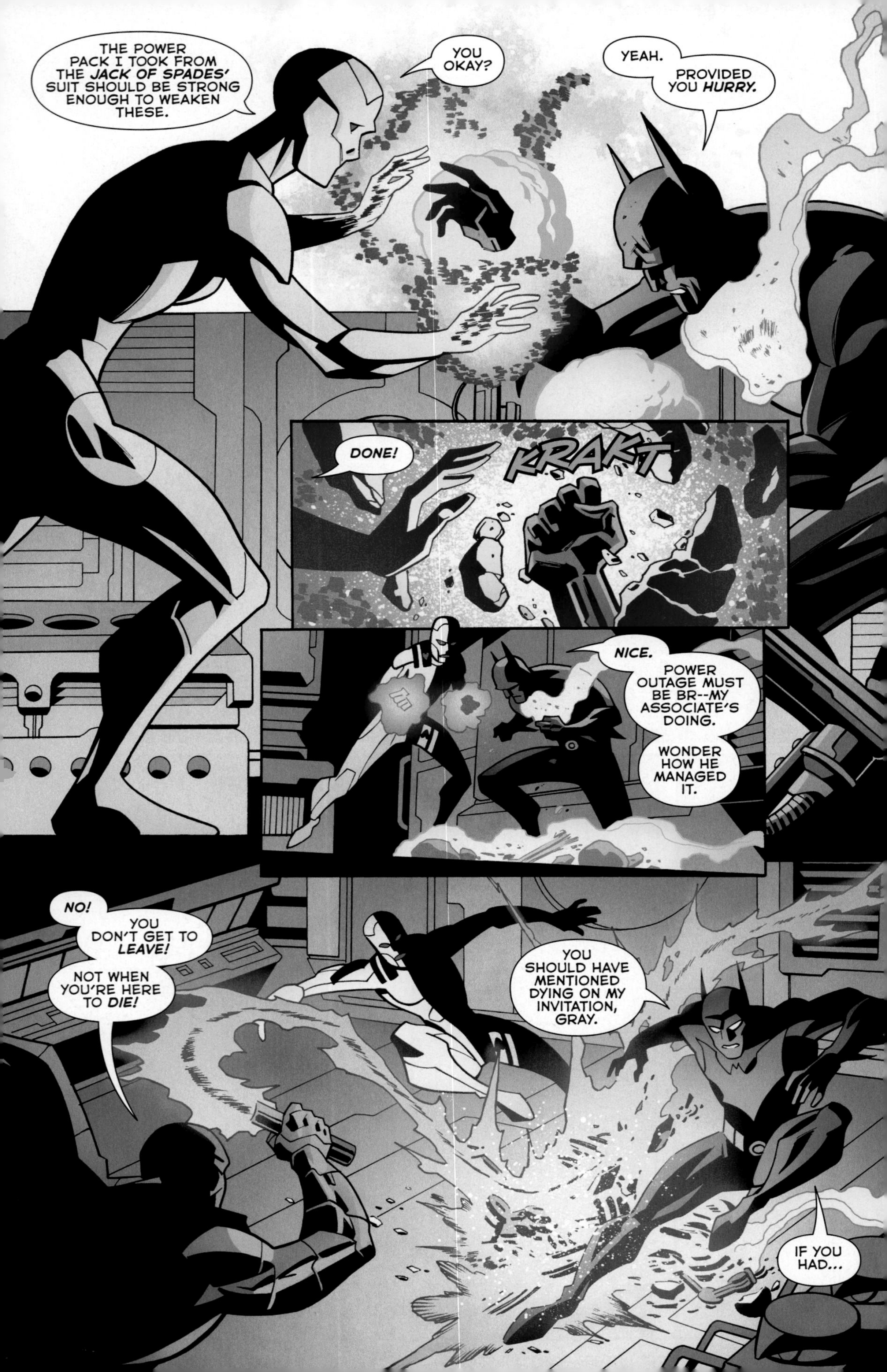
THE POWER PACK I TOOK FROM THE JACK OF SPADES' SUIT SHOULD BE STRONG ENOUGH TO WEAKEN THESE.
YOU OKAY?
YEAH.
PROVIDED YOU HURRY.
DONE!
KRAKT
NICE.
POWER OUTAGE MUST BE BR--MY ASSOCIATE'S DOING.
WONDER HOW HE MANAGED IT.
NO!
YOU DON'T GET TO LEAVE!
NOT WHEN YOU'RE HERE TO DIE!
YOU SHOULD HAVE MENTIONED DYING ON MY INVITATION, GRAY.
IF YOU HAD...

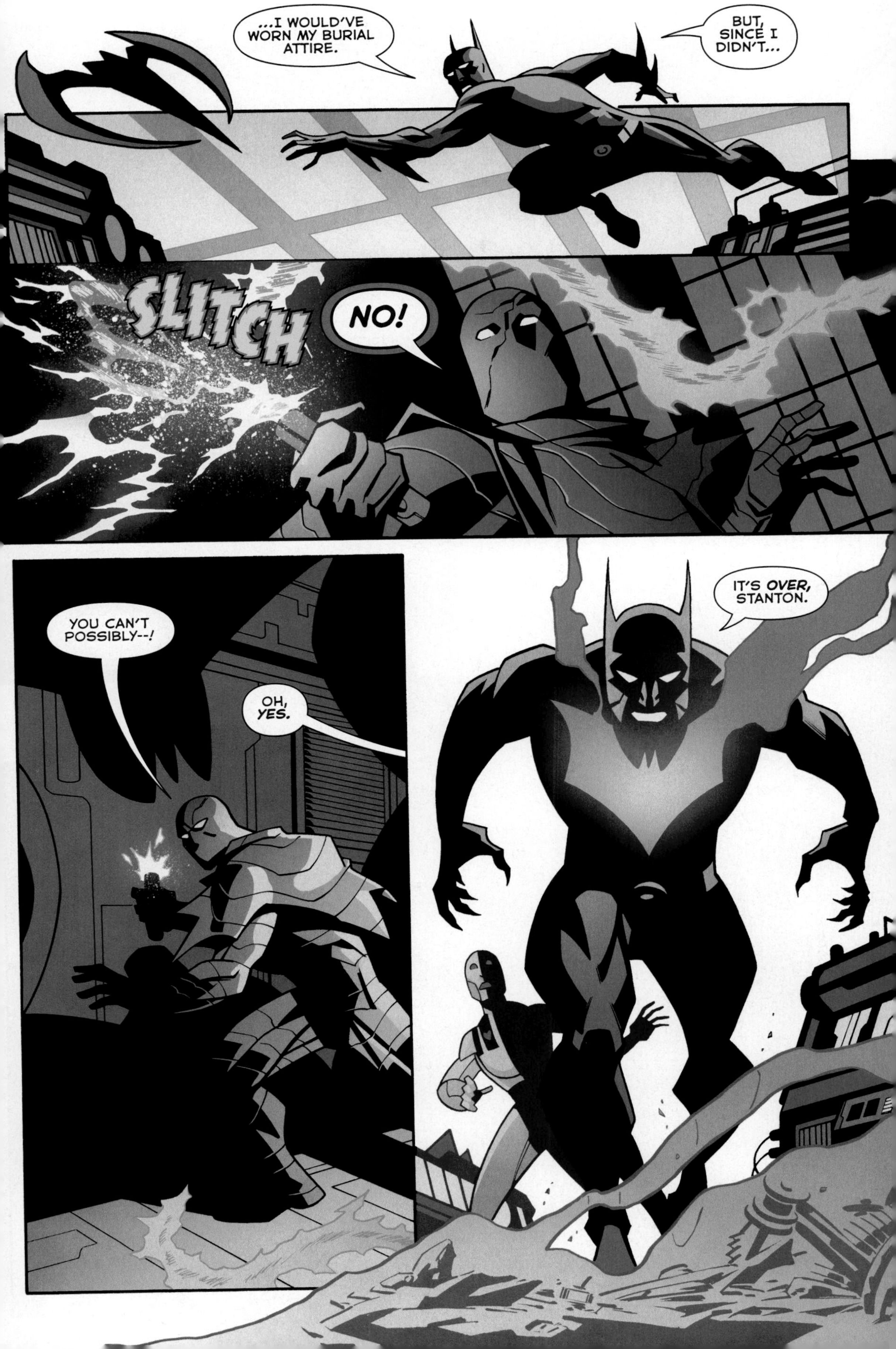
...I WOULD'VE WORN MY BURIAL ATTIRE.
BUT, SINCE I DIDN'T...
SLITCH
NO!
YOU CAN'T POSSIBLY--!
OH, YES.
IT'S OVER, STANTON.

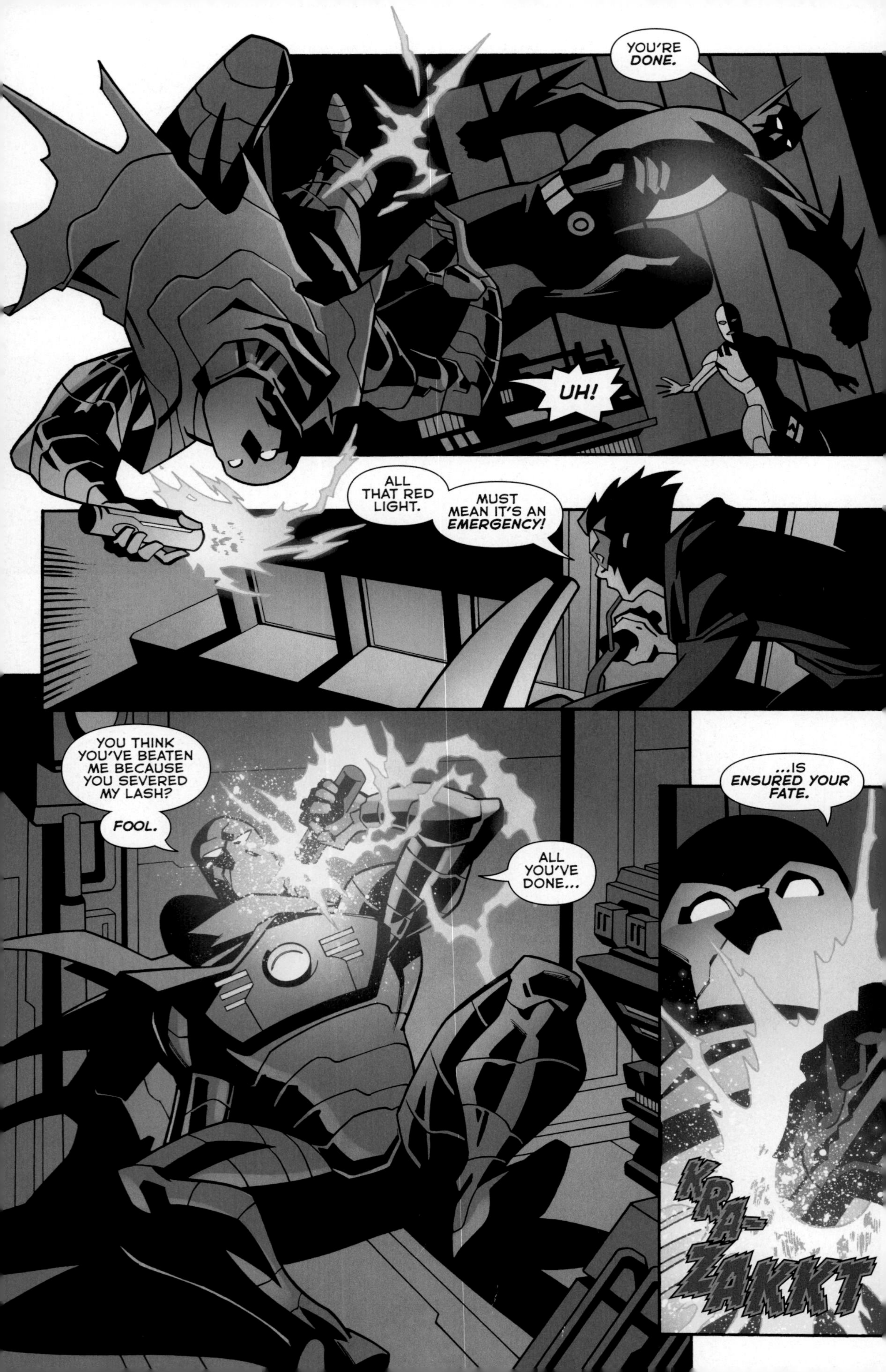
YOU'RE DONE.
UH!
ALL THAT RED LIGHT.
MUST MEAN IT'S AN EMERGENCY!
YOU THINK YOU'VE BEATEN ME BECAUSE YOU SEVERED MY LASH?
FOOL.
ALL YOU'VE DONE...
...IS ENSURED YOUR FATE.
KRA-ZAKKT

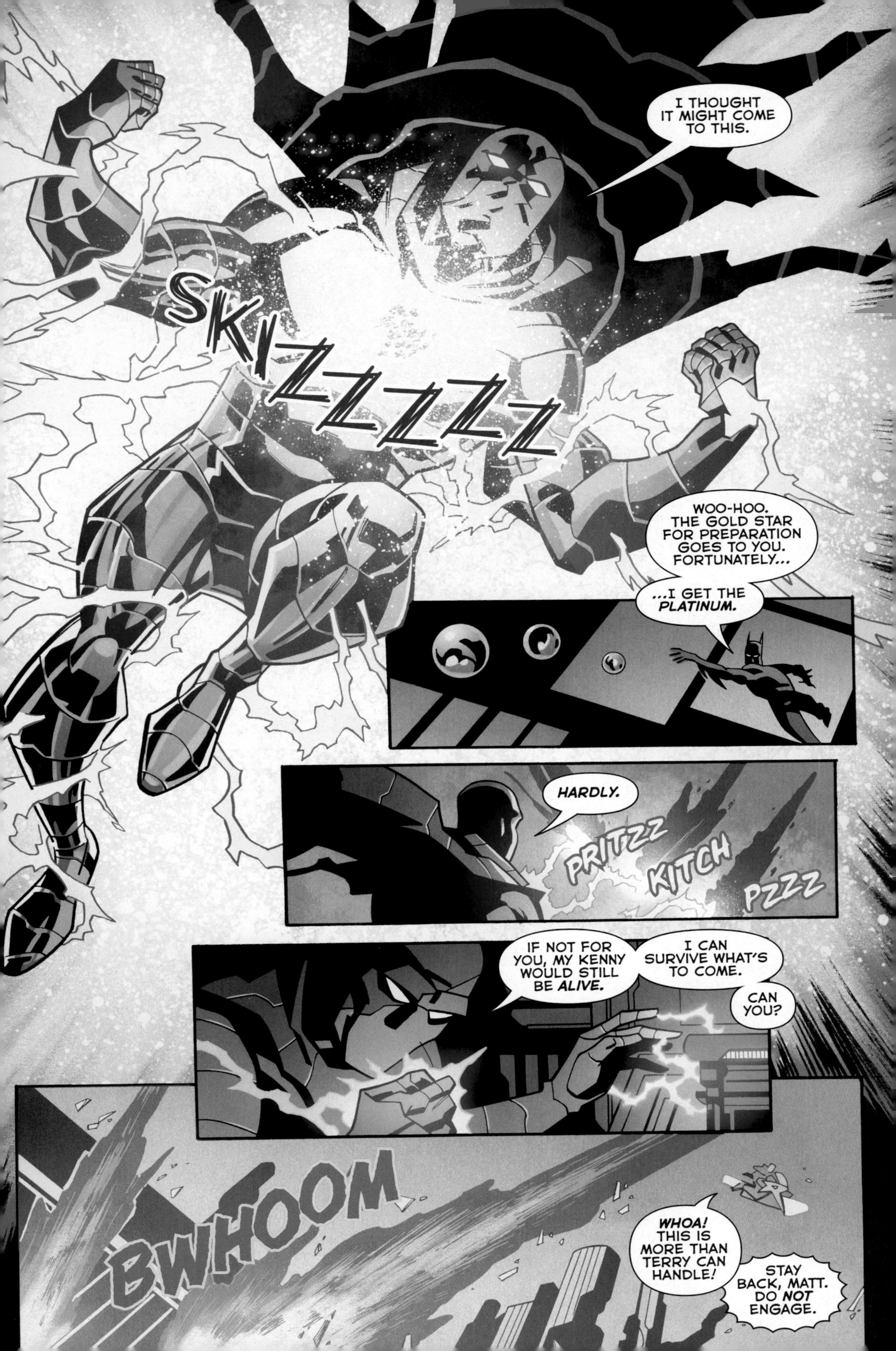
I THOUGHT IT MIGHT COME TO THIS.
SKIZZZZZZ
WOO-HOO. THE GOLD STAR FOR PREPARATION GOES TO YOU. FORTUNATELY...
...I GET THE *PLATINUM.*
HARDLY.
PRITZZ
KITCH
PZZZ
IF NOT FOR YOU, MY KENNY WOULD STILL BE *ALIVE.*
I CAN SURVIVE WHAT'S TO COME.
CAN YOU?
BWHOOM
WHOA! THIS IS MORE THAN TERRY CAN HANDLE!
STAY BACK, MATT. DO *NOT* ENGAGE.

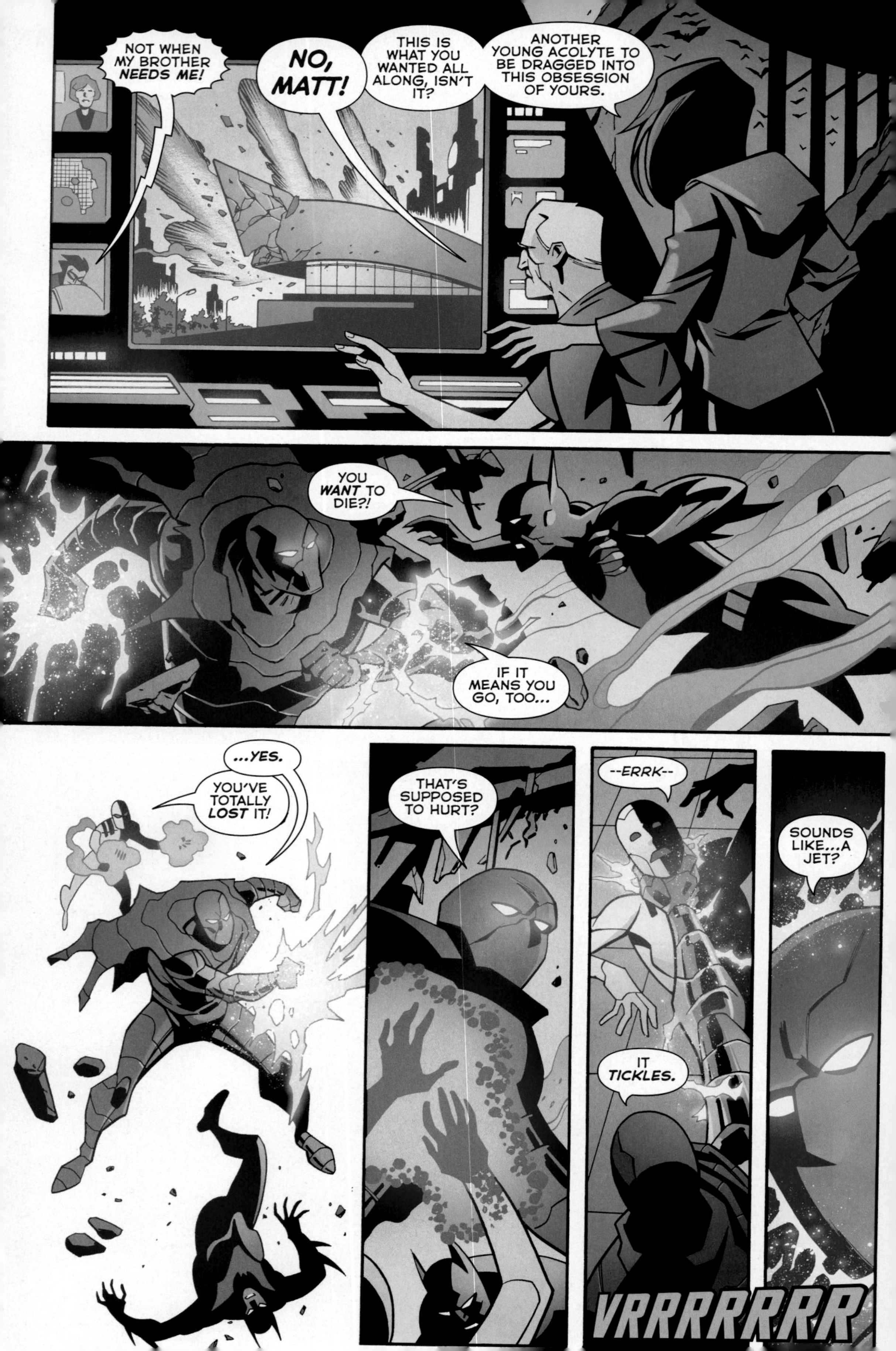

NOT WHEN MY BROTHER NEEDS ME!
NO, MATT!
THIS IS WHAT YOU WANTED ALL ALONG, ISN'T IT?
ANOTHER YOUNG ACOLYTE TO BE DRAGGED INTO THIS OBSESSION OF YOURS.
YOU WANT TO DIE?!
IF IT MEANS YOU GO, TOO...
...YES.
YOU'VE TOTALLY LOST IT!
THAT'S SUPPOSED TO HURT?
--ERRK--
IT TICKLES.
SOUNDS LIKE...A JET?
VRRRRRRR

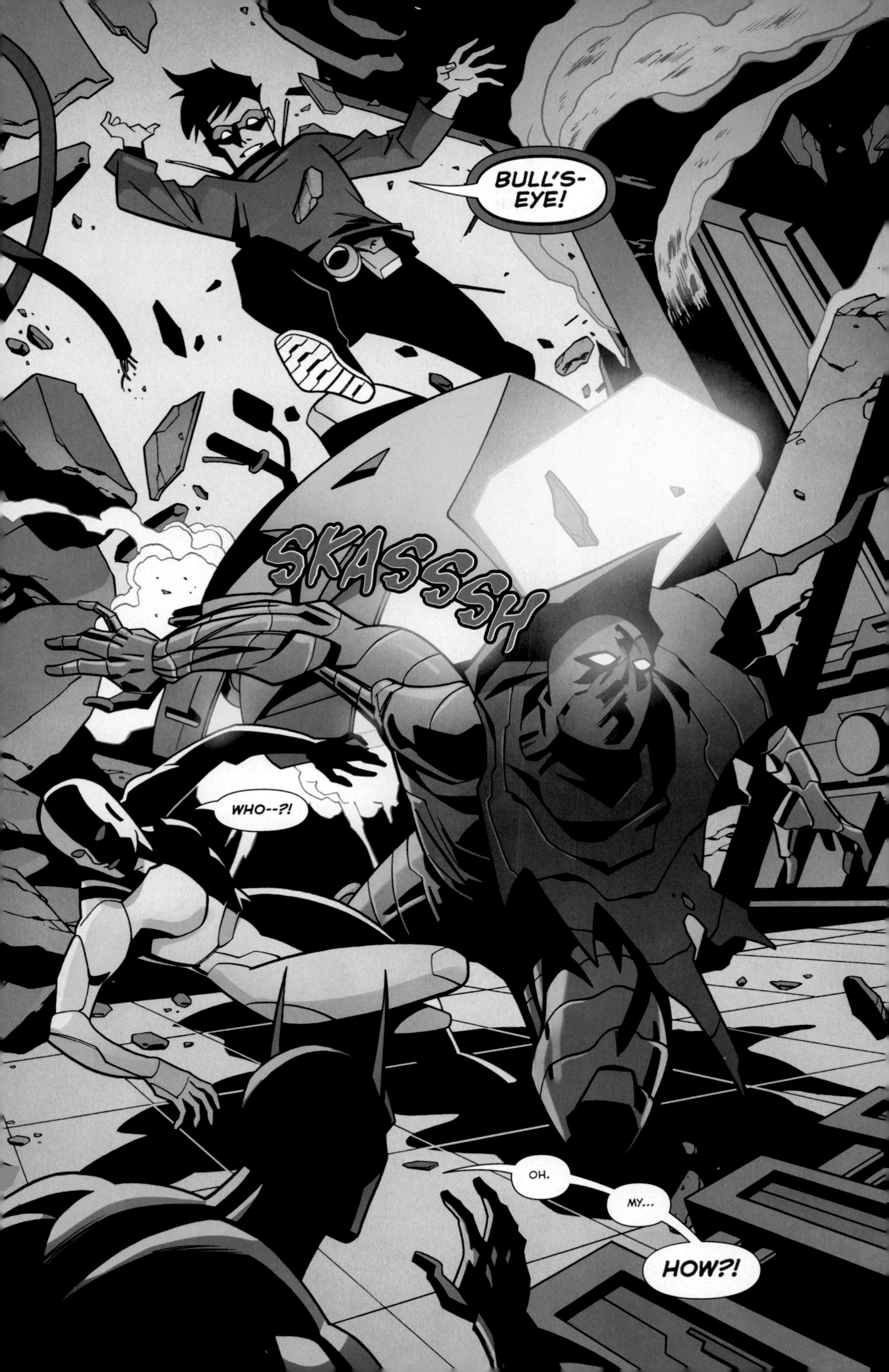
BULL'S-EYE!
SKASSSH
WHO--?!
OH.
MY...
HOW?!

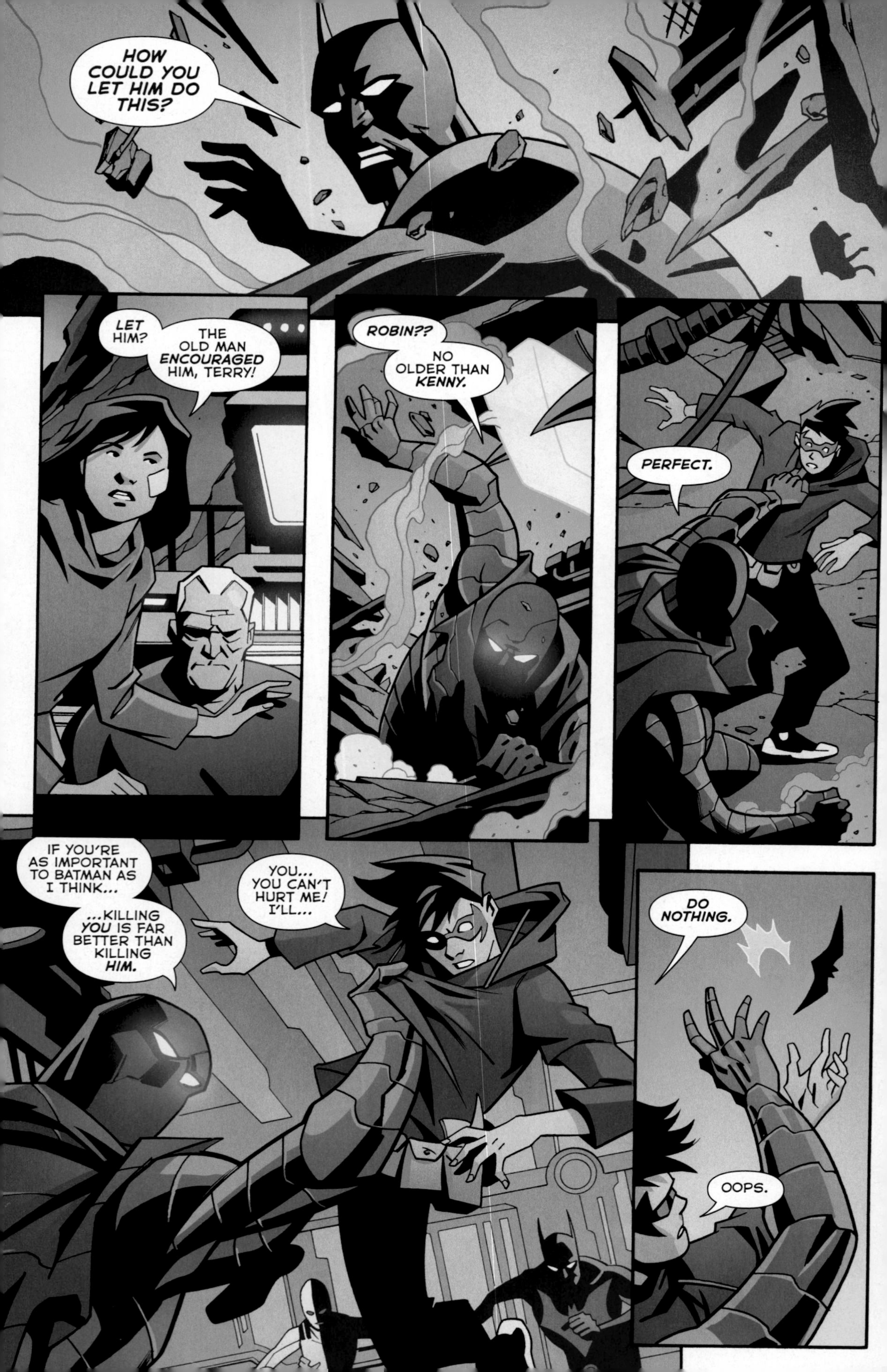
HOW COULD YOU LET HIM DO THIS?
LET HIM?
THE OLD MAN ENCOURAGED HIM, TERRY!
ROBIN??
NO OLDER THAN KENNY.
PERFECT.
IF YOU'RE AS IMPORTANT TO BATMAN AS I THINK...
...KILLING YOU IS FAR BETTER THAN KILLING HIM.
YOU... YOU CAN'T HURT ME! I'LL...
DO NOTHING.
OOPS.

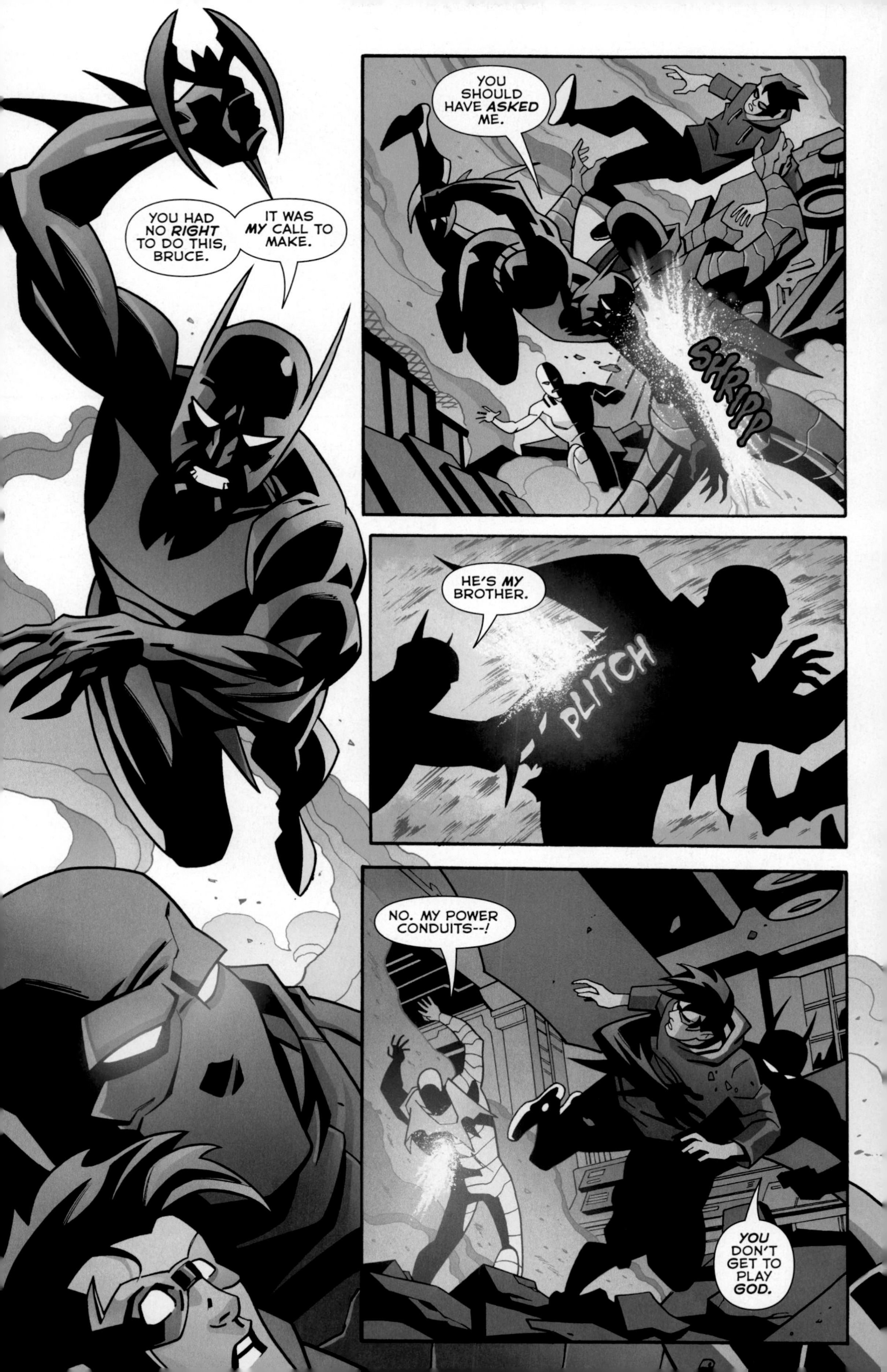
YOU HAD NO RIGHT TO DO THIS, BRUCE.
IT WAS MY CALL TO MAKE.
YOU SHOULD HAVE ASKED ME.
SHRIPP
HE'S MY BROTHER.
PLITCH
NO. MY POWER CONDUITS--!
YOU DON'T GET TO PLAY GOD.

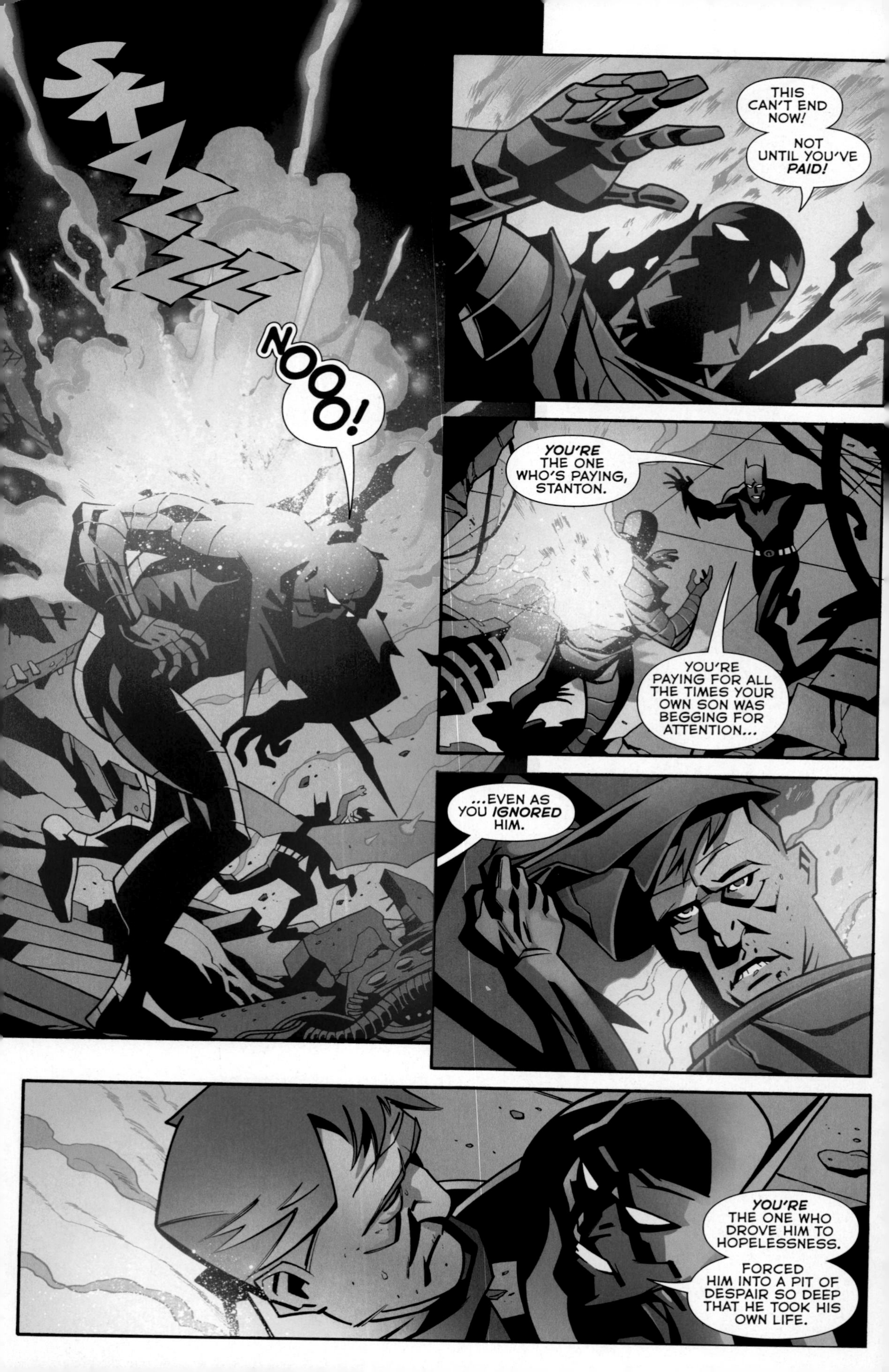
SKAZZZ
NOOOO!
THIS CAN'T END NOW!
NOT UNTIL YOU'VE PAID!
YOU'RE THE ONE WHO'S PAYING, STANTON.
YOU'RE PAYING FOR ALL THE TIMES YOUR OWN SON WAS BEGGING FOR ATTENTION...
...EVEN AS YOU IGNORED HIM.
YOU'RE THE ONE WHO DROVE HIM TO HOPELESSNESS.
FORCED HIM INTO A PIT OF DESPAIR SO DEEP THAT HE TOOK HIS OWN LIFE.

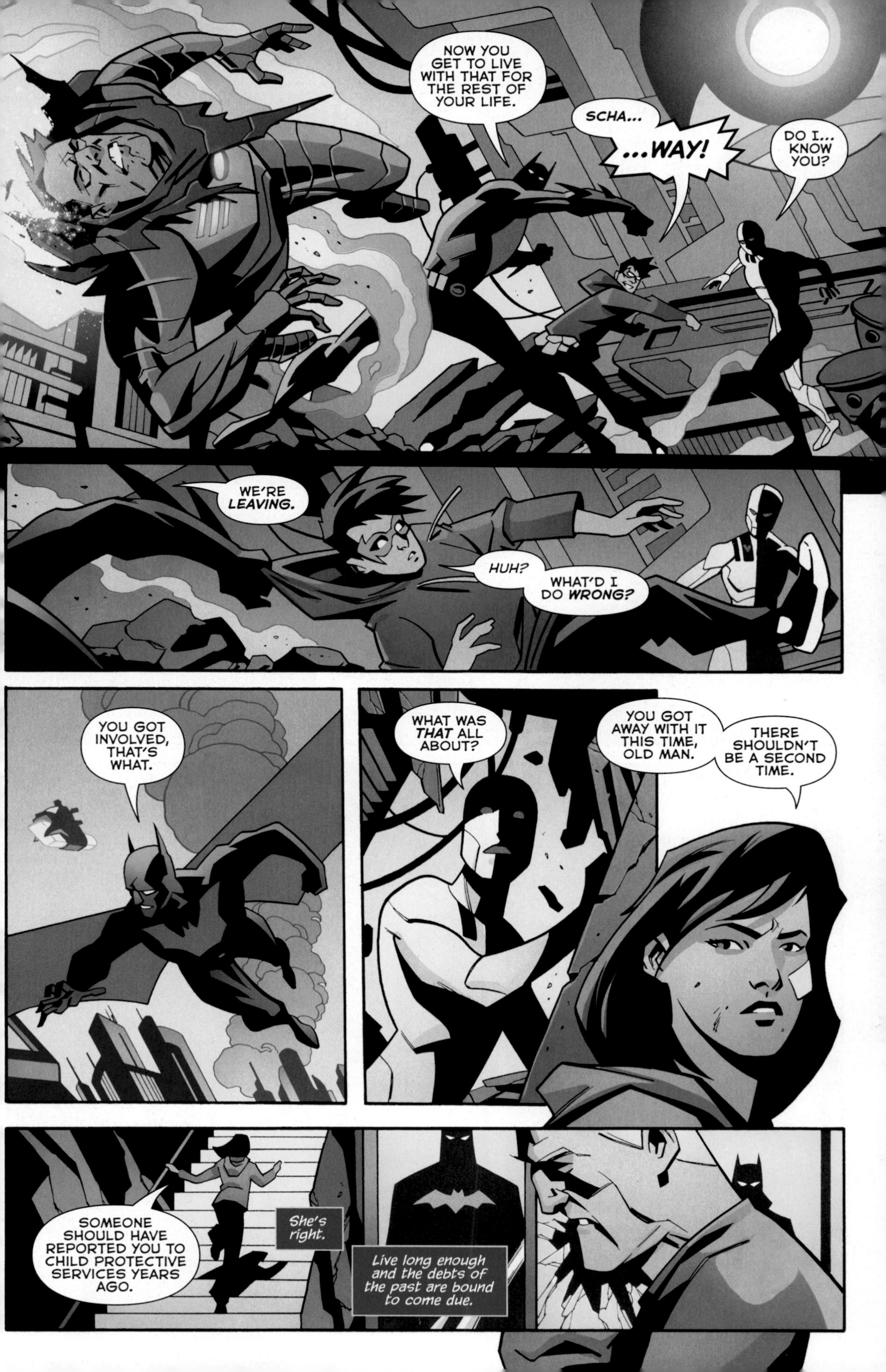

NOW YOU GET TO LIVE WITH THAT FOR THE REST OF YOUR LIFE.
SCHA...
...WAY!
DO I... KNOW YOU?
WE'RE LEAVING.
HUH?
WHAT'D I DO WRONG?
YOU GOT INVOLVED, THAT'S WHAT.
WHAT WAS THAT ALL ABOUT?
YOU GOT AWAY WITH IT THIS TIME, OLD MAN.
THERE SHOULDN'T BE A SECOND TIME.
SOMEONE SHOULD HAVE REPORTED YOU TO CHILD PROTECTIVE SERVICES YEARS AGO.
She's right.
Live long enough and the debts of the past are bound to come due.

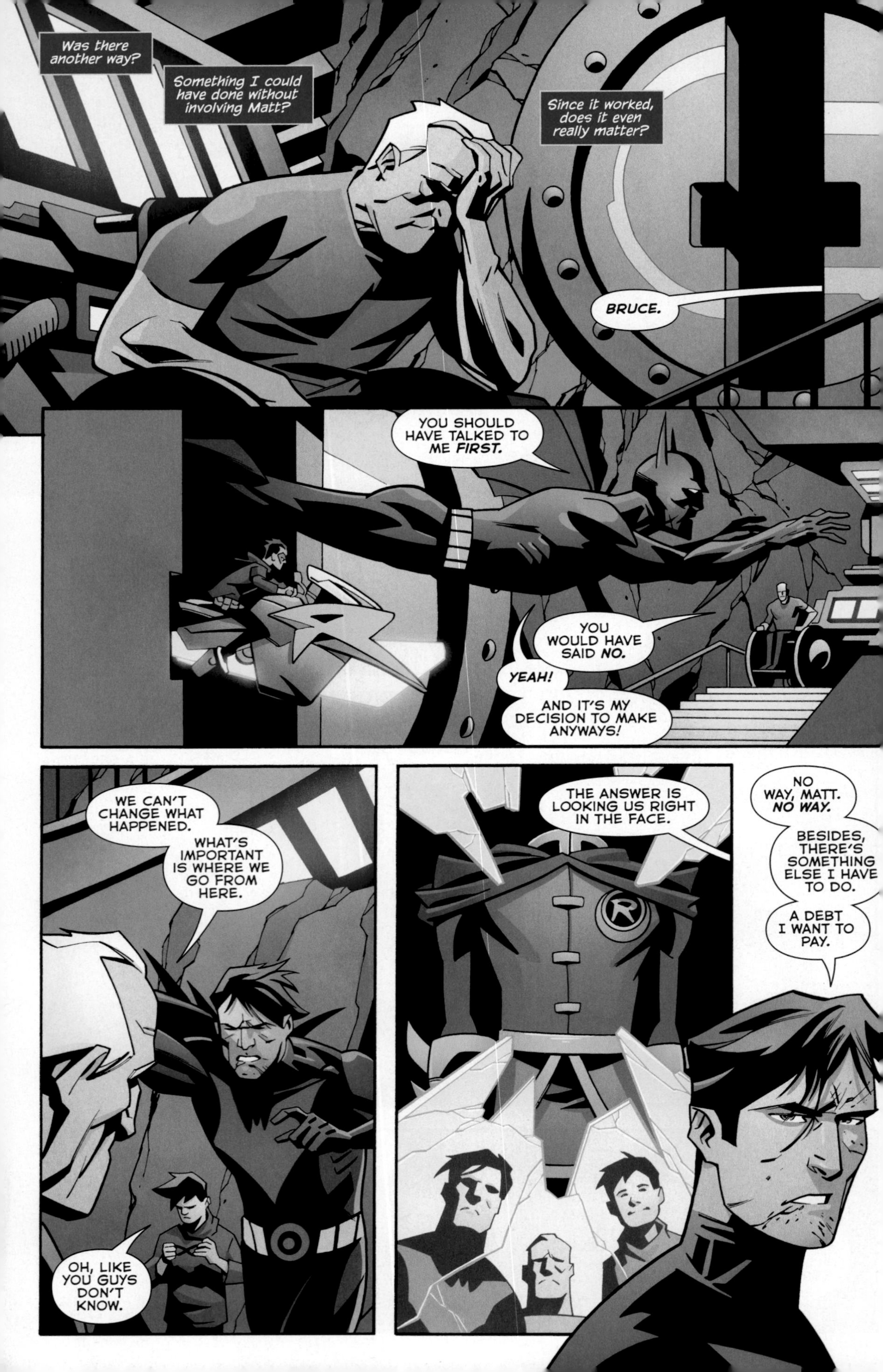

Was there another way?
Something I could have done without involving Matt?
Since it worked, does it even really matter?
BRUCE.
YOU SHOULD HAVE TALKED TO ME FIRST.
YOU WOULD HAVE SAID NO.
YEAH!
AND IT'S MY DECISION TO MAKE ANYWAYS!
WE CAN'T CHANGE WHAT HAPPENED.
WHAT'S IMPORTANT IS WHERE WE GO FROM HERE.
OH, LIKE YOU GUYS DON'T KNOW.
THE ANSWER IS LOOKING US RIGHT IN THE FACE.
NO WAY, MATT. NO WAY.
BESIDES, THERE'S SOMETHING ELSE I HAVE TO DO.
A DEBT I WANT TO PAY.

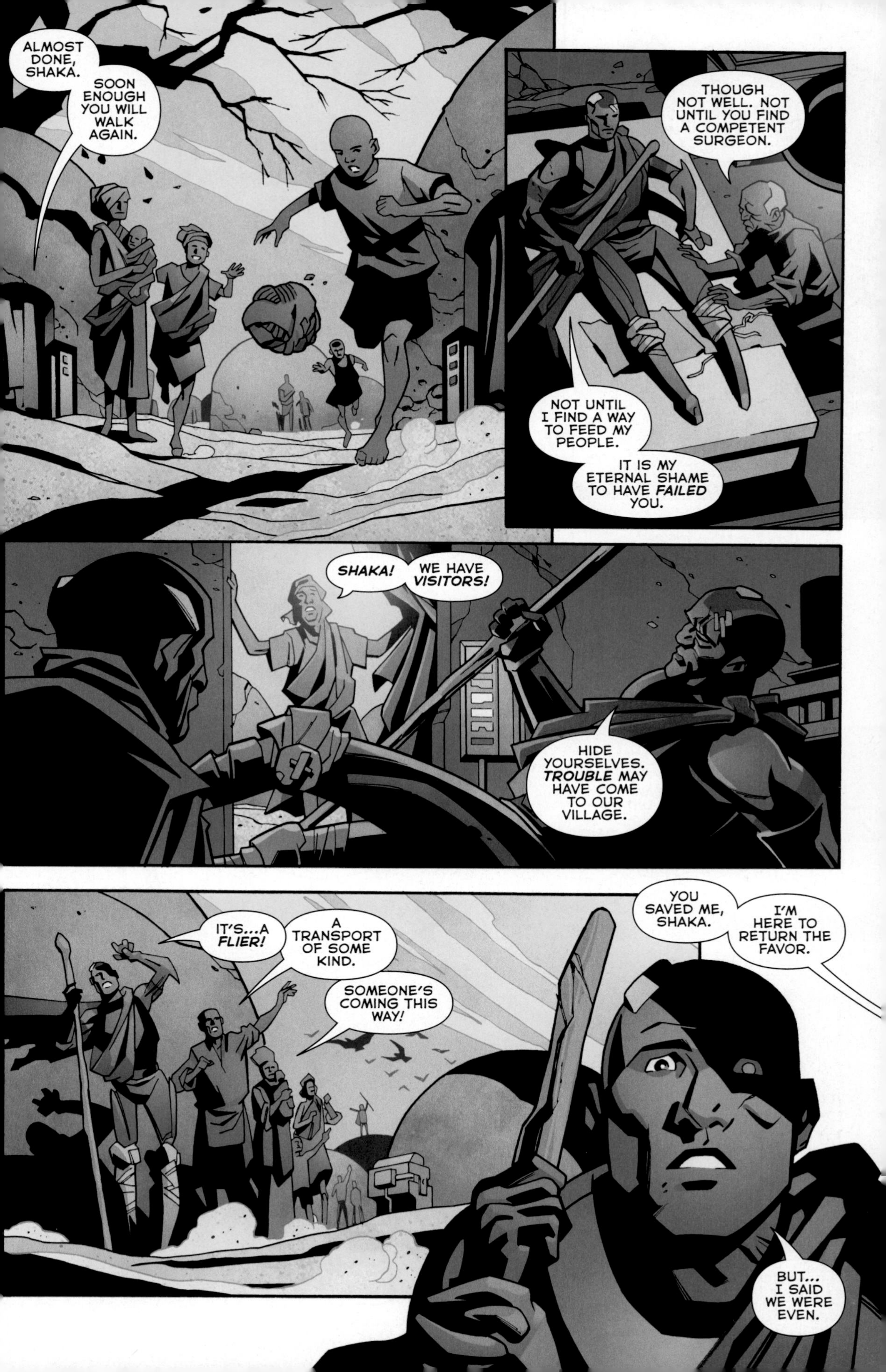
ALMOST DONE, SHAKA.
SOON ENOUGH YOU WILL WALK AGAIN.
THOUGH NOT WELL. NOT UNTIL YOU FIND A COMPETENT SURGEON.
NOT UNTIL I FIND A WAY TO FEED MY PEOPLE.
IT IS MY ETERNAL SHAME TO HAVE *FAILED* YOU.
SHAKA!
WE HAVE *VISITORS!*
HIDE YOURSELVES. *TROUBLE* MAY HAVE COME TO OUR VILLAGE.
IT'S...A *FLIER!*
A TRANSPORT OF SOME KIND.
SOMEONE'S COMING THIS WAY!
YOU SAVED ME, SHAKA.
I'M HERE TO RETURN THE FAVOR.
BUT... I SAID WE WERE EVEN.

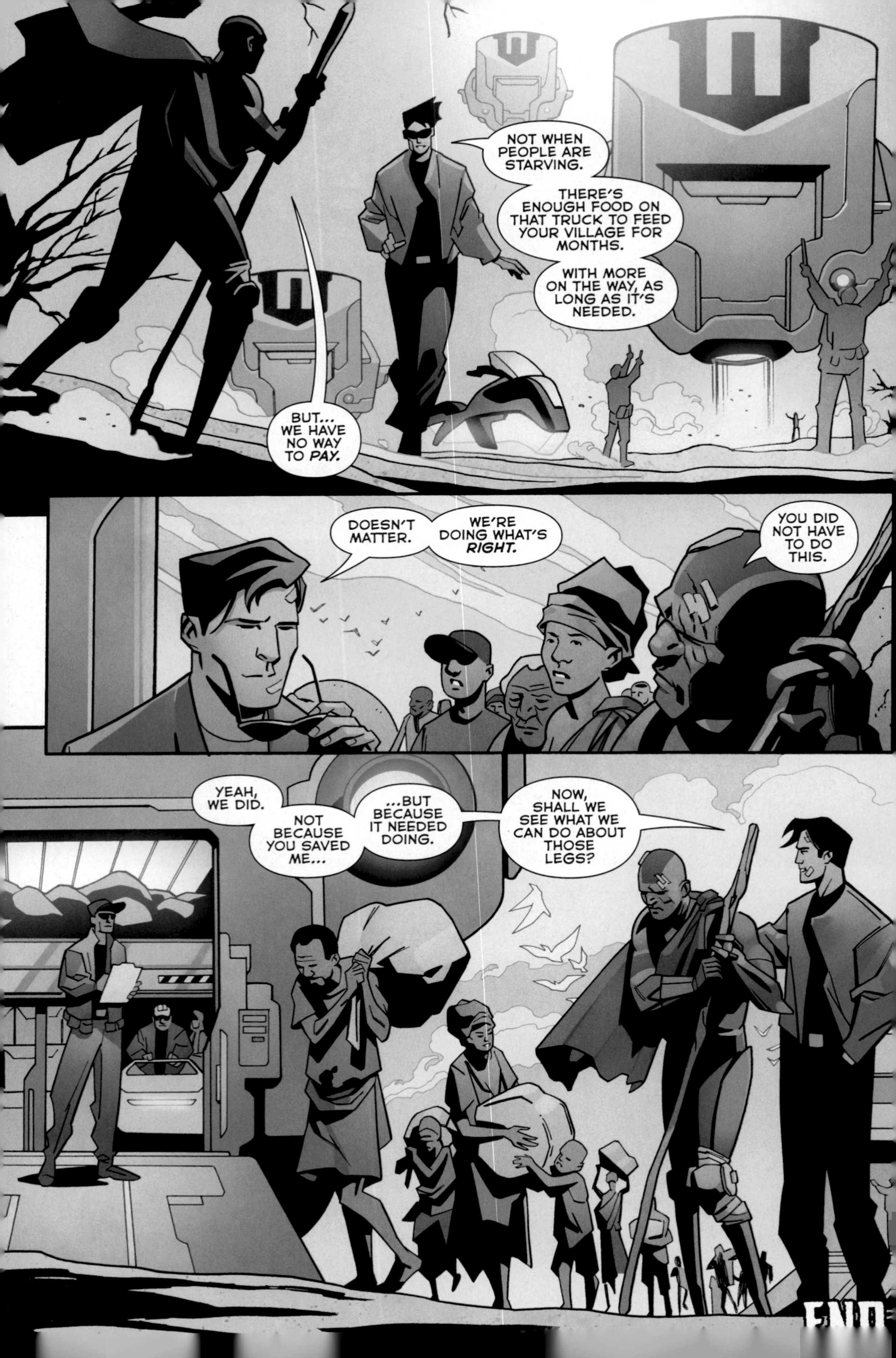
NOT WHEN PEOPLE ARE STARVING.
THERE'S ENOUGH FOOD ON THAT TRUCK TO FEED YOUR VILLAGE FOR MONTHS.
WITH MORE ON THE WAY, AS LONG AS IT'S NEEDED.
BUT... WE HAVE NO WAY TO PAY.
DOESN'T MATTER.
WE'RE DOING WHAT'S RIGHT.
YOU DID NOT HAVE TO DO THIS.
YEAH, WE DID.
NOT BECAUSE YOU SAVED ME...
...BUT BECAUSE IT NEEDED DOING.
NOW, SHALL WE SEE WHAT WE CAN DO ABOUT THOSE LEGS?
END

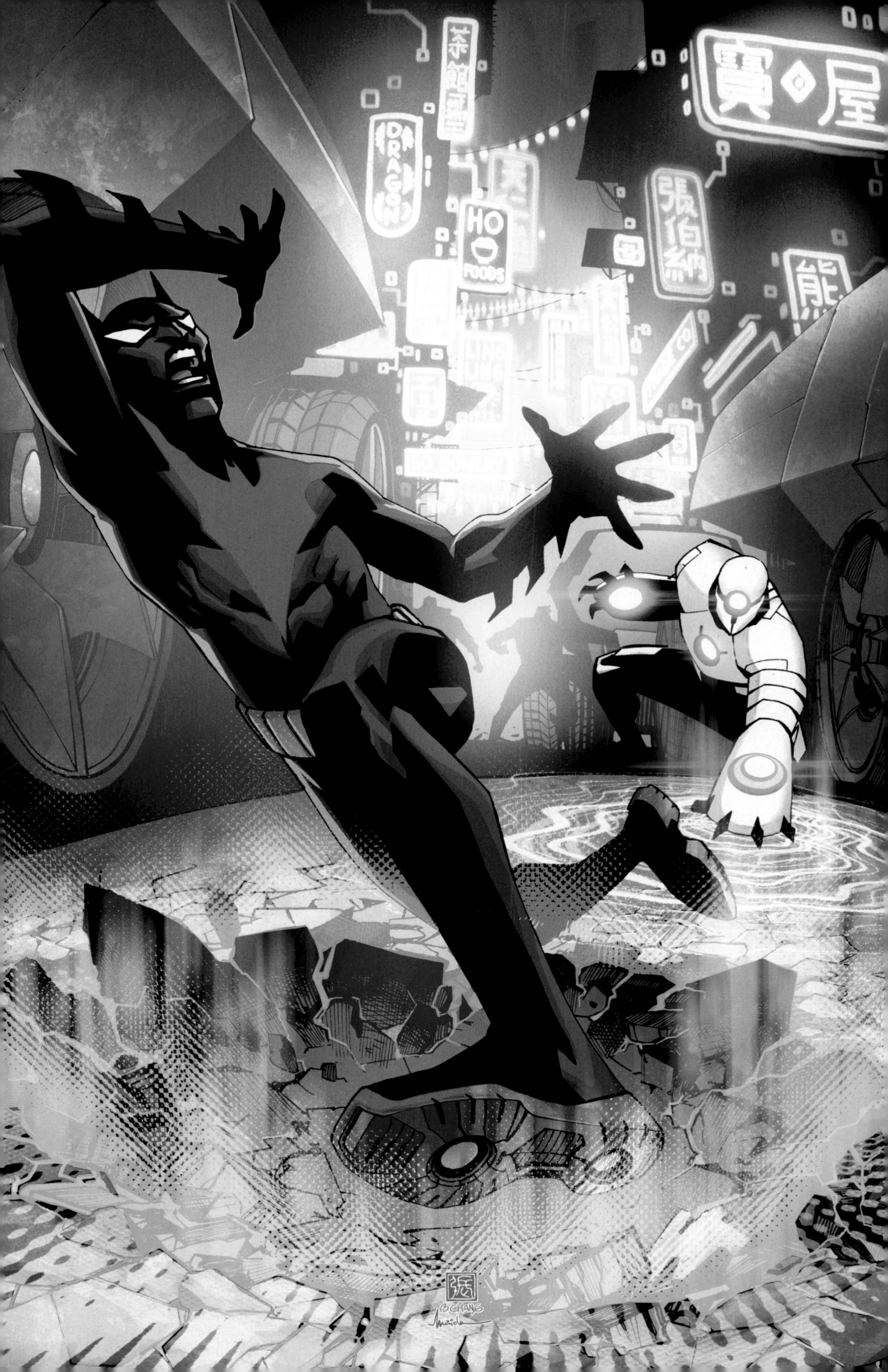

茶館
DRAGON
HO
FOODS
LING LING
張伯納
熊
B CHANG

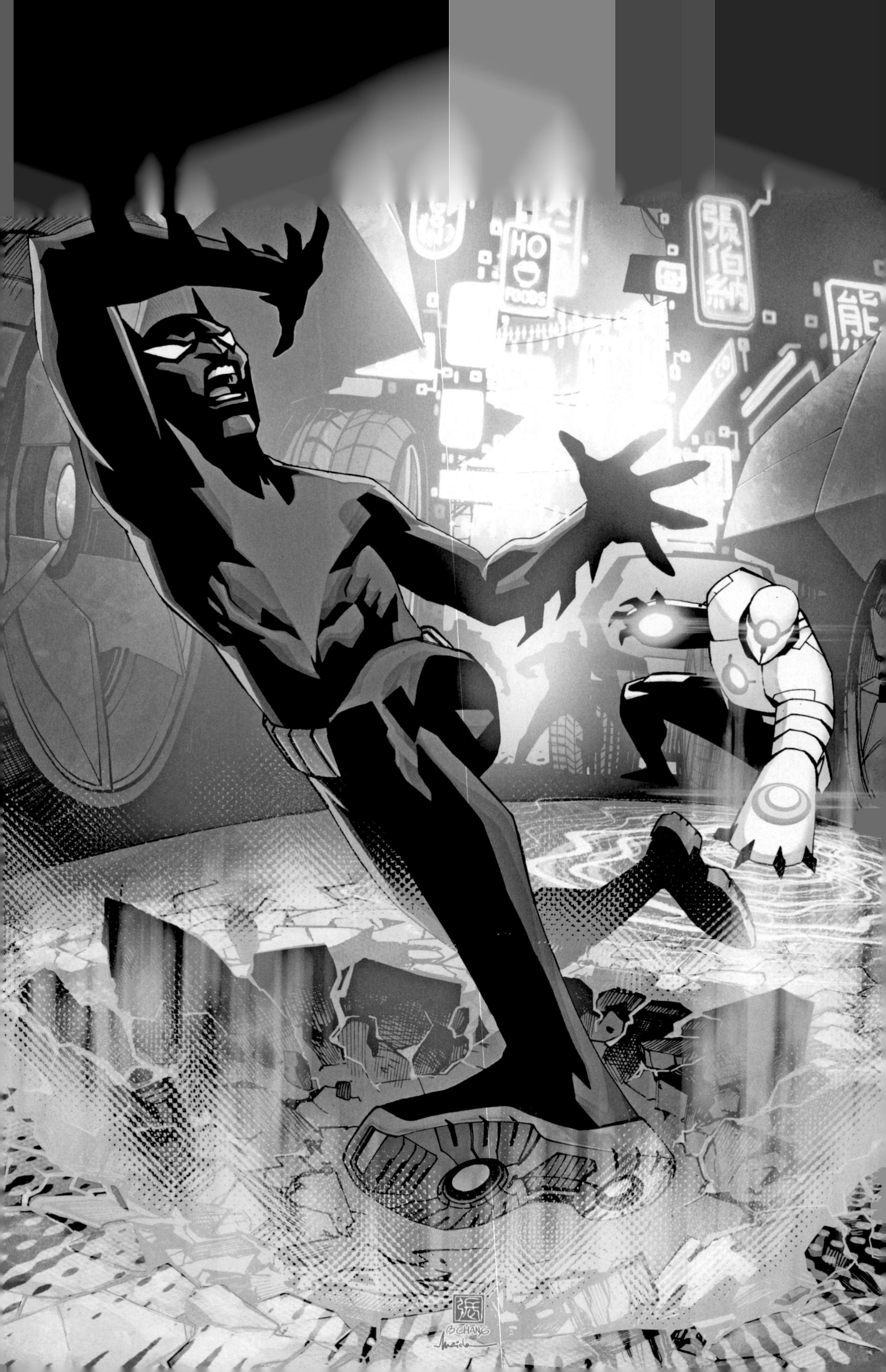
HO
FOODS
張伯納
熊
B CHANG

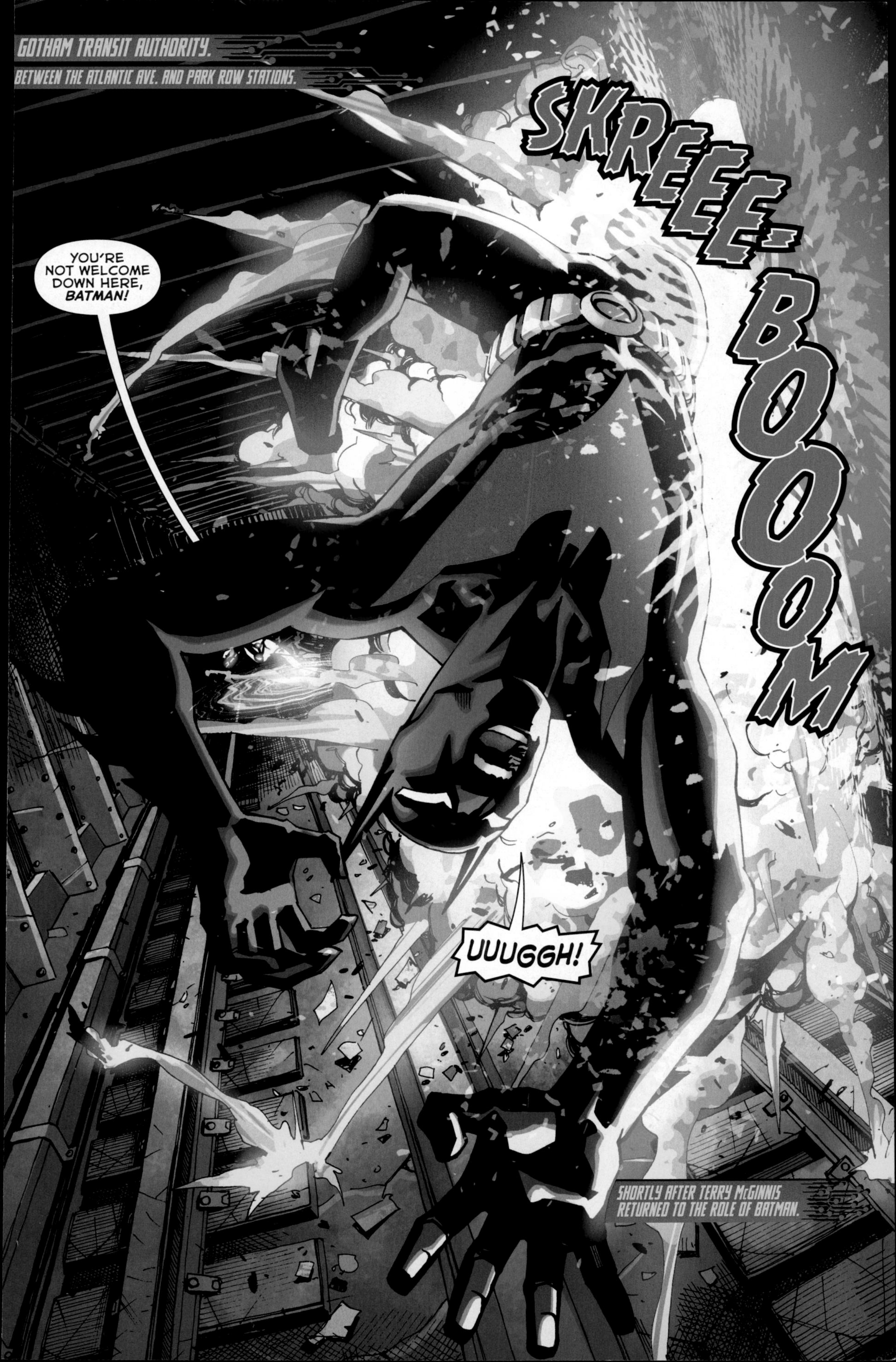
GOTHAM TRANSIT AUTHORITY.
BETWEEN THE ATLANTIC AVE. AND PARK ROW STATIONS.
SKREEEE-BOOOOM
YOU'RE NOT WELCOME DOWN HERE, BATMAN!
UUUGGH!
SHORTLY AFTER TERRY McGINNIS RETURNED TO THE ROLE OF BATMAN.

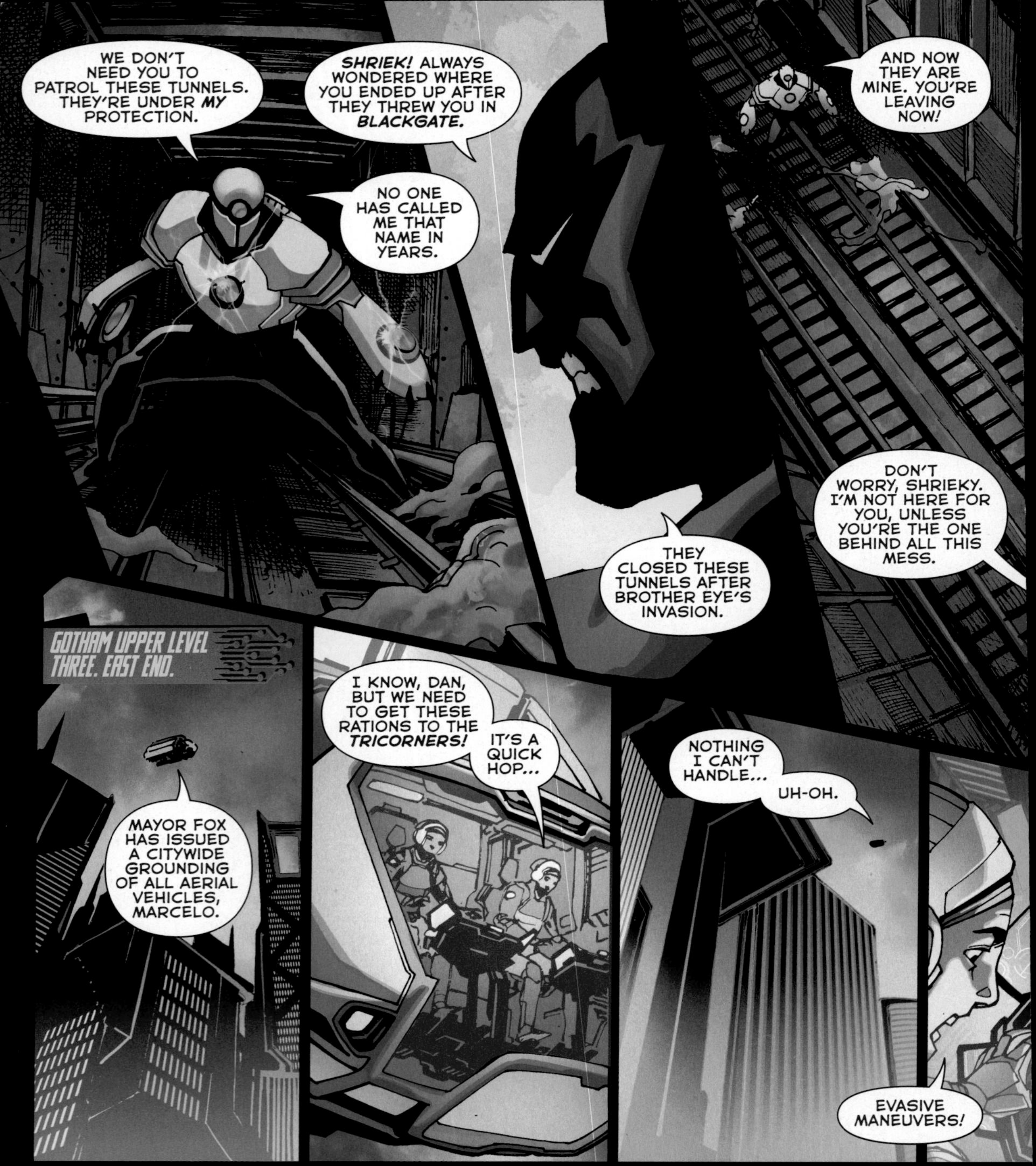
WE DON'T NEED YOU TO PATROL THESE TUNNELS. THEY'RE UNDER *MY* PROTECTION.
SHRIEK! ALWAYS WONDERED WHERE YOU ENDED UP AFTER THEY THREW YOU IN *BLACKGATE.*
NO ONE HAS CALLED ME THAT NAME IN YEARS.
AND NOW THEY ARE MINE. YOU'RE LEAVING NOW!
THEY CLOSED THESE TUNNELS AFTER BROTHER EYE'S INVASION.
DON'T WORRY, SHRIEKY. I'M NOT HERE FOR YOU, UNLESS YOU'RE THE ONE BEHIND ALL THIS MESS.
GOTHAM UPPER LEVEL THREE. EAST END.
MAYOR FOX HAS ISSUED A CITYWIDE GROUNDING OF ALL AERIAL VEHICLES, MARCELO.
I KNOW, DAN, BUT WE NEED TO GET THESE RATIONS TO THE *TRICORNERS!*
IT'S A QUICK HOP...
NOTHING I CAN'T HANDLE...
UH-OH.
EVASIVE MANEUVERS!

GOTHAM GAMES

BERNARD CHANG: writer/artist

MARCELO MAIOLO: colors
TRAVIS LANHAM: letters
CHANG & MAIOLO: cover
ROB LEVIN: associate editor
JIM CHADWICK: editor

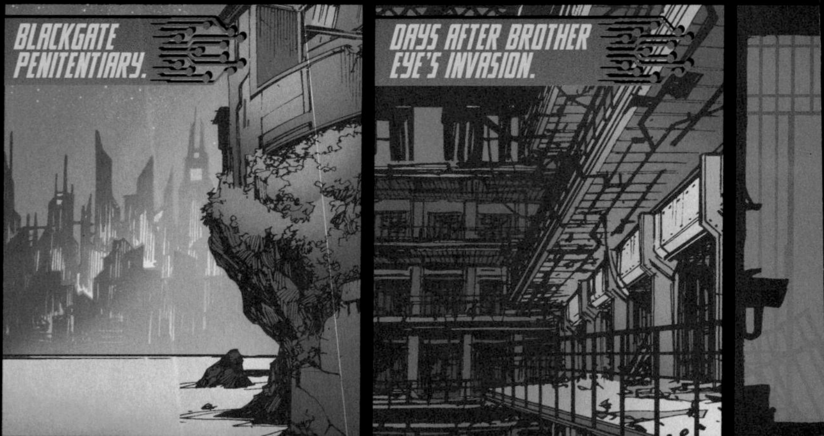
BLACKGATE PENITENTIARY.
DAYS AFTER BROTHER EYE'S INVASION.

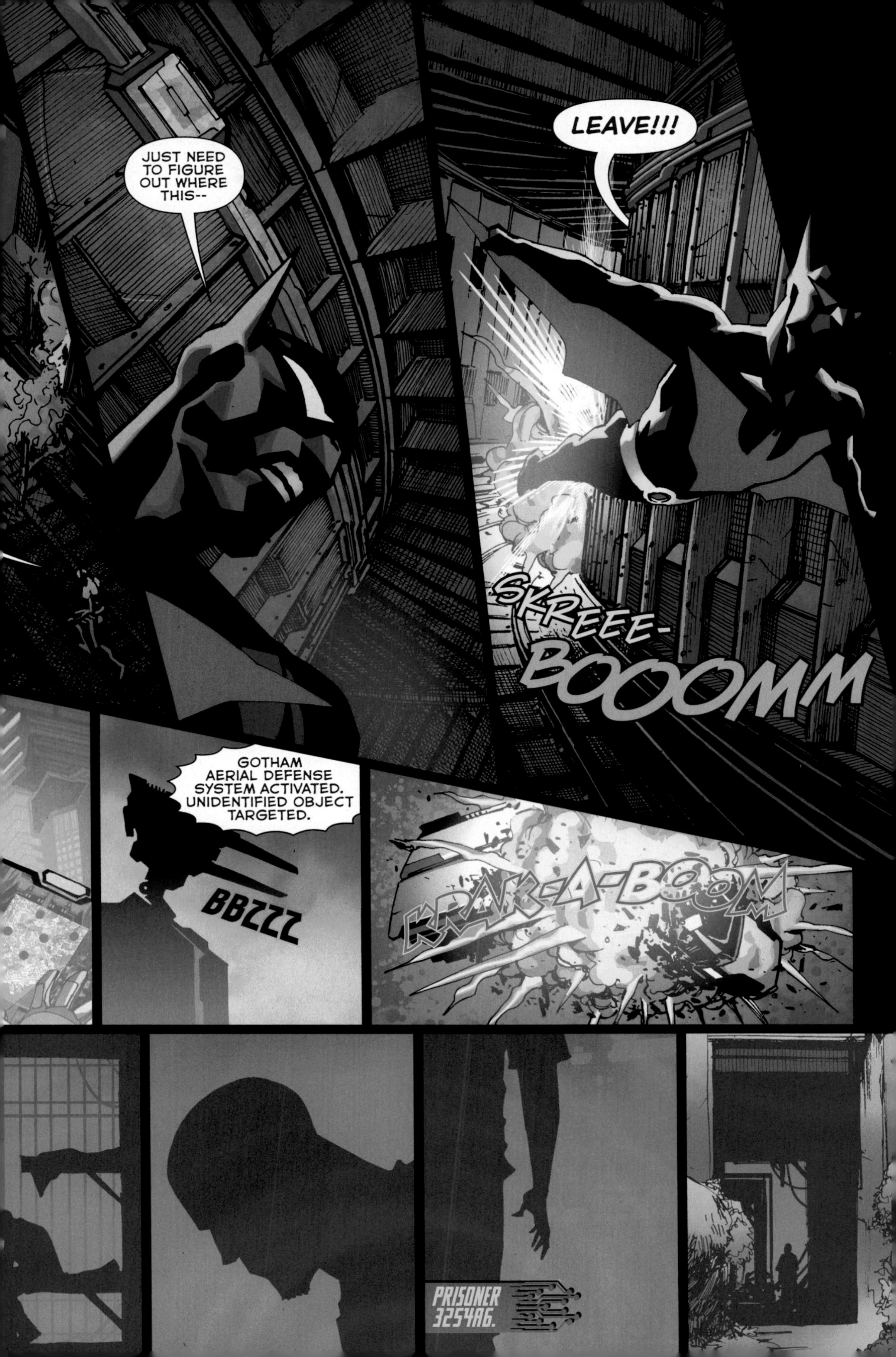
JUST NEED TO FIGURE OUT WHERE THIS--
LEAVE!!!
SKREEE-BOOOOMM
GOTHAM AERIAL DEFENSE SYSTEM ACTIVATED. UNIDENTIFIED OBJECT TARGETED.
BBZZZ
KRAK-A-BOOM
PRISONER 3254A6.

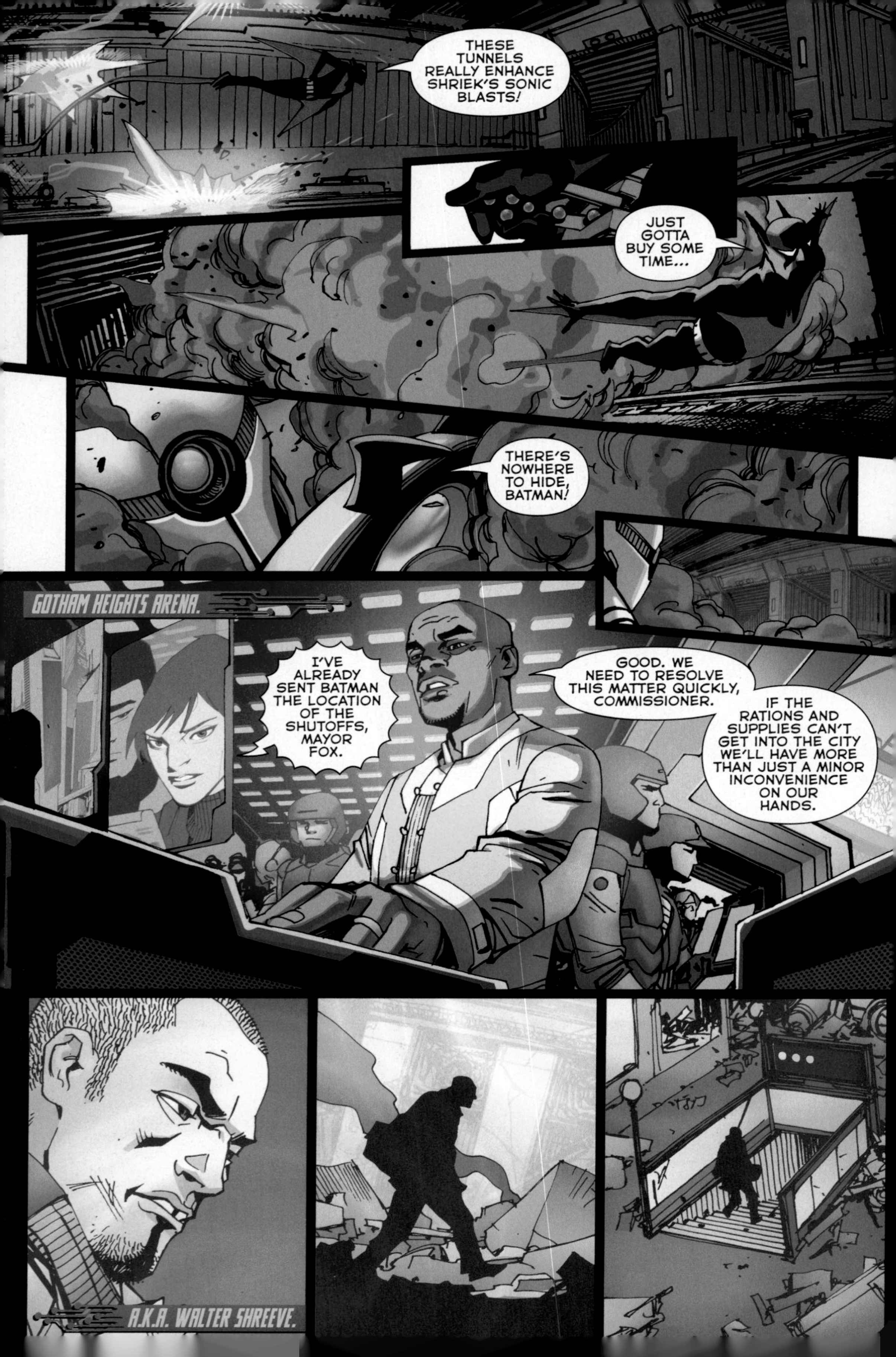
THESE TUNNELS REALLY ENHANCE SHRIEK'S SONIC BLASTS!
JUST GOTTA BUY SOME TIME...
THERE'S NOWHERE TO HIDE, BATMAN!
GOTHAM HEIGHTS ARENA.
I'VE ALREADY SENT BATMAN THE LOCATION OF THE SHUTOFFS, MAYOR FOX.
GOOD. WE NEED TO RESOLVE THIS MATTER QUICKLY, COMMISSIONER.
IF THE RATIONS AND SUPPLIES CAN'T GET INTO THE CITY WE'LL HAVE MORE THAN JUST A MINOR INCONVENIENCE ON OUR HANDS.
A.K.A. WALTER SHREEVE.

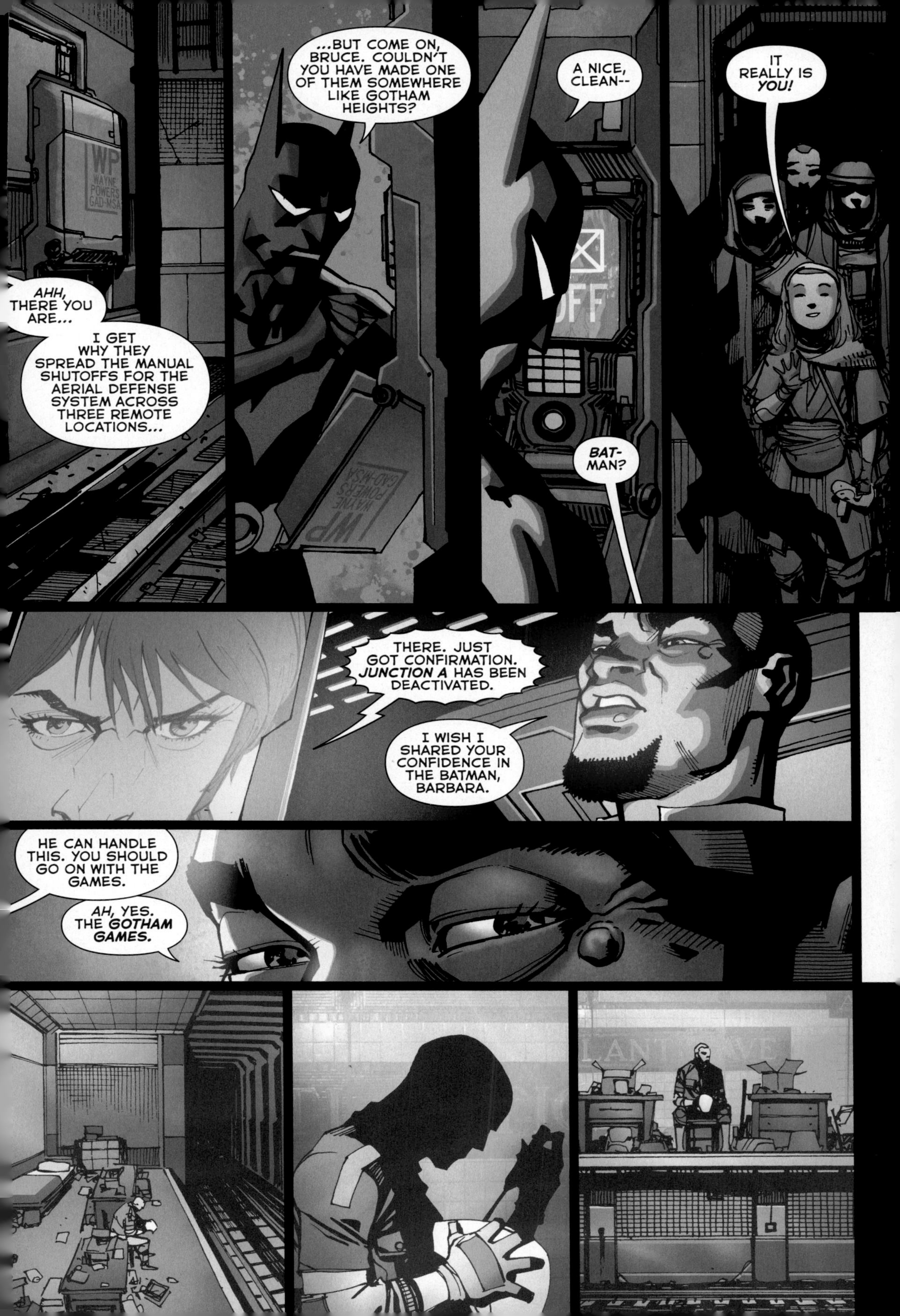
AHH, THERE YOU ARE...
I GET WHY THEY SPREAD THE MANUAL SHUTOFFS FOR THE AERIAL DEFENSE SYSTEM ACROSS THREE REMOTE LOCATIONS...
...BUT COME ON, BRUCE. COULDN'T YOU HAVE MADE ONE OF THEM SOMEWHERE LIKE GOTHAM HEIGHTS?
A NICE, CLEAN--
BAT-MAN?
IT REALLY IS *YOU!*
THERE. JUST GOT CONFIRMATION. *JUNCTION A* HAS BEEN DEACTIVATED.
I WISH I SHARED YOUR CONFIDENCE IN THE BATMAN, BARBARA.
HE CAN HANDLE THIS. YOU SHOULD GO ON WITH THE GAMES.
AH, YES. THE *GOTHAM GAMES.*

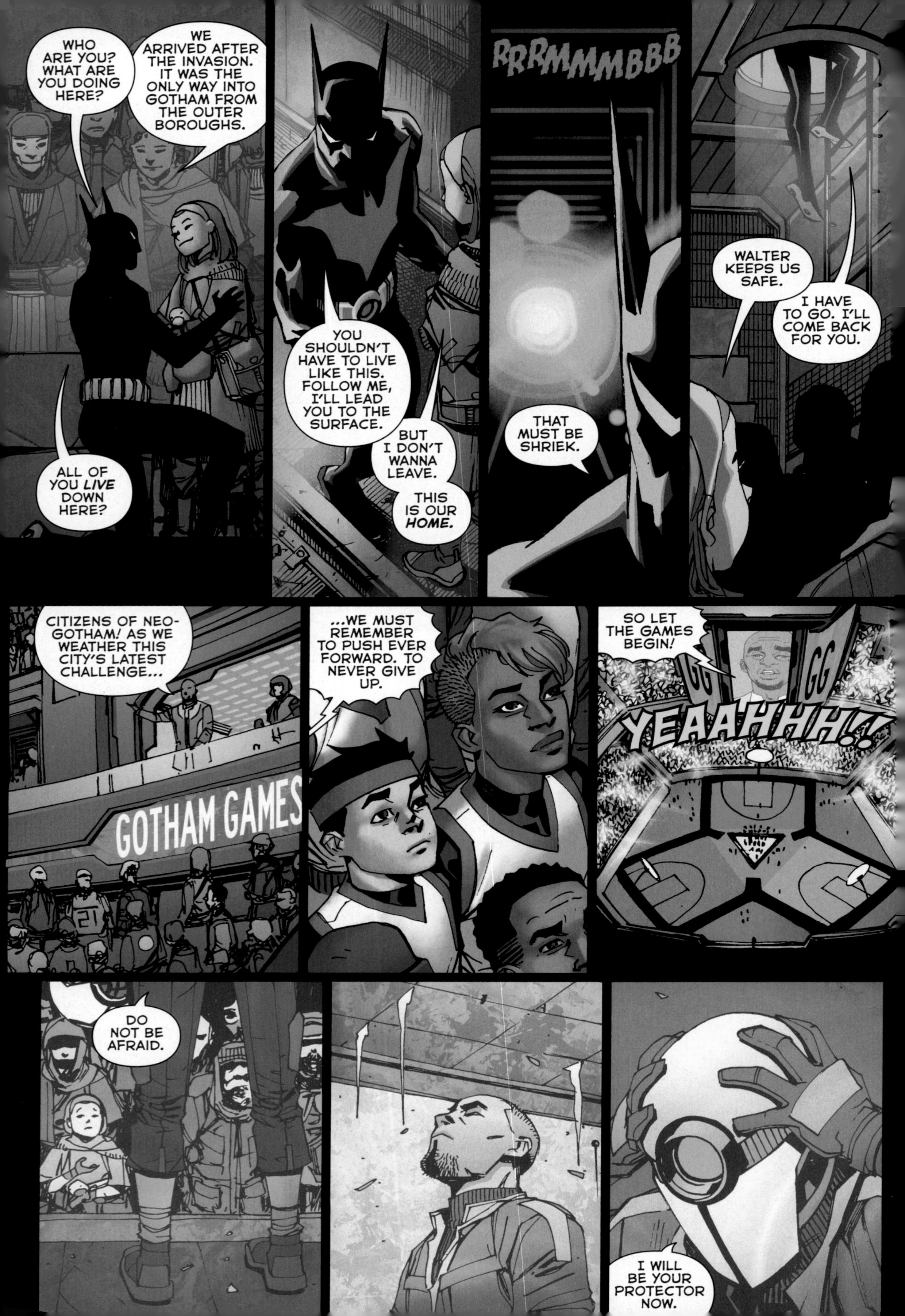
WHO ARE YOU? WHAT ARE YOU DOING HERE?
WE ARRIVED AFTER THE INVASION. IT WAS THE ONLY WAY INTO GOTHAM FROM THE OUTER BOROUGHS.
ALL OF YOU *LIVE* DOWN HERE?
YOU SHOULDN'T HAVE TO LIVE LIKE THIS. FOLLOW ME, I'LL LEAD YOU TO THE SURFACE.
BUT I DON'T WANNA LEAVE.
THIS IS OUR *HOME.*
RRRMMMMBBB
THAT MUST BE SHRIEK.
WALTER KEEPS US SAFE.
I HAVE TO GO. I'LL COME BACK FOR YOU.
CITIZENS OF NEO-GOTHAM! AS WE WEATHER THIS CITY'S LATEST CHALLENGE...
GOTHAM GAMES
...WE MUST REMEMBER TO PUSH EVER FORWARD. TO NEVER GIVE UP.
SO LET THE GAMES BEGIN!
GG
GG
YEAAHHH!!
DO NOT BE AFRAID.
I WILL BE YOUR PROTECTOR NOW.

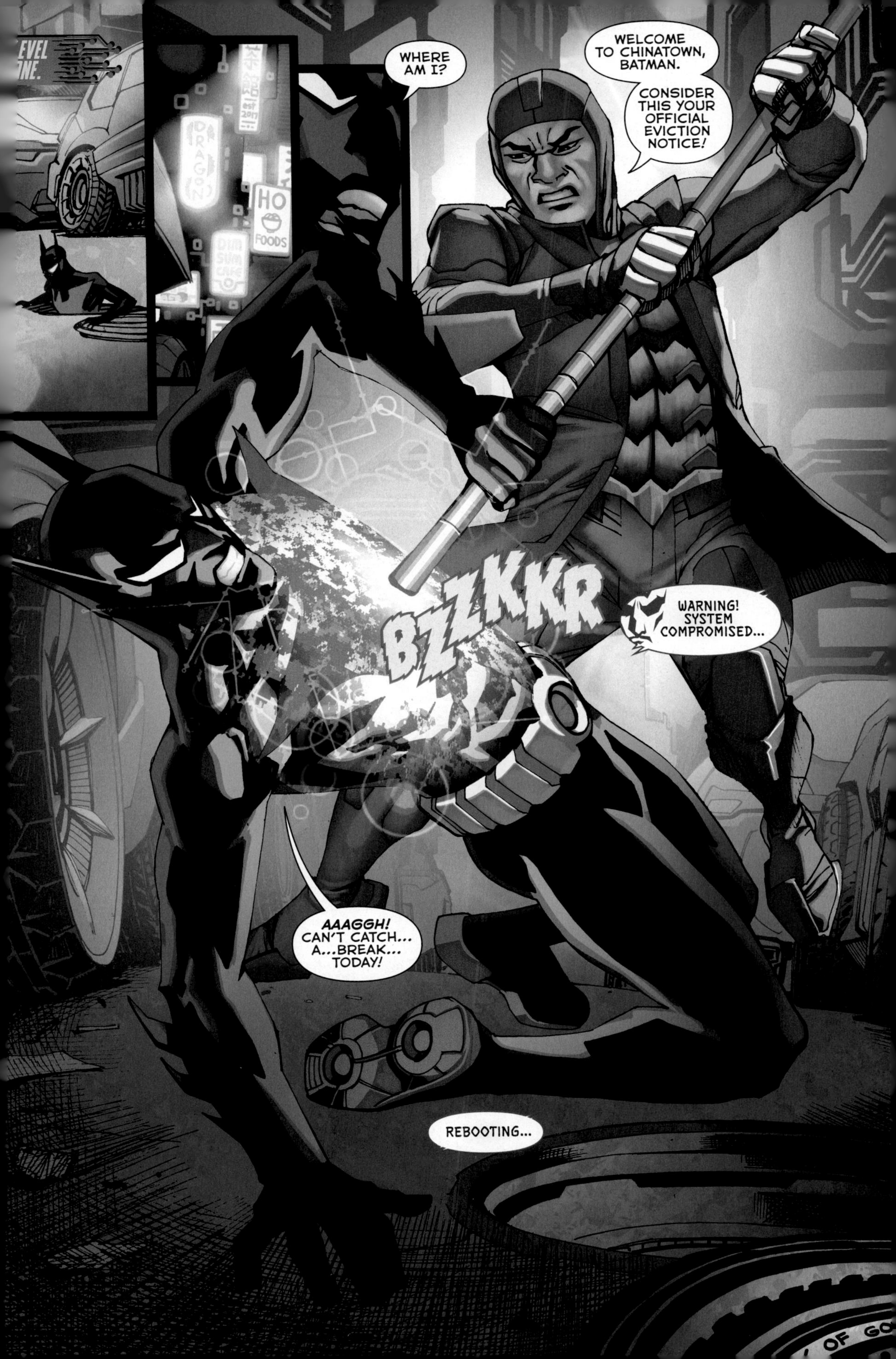
DRAGON
HO FOODS
DIM SUM CAFE
WHERE AM I?
WELCOME TO CHINATOWN, BATMAN.
CONSIDER THIS YOUR OFFICIAL EVICTION NOTICE!
BZZKKR
WARNING! SYSTEM COMPROMISED...
AAAGGH! CAN'T CATCH... A...BREAK... TODAY!
REBOOTING...

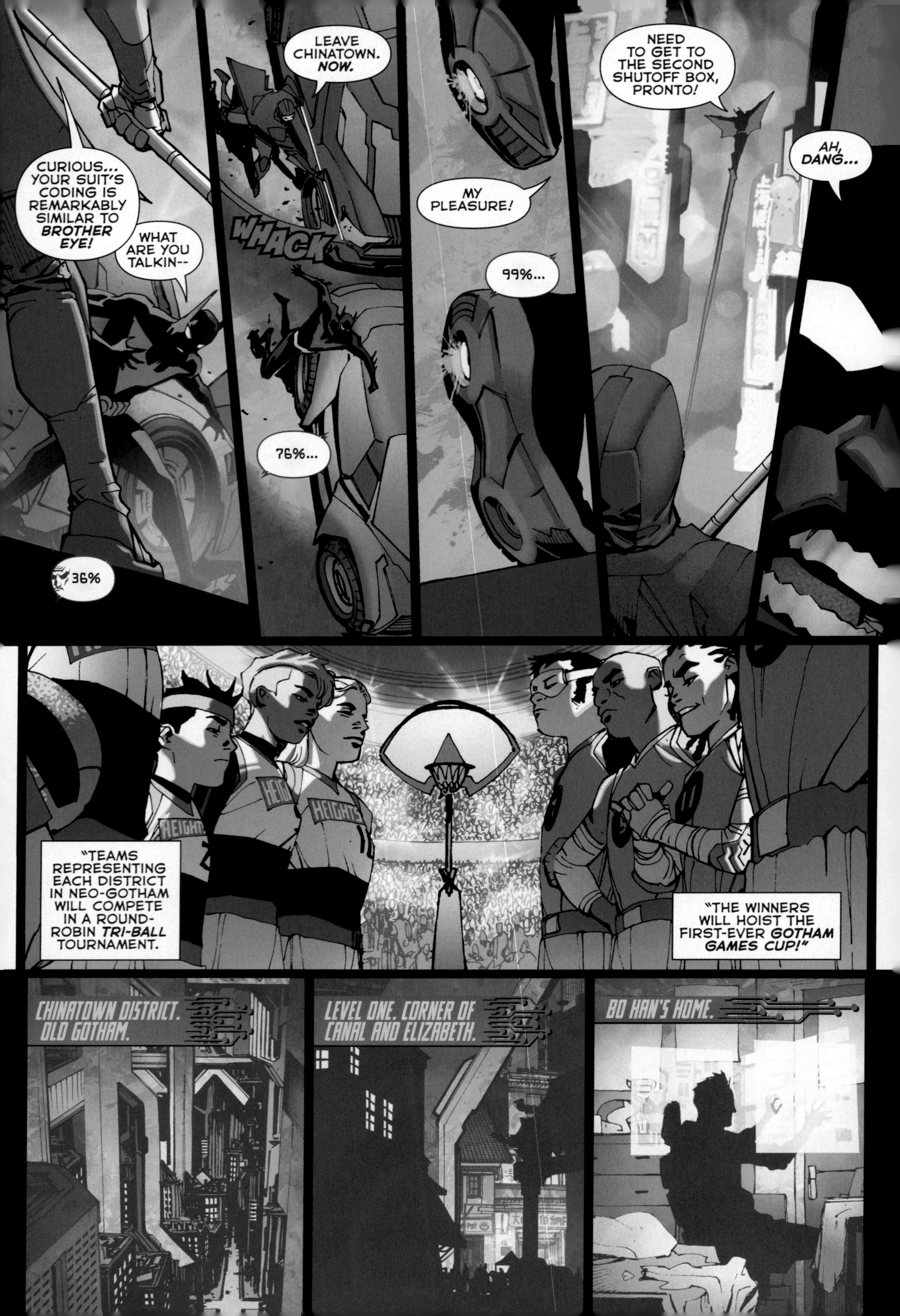

CURIOUS... YOUR SUIT'S CODING IS REMARKABLY SIMILAR TO BROTHER EYE!
WHAT ARE YOU TALKIN--
36%
LEAVE CHINATOWN. NOW.
WHACK
76%...
MY PLEASURE!
99%...
NEED TO GET TO THE SECOND SHUTOFF BOX, PRONTO!
AH, DANG...
"TEAMS REPRESENTING EACH DISTRICT IN NEO-GOTHAM WILL COMPETE IN A ROUND-ROBIN TRI-BALL TOURNAMENT.
"THE WINNERS WILL HOIST THE FIRST-EVER GOTHAM GAMES CUP!"
HEIGHTS
CHINATOWN DISTRICT. OLD GOTHAM.
LEVEL ONE. CORNER OF CANAL AND ELIZABETH.
BO HAN'S HOME.

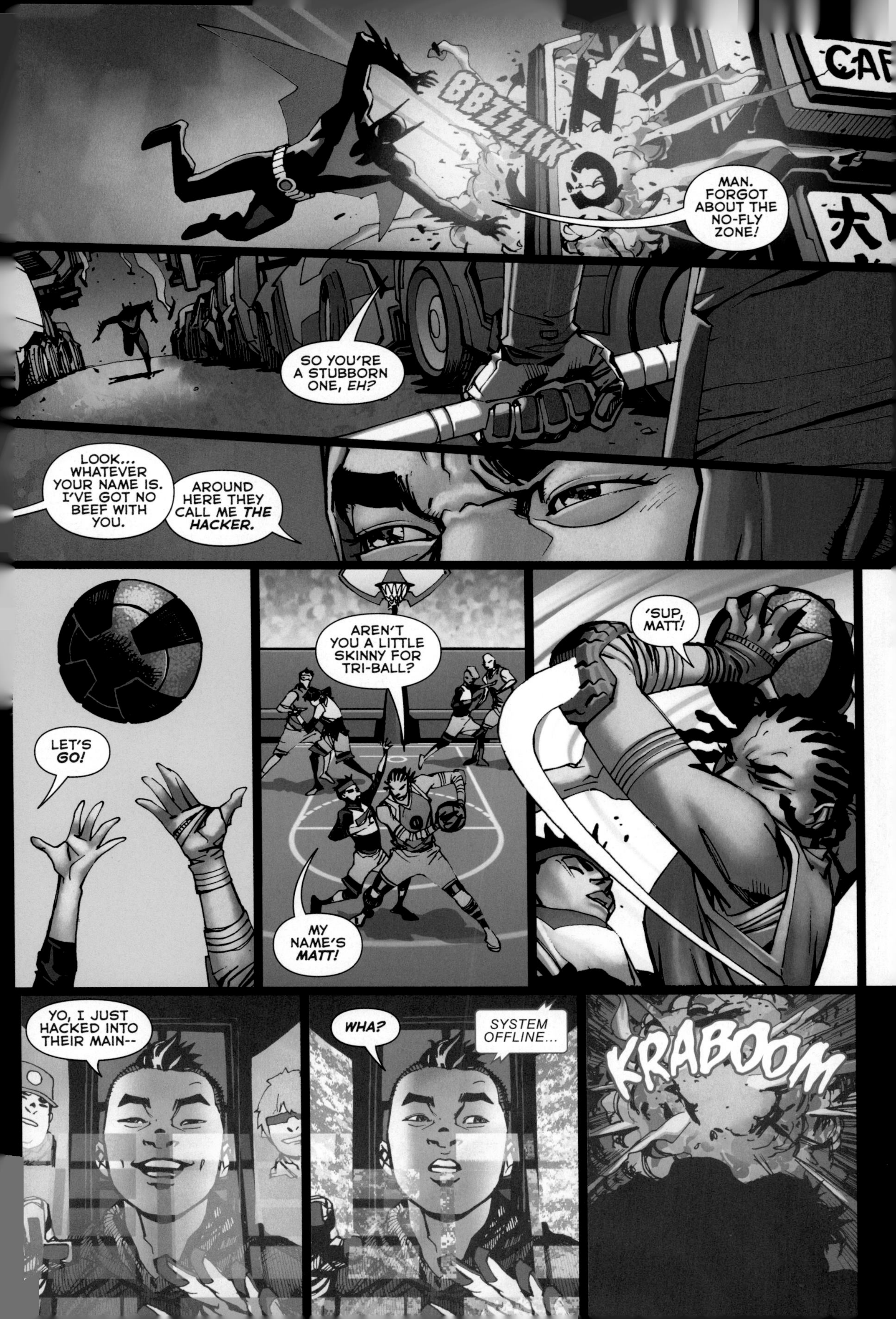
BBZZZKKK
CAF
MAN. FORGOT ABOUT THE NO-FLY ZONE!
SO YOU'RE A STUBBORN ONE, EH?
LOOK... WHATEVER YOUR NAME IS. I'VE GOT NO BEEF WITH YOU.
AROUND HERE THEY CALL ME THE HACKER.
LET'S GO!
AREN'T YOU A LITTLE SKINNY FOR TRI-BALL?
MY NAME'S MATT!
'SUP, MATT!
YO, I JUST HACKED INTO THEIR MAIN--
WHA?
SYSTEM OFFLINE...
KRABOOM

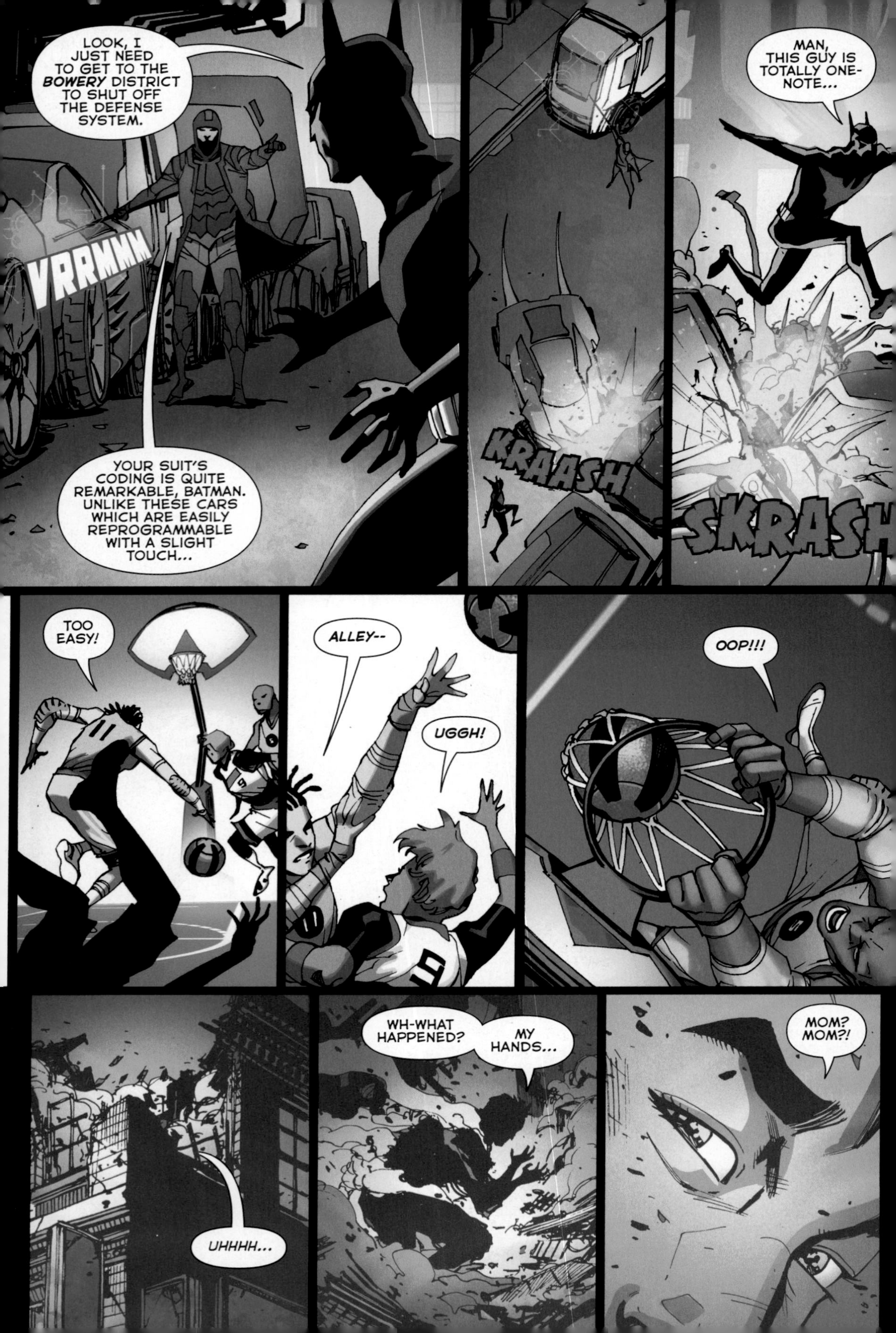
LOOK, I JUST NEED TO GET TO THE BOWERY DISTRICT TO SHUT OFF THE DEFENSE SYSTEM.
VRRMMM
YOUR SUIT'S CODING IS QUITE REMARKABLE, BATMAN. UNLIKE THESE CARS WHICH ARE EASILY REPROGRAMMABLE WITH A SLIGHT TOUCH...
KRAASH
MAN, THIS GUY IS TOTALLY ONE-NOTE...
SKRASH
TOO EASY!
ALLEY--
UGGH!
OOP!!!
UHHHH...
WH-WHAT HAPPENED?
MY HANDS...
MOM? MOM?!

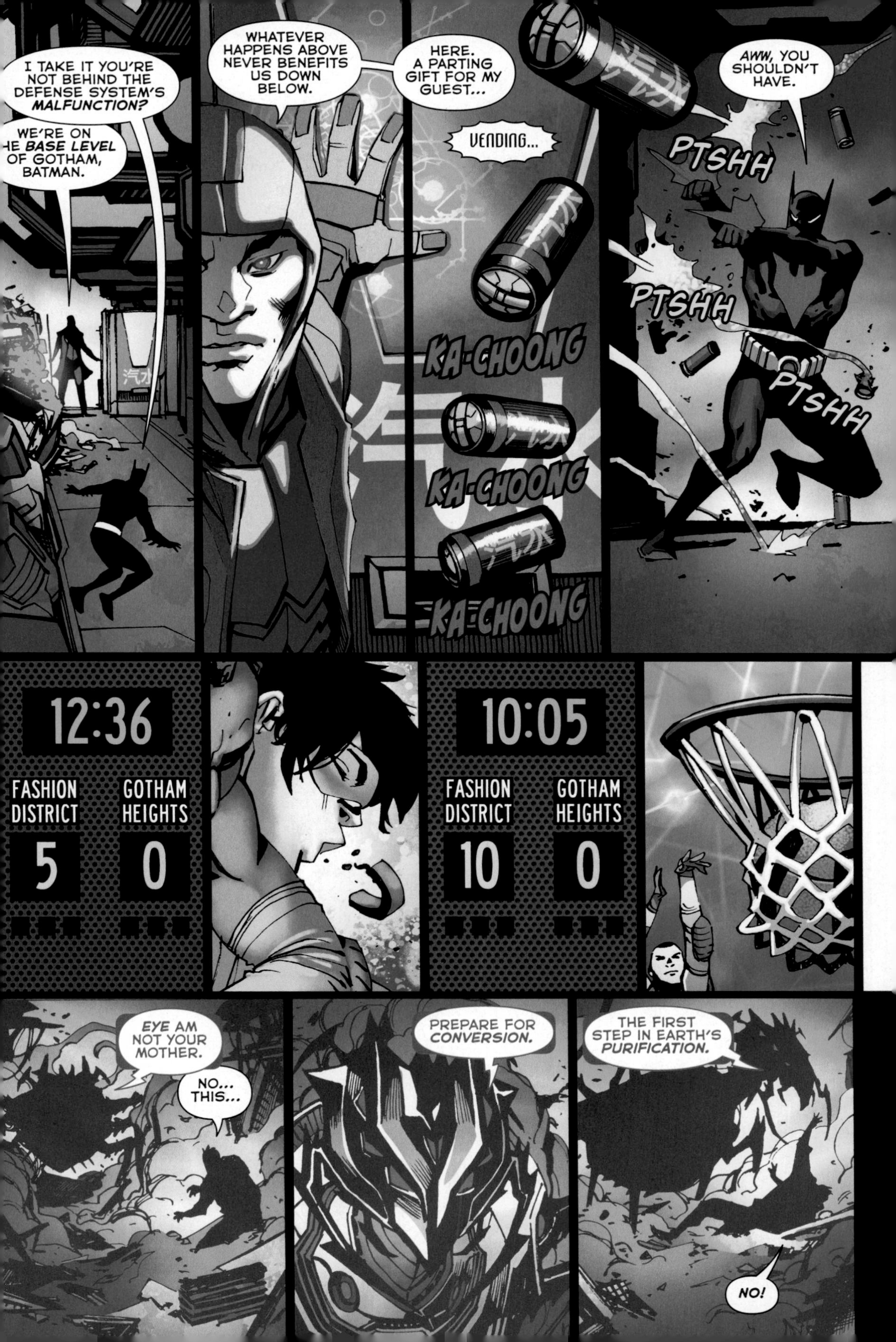

I TAKE IT YOU'RE NOT BEHIND THE DEFENSE SYSTEM'S *MALFUNCTION?*
WE'RE ON THE *BASE LEVEL* OF GOTHAM, BATMAN.
WHATEVER HAPPENS ABOVE NEVER BENEFITS US DOWN BELOW.
HERE. A PARTING GIFT FOR MY GUEST...
VENDING...
KA-CHOONG
KA-CHOONG
KA-CHOONG
AWW, YOU SHOULDN'T HAVE.
PTSHH
PTSHH
PTSHH
12:36
FASHION DISTRICT
GOTHAM HEIGHTS
5
0
10:05
FASHION DISTRICT
GOTHAM HEIGHTS
10
0
EYE AM NOT YOUR MOTHER.
NO... THIS...
PREPARE FOR *CONVERSION.*
THE FIRST STEP IN EARTH'S *PURIFICATION.*
NO!

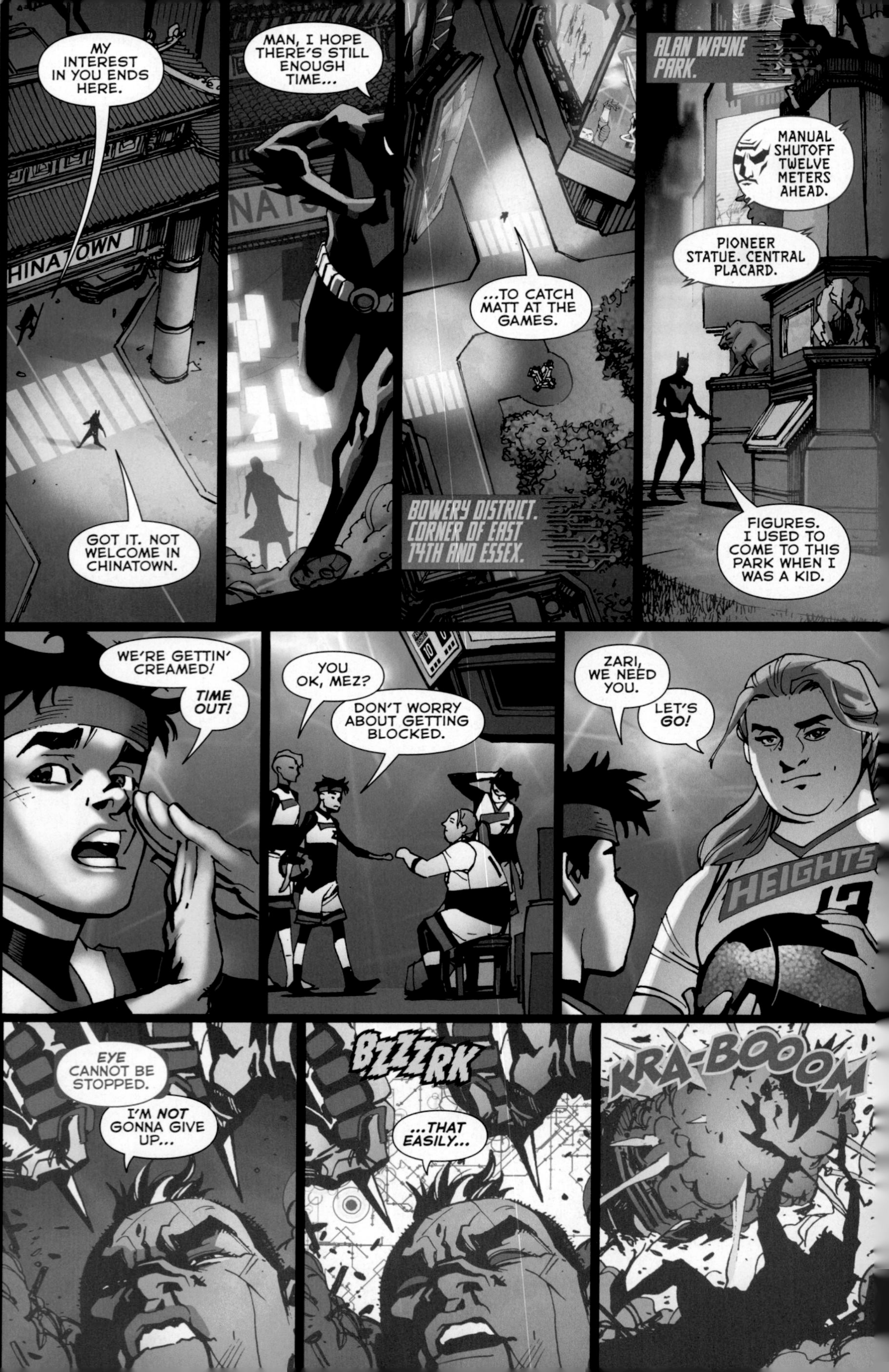
MY INTEREST IN YOU ENDS HERE.
GOT IT. NOT WELCOME IN CHINATOWN.
CHINATOWN
MAN, I HOPE THERE'S STILL ENOUGH TIME...
BOWERY DISTRICT. CORNER OF EAST 14TH AND ESSEX.
...TO CATCH MATT AT THE GAMES.
ALAN WAYNE PARK.
MANUAL SHUTOFF TWELVE METERS AHEAD.
PIONEER STATUE. CENTRAL PLACARD.
FIGURES. I USED TO COME TO THIS PARK WHEN I WAS A KID.
WE'RE GETTIN' CREAMED!
TIME OUT!
YOU OK, MEZ?
DON'T WORRY ABOUT GETTING BLOCKED.
ZARI, WE NEED YOU.
LET'S GO!
HEIGHTS
EYE CANNOT BE STOPPED.
I'M NOT GONNA GIVE UP...
BZZZRK
...THAT EASILY...
KRA-BOOOOM

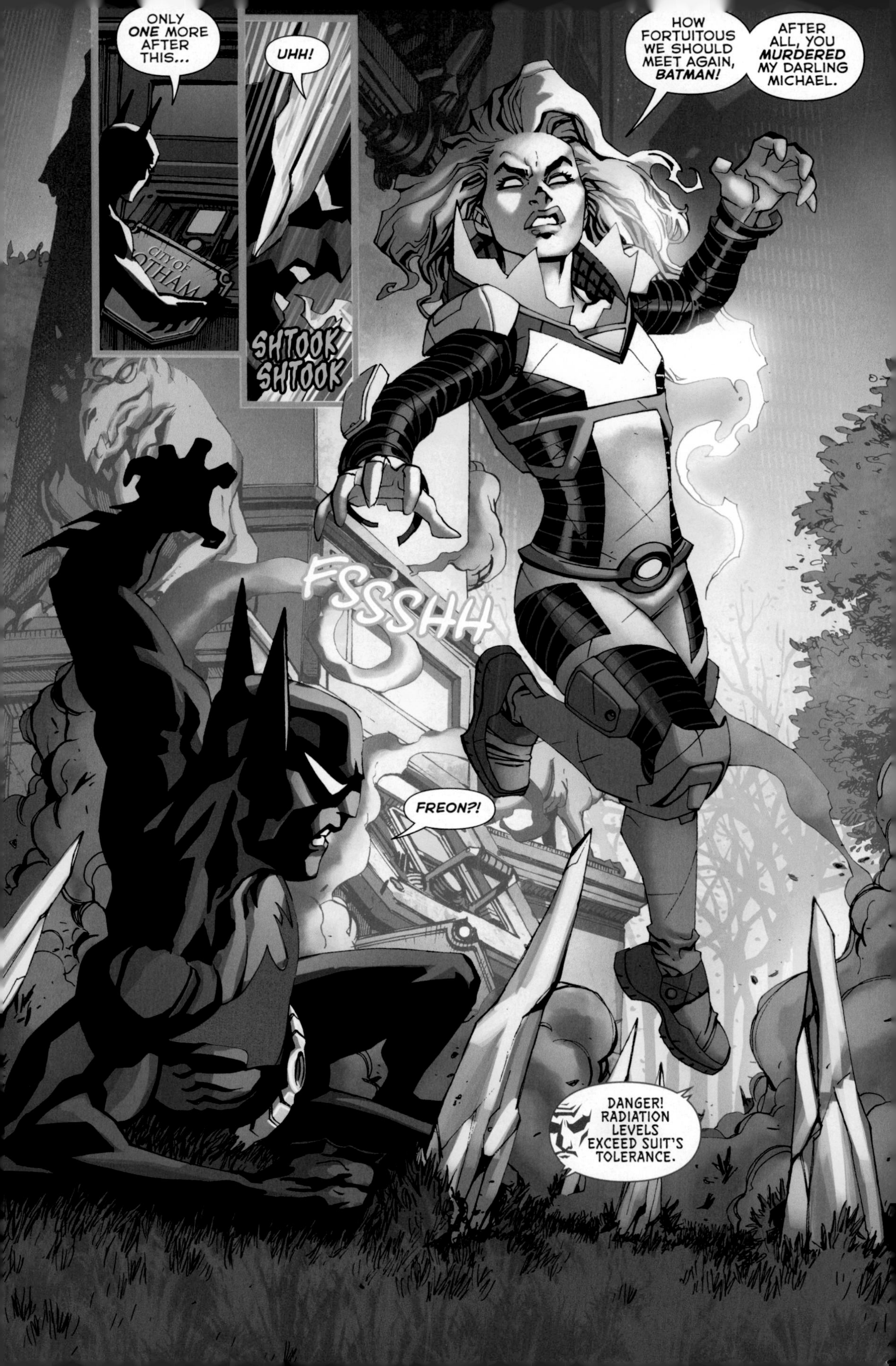

ONLY ONE MORE AFTER THIS...
UHH!
SHTOOK SHTOOK
CITY OF OTHAM
HOW FORTUITOUS WE SHOULD MEET AGAIN, BATMAN!
AFTER ALL, YOU MURDERED MY DARLING MICHAEL.
FSSSHH
FREON?!
DANGER! RADIATION LEVELS EXCEED SUIT'S TOLERANCE.

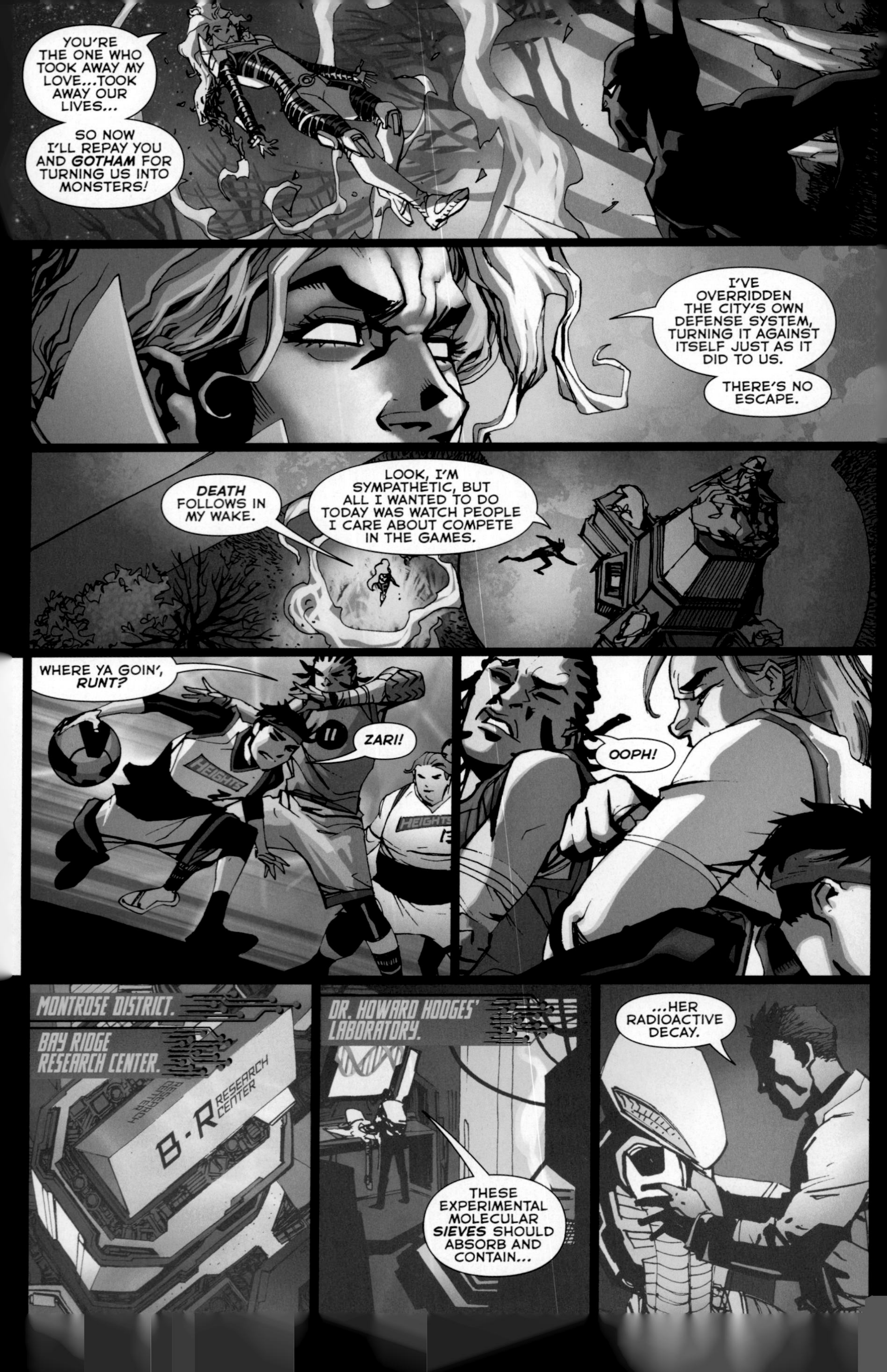
YOU'RE THE ONE WHO TOOK AWAY MY LOVE...TOOK AWAY OUR LIVES...
SO NOW I'LL REPAY YOU AND GOTHAM FOR TURNING US INTO MONSTERS!
I'VE OVERRIDDEN THE CITY'S OWN DEFENSE SYSTEM, TURNING IT AGAINST ITSELF JUST AS IT DID TO US.
THERE'S NO ESCAPE.
DEATH FOLLOWS IN MY WAKE.
LOOK, I'M SYMPATHETIC, BUT ALL I WANTED TO DO TODAY WAS WATCH PEOPLE I CARE ABOUT COMPETE IN THE GAMES.
WHERE YA GOIN', RUNT?
ZARI!
OOPH!
MONTROSE DISTRICT.
BAY RIDGE RESEARCH CENTER.
B-R RESEARCH CENTER
DR. HOWARD HODGES' LABORATORY.
THESE EXPERIMENTAL MOLECULAR SIEVES SHOULD ABSORB AND CONTAIN...
...HER RADIOACTIVE DECAY.

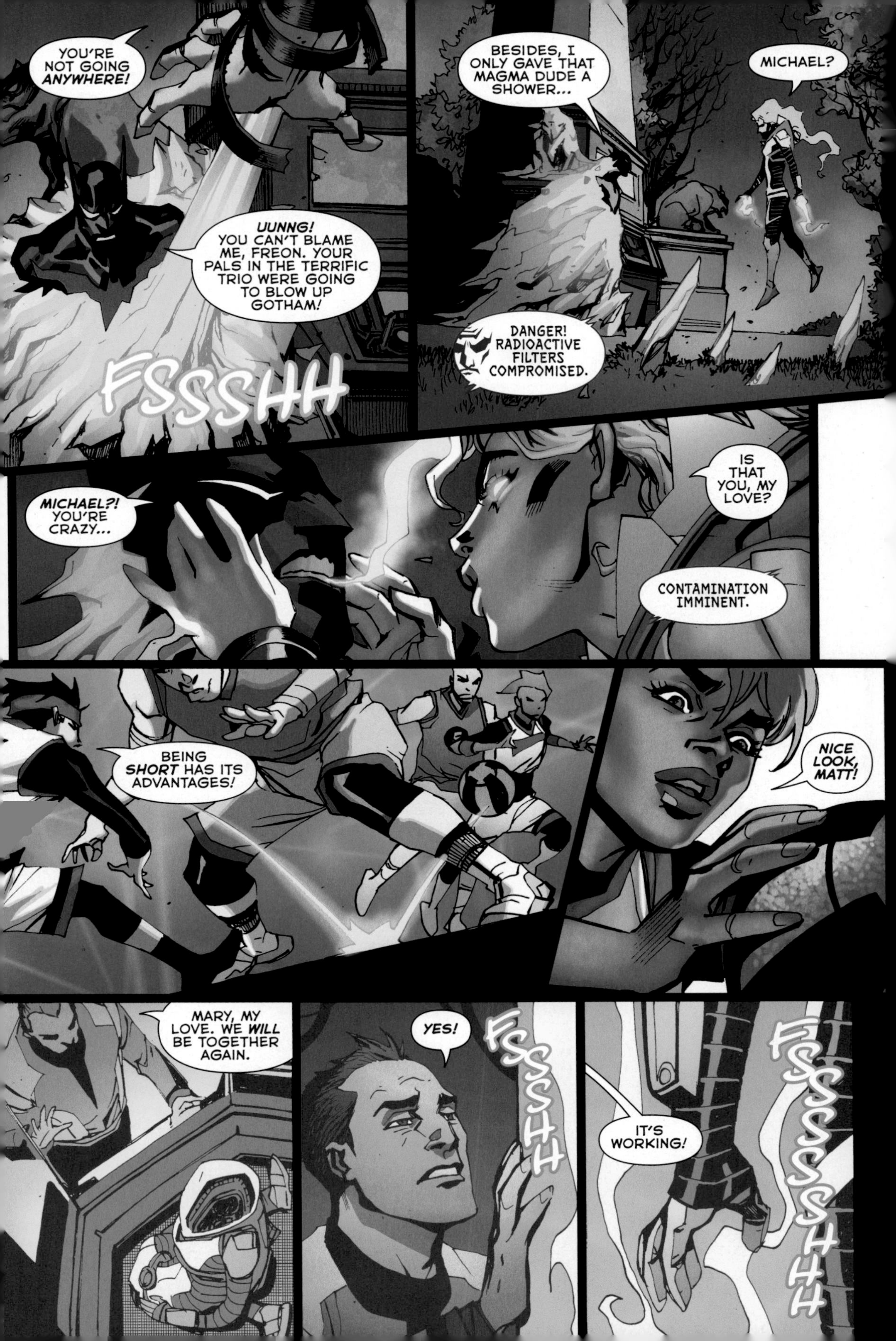
YOU'RE NOT GOING *ANYWHERE!*
UUNNG! YOU CAN'T BLAME ME, FREON. YOUR PALS IN THE TERRIFIC TRIO WERE GOING TO BLOW UP GOTHAM!
FSSSHH
BESIDES, I ONLY GAVE THAT MAGMA DUDE A SHOWER...
DANGER! RADIOACTIVE FILTERS COMPROMISED.
MICHAEL?
MICHAEL?! YOU'RE CRAZY...
IS THAT YOU, MY LOVE?
CONTAMINATION IMMINENT.
BEING *SHORT* HAS ITS ADVANTAGES!
NICE LOOK, MATT!
MARY, MY LOVE. WE *WILL* BE TOGETHER AGAIN.
YES!
FSSSHH
IT'S WORKING!
FSSSSSHHH

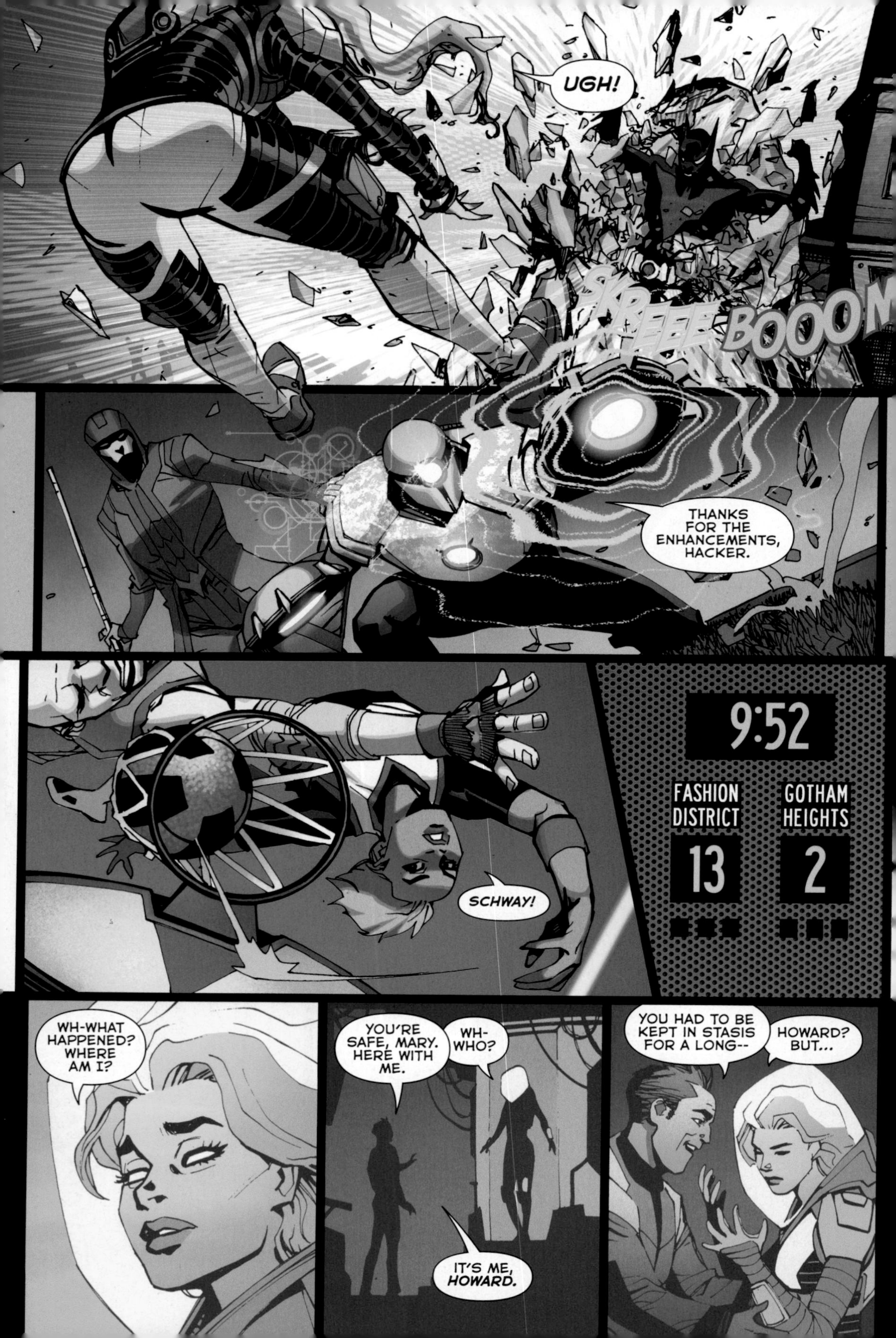
UGH!
SKREEEE
BOOOM
THANKS FOR THE ENHANCEMENTS, HACKER.
SCHWAY!
9:52
FASHION DISTRICT
GOTHAM HEIGHTS
13
2
WH-WHAT HAPPENED? WHERE AM I?
YOU'RE SAFE, MARY. HERE WITH ME.
WH- WHO?
IT'S ME, HOWARD.
YOU HAD TO BE KEPT IN STASIS FOR A LONG--
HOWARD? BUT...

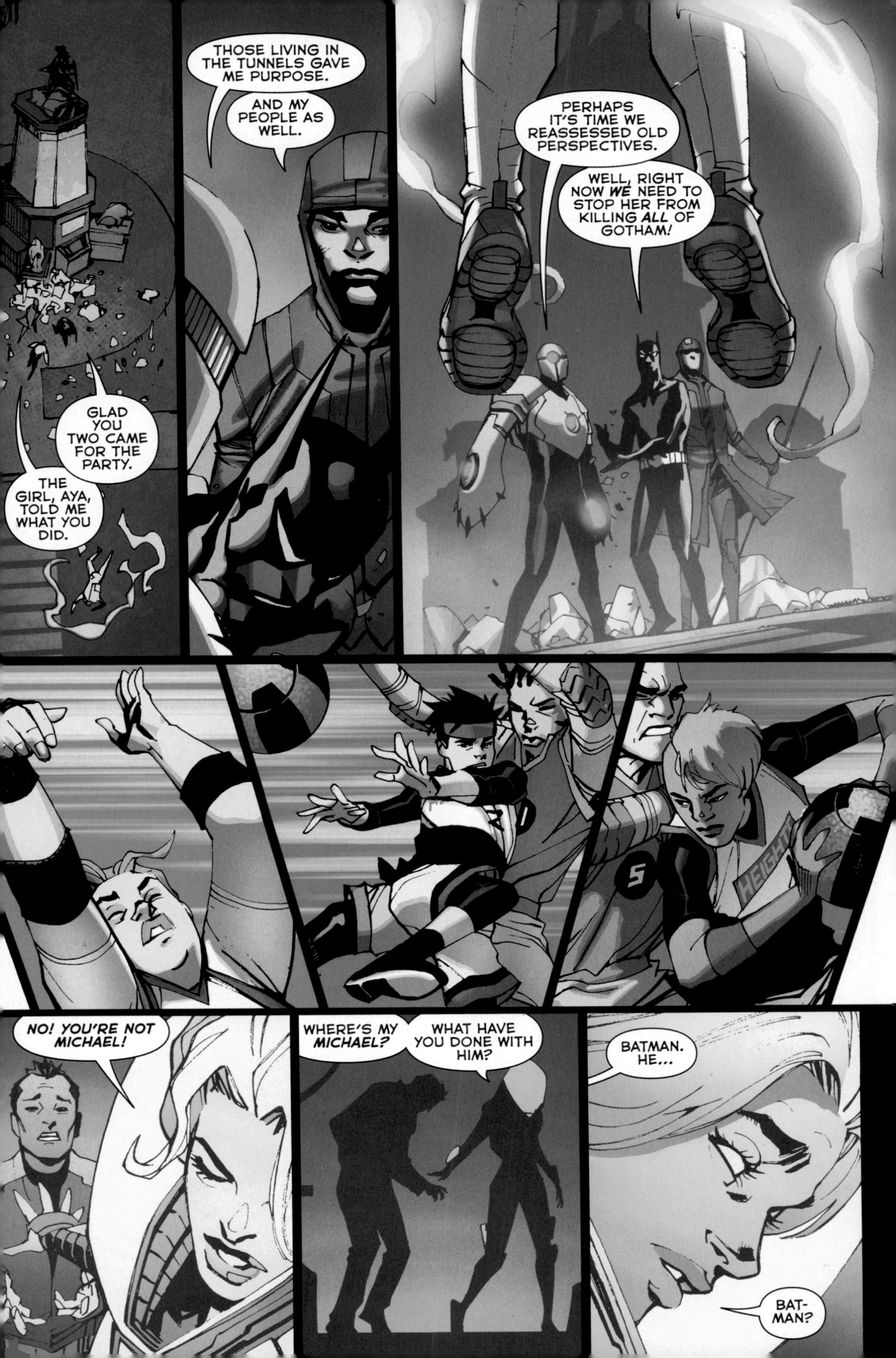

THOSE LIVING IN THE TUNNELS GAVE ME PURPOSE.
AND MY PEOPLE AS WELL.
GLAD YOU TWO CAME FOR THE PARTY.
THE GIRL, AYA, TOLD ME WHAT YOU DID.
PERHAPS IT'S TIME WE REASSESSED OLD PERSPECTIVES.
WELL, RIGHT NOW *WE* NEED TO STOP HER FROM KILLING *ALL* OF GOTHAM!
HEIGHTS
5
NO! YOU'RE NOT MICHAEL!
WHERE'S MY *MICHAEL?*
WHAT HAVE YOU DONE WITH HIM?
BATMAN. HE...
BAT-MAN?

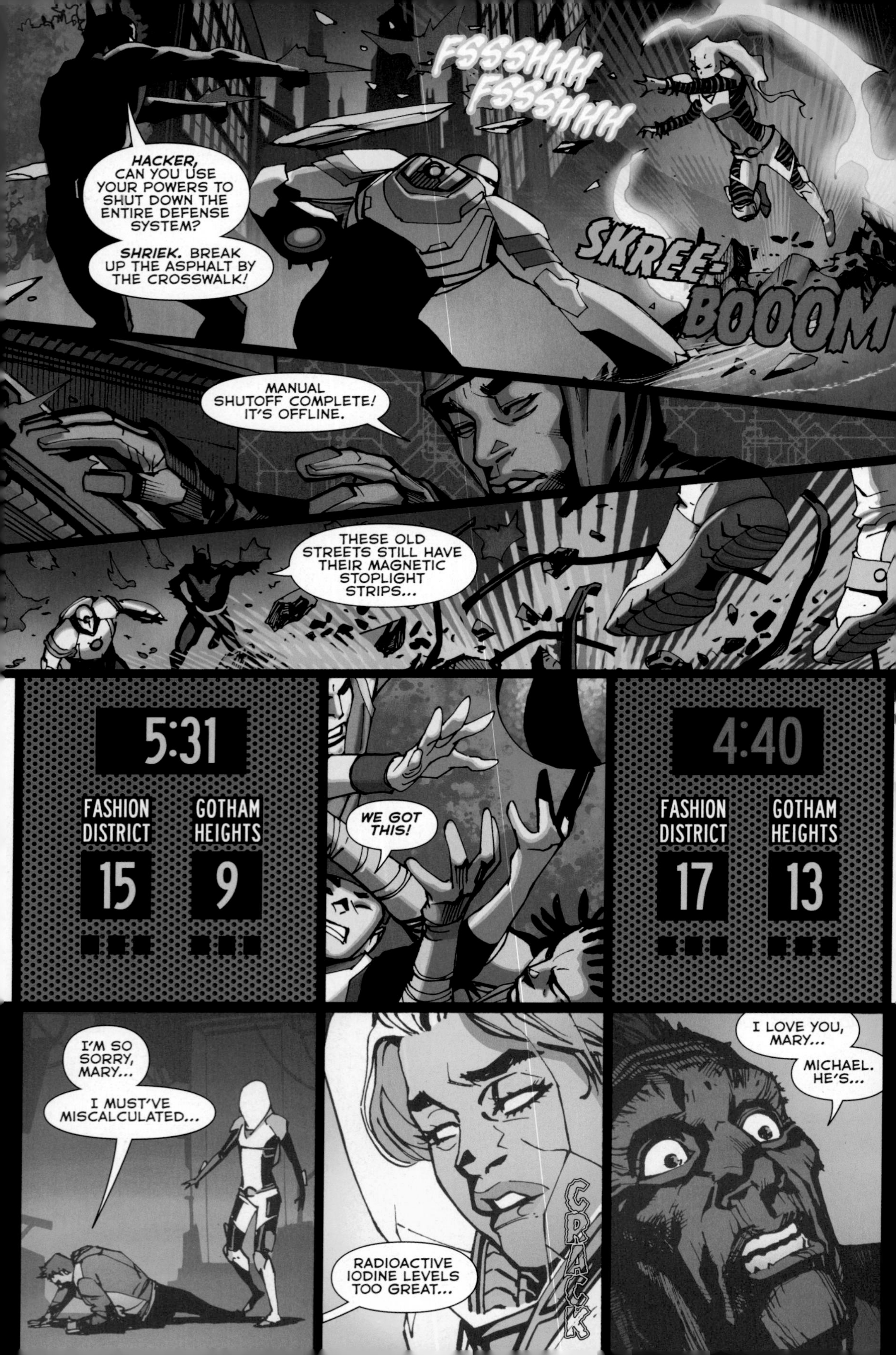
FSSSHHH
FSSSHHH
HACKER, CAN YOU USE YOUR POWERS TO SHUT DOWN THE ENTIRE DEFENSE SYSTEM?
SHRIEK. BREAK UP THE ASPHALT BY THE CROSSWALK!
SKREE-BOOOM
MANUAL SHUTOFF COMPLETE! IT'S OFFLINE.
THESE OLD STREETS STILL HAVE THEIR MAGNETIC STOPLIGHT STRIPS...
5:31
FASHION DISTRICT
GOTHAM HEIGHTS
15
9
WE GOT THIS!
4:40
FASHION DISTRICT
GOTHAM HEIGHTS
17
13
I'M SO SORRY, MARY...
I MUST'VE MISCALCULATED...
RADIOACTIVE IODINE LEVELS TOO GREAT...
CRACK
I LOVE YOU, MARY...
MICHAEL. HE'S...

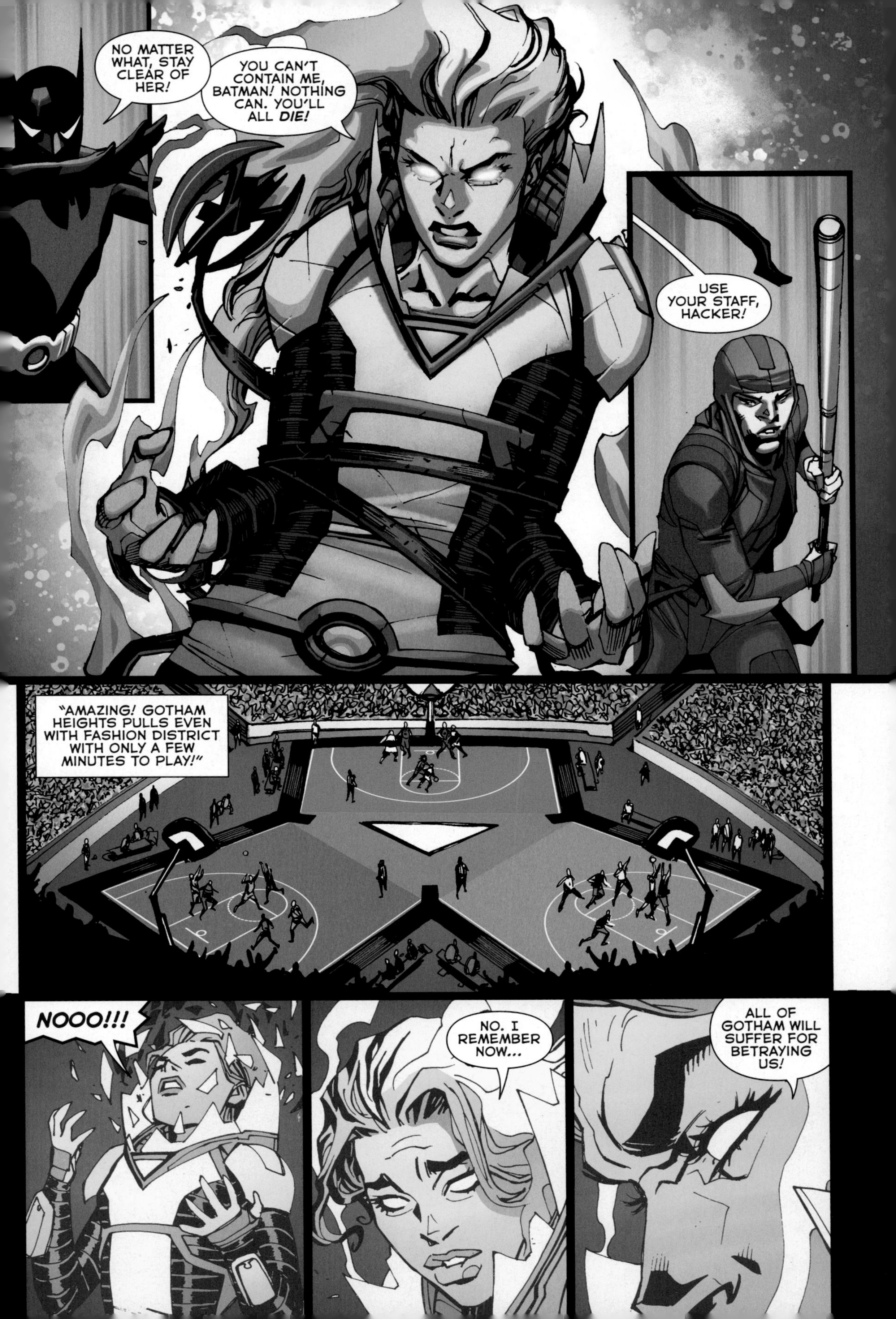
NO MATTER WHAT, STAY CLEAR OF HER!
YOU CAN'T CONTAIN ME, BATMAN! NOTHING CAN. YOU'LL ALL *DIE!*
USE YOUR STAFF, HACKER!
"AMAZING! GOTHAM HEIGHTS PULLS EVEN WITH FASHION DISTRICT WITH ONLY A FEW MINUTES TO PLAY!"
NOOO!!!
NO. I REMEMBER NOW...
ALL OF GOTHAM WILL SUFFER FOR BETRAYING US!

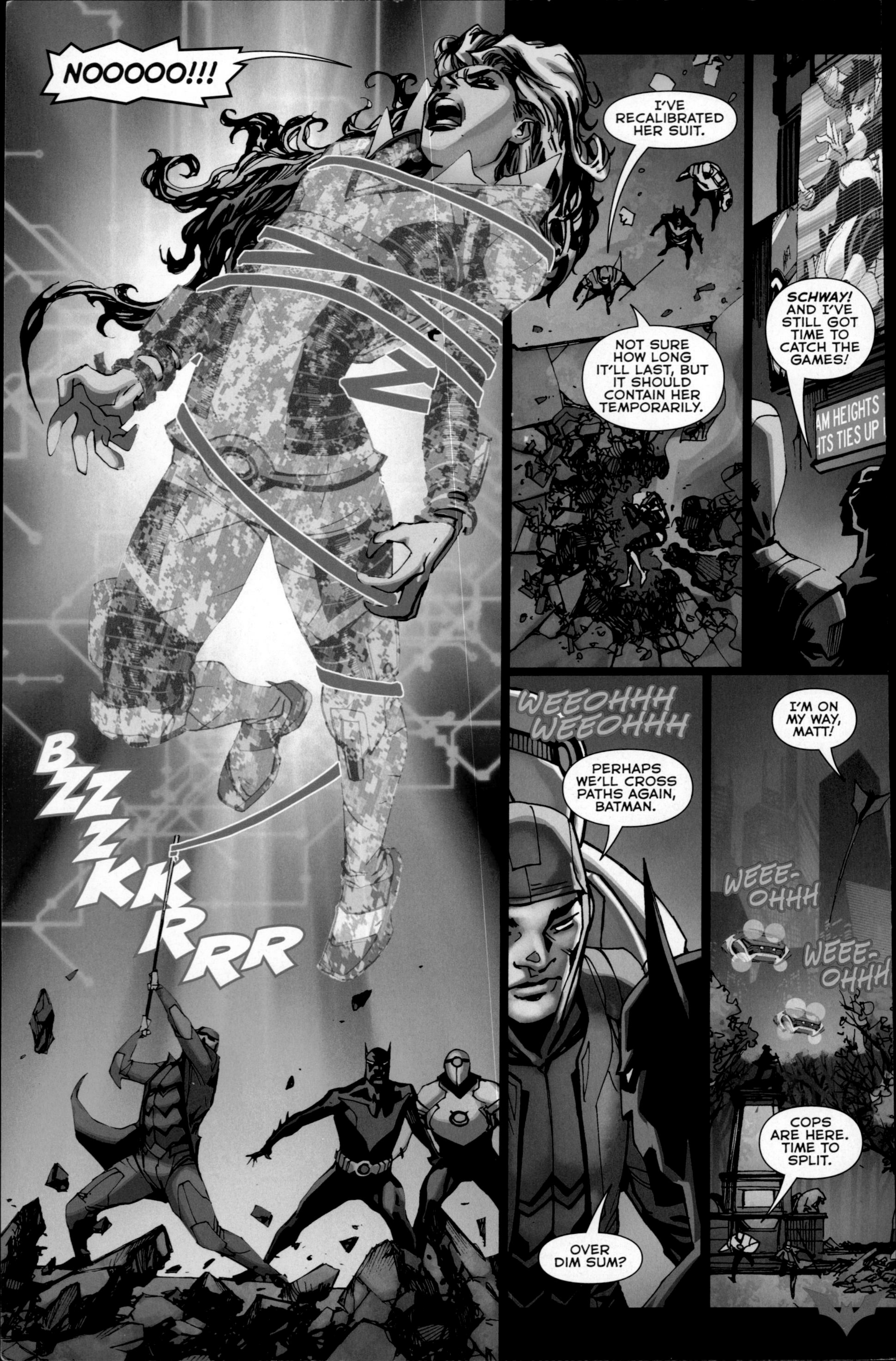
NOOOOO!!!
BZZZKKRRRR
I'VE RECALIBRATED HER SUIT.
NOT SURE HOW LONG IT'LL LAST, BUT IT SHOULD CONTAIN HER TEMPORARILY.
SCHWAY! AND I'VE STILL GOT TIME TO CATCH THE GAMES!
WEEEOHHH WEEEOHHH
PERHAPS WE'LL CROSS PATHS AGAIN, BATMAN.
OVER DIM SUM?
I'M ON MY WAY, MATT!
WEEE-OHHH
WEEE-OHHH
COPS ARE HERE. TIME TO SPLIT.

BATMAN BEYOND #14 Variant Cover by DAVE JOHNSON

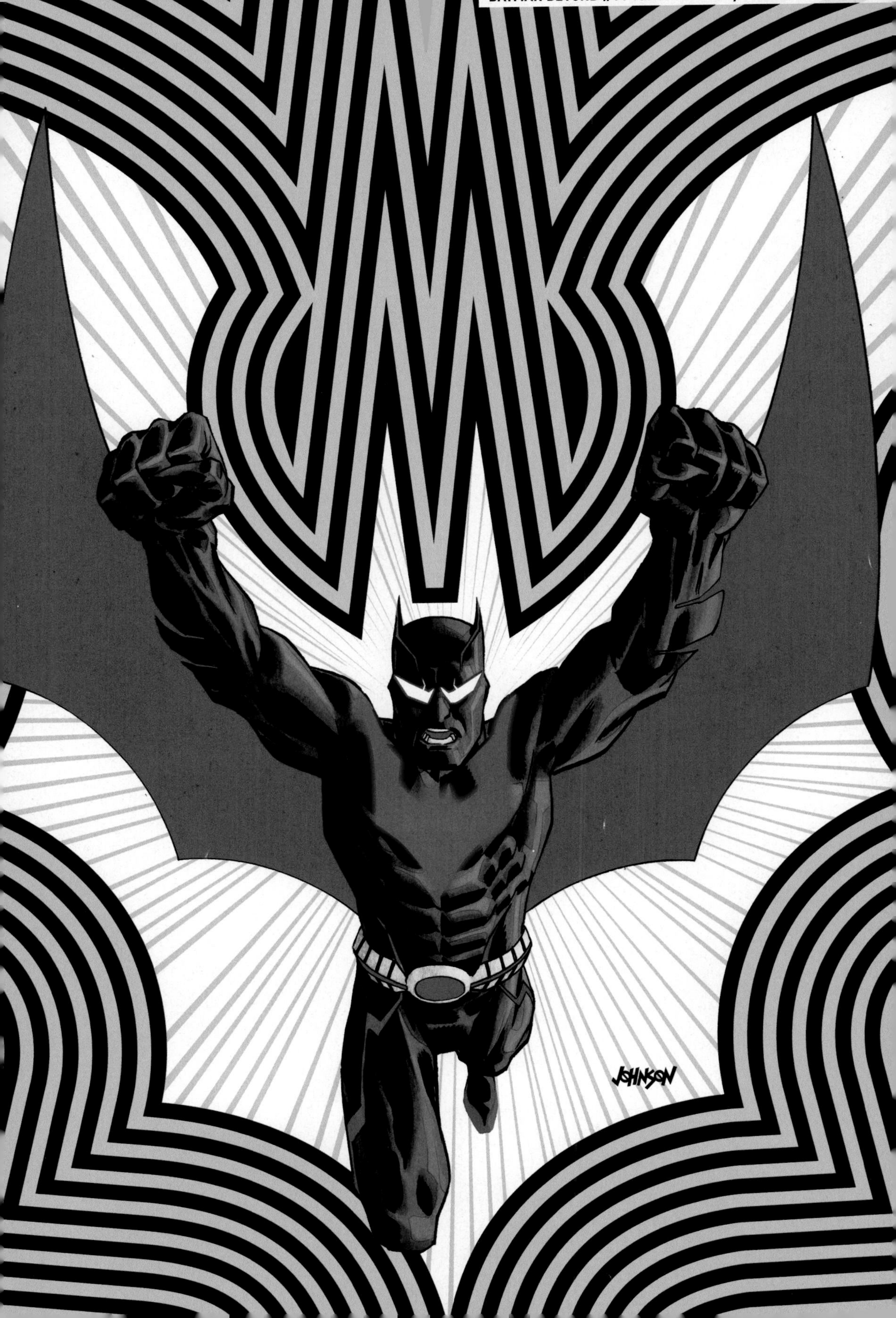
JOHNSON

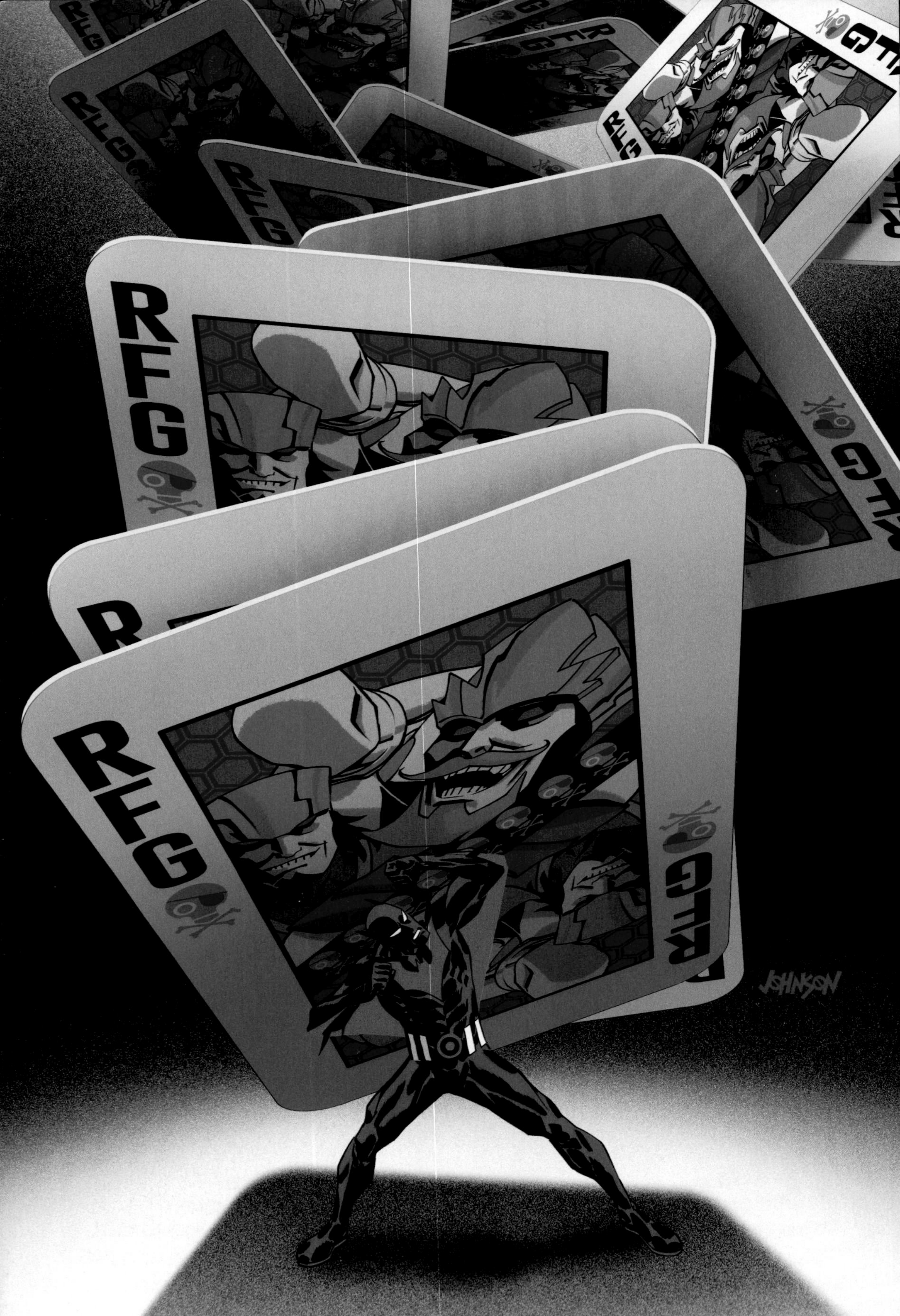
RFG
RFG
JOHNSON
BATMAN BEYOND #15 Variant Cover by DAVE JOHNSON

BATMAN BEYOND #16 Variant Cover by DAVE JOHNSON

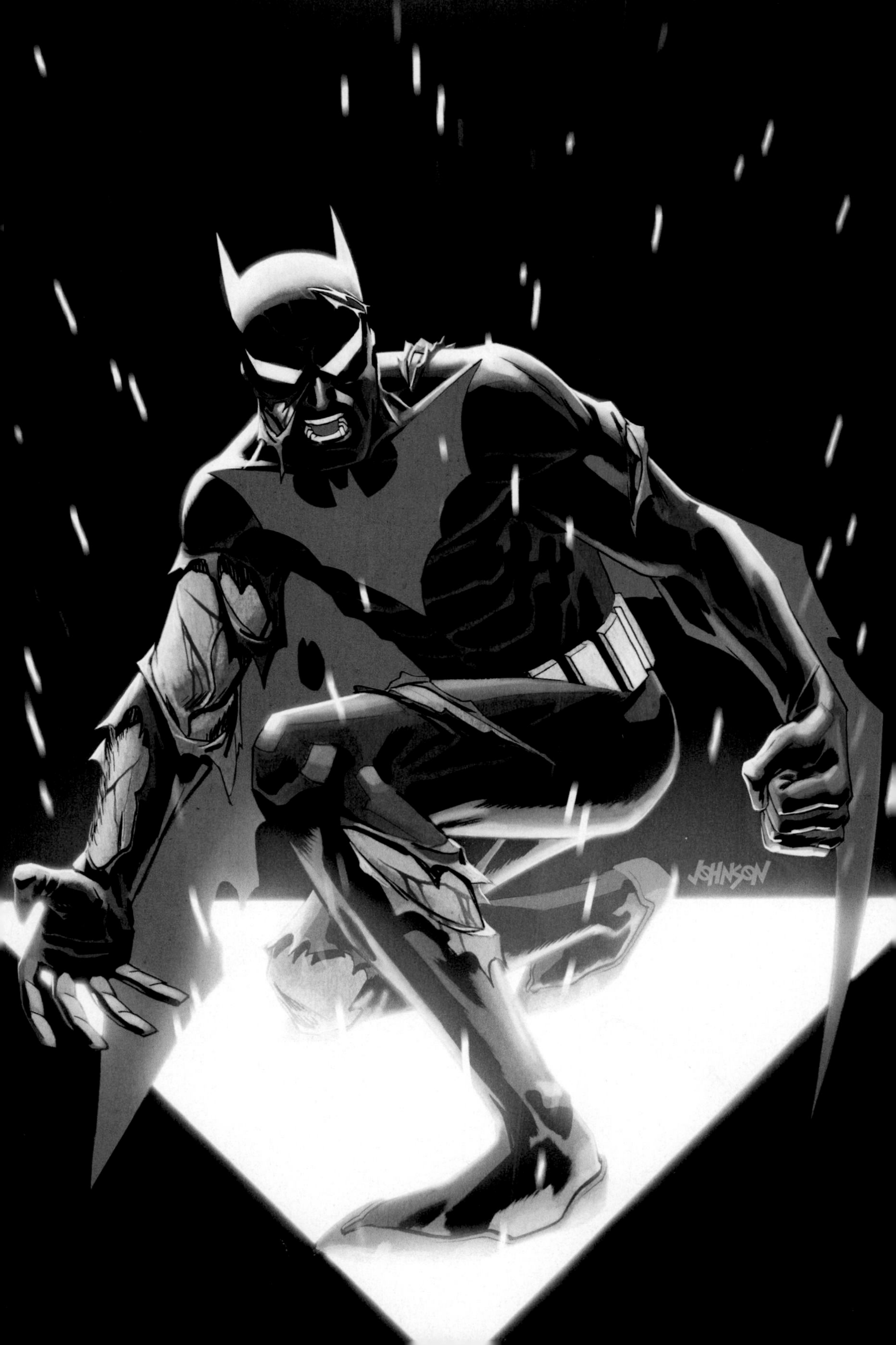
JOHNSON

BATMAN BEYOND #17 Variant Cover by DAVE JOHNSON

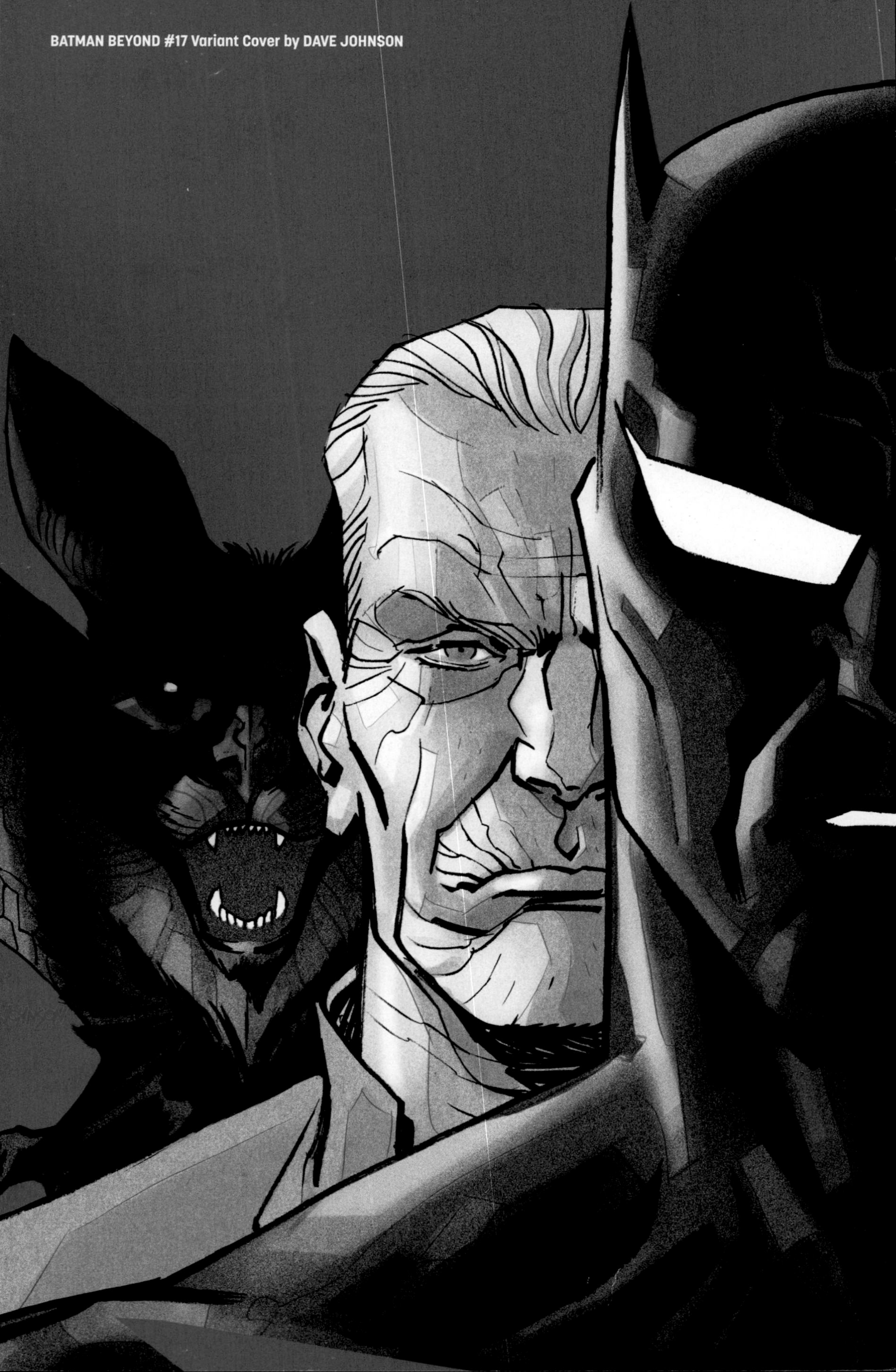

BATMAN BEYOND #18 Variant Cover by DAVE JOHNSON

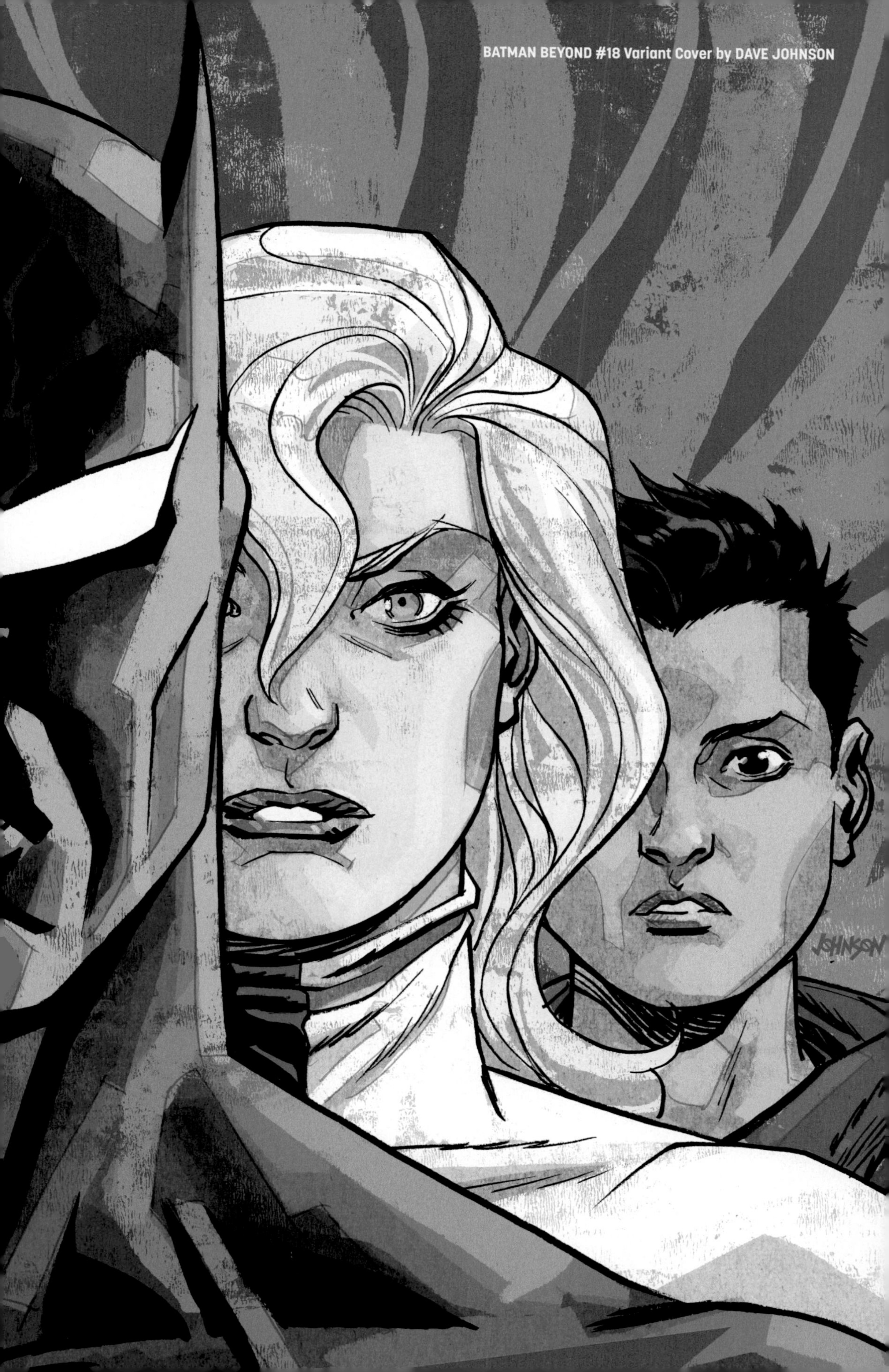
JOHNSON

BATMAN BEYOND #19 Variant Cover by DAVE JOHNSON

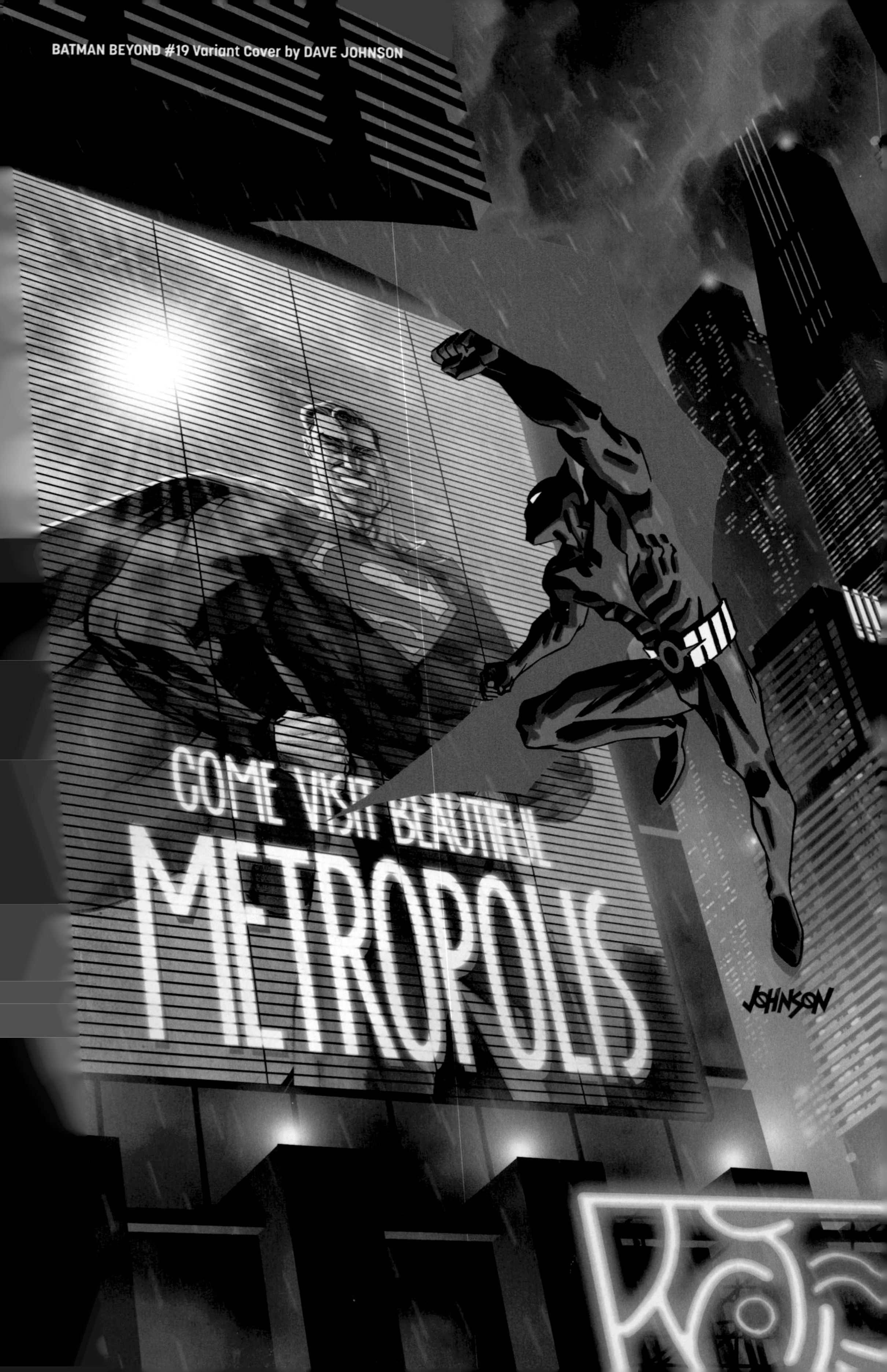
COME VISIT BEAUTIFUL
METROPOLIS
JOHNSON

BATMAN BEYOND #13 Variant Cover by DAVE JOHNSON

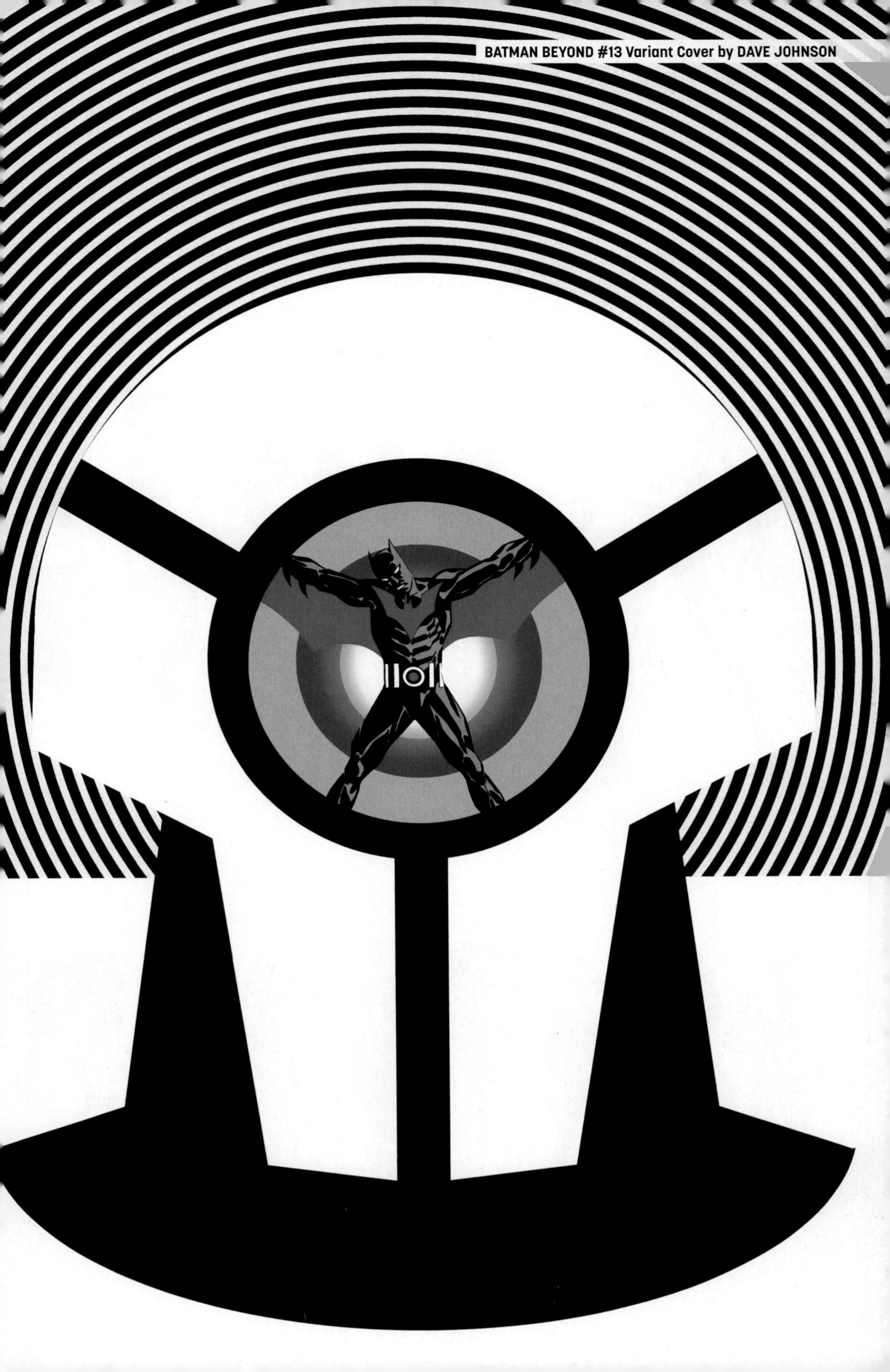

Beyond Rebirth Suit Design

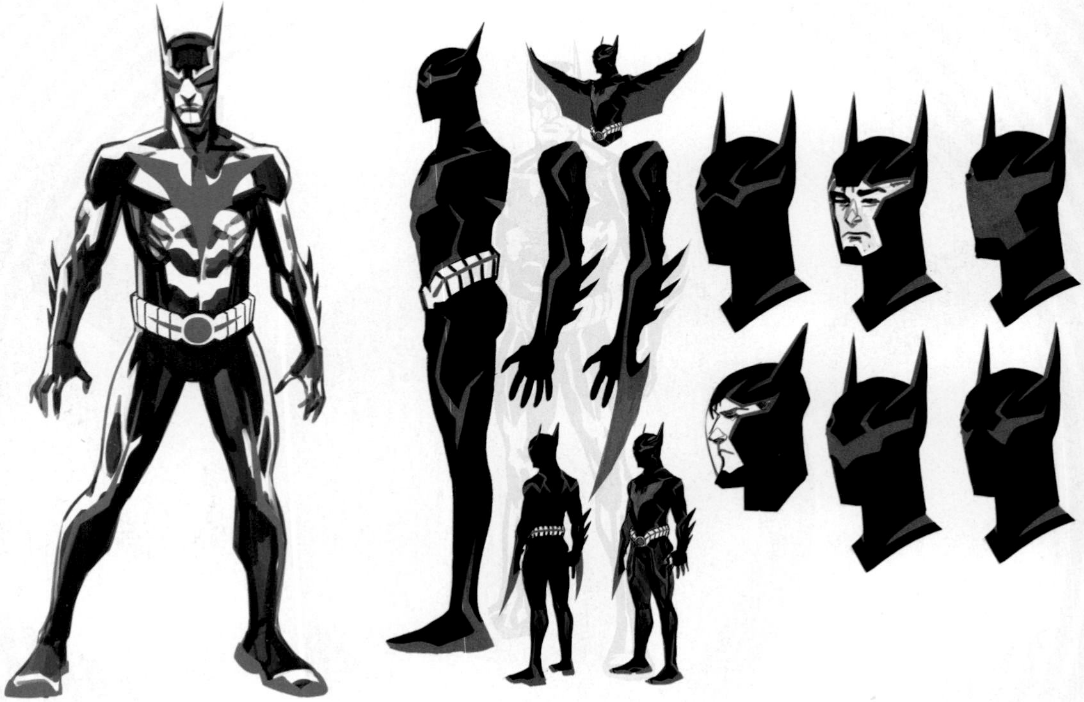

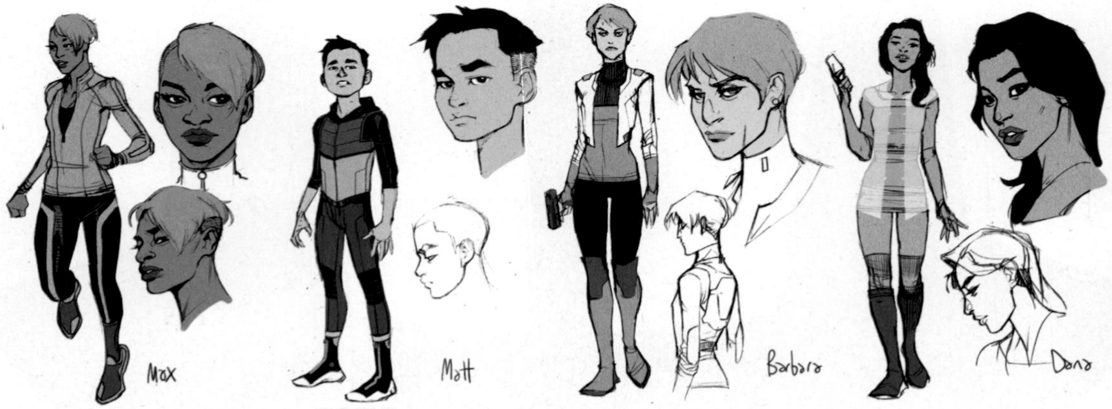
Max
Matt
Barbara
Dana

Updated Beyond Suit Design

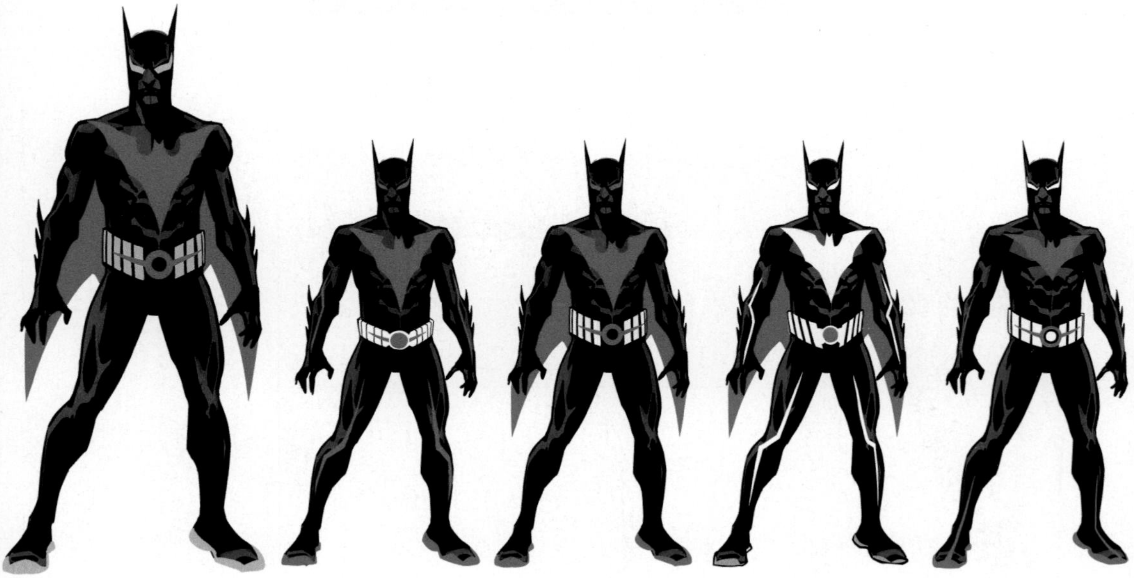

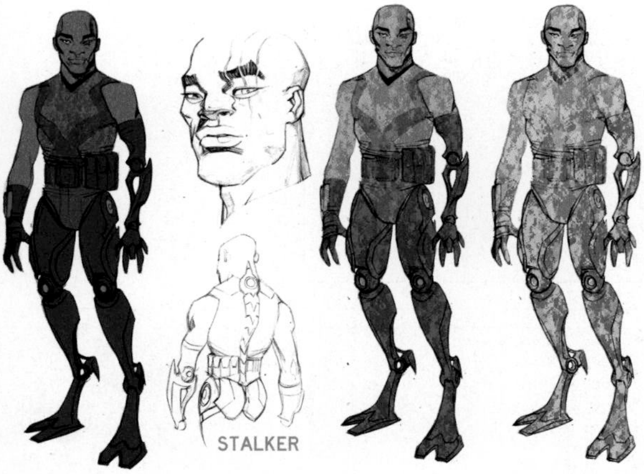
STALKER

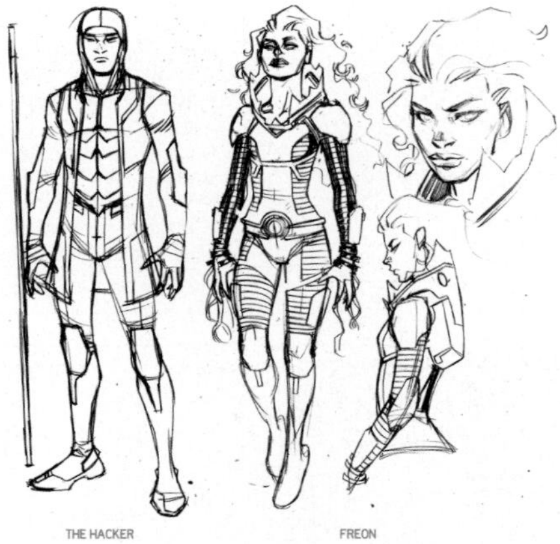
THE HACKER
FREON

Robin Cycle Design by Phil Hester

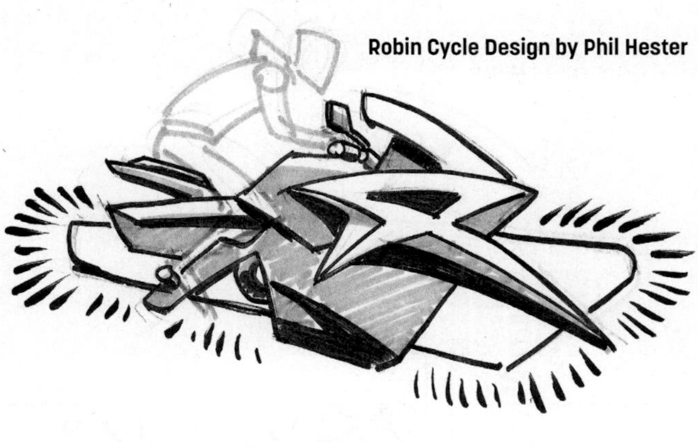

MAN BEYOND #13 BREAKDOWNS BY BERNARD CHANG

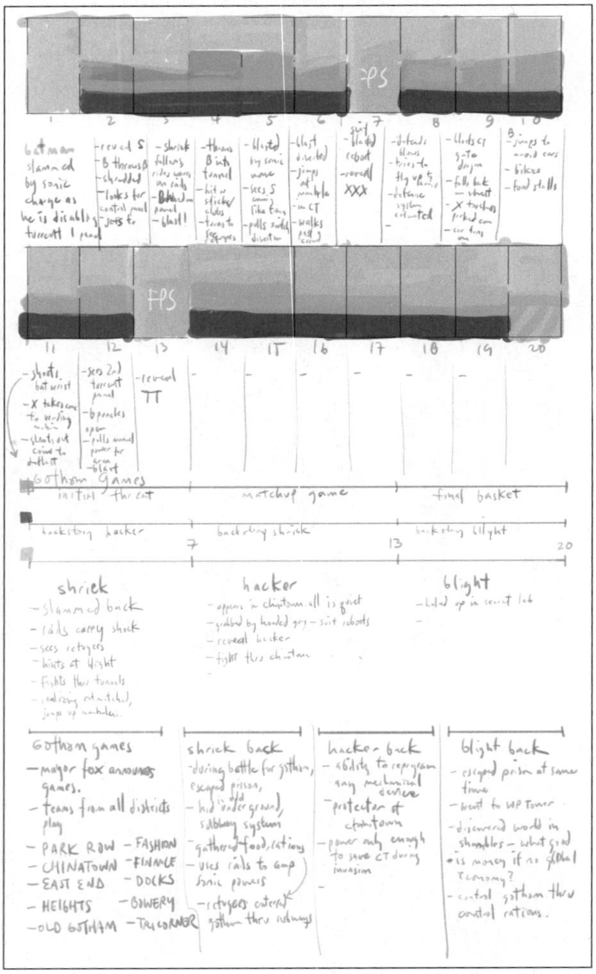
FPS
Gotham games
initial the cut
matchup game
final basket
shriek
hacker
blight
shriek back
hacker back
blight back
- PARK ROW - FASHION
- CHINATOWN - FINANCE
- EAST END - DOCKS
- HEIGHTS - BOWERY
- OLD GOTHAM - TRICORNER

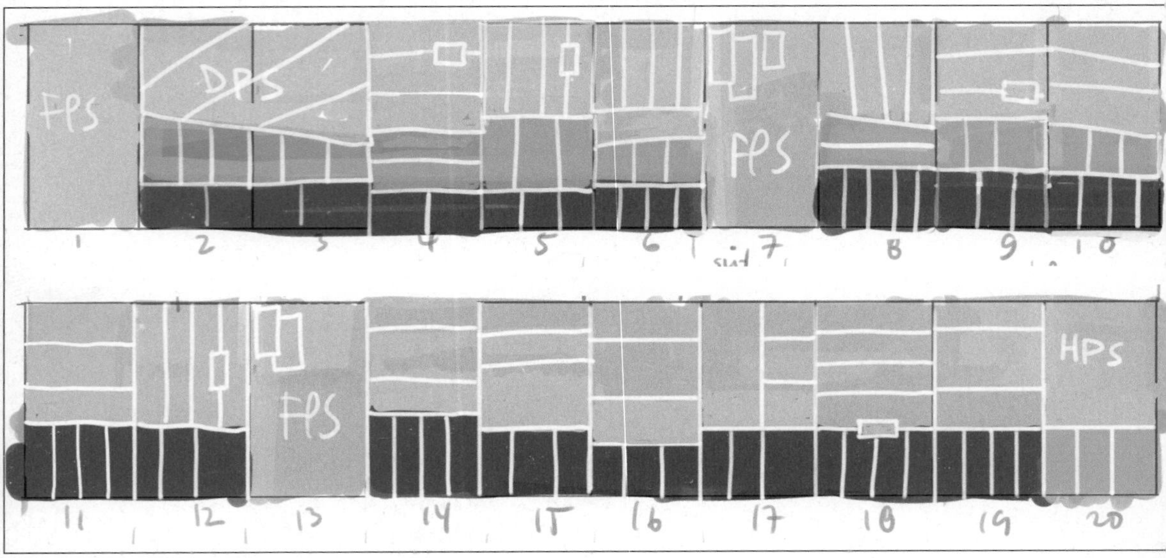
FPS
DPS
FPS
FPS
HPS

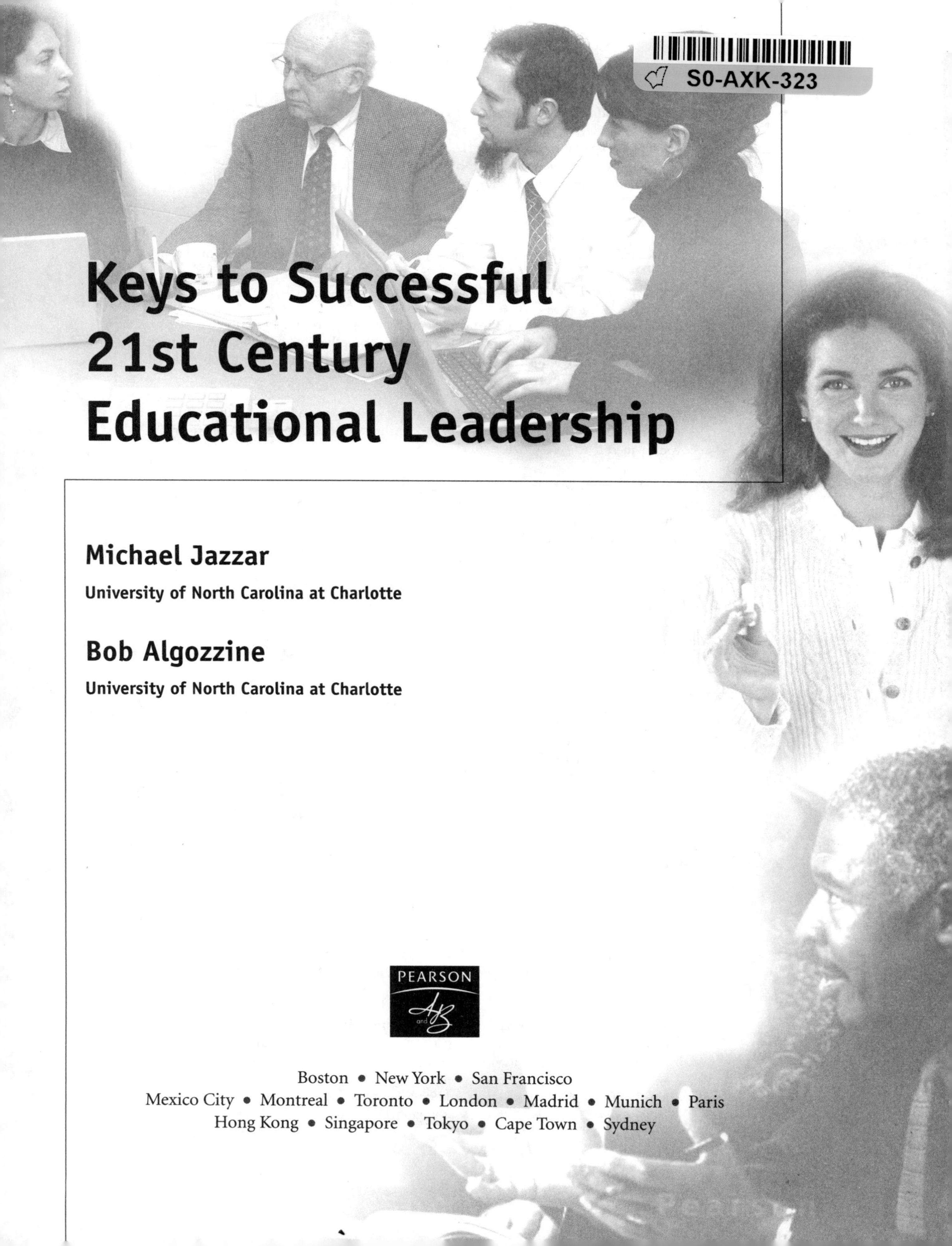

Keys to Successful 21st Century Educational Leadership

Michael Jazzar
University of North Carolina at Charlotte

Bob Algozzine
University of North Carolina at Charlotte

PEARSON

Boston • New York • San Francisco
Mexico City • Montreal • Toronto • London • Madrid • Munich • Paris
Hong Kong • Singapore • Tokyo • Cape Town • Sydney

Senior Series Editor: Arnis E. Burvikovs
Series Editorial Assistant: Erin Reilly
Marketing Manager: Tara Kelly
Editorial Production Service: Omegatype Typography, Inc.
Composition Buyer: Linda Cox
Manufacturing Buyer: Linda Morris
Electronic Composition: Omegatype Typography, Inc.
Cover Administrator: Joel Gendron

For related titles and support materials, visit our online catalog at www.ablongman.com.

Between the time website information is gathered and then published, it is not unusual for some sites to have closed. Also, the transcription of URLs can result in typographical errors. The publisher would appreciate notification where these errors occur so that they may be corrected in subsequent editions.

Library of Congress Cataloging-in-Publication Data

Jazzar, Michael.
    Keys to successful 21st century educational leadership / Michael Jazzar, Bob Algozzine. —
1st ed.
        p.   cm.
    Includes bibliographical references and index.
    ISBN 0-205-47375-X (pbk.)
    1. Educational leadership—United States.   I. Algozzine, Robert.   II. Title.   III. Title: Keys to successful twenty-first century educational leadership.

LB2805.J35   2007
371.2—dc22

2006045820

Printed in the United States of America

10 9 8 7 6 5 4 3 2 1   10 09 08 07 06

Credits: The Interstate School Leaders Licensure Consortium (ISLLC) Standards can be found on pp. xvi, 14, 27–28, 44, 59, 76, 94, 110, 131, 158, 176, 195–196, 213, 232–233, 254–255, 274, and 277–283.

The Interstate School Leaders Licensure Consortium (ISLLC) Standards were developed by the Council of Chief State School Officers (CCSSO) and member states. Copies may be downloaded from the Council's website at www.ccsso.org.

Council of Chief State School Officers. (1996). *Interstate School Leaders Licensure Consortium (ISLLC) standards for school leaders.* Washington, DC: Author. Used with permission.

CONTENTS

chapter 4   Successful Leadership Begins with You   45

PART II   FUNDAMENTAL KEYS

chapter 5   To Make It Great—Motivate   61

chapter 6   Making Decisions That Improve Education   77

chapter **7**   **Effective Instructional Leadership**   **97**

chapter **8**   **Curriculum Considerations and Implementations**   **113**

chapter 9   Legal and Moral Leadership: Doing the Right Thing   135

chapter **12** Developing New Millennium Assessments   197

Contents

PREFACE

Since the early 1970s, we, as educational leaders, have observed the effective and ineffective strategies used by others in our field. Our professional experiences—substantiated by theory—became our guidance for others. In turn, numerous researchers and theorists have challenged our educational leadership practices, strengthening what we hold as true. In other words, the many programs, processes, and initiatives that we have developed or provided oversight for in the last thirty years have been scrutinized by academicians, and this welcome scrutiny has added depth and substantiation to our guiding educational leadership principles and practices.

In writing *Keys to Successful 21st Century Educational Leadership*, we were continually mindful that our nation's schools face serious problems, ranging from student violence to deteriorating facilities to acute teacher shortages to substandard student achievement rates. We are deeply devoted to guiding, building, and supporting excellent educational leadership. After all, without highly effective educational leaders, our schools have little chance of overcoming the obstacles they face. We share wholeheartily this responsibility.

THE TEXT

Effective school leaders are essential to improving teaching, learning, and student achievement at the K–12 level of education. To be successful, legislators, board members, district superintendents, school principals, teachers, association leaders, and all other educational leaders need to know how to elicit support and create school structures and climates that foster the kinds of creativity, change, and innovation that will educate the heterogeneous group of children that make up America's schools. *Keys to Successful 21st Century Educational Leadership*, as a guide presenting critical, or *key*, lessons in leadership, is the "how-to" book for all educational leaders. This book serves as a guide to the successful preparation of (1) visionary educators, anchoring their work on improving schools, teaching, and learning; (2) moral agents and political-social advocates for the youth and the communities they serve; and (3) responsible leaders who make strong connections with diverse groups of people, valuing and caring for them as individuals and as vital members of the educational community. Our challenge, a complex and gratifying one not taken lightly, is grounded in a mix of contemporary practice substantiated by theory and processes that require continuing systematic analysis and review. In brief, *Keys to Successful 21st Century Educational Leadership* is the one book preparing and practicing educational leaders should have, as it presents educational leaders with the "how-to," or *keys*, for successful educational leadership.

Content

Keys to Successful 21st Century Educational Leadership is an original text addressing historical foundations, comprehensive guidance, new and exciting insights, and future considerations that shape best practices for school leaders. In each chapter, we comprehensively guide educational leaders through challenges that need to be identified, debated, and understood.

Topics and content are organized and presented in three sections. Part I, Foundational Keys, examines the study of theories, organizational structures, past educational reforms, the theoretical constructs of climate and culture, and the personal and professional individual convictions of educational leaders. Educational leaders who fail to understand and appreciate their own histories cannot fully understand the present or effectively manage the future. Part II, Fundamental Keys, presents current areas of challenge such as No Child Left Behind, reauthorization of IDEA, motivation, decision-making models, instructional and curricular leadership, and other imperative skills. The effectiveness of educational leaders comes from understanding the educational world as it is today. Part III, Future Keys, addresses current challenges such as renewal of schools, new millennium assessments, full-service schools, and essential reforms for school improvements in order to keep educational leaders prepared for rapid changes in the future. Educational leaders of the twenty-first century will generally fall into one of two categories: those protecting the status quo, therefore falling behind as education changes, and those with the knowledge and ability to lead and succeed in educational reform. *Keys to Successful 21st Century Educational Leadership* is dedicated to the latter.

Our goal is not only to present guidance on the many problems, concerns, and dilemmas that we identify but also to illustrate our ideas in a thought-provoking fashion that will provide clear directions for continuing dialogue that will foster development in the field. Jean Piaget taught us that the kinds of questions children ask reveal much about their development; similarly, we believe that the kinds of questions professionals ask tell much about the development of their field and provide a reasoned basis for review, reform, and progress. No current book in the area of educational leadership provides the scope, depth, or guidance of *Keys to Successful 21st Century Educational Leadership*.

Pedagogy

To support understanding and mastery of the content, we have included the following features in the text.

- The emphasis throughout the text on *keys* to success effectively meets the needs of ever-changing educational restructuring and reforming.
- The *Action Focus* features at the beginning of each chapter gently guide and bring light to the numerous theoretical constructs, concepts, and practices discussed throughout the chapter. To provide a greater depth, richness, and clarity of understanding, the Action Focus elements vary in length, depending on the complexity of the educational leadership fundamental presented in the chapters. For example, the Action Focus for Chapter 2 is brief, but the complexity of twenty-first-century curriculum based on Dewey's conceptualization (Chapter 8) and the intricacies of school finance (Chapter 10) required a continuous chapter-long Action Focus.
- *Praxis Preparation and Accreditation Readiness:* The full alignment of this textbook to ISLLC Standards can help students prepare to take the Praxis

Test for School Leaders and provides university professors with a textbook, activities, and artifacts suitable to meet and surpass accreditation requirements.

- The *In the News* feature connects the lessons of the text to the world of contemporary news. The feature deepens students' understanding of academic lessons by reproducing relevant news articles that illustrate linkages between topics discussed in the text and the world of media information. This feature also emphasizes the need for positive relations between educational leaders and the media.

- *Key Boxes* are intricately woven into the text. These boxes hold multiple keys, or guiding imperatives, to ensure the success of educational leaders.

- *The Reflective Practitioner* features presented at the end of each chapter provide a forum for integrating the Interstate School Leaders Licensure Consortium (ISLLC) standards into chapter fundamentals. See page xvi for a list of the ISLLC Standards and their corresponding chapter coverage. The Reflective Practitioner features also contain scenarios and discussion questions that provide opportunities for individuals, small groups, or large groups to review the content of the chapter. The Reflective Practitioner provides students and instructors with a basis for initiating dialogue and ample opportunities for reflection.

Supplements

Keys to Successful 21st Century Educational Leadership also features the following supplements:

- Research Keys throughout the book that direct students to additional resources found in the Research Navigator™ section of MyLabSchool™ and foster a deeper and more enriched understanding of the book's many principles and practices

- Attractive and effective PowerPoint™ presentations and a meaningful Test Bank of questions differentiated by levels of mastery that enhance the total teaching and learning experience. These supplements are available online by contacting your local Allyn and Bacon representative.

Keys to Successful 21st Century Educational Leadership represents perspectives derived from years of research and practical experience, providing guidance for effective educational leadership in public and private schools and successful preparation of competent educational leaders.

This book is not only designed for use in many college and university graduate courses, but it will also find its place on the desks of practicing educational leaders to help them meet the numerous and unexpected educational challenges they face.

Our intent was to provide an accessible, exciting, engaging book that is comprehensive, compelling, and highly prescriptive. We believe our combined experiences in providing leadership in public school systems and higher education institutions across the country have created a unique partnership that gave birth to an exceptional book. We also believe that our practical experiences in the field and our continuing deep record of academic research and scholarship provide a sound basis for considering issues guiding educational leadership in America's schools. We hope that *Keys to Successful 21st Century Educational Leadership* provides you with new views and beneficial comprehensive guidance.

ACKNOWLEDGMENTS

The enthusiasm of our colleagues and students who raved about our work and prompted us to finish so they could use this book was a welcome driving force. Numerous others, especially Arnie Burvikovs and Kelly Hopkins at Allyn and Bacon, were the wind beneath our wings—thank you!

We would also like to thank the reviewers for their helpful comments: Robert Anderson, Le Moyne College; Alicia Cotabish, University of Arkansas at Little Rock; John Daresh, The University of Texas at El Paso; Suzanne Eckes, Indiana University; Anthony Nomore, Florida International University; Perry Rettig, University of Wisconsin Oshkosh; and Angela Spaulding, West Texas A&M University.

We are also thankful for the unwavering support and encouragement of our families. Michael would like to thank Mary, Aaron, Danielle, and Jason, who made this book a very special labor of love. Bob would like to thank Kate for her continuing love and support.

ABOUT THE AUTHORS

Michael Jazzar (top) is an Assistant Professor at the University of North Carolina at Charlotte. **Bob Algozzine** (bottom) is a Professor at the University of North Carolina at Charlotte. Collectively the "ZZ Team" has invested more than five decades exploring and implementing cutting-edge practices in educational leadership. They have had opportunities to compare and contrast these practices in twenty-three countries. They have served as superintendent, principal, curriculum director, educational diagnostician, and teacher. Their efforts have earned them peer recognition in the form of outstanding educator of the year awards. As college professors for a collective thirty-nine years, they have prepared thousands of educational leaders around the world. They have also published more than fifty textbooks and over three hundred articles on research and educational practices, and they remain successful educational leaders today.

ISLLC STANDARDS

Standard	Covered in chapter(s)
1 A school administrator is an educational leader who promotes the success of all students by facilitating the development, articulation, implementation, and stewardship of a vision of learning that is shared and supported by the school community.	1, 2, 8, and 12–15
2 A school administrator is an educational leader who promotes the success of all students by advocating, nurturing, and sustaining a school culture and instructional program conducive to student learning and staff professional growth.	2, 3, 5, 7, 8, and 11–15
3 A school administrator is an educational leader who promotes the success of all students by ensuring management of the organization, operations, and resources for a safe, efficient, and effective learning environment.	2, 6, 8, and 11–15
4 A school administrator is an educational leader who promotes the success of all students by collaborating with families and community members, responding to diverse community interests and needs, and mobilizing community resources.	2, 8, 10, and 12–15
5 A school administrator is an educational leader who promotes the success of all students by acting with integrity, fairness, and in an ethical manner.	2, 4, 8, 9, and 11–15
6 A school administrator is an educational leader who promotes the success of all students by understanding, responding to, and influencing the larger political, social, economic, legal, and cultural context.	2, 8–10, and 12–15

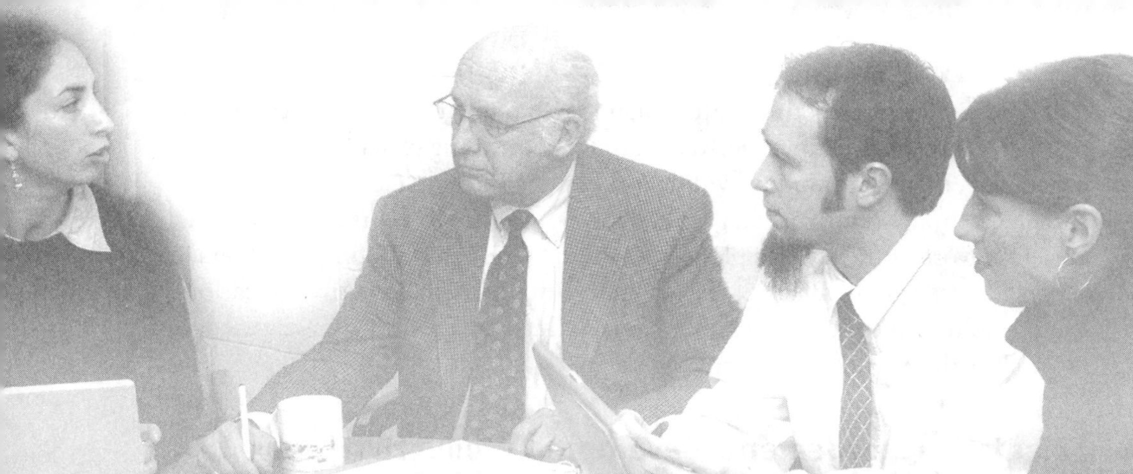

chapter 1

ISLLC *Standard* 1

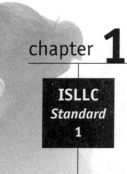

Leadership Theory and Practice

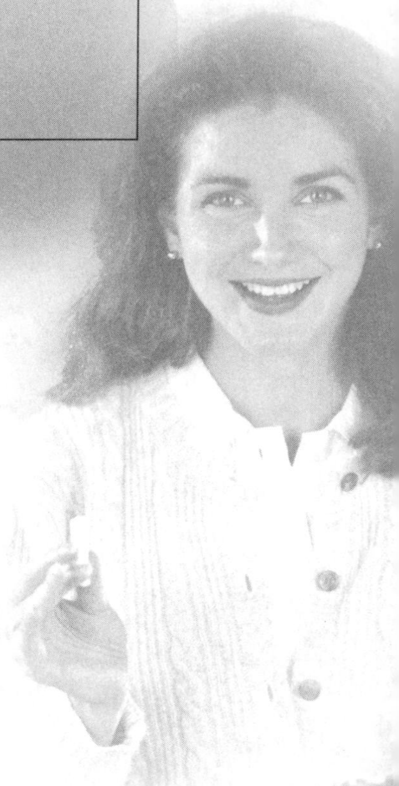

A key to a successful future is understanding the past.
—Anonymous

Welcome to your first Action Focus. Action Focuses will gently guide and bring light to the content of each chapter. By painting a broad-stroke picture of real-life situations, Action Focuses contribute meaning, purpose, and relevance to the many theories, concepts, and practices throughout the book. Similarly, our Action Focus in Chapter 1 portrays the theoretical foundation of Montessori education, casting light on the importance of the leadership theories and practices presented in this chapter.

Montessori (pronounced Mon-tuh-sore-ee) education was founded in 1907 by Maria Montessori, the first woman in Italy to become a physician. Montessori formed her educational theories from numerous *scientific observations* of children's learning processes. Guided by her beliefs that children teach themselves, Montessori designed a prepared environment in which children could freely choose from a number of developmentally appropriate activities. Today, nearly a century after Maria Montessori's first *casa dei bambini* (children's house) where the poorest of the poor children were educated in Rome, the number of Montessori schools continues to increase all over the world.

With over 4,000 certified Montessori schools in the United States and about 7,000 Montessori schools worldwide today, these schools have withstood the challenges of time, much due to their solid theoretical grounding. Maria Montessori's theories continue to guide, affirm, and support twenty-first century educators. Montessori educators throughout the world share a theoretical foundation and it is this foundation that unites, inspires and affirms their work globally.

As exemplified by Montessori educational leaders, numerous other educational leaders find support and affirmation when their decisions and actions are based on theoretical foundations.

FOUNDATIONS OF EDUCATIONAL LEADERSHIP FOR THE TWENTY-FIRST CENTURY

We begin our study of educational leadership in examining the foundations of the American educational leadership system and the key theories and practices that emerged from early times; after all, understanding the past is a key to success in the future. The principles derived from this beginning provide structure for organizing, managing, and providing successful educational experiences (Welcomer, Cochran, Rands, & Haggerty, 2003). Educational leaders are the caretakers and purveyors of these principles, using them to motivate and inspire others to achieve desired gains (Black & Hartel, 2002; Burris, 2001). Effective educational leaders hold the keys to education, many of which are grounded in knowledge as far back as the era of scientific management.

Scientific Management: Developing Productivity Keys

The late eighteenth century led to great changes in the production of textiles and other factory-made products. During this time, known as the Industrial Revolution, the factories that emerged created tremendous new challenges to organization and management (Columbo & Delmastro, 2002). Managing these new factories, and later new entities such as railroads, created the need for innovative and effective methods for resolving the emerging management issues.

The most well known of those who began to create a new science of management was Frederic Winslow Taylor (1856–1915), who was one of the first to attempt to systematically analyze human behavior in the workplace. Taylor's model was based on his view of the machine with its interchangeable parts, each of which performs a specific function. Taylor attempted to do to complex organizations what engineers had done to machines. He thought of the workforce in the same light as he did machines, analyzing each individual worker into the equivalent of a machine part (Lawson, 2001). Just as machine parts were easily interchangeable, cheap, and passive, so too should humans be likened to the machine model of organizations (Donaldson, 2001). This involved breaking down each task to its smallest unit and figuring out the one best way to do each job. After the most efficient practice was identified, it was the engineer's job to teach it to the worker and make sure the worker did only those motions essential to the task. Taylor attempted to make a science for each element of work and to restrict behavioral alternatives facing workers (Hansen & Mitchell, 2000). Taylor looked at the interaction of human characteristics, social environment, task, physical environment, capacity, speed, durability, and cost. The overall goal was to remove human variability. He believed that parts contribute to the whole and all are better for it.

The results were profound. Productivity under Taylorism went up dramatically. New disciplines and departments arose, such as industrial engineering, personnel, and quality control. There was also growth in middle management, as there evolved a separation of planning from operations (Kapstein, 2001). Rational rules replaced trial and error; management became formalized and efficiency increased.

Of course, Taylorism did not come about without resistance. First, the oldline managers resisted the notion that management was a science to be studied, not something one was born with (or inherited). Then, of course, many workers resisted what some considered the dehumanization of work (Marengo, Dosi, Legrenzi, & Pasquali, 2000). To be fair, Taylor also studied issues such as fatigue and safety and urged management to study the relationship between work breaks, the length of the workday, and productivity. He was able to convince many companies that the careful introduction of breaks and a shorter day could increase productivity. Nevertheless, the industrial engineer with his stopwatch and clipboard, standing over workers measuring each little part of the job and one's movements, became a hated figure and often led to much sabotage and group resistance during the *scientific management* era.

The *classical school* started to develop in France at the same time as Taylor's scientific management in the United States. Its father was a Frenchman, Henri Fayol, who regarded management as a universal process, and hence the school was often called *traditional* or *universalist* school. Fayol took the scientific approach, but he looked at organizations and productivity from the top down and laid down certain imperatives derived from his fourteen principles of administration (Fayol, 1949), as presented in Key Box 1.1.

RESEARCH KEYS

To enrich your understanding of **scientific management,** log on to www.researchnavigator.com and search Ebsco's ContentSelect.

Research Navigator.com

KEY BOX ▶ 1.1

Fayol's Fourteen Principles of Administration

1. Specialization of labor encourages continuous improvement in skills and the development of improvements in methods.
2. In justification of authority, Fayol asserted that the right to give orders and the power to exact obedience improves productivity.
3. Discipline was imperative, as Fayol believed the slacking or bending of rules is not productive.
4. For unity of command, Fayol argued that each employee has one and only one boss.
5. To achieve a unity of direction, a single mind was imperative to generate a single plan and all play their part in that plan.
6. When at work, only work things should be pursued or thought about with no subordination of individual interests.
7. Employees should receive fair payment for services, not what the company can get away with to the disadvantage of its workers.
8. Consolidation of management functions supports making decisions from the top down, in which centralization of decision making increases efficiency and therefore productivity.
9. A formal chain of command, running from top to bottom of the organization (like the military line of authority), comprises the most efficient way to maintain productivity.
10. All materials and personnel have a prescribed place and they must remain there.
11. Equality of treatment, but not necessarily identical treatment, is important.
12. Limited turnover of personnel and lifetime employment for good workers are important goals.
13. Thinking out a plan, and doing what it takes to make it happen, supports productivity.
14. Harmony and cohesion among personnel build strong organizations.

Out of the principles of management, Fayol prioritized the most important imperatives to be specialization, unity of command, a formal chain of command, and coordination by managers. We continue to see Fayol's fourteen principles of management practiced in many schools and school districts throughout our nation today.

Although Fayolism existed about the same time as the era of scientific management, it is a different approach—one that focuses on positions (administration) rather than people (administrators), as demonstrated by his fourteen management principles (Porter & Kramer, 2002). Furthermore, his impact on management in the United States continues to this day. His basic ideas that remain in twenty-first century practice include:

1. *Start at the top.* Problems of management stemmed from leaders being too far removed from an appreciation of the lifestyles and concerns of the average worker. Fayol believed that managers should come from the ranks of workers rather than from an elite class in society. He also believed that no formal education or training was needed and that even parents by virtue of having raised children would make good managers.

2. *Teach everyone management skills.* Fayol started trade schools and courses in the factories he supervised, not so much to afford workers a chance to move up, but to bring management and labor together in the workplace of ideas. Regular line-staff conferences and meetings were held periodically in the organization to discuss the ideas of management thinkers, and the purpose of these debates and discussions was intended to increase morale and esprit de corps.

3. *Eliminate paperwork without a purpose.* What productive organizations needed was careful forecasting, not guesswork, and focus on the vision and long-term (ten-year) goals of the organization. Fayol advocated periodically changing the organizational charts for no reason at all but to shake things up a bit.

4. *Exercise lateral (sideways or horizontal) communication.* Hierarchies created the problem of "middle management," ranks of people in the middle of the organization acting as buffers for vertical (up and down) communication. Since there was little to be done about innovating vertical communication (it would go on anyway), Fayol concentrated on horizontal (lateral) communication, inventing the now-famous gangplank principle, which means that there must be structured opportunities (not usually present in organization charts) for people at the same ranks to talk to one another, even if different departments are involved.

At about the same time as Taylor and Fayol, Max Weber, a German sociologist, was observing the organizational innovations of the German leader Otto von Bismarck. Weber identified the core elements of the new kind of organization that Bismarck labeled bureaucracy. The basic elements of bureaucratic structure included formal rules and behavior bounded by rules, uniformity of operations, division of labor, rational allocation of tasks, impersonal orientation, promotion based on technical competence, and employment based on merit rather than ascribed status. Breaking the Taylor and Fayol mold, Weber asserted that authority needed to be legally defined, the discretion of officers needed to be limited, competence needed to determine promotion, and tenure needed to be legally based (Arthur, 1996).

These elements, according to Weber, comprised an ideal *bureaucracy.* To achieve ideal bureaucracy, authority needed to be rational and legal as well as based on position and not the person in the position. In addition, the ideal bureaucracy could be achieved only if authority stemmed from the office and contained limits, as defined by the office. Positions needed to be organized in a hierarchy of authority if ideal bureaucracy was to be established (Black & Hartel, 2002). Also, Weber insisted that in order for organizations to attain ideal bureaucracy, _rules and regulations_ are needed to govern organizations.

Although many people think of bureaucracy in negative terms, this Weberian model in its pure form was a dramatic improvement over the previous management models based on fixed status and position by birth, not merit and unquestioned authority. The core elements of scientific management as asserted by Taylor and Fayol remain popular today. A picture of a factory around 1900 might look like something out of Dickens, but the core concepts of scientific management were not abandoned. Many were modified, updated, and implemented in the early schools of the United States.

IN THE NEWS

State Set to Start Hacking Away at School Rules

As Governor Blagojevich discovered, bureaucracies are known for their rules, regulations, and red tape.

"The most memorable moment of the state-of-the-state address 13 months ago was when Governor Rod Blagojevich produced a stack of paper more than five reams high—a copy of the Illinois State Board of Education's _rules and regulations_—and declared that it represented a _bureaucratic_ nightmare of biblical proportions," reported Eric Zorn, _Chicago Tribune_ journalist.

School bureaucracies often result in gigantic amounts of paperwork, including, but not limited to, rules, policies, procedures, notices, and other documents. To illustrate, the rule book for education in Illinois is over two thousand pages.

When the task of reducing all this bureaucratic red tape by even one ream is prioritized alongside more pressing problems in public education such as the state's funding of its schools, federally mandated programs and student learning, the bureaucratic dilemma is placed on the back burner.

Although bureaucracies have a negative image when it comes to overwhelming paperwork, there have been advantages.

Source: E. Zorn, "State Set to Start Hacking Away at School Rules," _Chicago Tribune,_ February 13, 2005.

Human Relations Management: Developing Resource Keys

Despite the economic progress brought about in part by scientific management, critics were calling attention to the "seamy side of progress," which included severe labor/management conflict, apathy, boredom, and wasted human resources. These concerns led a number of researchers to examine the discrepancy between how an organization was supposed to work versus how the workers actually behaved (Columbo & Delmastro, 2002). In addition, factors such as World War I, developments in psychology (e.g., psychoanalytic theory), and later the Great Depression all brought into question some of the basic assumptions of the scientific management era. One of the primary critics of the time, Elton Mayo, claimed that this "alienation" stemmed from the breakdown of social structures caused by industrialization, the factory system, and its related outcomes such as growing urbanization. Scientific research followed.

One of the most famous studies was conducted by Mayo. It showed how work groups provide mutual support and effective resistance to management schemes to increase output. Rather than responding to classical motivational approaches reflected in the scientific management model, workers were interested in the rewards and punishments of their own work group (Hansen & Mitchell, 2002). Sociopsychological factors that were not explained by classic theory were also important to the formal organization and formal leadership.

The Hawthorne studies from 1927 to 1932 added much to our knowledge of human behavior in organizations and created pressure for management to change the traditional ways of managing human resources. The human relations movement influenced managers toward gaining participative support of lower levels of the organization in solving organization problems. The movement also fostered a more open and trusting environment and a greater emphasis on groups rather than just individuals. Additional research gave us other paradigms for effective leadership.

In the 1930s, Kurt Lewin emigrated from Germany to the United States and laid the foundations for research in human behavior. Lewin was one of the founding fathers not only of social psychology but also of work and organizational psychology. He was one of the first to conduct a systematic analysis of an issue fundamental to social and personality psychology—namely, the relative contributions of personality and social environment to human behavior.

The principal characteristics of Lewin's theory reflect three fundamentals. First, behavior is a function of the field that exists at the time the behavior occurs. Second, analysis begins with the situation as a whole from which component parts are differentiated. Third, the concrete person in a concrete situation can be represented mathematically.

Lewin also emphasized underlying forces (needs) as determiners of behavior and expressed a preference for psychological as opposed to physical or physiological descriptions of the field (Chandler, McGraw, & Tedlow, 1996). A *field* is defined as the totality of coexisting facts that are mutually interdependent. Lewin used the language of physics, geometry, and mathematics in analyzing human behavior. He believed that social problems, including conflict, leadership, and adjustment, should be solved scientifically, for there "is no hope of creating a better world without a deeper scientific insight into the function of leadership and culture" and other essentials of group life (Lewin, 1948). Lewin's action research argues against the traditional distinction between basic and applied science by suggesting that scientific understanding will occur most rapidly if the efforts of researchers and practitioners are unified.

Lewin is best known for his development of the field theory—the proposition that human behavior is the function of both the person and the environment (Lewin, 1948). This means that behavior is a function of personal characteristics and the social worlds in which they operate.

The field theory may seem obvious to us now, but most early psychologists did not believe in behaviorism. Many psychologists at the time believed in the psychoanalytic theory that held human motives to be blind pushes from within. Lewin thought of motives as goal-directed forces. He believed that human behavior is purposeful; people live in a psychological reality or life space that includes not only those parts of their physical and social environment that are important to them but also imagined states that do not currently exist (Norton, 2000).

Lewin manipulated complex situational variables in natural settings. His approach has guided experiments in the field of social cognition, social motivation, and group processes. Most important, he helped the science of human behavior to develop by using empirical methods and controlled evaluation.

The works of Mayo, Lewin, and others kindled the vibrant and fiery exchanges of other human relations theories. The discoveries of client-centered therapy made by Rogers, the advancement of sociometric techniques by Moreno, human relations in the restaurant business with valuable implications for other organizations as asserted by Whyte, the small-group studies conducted by Homans, and human relations theories of Follet strongly influenced the behavioral science approach evident in many schools and organizations today.

Behavioral Science Approach

Many theorists added kindling to the fiery exchange known as behavioral science management approaches to leadership. Chester Barnard attempted to integrate human relations and the classical management principles in what he termed *cooperative systems.* E. Wright Bakke viewed organizations as a fusion of a personalizing process of the individual and a socializing process of an organization. Chris Argyris, in his optimal actualization construct, described the tendency of individuals to conform to organizational structures. Jacob Getzels and Egon Guba presented a theoretical formulation for studying administrative behavior. Douglas McGregor asserted two assumptions in Theory X and Theory Y, contrasting people's needs and management's strategies. Paul Hersey and Kenneth Blanchard provided insight into follower maturity, leader behavior, and leader relationships. Warren Bennis identified bureaucracy as the unconscious conspiracy. Many other behavioral management theorists, such as Victor Vroom (Expectancy Theory), Amitai Etzioni (Compliance Theory) and William Reddin (3-D Leadership), and others, created a vibrant exchange of ideas for all of humankind. Suffice it to say, numerous theorists have provided valuable keys to successful twenty-first century leadership.

Foundational Keys to Educational Leadership Thought

With vibrant ideas and inspiring thoughts, the founders of educational leadership thinking were as numerous as their ideas were diverse. From the scientific management, to the behavioral science, with the human relations between, one almost needs a program to keep the chief players organized. Therefore, we designed Table 1.1 to provide a graphic organizer of the foundational theorists presented in our first chapter.

The classical perspectives of scientific management, human relations, and behavioral science were ideas that were not only needed at the time they were developed but also essential to leadership strategies today. The founders of educational leadership thought provoked other great thinkers to assert their perspectives. The torch was passed. A flurry of thoughts flowed from the foundational concepts and principles. One such concept is total quality management.

Total Quality Management: Developing Continuous Improvement Keys

Riding on the coattails of the behavioral management researchers came a theory known today as *Total Quality Management (TQM),* also known as total quality control. Total Quality Management, widely recognized by its abbreviation as TQM since the mid-1980s, emphasizes the crucial role of management in the quality process. It uses a combination of theories, methods, techniques, and strategies for achieving exceptional processes and outcomes.

TABLE 1.1 Founders of Educational Leadership Thought

Classification	Key Components	Lead Contributor(s)
Scientific Management **1890–1930**	Efficiency, Maximizing profits, Minimizing costs, Specialized labor, Production-oriented, Impersonal, Economically driven, Autocratic, Coercive, Rigid lines of communication	Taylor Fayol Weber
Human Relations **1930–1960**	Group norms, Shared decisions, Empowerment, Inspiring human potential, Morale-centered, Valuing collaboration, Encouraging originality, Open channels of communication	Mayo Lewin Rogers Moreno Whyte Homans Follett
Behavioral Science **1960–Present**	Open systems, Interaction, Rational features, Natural features, Political motives, Contingency-driven, Interdependence, Integration of structure and individual	Barnard Bakkee Argyris Getzels & Guba McGregor Hersey & Blanchard Bennis Vroom Etzioni Reddin

The philosophies of Edward Deming represent the foundations for concern about quality. First implemented in Japan to boost its economy during the mid-twentieth century, TQM principles proved successful to the various Western businesses that had previously ignored them. The ideals summarized in what would be recognized as the Plan, Do, Check, Act (PDCA) cycle created by Walter Shewart were revised by Deming in 1990, creating the second well-known cycle of economic excellence known as the Plan, Do, Share, Act (PDSA) cycle.

It is generally agreed that Total Quality Management is a process and a set of disciplines that are coordinated to ensure that the organization consistently meets and exceeds requirements and expectations. It is a leadership process based on achieving customer satisfaction by carefully designing products or services and ensuring consistency in products. Acceptance of these two major objectives by all individuals within the organization is necessary, thus the term *Total Quality Management*. The TQM plan and strategy is to extend quality control efforts to every function of the company.

For an organization to achieve desired results through the implementation of TQM, four underlying criteria must be present: customer satisfaction, continuous improvement, respect for people, and managing with information and analysis. Deming developed fourteen points to bring his theory to life (see Table 1.2). The continued improvement fostered by Total Quality Management is based on a

TABLE 1.2 Deming's Fourteen Points of Management

Point I: Creating constancy of purpose for improvement of product and service
Point II: Adopting the new philosophy, one of zero defects
Point III: Ceasing dependence on mass inspection
Point IV: Ending the practice of selecting suppliers on the basis of only the price
Point V: Improving constantly and forever the system of production
Point VI: Instituting on-the-job training
Point VII: Adopting and instituting leadership
Point VIII: Driving out fear
Point IX: Breaking down barriers between staff areas
Point X: Eliminating slogans, exhortations, and targets for the workforce
Point XI: Eliminating numerical controls for the workforce
Point XII: Removing barriers that rob people of pride of workmanship
Point XIII: Encouraging education and self-improvement
Point XIV: Taking action to accomplish the transformation

circular system rather than a continuous single line because quality should not be thought of as having an ending.

Total Quality Management has focused leadership practices to create essential programs in the various sectors of public administration and management (GOAL/QPC, 2002). The principles designed by Deming over half a century ago continue to promote success for many different types of organizations. In order to view the progress of these advancements and to plan for future benefits, various means of organizing such data into charts, diagrams, and other useful tools are incorporated into the TQM programs. Deming's use of data to make decisions is the foundation for many effective leadership practices.

School-Based Management: Developing Schoolhouse Keys

In 1983, the report of the National Commission on Excellence in Education was the first of a series of critical reports on public schooling in the United States. *A Nation at Risk: The Imperative for Educational Reform* contained an open letter to the U.S. people, asserting that education has been eroded by a rising tide of mediocrity.

In a reaction to those reports, policymakers began reviewing the characteristics of the nation's best schools. Seminal research revealed that strong leadership on the part of the principal, high expectations for all students, and other essentials were evident in effective schools (cf. Brookover & Lezotte, 1979; Purkey & Smith, 1982). These findings started reform movements as many schools planned and began to carry out efforts using the principles derived from effective schools. In many cases, these school improvement efforts began at the single school level, largely ignoring the central office and bypassing the local school board (Lieberman & Miller, 1981; Neale, Bailey, & Ross, 1981).

Educational change tended to be viewed as a series of "prescriptions" that, if administered in correct doses, would result in more effective schools (D'Amico, 1982). As school improvement efforts became more seasoned, both researchers and policymakers began to realize that creating an effective school requires the leadership, collaboration, and support of the school board and the central office, as well as change at the building level, including a restructuring of personnel roles; the decentralization of the budget, instruction, and personnel; and shared decision making (Lezotte, 1989).

School-based management (SBM) has shifted decision-making authority to schools. The intent of SBM is to improve school performance by empowering faculty and staff to make decisions of educational significance instead of having decisions made by district leaders. The principal, under SBM, controls the school's resources and, in turn, is held accountable for the success of the school. Under school-based management, teachers are empowered, or given authority to participate, in the decision making of the school's finance, personnel, instruction, curriculum, and other meaningful areas. To fully implement SBM, parents form school-based management teams, or boards, vested with the authority to make policy to guide the education of their children.

Those school districts that have started the school-based management voyage by restructuring key personnel roles such as the superintendent, central office staff, the principal, and the faculty have encountered some tumultuous travels. From this road less traveled, it has been made clear that any attempt to change schools must clearly define and describe the intent for this reform. School-based leadership practices not only propose changes to curriculum and instruction but they also cause changes in the basic foundation

IN THE NEWS

Lessons for Leaders

School-based management brought changes in the very infrastructure of how schools conducted business.

Not long ago, a popular theory about school improvement went something like this: Put in strong principals and dedicated staff members, and then get out of their way. When it came to improving teaching and learning, the thinking went, the central office had lit- tle to add. The upshot was an era of policies that limited the role of district-level leadership in matters of instruction. *School-based management* and other school reform models flourished in the 1990s on the premise that individual schools could raise achievement.

If true school reform is to take place, studies reveal that school-based management needs exist.

Source: J. Archer, "Lessons for Leaders," *Education Week,* September 14, 2005.

and the mind-sets that underlie everyday behavior and functioning in school climates or cultures.

Cuban (2001b) refers to the complex changes associated with school-based reform as *second-order changes* that require the alteration, transformation, and modification of the basic character or identity of public education. Second-order changes require a fundamental renegotiation of cherished myths and sacred rituals by multiple constituencies, including citizens, local politicians, families, administrators, teachers, staff, and students (Cuban, 2001a). The entire community must reweave or reshape the symbolic tapestry that gives meaning to the educational process, and this takes time (Deal & Peterson, 1998).

We have learned from school districts and schools that have successfully implemented SBM that in order to avoid initial failure, they must manage change by providing sufficient development time, direction, and support. Because school-based leadership requires involvement from many, all expectations and end results must be explicitly defined. Schools that have successfully implemented SBM responded to the following questions in advance: Why the change to SBM? What is the purpose of the change? How will the change to SBM lead to improvements? What are the roles and responsibilities of each participant?

Leaders Make a Difference.   As roles and responsibilities change, the behaviors of superintendents, principals, and classroom teachers are inevitably altered to provide those educators who are closest to the students with a stronger voice in the decision-making process. All involved must substitute new skills, attitudes, and responsibilities for those in which they have grown accustomed and have gained comfort. Changes in roles do not come easily; however, bringing leadership closer to schools and classrooms leaves no other option.

In most cases, it is the *superintendent* who initiates leadership changes when hierarchical authority is replaced with decision making made at the school level. For a district to successfully initiate and maintain SBM, the superintendent must lead the innovation, overcome impediments to change, and provide professional development for others in making the transformation.

An important key to success for superintendents in this new era is to become good listeners and learn not only to give up some power but also to cope with the notion of shared decision making in which principals, teachers, and parents assume decision-making responsibility and control. Superintendents will need to collaborate with other district leaders undergoing similar changes.

Depending on the size of the district, a varying number of *central staff* positions are held, including business managers, personnel directors, curriculum specialists, special project directors, and special services personnel. Traditionally, these individuals have been authorized to make big decisions impacting schools, and when the SBM shift happens, it changes their lives. Principals, teachers, parents, and community partners also contribute to reform and change.

Financial matters, budgeting, and the allocation of funding have traditionally been placed in the hands of a *business manager.* This individual has been described as a money manager, a protector of district funds with a ready negative response to every request (Prasch, 1990). Financial decisions have been customarily centralized with the business manager. For this reason, the business manager has tended to gather power and may have the most difficulty in relinquishing authority over the school district's financial decisions. The role of the business manager in school-based management shifts to that of a facilitator, one who shares financial information so that school-based managers can best make their financial decisions.

The *personnel director's* role is transformed into an enabling relationship to school faculties and staffs that have decision-making authority for staff recruitment and selection. Under a centralized school system, the personnel director has a significant impact on the hiring of staff at the school site. Under SBM, the director's responsibilities focus on creating better selection and interviewing procedures throughout the district. The personnel director becomes a resource for leaders in schools by maintaining a comprehensive list of qualified applicants as well as current vacancies and results of exit interviews conducted with staff and faculty members leaving the school district.

Instructional and curriculum specialists provide important leadership as well. By encouraging the principal to serve as an instructional leader and by holding him or her accountable for doing so, SBM provides opportunities for others to be increasingly needed. In order for schools to be successful, the skills of the instructional and curricular experts in the central office take on a whole new purpose and meaning.

In successful school-based leadership, the *principal* assumes on additional responsibility as the primary change facilitator. The principal creates a climate that encourages maximum participation in school-based management in which all others—including teachers, custodians, food workers, parents, and others—feel ownership in sharing responsibility for the success of the school, including budget, discipline, textbook adoption, and cafeteria food and services.

The principal serves on a school council that includes parents, teachers, and often students. Each individual has equal voting power and is viewed as an essential colleague and fellow decision maker. The principal provides information to the school council regarding needs of the school, as well as information on federal, state, and district regulations. Although decisions made by the council offer strong direction, it is key to the principal's new role to establish that ultimately he or she is accountable and legally responsible for such decisions and may therefore vote on or veto decisions made by the council, taking care not to undermine the general authority granted to such councils.

In school-based management, *teachers* help to shape the decisions that affect the school. They become equals to administrators, other teachers, parents, and community members in the selection of goals and objectives for the school. Teachers' roles and responsibilities change, taking on new responsibilities as instructional specialists, mentors, coaches, and evaluators. They also take an active role in interviewing and selecting their school's personnel.

Initially, many teachers may be suspicious of the change to school-based leadership practices. Perhaps they will view their new "empowerment" as an additional responsibility with little to be gained. Typically, however, as teachers experience school improvements due to their own participation, the willingness to accept new roles and responsibilities generally and gradually increases.

From the traditional roles of band booster member, parent/teacher organization participant, and other restricted school roles, the most evident change in the role of *parents and other community members* is meaningful school involvement. As partners and stakeholders, they participate in establishing the school's mission and in making other important decisions. In some schools, parents and community members, through their roles on the council, make decisions on how the budget is spent and who is hired (David, Purkey, & White, 1989).

Key to "Local" Leadership and Management. One key to remember when it comes to successful implementation of SBM is that it requires a huge depar-

IN THE NEWS

Matter of Principals: Education Reforms Taking a Bite Out of Local Control

Principals need to be given back the rights to empower school-based decision makers.

Micromanaging state legislators, distrustful school boards, student rights' advocates, teachers unions and, yes, the federal government all have left their bite marks in the lonely principal's hide as reported by the *Arizona Republic*. If they were empowered, as they should be, principals would be ultimately accountable and responsible for school-based decision making that really increases student achievement. The drift of responsibility for the education of American students has continually been moving away from the schoolhouse. In a more logical future, perhaps we will return to a day when school principals, at the helm of the school, again will have the authority to inspire the actions and implement the decisions of school-based decision participants that actually make a difference in the lives of children.

In order for principals to lead effectively, they will need to be empowered to do so.

Source: "Matter of Principals," *Arizona Republic*, October 6, 2005.

ture from past tradition of the roles and responsibilities of school leadership. In necessitating large-scale change, SBM may generate large-scale confusion. The risks of misunderstanding are great; there is the potential for personal insecurity and feuding among staff. Districts opting for school-based management should ensure that each personnel role is carefully spelled out.

Additional keys to successful implementation of school-based leadership practices include clearly defining the shifts in responsibilities incurred from any initial changes. Educational leaders must provide for adequate preparation for new roles and responsibilities and this preparation may involve extensive training and retraining. In addition to the initial training required to transform centralized school structures, ongoing staff development and support for school needs and initiatives will be required.

Other more contemporary key players contributing to successful twenty-first century leadership include Bass and Leithwood with their transformational leadership findings; Bolman and Deal presenting reframing organizations; Irby, Brown, Duffy, and Troutman asserting the importance of synergistic leadership theory; Leithwood and Duke revealing the importance of instructional leadership, transformational leadership, moral leadership, and participative leadership; Shakeshaft, Grogan, Brunner, Tellerico, Irby, Brown, Skrla, Ortiz, Marshall, Dillard, and others arguing gender, race/ethnicity, and class imperatives; and Greenfield, Derrida, Foucault, Giroux, Bates, McLaren, English, Dantley, West, Young, and numerous other theorists providing critical theories and postmodernism constructs for today's successful educational leadership.

A CHAIN OF KEYS

All knowledge and practice is linked to what came before it. From the earliest industrial models to the systems used today, educational foundations have formed a chain, or series, of keys for the success of those who lead. If these keys help leaders achieve expected and desired outcomes, then the keys will be prized. If the outcomes are not achieved, then educational leaders need to continue their search. If educators keep on doing the same things over and over, the same results will be achieved, and doing the same things over and over while achieving the same unsatisfactory outcomes is a good definition of ineffectiveness. If the keys used are ineffective, it becomes the educational leader's job to attain, achieve, and implement replacements for the outdated, the insufficient, and the unacceptable. The making of new keys is exciting, as it may open an unlimited potential of impacting lives with greater benefit. In all honesty, making and using new keys may not be an option!

THE REFLECTIVE PRACTITIONER

Welcome to your first Reflective Practitioner containing your first scenario synthesis based on the ISSLC Standard 1 and your reading of Chapter 1. It is intended to provoke your thoughtful reflection and to stimulate

discussion among colleagues, classmates, and peers. The Reflective Practitioner provides opportunities to synthesize issues, make comparisons, and apply theory to practice. We hope it will motivate you to search for evidence, thus increasing your comprehension of the text and helping you examine your convictions and discover new and shared perspectives.

> **ISSLC Standard 1**
> A school administrator is an educational leader who promotes the success of all students by facilitating the development, articulation, implementation, and stewardship of a vision of learning that is shared and supported by the school community.

Scenario

It is fall term and the excitement, enthusiasm, and desire to learn are alive and ever so present! After all, students in the educational leadership program have been selected from numerous other applicants. From the very arduous completion of overwhelming application materials, to the challenging interviews and the meeting of testing requirements, twenty master's-level students survived and succeeded in gaining acceptance into a high-quality program of study.

These newly selected students admitted into the educational leadership program are seated in their first class, Administration 6100: Fundamentals in Educational Leadership, awaiting their professor. It was understood that Administration 6100 was the basic course in which concepts, principles, and preferred practices of educational leadership were drilled. From the spectrum of the development of administrative theory to the fundamentals of educational leadership, this course will be the very first experience and impression for the twenty bright-eyed and sparkling students.

Students in this educational leadership program are tomorrow's principals, superintendents, teacher leaders, technology directors, curriculum specialists, special education directors, counselor directors, and all other educational leaders. As diversified in educational leadership ambition as the twenty students are, each student has the following in common: their passion, commitment, collaborative skills, and vision for twenty-first-century school and school district improvements.

Dr. George Pullen, professor of Administration 6100, saunters into the classroom ten minutes late. Without outward verbal signs of humanness, such as a good afternoon, greetings, or even a welcome, Dr. Pullen, in a most condescending manner, challenges the class with the following question: Why is it important to know theory?

Regaining their composure, the students reflect on their professor's question, and moments later the brainstorm commences. They respond tentatively with the following:

- Theories are important because they serve as the framework and guides for educational leaders.
- Theories help with solving problems and stem from research in particular areas of need.
- Knowing theory can help us make decisions in different situations.
- Theories give us ideas that have been supported by evidence.
- Theories are like the "roots" and "heritage" of educators' belief systems.
- It helps educational leaders to define how a leader leads.
- By knowing theory we can create our own leadership style that is effective and that fosters positive relations throughout our organizations.
- Knowing theory provides a necessary foundation for building future success.
- Knowing theory provides educational leaders with a base on which to build their support and practice.
- Theories provide a basis by which people measure their own values and ideas.
- Theories provide us with a sound basis on which to form policies.
- Theories provide leaders with direction that is research based.
- Knowing theories gives us confidence that we are doing the right thing based on research and the experiences of others.
- Knowing theory helps us fit the pieces into a whole.
- Theories provide us with a tried and true option for leadership.
- Knowing theory provides us with research to support our decisions.
- Knowing theory provides knowledge about effective practices while making leaders feel secure in their practices based on evidence and proof.
- Theories provide foundations for educational leaders to use in developing their own philosophies.
- Theories provide a basis for sound practice.

Professor Pullen responds to this barrage of quality responses, "Well, then! I see we have given this question much thought. Open up your textbooks to Chapter 2."

QUESTIONS FOR REFLECTIVE THINKING

1. Which responses to Dr. Pullen's question, "Why is it important to know theory?" do you agree or disagree with and why? Please explain.
2. What should Dr. Pullen's next question to the class be and why?
3. How will your knowledge of the theories presented in Chapter 1 assist you in achieving success as an educational leader based on ISLLC Standard 1?
4. Based on your knowledge about past and current literature sources, why is it important to know theory?
5. How might knowing different approaches to leadership as described in this chapter contribute to your success as an effective twenty-first-century educational leader?

chapter 2

ISLLC
Standards
1–6

Educational Reforms—Recycling Keys and Opening New Doors

Shoot for the moon, for if you fall short, you'll still be among the stars.
—Anonymous

Your Chapter 2 Action Focus centers on new middle school principal, Ms. Martha McClean, in her first week at the helm of Hart Middle School. Much to the surprise of Ms. McClean, the faculty, students, parents, and community members, Mr. David Walter, a parent of one of Hart's sixth-graders, paid an unexpected visit to his daughter's teacher, Mr. Darrel. An argument over a grade dispute escalated, resulting in both standing up and Mr. Walter pushing Mr. Darrel against the classroom wall. The pressure was on Ms. McClean to act immediately!

Ms. McClean's thoughts rampaged as she questioned if she learned in her university principal preparation program something that would guide her in the here and now. After a thorough examination, she concluded that there wasn't a topic even remotely similar to this predicament discussed in her year-long internship program. Ms. McClean thought long and hard for something she could latch on to that she learned to guide her decisions and actions. She faintly recalled one of her professors stating that there were national standards that were developed to help educational leaders, even at times like this. Clearly, it was time to revisit the national standards to gain a perspective on the multidimensional ramifications of her situation prior to contacting her superintendent, planning a course of immediate action, and proceeding with her actions.

As briefly exemplified in your Chapter 2 Action Focus, educational leaders, such as Ms. McClean, are often bombarded by situations requiring decisions that they are requested to make often instantaneously. These decisions, whenever possible, should not be made on the fly or in the absence of sufficient understanding. Hence, prior knowledge is very important to successful twenty-first-century leadership. Making decisions without knowing prior issues, experiences, and actions can limit one's future leadership success. Furthermore, it is crucial to remember that if one does the same thing over and over, the same results will more than likely be the outcome. This is extremely troublesome when past results have been unsatisfactory.

Stated simply, the knowledge of the past is the key to successful educational leadership. It makes no sense to repeat the errors of prior practices. Worse yet, these repeated actions can lead to unsatisfactory performance and, in the most extreme case, job termination. Hence, it is imperative that educational leaders are well schooled in conventional wisdom along with cutting-edge theory. And this knowledge includes a deep understanding of not only the present but also the past—successes as well as shortcomings. A look back on the historical accomplishments and the trials and tribulations in education provides a valuable perspective from which to evaluate the future. As you think about the past, keep in mind that once answers were found, the questions often were changed in response to major historical and social events. The keys of educational leadership have been recycled time and time again.

The latest recycling efforts revolve around national standards for educational leaders. The Interstate School Leaders Licensure Consortium has set forth a new leadership paradigm, widespread throughout the United States, that provides a common core of knowledge, disposition, and performances that link leadership to productive schools and that enhance educational outcomes.

PASSING KEYS TO THE FUTURE

Successful twenty-first-century educational leaders need to have a keen awareness of the past for their decisions and actions to accomplish future gains. Therefore, this chapter will look back at educational reform and recycling. Our examination will begin by exploring the deficit column, as change comes from need, not abundance. Some argue that the story of public education has not been one of significant gains and accomplishments, and this perception at times has been supported by the media. Sadly enough, those who criticize education assert that education lacks a golden era when student achievement soared and educators were happy. Detractors of education emphasize that there is not a perfect prototype for public education to be discovered in history, held up as an exemplar, and bestowed on a supportive nation. Individuals and organizations sharing similar perceptions testify that public education in the United States is mediocre at best. Educational leaders need to recognize the existence of these perceptions and work diligently to change the perceptions held by detractors, knowing deep down inside that educators have made life-defining differences for the students they have educated. A look at the past history of educational reforms provides the cornerstones from which to build improved future schools and a baseline for educational leaders searching for keys to successful educational leadership today.

Opening the School Doors

The earliest organized effort to educate citizenry was the General Court of the Massachusetts Bay Colony in 1647, which passed a decree that every town of fifty families should have an elementary school and that every town of 100 families should have a Latin school (Murphy & Datnow, 2002). The goals of this schooling were simple and clear: to ensure that Puritan children learned to read the Bible and receive basic information about their Calvinist religion.

Over 100 years later, the highest quality education remained for selected students only. In 1779, Thomas Jefferson proposed a two-track educational system, which he termed *the laboring* and *the learned,* again resulting in increased scholarship for students tracked into higher academic studies. By the 1830s, the "selection of students" continued, with most of the southern states holding firm to their laws disallowing people in slavery to read. In 1851, the commonwealth of Massachusetts passed its first compulsory educational law for all students, in an effort to teach children of poor immigrants how to be civilized and obedient so they would make good workers. As if governmental control of education was sufficient, Congress in 1854 passed legislation making it illegal for Native Americans to be taught in their own native language. Children as young as age 4 were taken from their Native American parents and sent to off-reservation boarding schools to receive a civilizing education.

Public education in the United States continued to undergo one reform after another. However, it was not until after the Civil War that the government began funding public education. At the commencement of governmental funding of schools, student enrollments escalated. According to the National Center for Educational Statistics (2004), some 57 percent of the 12 million school-age children in 1870 were enrolled in public elementary or secondary schools, although only about 60 percent of those enrolled attended school on any given day, and the average school year was 132 days. By the turn of the century, the percentage of school-age children attending public schools had risen to 72 percent, with almost 70 percent of enrollees attending on any one of the 150 days in the school year. Most public education still occurred in the early grades—only 2 percent of the student population was in secondary school.

The most important boosters of the country's new public education system were what we today might call cultural conservatives (Senge, 2001). The turn of the century, after all, was a time of tremendous immigration. As more and more immigrants arrived in the United States, bringing with them a plethora of languages, cultural traditions, and religious beliefs, political leaders foresaw the potential dangers of diverse political agendas. The public education system, once designed primarily to impart skills and knowledge, took on a far more political and social role. The mission of public schools was to provide a common culture and a means of inculcating new Americans with democratic values.

Key Holders of Reform

Since the one-room school-house, individuals and groups of individuals have attempted to dominate public education up

IN THE NEWS

Special Education and Minorities

Tracking of students began over 200 years ago and it continues today.

In the debate of how to promote the success of all students and eliminate an achievement gap, the overrepresentation of black and Hispanic children in special education classes has been heatedly argued. It has become a heated argument that no race should have a disproportionate number of disabled children. Labeling of minority children as emotionally disturbed and intellectually disabled does not accurately describe them and is an atrocity. Investigations into this matter have revealed that students are being placed in special education because educators are misinterpreting behavior problems and misunderstanding cultural differences.

These actions and others have resulted in a two-track twenty-first-century educational system.

Source: A. Salzman, "Special Education and Minorities," *New York Times,* November 20, 2005.

to the present day. Such attempts have included instilling moral values into school curriculum, health lessons, and a myriad of other interests. Historically, education has been at the mercy and whims of those with influence. Even more confusing and frustrating for educational leaders were private agendas for public education that created a double standard, such as business leaders supporting a centralized approach to public education in stark contrast to what the same business leaders believed was appropriate in economic policy (Vecchio, 2002). For better or worse, the keys to education as posed by the business world were cast.

In the final analysis, diversified and numerous groups across the political continuum have attempted to persuade public schools to accomplish what they deem to be important, such as racial integration, social issues, civic responsibilities, or environmental concerns. Hence, the history of public education reform is a story in which individuals and groups jockey for position to assert their political agendas on public school policies of the day.

Reform efforts have appeared and reappeared so frequently that public school reforms seem to be recycled. In the 1940s, the teaching of social and human skills surfaced as a top priority, with social studies, psychology, and home economics considered of utmost importance. Driving these curriculum decisions were worries about a growing dropout rate, coupled by increased anxieties about a rapid pace following a world war and the commitment to help students adjust to an ever-changing world. Examples of classes provided by public schools during this period were titled Basic Urges, Wants, and Needs and Making Friends and Keeping Them (Darling-Hammond, 1997).

This humanistic development abruptly came to a close when the Soviet Union launched its *Sputnik* satellite into space in 1957. Again, prior educational efforts were lost, with new reforms emphasizing a return to the learning of basic subjects with emphasis on science and math. *Sputnik* wasn't the only craft sent into space. Public education in the United States launched new programs in accelerated math and programmed instruction that were taught in open classrooms in ungraded schools.

During the 1960s, reforms from the earlier decades began to impact the public education system. Some of these innovations may have worked in some schools; however, these innovations were clearly not the panacea that the nation had hoped for—unfortunately another common result of school reforms. In the 1970s, school reform led to new approaches such

IN THE NEWS

Annenberg Challenge Proves to Be Just That

Since the one-room schoolhouse, the need for educational reform has continued in the United States.

It was billed as a challenge to the nation: $500 million over five years, much of it to improve education in the country's largest and most intractable cities. Walter H. Annenberg announced his gift to the American people in late December 1993 and began funneling millions of dollars into Chicago, Los Angeles, New York, Philadelphia, and the San Francisco Bay area. He made grants available to several other urban areas.

A central assumption was that by giving money to reformers in the trenches rather than to the school bureaucrats, an improved public education for poor and minority students would prevail. More than three years later, some of the original cities could point to significant gains, such as 122 small schools in New York. However, the initial premise of circumventing district red tape by creating groups of schools and educators who drew their support from each other and from outside partners had proved unrealistic.

The search for educational reforms continues with interest in national standards.

Source: L. Olson, "Annenberg Challenge," *Education Week,* June 25, 1997.

as whole language, mastery learning, and the escalating of standardized testing of both students and teachers.

Finally, during the 1980s, the educational reform bandwagon was headed down the path of new ideas. Following the publication of *A Nation at Risk* in 1983, governors instituted all sorts of teacher training and testing programs, curriculum changes, and higher performance standards for students (Bennett, 2004). At the same time, state funding of schools dramatically increased. Also, President Ronald Reagan, who during his campaign vowed to eliminate the U.S. Education Department, increased federal spending for public education, with appropriations heavily directed toward programs for needy or minority students.

Politics of Reform

Successful twenty-first-century educational leaders will consider who is asking for what and why before launching off in a new direction. What has clearly been on the rise in recent decades is the use of U.S. public schools by political leaders to achieve some social outcome. Stemming from the 1950s and 1960s, the national focus on racial desegregation and the 1970s emphasis on socialism, humanism, spiritualism and environmentalism in education, the politics of reform have negotiated the ever-changing structuring of public education. Today, the nation's developmental psychologists and early childhood experts, stressing environmental conditions, are getting the attention of educators and political leaders (Certo, 2002). Hence, today we now have a strong emphasis on early childhood intervention programs, Head Start, in-school counselors and school psychologists, and a renewed interest in compensatory education.

No matter the reform, the nation's remaining monopolistic, bureaucratic, overregulated system of public schools needs unprecedented transformation to meet the challenges of the twenty-first century. Political, business, and education leaders need to team together harmoniously and work diligently and successfully to improve the current public education system. This reformation needs to include, perhaps first and foremost, successful twenty-first-century educational leadership!

Keys to National Leadership Reform

The field of educational leadership was initially informed by philosophy and religion, but neither provided a basis for the profession (Button & Provenzo, 1989). Rather, schools of the early twentieth century established their leadership on business and industrial models of the corporate chief executive officer. It was during the Cold War era that the search for the science of school administration was born. School administration was constructed almost entirely on a two-layered foundation built up during the nineteenth century: concepts from management, especially from the private sector, and theories and constructs borrowed from the behavioral sciences (Murphy, 2003, p. 4).

Although the field of educational leadership is relatively new, the concept of leadership is as old as civilization itself. The term didn't appear in literature on school administration until Elwood Cubberly's *1914 Rural Life and Education* (English, 1994, p. 102). Over the course of the twentieth century, our understanding of leadership slowly evolved as researchers began to define and describe leadership, in large part, by the character of those being led and the cultures of the organizations and communities in which they worked. Social systems theory suggests that these organizations are influenced by and, in turn, exert influence on the greater culture of which they are a part (Owens, 2004, p. 121). Within every school district, community, or classroom there might be dozens of different systems worthy of notice (Spring, 2005).

In the last half of the past century, educational leadership was examined from a variety of perspectives. Historically, it had been viewed as based on power (Etzioni, 1961). Early studies addressed leadership traits in which leaders were differentiated from nonleaders. Organizations were looked at as to how they might be structured differently (Gailbraith, 1973). It was believed that contingency or situational models explained the differences between effective and less educational effective leaders (Hersey & Blanchard, 1982). Leadership behaviors were believed to be driven by an individual's mindscape or mediation abilities (Gregorc, 1984; Sergiovanni, 2001). Effective leaders were described as visionaries (Bennis, 1989) or stewards (Sergiovanni, 1992). Recentering educational leadership in the humanities was considered (Hodgkinson, 1991). Transformational leadership was proposed as the central focus of school administrators (Cunningham & Gresso, 1993). More recently, a growing body of literature has discussed leadership (Elmore, 2000; Spillane, Halverson et al., 1999). However, educational leadership may be too young to have developed its own paradigms (Usdan, 2002a). Over the last quarter century, educational leadership has experienced considerable turmoil as it has struggled to grow out of adolescence (Murphy, 2003, p. 1).

A review of recent literature seems to support the position that the functions of providing directions lie at the heart of school leadership (Leithwood & Riehl, 2003, p. 2). In other words, leaders work through others to achieve shared goals. Leadership is a group function and intentionally seeks to influence others (Owens, 2004, p. 259).

WHAT WE KNOW ABOUT EFFECTIVE LEADERS

Although educational leadership may be hard to define, research reveals that there are common accomplishments that must be achieved by successful educational leaders. In his introduction to *On Becoming a Leader*, Warren Bennis (1989) asserts, "Having been a teacher and a student all my life, I am as leery as anyone of the idea of leaping to conclusions, or making more of evidence than is demonstrably true. So I have been forced, again and again, to qualify my answers" (p. 1). Effective school leadership needs to be qualified and quantified. Although sufficient empirical insight is absent, conventional wisdom argues that high-performing schools have effective school leadership and low-performing schools have weak leadership. Several questions emerge: What constitutes effective educational leadership? What is the correlation between successful educational leadership and student achievement? teacher retention? staff morale? These and other questions have been, and continue to be, of national interest.

National Framework

Over the past two decades, educational leadership has been part and parcel of school reform. In the mid-1980s, several influential organizations began producing models, principles, or frameworks for school leadership, certification standards, and leadership preparation programs. The National Association of Elementary School Principals (NAESP) sponsored a series of papers and publications, including *Principals for 21st Century Schools.* The National Association of Secondary School Principals (NASSP) sponsored the special report, *Performance-Based Preparation of Principals.*

In 1990, these organizations jointly sponsored the National Commission for the Principalship, which was charged with redesigning preparation programs and planning for a national certification process. The commission's first effort emphasized two dimensions of leadership: an overarching dimension of broad leadership influence on school culture, performance, vision, and innovation; and a more functional one of making things happen. The functional dimension included twenty-one performance domains divided among functional, programmatic, interpersonnel, and contextual headings. Following the publication of *Principals for Our Changing Schools,* specialists in each of the twenty-one performance domains were commissioned to define the knowledge and skills essential to informed practice within the boundaries of the separate domains. The result was *Principals for Our Changing Schools: Knowledge and Skill Base,* published in 1993 (Thomson, 1993). In the publication of the knowledge base, the National Policy Board for Educational Administration (NPBEA) represented ten national associations with a strong interest in school leadership. This massive document delineated the knowledge and skill base for each of the twenty-one performance domains.

The State of the States

Shortly after publication of the NPBEA knowledge and skill base, the Council of Chief State School Officers (CSSO) joined with NPBEA and its corporate secretary, Scott Thomson, to form the Interstate School Leaders Licensure Consortium (ISLLC). This initiative was funded by twenty-four member states and several foundations. An accomplishment of this consortium was the *ISLLC Standards for School Leaders* published in 1996. The Standards were drafted by personnel from twenty-four state education agencies and representatives of various professional associations and were forged from research on the linkages between research and productive schools from significant societal trends with implications for emerging views of leadership.

RESEARCH KEYS

To enrich your understanding of **ISLLC Standards,** log on to www.researchnavigator.com and search Ebsco's ContentSelect.

Research Navigator.com

The knowledge base for the ISLLC Standards was based, in part, on Scott Thomson's work in *Principles for Our Changing Schools: Knowledge and Skill Base* (Thomson, 1993). In addition to Thomson's work, Murphy recalls two guiding questions in developing the ISLLC:

- What do we know about schools in which all youngsters achieve at high levels?

- What do we know about the actions and values of the women and men who lead effective schools and productive school systems?

To answer the first question, the Standards-drafting team used a substantial body of research to define the word *effective* (Murphy, 2003). The team then reviewed the empirical findings from effective schools research. Members of the team looked at conditions of core technology that explained student learning and reviewed collective research dealing with perspectives and values. Their goal was to define *leadership* in terms of connections to conditions of schooling (Murphy, 2003, p. 9). To answer the second question, the development team reviewed the research on school leaders who consistently led high-performing organizations. The research revealed portraits of effective leaders who had a deeper understanding of and were more heavily invested in the core business of schooling (Murphy, 2003).

At the heart of the ISLLC Standards were seven guiding principles:

IN THE NEWS

Principals Receive Post Leadership Award

The seven guiding principles at the heart of ISLLC Standards were, by and large, the selection criteria for awarding three principals the prestigious Post Leadership Award.

Jerrold C. Perlet, an elementary school principal in Montgomery County, and Marlene A. Tarr, a high school principal in Frederick County, began their careers in education as classroom teachers. Perlet and Tarr were recipients of the Post Leadership Award. Both principals emulate the highest degree of care for their students, prioritize their students' achievement as tops, and demonstrate daily high energy, collaboration and creativity.

In receiving their Post Leadership Awards, both winning principals passed on advice to aspiring principals. Perlett emphasized that principals need to be well organized, save paperwork until after school hours, and get into classrooms as much as possible. Tarr asserted that educators must elicit parent support at all times, especially at times of discipline infractions. Tarr emphasized that failure to do so means that we, as educators, have not tried hard enough to change a child's behavior.

Being a principal can be one of the toughest jobs in education. That's why studying the performance of Perlet and Tarr, and other successful school leaders, is essential.

Source: L. A. Hernandez, "Principals Receive Post Leadership Award," *Washington Post*, December 8, 2005.

1. Reflect the centrality of student learning.
2. Acknowledge the changing role of school leader.
3. Recognize the collaborative nature of school leadership.
4. Upgrade the quality of the profession.
5. Inform performance-based systems of assessment.
6. Be integrated and coherent.
7. Be predicated on the concepts of access, opportunity, and empowerment for all members of the school community.

"Performances" and "dispositions" were developed for each of the ISLLC Standards. The development of dispositions was challenging to initiate. After development began, the dispositions shaped the development of the standards. Perkins (1995) stated:

> The inability to assess dispositions caused some of us a good deal of consternation at the outset of the project. As we became more enmeshed in the work, however, we discovered that the dispositions often occupied center stage. This is because dispositions are the proclivities that lead us in one direction rather than another within the freedom of action we have. (p. 278)

By 2003, the ISLLC Standards had been codified in forty states. University programs were compelled to align their preparation programs with the ISLLC Standards. The common standards were also created to promote collaboration among policymakers on topics of mutual interest, such as reciprocity of licensure and candidate assessment:

1. A school administrator is an educational leader who promotes the success of all students by facilitating the development, articulation, implementation, and stewardship of a vision of learning that is shared and supported by the school community.
2. A school administrator is an educational leader who promotes the success of all students by advocating, nurturing, and sustaining a school culture and instructional program conducive to student learning and staff professional growth.
3. A school administrator is an educational leader who promotes the success of all students by ensuring management of the organization, operations, and resources for a safe, efficient, and effective learning environment.
4. A school administrator is an educational leader who promotes the success of all students by collaborating with families and community members, responding to diverse community interests and needs, and mobilizing community resources.
5. A school administrator is an educational leader who promotes the success of all students by acting with integrity, fairness, and in an ethical manner.
6. A school administrator is an educational leader who promotes the success of all students by understanding, responding to, and influencing the larger political, social, economic, legal, and cultural context.

In turn, the ISLLC Standards were further broken down into Knowledge, Dispositions, and Performances, as presented in the appendix to this book (p. 277). Each reflects what professionals believe to be critical information for effective leadership in key areas, such as program development and review, licensure, and advanced certification. The ISLLC Standards—Knowledge, Dispositions, and Performances—provide a national framework for educational leadership. Support for the national standards is widespread throughout the nation and continues to expand in implementation and usage. We believe twenty-first-century usage of ISLLC Standards will continue, especially in this day and age of accountability.

KEYS TO LEADERSHIP PREPARATION
PROGRAM ACCREDITATION

Perhaps the most far-reaching effect of collaboration between the National Policy Board for Educational Administration (NPBEA) and the Council of Chief State School Officers (CSSO) was the adoption of the ISLLC Standards by the National Council for the Accreditation of Teacher Educators (NCATE) for the accreditation of preparation programs in school administration. Because NCATE institutions have policy-anchored connections with more than forty-five states, all programs in NCATE institutions fall under the professional and state-policy umbrella of the Standards (Murphy, 2003).

The Educational Leadership Constituent Council (ELCC), a specialty accrediting agency of NCATE—composed of the National Association of Elementary School Principals (NAESP), National Assessment of Educational Progress (NAEP), the American Association of School Administrators (AASA), and the Association for Supervision and Curriculum Development (ASCD)—accredited educational programs on the behalf of NCATE between 1995 and 1999. The emphasis during this period was on performance and the application of knowledge and skills. During 2000 and 2001, NPBEA and ELCC revised and recommended the ISSLC Standards to NCATE as the basis for accrediting university programs preparing school leaders. This recommendation was adopted by the full NCATE board in late 2001.

Today, leadership programs seeking NCATE accreditation are required to meet the revised standards as part of the institutional review process. Those programs that meet or exceed the standards receive national recognition by NCATE and NPBEA. The underlying assumptions of the NCATE standards are summarized as follows:

- The central responsibility of leadership is to improve teaching and learning.
- The purpose of the standards is to improve the performance of school leaders.
- The exercise of leadership in its various expressions constitutes the core function of the principal. . . . It is active, not passive. It is collaborative and inclusive, not exclusive. While leadership may be viewed as a process, it also requires the exercise of certain expertise and the expression of particular attributes.
- No overarching theory of leadership has proven adequate, but many of the skills and attributes of effective leadership are understood, can be taught, and can be practiced.
- Leadership preparation requires the cultivation of professional competence through bridging experiences and clinical as well as classroom performance activities.
- Many preparation programs fall short of developing the knowledge, skills, and attributes school leaders must use to take initiative and manage change.
- Leadership includes an ethical dimension.
- Preparation programs should be essentially an institutional responsibility, but design, delivery, and key learning experiences, particularly the application of knowledge and the practice of skills, must take place in school districts.
- The Standards should be assessed through performance measures.

Because the Standards are directed at institutions that prepare educational leaders, NCATE has added a standard to emphasize the importance of an extensive internship (field experience) component. In doing so, NCATE also strongly focused on student (candidate) and program assessment. The additional standard instituted by NCATE follows:

- Candidates who complete the program are educational leaders who promote the success of all students through substantial, standards-based, and integrated experiences in real settings that are planned and guided cooperatively by university and school district personnel for graduate credit.

HOLDING EDUCATIONAL LEADERSHIP KEYS

Although the national professional associations and accrediting agencies have been major forces in establishing standards for school leadership, they certainly have not been the only ones. The unique structure of public education in the United States provides multiple opportunities for input from governmental bodies, political entities, foundations, and special-interest groups. The major government participants have been politicians, administrative politicians, those who owe their allegiance to elected politicians, school boards, educationists (including intellectuals and writers who shape policy), and the courts (Spring, 2005). In addition, foundations, teachers unions, the corporate sector, and numerous other interest groups continue to impact educational leadership reform.

In short, the plethora of players today and yesterday has placed pressure on the federal government to link public schools to national policy issues. In the 1960s, it was civil rights issues. In the 1970s, businesses pushed for the establishment of career education and vocational education programs. The 1980s and continuing into the present saw the religious right wing's attempts to influence the federal government toward choice in education. During the 1990s, an increased emphasis on accountability for student achievement was legislated, with the No Child Left Behind Act signed by President George W. Bush on January 8, 2002. Increasingly, the federal government has continued during the twenty-first century to serve the role as a "Bully Pulpit," while leaving implementation to the states (Spring, 2005, p. 183).

THE REFLECTIVE PRACTITIONER

Welcome to your next Reflective Practitioner, which is based on all six ISLLC Standards, readings in Chapter 2, and your Chapter 2 Scenario. It is intended to provoke your thoughtful reflection and to stimulate discussion among colleagues, classmates, and peers. The Reflective Practitioner provides opportunities to synthesize issues, make comparisons, and apply theory to practice. We hope it will motivate you to search for evidence, thus increasing your comprehension of the readings and helping you to examine your convictions and discover new and shared perspectives.

ISLLC Standard 1
A school administrator is an educational leader who promotes the success of all students by facilitating the development, articulation, implementation, and stewardship of a vision of learn-

ing that is shared and supported by the school community.

ISLLC Standard 2
A school administrator is an educational leader who promotes the success of all students by advocating, nurturing, and sustaining a school culture and instructional program conducive to student learning and staff professional growth.

ISLLC Standard 3
A school administrator is an educational leader who promotes the success of all students by ensuring management of the organization, operations, and resources for a safe, efficient, and effective learning environment.

ISLLC Standard 4
A school administrator is an educational leader who promotes the success of all students by

collaborating with families and community members, responding to diverse community interests and needs, and mobilizing community resources.

■ **ISLLC Standard 5**
A school administrator is an educational leader who promotes the success of all students by acting with integrity, fairness, and in an ethical manner.

■ **ISLLC Standard 6**
A school administrator is an educational leader who promotes the success of all students by understanding, responding to, and influencing the larger political, social, economic, legal, and cultural context.

Scenario

At the national conference of the United States Association of High School Principals held in San Antonio in 2006, well-deserved recognition was given to Dr. Roberta Jimenez, principal of Caberalla High School in Los Angeles. At a breakfast ceremony on Sunday, the last day of the conference, a prestigious award was presented to Dr. Jimenez by the Honorable Richard Dwoling, a member of the U.S. House of Representatives. Representative Dwoling read from an already prepared manuscript containing the following words:

- Chairperson and delegation of the United States Association of High School Principals, I rise today to pay tribute to Dr. Roberta Jimenez, a distinguished leader from my hometown of Los Angeles who has made a positive impact on thousands of young lives in our community. I am proud to congratulate Roberta Jimenez, the principal of Caberalla High School in Los Angeles, who today was named the National Principal of the Year by the United States Association of High School Principals, the largest school leadership organization in the nation.
- Like those before her who have received this high honor as the nation's best principal, Roberta Jimenez has worked tirelessly for the benefit of every student enrolled at her school. Ten years ago, Caberalla High was best known for the crime-ridden neighborhood in which it was located and its excessive dropout rate of 13 percent.

- Then Roberta Jimenez took the helm. Today, Caberalla graduates 98 percent of its students. Caberalla's dropout rate of 2.3 percent is less than half of the average national dropout rate. Caberalla has been transformed from a school where dropping out was the norm to a flourishing environment where half of its students go to college.
- Roberta Jimenez has produced these results in an environment where students are faced with a host of challenges. Most students at Caberalla live in neighborhoods with high crime rates. Eighty-two percent of Caberalla students are poor. Ninety-three percent are immigrants or minorities, who speak a total of 30 languages.
- Roberta Jimenez has been so successful with these students because of her own challenging background. She grew up poor in Albuquerque, New Mexico, and in Los Angeles as the child of Spanish-speaking parents who taught themselves English and left school after the eighth grade. She and her family were discriminated against at every turn—a fact that motivated Roberta to succeed.
- She has put her credo—"all kids need equal opportunity"—into practice at Caberalla High School. With innovative alumni mentoring, student–teacher "academic families," and an on-site school clinic, Roberta Jimenez has brought the community together in the interest of educating its young people.
- Mr. Chairperson, the president this week called on the American people to work together, to realize that every student deserves the opportunity to succeed, and to improve America's educational system for the benefit of all students. Roberta Jimenez accomplishes this goal every day at Caberalla High School. I am pleased to see both her goals realized and her efforts recognized with the United States Principal of the Year award.

There was great cheer and support from the delegation assembled. Dr. Jimenez approached the podium to extend her deepest gratitude on behalf of the faculty, staff, students, parents, and community members of Caberalla High School.

QUESTIONS FOR REFLECTIVE THINKING

1. Dr. Roberta Jimenez was recognized for outstanding leadership as principal at Caberalla High School. After reading the words of Representative Richard Dwoling, what ISLLC Standards do you feel she mastered? Please explain your answer and be as specific as possible.
2. Likewise, what do you see as the advantages of national standards for future and practicing educational leaders?
3. Are the six ISLLC Standards, along with their knowledge, dispositions, and performances, adequate in sufficiently detailing effective educational leadership? Please explain your answer.
4. In review of the ISLLC Standards, which Standards do you feel best represent your leadership strengths? Which Standards represent your areas in need of improvement? Please explain your responses.
5. Let's say that one day you will be honored as Dr. Roberta Jimenez was, before your colleagues and country. What would you like to have mentioned about your leadership based on your achievement of which ISSLC National Standards, Knowledge, Dispositions, and Performances, and why? Please give professional and personal examples to help explain your response.

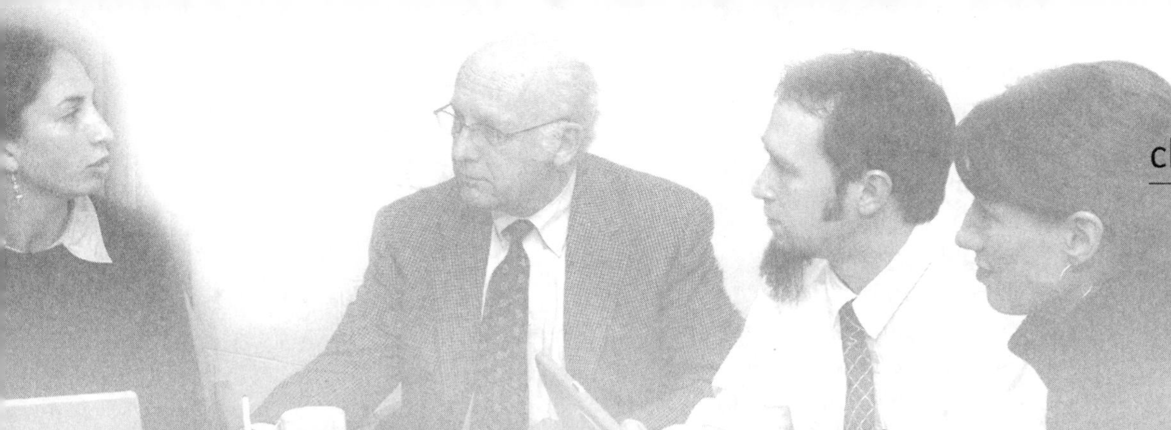

chapter **3**

ISLLC Standard 2

Navigating the High Cs—Climate, Culture, and Collaboration

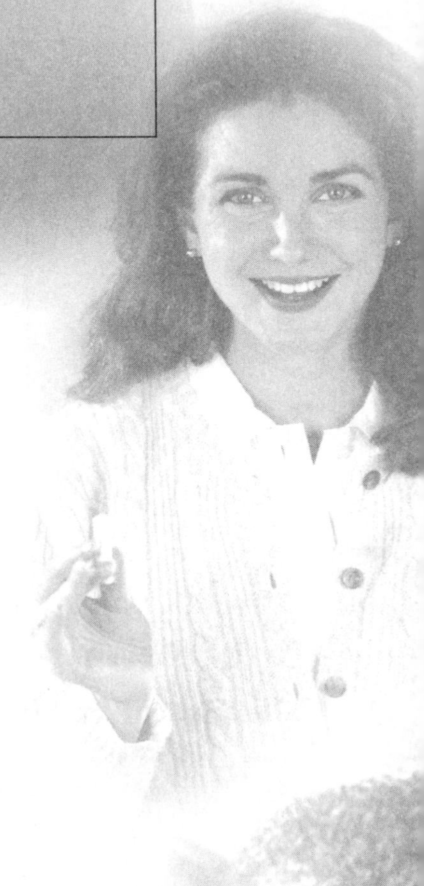

We discover our success as an educational leader through our relationships with others.

—Anonymous

You can "feel" the climate of a school as soon as you walk in the front door. The enthusiasm, cheerfulness, vitality, and welcoming relations of some schools are contagious. The climate of other schools may not be so invigorating. To set the stage for the importance of climate, culture, and collaboration, your Chapter 3 Action Focus invites you into Twenty-First-Century High School.

Welcome to Twenty-First-Century High School! We are located in a suburb of Bristol, Indiana, and educate 1,483 students in grades 9 through 12. Our school continues to experience annual student enrollment growth of approximately 12 percent annually. Approximately 40 percent of the student body is comprised of minority students, with 33 percent of students qualifying for a free or reduced lunch program. We have seventy-eight teachers and three administrators who serve students on practically a "shoe-string" budget.

Twenty-First-Century High School has been involved in a long-term, data-based school improvement process since 1993 to improve school climate and culture. The following school climate and culture imperatives have been established by our students, staff, parents, and community partners:

- We are student centered in all the decisions we make.
- Our school leaders are our instructional leaders.
- Our curriculum is based on the needs of our learners.
- The expectations for our students' achievement are realistically high.
- Our school is a "center of encouragement" for students, staff, and all others.
- Parents play an integral role in the education of their children, our students.
- Our collegiality and respect for one another is a hallmark of our faculty.

In addition to these imperatives, twelve norms enhancing the school climate and culture of Twenty-First-Century High School serve as the foundation for all actions of students, faculty, parents, and community members. These norms are:

1. Risk taking
2. Experimentation
3. Affirmation of one another as professionals
4. Trust and confidence
5. Tangible support
6. Data-driven decisions
7. Appreciation and recognition
8. Caring, celebration, and humor
9. Involvement in decision making
10. Selective abandonment of ineffective programs/practices
11. Maintenance of rich heritage and traditions
12. Honest, open communication

The twelve norms have helped us form what has been called our *professional family*. To illustrate this collaboration, teams are assembled to provide opportunities for students, teachers, parents, and community members to work together in a decision-making capacity to improve school conditions; therefore, school climate and culture are enhanced. Our staff, students, parents, and community believe a chief reason for our student achievement escalating from "cellar to stellar" is because of the tremendous gains in our imperatives and norms. The Twenty-First-Century High School welcomes visitors to stop by and share the positive edge evident where the school climate and culture are inviting and rich!

As illustrated in your Chapter 3 Action Focus, school culture and climate are essential to other school improvements. Before beginning the valuable lessons contained in Chapter 3, let's pause to visit Brookfield Elementary School.

IN THE NEWS

The End of an Era: Principal Says Farewell

One could literally feel the rich school culture when walking in the front door of Brookfield Elementary School.

With a tissue in her hand, Maxine Rithmire waved goodbye to the last Brookfield Elementary School busload of students. The students, with tears in their eyes, waved back and began in unison chanting that they would miss their principal. After thirty-two years, this successful twenty-first-century educational leader retired.

Rithmire commented on her last day in office that she felt proud of the wonderful culture that she and others established at Brookfield Elementary School. After all, Brookfield Elementary School was known for its child-enriched approach. The school was a center of encouragement for students, faculty, and parents. Volunteers were involved in meaningful activities and made wonderful contributions.

With Rithmire and thousands of others like her retiring, opportunities exist for aspiring principals to take the lead in developing rich school cultures similar to the established culture at Brookfield Elementary School.

Source: L. Diamond, "The End of an Era: Principal Says Farewell," *Atlanta Journal-Constitution,* December 1, 2005.

EDUCATIONAL LEADERS BEWARE: THE SCHOOLS—THEY ARE A-CHANGING

As prominent as school climate and culture are, as illustrated in Twenty-First-Century High School, too many educational leaders mistakenly overlook or minimize their importance. Educational leadership can no longer afford to underplay the impact of school climate and culture. Understanding and enhancing school climate and culture are essential keys for all educational leaders. Both climate and culture are vital to a school's quality of life and its ability to accomplish positive outcomes, including high achievement (Taylor, Pressley, & Pearson, 2002). In order for educational leaders to accomplish these desirable outcomes, they will need to become aware of and skillful in facilitating the powerful influence of school culture and climate.

Right from the onset and throughout this chapter, it is vital for today's successful educational leaders to have a clear understanding that school climate (institutional attributes) and school culture (psychological attributes) are the qualities that give an organization its personality (Bulach, Lunenburg, & McCallon, 1995). *Climate* consists of the environmental qualities within a school (such as opened or closed, warm or cold, easy-going or rigid, and friendly or hostile) and the attitudes of students, faculty, parents, and community members regarding these environmental qualities. *Culture* is the set of values, beliefs, traditions, and rituals built over time (Peterson & Deal, 1998). Both climate and culture have a vital relationship to one another. They are analogous to an iceberg, where the top part of the iceberg (environmental qualities) could not exist without the part that cannot be seen below the water (deep-rooted beliefs such as rites, rituals, heroes, and traditions).

Historical Perspectives of School Climate and Culture

Before educational leaders begin initiatives to improve school climate and culture, they need to gain a deep understanding of the magnitude of changes that have occurred historically in the climate and culture of U.S. schools. Starting with colonial times until the late nineteenth century, the context of schooling was little more than careful supervision by administrators who demanded conformity both in professional conduct and student behavior. Studies of the times revealed almost complete consistency of values within U.S. schools during this era (Hirsch, 1987).

During the post–Civil War period, instruction consisted mostly of transmitting factual information to rows of quiet, submissive students, many of whom were recent immigrants. Thus, the public schools in the United States functioned much like factories (Apple & King, 1983). Very little regard was given to the social, emotional, and physical needs of students. This paradigm was based on the "sit and get" paradigm that students were to sit compliantly, soak up every word of the teacher, and demonstrate (regurgitate) their mastery of taught material on a test.

From the late-nineteenth to mid-twentieth century, progressive educators such as John Dewey, William Kilpatrick, and Harold Rugg became the catalysts for changing public education in the United States. Religious teachings that were once common were largely removed from the public schools (Ryan, 1987) as courts held steadfast to Thomas Jefferson's assertion that there should be a wall of separation between church and state. As a direct result of this progressivism, teachers became uncomfortable with their traditional role as inculcators of values (Vallance, 1973). To adjust and share in this responsibility, the whole school population undertook the development of school climate and culture.

Beginning in the mid-1970s, the development of human resources management in business and industrial organizations began to strongly influence the practice of educational leadership. The scientific approach to educational goals—setting forth objectives in explicit, behavioral terms—was being challenged. This scientific approach in the management of schools was perceived as underestimating the importance of the dynamics of human interactions in educational performance.

In retrospect, if educational leaders are to neglect the fostering of rich climates and cultures, education in the twenty-first century will continue to be characterized by fractured relationships and a greater alienation of students. Closed, individualized, bureaucratic cultures typical of many schools have been unable to reverse these trends (Richardson, 2001). We have learned that collaboration within the schoolhouse is critical to meeting the individual needs of students and staff. Just as industry has moved away from mass production to mass customization, schools will need to similarly personalize the educational experiences of students and staff and to begin the restoration of relationships.

Regardless of numerous school improvement accomplishments in schools across the nation, unsatisfactory student achievement and violent student behavior continues. Due to the perceived failure of schools to improve, efforts to force change from outside education have led to an increasingly competitive market for education. The results of these forces have been home schooling, schools of choice, vouchers, charters, academies, and privatization of the enterprise. For public schools to compete with and succeed in the competition, educational leaders will need to build vibrant school climates and cultures that are enriching, encouraging, and motivating. There is no option!

Although school climate has been of interest since early colonial times, definitions and descriptions of school climate have been somewhat limiting. Research has interpreted *school climate* to be the atmosphere in a school. It consists of the attitudes shared by members of subgroups, such as students, faculty, and staff, and by the school population as a whole. Climate is generally considered to be positive or negative; some aspects of a school climate can be positive while others are negative. Factors that build or tear down school climate are presented in Table 3.1.

TABLE 3.1   Factors That Destroy or Create Positive School Climate

Factors That Destroy a Positive School Climate	Factors That Create A Positive School Climate
• Lack of effective leadership	• Sense of direction
• Lack of vision, mission, goals	• Positive attitude of faculty and administration
• Lack of firmness, fairness, and consistency	• Consistency and credibility
• Negative relations between school and community	• Positive, knowledgeable, energetic, and communicative leadership
• A continuous stream of controversy	• Removing fear and rewarding risk taking
• Highly bureaucratic management	• Team building where team members' decisions are not overridden
• Noncollaborative, noncooperative behaviors by school leaders	• Collaboration of individual groups
• Budget cuts of valued programs	• Adequate funding for programs and processes
• Using data for evaluation of school personnel rather than school improvement	• Fact finding and problem solving with maximized participation
• Disrespect for creativity and innovation	• Encouragement for creativity and innovation

Climate reflects what is happening today rather than the values, beliefs, and norms that have developed over a period of time (i.e., culture). Climate as an approach to school reform is rooted in the discipline of sociology, whereas culture is based on an anthropological approach. Climate and culture are similar in their powerful impact on a school and school district. Hence, the key to successful educational leadership is to respect, shape, and facilitate school climate and culture. Do not underestimate their powers!

WHY CLIMATE MATTERS

A plethora of studies have demonstrated the impact of school climate on morale, productivity, and satisfaction of persons involved in the organization (Hammond, 2000). These studies have revealed how staff, students, and community members feel about their school(s) and/or school district—whether it is a positive place to work and learn or one that is full of issues and conflict. When teachers feel good about their work, student achievement rises (Smith & Lindsay, 2001). Such studies as the effective schools research provide important keys for educational leaders in building positive school climates and cultures.

Effective Schools Research

Over twenty-five years ago a paper was written by James Coleman, a prominent education researcher who discussed the effectiveness, or lack thereof, of American education. Funded by the U.S. Office of Education, Coleman concluded that public schools have limited influence on student achievement. Coleman's report credited the student's family background as the main reason for student success in school (Smith & Stolp, 1995). He argued that children from poor families, broken homes, and dysfunctional families could not learn, regardless of what the school did. Coleman fanned the fires of other studies such as the effective schools research.

Ronald Edmonds, then director of the Center for Urban Studies at Harvard University, responded vigorously. Edmonds and others refused to accept Coleman's conclusions as final, although they acknowledged that family background does indeed make a difference. They searched and identified schools where students from low-income families were highly successful. Edmonds contended that schools can and do make a difference and that all children can learn.

Edmonds and other researchers examined the achievement data from large urban schools in several major cities—schools where students came from impoverished backgrounds. Across the nation, they found schools where poor children were learning. Although these findings contradicted Coleman's conclusion, Edmonds, Brookover, Lezotte, and other school researchers were left without an answer as to why students with similar backgrounds learned in certain schools but not others.

To answer this puzzling question, successful schools were compared to unsuccessful schools in similar neighborhoods. Suffice it to say, the success of a school was determined by the level of student achievement. Characteristics describing both types of schools were observed and documented. The findings of

TABLE 3.2 Essentials of Effective School Climate

- Staff members have a sense of purpose derived from a clear mission statement that is supported.
- A strategic plan to raise student achievement is established with administration, faculty, students, parents, and community members informed and involved.
- Teachers are empowered and feel a strong sense of efficacy.
- A school transformation has been brought forth by empowering students and staff on learning matters.
- Educational leaders are perceived as effective instructional leaders.
- High expectations for students are held and social promotion does not occur.
- Decisions are child centered.
- Well-organized, safe, orderly and secure schools are the rule.
- Parents and community members feel an engagement with the school and school system.

this comparative research were that school climate and culture make a significant difference in increasing student achievement.

Effective school researchers identified a number of climate- and culture-related essentials found in effective schools that were absent in schools with lower student achievement. The research of effective schools revealed that there were common essentials held by all successful schools. Table 3.2 presents these common essentials found in successful schools, or schools with higher levels of student achievement. The essentials are critical to today's educational leaders in improving and sustaining a productive and progressive school climate and culture. Everything flows from a commonly promoted vision statement, where all stakeholders understand and promote a common purpose. This impacts the cultural beliefs of an institution.

WHY CULTURE MATTERS

School culture, according to Fullan (2003), is the accumulation of many individuals' values, beliefs, and norms. It is the consensus about what is important over the long haul, with changes in culture taking just about as long to change as to form. It is the group's expectations, not just an individual's expectations. It is the way everyone does business.

School culture can also be described by the stories of a school revealing the way things are done. Examples of a school's culture can be found in the school's celebrations, customs, and traditions. Sergiovanni (1995) offers still another description of culture in general terms:

> School culture includes values, symbols, beliefs, and shared meanings of parents, students, teachers, and others conceived as a group or community. Culture governs what is of worth for this group and how members should think, feel, and behave. The "stuff" of culture includes a school's customs and traditions; historical accounts; stated and unstated understandings, habits, norms, and expectations; common meanings; and shared assumptions. The more understood, accepted, and cohesive the culture of a school, the better able it is to move in concert toward ideals it holds and objectives it wishes to pursue. (p. 89)

Successful twenty-first-century educational leaders have the ability to perceive a school's culture as the sum of several core values. Examples of collaborative culture include a school mission statement and leadership protocols. Shared leadership, relationships based on mutual respect and caring, collegiality, and a focus on performance and improvement, are additional core values in a collaborative culture (Peterson & Deal, 1998).

The culture of a school has escalated in importance since the advent of the accountability era and high-stakes assessment. School stakeholders have implemented a variety of improved culture efforts to achieve school improvement and promote higher levels of student achievement. In a democratic society, schools reflect the character of the culture. Many educators and researchers alike are discovering a "missing link" in the school improvement conundrum (Wagner & Hall-O'Phalen, 1998). This missing link is directly connected to culture. School culture is an important, but often overlooked, component to increasing student achievement through the implementing of school improvements (Freiberg, 1998; Levine & LeZotte, 1995; Peterson & Deal, 1998; Phillips, 1993; Sizer, 1988).

Beliefs centered on school improvement emphasize an individual's attainment of skills, almost to say "To improve schools, improve individual educators." This belief is based on the notion that individual professional development is the way to school improvements. However, in reality, negative cultures overwhelm the best teachers and increase teacher departures.

IN THE NEWS

Why Good Schools Are Counterculture

In a democratic society, schools reflect the character of the culture.

With all the spotlights on educational reform, we might just pause and shine a light on ourselves: In a democratic society, schools reflect the character of the culture. If we are unhappy with the character of culture, we may wish to turn to those schools that are countercultural—and allow more such schools to come into existence and flourish. If, in the garden of good and evil, flowers and weeds coexist, perhaps we should allow more flowers to bloom.

Successful twenty-first-century educational leaders work diligently to improve their school culture.

Source: P. F. Bassett, "Why Good Schools Are Counterculture," *Education Week,* February 6, 2002.

The paradigm of individual professional growth to school improvements has given way to a more culture-centered approach toward professional development in fostering collegial teaming—sharing and growing together—to enhance the school setting. Teaming leads to a collaborative community, greater productivity, and a sense of fulfillment among the people of a unit, department, company, or organization (Smith & Lindsay, 2001). Educational leaders should bear in mind that the key to improved student outcomes is based on improvements in the school culture.

Most successful school leaders will tell you that getting the culture right and paying attention to how parents, teachers, and students define and experience meaning are two widely accepted rules for creating effective schools (Sergiovanni, 2000a). Again, educational leaders are well served in being attentive to cultural values and how cultural values are manifested in school rituals, traditions, and stories.

Developing Collaborative Cultures

Educational leaders are wise to view culture as a jigsaw puzzle. The numerous individual pieces that are positioned together represent the interdependent core cultural values. If an educational leader attempts to get a better view of the puzzle by taking apart the pieces to look at them individually, he or she will lose sight of the entire puzzle. Similarly, if an educational leader tries to analyze a school culture by separating the core values and looking at each separately, he or she will lose sight of the entire culture. The key to understanding a culture of a school is through holistic vision. Through the lenses of holistic binoculars, educational leaders will discover a culture that is comprised of three interrelated parts: creating relationships, relevance, and responsibility.

Building Effective Relationships. Collaborative school cultures include visible, positive relationships and partnerships within and outside the school system. As a result of the trends leading into the twenty-first century and the resulting competitive educational environment, school culture must be more student centered in an effort to meet the needs of individual students. Relationships based on the beliefs that all students can learn and that teachers are responsible for student learning are fundamental in a collaborative culture.

Traditionally, teachers have done their work in isolation from the world beyond school as well as in relative isolation from colleagues (Hammond, 2000). Teachers who are accustomed to working alone must develop the mind-set to seek out partnering opportunities and the skills to make restorative partnerships work. In addition, teaching should focus on meeting individual student needs by developing multiple relationships with parents, social workers, psychiatrists, and other significant people in the child's life.

Effective relationships are at the core of a positive culture. Traditional school cultures inhibit collaborative relationships by isolating teachers from one another and by enabling a lack of respect between teachers and students. Schools that are committed to fostering productive relationships encourage teachers and students to team with each other as well as all others.

Fostering Relevance. Educational leaders need to provide guidance so that the instruction and curriculum are meaningful and relevant to student needs, both present and future. Relevance, meaning, and importance are essential to culture. A positive culture is characterized by work that motivates students because that work is relevant. Cynicism, poor student performance, strained relationships, and alienation from school are symptoms of a damaged school culture. The key to successful twenty-first-century leadership is for educational leaders to encourage teachers, support staff, students, parents, and the community to work together to create meaningful learning experiences for students. To this end, there is no alternative!

Sharing Responsibility. The third component of culture—responsibility—includes both the students' responsibility to learn and the school's responsibility for student learning. In such a school culture, students, staff, and parents act responsibly with each other. A culture based on responsibility rejects making excuses and pointing the guilty finger at one another. A culture based on responsibility emphasizes that each individual accepts responsibility for his or her actions and in turn receives the full support of others.

In an effort to improve school culture, educational leaders must persevere, with staff going beyond surface reform efforts and earnestly focusing on school culture. The bureaucratic school culture familiar in many school districts must give way to collaborative cultures established on relationships, relevance, and responsibility. The transformation to an improved culture will occur only with a sustained, focused effort on the part of the entire school community. The first key in this transformational process is for the educational leadership to be committed to building healthier relationships, followed immediately by training key school community members in the concepts of improved practices. A community in which young people are held accountable while being supported where they learn appropriate behavior without stigmatization is crucial (Ysseldyke & Christensen, 1993–96).

Principal Attributes for Culturally Effective Schools

School leaders shape the school culture by the things they pay attention to in the day-to-day life of the school. Where school culture is conducive to positive student gains, principals are aware of and attending to the 3 Rs. In addition, principals in culturally effective schools also demonstrate managerial, leadership, and general attributes that foster positive school climate, as presented in Table 3.3. Support, shared vision, and fair and consistent leadership seem to be keys of differentiation between a manager and a leader. A manager does the right thing; a leader does the things right.

In addition to the attributes of principals in culturally effective schools, several additional qualities need to be clearly understood. Good communication from the school leader(s) enhances culture by helping the staff feel they are part of a team (Gonder & Hymes, 1994). A kind word is nearly as valuable as hard currency, as teachers are profoundly motivated by the positive and often immediate feedback they receive (Ciruli Associates, 2002). This positive reinforcement supports the positive culture by building morale (Gonder & Hymes, 1994). Today's successful educational leaders know that in order to increase student achievement, the school culture needs to be positive (Bulach, 2001; Gallimore & Goldenberg, 2001; Gonder & Hymes, 1994).

TABLE 3.3   Exemplars of Principals in Culturally Effective Schools

Managing Exemplars	Leading Exemplars	General Exemplars
Manages operations	Instructional leadership	High expectations
Lives by "my way or the highway"	Staff builds vision	Shared decision making
Administers by instructions for others	Effective listener	Effective communication
Rules by the book	Individual basis for decisions	Professional accord
Disciplines when necessary	Rewards/recognizes others	Accountability
Presents objective, firm manner	Caring and considerate	Professional support and accord
Determines solutions to concerns	Positive response to concerns	Visible and dependable
Provides solutions	Collaborative and consensus building	Problem solving

KEYS TO BUILDING AND ENHANCING SCHOOL CLIMATE AND CULTURE

The key to building school climate and culture is for educational leaders to build a common vision. To create a school vision, school leaders must empower faculty members to change procedures and practices of the school. Faculty members need to feel confident in their ability to improve their performance, think critically, and gather data about where the school is at present. Strong convictions need to be communicated and used to guide school improvements.

Parents and teachers have the most direct contact with children. Educational leaders need to provide increased opportunity for teachers to help resolve learning issues. Teachers do not see themselves as belonging to an organization; rather, they feel they are at the outer reaches of a large bureaucracy (Donahoe, 1993). Traditional school has minimized collegial behavior among teachers. In an organization, the values and interests of all members are not always addressed, and this leaves many students and staff, once again, on the outside (Smith & Stolp, 1995).

Historically, the nature of the teaching profession has created a climate and culture where teachers' voices have not been heard. Teachers are psychologically alone, even though they are in a densely populated setting (Sarason, 1982). In any debate about school reform and improvement, the effectiveness of the teacher/ student relationship is frequently overlooked (Chaskin & Rauner, 1995). These concerns raise the question of how this situation can be remedied. In defining school climate and culture, it is key that educational leaders provide opportunities for all stakeholders to voice their thoughts, beliefs, and concerns. Teachers need to be empowered to make a difference in school culture and feel that they are "valued ambassadors" (Lane, 1992). Educational leaders must work diligently to transform a core of teachers into embracing the norms, values, and beliefs of a school climate and culture to encourage the critical mass of the staff to begin to follow suit.

Although all faculty members should be made to feel empowered to share in decision making, the role and the responsibility of enhancing school climate and culture rest greatly on school leadership. Indeed, no other school position has greater potential for maintaining and improving quality schools (Sergiovanni, 1995). This view of the principalship is echoed by other researchers as well. Only principals can provide the initial leadership needed to restructure and reculture the schools for problem solving (Peterson & Deal, 1998; Sizer, 1988; Smith & Lindsay, 2001). In other words, culture building is not meant to imply that the principal single-handedly constructs the school culture. Rather, it is meant to describe the principal's efforts to influence or shape the existing values and norms of the culture in a direction that best supports instructional effectiveness (Lane, 1992).

The principal is in the best position to orchestrate the blending of various internal and external elements into a coherent and accepted shared vision (Smith & Lindsay, 2001). Experienced principals may be the most capable people to assist with that necessary reflection-on-action that enlightens beginning principals (Roberts, 1993). In addition, it would appear necessary for the aspiring principal to have a personal belief system that can be incorporated into the new school culture.

Another challenge to educational leaders in the formation of school climate and culture is that school culture is faced with the challenge of trying to meet everyone's needs. Donahoe (1993), for example, explicates the historical changes facing schools since the 1960s:

> Those changes seem to fall into four categories: growth, diversity, inclusion, and social dislocations. First is the mismatch between growth and resources. Classrooms, schools, and sometimes districts are too large. They have grown beyond human scale for effective teaching, learning, and the management of these activities. Second is the phenomenal expansion of ethnic, linguistic, and cultural diversity in the classroom and the school. Third is the expectation of full inclusiveness. We have come to believe that all children can learn and should stay in school to do so. Fourth is the set of social changes or dislocations that have occurred over the past three decades: single-parent families, latchkey children, poverty and poor health, drugs, gangs and violence. (p. 301)

If school climate and cultural building and enhancing are to take place, educational leaders must first build schools that are centers of encouragement for all. Caring and nurturing will need to be so much more than words. These are values that have their roots in family relationships before they are brought to school. Schools should be seen as the "primary arenas" for caring and nurturing (Chaskin & Rauner, 1995). For lasting enhancements in school climate and culture, these crucial values must be grounded in relationships.

If school climate and culture are to be encompassing, faculty will need to reach out and welcome parents, community members, and all others. Visitors to the school need to be comfortable, heard, and understood. This level of encouragement is key so that all members of the school community are committed to excellence (Smith & Lindsay, 2001). Perhaps the best way to begin is to encourage an atmosphere where staff and students are comfortable offering visionary ideas (Smith & Lindsay, 2001).

Little research exists on parents and their influence on school culture. Recently, however, there has been an increase in such research because of the advent of school councils and parents' increasingly important roles within schools. Two potential problems with increased parental involvement exists that school leaders need to become aware of. One is the danger of special-interest groups forming in schools. These special-interest groups could have an unequal influence in schools and sway decisions in their favor, thus affecting school culture in a negative way. The second issue is that educational leaders will need to educate parents about the workings of schools so that they will understand the implications of their decisions on the school population as a whole.

If school climate and culture are to be transformed, the actual structure and organization of schools will need to change (Donahoe, 1993). The greatest impediment to improved school climate and culture may very well be the mere organizational structure of school.

Improving school climate and culture needs to be a high priority for all educational leaders. Research has revealed that the academic achievement of students is significantly higher in the schools where teachers recorded the highest levels of professional treatment than in schools where teachers recorded the lowest levels of professional treatment for three of the fours years studied (Gonder & Hymes, 1994). This proclamation should motivate educational leaders to work diligently to implement school climate initiatives.

First, the successful improving of school climate and culture by educational leaders needs input and support from its constituents. People who feel empowered tend to have higher morale. They are more personally invested in their work with an organization when they have a voice in what happens to them and when their work has meaning and significance in contributing to a higher purpose or goal (Lumsden, 1998). Without maximizing the participation of others, the development of climate and culture will be limited.

Second, good communication strategies are necessary to ensure that everyone becomes aware of the district's values and expectations and understands the role they play in improving the overall climate and culture (Berman, 1987). Another key to success in improving climate and culture is to establish a methodology that discovers and acknowledges others doing great deeds. Educational leaders should maximize gains through new employee orientations, which will provide an additional focus of the school's climate and culture. In addition, the educational leaders should institute many avenues of communication such as a website, weekly bulletins, faculty meetings, and department newsletters.

Educational leaders need to keep in mind that if employees feel they are not valued, they are "left in the dark" about what is happening in the school or district (Gonder & Hymes, 1994). Conversely, people who are rewarded have better morale and develop the needed motivation to perform at a high level (Ellenberg, 1972; Fredericks, 2001; Ingersoll, 2001a, 2001b; Johnson, 1998). In addition, people who feel needed, wanted, or appreciated can develop the type of morale that increases their level of performance (Lumsden, 1998). Therefore, educational leaders need to build on existing models of recognition and reward, such as student and teacher awards. Other forms of recognition include memos of recognition, personal letters of gratitude, certificates of achievement, and other sincere forms of appreciation.

IN THE NEWS

Grove Schools Win $500,000 Eli Broad Prize in National Contest

A change in a school district's climate and culture becomes the winning combination.

The five years of diligence and dedication in the Garden Grove Unified School District to improve student achievement despite poverty and language hurdles literally was rewarded. Garden Schools was recently awarded $500,000 from billionaire philanthropist Eli Broad's foundation. The school district was recognized as the most accomplished of the nation's impoverished urban school districts. Nearly all of Garden Grove's 66 schools met or exceeded performance targets mandated by No Child Left Behind.

If one improvement could be singled out as the catalyst for Garden Grove Unified School District's improvement in student learning, it would more than likely be the change in the district's climate and culture. Superintendent Laura Schwalm credits her school district's teachers who had to make some tough changes over the past few years in order to get everyone aligned and focused on the same goals, beliefs, and attitudes. This has meant many Garden Grove teachers dropping old classroom habits in favor of lesson plans based on data from student testing and state-mandated academic standards. In turn, Garden Grove teachers credited Schwalm with fostering what they call a rare climate and culture.

As superintendent Schwalm earned the respect and support of those she led, so too will other educational leaders venturing to improve culture and climate.

Source: J. Rubin, "Grove Schools Win $500,000 Eli Broad Prize in National Contest," *Los Angeles Times,* September 21, 2005.

Administrators can improve school climate and student achievement by understanding their roles in the school environment and working to improve them. Successful principals encourage risk taking and support good attempts. When principals back teachers, when they are fair and trustworthy, and when they are genuinely concerned about teacher growth, teachers go the extra mile (Sweeney, 1992). School leaders shape school climate by the things they pay attention to in the day-to-day life of the school. Principals need to be aware of and attend to the factors of respect, responsiveness, recognition, relationships, rites, and responsibilities. For example, giving positive feedback to staff promotes an achievement-oriented culture. This reinforces behavior that should be encouraged and focuses on the good things that are happening at school, while reducing and ideally eliminating discipline infractions, vandalism, and violent acts.

Profiles of Success

In summation, keep the following profiles of success in mind.

- Schools with positive climates and cultures are places where people care, respect, and trust one another and where the school as an institution cares, respects, and trusts people. In such a school, people feel a high sense of pride and ownership that comes from each individual having a role in making the school a better place.
- Schools with positive climates and culture are constantly changing as people reshape them in accordance with human needs. These schools are responsive to the times. There is a synergy that staff members feel. The faculty realizes that a team of educators is far greater than any single individual. In schools, school improvement is everybody's business.
- Schools with positive climates and culture are cohesive places. People know what their school stands for. In such schools the social groups (cliques) communicate with one another, respect one another, and work with one another for school improvement.
- Schools with positive climates and cultures are responsive to human needs. Procedures, rules, regulations, and policies serve the people in the school. Educational leaders know that education is a people business and "happy campers" stay where they are appreciated and go the extra mile for students and each other.

We have now had enough experience with climate and culture improvement to suspect that nothing improves until the school climate and culture does. How people see their school can either facilitate or sabotage change. School curriculum and instructional development is fueled by faculty members' emotions.

As the climate of the school becomes more positive, some highly undesirable symptoms of poor climate tend to disappear. Discipline problems, vandalism, defacing of property, and violence subside. Attendance and achievement improve. The number of dropouts declines. People smile more, are more respectful and helpful to others, and assume more responsibility for the well-being of the school.

THE REFLECTIVE PRACTITIONER

This Reflective Practitioner is based on the ISLLC Standards and what you have read in Chapter 3. It is intended to provoke your thoughtful reflection and to stimulate discussion among colleagues, classmates, and peers. The Reflective Practitioner provides opportunities to synthesize issues, make comparisons, and apply theory to practice. We hope it will motivate you to search for evidence, thus increasing your comprehension of the readings and helping you to examine your convictions and discover new and shared perspectives.

ISLLC Standard 2
A school administrator is an educational leader who promotes the success of all students by advocating, nurturing, and sustaining a school culture and instructional program conducive to student learning and staff professional growth.

Scenario

Central Elementary School is a large K–6 urban elementary school with a student population of 1,800 students. Over the past eight years, the school has experienced high faculty turnover, high faculty absenteeism, and low staff morale. This has led to an increase in student discipline problems and a decrease in student achievement. In fact, four students brought weapons to school last school year.

In an attempt to reverse this trend and build improved school climate and culture, Superintendent Johnson has appointed you to be the principal of Central Elementary School. He knows that you were instrumental as the assistant principal of Twenty-First-Century High School in promoting positive school climate and culture, leading to significant gains in staff morale and student achievement. He prizes your successful years of elementary teaching before you were appointed as the assistant principal at Twenty-First-Century High School. His final words to you are: "Whatever you do, increase morale and get those test scores up!"

You are appreciative of the superintendent's confidence in you and you are willing to take on this challenge to increase Central Elementary School's climate and culture. To help prepare you to be principal of Central Elementary School, please respond to the following questions.

QUESTIONS FOR REFLECTIVE THINKING

1. Based on your reading of Chapter 3, what actions would you take to improve the school climate and culture at Central Elementary School in efforts to improve staff morale?
2. If Central Elementary School were to improve school climate and culture based on the effective schools research, what programs, policies, and procedures would need to be implemented?
3. What keys to building and enhancing school climate and culture might be extremely beneficial in guiding you to improve school climate and culture at Central Elementary School?
4. In planning for your first staff meeting, what would you include on the agenda under school climate and culture as presented in "Keys to Understanding School Culture"? Please explain your response.
5. Create a realistic time line describing the school climate and culture changes you would implement along with the estimated time it would take to transform Central Elementary School to your level of satisfaction. Please explain your response fully.

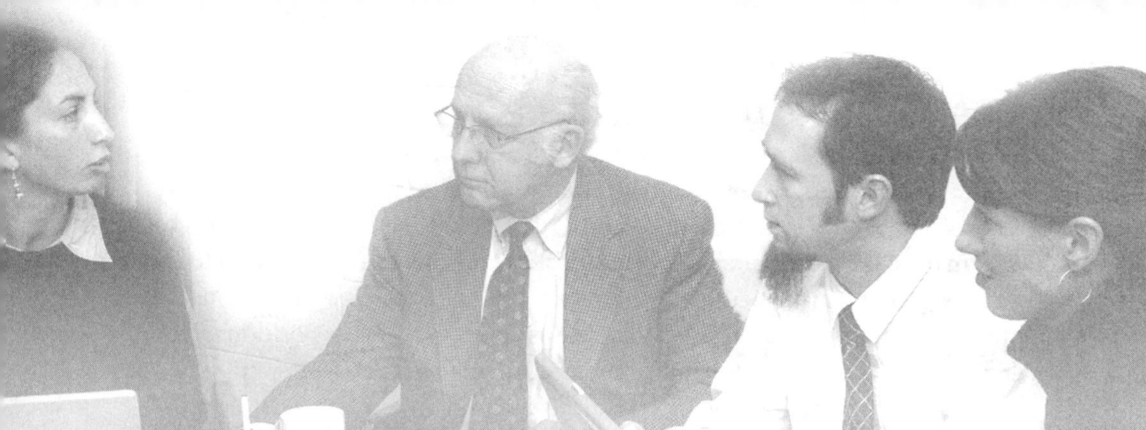

chapter 4

ISLLC
Standard
5

Successful Leadership Begins with You

The greater the obstacle, the more glory in overcoming it!
—Molière

Your Chapter 4 Action Focus brings to light the importance of interpersonal leadership skills.

It was one of those days, beginning in the wee hours of the morning with feelings of so much to do and so little time, no lunch, and meeting after meeting. The saving grace of the day was yet to come—the teaching of an introductory educational leadership class to thirty aspiring graduate students highly motivated to move forward in their careers.

As always, the three-hour class seemed to fly by. Students were grasping the numerous and diversified theories of educational leadership as evidenced by their contributions to class discussions, the critical questions they posed, and their active and spirited participation during small-group activities. They never ceased to amaze with their energy, especially considering that they were not full-time students, classes took place at the end of their working day, and their "get up and go" seemed revived each class period. In short, their enthusiasm, so contagious and energizing, was commendable.

Before class was over, students were reminded of their term paper assignments due next session, thanked for a great class, and wished a productive week. Before retiring for the evening, a quick e-mail check:

> Thank you for another great class tonight on the theories of leadership. Your enthusiasm and knowledge of the subject matter means much to us—future principals, curriculum leaders, technology directors, and other educational leaders. A number of us were talking after your class tonight and thought we would ask you if you would tell us the way it really is! That is, please give us advice that would help us become successful educational leaders. Help us examine our own personal and professional values. We recognize your success in the educational leadership positions you have held as a teacher, curriculum director, principal, and superintendent. Would you please share with us how it really is, especially interpersonal skills building! Please know we do appreciate all the theory we are learning and see its purpose and relevance. However, we believe that your thirty years of educational leadership experience is most valuable to us.

Reflecting on three decades of K–12 educational leadership and discussing real-world experiences and perspectives can make a difference in the professional lives of future educational leaders. Clearly, a little conventional wisdom mixed in with the academic side of leadership (e.g., Bennis & Nanus, 1985; Deal & Peterson, 2000; Drucker, 2002; Goleman, 2000; Goleman, Boyzatzis, & McKee, 2002) is extremely useful to the professional development of new leaders. Education is one of the few professions that relies more on book knowledge than experience as apprentices for its positions. The following is what the professor told his students during the next class session.

"Clearly, educational leadership positions are undeniably the most demanding and rewarding careers in education. Whether you are pursuing a leadership position in administration, curriculum, special education, technology, or any other area of education, you are needed. Interestingly, there are not long lines behind you pursuing these positions today. We thank you for your interest in taking the reins in your respective fields.

"As educational leaders, you will be in charge of our nation's greatest investment—our children. You will need to consider the interests of children and others whom you lead above self-interests, as stipulated in ISLLC Standard 5: A school administrator is an educational leader who promotes the success of all students by acting with integrity, fairness, and in an ethical manner. More specifically, your responsibilities as an administrator are established under the performances presented under ISLLC Standard 5, which include, but are not limited to: examining personal and professional values; demonstrating a personal and professional code of ethics; demonstrating values, beliefs, and attitudes that inspire others to higher levels of performance; serving as a role model; and treating people fairly, equitably, and with dignity and respect."

The professor went on to exemplify and affirm through his own practical wisdom how and why educational leaders need to act with integrity, fairness, and in an ethical manner.

Your Chapter 4 Action Focus reflects the importance of how successful educational leadership begins with you.

TO BE OR NOT TO BE, THAT IS THE QUESTION

Educational leadership is a tough job. The length of service for most positions is shorter today than years ago. Of course, there are a number of important personal skills that will benefit anyone who is, or aspires to become, an educational leader. We make no claim of originality in the identification of these and no guarantees about success. With gratitude and apologies to the Bard of Avon, our intent is simply to share a few personal keys to successful twenty-first-century educational leadership with you, the reader, as we have already shared with numerous future and current educational leaders.

To Thine Own Self Be True

It is critical for all educational leaders to develop a clear understanding of self (Sergiovanni, 2000a; Zaccaro, 2001). This includes understanding values, assets, and limitations as a leader, and commitment to students. Successful educational leaders need to develop clear and confident self-portraits that reflect what they can and will do.

The discovery of self as an educational leader is a never-ending journey, not a destination. The more you understand your role as an educational leader, the more successful and effective you will be in leading others. It is knowledge of self that helps an individual understand his/her dispositions and why and how he/she responds to people and challenges in the organization (DuBrin, 1996). Only when leaders are aware of their own beliefs do they become sensitive to the needs of others (McCowin, Arnold, Miles, & Hargodine, 2000). When they are sensitive to the needs of others, those who are led will contribute maximally to organizational goals, assuring the leader's success!

We, the authors, have constructed and implemented an exercise for educational leaders that exemplifies discovery of self. Select six qualities from the following list that are indicative of you as a leader. After selecting your "six pack," take a few minutes to think about the qualities that you selected and the reasons you selected each of them.

IN THE NEWS

Schools' Chief Suits Up for His Seasonal Job: Working as Part-Time Santa Fills Jim Watson's Schedule—and Heart

The more you as an educational leader come to grips with your convictions, the more successful and effective you will be in leading others.

Jim Watson, Lincoln County Schools Superintendent, brings good cheer to more than a dozen schools, churches, YMCAs, and neighborhoods each December playing Santa Claus. Watson has been a part-time Santa since 1998, a year after he took the reins for 11,867 students enrolled in 21 schools.

The responsibilities of Santa Claus are not taken lightly by Watson. He knows he has to meet the expectations of children and their parents. To succeed here, he knows he has to be a good listener and speak carefully. Above all, he understands his role as Santa means providing opportunities for others to relive their Christmas memories and to create new lasting thoughts.

Watson and other successful twenty-first-century educational leaders have a clear image of self, are sensitive to the needs of others, and are not hesitant to express what they value both on and off the job.

Source: J. DePriest, "Schools Chief Suits Up for His Seasonal Job—Working as Part-Time Santa Fills Jim Watson's Schedule—and Heart," *Charlotte Observer,* December 16, 2005.

I Am

Adventuresome	Fun	Playful
Approachable	Futuristic	Practical
Artistic	Generous	Precise
Capable	Gentle	Responsible
Caring	Genuine	Romantic
Communicative	Harmonious	Sensible
Compassionate	Helpful	Sensitive
Competitive	Imaginative	Skillful
Courageous	Independent	Spiritual
Curious	Innovative	Spontaneous
Dependable	Inventive	Supportive
Detailed	Knowledgeable	Thorough
Encouraging	Logical	Unique
Excited	Observant	Useful
Faithful	Optimistic	Versatile
Free	Organized	Warm
Friendly	Physical	Wise

Sharing the six qualities you selected and the reasons for your selections with others will help illustrate the importance of knowing yourself. There are plenty of other inventories, surveys, and questionnaires that can assist you in this awareness. You will need to acquire an understanding of self and your behavior to achieve effective relations with others. Otherwise, your continuous errors as an educational leader will erode the support of your followers. Hence, it is extremely important for you to know your convictions so that your beliefs can positively influence the beliefs and behaviors of others (Hammel, 2002; Siegrist, 1999). Again, know yourself (that's what you value) and act accordingly and consistently.

Likewise, your success as an educational leader in the twenty-first century will be dependent on coming to grips with your convictions and leading consistently and continuously. Colleagues and co-workers are more accepting of convictions and decisions rather than putting up with a leader who is arbitrary, cannot make a decision, or worse yet tells different things to different people.

Many years ago, a retiring superintendent shared a brief written message (author unknown) with a new principal. The statement is all about personal and professional conviction. Share it with someone you know:

Promise Yourself

Promise yourself to be so strong that nothing can prevent you from leading and achieving. To see the good in each person you meet. To make each person you meet feel important. To look on the positive side of all things no matter what the opposition may be, and to work diligently to make your dreams become your realities. To think only of the best, to work only for the best, and to expect only the best. To be just as happy about the success of others as you are about your own. To forget the mistakes of the past and press on to greater things of the future. To wear a cheerful smile at all times. To give so much time to the improvement of yourself that you have no time to criticize others. To be too large for worry, too noble for anger, too strong for fear, and too happy to permit the presence of trouble.

At your deepest and darkest times of challenge, call on your own promise to see you through. When your decisions go awry, when others disappoint you, and when you stare opposition in the face, keep your pledge to yourself first and foremost. Realize that how you react at the most difficult times of your professional life will reveal your leadership character (Tirozzi, 2001; Webb, 1990). The next personal key to successful educational leadership is set the example for others to follow.

Neither a Borrower nor a Lender Be

Once you are true to yourself as an educational leader, your actions must consistently support your beliefs. This may sound simple, but striking the right balance of respect, dignity, fairness, and consistency is both an art and a science for successful twenty-first-century educational leadership.

As problems grow, your leadership will continue to be challenged. School violence, student underachievement, sensationalized media reports, and a myriad of other attacks often test the patience and skills of the greatest leaders. These tests often result in burnout, causing promising professionals to leave the field. The antidote to these hazards of our profession lies in the ability to inspire trust, gain loyalty, attain commitment, and build collegiality among others. These qualities of relationships will be the glue that binds you to those you will lead, even at the most difficult times.

Again, the greatest building of binding relationships will not be found in what you say but rather in what you do. As an educational leader, you will need to demonstrate for others what is important through your actions. It is critical for you to know that your actions as an educational leader will determine the thoughts and actions of others. Proclamations without performance generally do not produce positive outcomes. If a principal calls for increased morale but does nothing to make it happen, change will be slow to come and improved morale may never be a part of the school.

Setting an example manifests itself in numerous actions. As the educational leader, you will need to demonstrate to others how to keep their cool in crisis situations and remain calm as panic occurs and tempers flare. In addition, your actions need to be true to your words; that is, do what you said you would do— to the letter! Nothing undermines the trust others have in their leader more than empty commitments. In setting the example for others to follow, there are eleven commandments to successful twenty-first-century educational leadership. The eleven commandments presented in Key Box 4.1 have been developed by theorists and others stated by the authors.

KEY BOX 4.1

The Eleven Commandments to Successful Twenty-First-Century Educational Leadership

1. Assume responsibility for your own actions. If you are unsuccessful, don't blame others. Set the example for others by owning up to your shortcomings, learning from them, and forming a plan of improved action for the future.
2. Assume responsibility for your emotional reactions (Cherniss & Adler, 2000; Goleman et al., 2002). It's not what happens to you that matters; it's what it means to you that determines your actions. Stand back and put matters in perspective.
3. Identify the potential in others. Remember, those you lead will tend to live up to your expectations of them (Kelleher, 2001). Set this example for all others to observe and hopefully follow. The potential and expectations as set by you, the educational leader, determine the accomplishments of those you lead.
4. Be positive! Your enthusiasm will be contagious—so will your lack thereof. If those you lead are going to develop a positive, can-do attitude, you will need to set the example.
5. Be available and visible to your staff. Communicate with those you lead as regularly and frequently as possible. This may mean saving federal and state reports until the end of the day. A presumption of an "open-door policy" is that others will walk through it to communicate. Establishing professional rapport with those you lead is more apt to take place away from your office in a more natural, inviting, and nonthreatening environment.

---

6. Treat others with empathy and respect—no matter what. Gain the self-respect that comes from doing the right thing, without regard to what others do. Keep in mind that obstacles are those frightful things you see when you take your eyes off your goals.
7. Leave your ego outside the school door. If you think it is your way or the highway, you may end up being the one who travels. Pride, ego, and self-centeredness are impediments to improvements (Greenleaf, 1998). Your leadership of others is dependent on your understanding and support of their goals when aligned with agreed educational outcomes.
8. Support others in public; discipline in private. Perhaps there is nothing more powerful than well-deserved praise nor as destructive as disciplining those you lead in public. Exemplify this key consistently and hold others accountable in doing the same.
9. Set an example—be a high performer. Work hard and smart. Others will model your leadership.
10. Be honest with yourself and your followers. Realize that eventually people who follow your lead will know you for who you are. Be open to their criticism and learn from it; after all, a mind is like a parachute—neither works when closed.
11. Set the example for others to follow based on someone you admire. That is not to say you should become a clone of another leader, as you will fail miserably in attempting to be someone you are not. However, emulate the quality characteristics of those who have inspired you.

In the final counting, educational leaders are responsible for someone else's performance. Those you lead may not follow your example at all times, opting instead to do things their own way. Sometimes they will make mistakes. Although those you lead are responsible to you for their mistakes, you need to lead by example that it is not your way or the highway. You should hold others accountable; however, at the same time you should encourage alternative approaches to the same needs. By setting an example for those you lead to follow, they in turn will provide innovative and creative opportunities for those they lead, coach, and serve.

And Lead Us All to Meditation

The bureaucratic model of leadership is quite simple. The boss told employees what to do and they complied. No one worried then if somebody's feelings were hurt along the way. Employees who failed to follow orders were issued ultimatums or terminated. Bureaucrats believed their authority should be obeyed at all times. Employees acted accordingly and without question. Fear dominated the work setting and the system was efficient—at least that is the story we have been told.

RESEARCH KEYS

To enrich your understanding of **bureaucrat,** log on to www.researchnavigator.com and search Ebsco's ContentSelect.

Research Navigator.com

Although fear as a management style can accomplish short-term gains, the long-term consequences can be devastating. With demand high and supply short of teachers and other school professionals, no educational leader today can afford to alienate others (Burnard, 1996; McDowelle, 2000; Skaalvik & Skaalvik, 2002). Disgruntled educators may vent their frustrations by being rude to students, parents, and community stakeholders. In addition, educators who are treated unfairly perform minimally, quit, or complain to upper leadership. Some educational leaders may even face lawsuits for treating their followers unfairly.

Although many autocratic managers still remain in some schools, today's educational reforms demanding higher efficiency and productivity will eventually drive them out of education. In short, motivational educational leadership produces improved long-term results. If you focus on positive reinforcements rather than fear and intimidation, you are far more likely to become a successful educational leader in the twenty-first century.

Your motivational leadership will allow you to assist or coach those you lead to maximize their potentials. Your coaching of those you lead should have four primary goals: (1) to promote honesty and integrity; (2) to ensure that the legitimate interests of those you lead are promoted as aligned to the school or school district's mission; (3) to encourage transparent and continuous communication among those you lead and between those you lead and you, their leader; and (4) to seek to develop channels of input that keep you firmly rooted in the needs and aspirations of those you lead.

At times, you will question your coaching outlook as an educational leader. Fear will play havoc with your convictions. Your fears of failing, fears of personal connections, and fears of losing control will continue to challenge your coaching philosophy. Even a belief that the short-term results are more important than the long-term development of team members will threaten your commitment to coach those you lead.

To achieve successful educational leadership based on coaching you will need to guide and support those you lead (Bradshaw, 2000; Daresh, 1997). You will need to set clear standards and expect the best. In addition, your success as a coach will be found in your leadership that is heart to heart, knowing that people really do not care how much you know until they know how much you care. Your persistence as a coach will determine the magnitude of accomplishments of those you lead.

Your success as the educational leader who provides coaching to those you lead will be dependent on the dispositions of those you're coaching. Their dispositions include their willingness to commit to a coaching experience, their setting of realistic expectations, their openness to coaching, their open participation in coaching, their willingness to take risks, and their involvement with others in the coaching experience.

The degree to which you, the educational leader, are willing to serve others within the coaching experience will also determine the success of those you lead. The greatest leaders that ever walked the earth were the greatest servants. They weren't hesitant to go into disease-infested areas and serve the sick and impoverished. They committed their lives to others so that others would benefit. Similarly, you're serving those you lead to help them achieve what they didn't realize they were capable of achieving.

Your serving others as an educational leader is commonly called *servant leadership*. Servant leadership stems from an ancient idea that has become the premier focus in leadership philosophy for the twenty-first century (Sergiovanni, 2001). As a servant leader, you will discover your true power and authority to lead.

In turn, your servant leadership will provide health, wisdom, and more autonomy for those you lead. By your very actions, you will encourage collaboration, trust, listening, and empowerment. Your servant leadership will provide long-lasting change instead of a temporary fix. We the authors, assert that you, as a servant leader, will no doubt practice the essentials presented in Key Box 4.2.

KEY BOX 4.2

Essentials to Successful Servant Leadership

- Devote yourself to serving the needs of those you lead.
- Focus on meeting the needs of those you lead.
- Develop the educators you lead to bring out the best in them.
- Coach others and encourage their self expression.
- Facilitate personal growth in those you lead.
- Listen and build an educational community.

As a successful educational leader of the twenty-first century, you will need to view leadership or "growing" people as foundationally more important than managing projects or processes (Pajares & Graham, 1999; Rayner & Devi, 2001). In this respect, you as an educational leader must capture the coaching and serving moment when those you lead act below expectations, hence transforming education in positive ways. Similarly, you must coach those individuals to realize that holding each other accountable is both acceptable and expected. In order to do so, you must uphold your credibility.

IN THE NEWS

Districts across the Country Are Struggling with How to Focus Efforts of Instructional Leaders

View leadership or "growing" people as foundationally more important than managing projects or processes.

Kelly Griffith's job description is most notable for what it doesn't include. The principal of Easton Elementary School in Easton, Maryland, doesn't handle maintenance. She doesn't help arrange field trips. She doesn't oversee her building's cafeteria workers. Nor does she supervise the buses before and after school. Instead, she spends her time in classrooms, observing educators and showing them new methods of instruction. She analyzes test scores. She plans professional development activities for her teachers aimed at boosting student achievement. Griffith can focus on teaching and learning because her school-district leaders made a conscious effort to let principals do so. Two years ago, the 4,500-student Talbot County system put "school managers" in its buildings to free principals of administrative duty and let them concentrate on *coaching* teachers while increasing student achievement.

School district leaders at Talbot County Schools, and other educational leaders across the nation, have prioritized teaching and learning and, in doing so, have established provisions for their principals to maximize their instructional leadership.

Source: J. Archer, "Districts across the Country Are Struggling with How to Focus Efforts of Instructional Leaders," *Education Week,* September 15, 2004.

Thou Canst Not Then Be False to Anyone

Your success as an educational leader will depend on the trust and belief in what you say and do as perceived by those you lead—in other words, your credibility. Conversely, skepticism of your honesty and integrity from those you lead will erode your effectiveness as a leader. If you lose the confidence of those you lead, pack it up and head out of Dodge. Your credibility is that critical to your leadership.

Effective communication is the first step to building credibility for your leadership (Castetter, 1996; Lezzotte & Pepperl, 1999). And, like other qualities of leadership, you must develop your credibility by remaining consistent in what you say and backing up your words with your actions. Although this sounds logical, many people don't follow these principles and lose their credibility—their ability to lead.

Why do educational leaders fail when their credibility is in question, worse yet, destroyed? If educational leaders lose their credibility, their communication falls on deaf ears. Just think about it: Without credibility, the content of communication loses all its value; without credibility, multiple processes for communication become useless; and without credibility, relationships fall apart!

To illustrate this erosion of credibility, let's imagine that you have just accepted the educational leadership position of your dreams. As you take over, you make a common mistake. You work exhaustively to please and support your superiors, not wanting to disappoint them. In fact, your eagerness to please causes you to hesitate in deciding on a clear direction because you believe you might be losing the support of your superiors. Hence, in your attempts to appease everyone, you waffle and take unclear positions when difficulties arise. Worse yet, you agree with one person one day and another person the next. You promise change but your actions do not follow your words. You lack clarity of purpose and consistency in your communication. Under this downward spiral, you lose your support day by day as a leader. Your ability to communicate as an educational leader is weakened. Your superiors and those you lead are not drawn to your leadership. In fact, they go to extra limits to avoid it and perhaps even work against you. Eventually, you lose your credibility—and your dream job, which is what you were trying to protect in the first place.

In this most unfortunate scenario, hopefully one that never happens to you, think about how those you lead would feel when you, their educational leader, fail to communicate clearly and consistently—in both words and deeds. Their trust disappears. Their motivation dissipates. They find excuses to give less or not at all. Those you lead feel demoralized and hurt. That's why you, the educational leader, need to work diligently, maintain guard, and uphold your credibility.

The impact of credibility goes beyond the individual level. When you as the educational leader are thought to have high credibility, those you lead will more likely be proud of the school, school district, and educational organization. When those you lead are proud of their school, they will speak positively to their colleagues and others because they feel a sense of ownership for high-quality results, chiefly increasing student achievement (Ash & Persall, 2000; Bong, 2002). Conversely, if you are thought to have a low degree of credibility, those you lead are more likely to produce only when watched and perform at the lowest level of expectation and often lose their sense of purpose. These disgruntled followers are motivated primarily by money and describe your leadership in less than positive terms while searching for another job.

Nothing Can Come of Nothing

Your key to successful educational leadership begins with your commitment to educational excellence and throwing out old leadership models that are no longer effective. You, as a twenty-first-century educational leader, must serve as a leader for student learning (Marshall, 1997). You must know academic content and pedagogical techniques. You must work to strengthen not only your teachers' skills but your skills as well. You must collect, analyze, and use data in ways that fuel excellence. You must be able to permit and encourage teachers to exercise leadership outside the classroom through efficacy and empowerment.

Your commitment to excellence will fulfill a variety of roles and responsibilities. First, you will become an instructional leader where you will focus on strengthening teaching and learning, professional development, data-driven decision making, and accountability (Fullan, 2000a; Hallinger & Heck, 1996). Second, you will be committed to community leadership imbued with a big-picture awareness of the school's (or school district's) role in society; shared leadership among educators, community partners, and residents; and close relations with parents and others. Third, as a successful twenty-first-century educational leader committed to excellence, you will be a visionary leader (Bennis & Nanus, 1985; Drucker, 2002; Mattocks & Drake, 2001). As a visionary leader, you will demonstrate commitment to the conviction that all children will learn at high levels, and you will inspire others inside and outside the school building with this vision.

A set of standards for your commitment and attainment of educational excellence is found in the embodiment of the ISLLC standards and your development of knowledge, skills, and attributes of an educational leader. Your capacity to galvanize the internal and external school communities in support of increased student achievement and learning is critical. Keys to educational leadership excellence have been the study of many. Researchers have revealed various insights into educational excellence accomplished through skillful educational leadership (Barnett, Basom, Yerkes, & Norris, 2000; Czaja & Lowe, 2001; Restine, 1997; Van-Meter & Murphy, 1997). Educational leadership preparation programs sponsored by universities and other organizations have strived to identify what excellent educational leadership really is. One such attempt has been made by the College of Education at the University of North Carolina at Charlotte, titled *Rising to the Challenge: Developing Excellent Professionals* (2004). This framework, like others, provides you with a snapshot to envision your role and responsibility to educational excellence. It follows:

RISING TO THE CHALLENGE: DEVELOPING EXCELLENT PROFESSIONALS

Executive Summary of the Conceptual Framework for Education of Professionals

What are the characteristics of excellent professionals?

1. Knowledgeable
   - demonstrate highly advanced knowledge of human development and of student needs
   - demonstrate highly advanced knowledge of curriculum and content
   - demonstrate highly advanced knowledge of expectations within a variety of educational environments for P–12 children/youth/young adults and their families, as well as state standards for P–12 learners, instructional contexts, social contexts, and societal goals
   - make links among theory, research and practice as well as between content and pedagogy
   - demonstrate knowledge, high regard, and adherence to the ethical standards of their field
   - expand their professional knowledge through the use of technological resources

2. Effective
   - use justifiable, appropriate strategies well grounded in research and the wisdom of practice within their respective disciplines
   - apply their knowledge to planning, goal-setting, implementation, and continuous assessment
   - use data to make professional decisions
   - demonstrate a positive impact on P–12 student learning either through teaching or through the establishment of educational environments that support student learning

3. Reflective
   - demonstrate excellence in their reflective educational decision-making
   - demonstrate reflective self evaluation skills
   - demonstrate flexibility and adaptability
   - engage in continuous improvement of professional practice

4. Responsive to Equity/Diversity
   - apply their knowledge and skills to foster educational environments that are respectful of diverse backgrounds and cultures
   - promote positive, supportive educational environments that are respectful of and responsive to individual differences
   - provide developmentally appropriate, age appropriate, individually appropriate, and culturally responsive instruction
   - practice inclusive professional practices that respond effectively to the educational needs of all children/youth/young adults
   - hold high expectations for all children/youth/young adults and provide high levels of support for high achievement
   - recognize that equity and social justice are enhanced through education

5. Collaborative
   - value the collective contribution of others in their efforts to provide excellent programs and services
   - demonstrate effective communication, decision making, problem solving and interactive teaming skills.
   - work in partnership with families, communities, and colleagues for the benefit of children/youth/young adults

6. Leaders
   - demonstrate leadership in the improvement of professional practice at a variety of levels
   - communicate effectively their professional knowledge to others
   - engage in policy decisions that have positive impacts on P–12 children/youth/young adults

Source: College of Education, University of North Carolina at Charlotte. Used with permission.

Successful twenty-first-century educational leaders will commit and insist on excellence and hold those they lead accountable. This accountability of others will not be accomplished with a chair and whip. The most meaningful and lasting assurance of increased student achievement comes from educational leaders and those they lead who regard each other as professional colleagues who have developed teams or professional families.

We Few, We Happy Few, We Band of Brothers (and Sisters)

For schools today to be considered successful, you must come to the realization that your efforts and those of only a few others will no longer suffice. Making schools successful takes more than just individual effort—it takes teamwork (Murphy & Shipman, 1999). Effective twenty-first-century schools will use teams of educators to accomplish improved results. Such teams will participate in improving instructional practices, implementing curricular reform, developing new programs, and restructuring (Atwater & Bass, 1994; Kowalski, 2003a). For team effort to be successful, you, as a future educational leader, will need to be skilled and committed to leading others in constructing clear, shared goals; developing commitment; motivating cooperative initiatives; instilling mutual accountability; and advocating and attaining the necessary resources and skills.

During the twentieth century, the vast majority of teachers worked in isolation, administration tried to accomplish tasks alone, and the responsibility of implementing new ideas fell predominantly on individuals. The lasting impact of school improvements was often limited to the duration of an educational leader's tenure. Once the educational leader departed, so too did the school accomplishments.

Your building of teams as an educational leader will result in more effective ways to accomplish important tasks (Fullan, 2001; Hanson, 2002). Teams have many advantages over individuals working in isolation when building ownership and empowering others. Teams tend to be better at solving problems. Those you lead will have a higher level of commitment if they are involved in the decision-making process and are more likely to implement an idea or plan right from the start. Moreover, consider the energy and interest in new initiatives you will be able to generate by the inclusion of others, which will carry over into a multitude of other projects and initiatives.

It is critical for you and those you lead to separate the members who contribute to the group from those who detract. School improvements that have taken years to build can too easily be destroyed. You, as the educational leader, will need to readily and rapidly distinguish constructive actions from destructive intentions to support those you lead in achieving enhanced standards. This message is clearly made in the following poem:

Which Am I?
I watched them tearing a building down—
A gang of men in a busy town.
With a ho-heave-ho and lusty yell
They swung a beam and a sidewall fell.
I asked the foreman, "Are these men skilled
And the men you'd hire if you had to build?"
He gave a laugh and said, "No indeed!
Just common labor is all I need;
I can easily wreck in a day or two what
Builders have taken a year to do!"
And I thought to myself as I went away
"Which of these roles have I tried to play?"
Am I a builder who works with care, measuring
Life by the rule and square?
Am I shaping my deed to well made plan,
Patiently doing the best I can?

Or am I a wrecker, who walks the town,
Content with labor of tearing down?

—Anonymous

As the lines of the poem depict, each member of the team needs to examine the contributions being made. It is your responsibility to lead all team members to be positive contributors. Your building of effective teams will not be an easy proposition (Noonan, 2003). It will take your time, commitment, support, and belief that *Together Everyone Achieves More (TEAM)*. Your development of effective educational teams will require skillful planning and skillful implementation. You will experience resistance toward team participation until the benefits of participating on teams are valued by those you lead. Be patient, as it does take time, skills, and knowledge to form successful teams. And last, the goal of your team building should carry you through the most challenging of times so long as your goal is centered on improving student outcomes. Remember: The challenges of team building and implementation are only obstacles to change if you take your eyes off your goals.

Our Remedies Oft in Ourselves Do Lie

For continued success as an educational leader, you will need to continue to engage in purposeful learning for improving your knowledge, skills, and competence. Your lifelong learning will be imperative in staying abreast of continuing technological and social changes. Your future needs will include updating obsolete skills and acquiring current skills and cutting-edge knowledge. Your understanding of the world and its conditions are critical to envisioning the needs for your continued professional development. In other words, you will need to develop yourself to your highest potential (Fullan, 2001; Knowles et al., 1984; Welton, 1995).

Imagine just for a moment three large-scale revolutions (technological, economic, and social) that have occurred in the last two decades alone. The rapid upgrading of computers and the development of a range of information technologies have resulted in enormous changes. These changes have been so great that the nature of work, skills, and knowledge have been transformed. In turn, the technological revolution has caused an economic revolution with the newer technologies outdating older models and resulting in new manufacturing processes and diversified methods of industrial organization (Cuban, 2001a; Hammel, 2002). As a result of the technological and economic changes, there have been major social changes, with new enterprises and sources of wealth, power, and status emerging.

So, what does this mean to you as an educational leader? Not only will you need to respond to this ever-changing world but you will also need to provide the much needed leadership that prepares students to live and contribute to these changes. This taught knowledge has been linked to effective economic production and the maintenance of a society's prosperity (Cullen, 1997). In order to provide meaningful education for all twenty-first-century students, your continued learning will be imperative to your effectiveness as an educational leader.

To maximize your life's pursuit of learning, you will need to continue to study formally at a college or university. Besides, the more academic degrees, certifications, and licenses you achieve, the more career choices will be available to you. It will be necessary to stay current in curriculum development, instructional practices, technology, law, and finance, as well as other content areas. You cannot afford to become incompetent in essential leadership areas.

Your participation in professional associations within your field is extremely advantageous. Participation in lectures, work sessions, and intercommunication with your colleagues provides vibrant learning opportunities. You will find that professional association participation will provide you with two major gains: first, an exchange of innovative ideas and second, an appreciation of the accomplishments in your school or school district that may have otherwise gone unnoticed. Professional associations with strong memberships have the ability to shape educational outcomes significantly.

Your involvement in national, state, regional, and local associations and organizations will provide you with learning opportunities that are targeted to common needs and challenges. Schools can no longer operate in the absence of other entities; don't remain the Lone Ranger. Common needs and unification make people more apt to stand, deliver, and succeed.

Do not underestimate your grassroots networking with colleagues. Maintain relationships with those you have met through your university programs. Make new professional ties as well. Who you know as educational leaders often will determine how far you'll go.

In retrospect, you must engage in lifelong learning for intellectual stimulation and professional and personal edification (Knowles, 1986; Noonan, 2003; Welton, 1995). Keep informed about current research and theories regarding effective schooling, continually expose your staff to cutting-edge ideas on how to be effective, systematically engage staff in discussions about cutting-edge advancements in education and society, and involve faculty in reading articles and books about effective practices.

BE NOT AFRAID OF GREATNESS

Yes, it is critical to come to know yourself, set the example for others to follow, coach and serve others, uphold your credibility, commit to educational excellence, build professional families, and engage in lifelong learning to lead successfully in the twenty-first century. There is one more key to successful leadership, and that is to begin with the end in mind (Covey, 1989). Throughout your educational leadership career, there is one person who will accompany you every day, every week, and every year, and that person is you! Whether you succeed or fail, win or lose, you need to remain true to your beliefs, convictions, and promises. As you look back at milestones in your career, your reflective visions truly need to be free of deceit on issues of personal and professional value. To emphasize this, we share a poem that has added tremendous meaning to our lives:

> **The One in the Glass**
> When you get what you want in your struggle for self,
> And the world makes you queen or king for a day.
> Just go to the mirror and look at yourself.

And see what that person has to say.

For it isn't your father or mother, husband or wife,

Whose judgment upon you must pass.

The one whose verdict counts the most in your life,

Is the one staring back from the glass.

Some people might think you're a straight shootin' chum,

And call you a wonderful girl or guy.

But the one in the glass says you're only a bum,

If you can't look her/him straight in the eye.

The one in the mirror is the one to please, not the rest,

For the one in the mirror will be with you clear to the end.

And you've passed your most dangerous, difficult test,

If the one in the glass is your friend.

You may follow the big world down the pathway of years,

And get pats on the back as you pass.

But your final reward will be a heartache and tears,

If you've cheated the one in the glass.

—Anonymous

This poem, written by an anonymous author on the wall of a death-row holding cell, was received with silence, contemplation, and reflection. The message is clear: Hold yourself responsible for your lifetime choices, beliefs, and convictions; your professional and personal actions; and how true you are to yourself.

THE REFLECTIVE PRACTITIONER

Welcome to your fourth Reflective Practitioner, which is based on ISLLC Standard 5, your Chapter 4 Scenario, and your reading of Chapter 4. It is intended to provoke your thoughtful reflection and to stimulate discussion among colleagues, classmates, and peers. The Reflective Practitioner provides opportunities to synthesize issues, make comparisons, and apply theory to practice. We hope it will motivate you to search for evidence, thus increasing your comprehension of the text and helping you examine your convictions and discover new and shared perspectives.

Standard 5
A school administrator is an educational leader who promotes the success of all students by acting with integrity, fairness, and in an ethical manner.

Scenario

Yesterday on the front page of your local newspaper a headline stated surprising news: Principal Retires, Leaves Huge Footsteps to Follow. In a tribute to a great leader, the front-page article described JoAnn O'Dwyer, principal of Union Middle School, as an educational leader who was committed to the success of each and every student and teacher. The article quoted Superintendent Smith in saying, "Principal O'Dwyer demonstrated the highest degree of integrity, fairness, and ethics! She will be missed."

Principal O'Dwyer began her lifetime career in education thirty-five years ago at Union Middle School, holding positions throughout the years as a teacher, counselor, assistant principal, and, most recently, principal. Principal O'Dwyer was best known for inspiring all others to higher levels of performance, serving as a role model, and treating others fairly, equitably, and with dignity and respect.

Dr. O'Dwyer's focus was always on learning and what people individually and collectively learn about themselves, each other, and the world in which they live. This was evident in her work in all aspects of education. In her science classroom, she challenged students to achieve excellence, while respecting the strengths of others. As an author and coach for numerous science fairs, she encouraged teachers to be creative and to design programs that engaged and stretched not only the minds of students but also their hearts. As principal, she challenged students to set their sights higher than their most recent behavior, helped teachers find ways to reach students who seemed reluctant, and supported parents with wise counsel through difficult times with their children.

Serving fifteen years as principal of Union Middle School, Principal O'Dwyer will be remembered for her quiet manner, her humanity, her humor, and her credibility as an excellent leader. In the most difficult circumstances, she made others feel dignified and respected—even when administering serious consequences for unacceptable behavior. For these reasons and others, Principal O'Dwyer will always be remembered as an important person in the lives of students, faculty, parents, and community members. In return, members of the faculty, graduating classes, parents, and community have arranged for the new community library to be named in her honor.

With big shoes to fill, Superintendent Smith has asked faculty, students, parents, and community members to share with her in writing the qualities, skills, and abilities they believe that Principal's O'Dwyer's successor will need to achieve a seamless transition.

QUESTIONS FOR REFLECTIVE THINKING

1. Please respond in writing to Superintendent Smith regarding the qualities, skills, and abilities you believe Principal's O'Dwyer's successor will need to achieve a seamless transition at Union Middle School. Base your response on ISLLC Standard 5 and the Performances established under ISLLC Standard 5.

2. Which of the seven keys to twenty-first-century leadership success do you feel depict your leadership strengths? Please explain.

3. Which of the seven keys to twenty-first-century leadership success do you feel address areas of need for your building of leadership skills? Please explain your response.

4. *Promise Yourself* is a personal and professional philosophy presented in Chapter 4 shared by a retiring superintendent with a new principal. Compose your own *Promise Yourself*, stating the personal and professional convictions that help you weather the most difficult of times. Keep your convictions displayed in a visible location (perhaps on your desk in view) and review them at times of conflict and challenge.

5. Write your own personal and professional "Ten Commandments of Leadership." Explain each of your commandments in terms of its importance to you to ensure your success as a twenty-first-century educational leader.

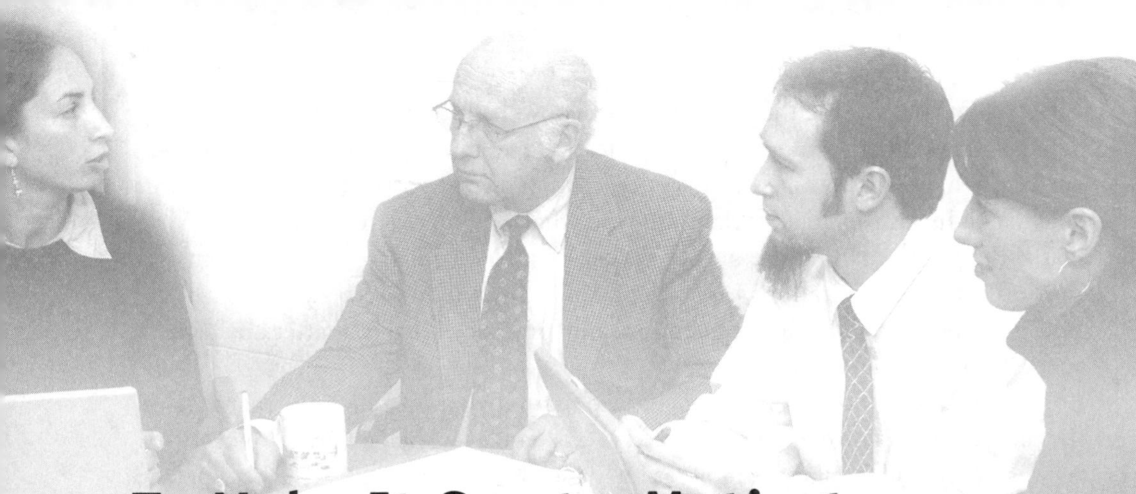

chapter 5

ISLLC *Standard* 2

To Make It Great—Motivate

Our chief want in life is somebody who will make us do what we can.
—Ralph Waldo Emerson

Your Chapter 5 Action Focus welcomes you to James A. Garfield High School, the fourth largest year-round high school in the United States, located five miles east of downtown Los Angeles. The vast majority of the 4,800 students enrolled at Garfield High School live in neighborhoods surrounding the school, commonly known as East L.A. More than 72 percent of high school students live in non-English-speaking homes where their family income average is $18,750. Twenty-four percent of Garfield High School's students annually go on to four-year colleges. Garfield High School was made famous by the true-life movie titled *Stand and Deliver.*

Enter Jaime Escalante. Born in La Paz, Bolivia, and much like the parents of Garfield High School students, Escalante immigrated to the United States. His mission for leaving his native country in 1964 was to teach students in the United States. Lacking both the ability to speak English and the credentials to teach in the United States were obstacles soon overcome by his tremendous motivation, diligent effort, and academic achievement in night classes at Pasadena City College. Upon successful completion of his college studies, Escalante accepted a teaching position at James A. Garfield High School.

The rest became history as detailed in a book titled *Escalante: The Best Teacher in America* by Jay Mathews and as portrayed in the movie *Stand and Deliver.* The 1988 book and movie extended tribute to Escalante's motivation of his Garfield High School students in 1987, as 73 of his first-year calculus students passed the advanced-placement calculus exam and 12 of his students passed the accelerated version of the exam usually reserved for second-year calculus students. Escalante's uncanny ability to inspire students to achieve their fullest potentials became an educational focus of our nation. To illustrate, Escalante encouraged 14 students to enroll in calculus in 1982. By 1990, the number of students Escalante motivated to study calculus grew to 400 students, with some of his class sizes increasing to over 50 students. In 2001, following an illustrious career in education, Escalante retired to his native Bolivia. Since his retirement, the Garfield High School calculus teacher has returned regularly to the United States to visit his former students.

When considering the magnitude, the power, and the magnanimous achievements of Escalante and other educators like him, questions naturally will surface. What explains an educator's powerful ability to motivate others? What inspires an educator to go above and beyond what was considered impossible? What is it about the human nature of motivation that drives educators and students beyond common limitations to replace fears with a will to succeed? Just exactly how do educators achieving tremendous outcomes, or for that matter any leaders, successfully motivate others?

Motivation of others is a challenge no matter what the task and regardless of the project or initiative to be performed (Herzberg, Mausner, & Snyderman, 1993). As was the case in Escalante's motivating his students to excel, motivating others to accomplish great things is the challenge of educational leadership. Inspiring others to work diligently and successfully are the ultimate tests of leadership.

As illustrated in your Chapter 5 Action Focus, successful educational leaders instill the will to succeed! Mindful of this, we begin our exploration of motivation with what is known about motivation.

WHAT WE KNOW ABOUT MOTIVATION

Do you ever wonder what specific strategies motivate people? The underlying motivational principles of theorists such as Maslow, Alderfer, Herzberg, and others represent perspectives for identifying what it is within an individual or the work environment that supports and sustains behavior. These theoretical foundations affirm and extend educational leaders' efforts to motivate others.

Needs Theories

Proponents of some theories of motivation assert that people in general share a common set of needs that orient and energize them. When needs are not fulfilled, an internal state of tension or discomfort occurs within any given individual. Only when tension and discomfort are present will individuals be optimally motivated to change (Gagne, Ryan, & Bargmann, 2003). This approach assumes that human beings constantly seek a state of equilibrium (i.e., when one is hungry, one eats). In essence, individuals are motivated to engage in behaviors that will satisfy a need or reduce associated tension. These theories of motivation based on needs are the most popular and widespread of all motivational theories.

Abraham H. Maslow's *hierarchy of needs* is the most well known theory of human motivation. Maslow's theory is most identifiable and supported because of its clarity and simplicity in message. The hierarchy of needs is based on two basic foundations. First, the constant state of all human beings is one of "wanting." Needs that are not satisfied are and remain as motivators. On the other hand, needs that have been achieved can no longer be motivators. Humans rarely reach a state of complete homeostasis or satisfaction (Deci & Ryan, 2000). As soon as one need is gratified, another surfaces to take its place. Maslow's research revealed that humans are always in a state of "wanting."

Second, Maslow argued that humans have five sets of needs that are arranged in a hierarchy. He contended that people started by trying to satisfy their most basic or compelling needs and progressed toward the most fulfilling. These needs are shown in the following diagram.

Self-
Actualization
Esteem
Social
Safety
Physiological

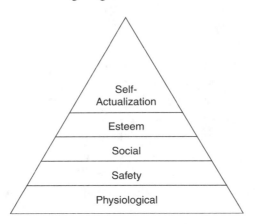

Physiological Needs. Physiological needs are very basic to the survival of the organism, including such things as food, water, rest, shelter, and air. Physiological needs will dominate when they are unsatisfied. As a result, no other need will serve as a basis for motivation until the physiological needs are met. To illustrate, a person who is in need of food, love, and esteem more than likely will select food before anything else.

Safety Needs. Safety needs include security, stability, and structured environment, free from threats to one's existence. Safety needs also include areas such as protection from ill health, economic disaster, physical harm, and unexpected harm. These needs may be manifested in an educational environment by faculty as job security, pension, and insurance plans (Koestner & Losier, 2002). Personal motivation may include the peace of mind that can be provided as a result of these needs being secured.

Social or Relational Needs. Social needs are comprised of relationships where friendship, affection, and affiliation are present. Social or relational needs are manifested in terms of a desire to belong or meaningfully be connected to other people and organizations. It is at this point that Maslow's hierarchy of needs separate from the physical or quasi-physical needs to higher-order needs. Failure to satisfy the needs at this level can adversely impact an individual's mental health.

Esteem Needs. Esteem needs include feelings of adequacy, competence, independence, confidence, appreciation, and recognition by others. These needs are concerned with the desire of individuals to have positive self-perceptions and to be respected by others. Satisfaction of esteem needs leads to a feeling of self-confidence and prestige.

Self-Actualization. The need of self-actualization is the most difficult to describe and define because different people have different ideas about what they need to achieve in order to obtain true happiness. For example, for a wealthy person, money may no longer be the greatest motivator. Self-actualization needs in general refer to the desire of individuals to achieve self-fulfillment, to develop one's potential to the fullest, to become everything that one is capable of becoming, and to achieve fulfillment of one's life goals.

Maslow argues that not only do unsatisfied needs motivate but they also follow a sequential hierarchy (Gollwitzer, 1990). That is, only when the physiological needs of a person are reasonably satisfied will the person be motivated by the next set of (safety) needs. When the physiological and safety needs are reasonably satisfied, the person will feel the urge of love, esteem, and self-actualization needs in that order—after each has been and continues to be satisfied. Maslow's hierarchy of needs also maintains that whatever level of needs may be motivating a person at a given phase of his or her life, there will occur a reversal or backslide to the needs of that lower level whose satisfaction has been blocked for a significant period of time.

In further consideration of this theory, it appears that the further up the scale an individual moves, the more the rewards or motivators move from the external environment to the internal need. It also becomes more difficult to influence motivation, since material rewards become less relevant and internal rewards become more difficult to identify and address. In order to enhance organizational performance, it is important that educational leaders recognize individual needs and provide opportunities for satisfaction.

Another needs-based theory, *existence, relatedness, and growth,* was developed by Clayton Alderfer. Based on Maslow's hierarchy of needs, Alderfer modified Maslow's theory by developing three basic needs instead of five. Alderfer sees his three levels consisting of existence, relatedness, and growth needs as also being hierarchical in nature, and thus influenced by personal growth.

Existence Needs.   Existence needs are satisfied by material substance or conditions. They correspond closely to the physiological needs identified by Maslow. Existence needs are satisfied by material rather than interpersonal rewards or conditions. These needs include food, shelter, money, and a safe and secure environment.

Relatedness Needs.   Relatedness needs may be satisfied by communication, or exchange and interaction with other individuals. There is a dependence on feedback from other organizational or community members to fulfill these needs. This feedback is dependent on accurate and honest communication, which may involve direction and advice rather than unconditional pleasantness or agreement.

Growth Needs.   Growth needs are fulfilled only by strong personal involvement that fully utilizes one's skills, abilities, and creativity. Growth needs include Maslow's self-actualization as well as esteem needs.

Both Maslow's and Alderfer's theories are similar because they are hierarchical and both concur that individuals will concentrate on the achievement of the lowest level of need that is not satisfied. Maslow contends that the lowest level of need must be satisfied before an individual can proceed to the next level. Alderfer argues that if a higher-level need is unsatisfied, the individual will regress to a desire to satisfy lower-level needs (Sheldon, Ryan, Deci, & Kasser, 2004). Maslow believes that once a need is met, it is no longer motivational. Alderfer argues that although an individual may have met a higher-level need, he or she may still be operating much lower on the scale where skills, aptitude, and knowledge may affect performance and confidence.

Herzberg's *two-factor theory* describes needs in terms of satisfaction and dissatisfaction. Frederick Herzberg examined motivation in the light of job content and context, asserting that motivating employees consists of a two-step process: maintenance factors and motivation needs.

Maintenance Factors. Herzberg believed that there are factors/conditions that serve primarily as dissatisfiers when absent. Herzberg called these factors/conditions *maintenance factors*. The presence of maintenance factors does not result in motivation. Rather, the absence of these maintenance factors leads to dissatisfaction. Stated another way, maintenance factors have the most impact when they are absent. Maintenance factors do not assure motivation when they are present (Gagne, Ryan, & Bargmann, 2003; Herzberg, 1968). They include salary, status, work conditions, job security, and the like.

Motivational Factors. Herzberg uses the term *motivational factors* for job satisfiers because they lead to high levels of motivation and job satisfaction when they are present. Examples of such factors include achievement, advancement, and recognition. When motivational factors are not present, they do not lead to "no satisfaction" or necessarily high levels of dissatisfaction. Herzberg viewed motivation as coming from the employee's feelings of accomplishment or job content rather than from the environmental factors or job context. Motivators encourage an employee to strive to do his or her best. Job enrichment can be used to meet higher-level needs. In practice, educational leaders wishing to enrich educational work for others may introduce new or more difficult tasks, assign individuals specialized tasks that enable them to become experts, or grant additional authority to faculty members.

Process Theories of Motivation

Additional theories of motivation purport to explicate and exemplify the process of how behavior is energized, directed, and sustained. Process theories include *equity theory, expectancy theory,* and *goal setting*. These theories provide much needed insight into the work environment resulting in increased motivation. These theories first attempt to define the major variables that increase motivation.

Equity Theory. A fair or equitable rewards system is one in which people with similar accomplishments and experience receive similar rewards. Equity theory reveals the importance of the fairness of rewards, as the rewards are compared by recipients and nonrecipients (Frunzi & Savini, 1997; Walster, Walster, & Berscheid, 1978). If there is a perceived inequity that exists, organizational members are likely to withhold their contributions, either consciously or unconsciously, to bring the situation into better balance.

A closer examination of equity theory holds valuable insight for today's leader. Equity theory argues that there should be an equitable distribution of

Teachers Unions Blast Governor's Merit Pay Plan. Some Educators Call Proposal Untenable, Costly; Others Say It May Help Attract Instructors

Equity theory argues that there should be an equal distribution of awards.

In his proposal to tie teacher pay to merit that is based on teacher performance, Governor Arnold Schwarzenegger drew harsh criticism from union leaders. Union leaders argued that linking pay to performance would wreak havoc contractually and be received by teachers as just another blast. In addition, other opponents to teacher merit pay criticized merit pay because of the uncertainty of establishing standards for awarding merit pay to ensure that all teachers were treated fairly. Furthermore, merit pay raised additional red flags, especially for teachers who work in difficult schools where using student achievement as the measure for merit pay would not present an equal distribution of awards.

Educational leaders need to make decisions and take actions that equally and fairly distribute awards.

Source: C. M. MiMassa & J. Rubin, "Teachers Unions Blast Governor's Merit Pay Plan. Some Educators Call Proposal Untenable, Costly. Others Say It May Help Attract Instructors," *Los Angeles Times*, January 10, 2005.

rewards based on an individual's input. The theory removes needs from their social isolation and makes the assumption that people engage in social comparison and are attentive to the process of exchanging their work contributions for organizational rewards (Heller, 1998).

A feeling of inequity will result in tension within the individual, and that individual will be motivated to reduce that tension for better or worse. The behaviors associated with this tension reduction provide the key for motivational strategy for leaders. The clear implication of equity theory for educational leaders is that they must ensure that there is a perception of fairness associated with the organizational rewards system (Hunt, Osborn, & Schermerhorn, 2000). If this sense of fairness does not exist, the educational leader must take steps to establish it in the minds of those they lead as well as within the objective reality of the rewards system.

Whereas equity theory was originally concerned with differences in pay, it has recently gained a larger application, taking into consideration other forms of tangible and intangible rewards. If any input is not balanced with some fair output, the motivation process will be difficult. Educational leaders need to manage the perception of fairness of each person they lead. If subordinates think they are not being treated fairly, it is difficult to motivate them.

In retrospect, equity theory involves the inputs a person brings to the work environment and the outcomes the person receives as a result of those inputs. It is the ratio of these inputs to outcomes in comparison with the perception of this ratio for other persons that is of importance to the leader. People normally compare themselves with others whom they see as being like themselves in terms of either similar past experience or similar interests.

The major underlying premise of equity theory is that the whole comparison process is based on the perceived situation, which may or may not reflect reality (Homans, 1961; Kelleher, 2001). The educational leader must be alert to perceived inputs by faculty members and others, as well as to the fairness of the outcomes provided for those inputs. Knowledge of equity theory provides the framework for a leader to discriminate in allocating rewards based on performance (Bong, 2002). Further, perceptions of inequity demand that the leader ensure that the objective reality of organizational reward systems is clear to all subordinates. Educational leaders should be able to analyze the reward system from a subordinate's viewpoint. In conclusion, equity theory tells educational leaders that organizational rewards must depend on level of performance so that there is perceived equity.

Expectancy Theory.   The anticipation of a reward or punishment also motivates people; this is called *expectancy theory*. When a person expects an important reward, there is an increase in the intensity and persistence of behavior directed toward that reward (Baard, Deci, & Ryan, 2004). The expectancy of a reward motivates behavior. The expectancy theory is based on four assumptions applied to educational leaders (Frunzi & Savini, 1997; Gagne, Ryan, & Bargmann, 2003; Heller, 1998; Noonan, 2003).

1. Student and faculty behavior in particular is caused by a number of forces in the work environment and in the individual.
2. Faculty and students consciously make decisions about their behavior.
3. Faculty members and others will have different types of needs, agendas, and desires.
4. Students, faculty, parents, community members, and others will do things that will result in favorable outcomes and will avoid those behaviors that lead to unfavorable outcomes.

As for rewards, there are two major classifications: intrinsic or extrinsic. It is vital that educational leaders realize that some individuals may be more motivated by extrinsic rewards such as pay, supervision, benefits, and job perks. Other individuals may be more interested in the gratification they receive from their contributions without the extrinsic rewards motivating their actions. More often than not, extrinsic and intrinsic rewards often exist simultaneously within a productive work environment (Frunzi & Savini, 1997; Heller, 1998; Noonan, 2003).

The expectancy theory is important because it provides insight into why some attempts to motivate others are successful and others fail. The key here is that leaders continue in efforts to reward outstanding accomplishments.

Goal-Setting Theory.   Simply stated, goal setting is a process in which educational leaders and faculty members jointly identify common objectives. During this goal setting, each faculty member's major areas of responsibility in terms of expectations are described (Locke & Latham, 1990). The agreed objectives then become guides for assessing the faculty member's performance.

The goal-setting theory has provided an effective approach to motivation for educational leaders through the establishing of clear goals and objectives. With a thorough understanding of expectations, each educational leader and faculty member will know what they need to accomplish. The faculty member feels a sense of ownership in the organization's goals.

The positive side of goal setting is that it places the educational leader's emphasis on results rather than handling daily crises. Teamwork is improved because of more clearly defined goals, established priorities, and planned resource allocation. Goal setting provides the potential for clear standards for performance evaluation and creates an environment for constructive and timely criticism, better communications, and greater team member development. Since faculty

Why the United States Should Look to Japan for Better Schools

Goal setting provides the potential for establishing goals, creating opportunity for constructive and timely criticism, increasing communication, and enhancing professional development.

The nation could again be at risk unless the United States can compete and surpass the educational performance of rival nations. To accomplish this goal, students in the United States will need to achieve the highest levels in math, science, and literacy. Leading the bandwagon for this goal setting are politicians, business leaders, and other elected officials.

Once the goal is set, chiefly the United States attaining world student achievement dominance, care must be given as to whether the goal is achievable. No Child Left Behind intended to achieve this goal of world-class student achievement but instead got bogged down in the quagmire of politics. Professional development has been varied, but teacher training is hesitant to formulize how teachers should teach what they teach. As long as there are fifty different sets of standards for fifty different states and within each state the quality of education depends upon the neighborhood in which students live, it is questionable whether the United States will rise to the pinnacle of world student achievement.

Goal setting provides opportunities to revise goals, establish conditions that enable goal achievement, and measure the success of goal attainment.

Source: B. Staples, "Why the United States Should Look to Japan for Better Schools," *New York Times,* November 21, 2005.

members know what is expected of them, understand what constitutes success, and agree to the objectives, they are motivated to accomplish their jobs.

There are numerous advantages and disadvantages of the goal setting theory for successful twenty-first-century educational leadership. The educational leader must be careful that the goal-setting process fits the needs and realities of the specific educational organization. Some educational leaders feel threatened by goal setting because they believe they lose control and authority when team members are allowed to help in setting goals and action plans. The educational leader must ensure that the goals are achievable by faculty members but are still challenging. Educational leaders must also be careful not to place too much emphasis on numerically measurable results. This creates a climate of leadership by statistics and involves an extraordinary amount of paperwork. If used well, the positive aspects of goal setting will outweigh the limitations. Even the periodic review of the progress achieved by the educational leader and faculty members greatly assists in the professional development of faculty members, improves communication, increases individual motivation, and improves the organization's planning capability.

In establishing goals, it is fundamental for educational leaders to keep many essentials in mind. First, goals that are both specific and difficult result in consistently higher effort and performance than when the established goal focuses on "do your best" type goals. Second, goal commitment is critical for both educational leaders and faculty members who are engaged in goal formation. Even though faculty member participation in developing the goals is one way to increase commitment, goals set by the educational leader or jointly between the educational leader and faculty members can both result in the accomplishment of the desired goal.

Regardless of the source of the goals, faculty members exert the greatest effort when goals are accompanied by feedback. In research dealing specifically with group performance, it was found that goal specificity is critical for improving group performance. Educational leaders with the highest-performing groups worked with followers to jointly set goals and give concrete feedback on goal progress. Educational leaders who didn't use participatory goal setting or provide feedback were not as successful. If time is limited, however, it may be preferable for the educational leader to establish challenging goals and provide ongoing concrete feedback instead of taking the time to engage the group in participative goal-setting efforts.

In summary, successfully completing goals provides teachers with a sense of accomplishment and satisfaction, and a greater sense of motivation (Hunt, Osborn, & Schermerhorn, 2000; Koestner & Losier, 2002). Educational leaders can achieve these goals by talking to their team members about goals held in common, involving the team members in establishing goals when possible, and providing team members with ongoing concrete feedback about the accomplishment of the established goals.

MOTIVATION MATTERS

Before proceeding with the actions that leaders take in getting others to do great things, we need to briefly define and describe the powerful phenomenon called *motivation*. Motivation, put into the simplest terms, is the combination of desire and commitment to attain maximum accomplishments. Numerous studies have examined motivation in the context of organizational behavior. Educational leaders have been obviously interested in getting the most from students and faculty members to improve academic accomplishments.

As a science and social phenomenon, motivation is an integral aspect of human behavior that psychologists have invested great interest in understanding better (Bono & Judge, 2003). The word *motivation* is derived from the Latin verb *movere,* which means to move. That which moves an individual or organization to act or behave in a certain way is the individual's or organization's motivation. The inner drive, the urge, or the desire of the person or organization constitutes their motives. If the motives causing an individual to act in a certain way can be identified, psychologists believe the individual will be better understood.

It is generally believed that motivation can be defined as the cause of action. Motivation energizes human behavior. It causes a person to act. Motivation often helps explain why a person performs at a particular level. People can be motivated to do just about anything, and conversely, they can be motivated to do absolutely nothing. It is the role and responsibility of today's educational leader to successfully motivate others.

Keys to Motivation

A closer look at the actions that have successfully motivated millions in the construction of human-made Wonders of the World provides us with insight for today's leaders considering actions and methods in motivating others. In general, five keys were implemented by leaders in motivating others to achieve monumental gains. First, leaders demonstrated the highest ethical standards in motivating others to attain what they thought was not possible. Second, the leaders developed unified teams where together everyone achieved more than any one individual. Third, leaders rewarded and disciplined those they led firmly, fairly, and consistently. Fourth, leaders recognized and met the needs of those they led. And fifth, leaders served as, and developed, positive role models.

Demonstrating High Ethical Standards. With construction beginning in 1631 and successful completion twenty-two years later, 20,000 workers were led with a fleet of 1,000 elephants to complete one of the most amazing architectural wonders of the world: the Taj Mahal. Such achievement was made possible only because workers held confidence in leaders such as Emperor Shah Jahan, the architect, and other leaders at that time. The workers needed their leaders to demonstrate the standards against which they could compare their own behavior and abilities (Bolman & Deal, 1991). The laborers of the Taj Mahal, like today, wanted to depend on their leadership to provide the moral force that the values of their society demanded. The common laborers wanted their leaders to be successful, but they also wanted their leaders to be decent and honorable. The purpose for constructing the Taj Mahal was indicative of these virtues, as it was built as a burial for Mumtaz Mahal, the emperor's wife. The confidence that the workers held in their leaders assisted in their development of discipline, direction, and determination.

Developing Unified Teams. The strength that comes from a unified team has been a powerful motivator throughout time (Bass, 1990). Such unification of teams resulted in the construction of the Panama Canal, one of the greatest engineering feats of the twentieth century. The mastermind leading this construction was Colonel George Goethals, one of the most famous engineers to wear the uniform of the U.S. Army. Of all the engineering feats of the twentieth century, the building of the Panama Canal was certainly one of the greatest. Furthermore, through Goethals's unification of teams, he was able to succeed in the completion of this human-made wonder of the world, whereas many distinguished American and European engineers had failed. Caring for laborers and working hard to make construction meaningful assisted in the development of a cohesive working force. It took much work to properly teach, coach, counsel, and train the workers but this created bonds that lead to cohesion, trust, and mutual respect. Followers of Goethals went above and beyond what other workers with different leadership even dreamed of accomplishing. Their performance as a team of laborers resulted in a passageway used extensively today. Where individuals failed, developing cohesive teams motivated all to succeed.

Rewarding Some and Disciplining Others. Although rather simplistic in nature, the outcomes of behavior are often manifested in rewards and punishments. The consequences of an individual's actions can become an effective motivational tool. The rewards or discipline one receives or expects to receive can be incentives or deterrents to motivation.

Such was the case in the construction of still another human-made wonder of the world: the construction of the Trans-Siberian Railroad. This railroad was perceived by the Soviet Union as a critical link between European Russia and the Pacific Coast. Construction began in 1891, taking place in some of the harshest conditions on earth. Successfully completed in 1905, the opening of this railroad greatly affected the history of the Russian Empire by opening Siberia to large-scale colonization. The labor of a relative few was recognized by many.

Rewarding Outstanding Achievement. The brave-hearted and successful achieved rewards for their contributions to the construction of the Trans-Siberian

Railroad. These rewards brought wealth, recognition, and other accommodations. No doubt, these rewards served as reinforcement for positive conformity, as the rewards were designed to promote desired behavior. Clearly, from the construction of this world wonder, it is safe to deduct that a well-developed system of rewards has the potential to impact performance favorably; in fact, rewards were used to increase motivation.

Upon his observation of well-deserved recognition, Napoleon asserted that the motivation incurred from a small piece of ribbon (for exemplary attainment) was spectacular. He concluded that if he had sufficient ribbon, he could conquer the world. As was the case in the construction of the Trans-Siberian Railroad and all other magnificent attainments, when using rewards it is imperative that such acknowledgment be fair, consistent, and equitable. Failure to distribute rewards accordingly will diminish the value of motivation.

From the construction of the Sydney Opera House to the Golden Gate Bridge and beyond, in order for leadership to increase workers' motivation through a rewards system, leaders must serve as positive role models.

Serving as Positive Role Models.   Successful leaders of the past who were not hesitant to join those they were leading, such as digging a ditch in building the Great Wall of China or working on top of the mountain peak of Machu Picchu, had followers who were more motivated to go above and beyond where others had failed. Because great leaders of all time were credible and competent, they were extraordinary motivators. Such leaders had followers that were confident in their leaders' abilities; therefore, these followers were willing to go into the most difficult situations.

Making Motivation Work

In addition to the five keys to successful motivation, leaders accomplished tremendous achievements throughout history because of very special key concepts to motivation. These key concepts, or skills and abilities, include clearly stating goals and objectives, developing unified teams, rewarding outstanding achievement, exemplifying expected behavior, developing meaningful rewards procedure and process, extending a well-deserved compliment, and accentuating the positive. These attributes are examined closely as each is a critical link to successful twenty-first-century educational leadership.

State Goals and Objectives Clearly.   The construction of still another human-made wonder of the world—the successful completion of Mount Rushmore—had clear goals and objectives right from the outset. Such objectives and rewards needed to be stated and understood clearly. In addition to clearly articulated goals and rewards, providing a definite process and procedure was critical in motivating accomplishments. The saying, "Just tell me what to do and what it's worth," may be rather simplistic, but it is facilitates motivation.

Develop Meaningful Rewards Procedure and Process.   The ribbon-cutting ceremony of the Golden Gate Bridge was held at its completion on May 27, 1937. This was a special time as a nation rejoiced. Acknowledgments were made, certificates were distributed, balloons were launched, and a world paid tribute to the laborers—those alive and the eleven workers who gave their lives in the line of duty. The rewards procedure and process with all its pomp and circumstance was clear from the very beginning. When the billionth vehicle crossed the bridge in 1985, the rewards of labor were again made clear.

As demonstrated by the process and procedure for rewarding successful completion of the Golden Gate Bridge, such accomplishments should be recognized by a rewards process and procedure whether it be a parade or some other appropriate unit ceremony. This rewards process and procedure is extremely beneficial in today's schools. Public recognition makes individuals feel special and serves as a motivator. The process and procedure needs to be commensurate with the magnitude of achievement.

Extend a Well-Deserved Compliment.   Rewards systems do not have to have all the fanfare as the celebration of the completion of the Golden Gate Bridge. From the completion of a human-made wonder of the world to an unselfish deed, everyone appreciates a pat on the back for a job well done. Verbal praise is free and easy to give and positively motivates an individual or a group. Educational leaders need to consider and practice this important key to motivation.

Accentuate the Positive.   The world is full of significant accomplishments, both yesterday and today. The world is lacking in leadership taking the time and effort to acknowledge diligent efforts, honor the achievement of expectations, and recognize the accomplishments of mission statements. The high performer is a positive role model and by virtue of his or her performance, he or she deserves recognition. When high performers receive a well-deserved compliment, certificate, or letter from their leaders in the presence of others, this gesture serves as a motivating factor for others. Educators all too commonly do not take the time to celebrate successes or even appreciate significant gains of other educators. The educational leader that breaks this cycle will inherit powers of motivation.

Deal with Unsatisfactory Performance.   It is commonly understood that rewards provide a source for motivation. It is less clear how discipline also motivates expected behavior. Angkor Wat, another human-made wonder of the world, was constructed between the eighth and the thirteenth centuries in Cambodia. The construction was accomplished under the strict scrutiny of the kings of Funan, Chenla, and Kambuja with punishments clearly known. Conformity and adherence to governance structure was expected; delinquency was not tolerated. Under this highly disciplined structure, the largest religious monument in the world was built. Today, with a lack of security in Cambodia and the continuing rebel insurgency around the Angkor region, the much needed restoration of Angkor Wat is not possible.

From Angkor Wat and other wonders of the world, educational leaders learn to hold others accountable by sanctioning appropriate disciplinary measures to those who do not perform to standard. Under the kings of Cambodia, if a worker assigned to the construction of Angkor Wat did not try, intentionally failed to meet expectations, or failed to follow directions, the behavior did not go unchecked. Punishment was designed to eradicate unacceptable behavior and prevent its recurrence. Kings punished followers in an attempt to change their behavior. Punishment also demonstrated to others what they could expect if they chose to perform in a similar manner. Hence, punishment was a motivation for all to walk the straight and narrow.

As depicted by the conditions at the time of construction of Angkor Wat, educational leadership has the responsibility to instruct, oversee, and discipline unsatisfactory performance. Successful educational leaders need to know and understand the governance structure such as policies, contracts, and specific instructions from superiors prior to sanctioning discipline. Of course, the type of discipline should be appropriate to the discipline violation. Examples of discipline or coercive tools of motivation for educational leaders are presented in Key Box 5.1.

KEY BOX ▶ 5.1

Coercive Tools of Motivation

- Give warnings about inappropriate behavior.
- Use verbal and written reprimands when appropriate.
- Conduct reprimands, counseling, and corrective action as privately and as quickly as possible after an offense.
- Direct the punishment or counseling at the behavior, not the subordinate.
- The faculty member must know the desired behavior and be able to perform it to standard.

The use of discipline as motivation in attaining human-made wonders of the world and other great achievements in the past by leaders has included actions as presented in Key Box 5.2.

KEY BOX ▶ 5.2

Using Discipline as a Motivational Tool

- Leaders let those they lead know they are disappointed about their followers' behavior, not about their followers as people. Similarly, leaders need to clearly state that their sanctions of discipline are in response to the unsatisfactory actions by those they lead and not the individuals themselves. Separating the actions from the individual is imperative in both instances, as the unsatisfactory actions of an individual do not necessarily make that individual unsatisfactory. Humans make errors.
- Leaders let those they lead know they care about their followers as people but expect improved performance from them.
- Leaders do not discipline their followers who are unable to perform a task. Leaders only discipline those unwilling or unmotivated to succeed.
- Effective leaders never lose control of their temper.
- Successful leaders do not hold a grudge after their disciplining is over.

Consider Group Rewards and Discipline.   From the construction of the Taj Mahal to the elevated city of Machu Picchu, leaders have effectively directed collective groupings of workers wisely and successfully. Although motivational strategies such as rewards and discipline sanctions apply similarly to both individuals and groups, a leader's motivation is more complex because of the diversities of the personalities involved and the interactions that are always part of group behavior. The double-edged leadership sword of praising and disciplining not only apply to the members collectively, but to each individual in the group. It is often difficult for even the experienced educational leader to forecast the outcomes of rewards and discipline sanctions that are applied within a group.

Clearly, the group is a powerful influence on behavior. As was the case in the construction of the Panama Canal, leadership cautioned groups of workers how they could avoid malaria by taking certain precautions. Informing the group in advance about the adverse consequence led the group to exert the internal pressure necessary to avoid the unhealthy conditions and attain favorable outcomes. Similarly, when leaders inform the group of consequential rewards or discipline sanctions for individuals or subgroups within a larger body, the leader must be sensitive to the resultant perceptions of importance, understanding, and responsiveness by group members. In this situation, the educational leader should also keep in mind that other organization members who were not involved in a particular situation may form their own perceptions of how the reward or discipline sanction was carried out.

Group rewards and discipline have been effective in making the wonders of the world. By using group approaches, the leaders were willing to sacrifice the unique achievements of individual effort. This means that educational leaders sometimes need to implement a group approach to accomplish monumental gains. To do so, they will need to recognize the needs of students and faculty members and develop positive role models.

IN THE NEWS

Protecting Mediocre Teachers

Successful educational leaders are mindful that other organization members who were not involved in a particular situation, such as the dismissal of a teacher, may form their own perceptions of how a discipline sanction was carried out.

Let there be little doubt, it is hard to fire incompetent teachers, at least in Chicago. With 95,000 tenured educators, only two teachers a year on the average are dismissed for incompetence. Five teachers get fired on the average annually for misconduct.

Scott Reeder who writes for papers in Moline, Rock Island, Kankakee and Ottawa reveals alarming data from his investigation of the Illinois Board of Education and 876 school districts. Seven percent of school districts made an attempt to fire a teacher in the last 18 years and only two-thirds of those school districts were successful. With costs averaging $100,000 to go through bureaucratic mazes, up red tape ladders and through legal hoops, educational leaders are often deterred. In addition, educational leaders have hesitated to proceed with teacher dismissal fearing that hearing officers are likely to toss a case out if they find a single mistake on any of the dozens of forms required for termination of employment. Reeder discovered that changes in state tenure laws prompted more than 2.5 million hours of administrative work for principals in the last two decades.

As for tenure, it doesn't seem to provide many advantages for teachers other than those that are incompetent. Elected officials need to consider the development of additional policies that permit the dismissal of bad teachers.

It is time for all stakeholders of public education to unite in doing what is best for children.

Sometimes educational leaders need to implement a group approach to accomplish monumental gains.

Source: "Protecting Mediocre Teachers," *Chicago Tribune*, December 9, 2005.

monumental gains. To do so, they will need to recognize the needs of students and faculty members and develop positive role models.

Recognize and Meet the Needs of Others.   All people have needs; food, water, and shelter are rudimentary. Beyond these basics, humans need security and need to belong to and be accepted by a group. Historically, humans have demonstrated that they need to feel that they make a difference. Social scientists have developed several motivational theories based on the concept of needs. The underlying concept of all need theories of motivation is that an unsatisfied need creates a state of internal wanting or disequilibrium. In order to restore equilibrium, humans will be motivated to do something that they perceive will satisfy a need or reduce the tension of an unpleasant situation.

Serve as, and Develop, Positive Role Models.   As Pharaoh Djoser during the third dynasty provided outstanding role modeling leading to the construction of the Step Pyramid in Saqqara (still seen today as the most spectacular site in Egypt), so have other role models throughout history motivated others to unparalleled heights. As role models, others learned from them through observation and imitation. History has taught us that each individual in an organization is a potential role model and has the potential to contribute to or detract from group motivation. We have learned that positive role models can be formal and informal leaders.

Support Formal Leaders.   Members of the formal chain of command—such as generals, captains, and other appointed or elected leaders—are obviously role models. In many of the human-made wonders of the world that were constructed over generations of time, the changing of formal leaders often took place to maintain continuity of the construction to successful completion. The actions of these formal leaders and the consequences of their actions were observed by others. Leaders were constantly under the scrutiny of their subordinates. Formal leaders who demonstrated initiative, took responsibility for their actions, and developed well-trained, cohesive groups were positive role models. Others emulated their leaders and ultimately improved their own performance. When this occurred, role modeling was a positive motivator.

Support Informal Leaders.   Within each construction of a wonder of the world, leaders who were not first part of the chain of command emerge. Such was the case when Colonel George Goethals, rising from within the ranks where others had fallen short, took over in leading others in building the Panama Canal. An informal leader is an individual whom peers look to for direction. He or she is both trusted and respected. Because the informal leader exercises a great deal of control and influence within an organization, it is essential that formal leaders identify the informal leaders as quickly as possible. Informal leaders can be used as excellent role models for their peers. However, formal leadership must be careful not to overlook the beliefs and values of the other members of the unit. If informal leaders have a negative impact on the motivation of a unit, they must be disciplined quickly by the formal leader.

Motivation has resulted in human-made wonders of the world. Leaders at the helm of these projects demonstrated the highest ethical standards, built cohesive and winning teams, effectively used rewards and discipline sanctions, recognized and satisfied individual needs, and developed positive role models. History has presented actions that future leaders can take to motivate their followers. But how do educational leaders decide which is the best action to take? Knowing actions you can take to improve motivation is important; however, understanding the underlying motivation factors can help you be an even more effective motivator to others.

WHAT DOES IT TAKE?

The grounding and grinding of twenty-first-century keys to motivation began when the first two people on earth met and one tried to influence the other into saying or doing something. From the wonders of the media's portrayal of the *Best Teacher in America* to the wonders of the world, superlative motivation has been the guiding force. Research of diversified and numerous motivational theories have been developed, providing affirmation for keys to successful twenty-first-century educational leadership motivation. Knowing and practicing these theories will support and assist educational leaders in gaining much needed school improvements through the release of human potential of educational members.

THE REFLECTIVE PRACTITIONER

Welcome to your fifth Reflective Practitioner containing your fifth scenario synthesis based on the ISSLC Standard 2 and your reading of Chapter 5. It is intended to provoke your thoughtful reflection and to stimulate discussion among colleagues, classmates, and peers. The Reflective Practitioner provides opportunities to synthesize issues, make comparisons, and apply theory to practice. We hope it will motivate you to search for evidence, thus increasing your comprehension of the text and helping you examine your convictions and discover new and shared perspectives.

ISSLC Standard 2
A school administrator is an educational leader who promotes the success of all students by advocating, nurturing, and sustaining a school culture and instructional program conducive to student learning and staff professional growth.

Scenario

Molick Park Elementary School, with a population of approximately 900 K–6 students, is located in the inner city of a large northern, urban area. Molick Park Elementary School has the lowest socioeconomic rated student enrollment in the state. The faculty composition is 40 percent Caucasian, 30 percent African American,

and 30 percent Hispanic American. Although the school district has been desegregated by court order, Molick Park Elementary School's student enrollment remains 92 percent minority and 8 percent Caucasian.

Although there is a school vision of learning that is shared and supported by school staff, staff morale is very low and staff are apathetic about contributing to achieve this vision. Conditions have been this way for the last decade. None of the faculty members like it this way—it's just the way it's been. It is known and accepted by faculty that this is the reason student achievement is in the cellar, with not only the lowest scores in the school district but also the second lowest in the state. Although Mr. Mulder, who has served as principal for the last fifteen years, is considered a really nice guy by faculty, staff apathy has escalated, absenteeism has steadily increased, and new teacher turnover is the highest in the four-state region.

With the appointment of a new superintendent, Mr. Mulder has submitted his retirement resignation effectively immediately. You are appointed as his replacement as principal of Molick Park Elementary School. In hearing of your appointment, several teachers, parents, and community members shared confidentially with you the urgency in increasing staff morale. Motivating those teachers! Having students, staff, and parents strive for great achievements! The new superintendent concurs and believes faculty and students have the potential.

QUESTION FOR REFLECTIVE THINKING

1. Write a strategic plan as principal for motivating the faculty of Molick Park Elementary School. Include as many strategies as you deem appropriate as presented in Chapter 5. In addition, apply a time frame to each action step. After all, the new

superintendent has requested your strategic action plan for motivating the Molick Park Elementary School staff and students on his desk in two weeks. Continued success!

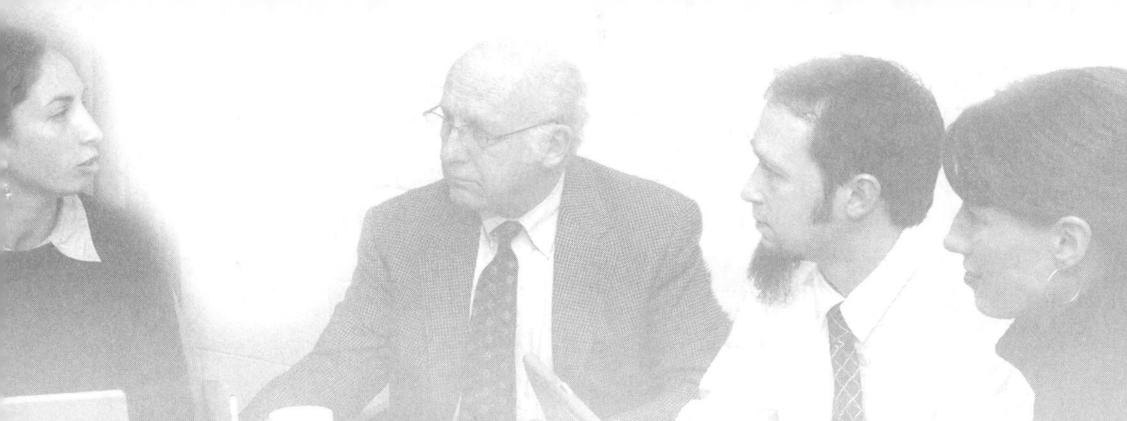

chapter 6

ISLLC
Standard
3

Making Decisions That Improve Education

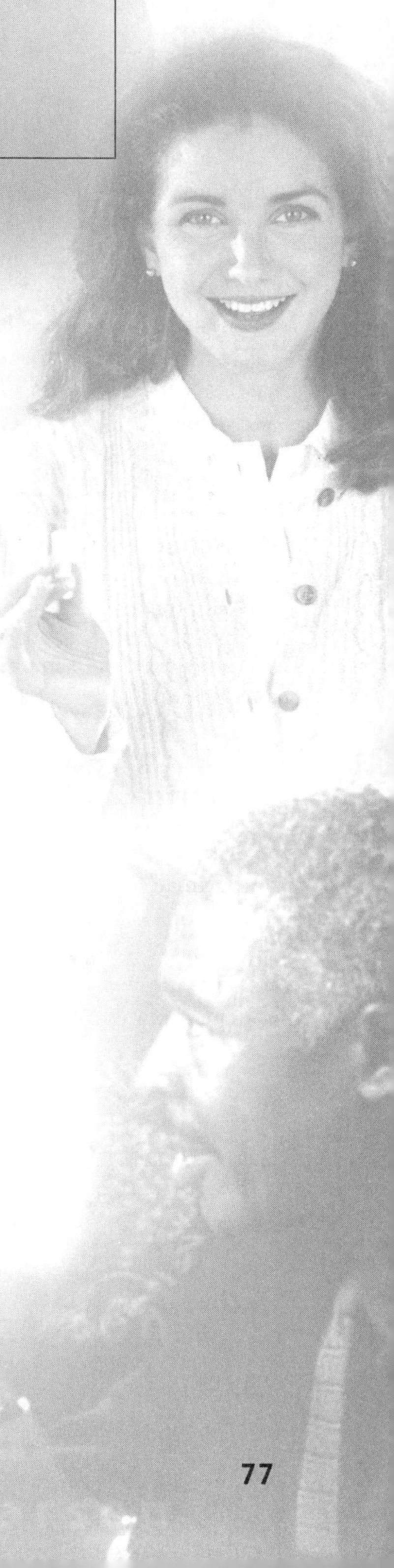

Today's decisions are tomorrow's companions.
—Anonymous

Your Chapter 6 Action Focus paves the path of importance of decision making beginning with a letter from two professors to one of their former students. Some student/professor relationships go far beyond graduation. Such has been the case with Sharyn, a graduate of our principal preparation program, and both authors. A recent letter sent to Sharyn describing *Keys to Successful 21st Century Leadership* follows:

Dear Sharyn,

It was wonderful receiving your letter. Congratulations on your appointment as principal of Sterling Middle School. Truthfully, this comes as no surprise to us. Your performance in our master's in school leadership program was extraordinary, as you excelled particularly in your ability to integrate theoretical foundations into cutting-edge leadership practices, understood and contributed significantly to the culture and climate of our university program, and demonstrated the personal and professional skills needed in twenty-first century leadership programs.

Thank you for asking about our current involvements. In addition to our teaching master's and doctoral classes, consulting, and writing reports for our department's accreditation, we continue to stay active and busy co-authoring books and articles for future and current educational leaders. The one we are writing currently is *Keys to Successful 21st Century Educational Leadership.* We affectionately refer to it as our *Keys* book as we speak heart to heart with our readers, providing them with practical directions for successful new millennium leadership. We think of it as "views they can use!" We present keys to successful educational leadership on important leadership topics based on our research, publications, teaching, and work in schools and school districts. In addition, our writing is aligned to national standards for student relevance and university accreditation. We have even included research links for additional exploration and investigation. We are excited about the promise of providing a book that future and current educational leaders will position within an arm's length to use as a "desk reference" as they provide effective, responsive, and innovative leadership as we know you will be doing at Sterling.

As you have stated in your letter, Sharyn, effective decision making is a foundation for successful leadership. There is no question that the whole art and science of decision making needs clarification, continuing analysis, and understanding. Like breathing, educational leaders often make decisions without much consideration of the process of how those decisions were rendered. Too often, educational leaders make decisions by the seat of their pants, on the run, and with too much haste.

Again, thank you for your letter, Sharyn. We wish you the best of continued success in all future endeavors. Please stop by and visit us whenever you are in the area, and above all, lead on!

Sincerely,
Your ZZ Team

As demonstrated in your Chapter 5 Action Focus, Sharyn, as well as her colleagues throughout the nation, constantly search for strategies that are effective in decision making. As educational leaders experience intense challenges requiring high-stakes decision making, decision-making strategies as presented in Chapter 6 are imperative for successful educational leadership. Hence, the intent of Chapter 6 is to provide educational leaders with technical assistance and guidance—the keys for successful decision making!

HISTORICAL VIEWS ON DECISION MAKING

The scientific management, the human relations movement, and the behavior science approach established the importance of decision making; that is, organizations of the many were guided by decisions made by the few, usually an individual or a board of trustees (Davis & Ashton, 2002). Under these theories, centralized decision making was seen as the best way to enhance productivity and develop human capital. By the middle of the twentieth century and beyond, there was much interest regarding human motivation and its impact on job satisfaction and productivity. Creating hierarchies resulted in inequality with limited evidence of increasing productivity. Clearly, much can be learned from the fundamentals of each of these decision-making strategies.

Keys to Classical Decision Making

The first model to be presented is the classical decision-making model, an approach that is centered on maximizing achievement of the organization by finding the best solutions. The classical decision-making model employs an optimizing strategy by seeking the best possible alternatives to reach goals and objectives (Gaustello, 2002). The keys to successful classical decision-making include the following:

- *Identify the problem.* The first step in the classical decision-making model is identifying the problem; after all, two-thirds of a solution to a problem is found in its proper definition and description. To illustrate, an educational leader confronted with a high teacher absenteeism rate resulting in student underachievement must first identify the reasons for teacher absenteeism. Identifying problems accurately may be most challenging, even for the seasoned educational leader, as this identification is often multifaceted, complex in nature, and difficult in gathering all pertinent information.

• *Establish reasons and rationale for decisions.* Establishing clear reasons and rationale for the decision to be made is critical before you make up your mind. Successful educational leaders should not make a decision in the absence of sound reasons and rationale. Just remember: Educational leaders will often be judged by the last decision they made.

• *Generate all possible solutions.* All possible options need to be understood. The more options within reason, the better the decision will be. The thoughtful consideration of all solutions is essential. Known commonly as *fact finding* and *problem solving,* the educational leader's journey for possible solutions is equally as important as the destination or act of deciding.

• *Consider all possible outcomes.* Successful twenty-first-century educational leaders need to envision the outcomes of their decisions before rendering a final determination. Recognizing all possible outcomes from each viable solution assists in choosing the best outcome. In addition, the successful educational leader will need to ascertain that his or her decision does not create additional problems, perhaps even greater than the first challenge necessitating the decision.

IN THE NEWS

Filling New Schools: An Intricate Equation

Following the keys to the classical decision-making model was advantageous for a school district that decided on its new school boundaries.

With a rapidly increasing population within the school district's boundaries, the Prince George County Board of Education needed to decide how to proceed when it came to establishing new boundaries for its newly constructed schools. In spite of the blessing of increased student enrollment, intense debate surrounded forthcoming decisions involving a complicated sequence of boundary moves.

The Prince County Board of Education wasn't about to tackle this decision in the absence of its community members. Public meetings were held to clearly *identify* the problem, *discuss* the rationale of many possible decisions, *generate* the best possible solutions, *consider* all outcomes, *align* solutions to educational imperatives, and eventually *select* the best decision. The board members felt that only with the support of parents and other community members would the best outcomes be achieved.

Although the classical decision making model was the model of choice for the Prince George County Board of Education, this decision-making model has its limitations.

Source: N. Anderson, "Filling New Schools: An Intricate Equation," *Washington Post,* November 24, 2005.

• *Align all possible solutions to what you value.* Clearly established solutions are helpful to the process of decision making—so are the values of the decision maker or the educational leader. When solutions are aligned to the values of the decision maker, the educational leader will be able to live with the results. This living with the results translates into ownership of the decision. An educational leader who is true to self is readily recognized by his or her followers with increased respect.

• *Select the solution that maximizes long-term gains.* Selecting the solution that maximizes long-term gains requires the educational leader to be farsighted. Too often educational leaders resolve one issue only to find themselves in a more difficult situation. Solutions that are far reaching and that maximize short- and long-term gains should be highly sought.

The classical decision-making model is not without its shortcomings. Implementing all six steps is time consuming and not possible when time is of the essence. Educational leaders are often limited by time constraints, cost, and opportunity to process information. In order for the classical decision-making model to be optimally used, the educational leader should at least gather input from others, particularly when there are several viable solutions (Baron, 2000). The use of this model has some limits, and many educational leaders consider the behavioral decision-making model as one of the better approaches to educational leadership decision making.

Keys to Behavioral Decision Making

The shortcomings of the classical decision-making model have enhanced the consideration of successful twenty-first century educational leaders of the behavioral decision-making model. The complexities of educational conflicts and the limited time to arrive at viable solutions reduce the chances for an educational leader to implement the optimizing strategy of a classical decision-making model. The behavioral decision-making model follows a chronological order of events as presented by the following keys to effective implementation.

- *Leaders make decisions based on all that is known at the time.* Timely decisions are often needed. All the factors may not be known at the time a decision needs to be made. Additional information may follow *after* the decision has been made. Such is life. Decisions can always be fortified, revised, or enhanced as additional information is known. Sometimes in education it needs to be "ready, fire, aim" instead of "ready, aim, and fire" when a decision has to be made in a timely fashion.
- *Making a decision is sometimes more important than collecting all the alternatives.* Consider, for example, the situation in which a decision has to be made as to which grade should be dismissed first to go to the assembly. Should it be the tenth, eleventh, or twelfth grade? Does it really matter as long as a decision is made with sufficient time to plan before the assembly? After all, the seating chart is known by all faculty members as to where students sit during the assembly. Making a decision is more important to faculty than taking the time to consider all possible options. Besides, educational leaders may never succeed in generating all possible alternative solutions for consideration in a complex organization such as a school or school district (DeGroot, 2004).
- *Expect the unexpected.* There is really no certainty as to all the consequences of an educational leader's decision. Viable options realistically are always evaluated incompletely because it is impossible to predict accurately all outcomes (Raiffa, 1997). A lesson to be learned for successful twenty-first-century leadership in decision making and all other situations is always expect the unexpected. The only certainty is change.
- *If it works, don't try to fix it!* If the decision that is made achieves a viable solution, let it stand and move on to another challenge. It is impossible at times, at least without great pains, to know which alternative is optimal. Be thankful that you've arrived at a decision that is workable. The idea here is not to be perfect. Rather, the educational leader needs to concentrate on what is most human and humane.
- *Select the first alternative that satisfies minimal standards of acceptability.* At times, educational leaders, especially when under time constraints, will select the first alternative that satisfies minimal standards of acceptability without

exploring all the known possibilities. This is commonly referred to as *satisficing*. Often, the decision making of educational leaders is concerned with a decision of *satisficing* rather than the discovery and selection of satisfactory alternatives (Goodman & Wright, 2004).

It is often difficult to make something rational out of the irrational. In behavioral decision making the same terms hold true, to a certain extent. There are four keys to rational behavioral decision making: bounded rationality, contextual rationality, procedural rationality, and retrospective rationality. Because it is important for successful twenty-first-century educational leaders to understand these concepts, we are describing these forms of behavioral decision-making rationality as follows:

- *Base your decisions on limited information.* Educational leaders too often need to make decisions on limited information. These decisions are called decisions of *bounded rationality.* Successful educational leaders will call on their prior experiences, intestinal fortitude, intuition, and related situations in coming to grips with making a decision. Time constraints, insufficient funding, and lack of precedents for decision making often result in bounded rationality. Accept bounded rationality at its face value, maintain your wits, and make the best decision you are able to make.

- *Maintain your perspective in making decisions.* Often, environmental influences create havoc and impede decision making. *Contextual rationality* is a term used to describe these environmental influences, including, but not limited to, internal and external politics, distribution of power and authority, and other environmental influences that impact decision making (Murighan & Mowen, 2002). Successful leaders strive diligently to render the best decisions, but realize that it is not their way or the highway! They realize that, due to contextual rationalities, their best decisions may be *negotiated renderings* or improved decisions.

IN THE NEWS

Superintendent Finds One Word Can Spell Trouble

A state superintendent, admitting her misjudgment of a situation, maintained her perspective and negotiated her renderings.

As a state superintendent of schools, Kathy Cox stated that the word *evolution* should be taken out of her state's new curriculum, making Georgia's public school system the target of scrutiny and ridicule across the nation. Cox stated her rationale for removing the *e* word was to give educators some leeway in teaching some of the concepts, but not having to use a word that upsets some parents.

Instead of avoiding confrontation, Cox started a heated national debate. Her actions were blasted by scientists, educators, and even a former president. What was an educational leader to do? Cox maintained her perspective and negotiated her response by issuing a public statement that she misjudged the situation and would recommend that the word be put back in the curriculum.

Whether her reversal will calm her opponents or cast dark clouds over her political career, Superintendent Cox thought she made the very best decision she could under the circumstances. She gave it her best *rendering* and went on to her next decision. Although critics will say that a leader is only as successful as his or her last decision, leaders are human and humans make mistakes.

Superintendent Cox thought is was a better decision to change her first decision in consideration of the established structures or an overwhelming majority of those favoring the usage of the word evolution.

Source: D. Togif, "Superintendent Finds One Word Can Spell Trouble," *The Atlanta Journal-Constitution,* February 8, 2004.

- *Use established structures as a basis for making your decisions.* Education has its share of federal mandates such as No Child Left Behind, state school codes, and local district policies. There is nothing insufficient about the established governance structures over education today. These structures comprise what is known as the *procedural rationalities* of decision making. Successful twenty-first-century educational leaders learn quickly that their decisions need to support established structures. Ignorance of these established structures is not an excuse for decisions that conflict with procedural rationalities.

• *Give it your best shot and go on to your next decision.* It is only wasted energy that goes into continual justification of the rationality of a past decision. Entitled *retrospective rationality,* this is another major form of decision making where considerable energy goes into justifying the rationality of decisions that have already made. Once a decision has been made, expending energy to find good reasons for an already made decision is counterproductive (Pelled, Eisenhardt, & Xin, 1999). Those who are arbitrary, insecure and defensive tend to spend inordinate amounts of time and energy justifying past decisions instead of concentrating on future needs. Make your best decision, let it go, and go on to the next decision.

The more educational leaders understand about decision-making processes, the more apt these educational leaders are to become more skillful decision makers (Drucker, 2002). Classical and behavioral decision-making models provide valued insight, but the incremental model is also useful.

Keys to Incremental Decision Making

Decision making characterized by the science of muddling through complex, uncertain, and conflict-entrenched issues is especially beneficial when a clear solution just simply does not emerge. Inasmuch as the incremental model of decision making considers only alternatives that are similar to the existing situation, it greatly reduces the number of alternatives. The process used while employing the incremental model of decision making is often referred to as the method of *successive limited comparisons.* Ignoring all alternatives that are outside the educational leader's specified range of interest, the incremental model of decision making analyzes differences between the current state and proposed outcomes (Lindblom, 1993). The incremental model reduces the complexities of decision making and makes arriving at a decision by the educational leader more manageable. Key Box 6.1 lists the advantages of the incremental approach to decision making.

KEY BOX 6.1

Advantages of the Incremental Approach to Decision Making

- Establishes goals and considers different solutions occurring simultaneously
- Renders the quality of the solution to be determined by the agreement of decision makers
- Considers only the options similar to the current state of affairs; the number of options and outcomes are significantly reduced
- Narrows the analysis of the differences between existing situations and options
- Deemphasizes theoretical analyses and increases the comparisons of concrete alternatives

Through the implementation of incremental decision making, educational leaders who focus on a reasonable set of alternatives on the basis of their experiences are able to make predictions of outcomes with accuracy and confidence. As problems become increasingly more complex, the inadequacies of reducing alternatives may prove insufficient in determining intricate decisions. Although widely used, incremental decision making has its limitations, one of which is that it can be too narrow and specific. Hence, successful twenty-first-century educational leaders should consider the following additional decision-making models before they enter a decision-making process.

Keys to Mixed-Scanning Decision Making

As a newly appointed educational leader, you will find that you have to make decisions with only partial information and while being bombarded with numerous other issues. The mixed-scanning decision-making model provides a pragmatic approach to complexities and uncertainties while meeting the needs of decision making under these conditions (Etzioni, 1967, 1990). This approach is actually a synthesis of the behavioral and the incremental models.

In using the mixed-scanning model, educational leaders will examine data that are of slight importance as well as data that are deeply entrenched in their school's culture. They will first consider data in general or scan a broad range of facts and choices. Their scanning will be followed by a detailed examination of the facts and choices. In this two-step process, they will consider matters of great importance to be considered in their decision making, such as mission statement or policy stipulations with lower-order matters. To more clearly see the utility of the mixed-scanning model of decision making, successful twenty-first-century educational leaders unite the rationalism and completeness of the behavioral decision model of decision making with the flexibility of the incremental model of decision making. The advantages of the mixed-scanning model of decision making emerge. The successful implementation of this model consists of the following seven keys (Russo & Schoemaker, 2002).

- *Arrive at your decision through trial and error.* The first step in arriving at your decision through trial-and-error methodologies begins with your search for reasonable alternatives. After identifying all reasonable alternatives, you then select, implement, and test them. Last, you adjust and modify as the outcomes become clear. You will use this trial-and-error method when you need to make a decision when important information is missing. In essence, you will make decisions with partial information and then carefully monitor and modify your decision in light of new data. Make sure you reserve the right to modify your decision as additional information is made clear.
- *View each decision you make as tentative.* Although the decision you make today may be the best at the time, as circumstances change and additional clarification is made known, you will soon learn to view your decisions as part of a continuous process, not a terminal end. Information during the twenty-first century is projected to double every thirty days (Luehrman, 1998). Not one educational leader, regardless of the number of successful years of experience, will be able to know everything. The best you can do is to respond positively to

changing conditions. In order to do so, remain tentative in making decisions, position yourself with those you lead in understanding a course of action you may have to change given a set of unforeseeable circumstances at the time. It is important to maintain the option of reversing a decision as additional information and clarification is revealed.

- *Buy more time if you can.* Sometimes patience is a virtue when more time is needed to make the very best decision. The best educational leaders have hurried to make a decision and that haste has made waste to say the very least (Harrison, 1999). Do not make a decision that results in a worse outcome than if a decision were not made in the first place. If additional time is needed to make the best decision, explain to others the importance of this additional time. Even giving others an indication of when a decision may be made is helpful. This is particularly the case in certain situations that are ambiguous. A delay to collect and analyze more information before taking action is crucial.

- *Reveal your decisions in stages.* Have a well-developed master plan comprised of goals that are both short term and long term. The successful achievement of these goals will be based on the quality of the decisions you make and how these decisions are communicated to others. Sometimes sharing numerous decisions all at once is overwhelming and confusing. It is better to stagger your decisions instead of shotgunning them out all at once. By revealing your decision in stages, you will be able to evaluate the outcomes of each decision before proceeding to the next revelation.

- *Don't put all your eggs in one basket.* By revealing your decisions in stages, you prevent the budget from being exhausted all at once. The development of stages of decision revealing also results in the development of budgeting stages. If a certain decision you have made leads to unfavorable outcomes of both conditions and expenditures, both outcomes and budgeting amounts will undergo revision more efficiently and with decreased formality. In other words, partial decisions allow the usage of partial resources until the consequences are satisfactory.

- *Diversify your alternatives, maximize your gains.* Through the decisions that educational leaders make, they implement several diversified alternatives. Before doing so, however, they ascertain that each alternative will result in an acceptable outcome. Treating each alternative as an investment, educational leaders make adjustments on the basis of the gains. To illustrate diversifying alternatives and maximizing gains, let's say that you are asked to establish the times and days for professional development for your faculty. Your first hunch might be to go with the same day of the week during the same week of the month in which faculty would be released from classes to attend. Instead, you might decide to have professional development for faculty on different days of the week, different weeks of the month, and scheduled at different times during the day. Varying the days, weeks, and times results in improved outcomes because the students would not be missing the same classes each time there is professional development. By diversifying your alternatives, you will maximize your gains— increase student achievement and provide a variety of professional development times for faculty.

- *Keep your options open.* Position yourself in the decisions that you make so that you are able to rescind, reverse, and improve your decisions when additional information is known. Decisions are not cast in stone. Keeping options open means that the decisions that are made are subject to reversal, revision, and even deletion as better courses of action are made known.

Knowing a variety of decision-making models will be of great advantage to educational leaders when they need to determine how best to make a decision. As circumstances readily change, so too will your implementation of different decision-making models. There is even a decision-making model that hasn't been shared yet called the *garbage can model*. (It isn't exactly what its name implies, so read on!)

Keys to Garbage Can Decision Making

The garbage can decision-making approach allows decision makers to store decisions even before problems occur. This idea comes from observation that decisions are made in organizations when particular decision-making opportunities or requirements arise (Rainey, 2003). In this model it may be unclear who has the authority to decide what and for whom (Stone, 2002). Garbage can decision making is unlike other classical decision-making models because solutions are developed before problems are determined (Kingdon, 2003). In other words, instead of waiting for a problem to respond to, decision makers are waiting for an opportunity to implement the decisions that already have been determined. Once attention is brought to a problem that is related to kept-on-the shelf decisions, decision makers then announce it at that time (Kingdon, 2003).

Decision makers should be aware of the limitations of using the garbage can decision-making approach. When decision makers use this approach with their decisions rendered before a problem occurs, their decisions will often lack consideration of unique circumstances surrounding each situation (Cohen, March, & Olsen, 1972). In addition, this approach to decision making relies on the chance that a certain problem will occur. The garbage can approach is most likely to occur in organizations that experience extremely high uncertainty without established board policies and administrator procedures.

Another way of looking at the limitations of garbage can decision making is to envision educational leaders using this decision-making model solely. These decision makers would not recognize that something is unsatisfactory and in need of a decision until a decision matches a problem. That is to say, when problems and solutions happen to match, then, and only then, a decision may occur. Furthermore, an educational leader who has an enlightening thought may cleverly find a problem to solve.

Undoubtedly, the garbage can metaphor contains elements of truth (Rainey, 2003). In numerous studies, the garbage can process seems to be an appropriate description of the way decisions are reached in some situations but not in others. The model has received support in a number of studies of different kinds of organizations, although other studies have questioned its value as a general model of decision making, even in organizations of complexity, uncertainty, discontinuity, and power politics. It needs to be clearly emphasized that although the garbage can metaphor may describe how decisions are at times made, it is not recommended as the only model for decision making.

Keys to Shared Decision Making

In addition to determining which decision-making model to employ, successful twenty-first-century educational leaders determine whether to involve others in the decision-making process or to make the decision independently. Who to involve in the decision-making process can be a challenging concern in itself.

In recent years, with the widespread pressures to increase student achievement, educational leaders have taken to *shared decision making* as one of the viable strategies. This approach maximizes participation in making decisions, whether it involves administrators, teachers, students, parents, and/or community members. The intent, whether directly or not, is to support and increase student learning.

RESEARCH KEYS

To enrich your understanding of **shared decision making,** log on to www.researchnavigator.com and search Ebsco's ContentSelect.

Research
Navigator.com

Shared decision making means different things to different people. Participants in the process vary from a few volunteers serving on a small committee to all members of the entire organization working together to solve a problem. At times, teachers will team together to review and decide on the best instructional and curricular practices. At other times, administrators, teachers, students, parents, and community members may decide on and implement large-scale school improvements such as school safety and security issues. The five keys to sharing a decision presented in the order of least participation to the maximum participation follow (DeGroot, 2004; Eisenhardt, Kahwajy, & Bourgeois, 1997).

- *Call others together to share a decision.* Educational leaders will call those they lead and others together for the sole purpose of sharing a decision that already has been made. The educational leader perhaps shares the rationale of an established decision, and maybe gives others a chance to ask questions, digest the implications of the decision, and prepare for the outcomes of the decision. In doing so, the educational leader hopes others will accept the decision more readily because the decision was communicated to them before implementation or hearing the decision elsewhere at a later date.

- *Call others together to seek input.* Although the educational leader who calls others together in efforts of procuring information is more than sharing an already made decision, it does not provide opportunities for others to participate in the making of a decision. The benefit of this participation is the facilitation of a more rational and logical decision. The educational leader who uses this shared decision-making model must ascertain that participants are aware that the educational leader will ultimately be making the decision based on the consensus of information he or she has attained from others. In addition, the successful educational leader will extend appreciation to others for their input, but explain that the thoughts of others will not necessarily be reflected in his or her decision.

- *Call others together to value their ideas.* Perhaps the chief reason why the educational leader calls others together is to demonstrate his or her care for their thoughts, concerns, and recommendations. It may be clear that the educational leader may have been lassoed into making the decision solely; however, the ideas of others are important and will help shape the decision. Educational leaders who use this shared decision-making model call together those they lead to share that they, as educational leaders, will need to make a decision but only after they have reflected on their followers' input.

- *Call others together to obtain a majority rule.* Educational leaders call others together to actually participate in the decision-making process. For whatever reasons, the gesture of including others in decision making seems noble; however, when it does not appear likely that unanimity or even consensus will prevail among those called to make a decision, what do educational leaders do? Successful twenty-first-century educational leaders use majority rules to determine the decision. It offers the great advantage of specifically encouraging opinions and shifting positions in time as ideas and values change. However, beware: The majority rule technique has the distinct disadvantage of creating winners and losers.

- *Call others together and use consensus to determine decisions.* When educational leaders call others together to participate in decision making, it is vital for educational leaders to explain the process for making decisions straight from the outset. If consensus is the technique that will be required for the group to make a decision, this needs to be made clear before the decision making begins. Consensus building is most often used when the issues leading to a final decision are most important. Consensus may create pressure; therefore, it is recommended that consensus building be implemented sparingly. However, when it is used successfully, keep in mind that consensus building is a powerful decision-making technique.

Although shared decision making empowers others, it also means increased responsibility on the shoulders of others. Being responsible for the outcomes of decisions can often be overwhelming. Therefore, participants in shared decision-making situations must be willing to risk emotional involvement in situations once perceived as off limits under autocratic paradigms (Senge, 1990a; Stacey, 1996). Hence, educational leaders need to encourage those they lead to step up to the plate and contribute to group decision making. Educational leaders need to bear in mind that regardless of ample encouragement, at times individuals may shy away from the opportunity to participate in decision making.

Successful participation in shared decision making requires skills that need to be learned and this learning is lifelong. The skills of shared decision making, such as collegiality, cooperative efforts, and respect for each other's viewpoints as professionals, have not had numerous opportunities to be practiced in education. To this day, some schools and school districts cling to their bureaucratic heritage. Yet, if shared decision making is to succeed, the mastery of decision-making skills by all participants is vital. More specifically, if shared decision making is to be successful, educational leaders will need to provide the following keys to develop shared decision-making processes (Clemen, 1996; Ghahramani, 1996).

- *Educational leaders need to build collaborative cultures.* Education in general has been a place for individual pursuits. Teachers arrive in their classrooms in the early morning, perhaps have lunch at their desks while helping students, and leave at the end of the day with little interaction among colleagues. Worse yet, educators for the smallest of issues and instances have built walls instead of bridges around themselves. Creating a collaborative culture that values others as capable contributors to the decision-making process is not an easy undertaking.

- *Educational leaders need professional development to bring this change.* Educational leaders must be trained to transform educational settings into collegial environments. They will become the teachers of faculty, necessitating understanding adult learning. The transitioning from traditional power structures to implementation of shared decision making holds issues that need to be resolved through newly acquired knowledge.

- *Educational leaders need to align personal values with organizational values.* Some educational leaders will have difficulty letting go of their power and authority and empowering those they lead. It is important that educational leaders establish congruence between personal values and organizational values when it comes to implementing shared decision-making strategies.

- *Educational leaders need to develop successful decision makers.* If educational leaders are to relinquish authority in some educational matters, the question surfaces as to who will lead shared decision-making initiatives? In other words, the question here is: Who will lead in developing content, process, and research information to be used by decision makers? Effective shared decision making requires successful decision-making leaders in the absence of formal educational leadership's authority.

- *Educational leaders need to sustain shared decision-making practices.* Too often in education, the "curricula de jour" is here today and gone tomorrow. These short-termed, often shortsighted, initiatives have left seasoned staff members with the thought, "Even this shall pass; why bother to get involved?" If shared decision making is to be successful, educational leaders need to establish mechanisms and procedures to initiate and sustain shared decision-making processes.

- *Educational leaders need to provide meaningful training for others.* Professional development should not be limited to educational leaders. Too often in education some sort of change is implemented without the proper training. As a result, the change is doomed to failure. Educational leaders need to provide skill acquisition for all staff members through meaningful, real-life training opportunities.

- *Educational leaders need to provide reflection and celebration.* Too often educators do not take the time to celebrate successes! Monumental successes are often taken for granted. This lack of

IN THE NEWS

What Do Good Leaders Do Right?

Kenneth Leithwood and a team of investigators will use metacognitive strategies to determine the links between, and future improvements for, educational leadership strategies and increased student achievement.

Researcher Kenneth Leithwood is confident that educational leaders affect student learning. But he's just as adamant that not enough is known about how they do so. And that's something he hopes to help change. With a new five-year study involving 180 schools in 45 districts and nine states, he and a team of other investigators plan to paint a clear picture of the links between student outcomes and the work of principals, superintendents, and other educational leaders. Claiming to be the largest study ever of those connections, the Learning from Leadership project will bring a team of investigators together to participate in *shared decision making* that promises to shed light on how schools should be managed, how administrators should be trained, and what state policies most help school leaders in raising student achievement levels.

As Leithwood unified a team of investigators, so too will successful twenty-first-century educational leaders do in forming shared decision-making opportunities.

Source: J. Archer, "What Do Good Leaders Do Right?" *Education Week,* September 8, 2005.

affirmation and acknowledgment for accomplishments often leads to frustration, apathy, and hopelessness. The successful implementation of shared decision-making strategies is no simple transformation. Educational leaders should provide training that includes opportunities for personal and organizational reflection and celebration.

- *Educational leaders need to provide assessment and awareness opportunities.* Educational leaders must ensure that training includes an understanding of the importance of assessment and an awareness of the change process and how it can be tailored to the different types of decisions that will need to be made. The more shared decision makers engage in metacognitive strategies to assess their gains, the more improvement through shared decision making will emerge.

Many leaders who have participated in shared decision making swear by it and its many advantages; others swear at it. What is startling is that these individuals are often employed in the same school. The point here is, shared decision making has been met with exceptional success and disappointing failure and sometimes touted as the new leadership paradigm to rescue schools (Bazerman, 2002). Shared decision making has also been named one of the most futile attempts to reshape U.S. schools. These divergent views are, in part, a result of insufficient orientation and training and a challenging movement from a highly centralized system with refusals in letting go of autocratic management to a decentralized, shared decision-making concept. An understanding of the advantages and disadvantages of shared decision making is key to your decision of whether to implement this decision-making model.

Advantages of Shared Decision Making.　Several studies have revealed benefits of shared decision making both in business and in educational organizations. Faculty member participation in decision making improves productivity in the following ways.

- *Shared decision making increases faculty morale.* We have noted time and time again that the opportunity for faculty members to participate in decision making seems to increase the morale of teachers and their enthusiasm for the school. Feeling engaged, connected, and affirmed comes from involvement and ownership.
- *Shared decision making fosters job satisfaction.* Participation in decision making is positively related to the faculty members' satisfaction with the profession of teaching. Again, if faculty members have a say, they are more apt to feel that their efforts are making a schoolwide or districtwide difference.
- *Shared decision making builds faculty support of educational leaders.* It is human nature for people to want to belong, to relate, and to contribute to the benefit of others. This is especially true for educators because participation is at the heart of why many educators entered their profession. The opportunity to be involved in meaningful decisions tends to result in increased support of educational leaders.
- *Shared decision making increases faculty support of decisions.* Ownership of decisions derived from the opportunity to engage in decision making results in greater support of decisions. Involvement in shared decision making will enhance the success of decisions regardless of what was decided. Decisions fail because

educational leadership chooses not to involve those in shared decision making whom the decision will impact.

● *Times for implementing are thoughtfully selected by educational leaders.* Even too much of a good thing can be bad. To illustrate, for every decision to be made in a school—such as lunch line configuration, bus routes, and breakfast menus—a group decision is not necessary. Some of these decisions should be made by the one in charge (e.g., cafeteria supervisor and transportation director). Faculty members neither expect nor want to be involved in every decision. Too much involvement can be as detrimental as too little.

● *Shared decision making positively impacts job satisfaction.* There is considerable research showing that shared decision making positively affects employees' job satisfaction. As we all know, satisfied employees are highly desired by educational leaders for several reasons. Satisfied faculty members are more likely to exhibit low absenteeism, contribute more fully to their schools, and treat others more positively.

● *Shared decision making benefits mental health.* Additionally, it has been our collective experience that shared decision making may be beneficial to faculty members' mental health and job satisfaction. When faculty members are engaged meaningfully, healthier conditions prevail. The degree that shared decision making benefits mental health and job satisfaction is contingent on individual and situational variables.

The Rusty Keys of Shared Decision Making. There is a downside of shared decision making as well. At times during shared decision making each faculty member's voice may not be encouraged and respected. Some faculty members engaged in group decision making may not always keep an open mind. Sometimes faculty members in group decision-making situations do not clearly hear and understand what is being said by another.

If these tendencies are allowed to dominate, the negative consequences of group decision making erodes other qualities of group decision making, such as innovation, creativity, and ownership (Drucker, 2002). The awareness of these disadvantages is critical to the harmony and cooperation of shared decision makers. Hence, successful twenty-first-century educational leaders need to intervene when impediments reduce or oppose group decision-making progress. Your ability to recognize the risks that impede group decision making, as presented in Key Box 6.2, is critical to the success of decision making.

KEY BOX 6.2

Risks That Impede Group Decision Making

● *Risk 1: Shared decision-making members drop their guard!* When shared decision-making members drop their guard, they ignore obvious limitations of their decision, take extreme risks, and are overly optimistic. Worse than impeding the progress of shared decision making, outcomes of dropping guard adversely impact future thoughts of group decision participation.

● *Risk 2: Shared decision-making members implement hidden agendas.* At times, faculty members may participate in group decisions for the very reason of implementing a hidden agenda, or something the faculty member desires that may not be in the best interests of others. It is essential that the educational leader recognizes this behavior early on.

- *Risk 3: Shared decision-making members are on a moral crusade.* Members believe their decisions are morally correct, ignoring all the other consequences of their decisions. Let's say a shared decision-making body decides that the topic of creationism is morally correct and decides that it needs to be taught, although board policy or state legislation may disallow it. Be vigilant in recognizing this tendency.
- *Risk 4: Shared decision-making members become "we" and "they" groups.* Those participating in group decision making at times feel superior to others who are not involved in shared decision making. This behavior leads to divisive measures that challenge the unity of the whole faculty. Successful educational leaders viewing this behavior should remind shared decision-making members of their mission and responsibility to the whole staff.
- *Risk 5: Shared decision-making members cave in to peer pressure.* Shared decision-making members may resort to pressuring other group members who express arguments against the group's collective vision or commitments, viewing such opposition as disloyalty. Individuality is key to successful shared decision making.
- *Risk 6: Shared decision-making members falsely view silence as golden.* Members perceive falsely that everyone agrees with the group's decision; silence is seen as consent. Educational leaders need to encourage each shared decision-making member to share his or her thoughts, ask questions, and voice concerns.
- *Risk 7: Shared decision-making members appoint themselves to superior positions!* Some members appoint themselves to superior roles within the shared decision-making group. Educational leaders need to ensure that shared decision-making members uphold an equal voice, equity, and an equal vote status.

The shift from more classical decision-making models to shared decision-making methods requires a new understanding of authority and a new sense of organizational wisdom. The transition to shared decision making will necessitate the educational leader's intervention at times to ensure the success of this decision-making model. Empowering teachers and other staff members to participate in shared decision making requires a paradigm shift from decision-making models that are less participatory to decision-making models that improve results, increase faculty morale, and lead to increased student achievement.

PERSPECTIVE ON DECISION MAKING

Our final words for now on decision making are: Simply following the keys of the decision making models that we've shared with you is not sufficient. Effective decision making depends on the skills, dispositions, and experiences of the educational leader. There are effective decision-making models; select one that is best suited to your situation, your leadership style, and your goals to be accomplished.

During the last three decades, American education has emerged to the front and center of campaigns waged by hopeful and seated

RESEARCH KEYS

To enrich your understanding of **educational decision making,** log on to www.researchnavigator.com and search Ebsco's ContentSelect.

Research Navigator.com

elected officials. Whether justified or not, widespread concern about the quality of public education was held in question. Reforming education became the rule rather than the exception as panels, task forces, and commissions convened over and over. The recurring theme commonly held, "Education is broken and we're going to fix it," continued into the twenty-first-century. In fact, one of the more alarming reports written in 1983, *A Nation at Risk: The Imperative for Educational Reform,* sensationalized education into terms of war and surrender!

With all of these attempts at school reform, one would think that the bureaucratic educational decision-making model would have left with the hula hoop. As you know, public schools have continued to promote a well-defined hierarchy of authority (where teachers and students remain at the bottom), where the board of education, with input from the superintendent, decides the rules that determine the behavior of educators through the development of policies and the creation of job descriptions. At times, the board of education even engages in deciding the hiring and firing of its staff through its micromanaging.

The classical approach of Weber is alive and thriving in schools today. The bureaucratic model, in emphasizing the formal distribution of authority, is not congruent with educational leaders being asked to lead with all their might while at the same time they are limited by board policy. There is need at this time for additional clarification regarding the relationship of bureaucratic decision making and professionalism in our schools and how this interplay influences governance and decision making.

At best, under a bureaucratic decision-making model, a fine line exists between centralized policies and decentralized autonomy extended to educational leaders in determining curricular, instructional, and personnel decisions. The complexity of these concurrent decision-making models, which are bureaucratic and decentralized in nature, needs to remain in a contentious perspective maintained with care and caution (Shapira, 2002). To illustrate, resource allocation and school policies have typically been the domains of the centralized decision makers (board of education and its designees). At times, decisions supporting instructional or curricular practices within limitations have included teacher input.

With two spheres of decisions operating concurrently, the educational leader must juggle the decisions from differing decision-making bodies to keep matters afloat and moving forward (Goodman & Wright, 2004). Walking a "tight wire" by educational leaders is especially prevalent in decisions involving the distribution of human and material resources in the school; security decisions impacting the preservation of physical and psychological safety of faculty and students; boundary decisions determining who controls the passage of materials, information, and people from one domain to another within the school or between the school and community; evaluation decisions when passing judgment on the quality of performance (teacher or student); and instructional decisions where classroom teaching/learning is determined. Awareness of these complexities is critical to your success as you lead and coordinate the efforts of all decision makers, as confusion, frustration, and acrimony need to be prevented or at least reduced.

The bureaucratic decision-making model implemented in education was not considered a panacea by all. Hence, efforts at restructuring continued. Those leading this parade argued that capacity building and shared decision making should drive the transformation of public schools. The virtues of learner-centered decision making, participatory decision making, collegiality, and collaboration were the driving forces for increased student achievement.

Although this expanded decision-making capacity seemed noble, educational leaders are yet to implement sufficient training for these increased roles and responsibilities of these new decision makers (Northouse, 1999). Without sufficient professional development and the creation of the affirming structures (board policies, finance, and noninterference), this lofty goal for decision-making change has been slow, if not impossible. This lack of preparation for decision-making transformations has been apparent since conception, and these shortcomings have left efforts of shared decision making with black eyes.

It is important for educational leaders to be aware that there are many "unhappy campers" that have worked diligently but not successfully in striving to share decision-making practices. They have hit walls of resistance, have felt that their efforts have gone in vain, and have turned apathetic, even cynical, toward additional attempts to maximize participation in decision making (Murnighan & Mowen, 2002). These individuals and organizations have adopted a "why bother" attitude that their decisions are going to be negated or overturned, so why bother to participate? This defeatist attitude needs to be overcome through successful twenty-first-century leadership if education is genuinely to progress. Today's educational leaders have the right tools to bring this change. "Accept the challenge so that you may feel the exhilaration of victory!" as General Patton has eloquently articulated.

It is imperative for your success as an educational leader to perceive decision making straight from the onset to be a systematic process of choosing from among alternatives. Selecting among alternatives may have far-reaching implications, some positive and some negative. For example, if educational leaders, hopefully with input from others, make the ultimate decision to implement block scheduling, they will need to ascertain that before their decision is made, they have certain necessities in place, such as adequately prepared teachers and sufficient finances for continued professional development before rendering a final decision. To enhance the faculty's support of an educational leaders' decision to implement block scheduling, or any other decision for which they ultimately will be held responsible, they will need to inform all the faculty of the advantages and disadvantages of their decision to minimize negative consequences and maximize positive outcomes. Successful educational leaders will need to be aware that their decisions will bring conflict from some, regardless of their decision, and they will need to resolve this conflict if the decision is to be successful. Preventing problems and solving conflicts by twenty-first-century educational leaders are commonly known as "putting out the fires" or "mending the fences" to ensure the success of their decisions.

Today's educational leaders have a repertoire of decision-making models to choose from when needing to make decisions. These professionals will continually be making decisions about individuals, groups, school structure, instructional and curricular programs, and many other facets that ultimately impact student achievement (Russo & Schoemaker, 2002). Student achievement is the most important indicator of successful twenty-first-century educational leadership. Therefore, educational leaders' understanding of the decision-making process and how to improve student learning will be greatly beneficial to those they lead.

The shaping and forming of keys to decision making began as a matter of trial and error, perhaps more error than trial. Leaders have searched endlessly for keys to help ease the pain of challenging decisions. They have attempted to reform education through transformations of decision-making models. Key concepts, keys to success, and even risky keys have been tried time and time again to improve decision-making processes. Knowing and practicing these decision-making keys will support and assist educational leaders in gaining increased student achievement and school improvements.

THE REFLECTIVE PRACTITIONER

Welcome to your sixth Reflective Practitioner based on ISLLC Standard 3, your reading of Chapter 6, and your Chapter 6 Scenario. It is intended to provoke your thoughtful reflection and to stimulate discussion among colleagues, classmates, and peers. The Reflective Practitioner provides opportunities to synthesize issues, make comparisons, and apply theory to practice. We hope it will motivate you to search for evidence, thus increasing your comprehension of the text and helping you examine your convictions and discover new and shared perspectives.

ISLLC Standard 3
A school administrator is an educational leader who promotes the success of all students by ensuring management of the organization, operations, and resources for a safe, efficient, and effective learning environment.

Scenario

The parents of Hilltop Middle School left the superintendent's office smiling because Superintendent Ferra had informed them that a new principal has been appointed to Hilltop with specific instructions to develop a mandated schoolwide middle school curriculum. For several years, the curriculum that was taught differed from class to class and from year to year. What was taught was left to the discretion of each teacher. The curriculum at Hilltop Middle School lacked scope, sequence, consistency, and continuity. The last two years, this situation had seriously escalated, particularly in science and math. Parents and students became concerned, the

PTO discussed this concern with the former principal, and letters were written to board members. Still, nothing was done.

The former principal had operated with a hands-off policy, viewing curriculum selection as a faculty matter. In fact, the curriculum guide had not been updated during his seven-year tenure there. The parents argued that curricular inconsistency was particularly apparent in terms of student achievement on statewide tests and adequate yearly progress (AYP) as stipulated under No Child Left Behind.

Principal Loyeral, having been appointed in late June, worked all summer planning and organizing how a consistent schoolwide curriculum for Hilltop Middle School could be developed. She read books, talked with other principals in the district, and studied several academic programs. Having discussed academic consistency with the superintendent and other principals, she felt as principal it was her responsibility to develop a workable plan for developing curricular consistency for the faculty.

When Principal Loyeral presented her completed curriculum consistency plan to the faculty at the first faculty meeting in August, she was immediately bombarded with a mixture of reactions. Those in favor of a consistent middle school curriculum voiced that curricular standards would increase statewide test achievement and be of great value, particularly to new teachers. Detractors of a consistent middle school curriculum alleged that the selection of what to teach should be left to individual teachers, that such a notion insults teacher professionalism, and that teachers know their students best and one size does not fit all. A debate ensued as to the value of a consistent middle school curriculum that all teachers would have to teach. The stream of positive and negative faculty comments continued to flow.

Then, Mr. Gorman, the teacher with the longest tenure at Hilltop Middle School, began to speak. Others listened. "It is time for a change. I believe we should form committees and study the situation, and then implement a plan that is acceptable to all faculty members," offered Mr. Gorman. Following his appeal, there was a long pause of silence.

Principal Loyeral, to say the least, was perplexed in hearing such diverse comments from her new faculty. It was clear that her first school year would be a year of important decisions, and curriculum consistency was first on her agenda.

QUESTIONS FOR REFLECTIVE THINKING

1. The very first disposition under ISLLC Standard 3 states "making management decisions to enhance learning and teaching." With this stated, which decision-making models presented in Chapter 6 would you recommend that Principal Loyeral implement at Hilltop Middle School in efforts of achieving academic consistency for all students? Please state your rationale.

2. Selecting a decision-making model is said to be situational. Please explain in writing a true-life experience that supports or negates this statement. What are the implications of this true-life experience to knowledge, disposition, and performance indicators of ISLLC Standard 5?

3. How might the risk keys of the shared decision-making models impede the progress being made by an educational leader in terms of ISLLC Standard 5?

4. Write your own professional platform selecting and explaining the decision-making models that are most aligned to your professional goals and personal convictions. State how your implementation of the selected decision-making models will maintain or elevate your integrity, fairness, and ethical manner as perceived by those you (will) lead.

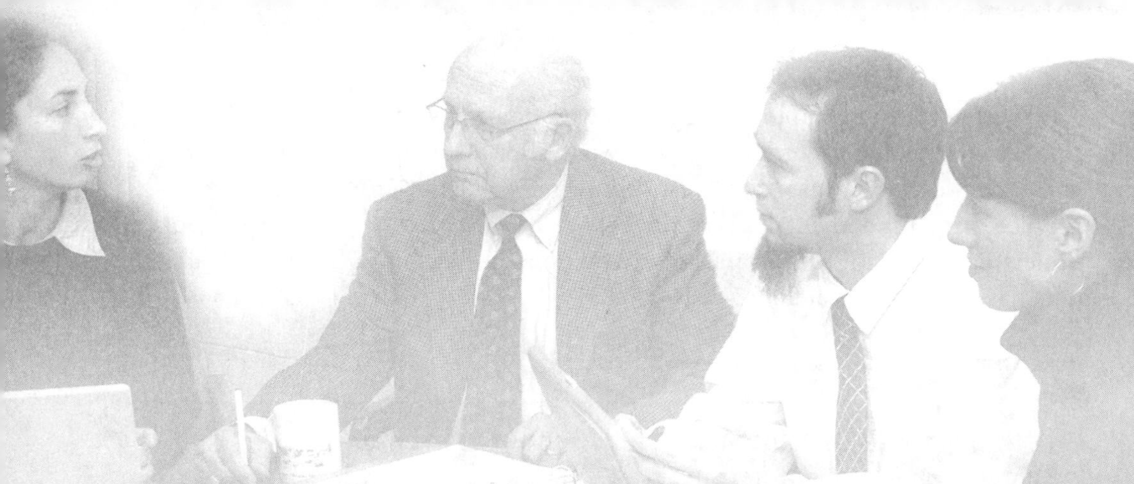

chapter 7

ISLLC *Standard* 2

Effective Instructional Leadership

One may receive the information, but miss the teaching!
—Jean Toomer

Your Chapter 7 Action Focus focuses on the importance of twenty-first-century instructional leadership beginning with an extensive search. Our Internet search, high and low, employing common research engines and inserting the words *Keys to 21st-Century Educational Leadership,* had zero results. Left empty-handed, we expanded our search by plugging in the two words *instructional leadership.* A mind-boggling 2,230,000 results were displayed. In a quick perusal of a few listings, *instruction* was defined, described, and detailed, and *leadership* received the same treatment with multiple descriptors. There were listings presenting findings from qualitative and quantitative research summarizing existing instructional leadership. In general, however, there appeared to be an alarming absence of "keys to follow" for improved instructional leadership. For example, none of the listings presented a step-by-step guide to improving instructional leadership for twenty-first-century board members, superintendents, principals, teachers, curriculum directors, union leaders, elected officials, or any other educational leaders.

Seemingly remiss, to say the least, particularly with respect to the numerous so-called holders of the keys who have not contributed to the shaping, defining, supporting, and guiding of educational leadership strategies, we rethought the themes. Jean Piaget left us with the lasting impression that "the types of questions determine the magnitude of learning." Frederic Winslow Taylor argued that scientific management was the most efficient manner of administration. Mayo (human relations keys), Lewin (behavioral science keys), and Deming (shared decision-making keys) were also developers, distributors, and purveyors of keys impacting educational leadership decisions and therefore, either directly or indirectly, directors of instructional leadership practices. The National Policy Board for Education Administration was comprised of many key holders from several states deciding on six keys: Interstate School Leaders Licensure Consortium (ISLLC) Standards.

As reflected in your Chapter 7 Action Focus, guidance is needed in "how" educational leaders could become successful twenty-first-century instructional leaders as if it was widely known, a "best kept secret" to be dispensed with special privilege, or a fundamental lacking in importance. To provide you with a deeper understanding to the importance of instructional leadership, a short true–false quiz has been constructed in Key Box 7.1.

KEY BOX 7.1

A True or False Quiz for Successful Twenty-First-Century Instructional Leaders

1. An educational leader will be dismissed for not developing and implementing a shared vision for learning.
2. It is a violation of federal law for educational leaders not to create a school vision.
3. It is a noncompliance with state legislation for an educational leader not to successfully improve the dilapidated facilities of his or her school.
4. It is against most school board policies for educational leaders not to provide an ongoing and continuous community relations program.
5. It has been decided by the courts that educational leaders shall not engage in double-talk (i.e., saying one thing to one person and something contradictory to another).
6. It is a federal law that educational leaders will increase the annual yearly academic progress of all students.

Although you may share strong beliefs about one or several of these statements, item 6 is the only statement that is legally binding (at the current time). It is vital, not lawful, that school vision (statements 1 and 2), schools conducive to learning (statement 3), an ongoing community relations program (statement 4), and consistency of message (statement 5) are present to increase student achievement. On the other hand, federal law, specifically the No Child Left Behind Act of 2001, necessitates that all educational leaders are successful instructional leaders first and foremost. In other words, instructional leadership is critical; there is no option, and it is required by the law! Consider the importance of instructional leadership in consideration of the No Child Left Behind Act, as presented in Key Box 7.2.

KEY BOX 7.2

The Importance of Instructional Leadership Regarding No Child Left Behind

- Under No Child Left Behind, passed by Congress in 2001 (Public Law 107-110) and enacted beginning in the 2002–2003 school year, every state must test all pupils in all schools.
- No Child Left Behind stipulates that the state must set the proficiency level for all testing.

- Each school must disaggregate students into a number of subgroups, including race, ethnicity, income level, second-language learners, and various categories of special education.
- Ninety-five percent of all students must pass statewide tests; otherwise a school is labeled as "failing," and by the school year 2013–2014, there shall be 100 percent proficiency achieved by all test takers.
- Every subgroup of students is expected to make adequate yearly progress (AYP) each year; otherwise, the school is labeled as "failing."
- If a local school district has one failing school, it is labeled as a "failing school district."
- In the first year, at least 20 percent of each group must have scores at or above the proficiency score in order for the school to meet the requirement of adequate yearly progress.
- Each state must set successively higher requirements each year for the percent of each group scoring "proficient" to meet adequate yearly progress.
- By the year 2014, 100 percent of students in all groups must score at the proficient level in reading, math, and science on an approved test.

If these mandated expectations do not cause the hair to stand up on the backs of the necks of our nation's finest instructional leaders angered by what these pressures do to students and their faculty, the mandates of No Child Left Behind illustrate the importance of all educational leaders becoming the very best instructional leaders. Consider these mandated punishments driven by No Child Left Behind:

- If a school is failing for more than two years, the school district is required to permit parents to request transfer of their children to a nonfailing school in the district at district expense.
- Parents of children in failing schools may also request the school district to provide private tutoring at district expense.
- If the school continues to fail annual yearly progress, drastic measures are required of the staff, faculty, and especially school leadership, including, but not limited to, making a contract for operation of the school to be taken over by the state.

And as if these discipline sanctions are not sufficient, the states are also required to punish educational leaders, the other educators, and, first and foremost, the students. No Child Left Behind stipulates that states will do the following:

- Defer programmatic funds or reduce administrative funds.
- Institute and fully implement a new curriculum, including provision of appropriate professional development based on scientifically based research.
- Replace district personnel.
- Remove particular schools from local jurisdiction, establishing alternative arrangements for such schools' policy governance and supervision.
- Appoint a receiver or trustee to administer the local school district's affairs in place of the superintendent and school board.

The adverse impact of No Child Left Behind is an excellent reason for educational leaders to rise up in arms to save the children. The overwhelming pressures from high-stakes testing, students labeled as failures at early ages, huge increases in dropouts, escalation of school violence by students who are considered unsatisfactory and disconnected from success, and teacher and educational leader departures from their profession will be on the rise.

These problems and many variations thereof will leave the most able twenty-first-century instructional leaders scratching their heads. The more an educational leader "will know" about instructional leadership, the further the educational leader "will go." As No Child Left Behind continues, other legislation joins ranks, judicial mandates jump in, and other significant pressures explode, today's educational leaders will need to sharpen their instructional leadership skills.

A glimmer of hope may be found in recent studies that have revealed strong correlations between schools with high student achievement and educational leaders who are highly engaged as instructional leaders (cf. Murphy & Louis, 1999). The nature of the relationship continues to be investigated. If student achievement is to increase significantly and school systems are to improve, then close, consistent, and coordinated communication between instructional leaders is essential (Murphy, 2002). Plain and simple, instructional leadership is second only to teaching among school-related factors in its impact on student learning (Leithwood, Seashore-Louis, Anderson, & Wahlstrom, 2004). This may be the last call, as far as instructional leadership is concerned, to either get on board or get out of the way, because it is coming through. There is no option. The time is now.

INSTRUCTIONAL LEADERSHIP KEYS FOR THE TWENTY-FIRST CENTURY

There has never been a time that instructional effectiveness has been put to a bigger test. Teaching is for learning and if students are not learning, teachers are not teaching. And if teachers are not effective, "Whose job is it, anyway?" Accountability is readily and heavily placed on the shoulders of educational leaders. Historically, the educational leader's effectiveness centered on his or her leadership skills, projects, programs, and other initiatives; the educational reform movements of the past decade have increasingly "turned up the heat" with cries for more impressive student achievement.

So, with all this high-stakes testing, pressures thrust on students and teachers, "do or die" contracts with educational leaders, and threats of school takeovers, what do educational leaders do to not only survive but also beat these instructional leadership challenges? Here are our views or keys for successful twenty-first-century board members, superintendents, principals, teachers, curriculum directors, union leaders, elected officials, and all other educational leaders.

Focus on Instructional Leadership

Leaders need to prioritize, make decisions, and demonstrate the importance of instructional leadership. This charge needs to be continuous, consistent, and highly encouraging of all others to join the march. What each faculty member does within a school needs to be appraised in how any given activity or initiative will increase student achievement. And the million-dollar question that should be asked time and time again without hesitation is: How will what you are teaching or planning to teach increase student achievement? Destiny is not a matter of chance; it is a matter of choice.

Develop Personal Instructional Leadership Skills

It is critical that all educational leaders keep abreast of current research, best practices, and cutting-edge theories that support and affirm today's practices. This also means that educational leaders will be committed to lifelong learning through university classes, workshops, conferences, and networking. It is important that these growth experiences are communicated with other professionals to solidify what has been learned and to enter into a vibrant exchange of ideas.

It is also our suggestion that educational leaders become prolific readers of everything from the local news to professional journals to stay ahead of what may be coming down the pike both in education and the world that education serves. The difference between ordinary and extraordinary is that little extra you need to do as an effective instructional leader.

IN THE NEWS

Content Matters in Preparing Educational Leaders

Today's superintendents want their principals to be instructional leaders.

Ominously, the evidence suggests that revolution in school account-ability, organization and manage-ment has so far left the nation's principals behind. In 2003, *Public Agenda* reported that today's su-perintendents want their principals to display prowess in everything from accountability to instructional leadership and teacher quality, but principals themselves say they are not equipped for these responsibil-ities. Just 30 percent of principals surveyed reported that they are factoring student achievement into their teacher evaluation. Why so few? From the principals surveyed, 96 percent reported that additional responsibilities have been added to their job descriptions without abandoning other less-meaningful tasks, leaving them with little time to tend to the bigger picture.

There has never been a time that instructional leadership has been put to a bigger test.

Source: F. M. Hess & A. P. Kelly, "Content Matters in Preparing Educational Leaders," *Education Week,* May 18, 2005.

Shape the Instructional Climate and Organization

Our collective years of research and practical experience reveal that leaders who engage in instructional leadership experiences, just by their mere actions, encour-age those they lead to do the same. Much is to be said for this *follow-the-leader model,* especially when the educational leader displays enthusiasm and passion for instructional leadership. It is more meaningful that the importance of in-structional leadership be "caught" by those being lead rather than only "taught." Qualities of spirit, energy, enthusiasm, and passion are contagious! By shaping the school's instructional climate and instructional organization, instructional leaders can best alter their followers' instructional practices by changing their attitudes.

Take Time to Celebrate Achievement

Increasing student achievement is a never-ending journey, not a destination. From the development of mission and vision statements, posters in hallways and on classroom walls, memos to staff, newsletters, and parent/teacher conferences and open houses, successful educational leaders will relentlessly instill the importance of student learning. A vital part of the importance of learning is taking the time to honor, acknowledge, and celebrate achievement. As Voltaire argued, "No problem can stand the assault of sustained thinking!"

Promote and Develop Effective Pedagogies

The science of instruction is the tip of the iceberg, and the needs of each learner constitute the foundation where the power and strength of each student emerges. Instruction should center on culturally relevant methods (Boykin & Cunningham, 2001; Dill & Boykin, 2000), brain research, multiple intelligences, authentic learning (National Commission on Service Learning, 2002; Newmann, Marks & Gamoran, 1996), critical thinking skills development, and other learner-centered preferences, styles, and strengths. Educational leaders must become instructional leaders where each child's individualized educational pedagogy is understood and achievement is maximized. They need to defeat any resistance with persistence in developing effective learner-centered pedagogies.

Value and Expect Differentiated Instruction

Successful twenty-first-century educational leaders know the importance of differentiated instruction; therefore, they will insist, persist, and hold their teachers accountable for varying instruction. No two ways about it: The "drill and kill"—only instruction leading to the sedentary "sit and get"—learning will lead to student achievement disaster. Proficiency tests determine the students' critical thinking skills, inquiry-based learning abilities, and skills in conceptualizing. Teachers need to cease using block scheduling as expanded opportunities to be the "sage on the stage" rather than the "guide on the side," at times providing students with inductive, inquiry, deductive, group interaction, and other differentiated learning opportunities that provide students with life-long skills—learning how to think. Teaching students how to think critically will allow them to soar on any test placed before them.

Provide Powerful Professional Development

Instructional leaders should provide, conduct, and/or facilitate meaningful professional development relevant to the improvement of instruction (Brown, Smith, & Stein, 1995; Cohen & Hill, 1997). This issue is critical. Our collective experience reveals that higher levels of student achievement are associated with teacher opportunities to participate in sustained professional development. This professional development needs to be grounded in content-specific pedagogy, often aligned with the curriculum the students are learning. As the school's instructional leader, the principal must provide opportunities for professional development, particularly to develop effective teaching practices targeted at increasing student achievement.

Restructure Schools to Improve Learning

Restructuring needs to include common planning times, additional planning time, looping, smaller class sizes, and smaller schools (Lee & Smith, 1997) as resources became available. Several researchers found that smaller class size improves instruction and increases achievement. Still other studies discovered that higher student achievement is associated with smaller high schools, suggesting that the ideal high school enrollment is between 600 to 900 students (Achilles, Harman, & Egelson, 1995). Today there are several grant and foundation funding opportunities to aid and assist in the downsizing of schools and classrooms. Keep in mind here: If you keep doing the same things over and over the same ways, you will keep getting the same results. If student achievement results are unsatisfactory, it is time to change the ways and methods you are educating students.

Make Student Achievement the Major Motivator

Cutting to the bottom line, student achievement needs to be the alpha and the omega, the beginning and the end, and the number-one educational priority for students, faculty, parents, and community. Successful twenty-first-century educational leaders will be those instructional leaders who have encouraged, motivated, and demanded excellence in student achievement. The emphasis placed on student achievement by educational leaders is critical to instruction and learning (Goddard, Sweetland, & Hoy, 2000; Hoy & Sabo, 1998). It has been our collective experience in the research and practical application of educational leadership that if you've made up your mind you can do something, you're absolutely right! Increasing student achievement is right; there is no option.

Keep Teachers at the Center of Instructional Improvements

In the final analysis, only teachers themselves can change and improve their instructional practices in the classroom. All that goes on behind the closed classroom door is known only to teachers, students, and very few others present. Nevertheless, instructional leaders must work diligently and successfully in motivating teachers and providing resources to make instructional improvements possible. Successful leaders will maintain firm, fair, and consistent accountability for teacher performance. Either improvements are made in

IN THE NEWS

Teachers Earn National Accreditation

The commitment of two states to the national certification of its teachers has been a rallying force for instructional improvements.

What two states wanted very much, they didn't hesitate to support. More than 2,000 Carolinas teachers achieved national certification this past year by passing a national exam and documenting their teaching skills. Broken down by state, North Carolina led the nation with 1,535 teachers certified by the National Board for Professional Teaching Standards. In South Carolina, 574 teachers achieved the same certification. Both states pay bonuses to their nationally certified teachers.

As the Carolinas provided constructive support for their teachers to achieve national certification, so too must today's educational leaders establish instructional goals and constructively support their teachers in their achievement of those goals.

Source: D. A. Helms, "N.C., S.C. Teachers Earn National Accreditation," *The Charlotte Observer,* December 6, 2005.

instruction or changes need to be made in instructors. Ultimately, teachers must decide their own destiny. On the other hand, commitment to instructional improvements can be a great rallying force.

Provide Constructive Support

Teachers not only want to hear praise for how they taught a lesson but they also want their instructional leader to share constructive support as to how they can improve their instruction. The two prerequisites to this constructive sharing are: The instructional leader is knowledgeable about instruction and the teacher is sincere about improving his or her teaching. To maximize the gains of this constructive sharing for the improvement of instruction, the following conditions need to be present between instructional leader and teacher: trust, respect, credibility, and professional accord. Keep in mind: Real leaders are ordinary people ✗ *like this* with extraordinary determination.

Provide Resource Support

It is paramount that successful twenty-first-century educational leaders are skilled and successful advocates and achievers of resources and materials to meet the needs of improved instructional practices. If established budgets do not allow for such expenditures, alternative funding sources (grants, foundations, business partnerships, etc.) need to be tapped. Resource support is a basic instructional leadership role. If instructional leaders do not take care of their instructors' needs, then private schools, parochial schools, charter schools, academies, and more affluent neighboring school districts look more desirable. Consider resource advocacy and attainment as opportunities.

Recognize and Celebrate Every Academic Success

Demonstrating their instructional leadership pursuit and passion, educational leaders should take the lead in recognizing and celebrating student achievement. Educators in general are notorious for achieving wonderful academic accomplishments but not taking the time to celebrate successes. Instead, following the achievement of a significant accomplishment, without pause the next feat is implemented. Taking time to smell the roses, for the thorns are many, and in recognizing and celebrating the success of students and teachers, such great academic gains continue to be reinforced in the pursuit of academic excellence.

Provide Honest, Courageous Leadership

Successful educational leaders will grasp reality for what it is, and be honest and open in admitting that improvement is needed. The first step to instructional improvement is for instructional leaders to admit that instructional methods need to be aligned to best practices. There are two kinds of instructional leaders—those working diligently and successfully to improve student achievement via instructional practices and those who are satisfied with past student achievements and therefore fall behind as the world rapidly changes. As Willa A. Foster asserted, "Quality is never an accident; it is always the result of high intention, sincere effort, intelligent direction and skillful execution; it represents the wise choice of many alternatives."

Use Teams to Boost Achievement

Successful educational leaders will promote the achievement of all students by engaging the support and commitment of all stakeholders. In order for schools and school districts to be successful, all individuals will need to be called on to help shape future policies and practices. The collective contributions of all individuals are far greater than any single individual's effort. Everyone, instructional leaders and those they lead—students, parents, community, board members, elected officials, businesses, agencies, the courts, and all others—need to be encouraged by educational leaders to roll up their sleeves and lend a helping hand to attack achievement gaps, deficiencies, and social promotions.

Develop Learning Communities

Knowing that tremendous student academic gains result from the formation of learning communities, effective lenders will work diligently to unify all staff members to improve student achievement. With this level of understanding in place, schools are transformed from an organization to a learning community (Sergiovanni, 2001). In turn, all staff members participating as members of a learning community will feel a sense of efficacy as they are empowered through a strong need to optimally educate students. Stated another way, as all staff members form a learning community, the synergy or fuel derived from working together will allow common people to attain uncommon results.

Plan Purposefully

Master plans need to be long-range and consistent. Successful instructional leadership programs of this new millennium need to be comprehensively prepared and implemented. Too many times in education, meaningful transformations in education have been positive from the start but short-lived (often labeled by doubters as "program de jour," meaning here today, gone tomorrow) due to the absence of thoughtful long-range plans. There are four steps to accomplishing an instructional leadership plan: plan purposefully, prepare thoughtfully, proceed positively, and pursue persistently.

Use Research to Inform Instruction

Successful instructional leaders will render decisions based on research. Research such as the effective schools stemming from one of its founding fathers, Edmonds (1979), has increased in importance in the past several decades largely because of its impact on increasing student achievement through instructional leadership. The research revealing a number of factors that directly influence academic achievement (Darling-Hammond, 1999; Ingersoll, 2001a; Woods, 2001) needs to remain front and center in all decision making by today's successful instructional leaders. Additional research, including, but not limited to, instructional leadership, performance standards, accountability, and participatory management, provide instructional leaders with a framework for decision making. Let the discoveries of the past be the key to improved decisions and actions.

Honor and Welcome Opportunities to Serve Others

The greatest of all leaders have been the greatest of servants. They have not hesitated to go into disease-infected areas, to wipe the feet of another, or to enter a war-torn area. This spirit of leadership applies to instructional leadership as well. Instructional leaders enter schools that are considered battlegrounds of underachieving students, and in some cases hope has departed with despair taking its place. This servant instructional leadership philosophy represents a significant departure from the hierarchical systems of prior leaders. The premise of servant leadership is deeply rooted in the leader's priority of serving others, to ensure that other people's highest priority needs are being served before one's personal needs (Fullan, 2001; Greenleaf, 1991; Hallinger & Heck, 1996). The servant instructional leader assists those they lead to achieve their instructional goals that increase student achievement. Thus, as instructional goals are being achieved, all students in the school or district move ahead.

Enhance Your Persuasiveness

Persuasive professional qualities, such as charisma, are a central component in leadership influence (Wong & Law, 2002). Instructional leadership qualities have positive influences on those the leaders influence (Kirkpatrick & Locke, 1996). Studies on the effects of attractive instructional leadership qualities such as vision, passion, and enthusiasm on staff members suggest that the influence of these qualities might be effective in improving motivation, performance, and therefore student achievement. The most bankrupt instructional leader is the leader who has lost his or her vision, passion, and enthusiasm.

Pay Attention to Emotional Savvy

Like all other leaders, instructional leaders who develop and maintain high emotional intelligence are better able to manage staff members' emotions and facilitate employee performance effectively (Ashkanasy, 2003; Ashkanasy, Hertel, & Daus, 2002; Goleman, 2000). Furthermore, successful instructional leaders know how to impact the emotions of those they lead. Emotional intelligence of instructional leaders has been associated with increased staff member satisfaction and "extra role" behaviors (Wong & Law, 2002).

Attract and Retain Quality Teachers

Successful twenty-first-century instructional leaders will exhaust all possibilities in attracting quality teachers into the schools and districts they lead. The single-most valuable investment in an educational system is the employment of a great teacher. Recruiting programs need to be continuous, active, and personalized. There is only one other single contributing factor to improving instruction that comes close to the employing of a teacher with excellent instructional skills, and that one factor is retaining that teacher.

Successful instructional leaders know and work diligently by positively impacting working conditions that support the recruitment and retention of teachers. Schools with patterns of highest teacher turnover are those schools where conditions, not characteristics of students, are the driving force of departure (Harris, 2002). Instructional leaders need to provide feedback and encouragement for new teachers in building positive working conditions that favorably impact the recruitment efforts of the school district (Hope, 1999). It is just the little differences between the good and the best working conditions that make the difference between a good instructional leader and the excellent instructional leader.

IN THE NEWS

Two Area Principals Win Post Leadership Awards

By adding important touches to their quality work environment, two area school principals are able to attract and retain quality teachers.

Two area principals were awarded the prestigious Post Leadership Awards. The Awards are sponsored annually by *The Washington Post*, recognizing area principals who provide exceptional educational environments. The winners are nominated by faculty, parents, and students and chosen by their school system's selection committee.

Robert Hindman, principal at Zachary Taylor Elementary School in Arlington since 1998, was honored with the Post Leadership Award for his constant communication with staff, students and parents. He also advocated and attained a partnership for his school and local university resulting in continuous professional development opportunities. Principal Hindman's teachers agree that he is an outstanding collaborator.

Deborah Thompson has been principal at Douglas MacArthur Elementary School in Alexandria for ten years. She has been selected as a Post Leadership Award recipient for her ability to mentor her assistant principals while demonstrating a thorough command of instructional strategies. Thompson provided leadership that led to her school being one of the first in her school district to achieve accreditation. Parents view their principal as a stickler for academic excellence and a wonderful caretaker for their children.

As both award-winning principals went above and beyond the call of duty, so too will aspiring principals need to do so in making their school environments inviting and encouraging.

Source: M. Wiseman, "Two Area Principals Win Post Leadership Awards," *The Washington Post*, November 18, 2004.

Provide Staff Professional Development That Improves Instruction

Professional development to increase student achievement through the improvement of instruction requires a minimal set of conditions. These conditions include prioritizing the learning of instructional models, relevant and meaningful training of authentic instruction, and ample and sustained professional development.

Education, unlike business, fails to adequately invest in its personnel by providing sufficient training. Today's successful leaders realize the importance of professional development and will prioritize each budgeted dollar, attempt to attain increased funding (again from alternative funding sources such as grants, foundations, and business partnerships), and direct every dollar possible to improving the instruction of their faculty members. The greatest accomplishment for continuous student achievement is not so much what has been attained, but in what direction teaching and learning are moving.

Provide Mentoring That Works

Successful twenty-first-century educational leaders realize that although there may be no short-cuts or cure-alls in recruiting and retaining new teachers, carefully designed mentoring programs can help meet the challenges inherent in teaching today. From the very beginning, new teacher induction should address the unresolved needs resulting in an inordinate rate of attrition existing among new teachers (Weiss & Weiss, 1999; Woods, 2001). Inasmuch as teaching is a stressful job, particularly as teachers' roles become more and more nebulous, the need for mentoring programs is imperative to focus on stress reducing conditions (Ingersoll, 2001b). Effective mentoring programs need to keep up with rising needs; the stresses of teaching today will not remain the same as the changes of a rapidly transforming society will require educators to meet increasingly complex challenges (Ingersoll, 2001a; Kelley, 2004).

In addition to raising the expertise of the new teachers in a school or those teachers changing assignments, successful educational leaders will also support mentoring programs for other reasons. Mentoring is one important mechanism for advancing the teaching profession as a whole. Effective mentoring programs contribute to the building of cohesive schools where teachers and educational leaders are encouraged to discuss the improvement of instructional practices that increase student achievement (Darling-Hammond, 1999). To increase student achievement, an expanding repertoire of skills will need to be developed and implemented by all teachers. The benefits of successful mentoring programs have been affirmed for quite some time by several theorists on several mentoring facets, including, but not limited to, mentoring functions, human development, personal networks, shared identity, information processing, power, social support, and transformational leadership (Hirsch, Koppich, & Knapp, 2001; Ingersoll, 2001a; Kelley, 2004; Weiss & Weiss, 1999). Instructional leaders know that the benefits of effective mentoring programs will be even greater as more and more teachers are entering the profession with less training.

Increase Achievement with Instructional Technologies

Successful instructional leaders will realize and implement the findings of research revealing how the powerful tools of technology increase student achievement. Research findings supporting increases in student achievement when technology is integrated into instruction will continue to provide vital insight for today's instructional leaders. Additional gains of computer-assisted instruction, such as students enjoying classes more and how teachers may develop more proficiency in using technology, will continue to shape instructional leadership practices. Successful instructional leadership practices should be implemented only when research is conclusive, not when additional research is needed, as is the case in instructional technology, with only 5 percent of the research being sufficiently empirical.

RESEARCH KEYS

To enrich your understanding of **instructional technology,** log on to www.researchnavigator.com and search Ebsco's ContentSelect.

Research Navigator.com

UNLEASHING YOUR INSTRUCTIONAL LEADERSHIP POTENTIAL

With more than a pocket full of keys for increasing student ach
the implementation of twenty-first-century instructional leade
100 percent proficiency looming ahead as enacted by No Child
advice is: Let's roll! Begin implementing your new-found keys
ine you saying, "But how?" Your next concern may be "How ca
with everything else I have to do?" After all, your due dates, de
requests, state report mandates, and other pressures keep you s
an inch deep and a mile wide. Here's the bigger question: Can
eventually implement instructional leadership keys with profi
dent achievement leaving much to be desired?

Well, with all this said, we would like to show you "how t
diately implementing the keys to twenty-first-century instruct
Change will be necessary! This change will be centered on wo
harder. Successful educational leaders will need to depart from
even their comfort zones. This change will involve risks, as yo
to second base until you take your feet off first. This change n
own choice, or you may have no choice but to change. We wa
meaningful change is not easy, but we will be with you every
following list presents keys to unleashing your instructional leadership potential.

- *Keep your "eye on the tiger."* Keep instructional leadership first and foremost in your mind always. Obstacles are only those frightful things we see when we take our eyes off our goals. Maximize your experiencing, demonstrating, modeling, evaluating, and celebrating of increased student achievement through improved instruction.
- *Prioritize your mission.* Prioritize your mission into six words: *Increase student achievement with improved instruction!* All decisions and involvements of instructional leaders need to be prioritized in relationship to this mission.
- *Abandon all that is not effective.* Traditionally, educators in general and educational leaders more specifically have added on one responsibility after another, layer by layer, without taking anything away! It is time to selectively abandon roles and responsibilities that are antiquated and that have little impact on student achievement. At times, less is more.
- *Attempt to be great—communicate.* Keep the dialog alive and ongoing with others as to how instruction and student achievement can be improved. Minimize time consumption on communications of lesser importance impacting student learning.
- *Keep time on your side.* Every minute is valuable and has inherent purpose. Keep a journal of time spent on your activities for a week. This can be a real eye opener! Many educational leaders do not realize how they misspend their time.
- *Empower others, don't overpower them.* Empower other educators with additional authority, such as handling routine issues without your daily involvement. Reduce the amount of time spent overseeing others by creating well-defined procedures with clear expectations. Create a mutually respectful

school climate so that staff members do not feel that they must come to you for all the answers. Delegate so that mini-crisis situations are handled at the lower levels.

- *Minimize meetings and eliminate unimportant ones.* Prioritize the meetings you attend, and condense the time spent at each meeting. Reduce the number of committees you're on, keeping in mind that committees may be those entities that save minutes but waste hours. Utilize administrative software to complete reports more efficiently and improve intraschool communication.

- *Hire a games manager.* Often the athletic director will hire a *games manager* to work with referees, provide crowd control, and cater to the needs of the contests. Similarly, tasks such as cafeteria and recess supervision, planning assemblies, and other operations need to be taken off the shoulders of the instructional leader, allowing him or her to lead the crusade of improving instruction and achievement.

HOW SUCCESSFUL TWENTY-FIRST-CENTURY LEADERS LEAD INSTRUCTION

Student achievement need not be an educational leader's bereavement. There will be no greater test of today's educational leader's success than student learning. Now is not the time to retire; it is the time to catch on fire as an instructional leader, taking part in a leadership so vital to the nation's children. The attitude here is not to just meet the requirements of No Child Left Behind but to surpass the mandates in every way possible. Unleash your potential as an instructional leader in developing your skills as highlighted in this chapter. Selectively abandon programs and practices that fall short of acceptable results, lead with honesty, be courageous, and develop communities of learners along the way.

THE REFLECTIVE PRACTITIONER

Welcome to your seventh Reflective Practitioner containing your Chapter Scenario based on ISLLC Standard 2 and your reading of Chapter 7. It is intended to provoke your thoughtful reflection and to stimulate discussion among colleagues, classmates, and peers. The Reflective Practitioner provides opportunities to synthesize issues, make comparisons, and apply theory to practice. We hope it will motivate you to search for evidence, thus increasing your comprehension of the text and helping you examine your convictions and discover new and shared perspectives.

ISLLC Standard 2
A school administrator is an educational leader who promotes the success of all students by advo-

cating, nurturing, and sustaining a school culture and climate and instructional program conducive to student learning and staff professional growth.

Scenario

On the first day of the 2012–2013 school year at an early morning back-to-school meeting, Principal Pamela Davis informed her Leland High School faculty of 81 teachers that the No Child Left Behind's adequate yearly progress says all test takers next year need to achieve 100 percent proficiency on the state test. She also clarifies for the faculty that she has concerns about Leland students achieving high enough test scores for Leland High School to pass proficiency levels. Principal Davis reminded the faculty that if Leland High School continues to fail, the state has legal provisions to take over the school and replace all faculty. She summarizes her comments with almost an apologetic overture, saying she just wanted the faculty to know.

After sharing No Child Left Behind's gauntlet hanging over the heads of Leland High School, Principal Davis informed her faculty that the time is long overdue that instructional methods change. She suggested that faculty members begin using inductive, inquiry, concept attainment, mnemonics, jurisprudential, and several other instructional models proven by research to increase student achievement. Principal Davis admit-

ted that she had not taken an active enough role as an instructional leader, but her time has come. She also advised the teachers that other things needed to change, but she did not specify exactly what changes she had in mind.

After sharing her new vision for Leland High School, Principal Davis extended best wishes for a successful school year and dismissed faculty members from the meeting, allowing them to return to their classrooms to prepare for the arrival of students the next day. Principal Davis returned to her office and finalized her instructional leadership strategies for the school year.

QUESTIONS FOR REFLECTIVE THINKING

1. Following your reading of Chapter 7, what keys to twenty-first-century instructional leadership would you recommend to Principal Davis? Please provide a rationale for each of the keys you selected.

2. Inasmuch as Principal Davis is a staunch believer in standards-based performance, explain how each of the keys you selected helps Principal Davis in achieving one or more ISSLC standard.

3. In your current or most recent school, how might the keys to twenty-first-century instructional leadership improve instruction and increase student achievement?

4. Do you believe that more educational leaders will be implementing keys to twenty-first-century instructional leadership as the ramifications of No Child Left Behind become greater? Please explain your answer.

5. What keys to improved instructional leadership will you implement to promote the success of all students achieving 100 percent proficiency as mandated by No Child Left Behind? Please provide rationales for your response.

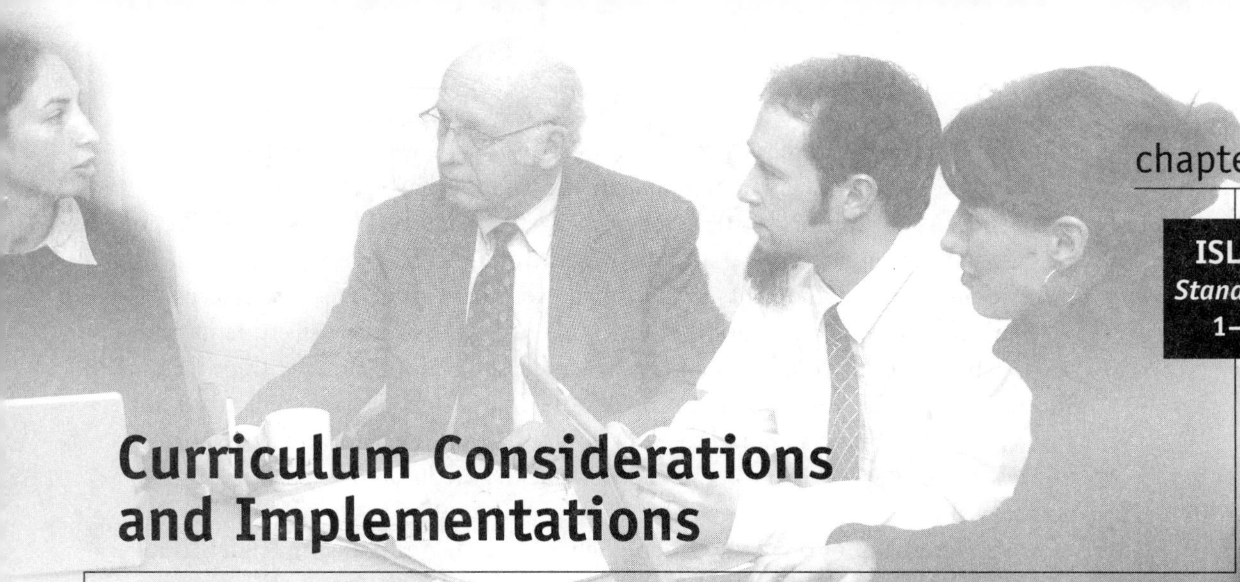

chapter **8**

ISLLC
Standards
1–6

Curriculum Considerations and Implementations

The future belongs to those who believe in the beauty of their dreams.
—Eleanor Roosevelt

Your Chapter 8 Action Focus is extended throughout this chapter to provide you with a deeper understanding of the complexities of twenty-first-century curricula. To begin, we are present at an awards ceremony where the honor of the Blue Ribbon School is presented to West Lansing High School, one of America's schools acknowledged for its excellent curricula. West Lansing High School is commended for its all-encompassing commitment to its curriculum that includes all the experiences children have under the guidance of their teachers (Dewey, 1938; Mash & Willis, 2003). This broad-spectrum approach to curriculum that includes all experiences of the learner (Cuban, 2001a; Ornstein, Pajak, & Bohar-Horenstein, 2003; Pinar, 1999) continues throughout Chapter 8 to provide, in the context of school operations, a thorough understanding through a deeper examination of excellent curricula in schools today. After all, the keys to outstanding curriculum are most often discovered by educational leaders who visit other schools and collaborate with other educational leaders. May your guided visitation of West Lansing High School increase your knowledge and skills as a successful twenty-first-century curriculum leader!

Ladies and gentleman, please join me in welcoming Dr. Mary Therese Williams, our United States Secretary of Education.

Thank you, Mr. Smith, for that kind introduction. I also want to thank Congressmen John Carthie and Stephanie Flowers for being here today. They both have been true friends of America's schools. And I want to congratulate Congressman Brownly on his reelection and Congressman Durr on her election to the United States Senate.

It is also good to see Governor Hendrick Moler here today. He has done so much for our schools, especially in my home state of Michigan.

And finally, I would like to thank a few more special people who have been true friends of education. We have singing sensation Tina Ike, movie star Darrel Lopez, and news reporter Leroy Jefferson with us today. I want to thank them for all the work they have done on behalf of our children.

It is a pleasure to be here with you today in Washington, D.C., at this year's Blue Ribbon School Ceremony entitled *A Series of Keys,* which provides an opportunity for educational leaders to focus on how schools have achieved curricular excellence. As educators, we strive for nothing less than excellence—excellence in every classroom and for every student. *A Series of Keys* will give all school leaders in the United States blueprints to follow, an exemplary guide to school success!

Although some question whether excellence is possible for all students and say we should settle for less, you, West Lansing High School, along with other Blue Ribbon Schools in America, have proven otherwise. Educational excellence is not just a dream; it can be a reality. You have seen it within the halls and classrooms of West Lansing High School. And today, we acknowledge and celebrate your accomplishments.

As a recipient of our Blue Ribbon School award, West Lansing High School is one of the very best in the country. Let me try to put your accomplishments into perspective. There are well over 100,000 public and private schools in the country. Of those schools, fewer than 500 can claim Blue Ribbon School status. That's less than half a percent. Congratulations.

Educators of West Lansing High School, your hard work and talents extend far beyond your community and even your state. You touch your students' lives so positively and they in turn touch eternity. Today's students will be tomorrow's lawyers, doctors, engineers, scientists, entrepreneurs, leaders, and hopefully teachers. By entrusting our children to your care each day, we entrust you with the future of our entire nation. You and others like you who are committed to student excellence are our nation's assurance of a more promising tomorrow!

I congratulate you for all of your success. Faculty, staff, and formal educational leaders—you have much to celebrate. Congratulations! Today, I also want to thank the parents, business partners, and community members that support your work. And of course, most important, we salute West Lansing students, who have worked diligently and successfully. We are very proud of each and every one of you. We are very honored to share the many cutting-edge ideas and practices that have emerged from your fine work in this wonderful school.

KEYS TO CURRICULUM FOR TWENTY-FIRST-CENTURY SCHOOLS

We are here today to celebrate your success, but we are also here to provide a road map for other schools to follow. The accomplishments of your work in curriculum should be emulated by educational leaders throughout our nation—every board member, superintendent, principal, curriculum director, teacher leader, union director, elected official, and all others taking leadership roles in education today. We want every school in America to achieve what you have achieved. By sharing your keys to successful twenty-first-century curriculum and by disseminating your strategies to all educational leaders, we will make excellence the rule for all of America's schools. And we can ensure that the success of every student will be achieved.

For many years, our nation turned a blind eye to the problems in our schools. While some students received a quality education, millions of others were mired in mediocrity (Doyle & Pimentel, 1999). The vast majority of these students were minority, low-income, and special-needs students. These students slipped through the cracks of our system. The result was a dangerous achievement gap, which left America's most vulnerable students behind their peers in school and in life.

In twentieth-century educational reform efforts, we tried to mend student underachievement by simply throwing more and more money at the problems. For example, from the 1960s to the turn of the last century, the federal government spent almost $130 billion on programs for disadvantaged students, but little changed (Romano, 2002). Test scores in reading were basically flat in the last decade of the twentieth century. There were some improvements in some areas, but the rate of improvement was slow and clearly did not reflect the money spent. The education system itself needed to be transformed.

The need for educational improvement was underscored by such programs as the Blue Ribbon School Program implemented in 2002–2003. The Blue Ribbon School Program that unites us today is a national program established to recognize schools around the nation for their pursuit of curricular excellence. Today, the Blue Ribbon School is an annual award program where schools such as West Lansing High School submit applications, winning schools are announced in September, and a recognition ceremony is held in Washington, D.C., in October. Schools considered for Blue Ribbon status must have either one of two criteria: having 40 percent of all students from disadvantaged backgrounds showing improvement or schools whose students and student achievement is in the top 10 percent on state tests. I am pleased to share with you that West Lansing High School meets both criteria.

Numerous twenty-first-century schools are excelling. Scores are improving and the achievement gap is closing. For example, the percentage of African American and Hispanic fourth-graders with basic reading and math skills increased more in the last four years than in the previous ten years combined. That's real progress!

Congratulations! West Lansing High School has earned one of

IN THE NEWS

Viers Mill School Wins Blue Ribbon

Excellence in curricula assisted the faculty at Viers Mill School in eliminating the achievement gap.

There is something unique about Viers Mill School in Montgomery County. What is unique is not its 35 percent student enrollment that lacks English fluency. It is neither the proficiency rate in third-grade reading on the 2005 Maryland School Assessment that rose 52 percent to 90 percent in 2003 nor students' achievement on the California Test of Basic Skills that rose from the 40th percentile in 2001 to the 64th percentile in 2004 in second grade reading and from the 52nd to the 79th percentile in math that makes Viers Mill School unique. What is unique about this school is the combination of all these factors and the Blue Ribbon flag that flies in front of the building for all to see, representing Viers Mill School's students and faculty uphill climb to success.

The Blue Ribbon Award is not only highly respected and appreciated by the students, faculty and community at Viers Mill School, it represents schools throughout the United States that have soared academically. To James J. Virga, principal of Viers Mill School, the Blue Ribbon Award meant a lot of people working together, making sure that instruction and curriculum were aligned to test standards, and believing that the kids could do it! Principal Virga and numerous other educational leaders have demonstrated a model of curricula excellence for all educational leaders to emulate.

Like Viers Mill School, other twenty-first-century schools and school districts need to develop and implement curricula excellence.

Source: D. de Vise, "Viers Mill School Wins Blue Ribbon," *The Washington Post,* September 29, 2005.

the most impressive distinctions of a Blue Ribbon School—curricular excellence. Over the last few months, I have had the chance to visit your school. I have seen your classrooms, spoken with your students, and listened to your fellow teachers. I have visited the businesses in your community and spoken to numerous parents and community members. Like all other Blue Ribbon Schools, West Lansing High School is such a very special place.

As a nation, we salute your curricular leadership today. If we are to give every child a quality education, if we are to give every child a chance to succeed in the twenty-first century, if we are to provide opportunity for every student to become a contributing member of society, we must learn from your success.

Today, I thank you for your dedication to our children and therefore our future. As you return to your community, share your skills, knowledge, and enthusiasm with others. And most important, continue your good work. There is no work more honorable. Congratulations. You have made the President of the United States and me proud.

Thank you, and God bless.

And now ladies and gentleman, it gives me great pleasure to introduce the Superintendent of West Lansing School District. Please welcome Dr. Richard Wisemore.

Dr. Williams, Congressmen Carthie and Flowers, Governor Moler, and other distinguished guests, on behalf of West Lansing School District, we thank you for the wonderful Blue Ribbon Award. West Lansing High School sets the standard for "Building a Foundation of Excellence," which provides high school students with the curricular basis for their lifelong quest for learning.

With a staff of 58 full-time and 20 part-time certified staff members and 948 students in grades 9 through 12, West Lansing High School continues to set the standard, especially in curriculum accomplishments leading to stellar achievement. In addition, one full-time and one part-time intervention specialist assist classroom teachers in meeting the needs of handicapped students through an inclusive model. Gifted education, guidance services, a program for second-language learners, and peer mediation also support individualized growth goals for West Lansing High School students.

KEYS TO CURRICULUM

It gives me great pleasure to share with you the "keys" to curriculum excellence that we believe are of national interest to board members, superintendents, principals, curriculum specialists, teacher leaders, union directors, elected officials, and all other educational leaders. Research reveals that student achievement is largely due to diversified and enriched curricula being taught by highly qualified teachers (Association for Supervision and Curriculum Development, 2002; Marzano, Pickering, & McTighe, 1993; National Education Association, 2001).

West Lansing High School curriculum is centered on the needs of all students! This may sound simple, but I have seen in thirty-plus years too many curricula based on politicians' whims, extremist group agendas, board member directives, and even teacher preferences. What the students need at West Lansing High School they receive, period! The accomplishment of this alignment of students needs to curricula is grounded in some key principles.

Effective Curriculum Is Interactive

The curriculum at West Lansing High School supports active participation of students, faculty, families, and the community (Carnegie Corporation of New York, 2001). Students' studies extend far behind the walls of their classrooms. Family engagement and community involvement enhances the curricula and provides a reality base fostering authentic learning experiences.

Effective Curriculum Is Challenging and Diverse

Learners are stimulated to achieve individual success within a challenging and diverse curriculum (Marzano, Pickering, & McTighe, 1993). West Lansing High School's curricula maximize students' engagement in developing critical thinking skills. Inquiry, deductive reasoning, concept attainment, mnemonics, synectics, and other higher-level thinking skills are integrated into the curricula.

Effective Curriculum Meets the Needs of All Students

A focus on meeting the needs of individual students is based on a collaborative goal-setting model in which students, parents, and teachers address the unique aspects of each student's academic, personal, and interpersonal curricula needs. An individualized curriculum plan for each student, including assessment measures, is constructed by a team of educators with each student and his or her parent(s) or guardian(s).

Effective Curriculum Is Relevant

Integrated curricula incorporating problem solving and decision making connects students to real-world applications for their learning. Our modules, scenarios, and vignettes have been thoughtfully prepared and field-tested before implementation.

Effective Curriculum Is Supported by Technology

At West Lansing High School, technologically visionary curricula enhance the learning experience. The power tools of technology are part and parcel of the curricula, as one cannot be taught apart from the other (Adler, 1999).

West Lansing High School's curriculum alignment to achievement indicators considered important is commendable. Social promotion occurs only during one of our many extracurricular activities. West Lansing High School has high aspirations for all its students.

Achievement Is an Important Indicator of Curriculum Success

Our students achieve high levels of academic success as evidenced on the ACT and SAT tests revealing a high correlation between West Lansing High School's

School Districts Expand Career Curriculum to Prepare Youths

Along with West Lansing High School, two other school districts are recognized by the media for prioritizing curriculum that is supported by technology as essential to preparing students for the twenty-first century.

Technology has become as essential as reading, writing, and arithmetic in the Katy Independent School District. More than 10,000 students in grades 7–12 in Katy are enrolled in some part of the district's career and technology education programs. With the twenty-first-century global economy expanding, it is felt by the educational leaders in the Katy Independent School District that curriculum that is aided by technology is critical to preparing students for their rapidly changing future.

The Fort Bend School District seconds the motion set by Katy Independent School District. Fort Bend students are offered curricula choices including telecommunications/electronic media, geographic information technology, automotive technology, computer drafting, health science technology, electronics, and digital electronics. It is felt by educational leaders in the Fort Bend School District that it is absolutely necessary that their curricula are supported by technology.

The key to curriculum success is implementing the technologies that support student achievement.

Source: D. S. P. Rosen, "School Districts Expand Career Curriculum to Prepare Youths," *The Houston Chronicle,* March 17, 2005.

curriculum and the content of these national tests. West Lansing High School students exceed all state and national performance levels in both proficient and advanced proficient categories without prompting or teaching to the state test prescribed by the curricula. International baccalaureate curricular expectations are exceeded by the students at West Lansing High School. Standard and alternative assessment methods embedded into the curriculum are utilized in the classrooms to accommodate varied learning styles. Outstanding curricular and noncurricular performances are recognized in announcements, in newsletters, and at assemblies throughout the school year.

Not only is parent involvement reflected in the curriculum, the curriculum of West Lansing Public Schools was designed with input from parents. From the planning stages, parents felt an ownership in designing the roles and responsibilities of parents in West Lansing Public Schools.

Parent Involvement Is Valued

West Lansing High School's parents are encouraged by all faculty members to hold their children's educational experience in high regard. Like other successful twenty-first-century educational leaders throughout the United States, the educational leadership of West High School ensures participation of parents in a variety of capacities comprised of meaningful educational opportunities (Ericson & Ellet, 2002). Parents serve on the school planning and design teams and actively volunteer in every classroom. Parents in classrooms are often seen tutoring, assisting students in self-discovery, and sharing their real-world experiences to support curricular goals. Parents are everywhere in the school and at school activities! The stigma of having parents participate in West Lansing High School's curricula is nonexistent. At the beginning perhaps there was a bit of indifference. However, after the students and faculty experienced the numerous contributions of parents, parents were considered a must. Today, parents help in the library, in the lunchroom, on field trips, with special programs, and in many other meaningful involvements in the high school's curricular experiences. Parents represent West Lansing High Schools on school curriculum needs. Single-handedly the parents earned sufficient funds to purchase three computers for each classroom. West Lansing High School parents are the greatest supporters and hardest workers on West Lansing School District's bond drives for additional facilities. The Parents Attacking Student Illiteracy (PASI) utilizes trained parent and community volunteers to provide quality reading intervention for identified at-risk students. This award-winning program focuses on developing reading and writing skills through the use of appropriate strategies and educational language to provide continuity during reading instruction.

Technology Prepares Students for Tomorrow

West Lansing High School's technology curriculum is dynamic! The technology that is embedded into the curricula provides enrichment and remediation on an individualized basis (Chen & Armstrong, 2002). Students are prepared to be effective, productive workers and citizens of the twenty-first century by using technology within the curriculum. The successful twenty-first-century educational leaders at West Lansing High School recognize that technology empowers students and staff to efficiently and effectively locate information, create and design products, and manage the teaching/learning environment (Fulton, 1999; Haertel & Means, 2000). At West Lansing High School, technology is implemented to facilitate communication between students, staff, parents, and the world community and extends the boundaries of the learning environment.

The educational leaders at West Lansing High School have formed business partnerships with American Consumers Power. An Internet link system was installed to allow students to monitor the amount of energy that is being used in their school building and to make comparisons to other schools of similar size.

A distance interactive project couples West Lansing High School with a school in a small village bordering Mexico, in Belize. Through this project, West Lansing High School students learn about impoverished conditions, yet gain a deep respect for cultural richness through open communication with the students in Belize. Students discover a common ground with one another and create an understanding and empathy for others.

West Lansing High School has been recognized as a leader in the state, the nation, and the world. The following awards and grants have been keys to building school pride.

- West Lansing High School was awarded the King-Chavez-Yamamoto Award acknowledging fifteen of its students' multicultural publications in professional journals.
- West Lansing High School was honored by the International Baccalaureate Association for advancements made in implementing seven foreign languages offered to students live and via communication technologies.
- The American Association of Curriculum Development awarded West Lansing High School with its most prestigious prize, the Curricular Process

and Procedure (CPP), for the 4 by 4 curricular review, revision, alignment, and implementation programs maximizing faculty and student involvement.

- West Lansing High School was selected as the nation's exemplary high school by the National Interagency Council for its integration of interagency involvements in curricular studies.
- West Lansing High School was acknowledged by the United Nations for West Lansing High School seniors who volunteered their services in Indonesia to help in the restoration following the tsunami in 2004.
- The International Cultural Alliance recognized West Lansing High School for its culture literacy curriculum instilling purpose, character, and positive virtues.

Thank you, Dr. Wisemore. Your presentation has been most helpful in the keys you have shared for the improvement of schools throughout our nation. At this time, please welcome Principal Phyllis Giaran.

KEYS TO CURRICULUM LEADERSHIP

Thank you, distinguished guests in honoring us by your presence this morning. First and foremost, West Lansing High School's faculty, students, parents, community members—I thank you for your conviction, diligence, and support of your high school! Yes, our curriculum remains the cornerstone of our academic success. The richness and diversity of our curricular offerings has not come about overnight. Each year the review and revision of our curricula has led us to the meeting of every student's needs, aspirations, and interests. In following the format of the day, I will continue to present our experiences as keys for other educational leaders, schools, and school districts to emulate.

Our early beginnings of full-scale curriculum development started at the dawn of the twenty-first century. Our first challenge then was deciding on a shared definition of curriculum (Barton, 2002; Mash & Willis, 2003; Pinar, 1999), much like nailing Jello to a tree. Our first key to understanding *curriculum* was our knowledge that the word was Latin for race-course, or the *race* itself—a place of deeds or a series of deeds providing us with a basic foundation. The second key to developing our curriculum emerged from our vision statement stating that our students needed to learn the skills that allowed them as adults to contribute to their communities.

Our curricular understanding stemming from our commonly held definition stemmed into concepts of keys leading to our success today (Dewey, 1938; National Institute for Literacy, 2002). There were many curriculum concepts we considered, but perhaps the one that exerted the most far-reaching influence on our programs as they actually developed was in connection with the nature of curriculum itself. And boy, did our thoughts about conceptualizations of curriculum abound. After much thoughtful deliberation, we decided on three keys that would represent our beliefs about curriculum, as presented in Key Box 8.1, 8.2, and 8.3.

Curriculum Is Subjects Arranged in a Sequence

This belief is grounded in elementary and secondary schools and colleges. The terms *classical curriculum, college preparatory curriculum,* and *general curriculum,* for example, refer to the subjects and sequence of subjects required of given groups of pupils for graduation. What is referred to as *mandated curriculum* is what is required by federal, state, or local board policy; whereas *curriculum* is specified sequentially with mandated testing affirming the specified curricula implementation. When this meaning is employed, the plural form is often used, reference being made to the various *curricula* of a school. In essence, this conceptualization of curriculum is the selection, organization, and administration of the subject matter designed to lead the pupil on to some definite life objective (Gould, 2002).

Curriculum Is What Is Taught

Our second belief is that curriculum is the subject matter or content that is to be employed in instruction. This concept extends the meaning of Key 1 to include, in addition to the selection and arrangement of subjects, the selection and arrangement of the content in these subjects. Curriculum making from this point of view consists largely in selecting and arranging the topics that are to be taught in various subjects (Bransford, Brown, & Cocking, 2000). This meaning is subscribed to by a number of students of educational problems. To illustrate this concept, teachers in the past decided and delivered, added or omitted, colored or discolored what they considered pertinent in the curricula, such as science labs and other inquiry-based curricula.

Curriculum Is Experiences for Learners

Our third belief about curricula is much broader, as it is based on the experiences of the learner. The curriculum under this concept involves all elements of experience rather than one only—that is, the content or subject matter that may be employed in experience. The task of curriculum making is very complex under this concept.

Pupil interests and activities, aims, method, content, in fact everything that influence the experience of the learner must be considered during the process of curriculum making. Hence, the curriculum should be a series of guided experiences so related and so arranged that what is learned in one experience serves to enrich and make more valuable the experiences that follow. The curriculum represents the experiences in which pupils are expected to engage in school and the general orders of sequence in which these experiences occur.

These three keys or beliefs about curriculum assisted us in our decision making leading to an enhanced and expanded offering of learning opportunities.

From the shared development and understanding of the three keys, curricular roles and responsibilities emerged for all educational leaders—board members, superintendents, principals, curricular specialists, teacher leaders, union directors, parents, community members, and all other educational leaders. These roles and responsibilities are reflected in keys to curriculum leadership.

Keep Current with Education Trends

As society changes, populations shift, information explodes, and the world gets smaller and smaller, educational leaders will need to stay abreast of these trends to prepare and provide curricula that are highly responsive to the needs of an ever-changing world (Murnane & Levy, 1996).

Understand What Is Being Taught

Educational leaders must be instructional and curricula leaders must know the curricula thoroughly and comprehensively. West Lansing High School has been gifted with knowledgeable educational leaders that not only know the curricula inside and out but due to their knowledge of our curricula are able to actively provide guidance in all curricular matters to those they lead.

Expect Curriculum to Be Taught

Leaders who know the curriculum expect and hold those they lead accountable for implementing it to the fullest extent intended. Curricula are the tools on which students need to build future knowledge. The scope, sequence, and continuity of the curricula are not optional at West Lansing High School.

Link Curriculum Objectives and Skills

Our educational leaders work closely with our teachers in developing curricular objectives that maximize learning opportunities (Means, Penuel, & Quellmalz, 2000). Our educational leaders work diligently and successfully to provide opportunities for faculty to participate in curricular development.

Support Diverse Interests

The faculty at West Lansing High School is dedicated to preparing students for a rapidly changing world. Student curricular interests have not remained the same in the last ten years. Furthermore, we believe that student interests in the future will continue to diversify. West Lansing High School believes if we don't take care of our students' curricular needs, another school will. The development of our diversified curricula is a never-ending journey.

Model Curriculum Implementation

West Lansing High School's educational leaders "walk their talk" by engaging in curricular development, professional development opportunities, and working alongside teachers to maximize the gains of every lesson.

Provide Continuous Feedback and Support

Our teachers seek continuous feedback and this feedback is shared in a professional and positive manner by our educational leaders. Where curricular support is needed, our educational leaders are highly responsive. The cornerstones of West Lansing High School's continuous feedback and curricular support are trust, passion, and respect for one another as professionals.

Prioritize and Work Diligently for Support

Knowing the high priority of curricula as held by faculty, students, parents, and community, our educational leaders have worked diligently and successfully in leaving no financial rock unturned. From maximizing appropriated dollars to attaining additional financial support for curricula through grants, foundations, and partnerships, our revenue for curricula has continued to grow. This strong financial base has been established through the efforts of educational leaders, faculty, parent organizations, community members, and donations from businesses and industries.

Maintain a Review and Revision Cycle

All faculty members participate in curricular review and revision along with students, parents, and community members. Participating members are empowered to make curricular decisions. The actual review and revision cycle consists of a four-year process in which each core curricular area (science, social studies, mathematics, and language arts) is considered for revision every four years. Additional curricular areas are scheduled alongside each of the core areas. New curriculum is introduced on an as-needed annual basis. Curricula are kept alive and well at West Lansing High School.

Promote Collaboration and Partnership

Our partnerships with our local businesses and industries, interagency councils, ministerial alliance, and community groups have infused curricular richness into our

IN THE NEWS

A Community Effort

Like West Lansing High School, collaboration and partnerships have also been created by Miami-Dade Board Officials, North Miami City Council, a culinary university, and community members to develop world-class educational programs.

Miami-Dade School Board Officials and the North Miami City Council have been developing massive plans for schools in North Miami. From rebuilding school buildings to reviewing and revising the public schools curriculum, their partnership has led to an ambitious charge. To illustrate, kindergarten classes will be focusing on marine animals native to Florida. The schools décor will mimic this theme. The first floor will look like an ocean, the second like the Everglades, and the third floor will look like mangroves. The architecture and design will enrich their world class curricula.

Enter Johnson & Whales University with their chefs in training providing meals for Miami-Dade's PreK–12 students. The plans for a twenty-first-century curricula have been as specific as the lunch menu where university culinary students will prepare meals from an organic, whole foods approach. The best educationally as well as nutritionally for the school district's students has become the mission as established by the collaborators and partners for improved schools.

Through collaboration and partnerships for Miami-Dade school improvements, curricula planning and other school improvements have been powerful.

Source: A. Martinez, "A Community Effort," *The Miami Herald*, October 29, 2005.

high school (Rothstein, 2002a). From donations of equipment for our nine labs to numerous volunteers working with our students, the curricula gifts and talents have been so powerful.

Again, thank you for the honor of this award. To all those who worked diligently to make this achievement happen, I am eternally grateful.

Ladies and gentlemen, please join me in welcoming Dr. Terry Landing, West Lansing High School's Curriculum Specialist extraordinaire.

Dr. Williams, distinguished guests, Superintendent Wisemore, Principal Giaran, students, parents, and community members—good morning and thank you! We are thrilled to have achieved this distinguished honor, the Blue Ribbon Award!

I have been asked to share my experiences as a nationally certified curricula specialist. I will attempt to present the accomplishments to date of the National Certified Curricula Association (NCCA), adapting the format used today in term of keys, or what and how educational leaders can readily and practically implement. After all, there are many schools and school districts today struggling to educate students who will be proficient and competitive in the international marketplace of the twenty-first century.

KEYS FOR FUTURE CURRICULUM DEVELOPMENT

Three years ago, the National Certified Curricula Association (NCCA), with a nucleus of interested educational leaders from twenty-three states, was conceived. We shared the common concern that if schools and school districts were to be judged by the federal government, then the playing field for schools throughout the United States needed to be leveled. Hence, our vision became the establishment of national curriculum standards aligned to federal mandates. Today, three years later, our membership has grown to all 50 states with NCCA's membership of over 3,000 educational leaders. We believe that interest in NCCA has stemmed from the desire and determination to achieve curricular excellence.

The notion of developing national curriculum standards was perplexing as each state's uniqueness of curricula and assessment prevailed. Our challenge was and continues to be exacerbated by the fact that school districts within many states are determining their own curriculum. The double-edged sword of local and state autonomy contrasted sharply and drastically in examination of national student achievement. Only recently, national curricular reform, out of agreement or druthers, was considered far and wide to be no option!

The ambition of the NCCA is grand—to describe what all students should know and be able to do upon completion of a thirteen-year public education. Many standards emerged from this ambition. Yet, it is important to note that none of these standards was meant to serve as a national test. Standards of the NCCA define the results expected but do not limit state strategies for how to ensure that their students achieve these expectations. To assist educators throughout our nation, NCCA has plans to eventually extend the standards into a curriculum framework. While also not a curriculum, this framework will bring to life the intent of the standards through classroom examples and a discussion of the underlying rationales.

State and local school district curriculum developers will then be able to use NCCA's framework as a resource to develop district curricula that best meet the needs of the students in each community. The curriculum framework of NCCA also can serve as a resource to classroom teachers and to staff developers throughout the United States who want to modify instruction in light of the NCCA's standards.

Since America's schools need to produce both excellent thinkers and excellent doers, the NCCA's curriculum content standards describe what students should know and be able to do in specific academic areas and across disciplines (Osher & Ward, 1996). Content standards are concerned with the knowledge students should acquire and the skills they should develop in the course of their K–12 experience. That is why each of the content standards is further described in terms of cumulative progress indicators. Over the next few years, the content standards will be further defined through the attachment of performance tasks and levels that will be determined as the standards are integrated into national indicators (such as ACT and SAT tests) and statewide assessment programs.

The NCCA standards emerged from the efforts of two different groups under the auspices of the NCCA that worked one after another for a total of fifteen months. Concurrently, panels of educators, business people, and other citizens developed preliminary draft standards in seven academic areas and career education. With increasing numbers of skilled labor positions being displaced to Asia and continued closings of businesses and industries in the United States, similarly constituted working groups built on these preliminary standards and engaged the public in a review process that resulted in several revised drafts.

Both working groups submitted a total of 105 standards comprised of 1,295 indicators to the NCCA; we reviewed the standards proposed for 7. Our review of the standards and indicators revealed five cross-content workplace readiness standards, as presented in Key Box 8.4.

KEY BOX 8.4

Five Cross-Content Workplace Readiness Standards for the Twenty-First Century

- *Key 1:* All students will develop career planning and workplace readiness skills.
- *Key 2:* All students will use technology, information, and other tools.
- *Key 3:* All students will use critical thinking, decision-making, and problem-solving skills.
- *Key 4:* All students will demonstrate self-management skills.
- *Key 5:* All students will apply safety principles.

Through these five cross-content workplace readiness standards, the knowledge and skills associated with career education have been elevated in importance for all instructional areas. The National Certified Curricula Association emphasizes the importance of every student linking school-based learning with a career major and of having both school-based and work-based learning experiences. Since one of the goals of public education is to prepare students for the world of work, NCCA stresses that these standards be addressed through all content areas.

The NCCA also underscores the achievement of proficient levels by all students in America in the key curricular areas shown in Key Box 8.5.

KEY BOX 8.5

Twenty-First-Century Curricular Areas

- *Key 1:* Comprehensive health and physical education
- *Key 2:* Language arts/literacy
- *Key 3:* Mathematics
- *Key 4:* Science
- *Key 5:* Social studies
- *Key 6:* World languages
- *Key 7:* Visual and performing arts

The listing of the seven key curricular areas is not in the order of priority or importance. The NCCA does not treat each curricular area as a separate content area because they are, by definition, interdisciplinary. Likewise, several other specific curriculum areas have not been designated as separate components of the core curriculum, including, but not limited to, the key areas presented in Key Box 8.6.

KEY BOX 8.6

Additional Curriculum Areas for the Twenty-First Century

- *Key 1:* Family and consumer science
- *Key 2:* Technology education
- *Key 3:* Business education and other occupational areas

These curricular content areas are seen by NCCA as critical as each can contribute to students' achieving the expected results set forth in NCCA's standards. It is also felt by NCCA that these curricular content areas provide students with opportunities to apply, and thereby reinforce, learning from the core curriculum content areas.

The National Certified Curricula Association has established its standards in curricular content areas that can be measured in a uniform and concrete manner. The standards do not include the affective domain, which addresses areas of self-esteem, emotions, feelings, and personal values. It isn't that NCCA doesn't recognize that students' intellectual growth is affected by their emotional disposition. However, NCCA purposefully excludes affective results from the content standards (which many states would formally assess) because of the following critical keys.

- *Key 1: A student's values or feelings are personal.* The NCCA considers it inappropriate to assess a student's values or feelings. Self-esteem, emotions, feelings, and values are personal and no attempt should be made to measure them in a uniform and concrete way. Not only are such attempts neither reliable nor valid, but evaluating a student's self-esteem, emotions, feelings, and personal values constitutes an intrusion and violation of privacy.

● *Key 2: Issues need to be addressed personally and appropriately.* Parents and local educators should make judgments about when and how these affective issues will be addressed in their communities. In doing so, NCCA upholds that such efforts maintain the confidentiality of each student.

● *Key 3: Self-worth is not an outcome or artifact to be comparatively measured.* Teachers, administrators, parents, and other community residents all have a responsibility to nurture and communicate the values, self-worth, and character development required for young people to succeed. Attempts at attaining empirical data—worse yet, comparing data school district by school district or state by state—are highly inappropriate and create false impressions as asserted by NCCA.

Although NCCA's standards have been constructed with formal education in mind, NCCA did not intend to imply that each standard could be met only through courses in a formal school setting (Berger, 2002). The application of knowledge from all content areas needs to be reinforced through experiences beyond the school walls. The NCCA views parents (or guardians) as the first and foremost educator in every child's life. The twentieth-century African proverb has carried over into the twenty-first century that it takes a whole village to raise a twenty-first-century child while implementing *twenty-first-century curriculum*!

RESEARCH KEYS

To enrich your understanding of **twenty-first-century curriculum**, log on to www.researchnavigator.com and search Ebsco's **Research Navigator.com** ContentSelect.

KEYS FOR CURRICULUM INTEGRATION

I cannot emphasize strongly enough that NCCA curriculum content standards need to be integrated across all curricular areas. Educators must deliver an integrated curriculum. To illustrate this imperative, please consider the exemplary keys to integrating curriculum content standards in Key Box 8.7.

KEY BOX 8.7

Keys to Integrating Curriculum Content Standards for the Twenty-First Century

● *Key 1:* Career education should be integrated into all curriculum content areas.
● *Key 2:* Language arts and literacy skills are keys to success in all areas of learning.
● *Key 3:* Science is an important part of health education.
● *Key 4:* Mathematics skills are tools for problem-solving in science and can be reinforced in vocational-technical areas.
● *Key 5:* The powerful tools of technology need to be used to support cross-curricular applications, bringing courses like physics and other studies to life.

- *Key 6:* Family and consumer sciences (home economics) must be integrated into health and science in providing students with lifelong skills.
- *Key 7:* The visual and performing arts provide an avenue for the understanding of science, social studies, language arts, world languages, and design technology.

In closing, NCCA curriculum content standards ascertain the academic accomplishments expected of all students. The curriculum content standards of our association serve as a foundation for all fifty states to unite to reshape our approach to education. Please join West Lansing High School's implementation of NCCA's curriculum content standards. Collectively, NCAA's approach to standards-based curriculum embodies a vision of the skills and understandings of all children's need for life in the twenty-first century! Thank you!

Please join me in welcoming our final presenter, Jennifer Lyons, a teacher leader, union director, and three-time recipient of Teacher of the Year as voted by the students and parents of West Lansing High School.

Good Morning, Dr. Williams, honored guests, Superintendent Wisemore, Principal Giaran, Dr. Landing, distinguished West Lansing High School faculty, students, parents, and community members. It is a privilege to receive the No Child Left Behind Blue Ribbon Schools Award. It is also a pleasure to share what I consider to be the keys to our success in developing and implementing excellent curricula.

The success of West Lansing High School is found in how we spell cooperation—*we!* It's our team approach that has led us to great accomplishments in curriculum and our other significant school accomplishments (Association for Supervision and Curriculum, 2002). With everyone pitching in, small curricular opportunities readily grew into great enterprises.

West Lansing High School Curriculum Council exemplifies our large curricular teamwork. Serving on the council are our principals, curriculum specialists, teachers representing each curricular area, parents, students, community members, interagency leaders, business and industry leaders, and even a minister from a local church. Meetings are posted and open to the public. In fact, we encourage participation at these meetings. We meet monthly and everyone has one equal vote and the council's decisions can be changed only by vote of the council. As you might well imagine, council members feel empowered as their choice, not chance, determines future curricula.

VISIONARY KEYS FOR CURRICULUM DEVELOPMENT

The twenty-first-century vision of the West Lansing High School Curriculum Council is to set the curriculum direction, make decisions that maximize this direction, and provide support to all faculty members implementing the direction of the Curriculum Council. Manifestations from the Curriculum Council's vision have resulted in child-centered outcomes where teachers' guidance as to what's best for learners is valued and supported. It is from the West Lansing High School Curriculum Council vision that the purposes of the council emanate. The purposes of the council are presented in Key Box 8.8.

KEY BOX 8.8

Visionary Keys for Twenty-First-Century Curriculum Development

- *Key 1: Provide for the development and implementation of curricula based on students' needs, learning styles, and preferences.* The development and support provided for implementation of curricula which takes into account the needs of students sets out the knowledge, understandings, skills, and attitudes that students are expected to acquire.
- *Key 2: Provide for the development and accreditation of courses.* Course development facilitates the adjustment of courses to ensure they are relevant to the continuously changing requirements of students' learning needs and accreditation requirements.
- *Key 3: Provide for the assessment and certification of student achievement* (Lazear, 1999). Accountability for student learning is critical to acquire, provide, and inform the community of valid and credible student assessment data.

KEYS FOR BUILDING CURRICULUM ORGANIZATIONS

Student learning is at the heart of everything we do at West Lansing High School, as demonstrated in our vision and purpose. In fact, the vision and purpose of West Lansing High School's Curriculum Council are underpinned by an unwavering commitment to the principles presented in Key Box 8.9.

KEY BOX 8.9

Keys to Building Twenty-First-Century Curriculum

- *Key 1: Provide comprehensive curricula.* The West Lansing High School Curriculum Council has worked diligently to provide students with comprehensive curricula that have scope, sequence, and continuity from ninth to twelfth grades, promoting meaning and purpose and bringing enjoyment to students' lives.
- *Key 2: Recognize the significance of learning outcomes.* Our Curriculum Council's learning outcomes represent an important means of describing the knowledge, understandings, skills, and attitudes that students are expected to acquire as a result of their schooling.
- *Key 3: Develop fair and explicit standards.* Our Curriculum Council assures that students and teachers know the criteria and standards by which achievement is judged. The council is committed to a fairness that provides students with equal opportunity to demonstrate their achievement and not be disadvantaged on irrelevant grounds.
- *Key 4: Provide students with a full and comprehensive curriculum.* Students are provided with the widest and most empowering range of knowledge and skills (Doyle & Pimental, 1999), as provided by West Lansing High School's Curriculum Council. To this end, the Curriculum Council recognizes and

accommodates the previous experiences of individual students and groups of students.

- *Key 5: Provide transparent decision-making processes.* Decisions made by our Curriculum Council are readily endorsed due to the fair and equitable reputation our council has earned. Meetings of our Curriculum Council are not only open to the public, but visitors are encouraged and welcomed.
- *Key 6: Collaborate with stakeholders.* A central function and obligation of the Curriculum Council is to listen, understand, and consider the implications of all stakeholders. West Lansing High School Curriculum Council has put in place structures and processes to promote wide and continuous collaboration with stakeholders.
- *Key 7: Demonstrate honesty and integrity at all times.* The West Lansing High School Curriculum Council demonstrates honesty and integrity at all times. Council members are held accountable and responsible for their actions. Their actions the last fifteen years have been ethical and truthful.
- *Key 8: Earn the respect of others.* By acting professionally, courteously, and with sensitivity and concern for the well-being of all others, the West Lansing High School Curriculum Council is respected. The council consistently treats others fairly and impartially, maintains confidentiality, and values the cultural diversity of others.

In closing, West Lansing High School is a wonderful school for students, faculty, parents, and community members. Much of this quality may be attributed to our Curriculum Council. However, the honest truth is that what we have in terms of our Curriculum Council can be achieved by other schools. Follow the keys, and if you build it, curricular excellence will come!

Thank you, Mrs. Lyons, and thank you for being with us at this Blue Ribbon Award Ceremony. It is the wishes of the good people at West Lansing High School that you practice the keys they have presented. The keys to successful twenty-first-century educational leadership need your implementation. May the schools you lead become Blue Ribbon Schools.

PERSPECTIVE ON CURRICULUM IN TWENTY-FIRST-CENTURY SCHOOLS

Keys, keys, and more keys to understand curriculum, how to develop it, and how to become a successful curriculum leader. National curricular standards, national curricular guidance, and step-by-step direction in building a curriculum council are presented with practical terminology based on conventional wisdom void of citations that often interrupt deep consideration and contemplation.

THE REFLECTIVE PRACTITIONER

Welcome to your eighth Reflective Practitioner, which is again based on all six ISLLC Standards, your Chapter 8 Scenario, and your reading of Chapter 8. It is intended to provoke your thoughtful reflection and to stimulate discussion among colleagues, classmates, and peers. The Reflective Practitioner provides opportunities to stimulate discussion among colleagues, classmates, and peers. The Reflective Practitioner provides opportunities to synthesize issues, make comparisons, and apply theory to practice. We hope it will motivate you to search for evidence, thus increasing your comprehension of the text and helping you examine your convictions and discover new and shared perspectives.

■ ISLLC Standard 1
A school administrator is an educational leader who promotes the success of all students by facilitating the development, articulation, implementation, and stewardship of a vision of learning that is shared and supported by the school community.

■ ISLLC Standard 2
A school administrator is an educational leader who promotes the success of all students by advocating, nurturing, and sustaining a school culture and instructional program conducive to student learning and staff professional growth.

■ ISLLC Standard 3
A school administrator is an educational leader who promotes the success of all students by ensuring management of the organization, operations, and resources for a safe, efficient, and effective learning environment.

■ ISLLC Standard 4
A school administrator is an educational leader who promotes the success of all students by collaborating with families and community members, responding to diverse community interests and needs, and mobilizing community resources.

■ ISLLC Standard 5
A school administrator is an educational leader who promotes the success of all students by acting with integrity, fairness, and in an ethical manner.

■ ISLLC Standard 6
A school administrator is an educational leader who promotes the success of all students by understanding, responding to, and influencing the larger political, social, economic, legal, and cultural context.

Scenario

You are the new principal of South Lansing High School. Although West Lansing High School and South Lansing High School are in the same school district, they are strikingly different. South Lansing High School is confronted by a number of challenges. The superintendent has requested a meeting with you for August 8, prior to the start of the school year for teachers and students. The purpose of the meeting is described in a memo from the superintendent (see p. 134). Other documents that will serve to establish a context for the meeting are also provided (see pp. 132 and 133).

- **School Improvement Goal:** Plan, construct, and implement a curriculum that will promote the success of all students.
- **Documents Provided:** School fact sheet, a memo from the teachers, a memo from the superintendent.

QUESTIONS FOR REFLECTIVE THINKING

1. As the newly appointed principal of South Lansing High School, please write a preliminary plan for curricular improvement to be shared with your superintendent.
2. What additional information would be helpful to you in preparing your preliminary plan for curricular improvement at South Lansing High School? Please explain how this information would be helpful.
3. Which ISLLC Standards are dependent on highly relevant, rich, and responsive curricula? From

the ISLLC Standards you have selected, present your rationale for the importance of curricula on a Standard-by-Standard format.
4. Who should be involved in the curriculum development process? Why?
5. Which keys presented in Chapter 8 will assist you in becoming a successful twenty-first-century curricular leader? Please explain your responses.

South Lansing High School Fact Sheet

South Lansing High School is located in a rural area of the Lansing School District, where population is rapidly growing and agriculture is the main source of income.

Although South Lansing High School is located in a rapidly growing rural area, student enrollment at South Lansing High School has not increased similarly. With a 2 percent increase in student enrollment each year in the last five years, South Lansing High School currently has 889 students enrolled in grades 9 through 12. Several parents and students, exercising the districtwide school of choice plan, have transferred to West Lansing High School, citing greater curricular choices.

Compared with other schools in the state, South Lansing High School has some unique challenges. For example:

- The student mobility rate is 23 percent, compared to the state average of 16.3 percent.
- The student/instructional faculty ratio at South Lansing High School is 28:1, compared with an average of 25:1 in the state.
- The faculty attendance rate is 88.8 percent at South Lansing High School, compared with a state average of 93.9 percent.
- The student/administrator ratio is 241:1, compared with a state average of 306:1.

The parents in the community served by South Lansing High School have been traditionally very supportive of the school and the school district. However, the support today seems to be eroding.

Although test scores at South Lansing High School are somewhat better than the state averages, they are lower than other high schools in the school district. This fact has caused some discontent among members of the public.

A Memo from the Teachers

TO: Principal, South Lansing High School
FROM: Teacher Education Association Officers,
          South Lansing High School
RE: School curriculum
DATE: August 3

Welcome to South Lansing High School. Congratulations on your appointment as principal of South Lansing High School. We look forward to working with you to improve South Lansing High School's curriculum.

As we embark on our joint effort, we would like to inform you of a problem—the curriculum at South Lansing High School. Every year, it seems as if more and more gets added to our curriculum, resulting in a reduction in time to do creative activities that used to make teaching and learning fun. Our students seem bored with all the emphasis on the basics and even the teachers at times feel stifled.

We would like to meet with you to discuss and hopefully resolve these issues.

A Memo from the Superintendent

TO: Principal, South Lansing High School
FROM: Superintendent of Schools
RE: Curricular planning for South Lansing High School
DATE: August 1

Welcome to the Lansing School District and to your first year as principal of South Lansing High School. On behalf of the entire board of education and administrative cabinet, it is a pleasure to extend to you our best wishes for a successful start to your administrative career.

As you learned during the interview process and our discussions, South Lansing High School faces some challenging issues. At the beginning of the summer, before you were selected as principal, several parents met with me to express their concern for the curriculum at South Lansing High School. Simultaneously, several faculty members indicated that they were interested in improving the curriculum as well.

I would like to work with you to develop a plan to improve the curriculum at South Lansing High School. I would like to tentatively schedule a meeting with you on August 7 at 11:00 A.M. to begin our work. Please prepare and present your preliminary plan for the improvement of curriculum at South Lansing High School when we meet on August 7.

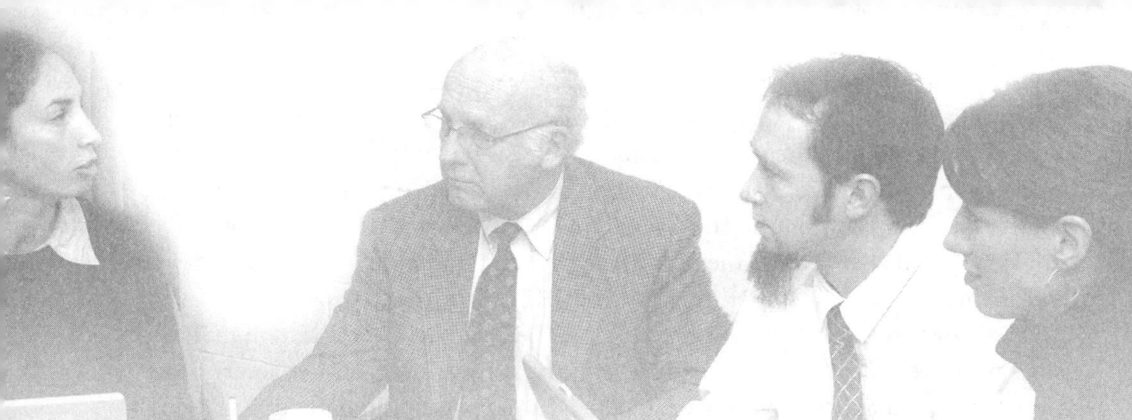

chapter 9

ISLLC
Standards
5 & 6

Legal and Moral Leadership: Doing the Right Thing

It is the procedure that spells much of the difference between rule and law of whim or caprice.
—William O. Douglas

Your Chapter 9 Action Focus begins with the appointment of a new superintendent to provide you with clarity in understanding the legal and moral challenges facing twenty-first-century educational leaders. Shortly following Dr. Jones's appointment to the superintendency, the board of education explained an ongoing lawsuit involving the school district. The board meticulously explained that the district was in court for the last four years for implementing a state-approved health curriculum. The board of education leaders shared that at the outset of the implementation of the health curriculum model, a few community members were dissatisfied with what students were being taught. Something about deep breathing to stay calm was equated with sexual overtones. A small nucleus of concerned citizens began to gain momentum as other community members joined their cause. As parents began pulling their children out of the schools, the community became divided. A recall election of the board members met a resounding defeat.

Two extremist organizations saw what was happening and marched into town. They first began supporting the community members opposing the health curriculum model. Soon they were leading the bandwagon. They pressed charges not only against the school district and intermediate school district but also the state. Wounds were opened with scars that would take numerous years to heal.

The board of education emphasized that the new superintendent needed to get the school district and community back on the same track. A day had not passed during the six years it took to resolve this judicial matter that someone did not threaten to press charges for something. If a community member or parent did not say each day that he or she was going to get an attorney, the silence was worrisome. The media sensationalized each judicial event every step of the way, as hundreds of thousands of dollars were spent, until a judge threw the case out of court.

As demonstrated in your Chapter 9 Action Focus, legal entanglements like this are all too common in the nation's schools. Why are people so bent on solving problems in court? Americans have turned into a highly litigious society; millions of lawsuits occur each year in the United States. And worse yet, it is not getting better, as one in every four Americans face having a potentially devastating lawsuit filed against him or her sometime in the near future (Gross, 1998).

So what are educational leaders to do? The best you can do to remain legally safe, to reduce the risk of costly litigation, to resolve legal issues apart from the courts is, in part, to have a plan in place. Laws protect and defend rights of individuals and the safest course is always to comply with rules and regulations defined by them. In addition, successful twenty-first-century educational leaders stay abreast of changes in laws such as those in IDEA implemented in 2005.

WHOSE IDEA IS THIS?

The most important federal laws related to the rights of students with disabilities are Public Law 94-142, or the Education of All Handicapped Children Act (EAHCA), enacted in 1975; Section 504 of the Rehabilitation Act (RHA) of 1973; the Americans with Disabilities Act (ADA) enacted in 1990; Amendments to the Individuals with Disabilities Education Act (IDEA) in 1997; and continual reauthorization efforts of IDEA, such as a major IDEA reauthorization signed by President George Bush on December 3, 2004. Of these federal laws, IDEA has had the most significant impact on public schools. Litigation, regulations, and judicial opinions have been continuous in defining important actions for educational leaders.

The most recent reauthorization of IDEA went into effect on July 1, 2005. Although it preserves the basic structure of prior legislation, Public Law 108-446 includes approximately twelve significant changes. These changes reflect keys to understanding and planning effective educational programs for students with disabilities in today's schools.

Employ Highly Qualified Special Education Teachers

An extensive definition of *highly qualified special education teacher* and the requirements of being a special education teacher are specified in the 2005 reauthorization of IDEA. In general, to be considered as highly qualified, new and veteran special education teachers who teach two or more core subjects exclusively to children with disabilities will need to fulfill the requirements in each core subject area taught under the Elementary and Secondary Education Act provisions providing compensatory education for disadvantaged students. In addition, all special education teachers must hold a Bachelor of Arts degree, obtain full special education certification or equivalent licensure, and cannot hold an emergency or temporary certificate. Careful recruiting and retaining of highly qualified special education teachers will be of utmost importance.

Expect Paperwork Reduction

Stipulations that are geared to reduce paperwork and other activity requirements have been established, such as the procedural safeguards notice requirements that have been amended to reduce the paperwork burden on schools. The new law requires that a copy of the procedural safeguards available to the parents of a child with a disability shall be given to the parents only one time a year. The only exceptions are that a copy be given upon initial referral or parental request for evaluation, upon first occurrence of the filing of a complaint, and upon the request of a parent. Change your procedures and curb expenses in staying current with paperwork reduction.

Provide for Homeless and Highly Mobile Children and Families

More detailed procedures have been added by the 2005 reauthorization of IDEA regarding the appointment of an individual to act as a surrogate for parents in situations where the child is a ward of the state or is an unaccompanied homeless youth. You will be required within thirty days after determination to provide such a surrogate.

Expect Increased Funds and Increased Requirements

The latest reauthorization of IDEA provides specific authorization of funding levels for FY2005 to FY2011 and establishes sums for succeeding fiscal years. Forecasting budgets for the next several years is possible with federal funding for 2007 at $16,938,917,714; 2008 at $19,229,188,286; 2009 at $21,519,458,857; 2010 at $23,809,729,429; and 2011 at $26,100,000,000. These dollar amounts may be deceiving inasmuch as when these large sums are disbursed throughout fifty states, the amounts received by some states may seem meager. The good news, however, is that the amounts are known and the amounts increase over time. This is very helpful when planning a budget.

Establish Risk Pools

Provisions of medical or other expensive services have resulted in very high costs for some school districts. The federal government in the 2005 reauthorization of IDEA provides states with the opportunity to establish and maintain a risk pool of dollars to assist local education agencies. Funds distributed from the risk pool must pay only for direct special education and related services for high-need children with disabilities and may not be used for legal fees or related costs. Be prepared to work alongside your state, as it will be the state that develops a risk pool with your school district.

Place Children with Disabilities in Private Facilities

A child with a disability may be placed in a private school by a local education agency or state education agency as a means of fulfilling the free and appropriate public education requirement. In short, you must be in compliance with five requirements for placing children with disabilities in private schools. First, the funds expended to private schools by the local or state agency must be no less than the dollar amount set by the federal government. Second, the local education agency, following meaningful consultation with private school leaders, shall conduct a thorough and complete process to determine the number of children with disabilities who are parentally placed in private schools. Third, services may be provided to children with disabilities on the private school premises, including religious schools. Fourth, state and local funds may supplement and not supplant the proportionate amount of federal funds required to be expended. Fifth, the local school agency must provide a report to the state school agency that states the number of children with disabilities served in private schools. When in doubt, it is highly recommended to seek legal counsel.

Implement Revised Performance Goals and Other Student Requirements

Before the 2005 reauthorization of IDEA, states were required to have performance goals for children with disabilities that were consistent to the maximum extent appropriate with goals and standards established by the state. Today, the provision requires that the state's performance goals are the same as the state's definition of *adequate yearly progress*. The reauthorization links performance indicators to measurable annual objectives for progress by children with disabilities. Last, under the 2005 reauthorization of IDEA, you will be reporting progress made toward performance goals every year instead of every two years.

Plan Offsets by Local Educational Agencies

The 2005 reauthorization of IDEA maintains the set-aside, or maximum reserve of 0.5 percent (or $25 million, whichever is less), for technical assistance to improve state data collection concerning assistance to children with disabilities. Educational leaders must contact the Bureau of Indian Affairs, the unit of government that maintains the set-asides, for additional information.

Use Funding for Early Intervention Services Effectively

States may adopt policies that permit parents of children receiving early intervention services to extend those services until the children are eligible to enter kindergarten. Before the 2005 reauthorization, in the states that chose not to adopt such a policy, children with disabilities were transitioned into a preschool program. Use this intervention effectively to reduce or eliminate the future need for special education for children who haven't qualified for special education in the past.

Implement Changes in Procedural Safeguards Prudently

The new IDEA has brought changes in procedural safeguards such as extending the due process hearing to the local educational agency to encourage parties to resolve a dispute, allowing school personnel the option to consider on a case-by-case basis any unique circumstances when determining whether to order a change in placement for a child with disabilities who violates a code of student conduct, and increasing a school's latitude to place a child with a disability who has inflicted serious bodily injury on another person into an interim alternative setting. In addition, it is important for you to know that the time limitation for placing a student with a disability in an interim educational setting has increased from "not more than 45 days" to "not more than 45 *school* days."

Link Performance Indicators to ESEA Requirements

To maintain compliance with the 2005 reauthorization of IDEA, successful educational leaders will link performance indicators to ESEA requirements. In addition, educational leaders will express these indicators in measurable annual objectives to determine the progress made by children with disabilities.

Comply with 2005 Reauthorization of IDEA

If a state does not meet the requirements of the 2005 reauthorization of IDEA, the federal government is required to take specific actions. The federal government's actions include, but are not limited to, requiring the state to prepare corrective action, withholding not less than 20 percent and not more than 50 percent of the state's funding, and making referrals to the Department of Justice.

As for the future of IDEA, one thing seems to be certain—change. As situations change, new presidents come and go, and the courts continue to shape public education, it is reasonable to say that future reauthorizations of IDEA will be forthcoming. Keep your ear to the legislative pavement and your eyes on elected officials; additional legislative revisions are certain to come.

IN THE NEWS

Legal Fight Over Special Education in Baltimore Enters New Phase

State selected administrators are partnering to resolve a 21-year-old special education lawsuit against Baltimore city school system.

In a 21-year-old lawsuit, a judge approved a plan for state-appointed administrators to intervene. After more than two decades of court battles over problems in the Baltimore city school system's special education programs and services, the district and the state of Maryland have embarked on a far-reaching intervention effort.

Under a federal judge's order, Maryland has selected nine administrators from school districts around the state to work directly with the Baltimore school district in personnel, information technology, guidance, transportation, and other departments. The five-year effort at $1.4 million a year is to be paid for with federal special education funds.

The move is the latest chapter in the lawsuit against the city school system that alleges the district does not provide timely services to students with disabilities. State officials are careful to call the work of the team a partnership with the 87,000-student school system and to note that state-picked administrators are working with Baltimore school district staff members, not supplanting them.

It is critical that successful twenty-first-century educational leaders keep abreast of legislative changes in IDEA as well as other legislative developments.

Source: C. A. Samuels, "Legal Fight over Special Education in Baltimore Enters New Phase," *Education Week*, September 7, 2005.

LEGAL FOUNDATIONS IN EDUCATION

With all the talk about No Child Left Behind and the 2005 reauthorization of IDEA, it is easy to get the impression that the federal role in public education historically has been heavy-handed. This actually has not been the case. In the following brief analysis of the Amendments to the Constitution as they pertain to education, you will discover that education receives a general framework from federal legislation but has been kept predominantly a function of the state.

For example, the First Amendment, *no law respecting an establishment of religion,* continues to be interpreted by the courts as to its impact on schools. The *freedom of speech* portion of the First Amendment in terms of students' and teachers' rights to freedom of expression has promulgated numerous court decisions. The *right of assembly* as stated by the First Amendment has also been a source of litigation involving student organizations and employees' rights to organize and bargain collectively.

In addition, concerning the Fourth and Fifth Amendments contentious battles have played out in court. The Fourth Amendment, as it pertains to *searches* of students' lockers and person and to teachers' *right to privacy,* continues to be center stage in the judicial arena. The first clause in the Fifth Amendment is relevant to cases where teachers have been questioned by superiors about their *alleged activities* with subversive organizations. The due process clause pertains specifically to acts of the federal government. The last clause is germane in instances where states or school boards *acquire property* for school building purposes.

Yet the Fourteenth Amendment, ratified in 1868, is the first amendment to delegate authority to the states. This amendment assures citizens that *no one should be deprived of life, liberty and property without due process of law.* Numerous education cases of noncompliance with this provision have kept judges and juries active. Compulsory school attendance laws, teacher tenure rights, educators' personal privacy issues, teacher dismissal cases, student expulsions, and a myriad of other legal matters have stemmed from noncompliance with the Fourteenth Amendment. This amendment also provides that no state shall *deny to any person within its jurisdiction the equal protection of the law.* The equal protection clause of the Fourteenth Amendment, as you can well imagine, has kept dockets of courts full, including matters of discrimination based on race, sex, ethnic background, age, handicaps, due process, equal protection, and state financing of public schools.

State Keys to Education

Clearly, the Tenth Amendment delegates powers to states for each of them to form and execute its own constitution that forms its basic laws, so long as these laws are not in conflict with the federal Constitution. State constitutions, which may be more specific than the federal Constitution, establish the state's funding structure and the conditions by which schools are to operate.

In addition to state constitutions, each state's legislature enacts, amends, and repeals laws. Laws passed by state legislatures are called *statutes.* The most abundant source of laws shaping public schools today are contained in statutes. School district policies, rules, and regulations are manifested in statutory law. Since education is considered a state function by virtue of the Tenth Amendment, courts tend to support the view that state legislatures' decisions prevail over public schools.

In turn, local school boards are granted the authority by the state to adopt and enforce reasonable policies and regulations necessary for the governance of schools and school personnel. However, let there be no mistake: local policies contain as much power and authority as state and federal laws. Once again, local school district policies may be more stringent than state or federal laws so long as those policies do not conflict. School officials must be able to demonstrate compliance with local policies as well as with state and national interests when allegations are brought forth.

Keys from the Courts

Another source of school law is judge-made or case law, or laws that have been shaped by court decisions. Clearly, case laws are dependent on the historical development of legal matters or precedents. Precedents established in past cases form the groundwork for decisions in the future. In the United States, the doctrine of precedent, otherwise known as the rule of *stare decisis,* or let the decision stand, is generally considered binding on subsequent cases that have the same or substantially the same factual situation.

The Supreme Court is the highest court in the United States and there is no appeal from a decision by this Court. Most cases that reach the Supreme Court have done so by appeal, or *writ of certiorari.* Most school cases that go to the Supreme Court are taken on *writs of certiorari,* meaning an original action whereby a case is removed from a lower court. The Supreme Court's ruling can be overturned only by an amendment to the U.S. Constitution. Supreme Court judges are appointed to life terms to provide consistency and avoid political infringement.

In the following pages, keys to compliance to keep you out of legal entanglement will be presented. Ignorance in a court of law is no excuse. These keys to legal compliance, or how to stay out of costly litigation and time-consuming judicial matters, covers the most frequently litigated issues. From the separation of church and state to frivolous lawsuits, the numerous keys presented will assist you in gaining compliance according to landmark court cases.

Keys to the Separation of Church and State

The separation of church and state has been argued feverishly since the first draft of the Constitution was drawn. In fact, the First Amendment states that "Congress shall make no law respecting an establishment of religion, or prohibiting the free exercise thereof." The interpretation of these general provisions and their application to public schools continue to be one of those hot topics in the field of education. School leaders need to maintain impartiality, neutrality, and objectivity regardless of preferences or affiliations.

Historically, it was common practice that many public schools began each day with a required prayer, Bible reading, or both. In support of this practice, Pennsylvania enacted a law in 1959 requiring Bible reading in the schools while at the same time providing an exemption for children who had written requests from their parents. In 1963, the Schempp children, who were Unitarians, challenged the law in *Abington School District v. Schempp.* Their case eventually reached the U.S. Supreme Court, which ruled in their favor.

The Supreme Court held that state-required Bible reading or prayer violates the establishment clause of the First Amendment when it is part of the required school curriculum. The Supreme Court stated, "They [children] are held in school buildings under the supervision and with the participation of teachers employed in those schools . . . such as opening exercises in a religious ceremony." The fact that students may be excused from the exercises does not change the fact that schools, which are extensions of the state, are involved. Although these principles were established close to forty years ago, challenges have continued to the present.

So what is an educational leader to do? On what safe judicial ground should educational leaders stand? What does an educational leader need to know regarding prayer and Bible readings in school today? Is meditation permissible in schools today? The following procedural keys to legal compliance regarding prayer, Bible reading, and silent meditation are presented here for your legal compliance.

Keys to Prayer, Bible Reading, and Silent Meditation in School

Under no circumstances can administrators approve school-sponsored prayer. It is a constitutional violation and cannot be justified based on First Amendment prohibitions. Educational leaders cannot allow school-sponsored reading of the Bible in school; however, the Bible studied as literature or used as an instructional document may be allowed. School-sponsored Bible reading in public schools is an illegal activity. It is highly recommended that ample description of the curriculum in which the Bible will be studied precludes students carrying a Bible to school. School-sponsored meditation is also not allowed. Silent meditation or any other type of devotional activity sanctioned by schools has not, and likely will not, be supported in the courts. Invocation at school-sponsored athletic events is also not be permitted, as it violates the establishment clause of the First Amendment. Educational leaders cannot prohibit students from voluntarily praying on their own accord, however. As in all questionable legal matters, successful educational leaders consult with legal counsel prior to sanctioning matters of private religious practices in public schools. Although prayer, religion, and faith sharing may be important to people as individuals, educational leaders must maintain neutrality, objectivity, and legal prudence when handling these matters. The same is true regarding prayer at school events.

RESEARCH KEYS

To enrich your understanding of **student-led prayer,** log on to www.researchnavigator.com and search Ebsco's ContentSelect.

Research Navigator.com

Keys to Prayer at School Events

The U.S. Supreme Court in a 6–3 ruling in 2000 in *Santa Fe Independent School District v. Jane Doe* banned student-led prayer at athletic contests. More recently, a federal court of appeals held that the recent U.S. Supreme Court ruling in the *Santa Fe* case does not prevent students in Alabama from discussing religion in public schools or praying publicly, so long as such activity is voluntary. This ruling was an outgrowth of a suit filed by the plaintiff Chandler in Alabama who challenged the practice of offering prayer at school-sponsored events. *Chandler v. McMinnville School District* constitutes the first interpretation by an appeals court of the Supreme Court's *Santa Fe* decision on voluntary student-led prayer.

Although the *Santa Fe* and *Chandler* cases appear be at opposite ends of the spectrum, *Lee v. Weisman* held that nonsectarian prayer at school graduation is unconstitutional. Adding complexity to the situation of prayer at a school-sponsored event, arguments in courtrooms continue to abound. What is an administrator to do, realizing court decisions, appeals, and further appeals will continue to keep a Philadelphia lawyer guessing? To keep you on solid legal footing, the keys to prayer at school-sponsored events are presented in Key Box 9.1.

KEY BOX ▸ 9.1

Keys to Legal Compliance Concerning Prayer at School-Sponsored Events

First and foremost and in light of recent court rulings, school administrators should ascertain that they have well-written rules and regulations in student and faculty handbooks to minimize legal challenges regarding prayer at graduation ceremonies. In addition, actions taken by educational leaders should address the critical issues of prayer in school.

- Establish legally defensible regulations incorporating the recent U.S. Supreme Court decision regarding student-initiated prayer at athletic contests and other school events.
- Resist the pressure of local customs and community expectations in governing student-initiated prayer at school events.
- Permit student-initiated prayer at school events when student-led and not endorsed by school officials. Voluntary student-led prayer will likely pass court scrutiny when it is initiated solely by students without involvement of school personnel.
- Provide immediate attention and follow through if staff members are encouraging students to engage in voluntary prayer at school-sponsored programs.
- Disallow prayer at school board meetings, as it violates the establishment clause.

The keys to the separation of church and state have been shaped, reshaped and will continue to be forever changing as influenced by societal trends and court interpretations. Successful twenty-first-century educational leaders will inform and hold those they lead in compliance with the separation of church and state. These legal matters are no easier when access to school facilities are requested, particularly by outside groups.

Keys to Equal Access

The Equal Access Act, passed by the U.S. Congress in 1984, states that it is unlawful for public schools that receive federal assistance and that have created a limited open forum to deny recognition of student-initiated groups on the basis of religious, political, or philosophical content of the speech at meetings. Limited open forum has been created when one or more noncurricular student groups are allowed to meet on school premises during noninstructional time. The Equal Access Act was based on the free speech determination of *Widmar v. Vincent*. In *Widmar*, the University of Missouri had refused to allow a religious group to use university facilities for fear of a possible violation of the establishment clause. The Court ruled that schools that used a limited open forum may not permit certain groups to use school facilities while denying others. The Reagan administration, using this case as rationale, applied the equal access concept to noncurricular high school activities in order to allow religious functions in public schools. The Equal Access Act provides that if a school district receives federal money and allows noncurricular activities and club meetings, then it is unlawful to deny the right to meet for religious activities.

Litigation emerging around the Equal Access Act has been a steady litigious stream, particularly when religious access is challenged. Although this legal hot potato has been tossed back and forth, the Supreme Court on June 4, 1990, upheld the constitutionality of the Equal Access Act. So, what are educational leaders to do? Procedural keys regarding equal access and use of facilities by outside religious groups are presented in Key Box 9.2.

KEY BOX 9.2

Keys to Legal Compliance for Equal Access and Use of Facilities by Outside Religious Groups

- If educational leaders allow some clubs with similar noncurricular functions to meet on school premises, all such clubs should be allowed the same privilege.
- Denying access because of an educational leader's disagreement with certain religious clubs' personal or philosophical beliefs is a court case waiting to happen.
- Extremely broad definitions as to what is considered curriculum should not be established by educational leaders if there is an effort to limit certain religious clubs.
- Educational leaders should consult the district's legal counsel regarding any questionable religious activities in their schools.
- If a limited open forum exists, educational leaders shall allow high school student religious clubs to use school facilities. Student religious clubs cannot be denied use if other noncurricular groups are permitted to use facilities before or after the school day.
- School leaders shall allow religious groups access to school facilities if other nonreligious groups are permitted to use them.
- Under a closed forum policy, then and only then shall school administrators disallow usage of school facilities by religious groups.
- Under an open forum policy, educational administrators shall remain neutral in allowing all religious groups regardless of denomination to use facilities.

The law must prevail in granting access to school facilities to outside groups. At times, this means that educational leaders must place mind over heart—that is, legal intellect over heartfelt sentiment for certain groups. You are cautioned here to remain consistent—if one group is granted access, all other groups have the same legal rights regardless of affiliation, agenda, or mission. Such is certainly the case in legal compliance regarding religious activities.

Keys to Legal Compliance Regarding Religious Activities

Is the posting of the Ten Commandments in public school buildings legal? Should educational leaders allow the posting of religious themes—the same theme inscribed on U.S. currency for over 100 years? Should the Bible be present on the shelves of a library of a public school? The lawful answers to these questions are yet to be conclusively agreed by the U.S. Supreme Court, as demonstrated as recently as June 27, 2005, in a 5-4 decision disallowing the displaying of the Ten Commandments.

Until the courts reach a decisive and lasting decision regarding the posting of the Ten Commandments, it is highly recommended that educational leaders, if they are going to err, err on the side of legal prudence. The procedural keys to religious activities presented in Key Box 9.3 are recommended to ascertain your legal compliance.

IN THE NEWS

Court Split over Commandments

Successful educational leaders soon learn the importance of maintaining legal prudence, especially in matters of separation of church and state.

A sharply divided Supreme Court issued a 5 to 4 decision on June 27, 2005, on the public display of the Ten Commandments on government property. Their decision specifically forbid framed copies of the Commandments on the walls of two rural Kentucky courthouses while approving a six-foot-tall granite monument on the grounds of the Texas Capitol in Austin. The Supreme Court saw the monument erected in 1961 as a less blatantly religious statement tinged with secular, historical, and educational meaning as one of several similar markers on the grounds.

Supreme Court decisions have been no less stringent when it comes to the posting of the Ten Commandments on school property. The Courts continue to apply the test of religious versus secular and historical purposes in determining the constitutionality of the Ten Commandments on school grounds.

It is critical that today's educational leaders keep current with regard to court decisions on the posting of the Ten Commandments as well as other judicial determinations.

Source: C. Lane, "Court Splits over Commandments," *The Washington Post,* June 28, 2005.

KEY BOX ▸ 9.3

Keys for Legal Compliance in Religious Activities

- Allow school-sponsored holiday programs if they are not conducted in a religious atmosphere.
- Allow released time for religious instruction if no public school resources are involved.
- Do not post the Ten Commandments or other references to God for meeting a purely secular purpose as this may be costly and time consuming to justify.
- Disallow religious pageants, displays, or symbols not meeting the constitutional requirement of neutrality unless used for a secular activity.
- Prohibit the distribution of religious material on school property. Students, on the other hand, are within their legal rights to distribute religious materials if the distribution of such materials does not interfere with normal school activities or create material or substantial disruption.
- Disallow the wearing of religious garb by faculty if stated garb creates a nonsecular atmosphere or creates a proselytizing effect on students.
- Disallow any behavior that would create an unclear line of separation between secular and nonsecular activities.
- Consult with legal counsel regarding any questionable religious activities in the school.

Educational leaders will continue to struggle regarding the display and demonstration of faith and religious principles. Posting "In God We Trust" seems perfectly legal considering that this inscription is found on U.S. currency. The operative word here is *seems.* What "seems" may very well not be what is legal, as the courts have ruled students to be too impressionable. Again, when in doubt, consult legal counsel in matters such as of freedom of expression.

Keys to Freedom of Expression versus Censorship

During the first half of the twentieth century when students challenged the lawfulness of school rules, the *reasonableness* test was used by the courts to judge school policies. If a reasonable relationship existed between the rule and some educational purpose, the rule would be upheld, even if most judges believed it was unwise, unnecessary, or restricted freedom of expression. Judicial support prevailed in providing school boards with legal latitude.

In a landmark case in 1969, the U.S. Supreme Court challenged the *reasonableness* test. In *Tinker v. Des Moines,* the Court ruled that students do not lose their constitutional rights to freedom of expression when they enter the public schools. This decision, however, should not be misconstrued to mean students can say or write anything they wish. *Bethel School District 403 v. Fraser* upheld in 1986 that students who use obscene, profane language or gestures that substantially interfere with student learning may be disciplined by school authorities. The courtroom has been an active place to weigh the rights of students and the authority of school administrators; it is the responsibility of the courts to weigh the legitimate rights in conflict and to determine when to limit and when to support the freedom of expression.

Before judicial decisions may be rendered in freedom of expression cases and all other legal matters, due process provided by school officials must have been provided. There are two types of due process: procedural and substantive. It is imperative for educational leaders to know and understand both types. *Procedural due process* refers to deprivation of life, liberty, or property as prescribed by constitutional procedure. In an educational context, the student or faculty member to be disciplined shall be told the reason for disciplinary sanction, provided an opportunity to be heard, and afforded a hearing that is conducted in a fair manner. Failure to follow procedural requirements will result in a violation of the person's constitutional rights. *Substantive due process* means that the state has a valid objective when it intends to deprive a person of life, liberty, or property, and the means used are reasonably calculated to achieve its objective.

Once due process is afforded, legal compliance with freedom of expression may be a sticky legal matter. However, there are several procedural keys that will assure educational leaders of actions to be taken in curbing or eliminating expression that is disruptive, offensive, or harmful. The following procedural keys to freedom of expression will assist you in establishing legal grounds for disallowing a particular form of expression. To remain legally compliant in critical issues regarding issues of freedom of expression, school administrators should consult Key Box 9.4.

KEY BOX **9.4**

Guide to Remaining Legally Compliant in Freedom of Expression Matters

- Do not prohibit a particular opinion merely to avoid the discomfort and unpleasantness that always accompany an unpopular viewpoint.

- Only prohibit freedom of expression when there is evidence that the forbidden expression would materially and substantially interfere with the work of the school or the rights of others.
- Restrict freedom of expression when there is evidence of material and substantial disruption, incident, or offensive speech; violation of school rules; destruction of school property; or disregard for authority.
- Prohibit buttons, pamphlets, and other insignia that communicate messages in a vulgar, obscene way or that mock others based on religion, race, origin, or sex.
- Regulate the time and place of the distribution of pamphlets, buttons, and insignia, preventing distribution in class during regular school hours.
- Establish lawful grounds to restrict the right of freedom of expression.

Keys to Legally Governing Student Newspapers

Educational leaders clearly have the authority to protect safety, property, and normal school operations by placing reasonable, nondiscriminatory restrictions on the time, place, and manner of freedom of expression. Such expression also includes communications through school newspapers. In fact, the Supreme Court decision in *Hazelwood v. Kuhlmeir* extended authority to educational leaders to control or censor a school-sponsored paper under certain conditions, as presented in the procedural keys to governing student newspapers contained in Key Box 9.5.

KEY BOX 9.5

Keys to Legal Compliance in Censoring Student Newspapers

- Construct a set of legally defensible policies governing publication of the school newspaper. It is highly recommended that the construction phase include representative students, teachers, parents, and other interested parties.
- Instruct faculty newspaper directors to select responsible student editors who will exercise high standards of responsible journalism.
- Decide and communicate whether the student newspaper is considered to be an open forum or a curriculum-based publication.
- Make certain that student editors know they will be held responsible that newspapers are free of libelous statements, profanity, and obscenity, as newspapers are subject to the scrutiny of the law in terms of libel.
- Do not impose policy restrictions on school-sponsored publications that cannot be defended on reasonable grounds.
- Develop procedures that certain regulations must be followed. These procedures include:
  - Time requirements for the review of materials before publishing.
  - The specific person who will be ultimately responsible for final editing.
  - The materials required for the final editing.

Proceed carefully: Parents of student journalists can be very vocal and judicially active! Again, have established procedures, agreements signed by students and parents, and continue to provide clarification of such structures. Another sticky wicket for educational leaders is search and seizure.

Keys to Search and Seizure

When it comes to censorship and other freedoms of expression, public schools have been commonly considered as a "marketplace of ideas." Equally as litigiously potent, student rights and responsibilities have comprised a limitless venue for court arguments. The Fourth Amendment of the United States Constitution proclaims, "The right of people to be secure in their persons, houses, papers, and effects, against unreasonable searches and seizures shall not be violated, and no warrants shall issue, but upon probable cause." School administrators need only to establish "reasonable suspicion," a standard of proof less rigorous than the requirement of "probable cause," in order to conduct a legal search. Suspicion itself implies a belief or opinion based on facts or circumstances that do not amount to proof. Probable cause, as implied in the Fourth Amendment, requires more than mere suspicion or even reasonable suspicion.

With reasonable suspicion, educational leaders have grounds to search a student's desk, locker, pockets, purse, book bag, coat, shoes and socks, and automobile on school grounds. It is key that educational leaders establish the clear need to maintain order, discipline, and safety prior to conducting a search and seizure. It behooves educational leaders to adhere to the procedural keys to search and seizure. To be in legal compliance regarding search and seizure, educational leaders are prudent to follow the guidelines presented in Key Box 9.6.

KEY BOX 9.6

Keys to Legal Compliance in Search and Seizure

- Only conduct a student search when there is a clear need to maintain order and discipline and to protect the health and safety of others.
- Consider factors such as the need for the search, the student's age, the history and record of behavior, the gravity of the problem, and the need for an immediate search.
- Decide on whether to conduct a search based on how detrimental to the school and its students the actions necessitating a search have been.
- Conduct a search independent of law enforcement officials. Searches involving law enforcement officials need probable cause and a search warrant.
- Secure evidence of student misconduct for school disciplinary purposes. However, the educational leader should be mindful that under certain circumstances, criminal evidence may be made available to law enforcement officials.
- Use strip searches only when imminent danger exists. Be certain that actions are fully justified with convincing information before conducting this intrusive search. Conduct the strip search in a private setting.
- Consider the magnitude of the offense, the extent of the intrusiveness, the nature of the evidence, and the background of the student before initiating a strip search.
- Conduct a pat-down search of students of the same sex and with other adult witnesses of the same sex present.
- Prohibit arbitrary searches or mass shakedowns, as they are illegal and cannot be justified as reasonable.
- Avoid the use of canines unless there is sufficient evidence to justify the need to employ these methods. The use of canine searches often is based on

the seriousness of incidents posing an imminent threat to students' safety. Although legal, the use of canines denotes imminent danger and is considered by the courts as intrusive.

- Use metal detectors only when there is evidence of student behavior that poses a threat to the health and safety of students in the school. Students and parents should be informed of the rationale for implementing metal detectors.

Our experiences as school leaders inspire us to pass on still another key to search and seizure. Discreetness is a virtue. Do not allow your school to turn into a guarded camp. The motives of search and seizure stem from a caring and passion for, not against, children. Even if law enforcement is accompanying educational leaders in search and seizure, it is vital that law enforcement be asked to comply with the educational leadership's requests in establishing humane and human transactions. Also drug testing of student athletes should be confidentially accomplished in a caring and empathetic manner.

Keys to Conducting Drug Testing on Student Athletes

In 1995, the Supreme Court in *Vernonia School District v. Acton* found that a school district's drug policy of conducting random urinalysis for athletes engaged in interscholastic athletics does not impermissibly invade a student's constitutional rights. Supreme Court Justice Scalia stated that the Vernonia School District's policy on drug testing was reasonable and constitutionally permissible for three reasons: student athletes have low expectations for privacy in communal locker rooms and restrooms where students must produce their urine samples; the testing program was designed to be unobtrusive, with students producing their samples in relative private with samples handled confidentially by an outside laboratory; and the program served the school district's interest in combating drug abuse, making sure athletes do not use drugs. It is important to note that the random testing of athletes involved in *Vernonia* was extended to the random drug testing of all students participating in extracurricular activities in 2002 by the *Board of Education of Independent School District v. Earls.*

Although drug testing of student athletes is permissible under certain conditions as deemed by the Supreme Court, it's the conditions that educational leaders need to be aware of and implement accordingly. Such practice will continue to be challenged with continuous accusations of constitutional violations. You need to be careful in making sure you implement the following procedural keys to drug testing of student athletes presented in Key Box 9.7:

KEY BOX 9.7

Keys to Legal Compliance in Drug Testing of Student Athletes

- Prior to initiating a drug testing program of student athletes, initiate a schoolwide program on drug education teaching the harmful effects of drugs.

- Develop school and district policies prohibiting the use and/or possession of drugs on school grounds. Specific discipline sanctions that will be taken when students are found guilty of violating school or district policy need to be specified.
- Provide a full due process procedure to facilitate a fair and objective opportunity for student athletes accused of drug use to share their side of the situation.
- Teachers, parents, student athletes, health officials, and community citizens should be involved in constructing drug testing procedures and programs that are reasonable and legally sound.

Drug testing programs should not be designed for punitive purposes. Effective educational leaders will provide support in cases where students are found guilty of drug use, as this is the time students need as much support as possible.

The jury is still out on the full extent of drug testing of student athletes as to the latitude of educational leaders. It is imperative to know the laws and court decisions and to follow legal counsel's opinion when implementing a drug testing policy and program. Zero tolerance is no exception.

Keys to Implementing Zero Tolerance

In 1994, Congress passed the Gun-Free Schools Act that mandates expulsion of students who bring weapons to school. This federal statute affects each state that receives federal funds, "requiring local educational agencies to expel from school for a period of not less than one year any student who is found to have brought a weapon to school under the jurisdiction of the local school district." The statute does not constitute automatic expulsion, as it places conditions on a case-by-case basis.

So the educational leadership question is, To implement zero tolerance or not to? If the answer to this question for whatever reasons is yes, key procedures to implementing zero tolerance must be followed to assure legal compliance, as presented in Key Box 9.8.

KEY BOX 9.8

Keys to Legal Compliance in Implementing Zero Tolerance

- When implementing zero tolerance, do so in a thoughtful and caring manner, weighing the severity of the offense, the student's history of past behavior, due process, and alternative educational options for students on long-term expulsion.
- Consider the delicate balance between safety in schools and the rights of students in the school.
- When implementing zero tolerance or "one strike, you're out!" provide flexibility based on discretion and caring.
- The only reason to use zero tolerance is to rid the school of disruptive students.
- Teachers, parents, community leaders, and student representatives should be included by educational leaders to develop zero tolerance policies.

- Draft policies that ensure the constitutional rights of students.
- Do not perceive zero tolerance as a cure-all for student misconduct.
- When it becomes necessary to expel students for an extended period of time, educational leaders will assist parents in seeking alternative education placements.
- Prior to implementing zero tolerance measures, consider the student's history of behavior in school, the seriousness of the offense, and the urgency of the discipline sanction.
- Make certain that all students are provided due process in all disciplinary matters.

A word to the wise from the experienced: zero tolerance is not the panacea that many may first consider it to be. We are reminded of a third-grader who brought a butter knife to the school cafeteria to cut a birthday cake and was expelled. The next day, major newspapers throughout the nation featured this discipline sanction by the school district with sensationalized expletives. Peer-peer student sexual harassment has been a hot potato tossed back and forth by the media too.

Keys to Peer–Peer Student Sexual Harassment Laws

In 1996, the Fifth Court of Appeals in *Rowinsky v. Bryan Independent School District* held that Title IX does not impose liability on a school district for peer-to-peer hostile environment sexual harassment unless the plaintiff can show that the school district directly discriminated on the basis of sex. Additionally, in *Davis v. Monroe County Board of Education* the court upheld that school officials have clear responsibilities in responding to peer–peer *sexual harassment* and that if a school district is able to demonstrate that its response to such harassment was not "clearly unreasonable," no liability will accrue. That is, school officials must not have had notice of the harassment and the harassment must not have the impact of denying a student's education. On the other hand, if school officials acted deliberately indifferent and if the harassment was severe, persistent, and objectively offensive, then the school may be liable for not responding appropriately to the harassment. If liability does exist, it remains uncertain as to the exact conditions that the courts would hold the school district liable.

So, educational leaders should not play with fire, as they may get burned litigiously. Hence, the following procedural keys to implementing and enforcing peer-peer sexual harassment laws are presented for compliance by educational leaders. As you review the procedural keys, keep in mind that the legal issues of classroom harassment are complex, even contradictory, and forever changing. It is best to consult with legal counsel whenever in doubt; also, consider the procedural keys presented in Key Box 9.9.

RESEARCH KEYS

To enrich your understanding of **sexual harassment,** log on to www.researchnavigator. com and search Ebsco's ContentSelect.

Research Navigator.com

KEY BOX 9.9

Keys to Legal Compliance in Matters of Classroom Harassment

- Formulate district policies and procedures to address the issue of sexual harassment of employees and students.

- Make certain that everyone—faculty, students, and staff—understands these policies and the consequences for violating them.
- To ensure the success of establishing zero tolerance policy, document that everyone—students, staff, parents, and community members—understands the school's position on issues involving harassment.
- Continuously provide training on current aspects of harassment.
- Encourage faculty and students to report all violations in accordance with established policies.
- Respond immediately to harassment complaints filed by students, parents, and staff to demonstrate the seriousness of such infractions.
- Create an environment where students and school personnel report complaints of harassment in confidentiality.
- Protect to the greatest degree possible the privacy of those filing complaints.
- Work diligently to provide and promote a school climate of respect void of harassment.

Vigilance is a virtue for educational leaders to maintain regarding peer-peer student sexual harassment. No matter is too small not to investigate. Place your students' needs as your first priority; in these litigious times, you cannot be too careful. It is with this same awareness that educational leaders will prevent school district liability.

Keys to Preventing School District Liability

The allegations against schools for negligence have constituted a never-ending stream of litigation. In one such case, *Peter W. v. San Francisco Unified School District* in 1976, a high school graduate who could read only at the fifth-grade level sued the school district for failing to provide him with adequate instruction in basic skills. The court dismissed the suit for the following reasons: (1) There were no clear standards to determine whether the school had been negligent, (2) there was no way to determine that a teacher's negligence was the proximate cause of the student's "injury," and (3) it would impose too great a financial burden on schools to hold them to an actionable duty of care in the discharge of their academic functions. More recent courts have supported this decision to refuse to undermine the professional judgments of educators in selecting programs for particular students.

Educational leaders are not to take for granted the courts support of their professional judgments. The day may be coming that the courts disagree with educational leaders on certain issues that were once considered legally safe. Again, school and district leaders must exercise judicial prudence at all times and understand and exercise a few fundamentals for preventing school liability, as presented in Key Box 9.10.

KEY BOX 9.10

Keys to Preventing School Liability

- Ensure that school buildings and grounds are safe for student use by maintaining the highest standard of care.

- Foresee potentially dangerous situations that may result in student injuries.
- Assume a higher standard of care during field trips and excursions involving students.
- Personal information regarding students should be kept confidential. Establish procedures that grant access to student personal information only to those who have a vested purpose in working with students.
- Do not allow students to be coerced to use equipment or perform physical activities for which they express serious apprehension. Inform school personnel that coercion of this type could result in liability charges against school personnel.
- Inform school personnel that the infliction of mental distress on students may result in personal liability charges.
- Prohibit unorthodox and indefensible practices aimed at disciplining students.
- Clearly state in school personnel manuals or district policy what is considered to be unacceptable behavior by school personnel, including discipline sanctions.
- Do not allow students to be detained after school for unreasonable periods of time for behavior that does not warrant that duration of detention.
- Maintain a higher standard of care in laboratories, physical education classes, and contact sports.

Educational leaders need to provide professional development, clearly written policies and procedures, and ample opportunities for question-and-answer sessions regarding liability issues. Again, not knowing the law is not sufficient reason for a jury to be swayed. The same holds true for all laws, including the following constitutional and judicial underpinnings of teacher freedom.

Keys to Protecting Teacher Freedoms

Teacher freedoms are protected under three sources: (1) constitutional rights and freedoms of the teacher as a citizen, (2) statutory relationships that govern the conduct of the public schools, and (3) contractual conditions of employment. These sources have substantial interdependence with each other in framing the rights and responsibilities of teachers. Under no provision do teachers lose their rights and freedoms when they become educators. Hence, the procedure keys for protecting teacher freedoms are essential for educational leaders to know and practice, as the burden rests with school authorities to demonstrate that their actions are not arbitrary, capricious, or motivated by personal and political objectives. To achieve compliance in critical issues regarding teacher freedom, educational leaders are prudent to adhere to the guidelines presented in Key Box 9.11.

KEY BOX 9.11

Keys to Legal Compliance for Teacher Freedoms

- Protect the constitutional rights of all educators, as educators maintain the same constitutional rights as do other citizens.
- Prohibit educators from verbally attacking others or making libelous and slanderous statements.

- Encourage teachers to report false information used to criticize a district's decisions or actions.
- Protect teachers and others under the First Amendment.
- Permit, perhaps encourage, teachers to introduce appropriate material in the classroom that is related to their assigned subject matter. On the other hand, do not allow teachers to use the classroom as a forum to advance their political or religious views.

As much as educational leaders need to protect teacher's freedoms, so too must educational leaders discipline teachers as well as other school personnel. At times, an educational leader's discipline of teachers is not optional. At these times of teacher discipline, it is imperative to ensure that teachers receive due process, as stipulated by the Fourteenth Amendment. When teachers hold tenure, the process and procedure is more complex than otherwise. Holding tenure is no reason for educational leaders not to administer discipline up to and including dismissal.

Keys to Teacher Dismissal

Tenure is a statutory right to hold office or employment and to receive the benefits of the position. After meeting designated academic and teaching requirements in a school district for a prescribed number of years, a teacher, if recommended for reemployment, may acquire tenure. The benefit of tenure is that it bestows on the teacher a right of continued employment, and dismissal cannot occur without a hearing and presentation of proof of sufficient cause to meet the statutory requirements for removal.

Grounds for dismissal may include incompetence, insubordination, immorality, misconduct, neglect of duty, and other good or just cause. Teachers not only must be moral persons but they also must conduct themselves in such a manner that others will know of their virtue. Again, consulting with legal counsel is advised right from the outset. Although court opinions are not uniform on the subject, the keys found in Key Box 9.12 will familiarize educational leaders with the planning of courses of action related to teacher dismissal.

KEY BOX 9.12

Keys to Planning Courses of Action Related to Teacher Dismissal

- Inform the teacher if an evaluation is conducted for any purpose other than the improvement of performance.
- Avoid any actions regarding evaluation for dismissal that constitute harassment or intimidation.
- Establish ample documentation prior to initiating teacher dismissal. Professional disagreements between educational leaders and those they lead do not constitute sole grounds for dismissal.
- In cases of alleged immoral conduct and dismissal, consider community norms and expectations regarding professional conduct of teachers.
- Understand that private acts of homosexuality and adultery may not be grounds for dismissal, unless this conduct adversely impacts an educator's performance.

- Before disciplinary action can be taken by the school district, be willing to bear the burden of proof in establishing that an educator's life choices adversely impact the performance of said educator.
- Understand that conviction for a felony or series of misdemeanors may form grounds for dismissal and revocation of the teaching certificate.
- Respond swiftly to sexual misconduct involving students by school personnel, as this will almost always result in dismissal.

The procedural keys to teacher dismissal are based on documentation, documentation, and more documentation. Furthermore, as important as it is to praise in public, it is also best to discipline in private, especially when dismissal is the end in mind. With teacher shortages looming, alarming percentages of teachers leaving the profession annually, and teacher certification lessening or being eliminated, decisions of teacher dismissal are made more difficult.

Moral Leadership

When discussions of lawfulness occur, consideration of ethics and morals needs more than ever to be an integral part of leadership (Beckner, 2004; Bolman & Deal, 1995; Osterman & Kottkamp, 1993; Sergiovanni, 1996b). At this time, when criticisms are being voiced about the eroding ethics of society, it is vital that the decisions and actions of twenty-first-century educational leaders be based on ethical and moral foundations. Successful leadership will involve moral choices (Cambron-McCabe, 1993; Rebore, 2001), emphasizing the importance of group membership, sense and meaning, morality, self-sacrifice, duty, and obligation (Sergiovanni, 1996b).

Just what might the successful educational leadership of the future be comprised of in terms of morality and ethics is one of the most basic questions in the field of educational leadership. In efforts to respond to these questions and others, several investigations into the importance of ethical leadership have been conducted following the turn of the twenty-first century (Normore, 2004; Quick & Normore, 2004; Shapiro, Poliner, & Stefkovich, 2001; Starratt, 2004). It is highly probable that today's educational leaders will need to be ethical and moral leaders (Pojman, 2002).

Recent writings reflect a distinct trend emphasizing that successful twenty-first-century educational leaders maintain an ethical orientation and moral dimension (Sahi, 2000; Sapre, 2000; Thomson, 2000). In order for school and district leaders to be successful in the new millennium, the pendulum must swing back to values and the moral dimension (Murphy, 1992; Schein, 1996). In addition, educational leaders will base their decisions and actions on their moral consciences, similar to the theoretical models that exist in business management (Bolman & Deal, 1995; Creighton, 1998). When moral authority overcomes bureaucratic leadership in a school, the outcomes are extraordinary (Pojman, 2002; Sergiovanni, 1997).

When morality and leadership are combined into a single, fundamental entity, there is no simple and straightforward definition. Moral dilemmas, such as quick-fix high school diplomas, stem from the context of situations that are often diverse and numerous. Therefore, moral leadership is difficult to define, and even

Poor Grades Aside, Athletes Get into College on a $399 Diploma

In order for educational leaders to be successful during the new millennium, the pendulum must swing back to values and the moral dimension (Murphy, 1992; Schein, 1996).

With a high school diploma from University High in hand, fourteen high school athletes were admitted to eleven universities with National Collegiate Athletic Association (NCAA) membership. The graduates of University High were awarded athletic scholarships to attend major universities.

As for their alma mater, University High held no classes. For that matter, it was not even accredited. University High consists of two small rooms on the third floor of an office building sandwiched between a Starbucks and an animal hospital in South Miami. Its promotional brochures feature diplomas that can be earned in four to six weeks with take-home exams, no classes, and no tests. A high school diploma costs $399, regardless of the number of courses taken. The publisher of what University High calls their textbooks referred to the materials as only study guides.

The actual work of University High's graduates consisted of picking up packets from University High's office, completing the packets at home and returning completed packets. The grades students received on the packets counted as the same grades on the students' transcripts for a yearlong course. Students admitted learning very little but were grateful for the opportunity to play sports in college.

At the same time the NCAA is pressing for academic reform and higher standards, its loopholes have been quickly recognized and exploited. The NCAA in 2000 shifted its power to high school administrators to determine which classes count toward a high school diploma. In doing so, the NCAA left schools with the authority to determine their own legitimacy.

It is critical that successful twenty-first-century educational leaders know that what may be legal may not be ethical or moral. Failure to know and understand both lawful and ethical matters and act properly have caused dismissals of educational leaders.

Source: P. Thamel & D. Wilson, "Poor Grades Aside, Athletes Get into College on a $399 Diploma," *The New York Times,* November 27, 2005.

more difficult to prescribe as to what behavior would be considered moral in any given situation. Moral dilemmas can arise between short-term and long-term goals, between autocratic leadership and servant leadership, and between institutional development and growth of society. Plain and simple, there is no mathematical formula to help one decide what is moral. There are, however, some guiding principles that can be followed to assist educational leaders in moral decisions, such as what is presented in the Knowledge, Dispositions, and Performances in ISLLC Standard 5.

ISLLC Standard 5, stating that *a school administrator is an educational leader who promotes the success of all students by acting with integrity, fairness and in an ethical manner,* has emphasized the importance of ethical educational leadership on a national level. Several codes of ethics have been constructed and aligned to the Knowledge, Dispositions, and Performances of ISLLC Standard 5 to ascertain the importance of moral and ethical leadership. One such Code of Ethics established by the American Association of School Administrators follows:

Educational leaders are expected to abide by the following Code of Ethics established by the American Association of School Administrators:

An educational administrator's professional behavior must conform to an ethical code. The code must be idealistic and at the same time practical, so that it can apply reasonably to all educational administrators. The administrator acknowledges that the schools belong to the public they serve for the purpose of providing educational opportunities to all. However, the administrator assumes responsibility for providing professional leadership in the school and community. This responsibility requires the administrator to maintain standards of exemplary professional conduct. It must be recognized that the administrator's actions will be viewed and appraised by the community, professional associates, and students.

To these ends, the administrator subscribes to the statements of standards presented in Key Box 9.13.

KEY BOX ▶ 9.13

Keys to Standards of Moral and Ethical Leadership

- Make the well-being of students the fundamental value of all decision making and actions.
- Fulfill professional responsibilities with honesty and integrity.
- Support the principle of due process and protect the civil and human rights of all individuals.
- Obey local, state, and national laws and do not knowingly join or support organizations that advocate, directly or indirectly, the overthrow of the government.
- Implement the governing board of education's policies and administrative rules and regulations.
- Pursue appropriate measures to correct those laws, policies, and regulations that are not consistent with sound educational goals.
- Avoid using positions for personal gain through political, social, religious, economic, or other influence.
- Accept academic degrees or professional certification only from duly accredited institutions.
- Maintain the standards and seek to improve the effectiveness of the profession through research and continuing professional development.
- Honor all contracts until fulfillment or release.

The successful twenty-first-century educational leader upholds a firm and consistent code of ethics. This means that educators of the new millennium will examine personal and professional values at all times and will demonstrate values, beliefs, and attitudes that inspire others to higher levels of performance. Successful educational leaders know that before they can expect and hold others accountable for demonstrating integrity, they need to treat others fairly, equitably, and with dignity and respect. Those who are not ethical leaders will experience shorter tenures and even termination, pending the circumstances.

LOOKING BACK, BUT NOT IN ANGER

It is imperative that educational leaders keep one eye to the courts and the other eye on legislatures to glean the most recent legal decisions and promulgations. Ignorance, as we have stated and restated, is no excuse in the court, frequently incurring costly litigation and huge unaffordable time consumption from the school district. As for the numerous legal keys we presented from the most frequently contested laws, follow them for your own legal protection and compliance.

THE REFLECTIVE PRACTITIONER

Welcome to your ninth Reflective Practitioner containing your Chapter 9 Scenario based on ISLLC Standards 5 and 6 and your reading of Chapter 9. It is intended to provoke your thoughtful reflection and to stimulate discussion among colleagues, classmates, and peers. The Reflective Practitioner provides opportunities to synthesize issues, make comparisons, and apply theory to practice. We hope it will motivate you to search for evidence, thus increasing your comprehension of the text and help you examine your convictions and discover new and shared perspectives.

- **ISLLC Standard 5**
  A school administrator is an educational leader who promotes the success of all students by acting with integrity, fairness and in an ethical manner.
- **ISLLC Standard 6**
  A school administrator is an educational leader who promotes the success of all students by understanding, responding to, and influencing the larger political, social, economic, legal, and cultural context.

Scenario

Mr. James Wilson is your assistant principal at Wehshore Middle School. He comes into your office with his head hanging low. He asks if you, his principal, have a few minutes for him to tell you something. Although you are up to your eyeballs in alligators, you look into Mr. Wilson's eyes and see distress, sadness, and remorse. You ask Mr. Wilson to make himself comfortable in the chair on the other side of your desk. You then encourage him to share his thoughts. Mr. Wilson shares the following with regret:

"Last night I went out on a binge. I was apprehended for drunk driving. It has been twenty years since the last time. I have attended Alcoholics Anonymous off and on and was really doing well. Last night I failed. I will be serving a prison term for two weeks, where I will be confined to jail and only allowed to fulfill my work responsibilities. My family is very disappointed, especially my two sons that attend our high school. Their friends are already harassing them for what their father has done."

Mr. Wilson then pauses for you to comment. You sit there, speechless, astounded, and alarmed. With *Keys to Successful Twenty-First Century Educational Leadership* opened up on your desk to Chapter 9, Legal and Moral Leadership: Doing the Right Thing, for unfortunate times like this, you scan the chapter and share applicable parts of Chapter 9 with Mr. Wilson.

QUESTIONS FOR REFLECTIVE THINKING

1. Following your scanning of Chapter 9, what did you share with Mr. Wilson regarding his unfortunate situation?
2. When Mr. Wilson asked you if he would be fired, what did you share with your assistant principal, as presented in Chapter 9?
3. Describe the ramifications of Mr. Wilson's drunk driving last night to the greater political, social, economic, and cultural context (as depicted in ISLLC Standard 6).
4. The best legal remedy is prevention—that is, preventing law infractions from occurring. Describe the orientation, training, and professional development that you would implement for the whole faculty if you were Mr. Wilson's principal. Which legal matters, as presented in Chapter 9, would you first present?
5. Compare and contrast legal and ethical decisions. If a law and ethic are contradictory to one another, what would determine your decision or action? Please state your rationale for each of your responses.

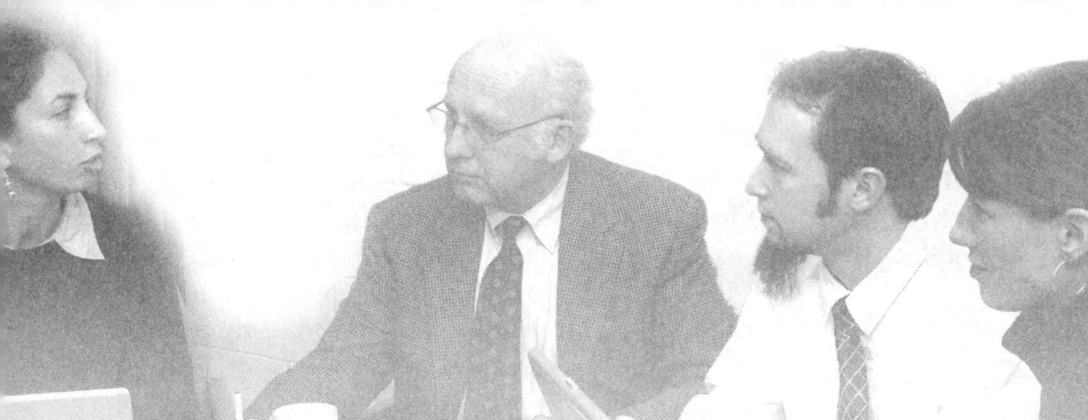

chapter **10**

ISLLC
Standards
4 & 6

Dollars and Sense: Funding America's Schools

An ounce of prevention may be worth a pound of cure!
—Anonymous

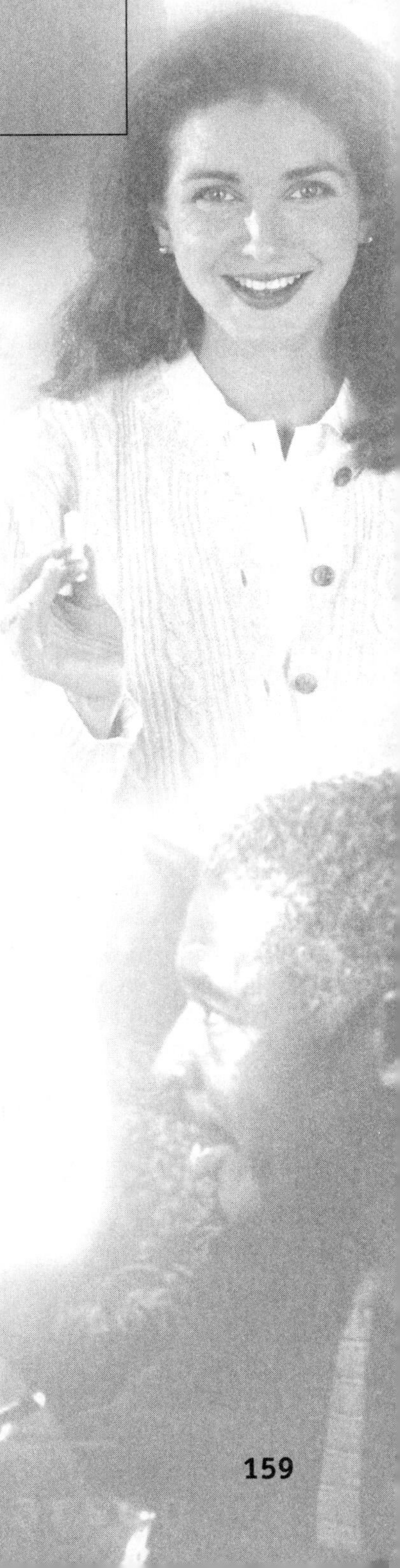

Your Chapter 10 Action Focus travels throughout this chapter to provide you with a keen understanding of the intricacies of twenty-first-century school finance. To begin, just imagine, after a long exasperating day as an educational leader, you return home, turn on your television, and suddenly the regularly scheduled program is interrupted with the following news alert:

EDUCATION IN CRISIS: FUNDING OUR NATION'S SCHOOLS

UNITED STATES CONGRESS

We interrupt your regularly scheduled program to bring you the following report prepared by the Bipartisan Staffs of the U.S. Senate Committee on Health, Education, Labor, and Pensions and the U.S. House of Representatives Committee on Education and the Workforce.

Our nation's schools are in a state of financial crisis, facing declining budgets, increased class sizes, and devastating choices as they struggle to provide a good education for our schoolchildren in the midst of a troubled economy. Throughout the United States, state education budgets are being slashed—an estimated $22.4 billion nationally (*Digest of Educational Statistics, 2004,* 2005)—and schools are taking drastic steps to make ends meet. They are beginning to lay off teachers, cut back on textbooks, cram more children into fewer classrooms, accept deteriorating buildings as a sign of the times, and eliminate professional development.

Legislative Logjam Blocking Textbooks: With Funding in Limbo, Schools Scramble to Find Some Subject Materials

The state of Texas is scrambling in efforts to establish a balanced budget.

Tattered old and outdated textbooks used for years awaited the return of students and staff to a new school year in 2005. Worse yet, glossy new replacements gathered dust in warehouses in the Dallas area and Lubbock.

Millions of new textbooks couldn't be delivered to school districts because the Texas Legislature was caught in a stalemate over school finance for months and hadn't authorized the purchase.

Principals and teachers were busy salvaging as many old textbooks as they could find, preparing to double and triple up on certain materials and photocopying pages.

As the state of Texas faced challenges in its funding of its schools, so too will other states continue to face school funding difficulties in the twenty-first century.

Source: R. T. Garrett & T. Stutz, "Legislative Logjam Blocking Textbooks: With Funding in Limbo, Schools Scramble to Find Some Subject Materials," *The Dallas Morning News,* August 4, 2005.

The devastating impact of shrinking budgets can particularly be seen in the nation's largest school systems in its most populated states, such as California, Michigan, Texas, New York, and Florida. The news will only get worse as states try to restore balance to their budgets, which are running a collective *$45 billion deficit* this year, and prepare next year's budgets under the worst fiscal conditions in the twenty-first century.

As millions of workers lose their jobs, the number of poor children in U.S. schools grows. An additional 650,000 poor children next year will require special help and additional resources (*Projections of Education Statistics 2011,* 2001). There is no clue how children will achieve the mandates of proficiency. Behind each dollar withheld or cut from our nation's schools is a child who gets less attention in a crowded classroom or a teacher trying to keep up without adequate training.

Immediately following the news commentary, a panel consisting of U.S. Senators, each sharing his or her perspective on the educational funding crisis, ensued. Telephone lines were opened to callers from throughout the United States, voicing frustrations and presenting questions on numerous problems in funding schools.

Problems in Funding Schools

The exchange between the panel of senators and individuals throughout America scrutinized the problematic conditions in school funding. Unless the federal government steps in quickly to financially assist schools, our children will continue to fail. The continuing improvement of the nation's schools could well rest on the actions of Congress and the White House. Funding of schools has reached rock bottom, especially when considering the following:

- The federal Constitution directs the financial responsibility of funding education to the states. Almost 50 percent of all funding of the nation's schools is derived from state budgets (*Digest of Educational Statistics, 2004,* 2005). Most of the state's revenue is generated from state sales tax, a tax dependent on *elasticity* (or proportionate change in demand given price changes) and a tax yield influenced by the average personal income in any given state.

- Local support of schools has steadily declined during the twenty-first century, decreasing to 45 percent of the 2002 school year's funding (Richard & Sack, 2003). Local tax is predominantly generated from property taxes, *sacrifice* taxes where people with more wealth are able to pay higher amounts of taxes. More affluent communities with greater property values tend to fund their schools increasingly, and those schools are able to provide enhanced opportunities and experiences for their students. Studies have revealed that the widening achievement gap is highly correlated with the widening funding gap among school districts (Mayer & Peterson, 1999).
- The federal funding role in education today is little more than 10 percent. Almost all federal school aid comes from income taxes. Income tax constitutes *vertical equity* for differing amounts of taxes where individuals with higher incomes contribute more taxes (Barrow & Rouse, 2004).
- What the federal government has mandated for education (i.e., No Child Left Behind and IDEA), the federal government has been reluctant to fund (Bracey, 2001). This has led to countless lawsuits contesting the adequacy of federal funding, and no change is foreseen.
- Other funding sources such as excise taxes on liquor and tobacco products, hotel taxes, real estate transfer taxes, taxes on insurance premiums, and casino taxes constitute a very small percentage of state revenue. These taxes are *inefficient,* meaning non-neutral, as they impact consumption in socially desirable ways (Archer, 2000).
- Lotteries were the promised panacea for school funding that never actually took place. Revenue collected from lotteries went into most states' general budgets, although voters were led to believe all dollars would be earmarked for education (Calonius, 1991; Garrett, 2001).
- The Golden Rule of funding applies regardless of the funding source: "The one (federal, state, or local) with the gold, rules!" This gold, or school funding, comes with a steep price tag of governmental mandates.
- State education cuts already total over 40 percent during the twenty-first century. State education budgets have failed to keep pace with inflation and growing enrollments.
- Further education cuts are likely. Fiscally prudent educational leaders should plan budgets for the worst and hope for the best.
- Already, seven state legislatures have called special sessions to address their budget crises.
- States are preparing to write the next fiscal year's school budgets "under the harshest fiscal conditions in a decade," according to the National Conference of State Legislatures.
- The demands on our schools are growing, even as their budgets are cut. As budgets continue to get cut, things continue to get increasingly ugly.
- Due to the economic slowdown, falling stock market values, and hurricane disasters, the number of children living in poverty is expected to increase by 950,000 during the next three years (National Center for Education Statistics, 1999).
- The mandates of No Child Left Behind cannot be accomplished with diminished resources.

- Three-quarters of schools reported needing to spend money on repairs, renovations, and modernizations to put the school's onsite buildings into good overall condition (Rothstein, 1998). The total amount needed by schools was estimated to be over $200 billion.

The news alert, "Education in Crisis," did not hold back any punches as to the dire straits in school funding. If America's children are to receive a quality education, government at all levels (federal, state, and local) must cooperate, support, and fund education adequately. Increased funding for schools is needed for increasing enrollments, renovation and repair of dilapidated buildings, as well as for salaries to attract and retain qualified teachers. In addition to a diagnosis, the panel of nonpartisan senators looked into their crystal balls to present a prediction for school funding.

Predicting Future Funding

Just to tread water, our schools will need a 5 percent increase in their budgets each school year to stay ahead of inflation and to meet rising costs. The Office of Management and Budget projects a 2.7 percent rate of inflation for the next fiscal year. The U.S. Department of Education expects enrollment to grow by 2.5 percent over the next year. Maintaining per-pupil expenditures, therefore, will require a 5.3 percent budget increase. Any progress in increasing our national investment in education will require increases above 5.3 percent (*Digest of Educational Statistics, 2004,* 2005).

It is difficult to know what states' fiscal conditions will be next year. However, many economists believe the economy will get worse before it gets better. More industries have gone overseas, particularly into China and India. As a result, the prognosis for increases in education funding is not favorable.

Federal Funding

In the next few weeks, Congress and the White House will decide the federal education budget for the coming academic year. In March, the president sent an official budget request for $3.8 billion in additional elementary and secondary education federal spending. The president's budget included the smallest increase for education in six years, and proposed only one-thirteenth as much spending on education as it did for tax cuts for the top 1 percent of taxpayers.

In October, the United States House of Representatives and United States Senate each passed federal elementary and secondary education budgets for the next fiscal year that will provide an increase of approximately $10 billion (or 19 percent) in federal school funding. This increase, combined with the proposals to increase federal higher education funding by approximately $4 billion and absent any additional commitment of resources, will increase school funding for the next academic year to a total of $12.14 billion.

The largest single federal K–12 education initiative is the Title I program for disadvantaged children. Title I, funded at $16.8 billion, fully serves 5.5 million needy children, 34 percent of those eligible. It provides 75 percent of all national compensatory education funding. Pending congressional approval, school budgets for the next academic year will increase funding for the Title I program by

$2.8 to $3.4 billion. Those funds will serve approximately 856,000 to 976,000 more disadvantaged children in poverty next year. But because the number of children living in poverty is expected to rise by 650,000, the funding increase will only allow Title I to keep pace with poverty instead of reducing the number of eligible children denied services (Bacon, 2001; Thurlow, Ysseldyke, Gutman, & Geenen, 1998). When considered in light of state education funding cuts this year, the worsening fiscal picture for states in the next academic year, and growing child poverty, the federal education budget commitment must more than double in order to respond fully to the needs of America's children.

Funding Follies and Foibles

This funding crisis comes on the heels of federally imposed student achievement mandates. Congress has nearly completed its overhaul of federal K–12 education programs. The education reforms aim high by expecting all children to meet challenging standards and holding schools accountable when they fail. But if the federal government is going to hold states and schools accountable for student performance, it must also provide some of the resources needed to meet new federal goals.

Schools will find it difficult to reach excellence while facing the most drastic cut in state funding to date. Worse yet, additional resources are needed to hire over 250,000 new teachers to reduce class sizes and counselors to reduce school violence (Barrow & Rouse, 2004; Bracey, 2001). These budgeted dollars would have been used to modernize 11,000 schools or build more than 1,000 new schools. Or they could make a real difference in raising teacher salaries and strengthening teacher professional development.

IN THE NEWS

Three Area School Districts Struggle to Reach New Pacts

Dollars are needed in three Michigan school districts to ratify contracts.

Teachers in three mid-Michigan school districts are working without contracts and no settlements are in sight. Wages and health care costs are the dividing issues that need to be agreed. Board members are quoted as saying that they want to pay their teachers more money but there are no more dollars. Others say the lack of money is the root of all problems and when there is a dollar shortage, everything turns ugly. The school districts are in dire financial straits and talks are only of more funding cuts. No one seems to know where all this will end.

Quality educational programs without adequate funding are like sailboats without wind.

Source: S. Trouth, "Three Area School Districts Struggle to Reach New Pacts." *The Lansing State Journal* (MI), May 21, 2004.

Education reform without adequate resources is an empty promise. We now know what works in education: well-prepared teachers with ongoing professional training opportunities; small class sizes; modern classrooms; after-school and summer help programs for extra help; and support services for troubled students (Darling-Hammond, 1999). And these investments require more resources, as failing schools cannot be turned around with declining resources.

FUNDING LOCAL SCHOOLS

With the shortfalls in funding schools, how do local school districts respond to this financial dilemma? What do twenty-first-century educational leaders do?

These answers and others will be presented in the authentic context of a school district. By creating a realistic template, it is our intent to provide greater depth, richness, and clarity in understanding school finance. The keys to successful budgeting will provide educational leaders with a strategy to emulate as they face similar financial challenges. Mindful of these gains, we turn to a meeting now in session being held by the Grand Public Schools.

Grand Public Schools welcome you! Thank you for coming to tonight's meeting. We can all be thankful for this lovely Kansas suburb in which we live. We educate approximately 7,700 students in grades K-12. In addition, our birth-to-5 Early Childhood Family Education Program serves families and children during the most critical developmental years. In all, more than 12,000 students of all ages take advantage of educational opportunities offered through our community education and summer recreation programs. Our relatively small size and commitment to quality means we can personalize each child's education to meet his or her unique needs.

We are pleased to share with you our Points of Pride or accomplishments. Please consider the magnitude of each as you review the following list:

- K–12 aligned curriculum in math, language arts, science, social studies, Spanish, integrated technology, integrated library media, physical education, and music
- Consistently high academic performance as demonstrated on the statewide tests, SAT, and ACT
- Champions of Diversity Team includes members of administration, staff, and community
- Online Board of Education Policies
- Districtwide staff development in differentiation of instruction
- Newly renovated buildings providing staff and community with enhanced facilities
- Districtwide wireless network
- Rigorous hiring process resulting in outstanding teachers
- Four scheduled collaborative planning sessions providing teachers with concentrated time for developing curriculum, technology training, school improvement, teacher evaluation, and department issues
- A Grand Public Schools Foundation that distributes over $50,000 annually in grants, scholarships, and awards to enhance programs not normally underwritten by the district
- Outstanding child-care and preschool programs that meet the needs of working parents in our community
- Careful administration of district funds and facilities.

It is this last point of pride that we need to discuss with you in greater detail.

Our Grand Public Schools will be facing a $3.4 million (5 percent) budget shortfall for the upcoming school year. Just today, Washington announced drastic reductions in school funding for the next school year. Our state will be facing a $380 million deficit. I give you my word that we will all work diligently to make fiscally prudent decisions that are educational sound! We will leave no financial rock unturned.

In examining ways to fix the budget imbalance, the district administration conducted an extensive review of all programs, services, and personnel in the district to identify potential reductions that can be made while maintaining excellence for students within the district's Vision and Strategic Plan.

A letter will be mailed to each community resident next month. I would like to share it with you at this time:

> The Grand Public School Board and administration are committed to becoming a world-class school district and will not compromise excellence. In some cases it may be better to eliminate a program or service instead of reducing it to mediocrity.
>
> When considering budget reductions, it is important to remember the keys to school district budgeting as presented in Key Box 10.1.

KEY BOX ▶ 10.1

Keys to Twenty-First Century School District Budgeting

- The budget deficit is the direct result of the state's inability to fulfill its commitment to fund education (Evans, 2001). The basic formula has not increased since 2005. Furthermore, the state has reneged on its commitment to special education funding and provided $780,000 less in special education funding last school year than is called for in state special education formulas.
- The budget imbalance is structural and cannot be fixed with minor adjustments. The adjustments require a strategic realignment of programs, service, and staff within the resources available.
- The shortfall in revenue is not a temporary problem, and the district cannot anticipate the adjustments made to ever be restored.
- A dollar saved is a dollar earned. A $1 cut this school year saves a $2 cut in the upcoming school year.

> Education is a people business. More than 80 percent of our budget goes toward salaries and benefits for employees. There is no way to make deep cuts in the operating budget without affecting staff and, foremost, our students.
>
> At what point is it enough? At what point will our community members, business partners, elected officials, and others say that we can't let our students lose more valuable teachers, staff, and programs? At what point will our legislators say that it's time to reform the way the state funds its schools?
>
> This district has made major gains in achievement. The process began before I was hired three years ago. It has accelerated since my arrival, because achievement has been a major emphasis of mine. It was one of the reasons I was hired. There are twenty academic areas on the state proficiency tests. During the time that I have been here, our district has improved on seventeen of those twenty. Our high school graduation rates are up, and last year's graduates received more than $1 million in college scholarships. Several high-performing students are earning college credit before graduating from high school, and advanced placement students are performing better than their peers on several areas of the international advanced placement tests.
>
> The loss to this district of more teachers and support staff would simply be devastating. It will have a terribly negative impact on student achievement.

The money from the bond issue that passed five years ago can be used only for the building program. It cannot be used for any other purpose. This is often confusing to our taxpayers. So while it may seem ironic that we are asking for funds while we're building new buildings, building them is the only prudent thing to do. That money has already been provided, and it's available, so we're going to use it. But we can't use it for salaries, textbooks, transportation, or other everyday operating expenses.

Further, about 16 percent of our budget comes from local sources, including levy money (Angulo, 2001). But that money does not adjust for inflation. It remains flat—which means that, over time, the rate of inflation outpaces about a third of our operating revenue.

Basic district expenses such as electricity, water, natural gas, and insurance have increased by 80 to 90 percent over the past decade (Barrow & Rouse, 2004). Costs have risen across the board. With local revenues remaining flat, a negative gap has been created.

This all has to do with the system of *school funding* that exists in our nation. Suffice it to say that because of this system, local districts are required to go back to voters every few years to request additional funds.

We cannot lose sight of the fact that although these times are trying, financially, it is an exciting time in terms of student achievement. I am confident that our teachers and staff will continue to put our children first and will continue to work diligently to provide them with the best education possible. But keep in mind, you cannot provide a world-class education on a shoestring budget. Therefore, your educational leaders have adopted a series of fundamentally sound budgetary measures, entitled *Keys to Financial Survival,* which will be implemented immediately. We will make every effort to keep you informed of our progress and continue presentations to our Grand Public School Board of Education.

RESEARCH KEYS

To enrich your understanding of **school funding,** log on to www.researchnavigator.com and search Ebsco's ContentSelect.

Research Navigator.com

KEYS TO FINANCIAL SURVIVAL

In efforts to be forward-thinking about financing our schools, the district has prepared a white paper illustrating its financial plans. The document defines fundamental actions that will make a difference in funding our schools.

Reducing Administrative Costs

For public school districts, as with any enterprise, fiscal responsibility starts at the top. This may mean reducing our administration costs. It is true that in the Grand Public Schools, central administration costs have increased more than twice as fast as instructional expenses, including teacher salaries. Building administration (principals, directors, facilitators, and supervisors) grew at about 5 percent, more than the 3 percent that teacher salaries increased over the same period. Combined, these administrative expenditures make up 10 percent of total annual education spending. This is very typical of school districts across our nation.

There may be ways of trimming administrative costs through outsourcing and making our operations more efficient. We need to realistically look at outsourcing our administrative functions such as payroll services, records management, benefits administration (flexible spending accounts, some insurance benefits, etc.), and perhaps even candidate recruitment.

Minimizing our administrative costs can reap savings for our school district and other school districts as well (Cox, Stewart, & Burybile, 2000). We will analyze our administrative expenditures first, before even considering reductions in classroom spending. We will attempt to make budgetary recommendations as far away from the classroom as possible.

Saving by Outsourcing Noninstructional Services

We must evaluate how we can save money and improve services by outsourcing noninstructional services such as transportation, janitorial, technology expertise, food services, landscaping, and maintenance. If there are private companies that can provide us with noninstructional school services cheaper and more efficiently than our own self-operating of these services, it behooves us to consider subcontracting these services. We must consider how these changes would impact our loyal and hard-working employees, many of whom live right here in our community.

Managing Health Benefits Effectively

Our school employee health benefits represent an enormous cost for Grand Public Schools. Behind employee salaries, health benefits are our second largest personnel cost in the school budget. We need to consider options in providing benefit levels at the lowest costs that enable us to recruit, reward, and retain the best and brightest employees.

Our health insurance costs have been rising faster than inflation nationwide over the past twenty years. Professionals believe that these costs can be controlled through a few effective management techniques. There are two keys to consider for improved coverage and lower costs: the structure of the benefits themselves (benefit design) and the company that will administer the benefit programs.

In doing a bit of research, we have discovered that health benefits should have a managed care element that connects cost with utilization of benefits. The vast majority of health maintenance organizations, preferred provider organizations, and point of service plans have some coinsurance rates, copays, and/or deductibles that bring some market incentives into health care utilization. If an individual knows that it will cost him or her $50 deductible to go to a relatively expensive emergency room but only $30 to see his or her regular physician for a common nonemergency ailment, that employee may opt for the cheaper alternative. A well-designed benefit structure can help contain costs, even in the absence of other cost-saving measures.

The health benefits we provide should include provisions for shielding employees against catastrophic losses due to illness and for covering uninsured dependents. It should also require a coordination of benefits if the spouse is working and has health insurance. In short, our personnel benefits should reward the good work of teachers and other school staff, and allow the Grand Public Schools to recruit and retain quality individuals, but not be so lavish that we price ourselves out of the insurance market. With just a few effective reforms, I believe districts can start to control their health benefit costs.

Structuring Capital Costs Effectively

The fourth key we need to investigate is the fiscal responsibility of our effective capital cost management. Our capital costs include a host of fixed school resources, including classroom buildings, administrative offices, some durable school equipment, and the land underneath school buildings. We are proud of our 100-year heritage; however, like your house, in time, our physical structures literally begin crumbling. Our infrastructure needs prompt us to push for voter support for building renovations and replacement. Our options at this time in dealing with our infrastructure issues are to purchase new land to construct additional facilities (or renovate existing facilities) or to lease space from private developers or property owners.

Both strategies have advantages and disadvantages. If our Grand Public Schools opt to purchase buildings and maintain full public control of school property, I recommend that we implement a sound debt/bonding policy. On the other hand, if our Board wishes to lease property from private landowners, we will need to properly negotiate the terms of the lease.

As we identify cost savings measures, we will recommend a fiscally responsible capital cost management system in terms of a solid debt policy. A debt policy is a formal document governing when, how, for what purposes, and to what extent school districts (or other government agencies) may issue debt (Garrett, 2001). A sound debt policy will provide many benefits for our school district to help us better manage our capital improvement programs. We as a school district should engage in competitive bidding for the site as well as the actual building. Instituting an effective debt policy can save us literally millions of dollars.

Our cost-cutting measures will investigate the effectiveness of the debt policies and procedures we are currently implementing. If beneficial, we will recommend refinancing our debt in a manner that will become a significant cost savings. We will use the following key principles to determine this cost savings feasibility.

1. Our long-term debt should not be used to finance our current operations or to capitalize expenses. Our operational expenses should be completely covered through the current-year budget. Our capital debt should not be used as a credit card to pay for teacher salaries, transportation services, or other recurring school district expenses.
2. Our long-term debt should be used only for our capital projects that cannot be financed from current revenue sources. Our capital debt should be used only for large "one-time" projects, such as school buildings, that will last for decades.
3. Our total district indebtedness should not exceed 15 percent of the district taxable valuation for any given year. Qualified school bonds are general obligations of the school district, whereas they are budgetary (sometimes called "moral") obligations of the state in the event of default. It is arguable as a matter of local district policy and of honesty to taxpayers and bond buyers that qualified bonds should be included in the limitation. This limitation is a maximum; however, fiscal prudence and the financial situation of the district may warrant a lesser percentage.

4. We will evaluate whether to retire 50 percent of the total principal on debt within ten years. Repayment of our debt in the shortest possible time without creating undue hardship for the taxpayers will save us millions of dollars.

5. We will determine if a reissuing of our current school mortgages will achieve a rate savings. If there is at least a three-percentage point savings, this recommendation will be part of our formal presentation.

It is our hope that by studying our debt policy and payback procedures we may incur savings to our school district and taxpayers. Although these savings will not help us with operational costs, we hope to gain enhanced support from our voters in future initiatives and other district savings initiatives once it is commonly known how our dollars are spent.

IN THE NEWS

Where Does All the Money Go?

Like educational leaders in Grand Public Schools, members of the Education Partnership in Rhode Island are discovering how dollars are spent in education.

In the small state of Rhode Island, as in many other others, there is a constant drumbeat of complaints that poorer communities lack adequate resources in education. Although very few would dispute this, a nonprofit group entitled the Education Partnership believes their question has to be answered as to whether current spending by Rhode Island schools is *appropriate?* In addition, this group believes answers to this question need to be present before lawsuits fly and more money is allocated to schools from increased property taxes.

How can policymakers and taxpayers be certain that local school districts actually need more money, if those districts have not taken the crucial steps of looking at how their money is being spent and asking the tough question of whether that spending is really helping students? The Education Partnership is recommending that communities and schools examine thoroughly the expenditures of schools before suing the taxpayers for more money.

In addition to examining their finances, local school districts need to examine improved ways for getting the greatest gain from existing dollars, such as site-based budgeting and several other budgetary measures.

Source: V. Forti, " Where Does All the Money Go?" *Education Week,* November 16, 2005.

Implementing Site-Based Budgeting

It may seem contradictory at a time of budget slashing to implement site-based budgeting where financial decisions are made at the building or program level. However, site-based budgeting has the potential to encourage innovation, enhance organizational effectiveness, and improve financial equity among schools and departments. By delegating a limited amount of dollars and "real" power over the budget as to where and how allocations are best distributed, a greater gain for each buck is achieved (Hunter, 2000). We are at a point of readiness for this change, as our school district's administrators for the last three years have been effectively using zero-based budgeting. That's the building and justifying of a new budget each year not based on the prior year's budget.

Creating Opportunities for Gifts and Contributions

We have many individuals and families who are interested in providing financial support for our schools while receiving tax savings, deductions, and shelters. We, like many schools throughout the nation, have not provided these programs for wills, trusts, and charitable gifts. Sure, we have our smaller gifts of books, computers, and even vehicles, but we are missing great opportunities to create win-win financial gains. We have begun discussions with our attorneys to discover the legal structure necessary to get these funding avenues established and communicated. Our alumni have already expressed interest and support in such programs.

Adapting Capital Expenditures

A few school districts have provided opportunities for individuals and businesses to provide financial support for school buildings, playgrounds, stadiums, and school grounds. In fact, a famous home improvement business has leased a high school football stadium for ten years, taking care of all utilities, renovations, upkeep, and even athletic equipment in exchange for advertising. We cannot rely on running our schools in the twenty-first century in the way we have in the prior century. We have learned that local businesses are paying top dollar to advertise on bill boards positioned on the sides of school buses.

Procuring Grants and Foundational Support

If there is a will, there will be a way! There is no such thing as a shortage of dollars; we are limited only by our own creativity and innovation. The district has been successful in attaining some grants; however, we have only scratched the surface. We must explore and attain foundational funding! In fact, several of our parents are employed by the large foundation in town. School districts today need to scramble to bring great educational opportunities to life through nontraditional funding sources.

Involving Policymakers

We need to develop continuous communications with our representatives and senators. In fact, our governor is a graduate of Grand Public Schools. We must remain politically active and persuasive. The programs we need to develop can no longer be just when we have a need. Education is in a state of crisis and our elected officials need to represent our interests. This also means that we need to become active participants in our professional organizations and affiliations. United, we form a power base of influence; divided, our needs are more likely to remain unaddressed.

Supporting Lobbying Efforts

We, the educational leaders of the Grand Public Schools, need to increase our participation, along with other educational leaders throughout the United States, to inform and influence our elected officials to fiscally support education (Manzo, 2001). Both through our professional organizations and individual letter-writing campaigns, it is time to step forward and work diligently to advocate and attain the needs of our students. These lobbying efforts will include invitations to our elected officials to participate in our school activities and programs.

Developing Distance Learning Opportunities

The initial cost of providing a distance interactive classroom where our students are able to take course offerings not available in our school district needs to be explored. As the world becomes smaller and smaller, we will need to provide a world-class education for our students just to keep their skills competitive. Such courses as Chinese, nuclear physiology, and space exploration may now be provided at a fraction of the cost through distance interactive and online courses.

Increasing Grants and External Funding

There are numerous grants and foundations that we will be investigating starting immediately. We, as educational leaders, need to ensure that the money we receive from funding sources does not create increased costs for our school district dollars in order to sustain programs or personnel. However, we are left with no choice but to go after the grants that will provide an advantage to our students, faculty, and community.

Providing Opportunities for Wills

We are currently seeking legal guidance in creating financial programs that would appeal to our alumni and other interested parties who are interested in naming Grand Public Schools in their wills. Such wills make for wonderful tax write-offs and carry the potential of positively impacting our schools. We will continue to keep you informed as this financial initiative progresses.

Increasing Support from Volunteers

The time has come for us to capitalize on our parents, community organizations, and philanthropic clubs in our community as volunteers. Even our teachers' union has pledged support, as it is better for our school district to be financially stable. We in turn have agreed that volunteers will not take over any responsibilities of current faculty. In fact, working relations with unions during the twenty-first century have been harmonious and cooperative in this regard, as there is really no option!

Conserving Energy

We are planning to meet with energy efficiency experts in the near future. Energy efficiency businesses have saved school districts substantial sums of money while in turn costing the school districts nothing. This is how they work: If a school district signs a contract with an energy efficiency business for five years, the business will regulate energy consumption in such a way that the school district's expenditures are less, even after the business draws its commission. Such contracts, on average, are for ten years and can turn into a win-win partnership for both parties. Again, we need to take a close look at this.

Forming University, Business, and Industry Partnerships

With a research-intensive university in our own backyard, it is about time that we create formal partnerships with them. Universities have the potential to provide current skills, advanced degrees, and teacher and administrator preparation and professional development. There are even exchange programs in which faculty from local school districts and university faculty teach each other's classes, spend time in each other's environment, and develop open channels of communication to confidentially share needs and challenges. And, I may add, all of this is made possible at a fraction of the cost we currently spend on professional development, conference travel, and consultants.

In addition to forming university partnerships, we will enhance our current business and industry partnerships as well as seek new relationships. Our businesses and industries have responded generously in the past and have continued to express their interest in helping the children in our school district.

Renting School Facilities for Special Functions and Financial Gain

Currently we do not charge for the use of school facilities by outside groups. We have had wedding receptions, church services, anniversary celebrations, and many other special occasions to use our facilities, and we have picked up the tab in paying our custodians to set up and clean up and the use of utilities (lights, air conditioning, heat, etc.). It is time to consider user-friendly fees that will at least cover our own costs. Our schools will still remain the best buy in town.

In addition, we have looked under every fiscal rock and have left no fiscal rock unturned. That is, we have literally spent hundreds of hours looking at our current budgets and considering what changes might incur what financial savings. Our investigations have provided us with the following costs incurred from following budget initiatives.

Implementing Fees for Transportation

RESEARCH KEYS

To enrich your understanding of **school transportation,** log on to www.researchnavigator. com and search Ebsco's ContentSelect.

Research Navigator.c☉m

A transportation fee would be set at $100 per year for each student living within the attendance area of the respective school attended and riding district-provided buses. Families with three or more students impacted would pay a maximum fee of $250. There would be no charge for students who qualify for free and reduced lunches. A public hearing will take place on this matter before final recommendations will be made. Approximate revenue from this school transportation savings and the feasibility of cutting dollars in this area has yet to be determined.

Enhancing Extracurricular Fees

A $60 fee for high school students and a $40 fee for a middle school students to participate in extracurricular activities would generate $340,120. The choice here would be to reduce the amount of extracurricular activities or charge the suggested fees. Those students on free or reduced lunches would be exempt from paying fees.

Increasing School Parking Fees

Access to high school parking is a privilege available to approximately 480 students. Historically, the demand for parking has exceeded available space. Fees, such as high school students paying for parking, are a viable source of revenue for our school district.

Reducing Travel

The travel for administrators and board members would be reduced significantly and supplies for offices would be reduced. This will impact the district's ability to have its leaders remain current with improvements, however. Keep in mind that the board of education needs to make their decisions based on current knowledge. One uneducated decision can potentially incur litigation and other costs several times more than what is saved.

Reducing Professional Development Funding

A discretionary fund for staff development across the district, directed by the superintendent to fund any special needs, has largely gone unused. A reduction in this discretionary amount can protect other programs, services, and staffing within the budget.

Restructuring Custodial Services

Four custodial positions will be reduced. Fewer custodians will be available during school hours to respond to faculty needs as they occur. Custodial services for direct cleaning during the evening will not be impacted. It is imperative that the resources of the district be used so that all buildings and grounds are safe, clean, and healthy. Furthermore, our buildings and grounds must remain attractive to encourage physical activities and provide essential gathering places for the community as a whole.

Eliminating the Assistant Superintendent for Personnel

There is a need to tighten districtwide administration and supervision in order to meet budget constraints. The responsibilities of the assistant superintendent for personnel will require additional shifts in assignments, including less contact with employees and less oversight of personnel matters by central office. The personnel office will report directly to the superintendent.

Reducing Positions

Budgetary constraints cause the school to restructure its administrative services for the future to best support students, staff, and parents. This reduction provides for equity across all employee classifications while it reduces administrative costs. The administration work will need to be accomplished by sharing the responsibilities with teachers and other staff in the building.

Returning High Schools to a Six-Period Day

This budget cut constitutes a return to a six-period day from the current seven-period day. This action reduces the possible choices of courses for students but increases the amount of time spent in each class and with each teacher. Therefore, these courses would be strengthened and supportive student–teacher relationships will continue to be formed. In fact, this budget initiative increases the equivalent amount of time for students to receive instruction by twenty to twenty-five days per year in the courses they do take. There will be about 1,211 minutes more time for instruction and individual help in each year-long course. This return to a six-period day will constitute a reduction of 7.5 teaching positions.

Adding Students to High School Classes

The challenge of raising class size an average of two students per class is that the final impact is not just two more students per class. Some classes cannot have more students, so the remaining classes would have to be increased much more than two. It is likely that this would result in some classes increasing by eight to ten students. Classrooms, science laboratories, and other instructional facilities will become more physically crowded. The addition of two high school students per class would reduce teacher positions by 6.4 full-time equivalences.

Restructuring the Middle School Day

One of the strongest movements in U.S. education was the transformation from junior high schools to middle schools. The middle school concept was driven by a middle school philosophy of focusing on students and meeting their unique needs and individual interests rather than focusing on subject matter as high school clones. Another philosophical underpinning was a vast and diversified array of exploratory courses important to middle school students who are discovering their interests and abilities. This budgetary option specifically would necessitate the following restructuring of the middle school day:

- The seven-period middle school day would be reduced to six periods.
- Class size would be maintained at current levels.
- Team teaching and common planning time for teachers would be eliminated.
- There would be a reduction of exploratory classes for students in physical education, health, world languages, music, and technology.
- With the reductions in exploratory classes and elimination of team planning time, there would be a compromise in middle school philosophy.
- There would be a reduction of 15 full-time equivalencies with eliminations in sixth-grade health education, reduction in music, and elimination of world language experiences.

- Students would have six fifty-four–minute classes each day, and teachers would teach five classes daily, with greater similarities to high school structure.

The cost of restructuring the middle school day, as you see, is far more than varying the lengths of class periods inasmuch as exploratory classes are reduced/eliminated, creating teams of students who are taught by a common group of teachers, using common planning time (team planning) for teachers in core classes, having no competitive activities, putting students in homogeneous groups, and eliminating advisory programs.

Eliminating Sixth-Grade Instrumental and Strings Music

Although sixth-grade instrumental and strings music is a very valuable experience for students, instrumental and strings lessons are more costly than Grand Public Schools can afford at this time. There are other options for providing lessons, such as community education night and weekend classes. Students will lose important opportunities to develop music talents with this 1.9 full-time equivalency reduction in teaching.

Restructuring Elementary Band and Orchestra

Instead of eliminating elementary band and orchestra, we are considering a fee-based system to partially fund these programs. This shift of partial program costs to the parent/guardian would reduce budget costs by $100,000.

Reducing the Technology Budget

The time has come for us to inventory how many of our teachers actually use technology beneficially. Although we have provided technology training for all staff members, very few have taken advantage of these learning opportunities. There is no doubt that the powerful tools of technology potentially can increase student achievement. However, technology can be some of the most expensive dust collectors. This is what I refer to as the double-edged sword. I believe we can shave $200,000 from our technology budget by placing computers only in the hands of those staff members who have competencies and who demonstrate usage of computers for more than glorified typewriters.

Providing Early Retirement Incentives

Grand Public Schools and the leadership of teacher and administrative bargaining groups are evaluating whether a modest financial incentive would encourage more staff to retire than are currently planning to retire at the end of this school year. Properly designed, this early retirement incentive would permit some cost savings between the cost of retiring employees and the cost of replacement employees. Further, additional retirements would reduce the number of staff who would be laid off and the number of staff who would be shifted from their current positions to other assignments.

Enhancing Media Relations

Last, but not least, we will enhance our relations with our media. We know that educational leaders need to establish and maintain positive relations with the media. Clearly, educational leaders need to respect the might of the pen, particularly when leaders of newspapers purchase their paper by the truckload and their ink by the tankload and simple headlines have the power to support or destroy. We will be inviting reporters to our school programs as well as welcoming reporters to our board of education meetings. It's communication, communication, communication with our media in building effective rapport.

In retrospect, we, your educational leaders, do not relish any of these budgetary measures. As we implement measures, we will act positively and with integrity in maintaining the financial integrity of our school district. We will continue to count every dollar, as every dollar counts. We welcome thoughts and ideas from our students, parents, faculty, community members, and all other stakeholders. We will keep you informed of all financial matters. Thank you for joining us this evening.

SCHOOL FINANCE MATTERS

As illustrated in your chapter-long Action Focus, the insufficient funding of schools in America may very well lead to the demise of the enterprise. Federal, state, and local funding during the twenty-first century will hit the rock bottom of despair as many school districts go financially belly-up. Elected officials on both sides of the aisle will need to put away political agendas to save our children. Public education has been the foundation of democracy and who will allow this foundation to erode will be identified. Which child will be left behind?

THE REFLECTIVE PRACTITIONER

Welcome to your tenth Reflective Practitioner containing your Chapter 10 Scenario based on ISLLC Standards 4 and 6 and your reading of Chapter 10. It is intended to provoke your thoughtful reflection and to stimulate discussion among colleagues, classmates, and peers. The Reflective Practitioner provides opportunities to synthesize issues, make comparisons, and apply theory to practice. We hope it will motivate you to search for evidence, thus increasing your comprehension of the text and helping you examine your convictions and discover new and shared perspectives.

■ **ISLLC Standard 4**
A school administrator is an educational leader who promotes the success of all students by collaborating with families and community members, responding to diverse community interests and needs, and mobilizing community resources.

■ **ISLLC Standard 6**
A school administrator is an educational leader who promotes the success of all students by understanding, responding to, and influencing the larger political, social, economic, legal, and cultural context.

Scenario

Congratulations, you are the newly appointed principal of Soaring Heights Elementary School, an exemplary school known throughout your state for its excellent faculty, wonderful academic programs, and soaring student achievement. Everything seems to be running smoothly. Approximately two months into the school year, the superintendent informs you that the budget of Soaring Heights Elementary School will need to be reduced by 25 percent for the upcoming school year due to reduced federal and state school funding. The superintendent also informs you that she would like you to present your strategic plan for reducing the budget of Soaring Heights Elementary School. The superintendent requests that your strategic plan for reducing the school budget includes, but is not limited to, collaborating with families and community members, as the budget reduction will impact them as well; responding to diverse community interests to understand their budget priorities; and influencing the larger political, social, economic, legal, and cultural context to fund education adequately.

QUESTIONS FOR REFLECTIVE THINKING

1. As requested in the scenario, write a strategic report for how you would reduce the budget of Soaring Heights Elementary School by 25 percent. Please include as part of your strategic plan what actions you would take to
   - collaborate with families and community members, as the budget reduction will impact them as well;
   - respond to diverse community interests to understand their budget priorities;
   - influence the larger political, social, economic, legal, and cultural context to fund education adequately.

   Include other actions in your strategic report that you would take to reduce Soaring Heights Elementary School's budget with the least amount of turmoil.
2. What strategies did the superintendent of Grand Public Schools present to influence what you might consider implementing at Soaring Heights Elementary School? What additional budgetary measures would you take to reduce the budget? Please explain your responses.
3. What do you think needs to occur to influence federal, state, and local elected officials to adequately fund education? How might you become a catalyst for this funding transformation?
4. Do the federal trends in financing schools as presented in Chapter 10 encourage or discourage your interests in becoming a twenty-first-century educational leader? Please explain your response fully.
5. Would you emulate the attitude and disposition of the superintendent of the Grand Public Schools given a similar contextual situation? How might your initiatives differ? How might your actions remain similar?

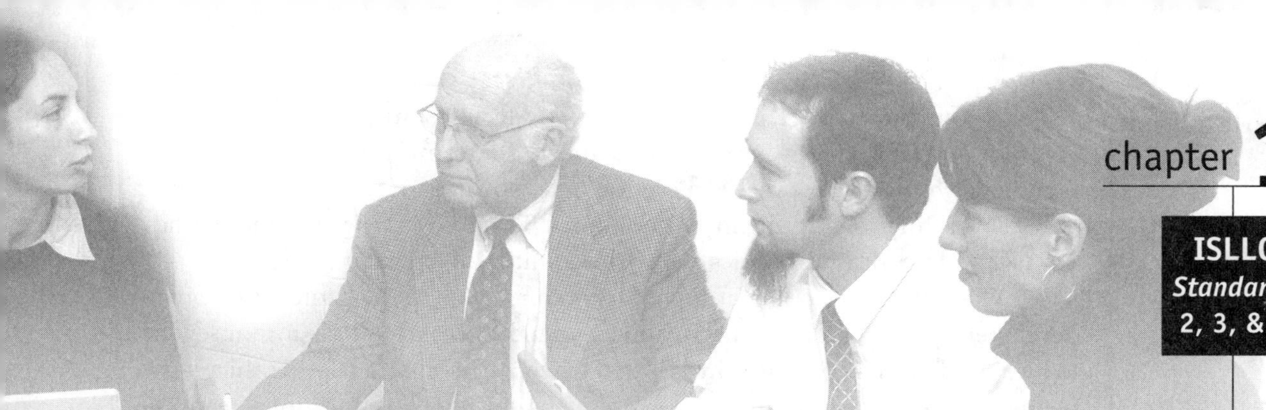

chapter 11

ISLLC *Standards* 2, 3, & 5

Keys to Renewing America's Schools

There is one thing stronger than all the armies in the world, and that is an idea whose time has come.

—Victor Hugo

The formula for successful twenty-first-century educational leaders for renewing America's schools may very well begin with breaking bad habits and emphasizing and enhancing what works in education. Suffice it to say, if educational leaders keep doing the same things over and over when the results are unsatisfactory, they will keep getting the same results. Chapter 11 begins with the demystification of micromanaging followed by the keys to curb this destructive syndrome. After all, if the gains of professional development are to be achieved, micromanaging must be stopped. Next, professional development, along with mentoring, are examined as methods to improve our new millennium schools.

Your Chapter 11 Action Focus sets the stage and brings to life the destroying and degrading impacts of micromanagement and the importance of its immediate cessation if the gains of professional development are to make a positive difference.

Welcome to the actual world of school system governance! The closed session of your school board has been going on for two hours. It is now midnight. Your ability to stay focused is waning. As each new question is hammered at you, you ask yourself, "How can this possibly be happening?"

When you finally emerge from the executive session, you figure there will be a 4–3 vote on the issue that never was on the agenda in the first place. A complaint about the cafeteria food planted by a staff member in the ear of a board member has resulted in behind-the-scenes havoc. You are sure the folks at the all-night coffee shop will know about it before you even have a chance to tell the principals.

Once you return to open session, you are relieved by the thought that the board meeting is almost over. Then a board member announces, "Teachers have told me that the food in the cafeteria is awful. Superintendent, what are you doing about that? The next time you interview candidates for food service manager, I want to be there!"

As you approach 1:45 in the morning, you feel two inches high. "My gosh," you ask yourself (perhaps in stronger language), "how much more can the board members whittle away at me? Am I in the wrong business?"

This is micromanaging in its finest hour. There is nothing about it that has not taken place in communities across the country on a regular basis.

Why is it that school board members cannot stick to their roles as policy developers? Why is it that board members with concerns don't ask for those items to be placed on the agenda? Why is it that when a person sees another micromanaging, he or she is more prone to do the same? Why do educational leaders micromanage? More important, what needs to be done to stop micromanaging? Micromanaging destroys and degrades and is highly destructive.

As demonstrated in your Chapter 11 Action Focus, school renewal and rehabilitation (or restoring to good condition, operation, and capacity) are dependent on the immediate cessation of micromanaging. This stopping of micromanagement begins with the demystification of its propensities.

DISPELLING A MYTH OR TWO

Micromanagement is the interference, involvement, or conflict with a subordinate's work, performance, or decision making that fosters employee apathy and disrespect; if educational leaders don't trust those they lead, why should their staff trust them? The result is low morale, a consistent failure to meet goals, impeding of professional development efforts, and high turnover.

Micromanagement is necessary to maximize productivity—false, and a myth at best! Nothing could be further from the truth. Micromanagement always degrades improvements, growth, and accomplishments. If board members and other educational leaders believe they must check on every detail, their style is symptomatic of insecurity or paranoia.

Micromanaging is based on a lack of faith and trust in other people (Fisher, 2004). It is repressive. It leads to little growth, it discourages any human resource development, it focuses on problems of detail, and it discourages teamwork. Eventually it may bring failure to an organization.

To illustrate, please meet Sally and Donald, two first-year educational leaders.

Sally, a newly appointed high school principal, believes that if a job is to be done right, she needs to direct it herself. Sally has arrived at this perception mainly because she felt she had to do it all as a high school teacher if things were to get done. She believes that she is in the position to make the best decisions. Sally keeps her hands in all facets of the organization, not allowing the decision-making process to flow down to capable subordinates.

Donald, a newly appointed assistant superintendent, represents another group of micromanagers, an individual who has been promoted beyond his capabilities. He sees subordinates as tools for getting a job done. He is happy so long as expected results are met. Donald turns into a tyrant if his expectations aren't reached, and he will use fear as a motivator. Knowing that he is over his head in capabilities, Donald reacts like a trapped animal and lashes out at the superintendent.

The end results are quite similar in each scenario, as both Sally and Donald are chronic micromanagers. Staff members in the school districts they lead reach a point that they do not feel supported or appreciated and are no longer willing to make sacrifices. Even parents and community members cease to support Sally and Donald as they view each as power-hungry micromanagers that are in conflict with school personnel.

Determining Levels of Micromanagement

It is clear that educational leaders' micromanaging diminishes the value of school personnel, poisons the work environment, and damages their own credibility as leaders. Renewing today's schools is impaired so long as micromanaging prevails. What may not be as clear is the intensity or degree of micromanaging (Chang, 2003). The questions presented in Key Box 11.1 are useful in determining levels of micromanaging (Anft & Williams, 2004; Boice, 2004; Jazzar, 2005).

KEY BOX ▶ 11.1

Questions That Determine the Level of Micromanging

- Do educational leaders spend time showing those they lead how to do a job right, specifically telling them what to do?
- Do educational leaders devote a lot of time to overseeing school projects?
- Are educational leaders irritated when decisions are made without consulting them first?
- Are educational leaders spending more time "in the trenches" instead of sticking to their own areas of responsibility?
- Do educational leaders prefer directing staff members rather than empowering them?

If the answer is *yes* to one or more of these questions, there may be a serious micromanagement problem. Overcoming these tendencies is possible, but it takes courage! Board members, superintendents, teacher leaders, legislators, and all other educational leaders will need to come to the realization that their delegating, by overcoming their feeling to micromanage, will gain them power. Genuine power is the ability to influence others by persuasion instead of coercion. In essence, when educational leaders do not micromanage, these leaders say to those they lead, "I trust you as being competent professionals. I don't look over your shoulder. That would be micromanaging. I will provide support and technical assistance for you to succeed." So why do leaders fear the loss of control?

OVERCOMING THE FEAR FACTOR

Understanding a primary cause of micromanaging, fear, is in itself a great way to begin understanding the driving forces of micromanaging. Strong feelings of feeling threatened, a personal attack, denial of fear, and an ill response to fear are all explanations, not excuses, for micromanaging. Here is a closer look at each of these keys to understanding fear (Jackson & Fogarty, 2005; Jazzar, 2005; Schuerman, 2004).

- Fear, concern, and worry are, more often than not, responses to feeling threatened. These feelings arise from one's natural instinct for self-preservation. To illustrate this fear, concern, or worry, envision a school district about to plan a deficit budget. This single condition could make educational leaders fearful, as impending cuts in programs and services may lead to a decline in student enrollment or disassembling of school improvements. Instead of working these threats out through established protocols and channels, micromanaging shows its ugly head.

- Fear can also be personal. An individual may be afraid that his or her position as an educational leader will be threatened by a particular view or action. Or perhaps the person feels insecure about his or her own role within the organization. Regardless of the cause, as a general rule, when educational leaders act improperly, they often feel threatened in some way, either personally or on behalf of the organization.

- Western culture doesn't put much stock in fear; in fact, it often denies fear. Most people prefer to see themselves as fearless, and because of that, many write off "fears" as being irrational. But in the case of many educational leaders' concerns, that is not necessarily so. Educational leaders are right to be concerned that the organization may be financially unstable. They are right to be concerned that there is no succession plan if the superintendent suddenly leaves. They are right to be concerned that equitable salaries are not being paid, especially at times of teacher and administrator shortages. These are important issues that impact all educational leaders. Educational leaders are right to be concerned, worried, and even fearful. For micromanagers to micromanage only compounds the problems and erodes potential support. The key here is not to rationalize micromanaging by thinking our fears justify it. The important realization is to recognize that micromanagement is a sign that

IN THE NEWS

More Boards Mulling Policy Governance

In order for the gains of twenty-first-century professional development to be beneficial, successful educational leaders, like the Clark County School Board members, will need to eliminate micromanaging.

In a brave departure from past practices, the Clark County (Nevada) School Board pledged four years ago to avoid micromanaging the district. Instead it announced its commitment to focus on the big picture of improving student achievement. For board members and other educational leaders accustomed to dealing with what one described as convoluted policies that filled several six-inch notebooks, the streamlined approach to governance was a welcomed change. In doing so, the Board spawned a countermovement to restore a more activist approach—an approach called Policy Governance.

Policy Governance has become a popular set of principles for effective boards. Its developer, John Carver, has inspired many boards of education to consider his activist approach to school district governance.

This activist approach has been implemented by many other school boards that have traditionally been plagued with infighting, lack of focus, and a propensity for micromanagement that has limited their effectiveness. In a sign of interest among boards and district administrators, national associations have emphasized the importance of Policy Governance.

In addition to the strategies used by the Clark County School Board, there are seven professional development keys to eliminate, or at least help curb, micromanagement.

Source: J. Gehring, "More Boards Mulling Policy Governance," *Education Week*, February 16, 2005.

educated leaders are reacting to those concerns and fears. So, the key to curbing micromanagement and moving the educational leaders forward is to *recognize* that their fear is guiding their response and to begin preventing micromanaging rather than working reactively.

In addition to recognizing that fear is the driving force of micromanaging, what else can educational leaders and those they lead do to eliminate—well, all right—at least reduce micromanagement? See what the Clark County, Nevada, School Board did to end micromanagement.

SEVEN PROFESSIONAL DEVELOPMENT KEYS TO CURBING MICROMANAGEMENT

Understanding the motives of micromanagement provides insight in how to curb this destructive activity (Alnoor, 2005). If educational leaders micromanage because they don't know what else to do, they need to be shown a different role. And if educational leaders micromanage because they are concerned and/or fearful, then the obvious solution is to allay those fears. And finally, if educational leaders have asked others to act as staff, then the obvious solution is not to ask them to perform staff functions. In addition to these recommendations, there are seven keys to curbing micromanaging that need to be incorporated into professional development. An examination of these seven keys to curbing micromanaging follows (Jazzar, 2005; Pearce, 2004; Schweitzer, 2004; Sinclair, 2004).

Find a Different Role for Micromanagers

Help micromanagers see what work is not getting done because they are spending their time micromanaging. Many micromanagers earnestly believe micromanagement is the appropriate role, arguing, "If we do not manage and do the work, then how will the work get done?" And so, the first step is to show them an alternative.

Educational leaders are responsible for creating the future, not watching if the pot boils. When they get stuck in the day-to-day routine, educational leaders are watching for a boiling pot, and that is not nearly as productive as helping them create the future. Creating the future means making a real educational impact. It is the very reason schools exist. After reviewing this exercise with your micromanager, he or she far is more likely to want to start creating that future.

Show Micromanagers How Focusing on Results Can Get the Job Done Better

Educational leaders must keep sight of the forest, not get caught up in the chopping down of a single tree. This is to say, educational leaders must focus on wholeness of the organization (department, school, or school district, etc.) and what the organization is about. They are to support, maintain, and even guard the process and flow of the whole organization they lead and not be deluged in minutiae. Stated differently, educational leaders should hire the most qualified and skillful individuals and resist the temptation to interfere in their work by micromanaging.

Clearly Define the Roles of Educational Leaders and Those They Lead

Policies, by-laws, procedures, job descriptions, and other structural forms need to be in place, marking clearly appropriate versus inappropriate behavior. The outcomes of this structure must be measurable. We cannot expect educational leaders to know how to productively lead until the expectations are clearly and formally articulated and agreed on by all stakeholders. Anything less than this will result in confusion and the perpetuation of micromanaging.

Invest in Continuous Professional Development

Giving a new educational leader a handbook about his or her roles and responsibilities is insufficient at best. An organization should invest in continuous professional development. Furthermore, educational leaders need to know the most current laws, financial forecasts, personnel trends, and the like to make wise decisions. The same is true for educational leaders to implement best practices instead of micromanaging. Continuous professional development helps educational leaders to keep their focus and simply become the best leaders they can become.

Ensure that Leaders Receive Necessary Information

The distribution of essential leadership and performance information in a timely manner is crucial to building understanding. Furthermore, educational leaders should be allowed to disagree with one another without becoming disagreeable. Educational leaders should be expected to challenge one another when their opinions differ. Those who merely rubber-stamp other educational leaders' decisions do little good for twenty-first-century school improvements, such as reducing micromanaging.

Build a Strategic Plan with Goals and Objectives

Performance measures should be developed and implemented to monitor progress toward objectives. Said another way, educational leaders should project a vision, infuse the schools with a mission, encourage and hold staff accountable in reaching their fullest potential, and develop professionally in the process.

Attempt the Great—Communicate!

It is imperative that educational leaders and those they lead constantly and continuously communicate. Micromanaging is less likely to occur when needs, goals, and desires are communicated, a plan of action developed, and sufficient follow-through provided. It is when communications are ineffective that others feel more prone to micromanage. Effective communication based on understanding and trust is the antidote to micromanaging.

Not only is micromanaging counterproductive but it is also destructive. The seven keys leading to effective professional development in curbing micromanagement are critical to the welfare, accomplishments, and future gains by staff, students, parents, and other community members. Educational leaders, like other individuals, too easily slip into micromanaging instead of effectively leading (Anft & Williams, 2004; Jones, 2004). Be on guard, be vigilant, and implement the seven keys!

Today's school districts are and will continue to be under public scrutiny. Successful leadership will be highly desired, but often ridiculed. School districts, as multicomplex organizations, will continue to compound the difficulty of successful leadership at all levels. It will be imperative that educational leaders stop micromanaging, as it erodes quality educational programs, increases personnel turnover, and negates professional development goals. The curbing of micromanaging and other ills that have plagued education will need continuous and rich professional development to rehabilitate twenty-first-century schools. The prevention of micromanaging is a prerequisite for gains to be made from world-class professional development.

KEYS TO REHABILITATING TWENTY-FIRST-CENTURY SCHOOLS: WORLD-CLASS PROFESSIONAL DEVELOPMENT

As we approach the year 2014 under No Child Left Behind and other imposing benchmarks for twenty-first-century education, there is increasing need not to allow education to carry on in a "business as usual" mode. In addition, overwhelming research, as well as practical wisdom, reveals the danger of continuing along the same educational path of destruction. Schools cannot keep doing the same things over and over, particularly when the results are unsatisfactory. There will be no option.

A full-scale systemic change of the whole educational enterprise is needed (Barchfeld-Venet, 2005). That is, the replacing of traditional strategies will be required, not just getting by with simply improving the structures that currently exist. Therefore, twenty-first-century education will require a total "checkup"—a *rehabilitation* of sorts that will reinstate the respected importance of education if progress is to be made.

In order for a full-scale systemic transformation to occur, educational leaders and those they lead will need to develop new attitudes, beliefs, knowledge, and skills. This large-scale rehabilitation, or attainment of a healthier and more effective state by educational leaders, is dependent on twenty-first-century *leadership professional development* (Bybee & Kennedy, 2005). This professional development will constitute a vast departure from traditional educational training, which in the past focused primarily on helping teachers and administrators develop isolated skills for a single or often short-sighted need.

Today's professional development will be built on yesterday's efforts. We now know that past approaches to professional development relied too heavily on the industrialist approach—that is, viewing schooling as simply a composite of single parts or discrete skills that should be taught separately with the hope that somehow each separate skill will be put together identically by educators into a coherent and

RESEARCH KEYS

To enrich your understanding of **leadership professional development,** log on to www.researchnavigator.com and search Ebsco's ContentSelect.

Research Navigator.com

meaningful whole. As a result, we learned that professional development cannot remain fragmented (Loucks-Horsley, Hewson, Love, & Stiles, 1998). Successful twenty-first-century professional development will present a true reflection of the complex relationships and interconnectivity among all aspects of the overall educational enterprise.

Keys of Commitment to Twenty-First-Century Professional Development

In rehabilitating the training of educators in the past into successful twenty-first-century professional development, commitments need to be kept. These commitments include but are not limited to quality, time, growth, prioritization, and long-term continuation (Chang, 2003). The keys of commitment to professional development presented in Key Box 11.2 are critical to successful twenty-first-century professional development (Barchfeld-Venet, 2005; Bybee & Kennedy, 2005; McLaughlin & Yocom, 2005).

KEY BOX 11.2

Keys of Commitment to Successful Professional Development

- Meaningful professional development needs to be established as a priority for the school or school district.
- Effective professional development must be a requirement of the school improvement plan.
- Professional development must be a rich integration of research and highly practical and useful experiences.
- Responsive and relevant professional development needs to be directly correlated to increasing student achievement.
- Time needs to be invested for high-quality professional development activities and this time must be free of distractions.
- High-quality professional development must provide news and views of what participants can use—the very next day.
- The importance of professional development is known by students, parents, and community members as continually and consistently shared by educational leaders.
- High-quality professional development is systemic, research based, holistic, continuous, and sustained.
- For effective implementation, professional development must be allocated the necessary resources, time, budget, follow-up, and support by educational leaders.
- From the very outset in deciding the topics and emphasis for professional development, educational leaders shall use data to drive their decisions.
- A school's mission or vision statement needs to contain a provision stating that high-quality professional development is vital to professional growth and increasing student achievement.
- Participants should embrace professional development wholeheartedly and with appreciation for such opportunities.
- Educational leaders need to be congenial and creative in designating times and resources that provide for professional development.

Professional development is essential for the improvement of today's schools. Also, professional development will need to be prioritized more highly than it has been in the preceding century if schools are to meet the needs of faculty and students. Critical to quality professional development will be selecting training that is useful, meaningful, and relevant to the needs of the professional development participants.

The keys of commitment to twenty-first-century professional development stress *quality*. There is nothing more disheartening in terms of professional growth than to end up with irrelevant, meaningless, and impotent professional development. Certain conditions need to be considered in planning high-quality professional development (National Education Goals Panel, 1999). These conditions are found in the keys to high-quality, twenty-first-century professional development that follow.

IN THE NEWS

Science Chief Says Schools in New York Are Failing

The commitment to quality professional development was made evident during a New York City Council Committee Hearing.

Dr. Judy Rankin, the Department of Education Official in charge of science programs, gave her own program in New York City a failing grade at a City Council Committee Hearing yesterday. She said that the state of science in the city was horrendous. She then added that steps were being taken to turn things around.

With that, the science chief spoke proudly about the outstanding professional development for science teachers that has taken place this past year. Council Members applauded the training efforts of science teachers, knowing that the school system suffered from a lack of qualified science teachers. Council Members agreed that science education is the foundation of our global economy and the professional development of science teachers was long overdue.

The City Council Committee Hearing members requested that Dr. Rankin present a follow-up report in a year on the progress of the professional development of science teachers.

Efforts undertaken by the Department of Education to provide high-quality professional development for science teachers received utmost attention and support.

Source: S. Saulny, "Science Chief Says Schools in New York Are Failing," *New York Times,* November 11, 2005.

Professional Development Must Incorporate Global Issues. High-quality professional development must include world issues. Inasmuch as the United States is a major player on the international playing field, education needs to align its professional development to the state of the world if tomorrow's leaders, our students today, are to be prepared to contribute to global welfare instead of warfare. In turn, legislatures need to appropriate the funds necessary to provide the resources (time and money) to support continuous professional development.

Professional Development Must Capitalize on Colleges and Universities. Across the nation, summer school, evening courses, weekend courses, and distance and online courses for teachers to upgrade their knowledge and skills to perform more effectively are available. High-quality professional development necessitates school districts and higher education institutions to maximize their unified efforts (McLaughlin & Yocom, 2005). Doctors, lawyers, engineers, and other professionals attend continuing-education courses for their professional development at colleges and universities; educators need to do the same.

Professional Development Must Be Standards Based. As curriculum and instruction are driven by standards, so too will high-quality professional development. Selection of professional development topics will be decided by aligning the needs of a school in terms of student achievement with the required standards of achievement. The greater the alignment of established standards to professional development, the higher the quality of professional development that will emerge (Stanovich & Stanovich, 2003). To illustrate, let's say that Greenway High School has identified a deficiency of underachievement by the ninth-grade boys on the state's required writing standards. Therefore, the educational leaders of Greenway High School deem it a priority to provide professional development for faculty based on the state's required writing standard.

Professional Development Must Work Down the Hall and Across the Hall.

High-quality, twenty-first-century professional development will dispel the myth that the finest professional development needs to be imported from more than fifty miles away with the trainers descending on school districts with attaché cases firmly placed under their arms. Some of the most meaningful professional development comes from colleagues in the classroom next door or down the hall. Unique skills that have been developed by faculty members can be shared with other faculty members to achieve high-quality professional development. Colleague trainers are not "here today, gone tomorrow" and are able to provide continuous support and assistance for the whole staff. As for those faculty members who are selected to share and show their skills, they become empowered to achieve even greater accomplishments.

Professional Development Must Be Collegial.

High-quality professional development will carry with it one additional requirement: sharing the gains of the professional development with colleagues (Tugel, 2004). Past practice in professional development has been that some educators leave their schools to attend off-site professional development seminars. The content might have been extraordinarily meaningful, yet as those participating in the professional development returned to their schools, there was a void—no sharing, no benefit to others, no exchange of ideas—simply a void. Professional development today must provide avenues, opportunities, and even requirements for this sharing to take place. Besides, endorsements by colleagues of professional development skills go a long ways in underscoring its importance to the total faculty.

Professional Development Must Focus on Increasing Student Achievement.

Professional development is targeted at increasing student achievement. Said differently, professional development that achieves the "greatest bang for the buck" in terms of increasing student achievement is what will constitute the highest-quality, twenty-first-century professional development. Hence, it is critical to engage teachers in selecting professional development that is highly correlated with increased student achievement. Besides, involving teachers in shared decision making regarding the selection of professional development will build ownership and will less likely be perceived by teachers as the "p.d. de jour," "irrelevant to what's needed" or "flavor of the month."

Professional Development Must Support Partnerships.

Local businesses and civic organizations will continue to extend a red carpet to educators to participate in their organization's twenty-first-century professional development. Such partnerships will provide educators with professional development opportunities that might not otherwise be possible. Much more may be gained through these partnerships besides the professional development itself. The forming of these partnerships will have the potential to grow into other shared initiatives, including but not limited to technology, fund raising, grants potentials, and other mutual gains (Weiss, Knapp, Hollweg, & Burrill, 2001). Educational leaders are reminded that the door needs to swing both ways and business and civic leaders should also be invited to participate in professional development sponsored by school districts.

Professional Development Must Support Paid Summer Internships.   Fellowships, grants, endowments, and other funding mechanisms will continue to support educators to work at a company or shadow a business partner for six to nine weeks during the summer. For example, a chemistry teacher might intern with a chemical company, a journalism teacher might work with a magazine or newspaper staff, or an auto mechanics teacher might intern with an auto manufacturer. These teacher-related experiences add much depth, breadth, and understanding of real-world applications to the teacher's instruction (Barchfeld-Venet, 2005). Hence, high-quality professional development will take on many shapes and forms. What will be important is the commitment and engagement in professional development by *all* educators.

Professional Development Must Support Opportunities for Educational Leaders.   On a special note, it behooves today's educational leaders to participate in professional development opportunities sponsored by businesses and companies offering on-site training for their personnel in leadership positions. Professional development opportunities sponsored by businesses and companies will continue to include highly qualified and sometimes well-known speakers (Bybee & Kennedy, 2005). Such high-quality professional development opportunities will strengthen educational leader–business partnerships while educators receive top-quality training on a shoestring budget. The networking that will follow this shared professional development opportunities may very well be equally as advantageous in the long term.

Professional Development Needs a National Focus and Concern.   Although not new in development, the National Board for Professional Teaching Standards (NBPTS) has resurged in activity during the twenty-first century. Following the ringing of a national siren in 1983 with *A Nation at Risk,* responded to by the Carnegie Task Force reply in 1986 with *A Nation Prepared: Teachers for the 21st Century,* the National Board for Professional Teaching Standards was originated one year later. Today, with increased intensity on student achievement caused by No Child Left Behind, the NBPTS has arisen. The mission of the NBPTS is to advance the quality of teaching and learning by maintaining high and rigorous standards for what accomplished teachers should know and be able to do; provide a national voluntary system of certifying teachers who meet these standards; and advocating related education reforms to integrate National Board Certification in U.S. education and to capitalize on the expertise of National Board Certified Teachers. At a crucial time, when developing high-quality teachers is essential

(Darling-Hammond & Youngs, 2002), educational leaders throughout the United States have supported the NBPTS and its professional development initiatives by encouraging their teachers to become nationally board certified.

Professional Development Must Incorporate Technology.   Twenty-first-century professional development via technologies will be far greater than what we have experienced in the past (McLaughlin & Yocom, 2005). Improvements in professional development via technology will be huge during this century, including online, course-based, distance learning, and various combinations of media. Virtual reality in just about every curricular area will emerge, bestowing professional development participants with extraordinary skill development. To illustrate, content-area teachers located all over the world will link together to swap ideas through language translation software and with greater comfort levels than face-to-face interaction. This vibrant exchange of curricula ideas will result in a networked community for real-time sharing among community members.

Educational leaders will need to participate in high-quality professional development in order to provide successful technology leadership. Additional roles and responsibilities of educational leaders as technology leaders are presented in Key Box 11.3 (Barchfeld-Venet, 2005: Cuban, 2001b; Weiss et al., 2001):

> **KEY BOX 11.3**
>
> ### Successful Educational Leaders' Responsibilities as Technology Leaders
>
> - Establish goals and visions of learning with technology.
> - Emphasize the correlation of instructional technology to student achievement.
> - Provide training that offers ongoing rather than "one-shot" professional development activities.
> - Maximize times to learn and access new technologies.
> - Spearhead the focus on the integration of technology tools into instruction.
> - Provide modeling of best practices of instructional technology in school performance.

Research of instructional technology and the need for increased student achievement underscore the vital roles and responsibilities of twenty-first-century educational leadership. The powerful tools of technology will be essential in meeting federal accountability measures of student achievement (Reauthorizations of IDEA, No Child Left Behind, etc.). Today's educational leaders will need to lead in narrowing the great digital divide.

KEYS TO THE LAST CALL

The emphasis on high-quality, twenty-first-century professional development does not adequately address the need for educational leaders to rehabilitate or revive a dwindling population of teachers (Ingersoll, 2001a, 2001b; Jazzar & Algozzine, 2006; United States Department of Education, 2000). After all, a teacher shortage of national concern is escalating, stemming from low teacher retention rates, high teacher retirements, changing teaching assignments, and fewer teachers joining the profession. With approximately one-third of new teachers leaving the classroom within three years and nearly one-half within five years (National Commission on Teaching and America's Future, 2003), educational leaders are actively implementing and enhancing mentoring programs.

Another form of high-quality professional development, teacher mentoring programs, although not the only answer, will be even more crucial in the years ahead in recruiting new, and retaining current, quality teachers (Kelley, 2004). To construct effective teacher mentoring programs, the following keys to effective teacher mentoring programs are presented to guide educational leaders in building successful teacher mentor selection criteria, developing enhanced training, and evaluating teacher mentor effectiveness. This may be the last call to support and improve teacher mentor programs.

IN THE NEWS

High-Tech Boards at Head of the Class

Demonstrating best practices of instructional technology in school performance, teacher Jill Gough implements the whiteboard to its fullest capabilities.

When Westminster teacher Jill Gough wants to search webpages, display class notes, conduct an Internet search, illustrate lessons with true-life examples, and more, she simply taps the whiteboard behind her. It springs to life like something out of a science fiction movie.

Gough is able to use the latest in classroom technology to maximize her students' learning because of her participation in comprehensive professional development programs. Furthermore, her training has been ongoing rather than a one time event. Such professional development is imperative to keep up with the rapid changes in technology.

As for the whiteboard, there are numerous advantages for those who have been trained to use it. On the chalkboard, notes were lost forever. With the interactive board, notes can be saved and scrolled to at a tap on the whiteboard. As one of the most exciting technology developments, it is well worth the time invested in professional development to learn the capabilities of this new technology.

Technology training is imperative for increasing student achievement.

Source: P. Donsky, "High-Tech Boards at Head of the Class," *The Atlanta-Journal Constitution,* October 3, 2005.

Teacher Mentoring Programs

A teacher shortage will enter crisis levels during this century (Ingersoll, 2001a, 2001b). This teacher dilemma will be compounded by the uncounted numbers of experienced teachers who will assume new assignments. Far too few teacher candidates are enrolled in university teacher preparation programs, and even fewer are projected. Many more states will deregulate teacher certification requirements. Increasing numbers of teachers will enter schools with far less training. Nobody should simply be thrown into a classroom without the support needed to be successful (The Teaching Commission, 2004). Immediate solutions are needed to ensure that no twenty-first-century classroom is left behind.

Although not the cure-all, carefully designed mentoring programs can help to meet the challenges inherent in recruiting, in-servicing, and retaining qualified teachers. Educational leaders who have constructed successful mentoring programs will have an advantage when vying for top-quality new teachers from a shrinking pool (Darling-Hammond, 2003; Hirsch, Koppich, & Knapp, 2001; Kelley, 2004; O'Neill, 2004). When new teachers know they will receive support and guidance from well-trained mentors where other employment benefits are similar, they will choose schools and school districts where a greater assurance of their success is present. In essence, effective mentoring programs may be one of the reasons why new teachers apply and stay teaching at selected schools.

At the heart and soul of each successful teacher mentoring program is an effective mentor. Successful mentors help their less experienced colleagues make sense of the realities to be faced in teaching (Peske, Liu, Johnson, Kauffman, & Kardos, 2001). Mentors provide protégés with access to instructional knowledge and expertise in ways that contribute to their success. The bottom line is when new teachers benefit from great mentors, they are able to make significant student gains.

The forming of mentor–protégé relationships premised on trust, collegiality, confidentiality and the sharing of instructional skills is critical. Mentors need to be more than someone to help protégés meet academic, professional, and social needs. Mentors should be someone who can be trusted, who will hold concerns confidentially, or who will listen to venting of frustrations. Such binding relationships often mean the difference between new teachers staying or leaving their profession.

Although the value of teacher mentoring may be clear, the criteria for selecting, training, and evaluating effective mentors needs clarification. Educational leaders need to strive continually to improve the criteria for selecting, training, and evaluating their mentors (Portner, 2001). Keys for selecting mentors are critical to identifying teachers to guide other teachers.

RESEARCH KEYS

To enrich your understanding of **teacher mentoring**, log on to www.researchnavigator. com and search Ebsco's ContentSelect.

Research Navigator.com

Keys for Selecting Mentors

The selection criteria in identifying a mentor are critical to the success of the mentor–protégé relationship (Carroll & Fulton, 2004; Darling-Hammond, 2003; Hirsch et al., 2001). The selection criteria should include communication skills, knowledge of politics, positive attitude and attributes, professional competence, and trustworthiness. Before proceeding, it is important to note that each criterion is equally important in selecting teacher mentors.

Mentors Have Excellent Communication Skills.   In describing the ideal mentor, teachers, school administrators, and higher education faculty most often have in mind a highly skilled teacher (or someone with close connections to the classroom) with excellent peer communication skills. Equally important is the ability of a mentor to offer criticism and critiques in positive and productive ways. The mentoring relationship needs to be a skillful sharing of views. Effective mentors exercise diplomacy in collegial relationships and model a dedication to teaching.

Mentors Have Knowledge of the Political Landscape.   In addition to exemplary communication skills, effective mentors know the "ins" and "outs" of a school, school district, and community. Mentors who understand the culture of the school community, as well as know how to acquire instructional resources, are a bonus to their protégés. A mentor who is respected and knows several others has many advantages. These qualities are less a function of years of service and more a matter of insight and knowledge.

Mentors Have Positive Attitudes and Attributes.   Attitude and character are comprised of a willingness to serve, a commitment to teaching, and a belief in mentoring. Positive attitude is the single-most important quality in a successful mentor. The credibility of a mentor is critical to the mentor–protégé relationship. Honesty, integrity, and pride are very important qualities of mentors. In addition to the stated criteria, a commitment to lifelong learning, the ability to be reflective, and the desire to share ideas are also qualities of attitude and character.

Mentors Have Professional Competence and Experience.   Professional competence and experience include excellent knowledge of pedagogy coupled with strong classroom management skills. What is learned from a mentor about teaching often makes a lasting impression. When the mentor does what he or she should in terms of instructional recommendations, the protégé will be off on the right foot. This professional competence and experience of the mentor also include exuding confidence and feeling comfortable while being observed by other teachers.

Mentors Are Trustworthy.   Improved criteria for the selection of effective teacher mentors need to include the mentor's ability to maintain a trusting professional relationship. In doing so, an effective mentor knows how to express care for a protégé's emotional and professional needs. Mentors need to be approachable, establish rapport with ease, and always be patient. Mentors who are sensitive to political issues and work well with individuals from different cultures are a premium.

KEYS TO ENHANCING TRAINING AND SUPPORT FOR MENTORS

Once mentors are selected in accordance with the school district's policies and contractual agreements, the professional development provided for mentors cannot be overstated. Mentoring can be difficult, challenging, and even awkward at times for the mentor as it is for the protégé (Holloway, 2001; Hull, 2004). Often, mentors do not have an easier role than the protégé, as it may be more difficult on the other side of the desk. Mentor training must be ongoing, meeting the ever-changing needs of schools. In addition, monthly planning and informational meetings throughout the school year need to be scheduled to support mentors and keep them abreast of recent developments. Furthermore, training for mentors needs to include relevant and meaningful content and ample opportunity for networking (Meyer, 2002).

Provide Relevant Professional Development

Professional development relevant to the needs of mentors includes developing reflective practice, understanding state mandates, and forming collaborative relationships. Before becoming a mentor, the training needs to be thorough, including classroom observation skills, creating long-term professional development plans for new teachers, and understanding the academic, professional, and social needs of new teachers.

Provide Opportunities for Networking with Other Mentors

Some professional development programs provide mentors with ready access to the guidance of higher education faculty. In addition, professional development for mentors includes meeting with other mentors on a regular basis to discuss coaching strategies, share instructional resources, and plan additional ways to assist protégés.

With numerous and diversified strategies, it still must be said that there are no easy solutions to preparing effective mentors. Preparing mentors necessitates cooperation between a school district and its teachers. The way a district supports its mentors requires systemic changes that affect school climate, conventional definitions of the job of teaching, and a host of policies and procedures governing school business. With immediate improvements needed in teacher recruitment and retention, there is no other option!

KEYS TO MEASURING THE EFFECTIVENESS OF TEACHER MENTORING

Effective mentoring programs evaluate the performance of their mentors. Good programs also hold mentors themselves accountable. Protégés often participate in evaluating their mentors at the end of the year. Other educational leaders evaluate certain facets of mentors. The evaluations of mentors should not be confrontational; after all, the very best candidates have been selected to do very important work (Sparks, 2002). The two keys to measuring the effectiveness of teacher mentoring programs follow to aid and assist educational leaders everywhere.

Document Improvement and Results

At the program level, careful documentation needs to be maintained to improve the effectiveness of mentoring and to encourage policymakers, as only fifteen states require and fund mentoring programs for novice teachers (*Education Week,* 2004). Participating districts, teacher associations, higher education institutions, and other partners should generate data indicating a mentoring program's success or shortfalls. Student time on task, parent satisfaction, teacher absenteeism, morale, and other school improvements are important sources of data. Mentoring programs need to be evaluated and documented—if only to construct a convincing argument that demonstrates that mentor programs offer a significant return on investment and that the cost of mentoring and retaining new teachers is less than the combined outlay for large-scale recruitment and long-term remediation (The National Commission on Teaching and America's Future, 2002; Zuckerman, 2001). As part of the mentor evaluation documentation, mentors are often required to keep a portfolio.

Use Achievement to Monitor Success

Student achievement may be the most valuable indicator for evaluating a mentoring program. Educational leaders need to implement mentoring programs such as the Pathwise Series that are tied to research-based standards using common language, clear and concrete levels of performance, and structured events for mentors and protégés (Educational Testing Service, 2002), providing opportunities to monitor the success of mentoring programs using student achievement. However, it is noteworthy to say that there is insufficient research at this time revealing the direct connection between teacher mentoring and student achievement. Additional studies are needed to determine the cause and effect of increased student achievement and effective mentoring programs.

LAST CALL FOR TEACHER MENTORING

Selecting, training, and evaluating teacher mentors are critical because changes in society require educators, like the scientific community, to meet increasingly complex challenges. The advancing of teacher mentors through improved criteria for selection, enhanced training, and proper evaluation will support the creating of cohesive schools where teachers and administrators constantly discuss instructional practice and student learning (Jenkins & Veal, 2002). The last call is for all educational leaders to support and improve teacher mentoring programs as if teacher recruitment and teacher retention depends on it—because it does!

The enterprise of education will reach rock bottom during the twenty-first century. Micromanaging will lead to its demise. There will be only one direction for education to move—to get better, healthier, and more efficient. It is sad but too often true that before education gets better, or rehabilitates, education will take a hard nosedive. This rehabilitation will be facilitated by high-quality, twenty-first century professional development led by all educational leaders. In addition, meaningful mentor–protégé programs will be developed and sustained by educational leaders to attract and retain quality teachers.

THE REFLECTIVE PRACTITIONER

Welcome to your eleventh Reflective Practitioner containing your Chapter 11 Scenario based on ISLLC Standards 2, 3, and 5 and your reading of Chapter 11. It is intended to provoke your thoughtful reflection and to stimulate discussion among colleagues, classmates, and peers. The Reflective Practitioner provides opportunities to synthesize issues, make comparisons, and apply theory to practice. We hope it will motivate you to search for evidence, thus increasing your comprehension of the text and helping you examine your convictions and discover new and shared perspectives.

ISLLC Standard 2
A school administrator is an educational leader who promotes the success of all students by advocating, nurturing, and sustaining a school culture and instructional program conducive to student learning and staff professional growth.

ISLLC Standard 3
A school administrator is an educational leader who promotes the success of all students by ensuring management of the organization, operations, and resources for a safe, efficient, and effective learning environment.

ISLLC Standard 5
A school administrator is an educational leader who promotes the success of all students by acting with integrity, fairness, and in an ethical manner

Scenario

Ms. Grownlee is in her second year of high school teaching and is highly regarded by the faculty. She teaches gifted and talented students and helped write the present gifted and talented curriculum four years ago. Ms. Grownlee follows the curriculum without variation.

School is now in the fourth month. Ms. Grownlee has established her routines and expectations for her ninth- and tenth-grade students. She teaches, as do all other high school teachers at her school, using block scheduling, now in its third year of implementation. She uses all ninety minutes to lecture, nonstop. All students have received As on their first two report cards. However, both students and parents have expressed dissatisfaction to you about her teaching.

Ms. Grownlee's students refer to her teaching as "Ms. G's drill and kill only method." Students have gone so far as to draw caricatures of Ms. Grownlee as a "sage on the stage" and never the "guide on their side." Students breeze through their assignments with little to no effort. They describe their class as "the same thing every day," "the only thing we do is paper and pencil work," "we don't get opportunities for discussion," and "we never get to work together."

You have observed Ms. Grownlee's class several times, and although students are not misbehaving, they really are not involved in the class. There is a quiet pall that falls over the classroom as class begins. Higher-level thinking skills, challenging objectives, and motivational strategies are absent. In Ms. Grownlee's defense, since the high school went to block scheduling, the increase of forty minutes in each class period has thrown many teachers for a loop.

Ms. Grownlee's mentor has shared with you, the building principal, that she and several other teachers have seen the superintendent and board president, both of whom have children in one of Ms. Grownlee's classes, regularly standing in the hall outside Ms. Grownlee's classroom door to eavesdrop. Ms. Grownlee's mentor shared that she has heard rumblings from numerous other parents that they feel students are not being prepared for advanced courses. In addition, Ms. Grownlee's mentor asks you for advice on how to become a more effective mentor.

The eavesdropping on Ms Grownlee's class by the superintendent and board president needs to stop, as it destroys the efficient and effective learning environment as stipulated in Standard 3. Therefore, upon your request, the superintendent agrees to meet with you. Based on your reading of micromanaging in Chapter 11, what request would you like to present to your superintendent? Please provide a rationale for your request. Be careful!

QUESTIONS FOR REFLECTIVE THINKING

1. Teachers do not seem to be gaining the fullest potential of block scheduling in your school. Develop a high-quality professional development plan that you would recommend to the faculty to achieve a successful implementation of block scheduling. Substantiate your high-quality professional development with your reading of Chapter 11.
2. Ms. Grownlee's mentor awaits your advice as to how she can become a more effective mentor. Based on your reading of the keys to improved mentoring, what will you advise Ms. Grownlee? State the reasons for your advice.
3. Describe your school mentoring program. Based on your reading of Chapter 11, what recommendations for improvement of your mentoring program would you suggest and why? If you do not have a mentoring program, please describe what you would include in a successful mentoring program.

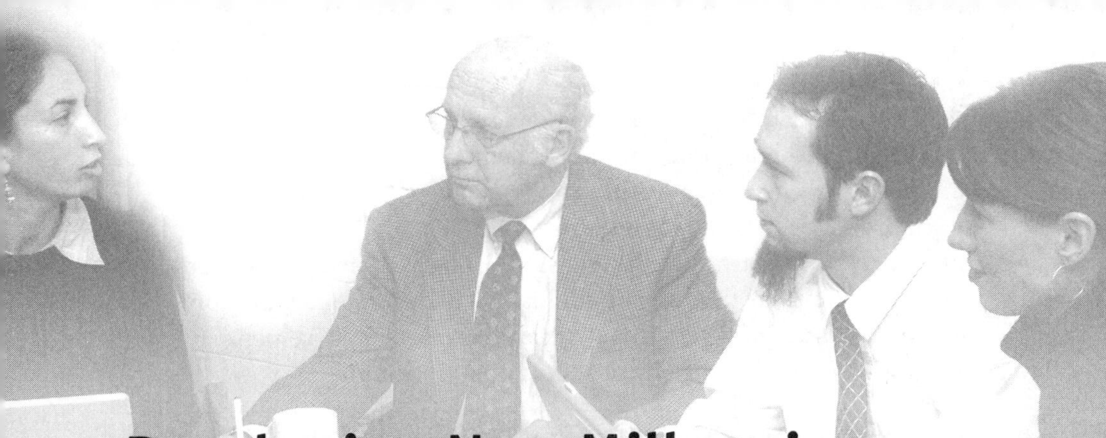

chapter **12**

ISLLC
Standards
1–6

Developing New Millennium Assessments

Assess for success, not school digress.
—Anonymous

Our Chapter 12 Action Focus welcomes you, the newly appointed principal of Christa McAuliffe Elementary School, into one of your fifth-grade classrooms taught by Mary Michaels. You view the following:

Working intensely in groups of five or six, students are actively categorizing and evaluating personal and political views of outstanding leaders. The facts and figures each group has collected have been compiled in an outstanding leaders' facts database used to enhance student understanding of leadership characteristics. Students were discussing the multimedia presentations and informational webpages that they soon will be presenting to the whole class. The culminating activity will be the annual wax museum in which each student will impersonate an outstanding leader by giving a short speech while dressed up in the leader's attire. Parents and other community members have already received their invitations to attend this program and have responded affirmatively in large numbers.

Before leaving her classroom, you share with Ms. Michaels how impressed you are with her students' motivation in their learning, and, wanting to know more about her lesson, ask her to stop by your office during her planning period later that day.

At the requested time, Ms. Michaels knocks at your office door. You invite her to enter your office and be seated. You begin by expressing your pleasure in seeing her students so intently engaged in the lesson. You ask Ms. Michaels to share with you additional information about the lesson you observed.

Ms. Michaels, sensing your genuine interest in her teaching, extends her appreciation to you for your desire to know more. She then describes her students' motivation for learning as stemming from a shared opportunity to decide on their learning outcomes. Self-evaluations, along with peer evaluations, help to guide their learning. Authentic assessments, including a multimedia presentation, a webpage, and participation in the wax museum, add purpose and meaning to student learning. The family and community involvement in attending the wax museum has given her students a sense of importance for their learning. These assessments have resulted in substantial gains by all students, virtually eliminating racial differences and greatly reducing socioeconomic differences. In creating an even playing field for testing, all students have become equal learning partners and the achievement gap has begun to narrow.

Time seems to race by; only minutes remain in Ms. Michaels's planning period. You thank your star teacher for a most informative sharing, wish her a great remaining day, and say that you would like to visit with her again soon.

Developing assessments that actually measure student achievement are critical to the success of twenty-first-century educational leadership.

As exemplified in your Chapter 12 Action Focus, assessment that includes self and peer assessments, authentic assessment, and family and community involvement will be critical to new millennium education. In addition, assessment that is based on research in emotional intelligence and developmentally appropriate practices are essential. It all begins with effective early childhood assessments.

EARLY CHILDHOOD ASSESSMENT

There is no greater period of human development than conception through early childhood in maximizing the potential for living a healthy and full life. These years in an individual's life are highly impressionable. The importance of educational leaders focusing on early childhood assessment and intervention for infants, toddlers, and young children constitutes a window of opportunity for the individual, educational experiences, and the community at large (Epstein, 1996; Helm & Gronlund, 2000). For every dollar invested into early childhood assessment and intervention, that one dollar will be multiplied in value a hundred times over in terms of childhood and teenage gains. It is an old Greek anthropomorphic illustration revealing the importance in early childhood assessment and intervention in saying if the young slanting sapling is not stood erect, the tree as it gets older will be several times more difficult to stand straight.

To make assessment more meaningful, keys to implementing successful early childhood assessments need to be understood. These considerations include test results, test result interpretation, lifetime importance, appropriateness of assessments and interventions, and determination of strategies. The value of each is underscored in the following sections.

Test Results Reflect Distributions, Not Individuals

Whenever a measurement is applied to a group of people of any age—especially a group that is diverse in background, experience, aptitude, development, culture, language, and interests—some will rank higher and some lower than others on any item assessed. Caution is advised in discussing bell-shaped curves at the early childhood level: The younger the child, the greater sensitivity is required in interpreting test results to parents of children (Bandura, Pastorelli, Barbaranelli, & Caprara, 1999). The younger the infant, the more defensive the parents are and the more sensitive educational leaders need to be!

Interpretations May Reveal Limitations

Educational leaders should clearly understand that assessments at the early childhood level will yield vast differences. It is statistically impossible for all children measured by the same assessment to be above average. It is best for educational leaders to implement assessments that determine achievement on an individual basis, rather than compare infants, toddlers, and young children. Furthermore, all test results at all ages and grade levels should be interpreted on an individual basis. Test results that are used to compare students, schools, and school districts are ludicrous.

Successful Schooling Begins in Early Childhood

Failure to assess and intervene early in children's lives might mean that some children will be deprived of needed intervention with special services at a time when these services can do the most good. Conversely, the more early childhood assessing and intervening at younger ages, the less special education services will be needed in the elementary school (Schweinhart & Weikart, 1997b; Wasik, 2001). Fewer special education services at the elementary school level mean significantly reduced financial costs as well. Hence, we assert again that the more dollars invested into early childhood assessment and intervention, the greater the gains for individual students and the school system.

Developmentally Appropriate Assessments Are Essential

Although educational leaders cannot be accountable for all children being above average or for all children being below average, educational leaders *are* accountable for applying all developmentally appropriate assessments and interventions for the learning situation at hand. The operative words here are *developmentally appropriate*. We have sufficient research today that accurately reveals children's capabilities, needs, emotions, academic potentials, social development, and physical capacities (Schweinhart & Weikart, 1997a). Assessment, interventions, and other practices that are not aligned with this body of research are inappropriate, damaging, and destructive.

Assessment Informs Instruction

Developmentally appropriate assessment procedures should indicate which of the strategies and resources are available and judged appropriate. Like pediatricians, educational leaders should know, prescribe, and oversee that the appropriate strategies and resources are provided for each child. The more successful educational leaders are in meeting the needs of each individual student, the greater the success will be for the whole school. Educational leaders build great schools one student at a time.

Early Assessment Narrows the Achievement Gap

With increased academic requirements and testing mandates, the achievement gap may be widening. Students who are high achievers will continue to succeed academically. Those students at academic risk may get further "left behind." The key to narrowing the achievement gap is early childhood assessment and intervention. Early childhood assessments and interventions have resulted in enduring effects on the life-course development of low-income children (Dunn & Kontos, 1997; Marcon, 1995; Sherman & Mueller, 1996; Snow, Burns, & Griffin, 1998), as presented in Key Box 12.1.

KEY BOX ▶ **12.1**

Keys to Narrowing the Twenty-First-Century Achievement Gap

- Enhance cognitive development and school achievement.
- Reduce the need for remedial education services.
- Reduce rates of delinquency.
- Increase educational attainment and economic well-being.
- Improve the children's well being.

In addition to the aforementioned gains in narrowing the achievement gap, early childhood assessment and interventions gauge the needs of the young, result in greater parent involvement in and satisfaction with children's schooling, and increase expectations for children's educational attainment (Reynolds, 1994, 2000). Such gains are also associated with greater school achievement and lower rates of school remedial services (Reynolds, 2000). Early childhood assessment and interventions were consistently associated with higher rates of high school completion and lower rates of juvenile arrest for violent and nonviolent offenses (Reynolds, Temple, Robertson, & Mann, 2002).

IN THE NEWS

Why the Public Is Losing Faith in the No Child Act

With increasing family involvement as a primary intent of No Child Left Behind, why has family participation been left behind?

In the nearly four years since Congress enacted the No Child Left Behind Act, states have been under considerable pressure to comply with certain requirements such as implementing a high stakes statewide testing program. But another of the law's goals—increasing parent and community involvement in the public schools—has received far less scrutiny even though it was mentioned over one hundred times in the legislation.

Explicitly, the No Child Left Behind Act promised to give citizens more opportunities to see what goes on in local schools, to become well informed about how schools work, and to become more involved in education policy debates, decision-making, *assessments* and accountability in general.

But policymakers have turned their backs on the promise of increased *family involvement* in the schools. Having listened to the concerns of thousands of citizens across the country, the Public Education Network agrees. Rather than bringing people closer to their schools, No Child Left Behind is causing many Americans to feel increasingly distrustful of, and marginalized by, professional educators.

Developing assessments needs to include family involvement.

Source: W. D. Puriefoy, "Why the Public Is Losing Faith in the No Child Law," *Education Week*, June 8, 2005.

Family Involvement Should Begin Early

Whereas interventions for older children and adults with similar limitations focus on the individual, a critical issue in early childhood interventions emphasize the *importance of the role of the family*. Without involvement of family, interventions are unlikely to be successful (Lally, Lerner, & Lurie-Hurvitz, 2001). Strategically, the target of the intervention must be the family, even though the primary concern is about the infant's poor growth, atypical behavior, or delayed development. A child is unlikely to thrive in any of these domains if the family is stressed by such factors as parental unemployment, unsanitary living conditions, or neighborhood violence.

MOVING FROM ASSESSMENT TO INTERVENTION

It is difficult to determine the recipe for successful early childhood assessments and interventions as to what ingredients, or testable items, should comprise a valid and comprehensive assessment. We know that the *items and behaviors assessed* should have demonstrable relationships to significant human functioning. For example, the child's knowledge of the names of shapes or of the calendar at age 4 or 5 is not developmentally appropriate because there is no meaning beyond test performance itself. In addition, it is widely recognized (Haller, 2001; Jacobson, 1996; Katz, 1999; Nel, 2000; Neuharth-Pritchett, 2001) that additional ingredients in early childhood assessment and intervention should include the following keys:

- *Key 1: Dispositions, feelings, skills, and knowledge.* In addition to assessing young children's social competence, adults should include the assessment of individual children's progress in acquiring desirable dispositions, feelings, skills, and knowledge.
- *Key 2: Documentation.* Documentation is the primary strategy for recording and presenting such assessments. This documentation is based on ample observation. Educational leaders are to bear in mind that their documentation needs to be free of cultural, racial, social, economic, gender, and all other biases.
- *Key 3: Eventual self-assessment.* Preschoolers and children in the primary grades can be encouraged to assess their own work according to specific criteria such as the clarity, inclusiveness, interest level, comprehensiveness, or aesthetic qualities of the work.
- *Key 4: Understanding by the assessed subjects.* Those tested should be informed about the standards on which the assessments are based. Such understanding by children is developmentally appropriate so long as the children have the ability to understand the standards.
- *Key 5: Metacognitive understanding of learning.* From third grade on, most children should be taught how to assess the general progress of their own learning. During teacher–child or teacher–parent–child conferences, children can be encouraged to indicate what mastery and learning they want to focus on during a given period.
- *Key 6: Self-evaluation.* From time to time, children can be asked to judge their own progress, using three or four categories. For example, children can be asked to discuss the work they think they are making good progress on, what they think they need to concentrate more on, what they want help with, and other categories nominated by the children. Most children will be quite realistic and sensible when engaging in such self-evaluation. The teacher can help by expressing her or his own realistic evaluation in a serious and supportive way. In principle, unless children are consulted about their own views of their own progress, they cannot learn to assume some responsibility for it.

- *Key 7: Contributing to class ethos.* Depending on their ages, children as a group can be encouraged to develop some criteria concerning what they want their classroom life to be like. These criteria are not simply lists of classroom rules. Rather, they should be a thoughtful examination of what kind of community the class should be, such as the extent to which it is a caring, cooperative group, respectful of individual differences; the extent to which it is a helpful community of scholars; and the extent to which it meets any other dimensions of classroom life the children and their teacher think are important.

- *Key 8: Student-led discussions.* Periodically, the teacher or a child can lead the group in a discussion concerning how well they are doing on these criteria as a class, and what additions or modifications of the criteria might be tried. Such discussions should be directed toward the development of positive and constructive suggestions. The more participation in developmentally appropriate activities, the greater will be the likelihood for student learning.

In many instances, children will thrive only if society cares enough to support their families. There is a high correlation between a child's achievement and the degree of which a family feels supported (Hoyt, 2000; Jones & Gullo, 1999). With family support, early childhood interventions have resulted in significant gains, as presented in Key Box 12.2.

KEY BOX ▶ 12.2

The Gains of Early Childhood Interventions When Family Support Is Present

- Gains are seen in emotional or cognitive development for the child, typically in the short run or in improved parent–child relationships.
- There are improvements in the educational process and outcomes for the child.
- Economic self-sufficiency, initially for the parent and later for the child, is increased through greater labor force participation, higher income, and lower welfare usage.
- Levels of criminal activity are reduced.
- There are improvements in health-related indicators, such as child abuse, maternal reproductive health, and maternal substance abuse.

Much is still unknown about early childhood intervention assessments, and this limits the degree to which these conclusions can be generalized to other early intervention programs. For example, the following remain unknown:

- How can early interventions best be targeted to those who would benefit most? It is not yet known which eligibility criteria would generate the most positive benefit/cost ratios.
- Will the model programs evaluated to date generate the same benefits and savings when implemented on a large scale? The demonstrations have been undertaken in a more resource-intensive context than is likely to be achieved in full-scale programs.

- What are the implications of changing the social safety net? Previous demonstrations were carried out under the now-superseded welfare system.

These unknowns will have to be resolved if wise decisions are to be made among early intervention alternatives and if the programs chosen can be designed to fully realize their potential for promoting child development—and saving money. In particular, research is needed to determine why certain programs work.

In reflection of the research, progress has been made in the development of effective early childhood intervention assessments. A large amount of data and systematic program development over the last two decades have indicated that highly effective intervention assessments will likely result in the functional prevention of serious problem behaviors (National Association of Early Childhood Specialists in State Departments of Education, 2000; Rathbun, Walston, & Hausken, 2000). The challenge is to create even more effective intervention assessments, as assessment-based positive behavior support provides the technical basis for effective early intervention. Family centeredness and the development of constructive partnerships and behavior support plans to be implemented in a manner that will produce meaningful and durable outcomes for the child and family are imperative. If these elements are in place during the first crucial years of early childhood intervention, then the prospects for positive experiences during the subsequent years of elementary and secondary schooling will be greatly enhanced.

AUTHENTIC ASSESSMENT

Of all the academic challenges facing educational leaders in today's political climate, perhaps the most significant are the assessments used to determine student proficiencies. Although tests have always been a part of the traditional educational enterprise, today's high-stakes testing has aborted all care and concern for an individual student's learning (Stefonek, 1991).

IN THE NEWS

Candidates Sound Off—Where They Stand on Overcrowding, the Gifted

Assessments that are used to determine student proficiencies need to be aligned with what is meaningful and relevant to a student's life.

Three school board candidates for the Cherokee County Board of Education were seated before the auditorium that was filled with community members. They were preparing for the rapid fire of questions soon to be presented by an *Atlanta Journal-Constitution* staff writer.

The questions were varied, including overcrowding, new building construction, and curricula. The one question that seemed to cause the most concern for the candidates was, *How can Cherokee improve its offerings to gifted and talented students?*

The first school board candidate's response captured the attention of those in attendance; you could actually hear a pin drop in the auditorium. He replied that

the way to improve the offerings to gifted and high-achieving students and all other students is accomplished by providing students with opportunities for authentic inquiry and assessments where the teacher is the facilitator and not the sole source of knowledge. Traditional assessments are antiquated and so is the overtly and covertly authoritarian style of leadership. Teachers must be allowed as well as encouraged to use their imaginations to design curriculum including authentic assessments and create lessons that are relevant and actively engage students.

After a long pause and supportive applause, several more questions and answers brought final closure to the forum.

Authentic assessments, where students are evaluated on their performance of real-world tasks, received a positive response to a twenty-first-century education question at the Cherokee County Board of Education candidate forum.

Source: C. Reinold, "Candidates Sound Off—Where They Stand on Overcrowding, the Gifted," *The Atlanta-Journal Constitution,* October 28, 2004.

High-stakes testing has been more concerned with sensationalizing test results to beacon the existence of exemplary schools and deplore the existence of schools with lower test scores, labeling them as "failing." Today's obsession with testing has gone berserk.

For today's schools to be successful, meaningful, and potent, student assessment will need to keep up with the times. The diversified skills and knowledge needed for twenty-first-century success needs to be a driving force for educational assessments. *Authentic assessment* is known generally today as the form of assessment in which students are asked to perform real-world tasks that demonstrate meaningful application of essential knowledge and skills. Authentic assessments need to be based on the following criteria (Karoly, 1996; National Schools Network, 1997; Sloan, 1996):

- *Key 1: Assess what is important.* If educational leaders have prioritized topics such as character education, the ability to work cooperatively, community service, or math principles needed in engineering, then the assessments used to appraise student learning of these priorities should be aligned. Paper-and-pencil tests in which students bubble in their responses do not adequately nor proficiently determine mastery of content. The fundamental argument here is if what we want students to learn is true to life, so must the assessments be true to life for the same reasons.

- *Key 2: Assess what schools teach.* Extending Key 1, educational leaders of the twenty-first century need to engage in designing assessments that measure more validly what schools try to teach. Rote memorization for a standardized assessment will have short-term gains at best. As to the preparation for these standardized or state-mandated tests, the "drill and kill" and "sit and get" from the "sage always on the stage" following direct and highly scripted instruction needed for high-stakes testing won't survive the twenty-first century.

- *Key 3: Assessments should not be trivial pursuits.* What counts for success in school is often considered trivial, meaningless, and contrived—by students and adults alike—particularly when this means the forfeiture of learning critical thinking skills. Lifelong skills are not measured by standardized and state tests. Assessments today must promote students' understanding of the learning process, will result in students knowing how to think, and will result in graduates being more than good test-takers.

- *Key 4: Assessments should be worthy of accomplishing meaningful achievement.* Outcomes measured by assessments will represent appropriate, meaningful, significant, and worthwhile forms of human accomplishment. Anything less will continue to limit and undermine a quest for knowledge, a quality education, and a worthwhile learning journey.

- *Key 5: Assessment should be authentic.* Authentic assessment requires students to demonstrate specific skills and competencies by engaging in a complex performance, creating a significant product, or accomplishing a complex task using higher-order thinking, problem solving, and often creativity. Such accomplishments prepare students for their futures by presenting relevance and meaning to learning.

- *Key 6: Assessments should be contextual.* Authentic assessments need to be based on the knowledge and processes learned and practiced in the context of thematic curriculum. This assessment allows students to develop a sense of competence and pride in their work.

Essentials of Authentic Assessment

So how do today's educational leaders determine quality authentic assessments? Furthermore, what guidance should educational leaders as instructional leaders provide for those they lead in developing authentic assessment? Research (Cumming & Maxwell, 1999; Freeman & Lewis, 1998) reveals there are five key essentials to twenty-first-century authentic assessment that need to be part and parcel of high-quality authentic assessments.

- *Key 1: Knowledge, skills and dispositions are embraced.* Authentic assessments are aligned to the knowledge, skills, and dispositions desired by educational leaders and measured in terms of student mastery. Furthermore, students need to demonstrate in their response to authentic assessment the required integration of knowledge, skills, and dispositions and provide actual artifacts of their achievement.
- *Key 2: Align content, outcomes and instructional practices.* High-quality authentic assessment constitutes a seamless alignment to the program's content, desired outcomes, and instructional practices. The point here for educational leaders is that what assessments tend to measure, students tend to learn so long as expectations are clearly stated.
- *Key 3: Provide multiple opportunities.* A single one-time assessment is inadequate. High-quality authentic assessments provide multiple opportunities for learning, practicing, and assessing the desired outcomes. Competence is the aim, not mastery of a test. As life is a matter of redoing, reworking, and revising to improve the outcome, so too do high-quality assessments need to provide multiple opportunities at demonstrating mastery.
- *Key 4: Authentic assessment includes feedback and reflection.* Authentic assessment engages the learning in highly reflective learning opportunities. Both feedback and reflection are considered by educational leaders as wonderful growth opportunities.
- *Key 5: Authentic assessment is highly contextual in nature.* Authentic assessments allow students to exhibit the desired knowledge, skills, and dispositions in differing contexts. To illustrate, the learning of a geometric equation is all well and good cognitively, but until it is applied to varying contexts, such as building a home, determining the shortest distances between locations in travel, and perhaps how to maximize the seating arrangement in an auditorium, authentic assessments will not maximize learning opportunities.

Best Practices/Current Practices

Authentic assessments and traditional assessments have quite dissimilar impacts on learning. Comparing the impacts between authentic assessments and traditional assessments provides understanding of authenticity and insight into assessment design and use. Therefore, the keys of comparison between authentic and traditional assessments are presented here.

- *Key 1: Perform a task rather than select a response.* Authentic assessments require students to be effective performers with acquired knowledge. Students are asked to demonstrate understanding by performing complex tasks. In contrast, traditional assessments tend to reveal only whether students can recognize, recall, or plug in what was learned, out of context. Students are typically given questions with one correct answer (such as "true or false" or "matching answers" tests).
- *Key 2: Provide real-life, not contrived, tasks.* Authentic assessments present students with the full array of tasks that mirror the priorities and challenges found in the best instructional activities: conducting research; writing, revising, and discussing papers; providing an engaging oral analysis of a recent political event; collaborating with others on a debate; and other true-to-life experiences. Authentic assessments are indicative of real life in which one demonstrates proficiency through one's performance. Conventional tests are usually limited to paper-and-pencil, one-answer questions. Very seldom in life does a selection of one response from four or five determine mastery of learning, as is often the case with traditional assessments.
- *Key 3: Construction and application are more important than recall and retention.* Authentic assessments attend to whether students can craft polished, thorough, and justifiable answers, performances, or products. Authentic assessment tests engage students in analysis, synthesis, and application while students create new meaning in the learning process through their construction of a project of performance from facts, ideas, and hypotheses. On the other hand, traditional assessments impact learning at lower critical thinking skill levels—recall and retention. Conventional tests typically ask students to select or write correct responses—irrespective of reasons. There is rarely an adequate opportunity to plan, revise, and substantiate responses on traditional assessments.
- *Key 4: The curriculum should be learner driven, not teacher driven.* Authentic assessments involve ill-structured challenges and roles that help students rehearse for the complex ambiguities of the game of adult and professional life. Conversely, the assessing of all students at all schools should at its very minimum measure what students have learned (Kozol, 1991). Authentic assessments such as *student inquiry* provide more student choice, multiple acceptable means to be taken to the successful culminating performance or product. Traditional assessments are more like drills, assessing static and too-often arbitrary discrete or simplistic elements of activities. Traditional assessments are carefully controlled by the creator of the tests.
- *Key 5: Direct, not indirect, evidence is best.* Authentic assessments offer more direct evidence of application and construction of knowledge than taking multiple-choice traditional tests. For example, an assessment of student mastery in playing a certain tune on the piano is best evaluated by playing the piano rather than taking a paper-and-pencil test on how to play that tune on the piano. Authentic assessments achieve validity and reliability by emphasizing and standardizing the "appropriate criteria" for assessments; traditional assessments standardize "objective items" and hence the right answer for each.

RESEARCH KEYS

To enrich your understanding of **student inquiry,** log on to www.researchnavigator.com and search Ebsco's ContentSelect.

Research Navigator.com

Beyond these keys of comparison between authentic and traditional assessments, the move to reform assessments needs to be based on the premise that assessments should primarily support the needs of learners. Thus, the secretive tests composed of proxy items and scores that have no obvious meaning or usefulness undermine teachers' ability to improve instruction and students' ability to improve their performance. In an attempt to quell their dissatisfaction with traditional testing methods, there have been numerous attempts by teachers to construct and implement authentic assessments in the shadow of high-stakes testing.

Critical Keys to Implementing Authentic Assessment

Authentic assessment and its implementation has increasingly gained acceptance (Darling-Hammond, 1994; Fullan, 1996, Kohn, 2001). Yet, this assessment is not the panacea that some may think it is. There are *critical keys to implementing authentic assessment* that educational leaders need to consider prior to delving into large-scale assessment reform.

- *Key 1:* Authentic assessments touched reformists' nerves by appealing to the need to make assessment more relevant. Yet, it is difficult to characterize authentic assessment; it seems to be defined primarily by what it is not. Authentic assessments seem to describe just about any alternative to a standardized multiple-choice test.
- *Key 2:* Authentic assessment is time and cost intensive. It requires educators to identify the essential learning competencies by grade level and discipline, and in some cases, across disciplines. These are difficult tasks. They require a consensus among educators that may be problematic.
- *Key 3:* The emphasis on authenticity gives rise to a contradiction. By advocates' definition, authenticity is learner specific. If an activity is selected because it is authentic, who is to determine its authenticity? A related problem is the difficulty inherent in making reliable judgments about different kinds of performances from different students. There has been little study of judgment reliability in authentic assessment.
- *Key 4:* Authentic assessment is a movement in process, and both its role and its relationship to standardized testing are still being defined. Part of the authentic assessment strength is the greater ease with which it can be integrated into instruction to some degree. Authentic assessments' focus on a wide range of skills and abilities may provide a basis for instructional decision making.
- *Key 5:* There is a dark side to instruction driven by assessment. Even authentic measures can create havoc, distorting curriculum and undermining professional autonomy. Evaluators of authentic assessment need to refuse to make the type of assessment an "either or" proposition and find ways to integrate a diversity of authentic assessments.
- *Key 6:* Authentic assessments provide parents and community members with directly observable products and understandable evidence concerning the students' performance. The quality of student work is more easily understood to laypersons than translations of stanines and renorming.
- *Key 7:* If properly initiated, authentic assessment should bring the students' learning out into the open where the teacher can see what is going on within the students' minds. Authentic assessments give the teacher useful data

on a daily basis. Such data may be used to suggest changes in teaching strategy or modifications to school pedagogy.

- *Key 8:* Advocates of authentic assessments connect the classroom to life beyond the school while advancing the quality of teaching in the process. The claims are enticing, but such authentic assessment reforms are limited to reforms within a school. Authentic assessments have been rarely developed by outside sources in place of standardized tests.

- *Key 9:* All too frequently, discontinuity occurs between the classroom and what students must do outside their schooling. This discontinuity provides a primary rationale for authentic assessments, but it is only one call for school reform. To provide relevance and meaning for life into learning is an arduous challenge. Making this challenge even greater, there are no silver bullets or quick fixes.

- *Key 10:* Authentic assessment practices not only give the educator a richer evaluation of student achievement but they also transform the processes of teaching and learning away from drill and recall. Authentic assessment is a conscious decision to connect real-world experiences with in-school learning and evaluation.

- *Key 11:* In order to withstand scrutiny yet maintain the virtues of authenticity, authentic assessments will need to be based on standards, provide multiple indicators of appraisal, and pass the tests of reliability and validity.

- *Key 12:* Authentic assessments neutralize some of the disadvantages that culture and language minority children must shoulder. Advocates of authentic assessment argue that this method of appraisal narrows the achievement gap, allowing all students to draw from their own life experiences in responding to the assessment.

- *Key 13:* The costs and feasibility of using authentic assessment instead of high-stakes standardized tests determining such matters as graduation and professional licensing is unknown. In addition, time and space constraints pose problems that will need to be resolved before standardized tests are replaced by authentic assessments.

In retrospect, unlike standardized testing, authentic assessments provide students with authentic texts of appropriate difficulty and a variety of types of support to meet their needs. Because teachers are focused on what they are teaching and therefore on what they want to access, the assessments are aligned with instruction and with individual students' needs. The assessment fits the child rather than trying to make the child fit the assessment.

For these reasons and others, twenty-first-century assessment must change. The diversified skills and knowledge needed for success today is a driving force of testing alternatives. Recent studies have provided insight into how students learn, and the relationship between assessment and instruction is changing the ways achievement has been appraised. Assessment strategies need to be tied to new outcomes of content. Hence, authentic assessment will gain widespread use in twenty-first-century education.

ASSESSING EMOTIONAL INTELLIGENCE

Currently, emotional intelligence is touched on in such courses as health, physical education, personal development, but across-all-curricula. Daniel Goleman, author of *Emotional Intelligence: Why It Matters More Than IQ* (1995), suggests that emotional intelligence assessments must be developed as part of an ongoing curriculum that is taught daily in our schools. Not only is this twenty-first-century curricular approach advisable, but emotional intelligence needs to be modeled by educational leaders and those they lead on a daily basis. This modeling is the most powerful form of teaching and assessing emotional intelligence both in and outside the classroom. As a guide to assessing effective emotional intelligence, Goleman (2000) suggests that a curriculum should encompass the contextual keys shown in Key Box 12.3.

KEY BOX ▸ 12.3

Keys to Building a Sound Curriculum Based on Emotional Intelligence

- *Self-awareness:* Building a vocabulary for feelings; knowing the relationship between thoughts, feelings, and actions; knowing if thought or feeling is ruling an action.
- *Decision making:* Examining actions and knowing their consequences; a self-reflective view of what goes into decisions; applying this to issues such as sex and drugs.
- *Managing feelings:* Monitoring self-talk to catch negative messages such as internal put-downs; realizing what is behind a feeling (e.g., the hurt that underlies anger).
- *Self-concept:* Establishing a firm sense of identity and feeling esteem and acceptance of oneself.
- *Optimism versus pessimism:* Recognizing that life can have setbacks but that through adversity individual strengths and self-reliance can triumph.
- *Handling stress:* Learning the value of exercise, guided imagery, and relaxation methods.
- *Communications:* Sending "I" messages instead of blame; being a good listener.
- *Group dynamics:* Cooperation; knowing when and how to lead and follow.
- *Conflict resolution:* Knowing how to fight fair with other kids, with parents, and with teachers; a win-win model for negotiating compromise.
- *Empathy:* Learning how to recognize the feelings and needs of others.

Historically, much emphasis has been put on certain aspects of intelligence, such as logical reasoning, math skills, spatial skills, understanding analogies, verbal skills, and so on. Historically, researchers were puzzled by the fact that although IQ could predict to a significant degree the academic performance and to some degree professional and personal success, there was something missing in the equation. Contemporary debate argues that IQ scores are racially biased (Fish, 2001; Goleman, 1995; Mayer & Salovey, 1993). The controversy surrounding IQ test scores as single indicators may boost interest in considering emotional intelligence as a factor of ability during the twenty-first century.

Building Achievement with Emotional Intelligence

Broadening the existing notion of intelligence so that it incorporates many significant faculties will lead to increased student achievement. The more educational leaders know about emotional intelligence, the further they will go in terms of

The Notion of Intelligent Emotion

Professional and personal successes are dependent on emotional intelligence.

Move over, IQ, a growing body of empirical discoveries reveal that emotional intelligence counts for more than innate brain power. Rather than the ability to perform well on standardized tests, emotional intelligence provides qualities like zeal, persistence, motivation, and self-control that passes real life tests.

Daniel Goleman, who made the term *emotional intelligence* well known, states that emotional intelligence accounts for eighty percent of what it takes to be as successful human being. Further disproving a single IQ factor, researcher Howard Gardner concurs with Goleman in saying that human beings have eight intelligences—linguistic, logical-mathematical, spatial, musical, bodily-kinesthetic, interpersonal, intrapersonal, and naturalist.

These concepts were further advanced by a major symposium called "Emotional Intelligence, Education at the Brain," held at the Art Institute of Chicago.

Additional twenty-first-century discoveries of emotional intelligence will provide opportunities to increase student achievement.

Source: G. Wisby, "The Notion of Intelligent Emotion," *The Chicago Sun-Times,* November 30, 1997.

student learning. The last and greatest twenty-first-century frontier will prove to be our understanding of emotional intelligence. Emotional intelligence keys to increasing twenty-first-century student achievement will increase student learning beyond former capacities:

- *Key 1: Potential for isolation by studies of brain damage, making it separable from other abilities in the functioning of the brain.* Studies have indicated that trauma to the brain's emotional circuitry and that circuitry's connections to the prefrontal areas can have significant consequences for the performance of competencies associated with emotional intelligence, such as empathy and collaboration. Yet, the abilities associated with pure intellect will remain entirely intact.

- *Key 2: An evolutionary history and evolutionary plausibility.* The limbic structures in the brain that govern emotion integrate with neocortical structures, particularly the prefrontal areas, in producing the emotional responses that have been essential for survival throughout human evolution. The bulk of the emotional intelligence competencies appear to be held by the prefrontal limbic structures with transference through its underlying circuits.

- *Key 3: An identifiable core operation or set of operations.* A universal characteristic of emotional intelligence is a two by two core set of operations constituting the overall ability to recognize and regulate emotions in oneself and others. Realization of this phenomena leads to instructional practices implementing a two by two core set designed to increase student achievement.

- *Key 4: Susceptibility to encoding in a symbol system.* People are able to articulate their feelings and operations of the core emotional intelligence abilities. Discoveries such as this will lead to greater learning potentials, particularly when genetic intervention is commonplace.

- *Key 5: A distinct developmental history, along with a definable set of expert, or end state, performances.* Emotional skills range from the simple (recognition of being upset) to the complex (artfully calming down an upset colleague). Emotional skills tend to develop in children at specific and recognizable stages.

The *emotional intelligence* model seems to be emerging as an influential framework offering a language and structure capable of integrating a wide range of research findings, particularly in psychol-

RESEARCH KEYS

To enrich your understanding of **emotional intelligence,** log on to www.researchnavigator. com and search Ebsco's ContentSelect.

Research Navigator.c☻m

ogy. Like many positive models, emotional intelligence has implications for the ways others might tackle many problems of the day—for prevention activities in physical and mental health care and for effective interventions in schools.

Keys to Emotional Intelligence Assessments

The conditional keys to twenty-first-century widespread emotional intelligence assessments begin with a lack of precision, speaking to the crux of what is meant by emotional intelligence. Educational leaders must view the hurdles and impediments to widespread implementation of emotional intelligence assessment as found in the following conditional keys.

- *Conditional Key 1: Acceptance of emotional intelligence as a science.* There is little argument that the attributes frequently associated with emotional intelligence—frustration, tolerance, empathy, persistence, regulation of mood, optimism, and impulse control, to name a few—are all important human qualities that contribute to making good life decisions. Of course, simply because they are all socially relevant psychological phenomena does not make them a legitimate type of intelligence as perceived by many scientists. For emotional intelligence to do justice either in theories of intelligence or as established personality traits in special talents, consensual definitions of intelligence will need agreement.

- *Conditional Key 2: Need for empirical data on emotional intelligence.* Emotional intelligence currently lacks scientifically sound, objective measures, making it difficult to interpret test scores with any confidence. It is simply impossible to know the legitimate parameters of emotional intelligence without objective, reliable, and independently validated measures. The development of scientifically acceptable measures will need very serious consideration, and the process of making assessments available to faculty and staff within a school may "stop the train."

- *Conditional Key 3: IQ or EQ or both?* If one indicator is insufficient, does emotional intelligence (EI) predict success more than IQ? In one sense, this question is purely academic: In life, cognitive abilities and emotional intelligence always interplay. In another sense, the comparison of EI and IQ reveal questions as to their importance in educational programs and assessments (Bradberry & Greaves, 2005). Data establishing the relative contribution of EI and EQ to effective student performance would be both of theoretical and practical importance—for instance, providing a scientific rationale for making decisions on educational assessments.

- *Conditional Key 4: Need for longitudinal studies.* The EI concept has been articulated relatively recently, and there has not yet been time to conduct longitudinal studies designed to assess the predictive power of EI relative to IQ in distinguishing student performance and career success. Never has a time been more critical to address the needs of children when depression and related illness threaten to become major health issues for the future (Bar-On & Parker, 2000). Development of curricula, particularly assessment, in an emotional literacy program is seen as essential in the light of events occurring in schools where youth suicide, bullying, drug and alcohol abuse, isolation and alienation, increasing competitiveness, and sexual activity all speak for the need for emotional awareness and a healthy dose of optimism.

- *Conditional Key 5: Devaluation of emotional intelligence.* Interpersonal and intrapersonal emotional intelligence has been neglected and devalued in society in seeking cognitive solutions through recognition of high intellectual achievement. There is concern in the academic world that education at all levels is gearing toward developing vocational and employment opportunities for students in a competitive market while neglecting development of the whole person and instilling values of compassion for community which is the hallmark of a civilized society.

- *Conditional Key 6: Redefining "smart."* Because our culture has evolved into its present state, the cognitive process and activity has come to be valued above emotions. In reality, both are partners in the evolution of learning. Emotional intelligence focuses on emotions as another measure of intelligence, refining what it means to be smart (Merlevede & Bridoux, 2001).

In retrospect, we are well aware that success at school does not necessarily indicate future successes in life, as exemplified by people such as Albert Einstein, Winston Churchill, and Australian Dick Smith who were all "failures" at school. Extensive research now indicates that only 7 percent of leadership success is attributable to intellect and technical skill, whereas 93 percent results from other qualities that encompass emotional intelligence: trust, integrity, respect, authenticity, honesty, empathy, persistence, and optimism. Successful twenty-first-century educational leaders will greatly capitalize on emotional intelligence in increasing student achievement.

ASSESS FOR SUCCESS!

With a genuine intent to engage in early childhood assessment, authentic assessment, and emotional intelligence assessment, for many school districts the fly in the ointment seems to be federally mandated testing. No Child Left Behind has left school districts behind in trying to figure out what to do with high-stakes testing to show adequate yearly progress. Worse yet, the high-stakes testing mandated by the federal government has continued to expand to grades 3 through 8 as well as in high school, creating even wider achievement gaps. The science content standards developed and assessed by 2007–2008 will not be the end of this complex menagerie.

Around and around governmental high-stakes assessment goes! Where it will stop, we think we know. It is our belief that assessments such as those we've discussed in this chapter and implemented in Mary Michaels's classroom will be implemented during this century. Educational leaders will be able to replace high-stakes testing for what is educationally appropriate and best for children. Early childhood assessments, authentic assessments, and emotional intelligence assessments provide educationally sound and humane solutions.

THE REFLECTIVE PRACTITIONER

Welcome to your twelfth Reflective Practitioner containing your Chapter 12 Scenario based on all ISLLC Standards 1 through 6 and your reading of Chapter 12. It is intended to provoke your thoughtful reflection and to stimulate discussion among colleagues, classmates, and peers. The Reflective Practitioner provides opportunities to synthesize issues, make comparisons, and apply theory to practice. We hope it will motivate you to search for evidence, thus increasing your comprehension of the text and helping you examine your convictions and discover new and shared perspectives.

◼ ISLLC Standard 1

A school administrator is an educational leader who promotes the success of all students by facilitating the development, articulation, implementation, and stewardship of a vision of learning that is shared and supported by the school community.

◼ ISLLC Standard 2

A school administrator is an educational leader who promotes the success of all students by advocating, nurturing, and sustaining a school culture and instructional program conducive to student learning and staff professional growth.

◼ ISLLC Standard 3

A school administrator is an educational leader who promotes the success of all students by ensuring management of the organization, operations, and resources for a safe, efficient, and effective learning environment.

◼ ISLLC Standard 4

A school administrator is an educational leader who promotes the success of all students by collaborating with families and community members, responding to diverse community interests and needs, and mobilizing community resources.

◼ ISLLC Standard 5

A school administrator is an educational leader who promotes the success of all students by acting with integrity, fairness, and in an ethical manner.

◼ ISLLC Standard 6

A school administrator is an educational leader who promotes the success of all students by understanding, responding to, and influencing the larger political, social, economic, legal, and cultural context.

Scenario

A Community where parents and staff work together as partners for the development of the whole child is the vision statement of Christa McAuliffe Elementary School, a school nestled in a suburb of a large metropolitan area. With 500 students in grades pre-K through fifth grade, the faculty is committed to excellent education for all students through *developmentally appropriate practices.* The special programs at Christa McAuliffe Elementary School include Spanish instruction, a daily book swap for kids, and a program for the deaf and hard of hearing. Numerous field trips and assemblies enrich the everyday school experience.

It is a wonderful elementary school, at least so it is written in Christa McAuliffe Elementary School's faculty and student handbooks, parent newsletters, and material displayed on the school's website. Perhaps in 1993, when the school was built and faculty hired, these qualities were more than just media sound bites. Like many schools, Christa McAuliffe Elementary School left its heritage behind and joined the bandwagon of schools vying for national acclaim based on high-stakes testing. Students' positive attitudes and faculty morale eroded and parents' attendance at school functions dwindled. The excitement and adventure for learning were absent. Teachers like Mary Michaels were too few and far between.

That is why you were appointed to be principal of Christa McAuliffe Elementary School—to promote the success of students and staff through developmentally appropriate practices as exemplified by Mary Michaels in this chapter's Action Focus. Your proven leadership skills, commitment to doing what is best for all children, positive faculty and parent relations, and talents as an instructional leader led to your selection as principal. There is no question that you certainly have your work cut out for you. You have the requisite skills and talents to succeed! Your journey begins by answering the following questions.

QUESTIONS FOR REFLECTIVE THINKING

1. Based on your understanding of learning, teaching, and larger educational issues, how would you characterize the broader challenges faced by Christa McAuliffe Elementary School?
2. Describe the specific actions you would take to implement assessments that are in the best interests of elementary schoolchildren.
3. Outline the strategies you would implement to restore the school to a place where parents and staff work together as partners for the development of the whole child.
4. The Christa McAuliffe Elementary School Parent-Teacher-Student Organization has asked you to share your philosophy on assessments. As there is no time like the present, write your philosophy of assessment to be presented to your parent group. Include the assessments contained in Chapter 12 and other assessments based on your own experience.

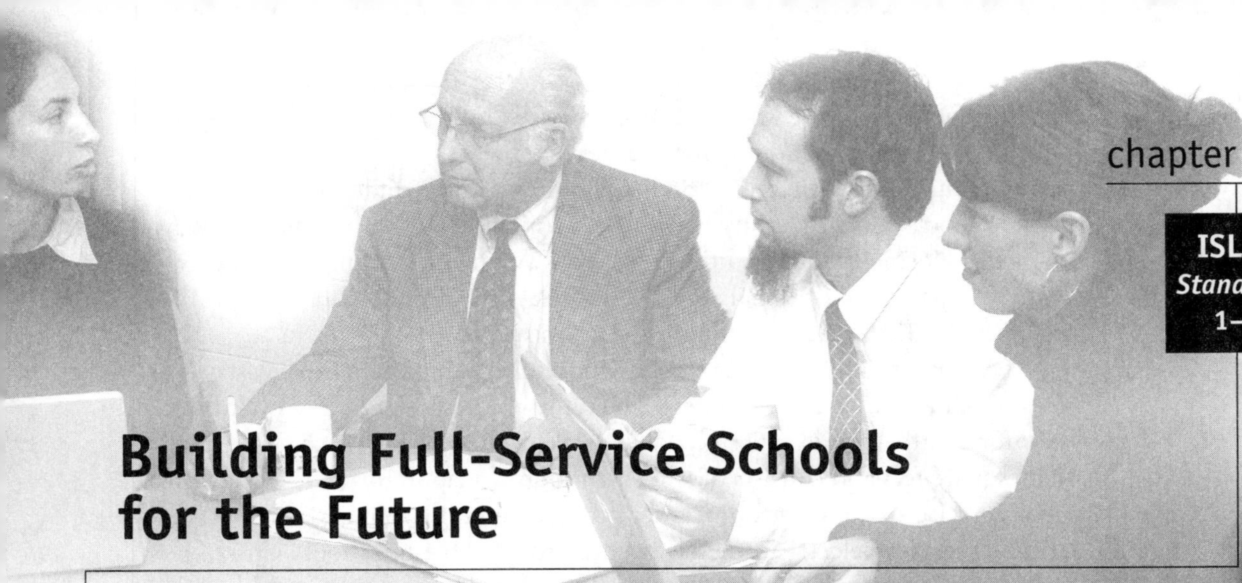

chapter 13

ISLLC *Standards* 1–6

Building Full-Service Schools for the Future

Man's mind, once stretched by a new idea, never regains its original dimensions.

—Oliver Wendell Holmes

Your Chapter 13 Action Focus paves the path to your understanding of twenty-first-century, full-service schools. To begin our studies, we travel to the Wayne County Public Schools in North Carolina to view how this school district improves adolescent health. In an initiative that began in 1979, the Wayne Initiative for School Health (WISH) has improved health-care accessibility in the rural, economically depressed county by setting up medical centers in four county middle schools. With grants from such organizations as the Duke Endowment and the Robert Wood Johnson Foundation, local and federal funding and local in-kind contributions, WISH school-based health centers are devoting attention daily to well-child care, acute and chronic health problems, and psychological issues.

The idea for WISH began taking shape in 1996 when the local hospital chief executive officer and a local pediatrician, with a vision for school-based health care, established a planning team consisting of community group leaders. State statistics showed that Wayne County ranked ninth out of 100 counties in North Carolina in the largest number of uninsured children. Children from birth to age 6 received medical care on a regular basis, but, according to state data, the early adolescent group received little to no health-care services.

With that information in hand, the planning team aimed to improve the physical and mental well-being of middle school students by increasing access to comprehensive health care in certain communities. Areas to be targeted would be those with high levels of ethnic minorities and poverty, those with uninsured children, and those where access to health care was hindered. The four schools selected to house centers were strategically located within the county.

Parental surveys helped determine adolescent health priorities. The top three needs were deemed to be basic health care, teen pregnancy prevention, and mental health issues. Eighty-two percent of respondents said it was difficult to obtain health care for their families because of the high cost of medical services and insurance, other financial issues, lengthy waiting periods to receive services, and the inability to leave work to get health care for their children. Many said they were unsuccessful in obtaining medical services.

Organizations represented on the planning team included Wayne County Public Schools, Wayne County Health Department, Goldsboro Pediatrics, Wayne Memorial Hospital, Communities In Schools, Wayne Community College, Wayne County Department of Social Services, and Wayne County Mental Health. They established WISH as a 501c3 nonprofit organization.

Leaders of Wayne County Public Schools were among the strongest advocates of school-based health centers. The centers were designed and built through the efforts of the school superintendent and a dedicated staff. Each center is about 1,000 square feet and consists of two exam rooms, a laboratory, a reception area, medical office space, a restroom, and a group counseling room. Maintenance, custodial services, electricity, and water are provided by the school district.

A school board member is on the WISH board of directors, and an additional central office staff member also meets with the board. The community partner organizations provide most of the staffing for the centers, including a registered nurse who is the clinical director, health educators, nutritionists, and mental health counselors. The county government has provided significant annual financial support for the program.

Successful endeavors documented at the centers include:

- A 75 percent decrease in teen pregnancies
- Improved performance on required standardized tests
- A 4 percent improvement in school attendance
- A dramatic decrease in emergency room visits by adolescents
- Enrollment in the WISH centers of 85 percent of the student body at each school

The WISH board of directors believes Wayne County's experience should be widely replicated.

Wayne County Public Schools received the distinguished 2005 National Civic Star Award in San Antonio at the AASA National Conference on February 19, 2005. Superintendent Steven Taylor affirmed, "The WISH initiative is a true collaborative effort among private and public entities and agencies in Wayne County doing what is good and right for children. The end result has been a healthier child, one better prepared to learn and individual specific health needs of our students being met in a positive and effective nontraditional approach. Our goal for the future is to further expand and enhance this program."

And WISH did expand! The first Wayne County high school, Goldsboro High School, opened its doors to WISH. Care for chronic conditions has reduced absences by 5 percent and reduced the number of emergency room visits. Close to 2,000 students a year are served by WISH. Acute health needs such as minor injuries are handled routinely. Students are also seen for chronic health needs, mental health services, and health education. No student is ever turned away for inability to pay.

Wayne County Public Schools (WCPS) is the nineteenth largest school system in North Carolina, serving more than 19,300 students. Located in eastern

North Carolina, WCPS has more than 2,500 employees in 31 schools. It educates all children by providing a stimulating learning environment ensuring they are lifelong learners who are self-sufficient, productive citizens. WISH has proven to be a school–community partnership that works. Wayne County Public Schools is a shining star example of what a full-service school is all about.

As demonstrated in this Action Focus, a full-service school, such as the award-winning schools in Wayne County Public Schools, is a center for care of the emotional, social, physical, and academic needs of students, parents, and community members. Services that are provided at a full-service school are rendered from the combined and coordinated efforts of educators, doctors, dentists, psychologists, and other skilled professionals.

KEYS TO FULL-SERVICE SCHOOLS

Offering services on school grounds alleviates many of the problems that interfere with families obtaining assistance for their children (Blackorby, Newman, & Finnegan, 1998; Dryfoos, 2002), such as no transportation, lack of understanding of public health and social service systems, inability to take time away from work, and lack of health insurance. The services offered by full-service schools may be numerous and diversified, as presented in the four service keys to twenty-first-century full-service schools.

- *Service Key 1: Preventive services.* Full-service schools provide preventive services for students, parents, and community members. These services may vary from center to center, depending on the needs of those served. Preventive services of twenty-first-century schools are presented in Key Box 13.1 (Adelman & Taylor, 2004; Nabors, Leff, & Power, 2004).

KEY BOX 13.1

Preventive Services for Students, Parents, and Community Members Provided by Full-Service Schools

- Adult education
- Immunizations
- Family planning
- After-school care
- Social services to access basic living resources
- Economic services/Job placement
- Quality early childhood education
- Mental/physical health screening
- Drug and alcohol prevention
- Dropout prevention
- School meal programs
- Child care

- *Service Key 2: Early intervention services.* Early intervention is critical to health and wellness during the later years of development into adulthood (Hanson & Autin, 2003). It is a far smaller price for society to send an individual to Penn State than to the "State Pen." Hence, full-service schools often provide the early intervention services shown in Key Box 13.2.

> ### KEY BOX ▶ 13.2
>
> Services Provided by Full-Service Schools
>
> - Guidance and counseling
> - Tutoring
> - Public health care
> - Conflict resolution
> - Child abuse education
> - Juvenile alternative services
> - Latchkey services
> - Mental health counseling

- *Service Key 3: Intensive treatments for chronic disabilities.* Full-service schools provide treatment for those with chronic disabilities. Often, through private practice these services are expensive and beyond the affordability of lower socioeconomic status families. Full-service schools with coordinated efforts of health-care providers offer treatments for chronic conditions such as those presented in Key Box 13.3 (Brown & Bobrow, 2004).

> ### KEY BOX ▶ 13.3
>
> Services Provided by Full-Service Schools in Treatment of Chronic Conditions
>
> - Special education services
> - Related services
> - Emergency, crisis treatment
> - Case management

- *Service Key 4: Additional support services provided.* The services provided at full-service schools will vary in accordance with needs. Full-service schools in high population urban areas will not only vary in needed services (compared to a rural area) but will also vary in the manner in which these services are provided, especially when considering language barriers, cultural uniqueness, and the like (Barrett & Ollendick, 2004; Bruns, Walrath, Glass-Siegel & Weist, 2004). All in all, however, additional support services provided by full-service schools will be based on need (see Key Box 13.4).

Additional Support Services Provided by Full-Service Schools

- Comprehensive health screening and services
- Dental services
- Family planning
- Individual counseling
- Substance abuse treatment
- Mental health services
- Nutrition/Weight management
- Referral with follow-up
- Basic services: Housing, food, clothes
- Mentoring
- Family welfare services
- Parent education, literacy
- Employment training/Jobs
- Case management
- Crisis intervention
- Neighborhood Watch crime prevention

The potential of full-service schools for students, parents, and community members will become greater in this century. School districts such as Wayne County Public Schools will continue to provide for the general welfare of those who reside within its district's boundaries (*Boston Excels Full Service Schools*, 2000). In turn, Wayne County Public Schools and other twenty-first-century school districts will gain the respect and appreciation of students, parents, community members, and all service providers. It does take a whole village to raise a child, but the whole village is most effective and efficient when it is coordinated, unified, and teamed for action.

KEYS TO FORMING FULL-SERVICE SCHOOLS

We believe that full-service schools will increase during

IN THE NEWS

Proponents of Community Schools Argue for Wider View of Education

The following Chicago model and other school and community partnerships throughout the nation provide valuable prototypes for today's educational leaders.

Educators, community leaders, and parents gathered in Chicago to promote stronger partnerships between schools and community-based groups as a powerful way to expand traditional paradigms as to how schools should operate.

The Coalition for Community Schools, a Washington-based organization that represents more than 100 state and national partners, hosted the national conference March 9–11, 2005. Community schools work with local organizations and social service providers to offer after-school programs,

health services, counseling, and continuing education classes.

More than 900 participants from across the nation—and several groups of international visitors from Quebec, the Netherlands, and Japan—filled seminars on *full service schools*, school-based health clinics, visited schools in Chicago that are working with community organizations, and heard researchers tout the academic and social benefits of having schools and communities share space and services.

To form successful full-service schools, school–community partnerships are essential.

Source: A. Duncan, "Proponents of Community Schools Argue for Wider View of Education," *Education Week,* March 23, 2005.

this century for many reasons. Education is in need of a silver bullet of school reform. There is no more powerful way of restoring respect and appreciation for the educational enterprise than to serve others, and this service includes the holistic needs (emotional, social, physical, as well as academic needs) of individuals (Chatterji, Caffray, Crowe, Freeman, & Jensen, 2004). More than just another passing curricular effort, twenty-first-century schools that respect and serve the needs of others will in turn gain respect from others.

Educational leaders who are considering forming a full-service school need to establish a clear vision and purpose for a successful one-stop service center. First, a needs assessment should be conducted regarding how students, parents, and community members might be greatly benefited (Bruner, Bell, Brindis, Chang, & Scarbrough, 1993). Whether the needs are determined to be adult education or comprehensive health services or violence prevention programs, the success of a full-service school is dependent on the needed services it provides. Second, setting goals for each of the identified needs is vital to the success of full-service schools. To illustrate, feasible needs and goals of full-service schools are presented in Key Box 13.5 (Hunter et al., 2005).

KEY BOX ▸ 13.5

Goals of Full-Service Schools

- *Adult education and parenting programs* that increase all participants' ability to assist in their children's education and improve their own status in the workforce.
- *After-school and weekend programs* that provide students with ample opportunities for tutoring and homework assistance as well as enrichment studies.
- *Family support programs* that strengthen family relationships by providing skill building and family counseling.
- *Comprehensive health services,* including school-based health promotion, prevention, and intervention services and programs.
- *Mental health programs* in schools that help students overcome challenges to learning.
- *Pregnancy prevention programs* to reduce teenage pregnancies.
- *Student support programs* that provide effective school-funded services and supplement them with resources from the community.
- *Substance abuse prevention programs* that prevent alcohol, tobacco, and other drug use.
- *Violence prevention programs* that reduce violence, bullying, and other disruptions, while building skills for conflict management.
- *Youth development programs* that build students' skills and abilities so they become productive and contributing members of society.

Millions of educational leaders with interest in forming full-service schools will be pursuing this vision in every state in the country, serving urban, rural, and suburban communities (Evans, Axelrod, & Langberg, 2004). And an even larger number of educational leaders will have parts of this vision in place. They will continue to involve just about every sector of the community: school districts, teachers unions, parks and recreation departments, child- and family-services agencies, Boys and Girls Clubs, local United Ways, YMCAs, Girl and Boy Scout chapters, small and large businesses, museums and zoos, hospitals and health clinics, and more. In some communities, even the forest service and police and fire departments will be involved.

Keys to Full-Service Educational Reform

Some of the better-known programs will be national in scope, but the true hallmark of this movement will be the diversity of the approaches. Full-service schools will be much more likely to be home grown, built on local needs and expertise and drawing on national experience.

In the vision of community schools, educational leaders and those they lead will be major partners but not always in the lead role. A capable partner organization—a child- and family-services agency, for example, or a youth-development organization, a college, or a family-support center—will serve as the linchpin for the community school, mobilizing and integrating the resources of the community so that educational leaders and those they lead can focus on teaching and learning (Dryfoos, 1994; Hanson & Austin, 2003). In some communities, schools themselves will be best equipped to provide the necessary leadership and coordination.

A full-service school will not be just another program being imposed on a school. It will be a way of thinking and acting that recognizes the central role of schools in communities—and the power of working together for a common good. Educating children and also strengthening families and communities, so that they in turn will help make schools even stronger and children more successful, will fortify full-service schools for the twenty-first century.

Keys to Health Care

Education has been perceived by many as the foundation of democracy. When those living in a democracy have had needs, education has responded affirmatively. Student health needs during the twenty-first century will, more than ever, include social, emotional, physical, and academic needs. It is only right for educational leaders to respond once again (Nabors, Leff, & Power, 2004). Specifically, the need for health care is quite evident and will get more important as the century progresses.

RESEARCH KEYS

To enrich your understanding of **student health,** log on to www.researchnavigator.com and search Ebsco's ContentSelect.

Research Navigator.com

Just imagine that your child risked dying from an allergic reaction to a hornet's sting because you couldn't afford the doctor visits and medicines that could prevent a life-threatening reaction. What if you had to choose between losing your only car and paying up front for your spouse's psychological testing? What if you ended your cancer treatments because you were afraid that your staggering bills would create devastating financial hardship for your family? Our nation's failure to provide Americans with affordable health care has made such heart-breaking choices commonplace. Millions of Americans face insurmountable financial burdens when serious illness strikes. And the worse news is that it is going to get worse.

The widening twenty-first-century health divide will be comprised of the "haves" and the "have nots" when it comes to health insurance. Approximately 53 million Americans lacking health insurance will face these hardships during

2007 (U.S. Census Bureau, 2003). And those numbers tell only part of the story. Millions more Americans are uninsured for short time periods or have skimpy coverage with low benefit limits or high deductibles. Lifetime benefit limits of $1 million or less are quickly exhausted when catastrophic illness or injury occurs.

Lacking health-care benefits harms individuals and families. Minority-group members, young adults, and people with modest incomes are much more likely to be uninsured than others. The lack of insurance often means people simply do not get care for serious medical conditions (Blackorby, Newman, & Finnegan, 1997). To fully understand the magnitude of the health-care crisis, educational leaders need to consider the following key impacts:

- Uninsured children in the United States face a higher risk of developmental delays than those with health coverage.
- Uninsured women with breast cancer, for example, are 30 to 50 percent more likely to die from it than are insured women.
- The uninsured are more likely to seek care in health clinics and the emergency room than those with insurance.
- The uninsured are more likely than the insured to put off seeking care, to not receive care when needed, and to not fill a prescription or get a recommended treatment because of the expense.
- The uninsured are more likely than the insured to have problems paying their medical bills, change their way of life significantly to pay for medical bills, or be rendered homeless.
- The uninsured are more likely to be hospitalized for a preventable condition than the insured.
- Uninsured adults who have been hospitalized for heart attacks are more likely to die while in the hospital than privately insured adults. The uninsured are just as likely to improve blood flow to their hearts in the acute stages of their heart attacks, but they are less likely to undergo further costly diagnostic and therapeutic interventions.
- Uninsured adults hospitalized for a traumatic injury are more than twice as likely to die in the hospital as insured adults—even after controlling for the severity of the injury.

The impact of a crisis in health care for Americans not only affects those without adequate medical care. Those who may have adequate medical care, as determined by insurance and personal wealth, feel the impact of a nation at health risk. Educational leaders need also to be aware of the adverse impact cast on those with adequate health care, as presented in the following impact keys (American Academy of Pediatrics, 2004; Evans & Weist, 2004).

- The cost of medical care for uninsured Americans in 2007 is projected to be over $100 billion.
- The United States spends billions of dollars per year to provide uninsured residents with medical care, often for preventable diseases or diseases that physicians could treat more efficiently with earlier diagnosis.
- Americans who lack health insurance cost the United States between $65 billion and $130 billion per year in lost productivity.

- The cost of state health-care programs fall disproportionately on the local communities where care is provided.
- High rates of uninsured residents can affect the financial viability of providers in local communities and can result in reduced access to medical care.

Although politicians will continue to strive for health-care relief, proposals before Congress will only close little gaps in the health-care void. There is a lack of unified vision and leadership when it comes to forging a comprehensive solution to make health care affordable for everyone (Institute of Medicine, 2003). Congressional budgets have only slightly reduced the number of uninsured—barely one-tenth of what economists say is needed to make sure that everyone is covered. What do we do?

This is not a new debate. In February of 1939, the first call was made for extending health-care coverage to all Americans. It was believed then that health-care coverage needed to be extended to all. Today, almost 70 years later, millions of Americans believe the same need exists. The only question is how should a sensible and humane health program be accomplished?

The time is ripe for a robust national reform on health benefits for all Americans. As more Americans are added to the uninsured, and as even those who have insurance find gaps in coverage that impose financial burdens, it is hard to imagine an issue that could be more pressing to so many Americans and their families. It is time for education to step up to the plate in forming full-service centers!

IN THE NEWS

A Washington Roundup: Wide School Role Urged

The twenty-first century will be the time that full-service schools increase if two elected officials can help it.

Two Democrats in Congress have introduced legislation to support full-service community schools. The measure, offered by Representative Steny Hoyer of Maryland and Senator Ben Nelson of Nebraska, would authorize $200 million to help public schools function as such schools, which coordinate educational and social-service programs for communities.

Successful twenty-first-century educational leaders should know the keys to large-scale full-service schools.

Source: E. W. Robelen, "News in Brief: A Washington Roundup. Wide School Role Urged," *Education Week*, May 18, 2005.

Keys to Large-Scale Full-Service Schools

Although examples of successful full-service school services exist in part in a few schools throughout the United States, we believe large-scale full-service schools will occur during this century. Currently, the partial full-service schools serve only a minuscule fraction of the 48 million schoolchildren (Dryfoos, 2002). In order for large-scale school reform to occur, the keys to large scale full-service schools as presented in Key Box 13.6 will need to ensue.

KEY BOX 13.6

Keys to Building Large Scale Full-Service Schools

- Develop deeper and more focused partnerships extending and strengthening communities and school districts across the country.

- Create more intentional linkages between community resources, including after-school activities and the school-day program.
- Change the mind-set of policymakers and professionals in different fields about the interwoven relationships of school, community, and health care.
- Develop state policies and funding that promote full-service schools.

The widespread adoption of this profoundly important approach to learning will happen only if educational leaders, together with business and political leaders, parents and families, and those who work with children and families every day, think carefully about what it takes for all of our children to succeed. The goal is not to heap additional responsibilities onto already burdened educators. The aim is for schools and communities working together to find creative ways for the communities, with so many assets, to share the responsibility (Bond & Keys, 1993; Fox, Leone, Rubin, Oppenheim, Miller, & Freidman, 1999). In that way, schools will no longer be isolated, and entire communities can be engaged in the most vital work of a vibrant democracy: the full care of all its children.

KEYS TO SCHOOL–COMMUNITY COLLABORATIONS

To the degree that full-scale schools will be successful will be the amount of success schools experience in forming collaborations. Schools have formed collaborations across the United States with their students' families and communities to support school improvement efforts and student achievement. Schools have been linked with a variety of community partners for recreation, presentations, fairs, and other activities. The ten major categories of school–community collaborations are presented in Key Box 13.7 (Adelman & Taylor, 2004).

KEY BOX 13.7

Ten Major School Collaborations for the Twenty-First Century

- Businesses and corporations
- Universities and educational institutions
- Government and military agencies
- Health-care individuals and organizations
- Senior citizen individuals and organizations
- Faith individuals and organizations
- National service and volunteer organizations
- Cultural and recreational institutions
- Community-based organizations
- Individuals in the community

Keys to Implementing Collaborative Partnerships

For interpersonal–collaborative partnerships to be successful, professionals serving the same people and communities will need to communicate better, coordinate their efforts, and cooperate effectively (Barrett & Ollendick, 2004; Stone, 1995). From this perspective, the idea of interpersonal–collaborative partnerships may be introduced simply and clearly. Every professional working with the same child, adult, and family will need to be engaged in cooperative and synchronized efforts.

In addition, there are seven interrelated keys to effective collaborative partnerships: interdependence, conditional equality, unity of purpose, shared responsibility for results, enlightened self-interest, reciprocity, and generativity. Each key needs a closer examination by educational leaders who are voyaging to the formation of full-scale schools. Closer scrutiny follows (Chatterji et al., 2004; Hunter et al., 2005).

- *Key 1: Interdependence.* The first key to implementing collaborative partnerships is interdependence, which is manifested in two ways. First, children's well-being will depend on their peer relations and networks, families, and community systems. Second, human needs and problems should not be neatly isolated from one another, as human needs and problems often nest in each other (e.g., domestic violence is often a condition of substance abuse).

These interdependent, co-occurring essentials will be especially challenging to the system of professions. Challenges make it difficult, if not impossible, to effectively address one need unless the others also are addressed. As a result, collaborative relationships depend on each other. That is, any one person (and his or her organization) will not likely achieve established goals and meet accountability requirements without the assistance and support of other individuals (and possibly their organizations). To put it another way, when humans depend on their peer networks, families, and community systems, and when human needs and problems co-occur and nest in each other, the specialized professions and all other stakeholders need to be interdependent (Chynoweth, 1994; Senge, 1990a). Each will require the other for students' health, well-being, and education.

- *Key 2: Conditional Equality.* The second key to effective collaborative partnerships will be conditional equality. Power, authority, and expertise will need to be shared, and democratic relationships formed, if schools of the twenty-first century are to prosper. Mindful of their equality, everyone, including individuals and families seeking service, must know that they are either part of the problem or part of the solution.

- *Key 3: Unity of Purpose.* The third key, unity of purpose, will need to be grounded in an understanding of the value of relationships—simply put, "working together, works!" When individuals come together under the schoolhouse roof, they will need to communicate more effectively, improve their working relationships, and develop unity of purpose. They will be able to coordinate their efforts, sharing the same forms and information systems and addressing confidentiality issues together.

On the other hand, unity of purpose does not mean that individuals will deny or sacrifice their special expertise. To the contrary, needs and problems will be assigned to them based on their special expertise. The most appropriate professional (the one whose specialization corresponds to the need) will need to be assigned lead responsibility for addressing a risk factor, or for meeting a need, if interpersonal–collaborative partnerships are to benefit children maximally.

• *Key 4: Shared Responsibility for Results.* To achieve unity of purpose, all individuals joined by interpersonal–collaborative partnerships will need to assume shared responsibility for results. This focus on the shared responsibility of results should include related activities such as progress charting, learning and improvement systems designs, and barrier busting. This results orientation, framed by unity of purpose, will guide data gathering and the development of data systems, including practitioners' action research methods.

With unity of purpose and a focus on results, learning and improvement, through data and data systems, may be facilitated in the twenty-first century. Everyone will be more likely to know what data are important; why they are important; how, when, where, and why to collect data; and how to use these data in support of strategic improvements, learning, and capacity building. They will come to know that these activities are in their best interests, as well as in the interests of those they serve.

• *Key 5: Enlightened Self-Interest.* The key to forming collaborative partnerships will be the enlightening of self-interest. At first this concept may seem contradictory because many conversations about collaboration convey the impression that everyone should put aside their specialized needs and interests. In actuality, only when all participants believe that interpersonal–collaborative partnerships will improve their jobs and lead to improved results will partnerships be enhanced (Senge, 1990). So, when professionals acknowledge their interdependence and agree to collaborate to improve results, they will be enlightened because they know that, by joining forces, they will gain "the collaborative advantage."

• *Key 6: Reciprocity.* The sixth key to forming collaborative partnerships is reciprocity. When professionals collaborate to achieve goals with enlightened self-interest, they will be more willing to give and share as well as to receive. Reciprocity will imply mutuality, and mutuality will mean developing common grounds for working together. Reciprocity also suggests an exchange system built on these common grounds. In this sense, effective collaborative partnerships will include reciprocal exchange relationships where give and take actions enable one another to achieve.

• *Key 7: Generativity.* True collaborative partnerships will generate creative, innovative approaches to the theory of the problem and to intervention and improvement strategies. These partnerships will generate learning, development, and systems change in relation to professional and organizational boundaries and boundary relationships. Last, but not least, when collaborative partnerships become communities of practice, they will generate affective commitments and identity empowerment. Effective and appropriate collaboration will change people's lives, not just their jobs.

In addition to the seven keys to forming collaborative partnerships, our experience in this area has taught us that the conditions presented in Key Box 13.8 will enhance effectiveness of twenty-first-century relationships and improved outcomes.

Enhancements for Building Collaborative Partnerships

- Reasonable people will listen, learn, compromise, adjust, and adapt.
- Effective collaborative leaders and facilitators will cross professional, community, and organizational boundaries to build relationships and serve those in need.
- Effective leaders engaged in collaborative partnerships will prevent applications of blame and maltreatment dynamics while improving the quality of mutual treatment and interaction.
- Special settings (places and environments) that support joint performances, learning, and development will need preparation and implementation by collaborative partners.
- Supportive organizational climates and structures will need to be encouraged by all partners engaged in collaboration.
- Organizational incentives, rewards, supports, and resources for joint work and ventures will be presented by collaborative leaders.
- Communicative and linkage mechanisms such as e-mail and conference calls will be used to support various shared initiatives.

Golden Keys to School Collaborative Partnerships

Despite increasing interest to schools to form collaborative partnerships by necessity, the road will not be well paved, as this means a departure from past traditions. Today's schools will need to come to the realization that collaborative partnerships do not automatically form (Ellis & Hughes, 2002). In fact, there may be impediments to forming these much needed collaborative partnerships. For example, a large, highly challenged, low-performing urban school with a high teenage pregnancy rate will stress the importance of mutual awareness and understanding in collaborative partnerships.

A school paradigm, as old as industrial America, will be broken during this century. Schools will come to the realization that their strength is found in the services they provide for students, parents, and community members, not as an exclusive academic island unto themselves. For educational systems to survive the twenty-first century, the school as a stand-alone institution in which educators do it all alone will become extinct—without exception. United schools will stand; divided (or nonpartnered) schools will fall short in taking care of their students, parents, and community members (their stakeholders). Educational leaders must know that if they elect not to take care of their stakeholders, then other educational leaders, in other school systems, will welcome the opportunity.

Multiple forms of collaboration will be promoted. Collaborative partnerships will be part of the planning frame but they will not stand alone. Family-centered collaboration, interorganizational collaboration, and broad-based community collaboration may add to the complexities of how educational leaders are to best form meaningful relationships (Fox, 2005).

Collaborative partnerships will share a simple yet compelling logic that school improvement and renewal processes will not accomplish full potentials until the family and community contexts for children's learning and health and wellness development are addressed simultaneously (Hiatt-Michael, 2001). In other words, today's schools will need to start the factors and forces known to influence and determine children's learning such as healthy development, academic achievement, and success in school and then ask how professionals, parents, and other diverse stakeholders in school communities can work collaboratively to address them. This work will entail institutional change involving schools in building expanded collaborative partnerships.

The dominant institutional definition of schooling will radically change during the twenty-first century. The American public school, as a stand-alone organization, will open its schoolhouse doors and embrace collaborative partnerships. Schools of the future will be designed for children and youth to enable their learning and academic achievement. Educators will join ranks collaboratively in sharing responsibility for this learning and academic achievement, and accountability will become a shared proposition. In this institutional definition, educators and their colleagues teamed collaboratively at school will focus on children's health, wellness, and academic achievement, and educators will be expected to act together with others.

TRANSFORMATIONAL KEYS FOR TWENTY-FIRST-CENTURY SCHOOLS

Collaborative partnerships will be needed because no one educational leader will achieve his or her goals maximally and meet accountabilities efficiently without the collaborative support of others. Professions and organizations will therefore collaborate out of practical necessity while reflecting their self-interest (Edyburn, Higgins, & Boone, 2005). As they develop common grounds, especially unity of purpose, they will also develop norms and procedures for reciprocity. For example, the school is well served when collaborative partners prepare children and youth to come to school ready and able to learn. In turn, collaborative partners will be supported and reinforced when children and youth succeed in school. Each system improves and gets stronger because of its new boundary relationships and exchanges.

In fact, the case will be made that the most important school-related, peer-related, family-related, and community-related factors for improved academic achievement, learning, and success in school will be the very same factors that predict success in the child welfare, juvenile justice, mental health, health, and employment sectors. The keys to educational improvement and renewal, then, will be the keys to improvements and renewal in other child and family-serving systems. By addressing school-related needs, other systems' needs also will be addressed (Dryfoos, 2002; Hanson & Austin, 2003). Needs analysis will serve as the cornerstone of collaborative partnerships, results-orientation for collaboration, and persistence on making certain that connections with and at schools are strategic ones.

Collaborative partnerships are so simple and basic in one sense, yet building these partnerships will be incredibly difficult because it will require new job descriptions and orientations, along with supportive organizational structures, cultures, and accountability requirements. Unfortunately, few professionals and community leaders will be prepared for this kind of boundary-spanning and -crossing work. Whatever their name—school–family–community coordinators, facilitators, resource coordinators, family advocates, community–school coordinators, or more plainly social workers, counselors, and special educators—their functions will be much the same. They will help orchestrate diverse people and they will help structure school community settings for collaboration. Proponents of collaborative partnerships enable educational reform and renewal because they support principals, teachers, and parents to engage in shared problem solving.

Educational leaders' roles and responsibilities will need to change, too. For example, educational leaders will learn to detect risks and needs, work with referral agents and systems, and partner with service providers and parents (Cunningham & Cordeiro, 2003). The firm dividing line between pedagogy and service integration will dissolve, and so will the ethnic and cultural lines that divide a growing number of children and families from educational leaders and those they lead.

IN THE NEWS

Students Shadow Area Doctors—Troy High Advanced Placement Teenagers See Medical Careers from Physician's View

The collaborative partnership between Troy High School and Henry Ford Hospital has provided valuable gains for all.

Troy High School advanced placement biology students are encouraged to complete a letter of application expressing their desire to participate in a partnership program between their high school and the doctors at Henry Ford Medical Hospital. The program was first initiated five years ago with doctors at the West Bloomfield clinic for high school students at West Bloomfield High School. Troy High School is the second school to get on board starting during the 2005 school year.

The collaborative school–hospital partnership allows students to gain valuable insights into what doctors may encounter on a day-to-day basis. From interactions with patients to working with other physicians, students are privy to seeing a doctor's work close up. This partnership has resulted in a win-win gain for students and the medical profession as many of the high school students enrolled in pre-med programs.

Developing collaborative programs like the Troy High School and Henry Ford Hospital partnership will escalate during this century.

Source: J. Sugameli, "Students Shadow Area Doctors—Troy High Advance Placement Teenagers See Medical Careers from Physician's View," *The Detroit News,* May 16, 2005.

Transformational Keys to Collaborative Partnerships

Educational leaders' roles and responsibilities will change as they and their schools accept new challenges. Although collaborative partnerships have not traditionally fit into the industrial models of top-down leadership, educational leaders of the twenty-first century will need to form effective relationships with all stakeholders. Failure to form collaborative partnerships will motivate parents to withdraw their children from closed-door schools, and choose a school with rich collaborative partnerships while taking the state per-pupil funding with them. All educational leaders will need to form these partnerships with others or watch others depart as increasing numbers of schools will be providing for their children's health, education and wellness. Of particular interest to all educational leaders, we believe that forming effective collaborative partnerships will depend on the following transformational keys.

- *Transformational Key 1: Facilities challenges.* Although some school facilities will be conducive to building collaborative partnerships, in most, educational leaders will have to work within the confines of existing school facilities. Educational leaders will need to find space for collaborative partnering, such as a community room, an adult resource area, or other supportive facilities. If facilities are used during the nonschool hours (evening functions, after-school activities, and weekend workshops) they must be returned to normal conditions after usage.

• *Transformational Key 2: Funding challenges.* To fiscally support collaborative partnerships, a change in financial priorities will need to occur. Successful leaders will need to consider Title I funds, Title IV-E and Title XIX of the Social Security Act, and IDEA funds to support these partnerships where permissible. Alternative funding sources such as grants, foundation support, and certain partnerships that will provide financial support may need to be attained.

• *Transformational Key 3: Selective abandoning.* Because educational leaders will be tapped as the primary facilitators for the building of collaborative partnerships, specified educational leaders' duties will need to be assigned to other personnel. In addition, this will ultimately mean that responsibilities of lower priorities will need to be selectively abandoned. Adding increased job descriptors while not discontinuing others will lead to the inability to perform any one responsibility with quality.

• *Transformational Key 4: Time challenges.* Educational leaders will have to empower others to find the time needed to help coordinate all collaborative partnerships at the school. Faculty members may initially express frustration because an educational leader is not readily available to them. It will be important for all staff members to understand why other key people, such as community leaders, parents, and others, constitute worthy time investments.

• *Transformational Key 5: People challenges.* Educational leaders will need to provide effective leadership for all stakeholders to change their mind-sets about collaborative partnerships and to change their paradigms for school reform. Collaborative partnerships will increase people traffic at the school. More people will bring more challenges, at least initially. Identified educational leaders will have the lead responsibilities for working out rules, roles, and responsibilities and for promoting positive interactions among people and for ensuring safety and security. Liability issues will become an additional area of concern.

• *Transformational Key 6: Collaborative leadership.* A new style of leadership, *collaborative leadership,* will be required—one that will foster voluntary commitments, develop a sense of empowerment, be results focused, and rely less on rule enforcement and compliance. Collaborative leadership will involve new school–community connections. These new connections will need planning, training, continued support, and proper evaluation assessments.

RESEARCH KEYS

To enrich your understanding of **collaborative leadership,** log on to www.researchnavigator.com and search Ebsco's ContentSelect.

Research Navigator.com

• *Transformational Key 7: Resource generation and effective use of all available dollars.* Especially in high-poverty communities, prioritizing resources will continue to provide overwhelming challenges. Educational leaders, as the key resource brokers, will need to secure new financial resources for the school. Collaborative partners may shed some light and promise in dealing with this issue.

• *Transformational Key 8: Advocacy for children and youth.* Educational leaders, more than ever, will need to be tireless, passionate advocates for kids' learning, success in school, and healthy development. In addition, educational leaders must set the tone in the school community and be willing to help others set and achieve high performance standards for all children and youth. The educational leaders' advocacy will need to be broad based and family centered. In short, educational leaders will be key leaders for the development of collaborative partnerships.

BLUE RIBBON KEYS TO SUCCESSFUL FULL-SERVICE SCHOOLS

Although a school community, agency, and business partners may bring any number of eagerly welcomed talents to a full-service school arena—from quality health care to expertise in building community support—the bottom line will be that each new partnership will need to be defined and described explicitly. In fact, the success of all new partnerships is dependent on a clear and definite understanding of what the partnership will entail. Although the formalizing into contractual language at the beginning may seem unnecessary, too many partnerships have come to an abrupt ending because of job and program descriptions, role definitions, and procedural concerns not spelled out from the beginning.

For schools and their partners forming a full-service center and wishing to get the most out of working together, paying attention to a few vital dynamics will go a long way toward increasing accomplishments and preventing potential problems. There are three blue ribbon keys that will be particularly crucial to making school partnerships successful in forming full-service centers. All educational leaders about to enter into a full-service partnership should consider these blue ribbon keys carefully.

- *Blue Ribbon Key 1: Know your potential partners.* Educational leaders should do their homework regarding potential partners. Know what potential partners will be willing to offer and what their expectations will be in return. Schools and partners often feel awkward about initially setting terms; however, the mutual understanding of new partnerships is crucial to the success of the union. It will be critical that both school and potential partners bring to the table in clear terms what each will be willing to offer (as well as what each will not) and what assurances are wanted in return (Dryfoos, 2002; Hank, 2000). If a potential partner has only one clear area of expertise to offer, it should be stated specifically. If there will be an expected level of communication and procedure, this also needs to be spelled out. All terms must be agreed on beforehand to avoid impeding and detrimental surprises later.
- *Blue Ribbon Key 2: Enter a give-and-take relationship.* School and potential partners forming a full-service center need to be ready to enter a give-and-take relationship. Although terms may be established before partnering, once the knot is tied, challenges that necessitate discussion, occasional disagreement, and careful consideration of solutions will test each other's partnering convictions. For example, a school district's partners may bring many points of view and differing priorities to the table. The challenge is

for the group to channel its cumulative judgment into making the right decisions for care receivers. Coming to an understanding of one another's perspectives is critical.

- *Blue Ribbon Key 3: See Eye-to-Eye.* Agreement needs to take place as to what is to be accomplished. Before a partnership can succeed, its members must define success. It will be crucial to agree on desired outcomes and the benchmarks that will be used to measure them. Such outcomes may include desired child-care costs, level of health care, and method of measuring achievements.

In summary, knowing your potential partners, entering a give-and-take relationship, and seeing-eye-to-eye are vital to forming partnerships resulting in full-service centers. The forming of full-scale schools through effective partnerships is both a science and an art, as complex as human nature itself. Forming full-service schools by creating effective partnerships will be a never-ending journey.

GO SOFTLY INTO THE NIGHT

It is this journey to successful twenty-first-century, full-service schools that will allow educational leaders to become the greatest of servants in catering to the sick, poor, and needy. The greatest leaders who walked on planet Earth were the greatest of servants not hesitant to go into a disease-infected area or wash the feet of another. In turn, it is only through this transformation of educational leadership (in caring for the sick, oppressed, and needy) that will restore education to a profession that is respected, appreciated, and supported.

THE REFLECTIVE PRACTITIONER

Welcome to your thirteenth Reflective Practitioner containing your Chapter 13 Scenario based on all six ISSLC Standards and your reading of Chapter 13. It is intended to provoke your thoughtful reflection and to stimulate discussion among colleagues, classmates, and peers. The Reflective Practitioner provides opportunities to synthesize issues, make comparisons, and apply theory to practice. We hope it will motivate you to search for evidence, thus increasing your comprehension of the text and helping you examine your convictions and discover new and shared perspectives.

■ **ISLLC Standard 1**
A school administrator is an educational leader who promotes the success of all students by facilitating the development, articulation, implementation, and stewardship of a vision of learn-

ing that is shared and supported by the school community.

■ **ISLLC Standard 2**
A school administrator is an educational leader who promotes the success of all students by advocating, nurturing, and sustaining a school culture and instructional program conducive to student learning and staff professional growth.

■ **ISLLC Standard 3**
A school administrator is an educational leader who promotes the success of all students by ensuring management of the organization, operations, and resources for a safe, efficient, and effective learning environment.

■ **ISLLC Standard 4**
A school administrator is an educational leader who promotes the success of all students by collaborating with families and community members,

responding to diverse community interests and needs, and mobilizing community resources.

■ **ISLLC Standard 5**
A school administrator is an educational leader who promotes the success of all students by acting with integrity, fairness, and in an ethical manner.

■ **ISLLC Standard 6**
A school administrator is an educational leader who promotes the success of all students by understanding, responding to, and influencing the larger political, social, economic, legal, and cultural context.

Scenario

The national winner of the 2004 Civic Star Award, as sponsored and selected by AASA and Sodexho School Services, is Frederick County Public Schools in Maryland. The school district took top honors in the annual awards program for replicable school–community partnerships for a comprehensive program to strengthen families and build stronger communities.

The winning program, Community Agency School Services (CASS), was formed when the school district's associate superintendent brought together public and private agencies, local and county governments, law enforcement officials, and businesses to work with the local school system to develop a collaborative model to increase student achievement. The goal was to provide affordable, accessible resources and support to families to help them overcome barriers to student success.

Collaboration and cooperation among schools, private and public agencies, local governments, businesses, organizations, churches, and families have assisted CASS in

working with 700 families of at-risk students from infancy to age 18 to provide accessible resources and support.

The first CASS pilot program was funded through grants from Maryland Department of Education and the Carnegie Foundation. When start-up funding ended two years later, the demonstrated success of the program led to salaries of CASS coordinators being paid by the school district and operating expenses by the Frederick County government.

Financial and in-kind support followed. Local municipalities and schools provide donated space for CASS services, which include health clinics, mental health counseling, outreach social services, evening high school programs, school-supply and holiday gift distribution centers, legal and mediation services, and job training. The state awarded Frederick County a bond bill for expansion and renovation of a building donated by a local municipality for CASS use. Community Agency School Services was awarded the HOPE VI public-housing revitalization funds and expansion funds through a competitive Community Partnership Agreement. In addition, CASS received $1.2 million in in-kind donations.

Judith H. McFadden, a school counselor, described CASS: "The home and family contact that CASS initiates with some of our families plays an important role at our school. As you know, children do not check their baggage at the door as they enter the school, they carry it with them. Children who are hungry, sick, tired, and worried about a family crisis are children who are not available to learn. CASS helps children learn!" In addition, the annual client satisfaction surveys have resulted in a consistent rating of 96 percent good to excellent service for its work with families.

QUESTIONS FOR REFLECTIVE THINKING

1. Based on your reading of Chapter 13, how might you develop such collaborations in your school and school district? What strategies would you implement to successfully create and sustain these collaborations?
2. How do you suppose CASS impacts each of the following actions contained within each of the following ISLLC Standards as presented?
   - "shared and supported by the school community" in ISLLC Standard 1
   - "conducive to student learning" in ISLLC Standard 2
   - "effective learning environment" in ISLLC Standard 3

   - "responding to diverse community interests and needs" in ISLLC Standard 4
   - "mobilizing community resources" in ISLLC Standard 4
3. How might ISLLC Standards 5 and 6 be very important principles for educational leaders in the Frederick County Schools engaging in the enhancing of collaborative partnerships? Please explain.
4. Did the implementation of CASS by the Frederick County Public Schools earn increased respect, appreciation, and support from students, parents, community, the state and federal government? Please explain.

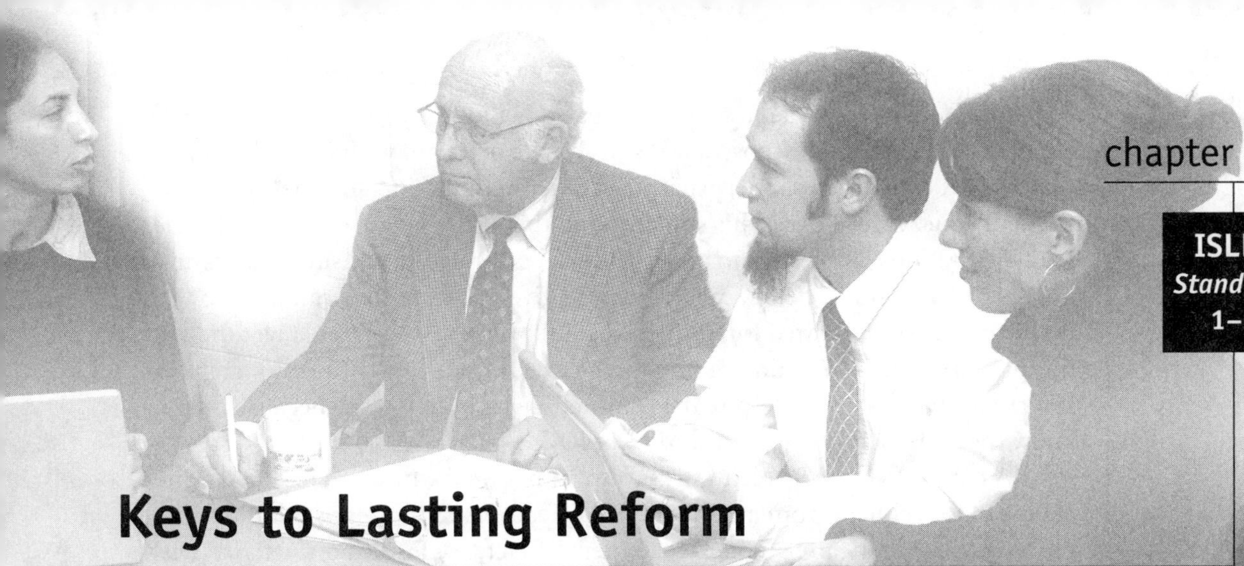

chapter 14

ISLLC *Standards* 1–6

Keys to Lasting Reform

Obstacles are those frightful things we see when we take our eyes off our goals.

—Anonymous

To bring light to the twenty-first-century need for lasting reform, your Chapter 14 Action Focus joyously guides your consideration of school transformation by taking you to a National Teacher of the Year Ceremony in Washington, D.C., where Miguel Rodriguez is being honored. (Actually, before the ceremony begins, you should know the following about Dr. Rodriquez.) Taking the advice of his parents to stay in school so he wouldn't be confined to working in a factory the rest of his life like his immigrant parents, Miguel Rodriguez has taken that "defining moment" in his life to heart as he, in turn, instills the importance of education within his students.

"In spite of their lack of formalized education, worldly poverty, and limited English-speaking ability, my parents spoke openly about the importance of school," Miguel commented upon accepting the National Teacher of the Year Award. "My father repeatedly reminded me, 'Education is your ticket to a better life. The more you know, the further you will go.' I dedicated my dissertation to my parents and since then I have built on my parents' perspective, attempting to instill the importance of education within each of my students."

For his philosophy and inspiring his students to engage wholeheartedly in learning, Dr. Miguel Rodriguez was presented the National Teacher of the Year by the United States Secretary of Education last night at a White House ceremony.

As a science teacher at Jefferson High School in New York City for the last twenty-nine years, Dr. Rodriquez has remained at the forefront in his field of teaching, providing cutting-edge learning practices in teaching and learning. Dr. Rodriquez describes the currency of his teaching as dependent on his lifelong learning leading him to implementing research discoveries such as conducting brain research, integrating technology into his instruction, and providing mastery learning opportunities for his students. Dr. Rodriquez encourages others to enter the teaching profession, as a shortage of teachers is escalating, and applauds the efforts of educational leaders in recruiting and retaining teachers.

One of Dr. Rodriquez's colleagues, Patricia Wong, describes him as "single-handedly developing the most successful science program we have and being a tireless advocate for the underprivileged student population and their families. Dr. Rodriquez's deep ties to his students and their families are evidenced by the many invitations he receives to attend special cultural events inside these families' homes," Wong says. "These families yearn to give whatever they can back to the man who has deeply cared for, respected, and loved their children. Over the years our parents have risked coming into our schools because of the relationships Dr. Rodriquez has fostered. Despite their limited English they come because they know they'll be safe, welcomed, and respected."

A committee of representatives from 14 national education organizations chooses the recipient from among the State Teachers of the Year, including those representing American Samoa, Department of Defense Education Activity, District of Columbia, Northern Mariana Islands, and U.S. Virgin Islands.

ATTRACTING AND RETAINING HIGHLY QUALIFIED TEACHERS

Unfortunately, teachers like Dr. Rodriquez are too few and far between. It is estimated that during the first decade of the twenty-first century the public schools of the United States will need to hire more than two million teachers to meet the demands of increasing student enrollment (Hussar, 1999). However, it is estimated that only about 100,000 people per year will enter the teaching profession during this period of time (Antonucci, 2001; Grant, 2001). The harsh realities of this impending teacher shortage will make it increasingly difficult for school districts to hire and retain quality teachers.

What may begin to explain the shortage of teachers today is that teaching is a difficult and complex job (Gewertz, 2002; Ingersoll, 2001a; Walsh, 2001). Teachers during the twenty-first century will face a multitude of challenges as they attempt to maximize student achievement. These challenges will be particularly daunting for new teachers as they adjust to their responsibilities in a new work environment (Darling-Hammond, 2000). Managing a classroom, becoming familiar with the school district's curriculum, acquiring information about the school and school district, and engaging in communication and collaboration essential to becoming a member of the school team are all challenges that must be met successfully by the new teacher (Gewertz, 2002). And that is just half the problem, as recruiting more new teachers will not address the teaching shortage but will make it worse until work environments are conducive to retaining current new teachers.

All educational leaders, not just the principal or human resource director, will need to strategically team together to play a critical role in attracting and retaining new teachers (Normore, 2004). Educational leaders will need to provide the resources that are necessary to achieve school goals and to demonstrate knowledge and skill in curriculum and instruction. In doing so, educational leaders will need to be skilled in communicating expectations to staff and creating a visible presence in fostering the school's vision. Because of these factors, all educational leaders play a key role instructionally, particularly with new teachers (Joravsky, 2000). Therefore, it is important for educational leaders to provide support, feedback, encouragement, and direction to new teachers.

There are key roles for twenty-first-century educational leaders to perform that will facilitate the success of new teachers (Starratt, 2004). Failure to provide new teachers with the needed support will throw education further into a downward spiral of teacher shortages (Kaplan & Owings, 2002). Failure to support new teachers will result in the following three outcomes.

- *Key Outcome 1: High attrition.* First, failure to provide support and guidance will contribute to a high attrition rate of new teachers. The learning curve new teachers incur is huge, almost insurmountable,

IN THE NEWS

The Dropout Problem: Not Students, but Teachers

The following study conducted by the Austin Chronicle underscores the importance of providing support, feedback, encouragement, and direction for the new teachers.

Consistent with reports from across the country, teachers in Texas are quitting for three big reasons: *pay, administrative (or administrator) hassles,* and *classroom management issues.* In a 2003 study of why Texas teachers leave the profession, 61% cited salaries, 32% mentioned poor administrative support, and 24% referred to problems with student discipline. Another recent survey by the Texas Federation of Teachers found that 45% of teachers were considering quitting. Of those, 58% cited classroom management issues and 34% cited paperwork as influencing their decisions.

The *Austin Chronicle* reports that in five years, nearly half of the new teachers starting today will be gone. This churning has financial implications too as various sources estimate that statewide, teacher attrition costs between $329 million and $2.1 billion a year in recruitment alone. The schools with the largest turnovers are those with the highest percentages of poor and minority students. These schools have the most difficulty and greatest expense in recruiting teachers.

With costs of recruiting soaring, supporting the success of new teachers is critical.

Source: R. P. May, "The Dropout Problem: Not Students, but Teachers," *Austin Chronicle,* August 12, 2005.

if support and guidance are not present (Bracey, 2002). Mentoring programs are most effective when all educational leaders and those they lead support and contribute to these programs (U.S. Department of Education Initiative on Teaching, 2000). The twenty-first century, doomed by unprecedented teacher shortages, will necessitate that all educators lend a helping hand to new teachers or face overcrowded classrooms caused by too few teachers.

- *Key Outcome 2: Recruitment problems.* Second, educational leaders who neglect to provide feedback and encouragement for new teachers could negatively impact other recruitment efforts of the school district (Linn & Haug, 2002). Those school districts that will be most successful in recruiting quality teachers will be those where encouragement is perceived by teacher candidates (Allen & Palaich, 2000). The truth of the matter is that this feedback and encouragement does not cost educational leaders in any one school district anything extra to provide. Conversely, the absence of feedback and encouragement will cost school districts' dearly, as teacher shortages will become disabling.
- *Key Outcome 3: Negative Influences.* Finally, when educational leaders do not provide early support to new teachers, the novices may fall prey to the negative influences that exist in every school (Rothstein, 2002a). Teachers' lounges have been notorious places for negativism, hostility, and often hurtful words and actions. Without adequate and appropriate support, new

teachers easily succumb to this negativism, low morale, and disheartening feelings without thoroughly understanding the reasons for what is being said and done by more senior teachers (Mantle-Bromley, Gould, McWhorter, & Whaley, 2000).

The effectiveness of twenty-first-century educational leaders in providing leadership for the recruitment and retention of new teachers is critical for the effective staffing of schools. An examination of key roles and responsibilities of all educational leaders is beneficial. The quantity of the application of the keys, as presented in Key Box 14.1, by educational leaders are commensurate with teachers' years of teaching, with less experience often requiring more frequent application of the indicators (Darling-Hammond, 2000; Grant, 2001; Joravsky, 2000; Normore, 2004).

KEY BOX ▶ 14.1

Keys to Increasing Teacher Retention by Educational Leaders

- New teachers need to receive frequent feedback.
- New teachers need to receive encouragement.
- New teachers must be informed of expectations in the area of lesson planning.
- New teachers must be informed of the expectations in the area of instruction.
- New teachers must be informed of the expectations in the area of classroom management.
- New teachers must be informed of the expectations in the area of school rules and regulations.
- New teachers must be formally evaluated annually with periodic checks throughout the school year.

In consideration of the fulfillment of these indicated keys, new teachers have certain perceptions and expectations of all educational leaders. New teachers often are ambivalent about educational leaders (Benham & O'Brien, 2002). Although they feel indebted to them for the job, they experience some anxiety because educational leaders exercise authority over them. They often perceive educational leaders as the persons who watch over teachers and many times the roles of educational leaders are not completely understood. Discussions initiated by educational leaders centered on these issues can provide significant gains.

Effective educational leaders can affect the retention and recruitment of new teachers by positively impacting working conditions (Odden, 2000). Schools with patterns of highest teacher turnover are those where conditions, not the characteristics of students, are the driving force for departure. Educational leaders need to provide feedback and encouragement for new teachers in building positive working conditions that favorably impact the recruitment efforts of the school district.

The collective portrait of teachers who have departed teaching reveals an interesting picture. Recognizing factors that lead to increased teacher attrition is advantageous for educational leaders desiring to improve conditions. The following are factors causing an exodus of teachers from their chosen profession (Darling-Hammond, 2000; Gewertz, 2002; Ingersoll, 2001a, 2001b; Normore, 2004; U.S. Department of Education Initiative on Teaching, 2000):

• Teacher attrition is high in the first years; mature women stay and younger women leave; elementary school teachers stay the longest periods, whereas chemistry and physics teachers stay the shortest times; teachers with highest test scores are more likely to leave earlier; teachers who paid more for college stay longer; regardless of race, teachers who work in large urban districts tend to have shorter teaching careers than do teachers working in smaller suburban districts; after controlling for district differences, black teachers are less likely than white teachers to leave teaching.

• In addition to gender, subject area, and academic ability, other personal variables that were studied include age, race, family factors, and initial teaching experience. The teacher attrition pattern follows a U-shaped curve over the life cycle. The attrition rate is high again for older teachers approaching retirement. Race is unrelated to teacher attrition. As for family factors, women with children are more likely to remain in teaching or reenter teaching than those who are not married and have no children; teachers from higher social classes are more likely to leave teaching (National Association of State Boards of Education, 1998). Another important factor in teacher retention is teachers' initial field experience. A rewarding experience was found to be positively correlated with teacher retention.

• Other school-related factors studied include teacher/student ratio, teachers' involvement in decision making, administrative support, teaching level, student characteristics, and school location. Teacher retention was found to be positively correlated with a larger teacher–student ratio, more involvement in decision making, and having more support from the administration. Also, in those instances where new teachers have difficulty learning how to work effectively with urban students, teachers at the secondary level leave teaching sooner than those at the elementary level.

Finding and Keeping Teachers

New teachers encounter many situations that generate conflict and stress. If not managed productively, conflict and stress affect physical health and psychological well-being, possibly leading to changes in self-esteem, altered patterns of sleeping and eating, depression, declining job satisfaction, and increased vulnerability to illness (U.S. Department of Education, 2002). Certain school conditions need to counteract these vulnerabilities to encourage good teachers to remain in teaching and to attract new promising candidates to the teaching profession. Hence, we emphasize that educational leaders need to promote and maintain the following keys.

• *Key 1: Establish meaningful relationships.* Meaningful relationships bind teachers to each other, educational leaders, students, parents, community members, and their profession. Educational leaders need to encourage and participate in meaningful professional relationships. Collaborative efforts may include involving administrators and teachers in determining the agenda for faculty meetings, having teachers participate in meaningful roles in matters of curriculum and instruction, and coordinating teacher schedules so that teachers may observe one another and take part in professional development activities with colleagues.

- *Key 2: Provide administrative support.* Educational leaders' support of teachers is even more critical today, considering the issue of retention of teachers. It takes a whole school, and all within, to educate students maximally. This support needs to be unwavering, particularly in times of opposition. An effective educational leader praises teachers in public and disciplines teachers in private. Leadership support means that teachers never have to lose dignity and respect (Deal & Peterson, 2000).

RESEARCH KEYS

To enrich your understanding of **teacher retention,** log on to www.researchnavigator.com and search Ebsco's ContentSelect.

Research Navigator.com

- *Key 3: Foster Parent/Teacher Relationships.* Parents and teachers working together promote longevity among teachers. Parents can provide support for teachers through personal involvement and frequent communication, and many teachers feel validated by constructive feedback from parents (Darling-Hammond & Youngs, 2002). Educational leaders need to encourage positive parent/teacher rapport and intervene in destructive relationships between parents and teachers.
- *Key 4: Supporting quality instruction.* Criticisms regarding the placement of unqualified teachers in classrooms have led to departures from the teaching profession. All efforts need to be put forth by educational leaders to assign teachers to classes for which they are academically prepared. With increasing student needs at younger ages, teachers must have the knowledge and skills in their assigned areas of teaching to meet these student challenges (Gewertz, 2002).
- *Key 5: Provide advancement opportunities.* Educational leaders need to provide concrete ways for teachers to experience advancement if they are to commit to long-term careers. Promotion within schools leads to an increase in morale and motivation (Fullan, 2001). A well-articulated promotion ladder using pay, position, and level of responsibility to denote progress through various stages of their careers provides teachers with a broader and more visible range of opportunities that aid retention.
- *Key 6: Keep workplaces positive.* A sense of humor is vital in twenty-first-century schools as pressures mount. Doom and gloom too easily replace hope and synergy. Through the use of appropriate humor, teachers will be able to diffuse volatile situations and factfind and problem-solve in a less threatening manner. Humor also functions as a means of escape from the monotony of our daily lives. Educational leaders should work continuously to create an atmosphere of caring, support, and fun in the workplace (Lezotte & Pepperl, 1999; Mattocks & Drake, 2001). When teachers are having fun, they work more effectively and efficiently and tend to value the work they are doing and where they are doing it.
- *Key 7: Center encouragement.* Schools must remain as centers of encouragement for teachers, students, parents, and community members. The educational leaders' role is to encourage others as well as hold all others to do the same (McCowin, Miles, & Hargodine, 2000). Feelings of encouragement empower individuals to achieve far greater accomplishments. Encouragement is a propelling

force for increasing student achievement. The opposites of encouragement—apathy and discouragement—are equally as forceful but highly counterproductive, destructive, and often cause early departure from employment.

RESOLVING TEACHER SHORTAGES

The U.S. teacher shortage did not occur overnight. Because of this critical challenge of new teacher recruitment and retention, it is important that educational leaders take steps to make and communicate research-based solutions. Many of the keys are organizational in nature and include interpersonal relationships, salary, school governance, trust, stability, safety, and the principal's job description and workload. However, there are policy keys that need to be attained to improve the recruitment and retention of new teachers. From the research of many (Darling-Hammond, 2000; Farkas, Johnson, & Foleno, 2000; Joravsky, 2000; Nelson, Drown, & Gould, 2000), these policy keys follow:

- *Key 1:* Research needs to remain the basis for decision making. Turbulent times are ahead for twenty-first-century education. Teacher recruitment and retention lead the parade of issues because without a qualified teacher in every classroom, education will falter. Research-based decisions need to determine the decisions and actions of today's successful educational leaders.
- *Key 2:* State Boards of Education need to take an active role in school reform. Research-based expectations that are clearly established and articulated by educational entities may have positive gains.
- *Key 3:* State Boards of Education need to develop a new policy framework for all educational leaders that supports the recruiting and retaining of new teachers through effective leadership for new teachers. Board members must understand their roles and responsibilities and the complexity of other educational leaders as instructional leaders. Recruitment and retention needs to be stressed; barriers need to be reduced. There are no magic bullets. Creating a transformational school climate requires the board's attitude, policy, and governance.
- *Key 4:* The educational leader's description needs to be reengineered. Very few dispute the importance of educational leaders. The effective leadership of new teachers is imperative. Educational leaders must be held accountable for reasonable accomplishments.
- *Key 5:* Compensation for new teachers and educational leaders needs to be adjusted. Incentives for recruitment and retention and other educational initiatives must be supported. Although salary has increased over the years, teachers' and educational leaders' counterparts in business and industry with equivalent education, training, and experience earn significantly higher incomes. Society values a quality education, and it needs to be willing to financially support it.
- *Key 6:* Boards and superintendents must understand that their actions contribute to their respective reputations. Trust, credibility, and support need to be demonstrated from the highest governance level of school districts, the boards of education, and superintendents. Teacher candidates are more likely to recruited and retained by school districts with quality interpersonal relationships.

IN THE NEWS

IBM Wants to Stem Slide in Math, Science

The active marketing, recruiting, and training of new teachers will hold surprises during the twenty-first century, such as the IBM Corporation carving out its own piece of the pie.

IBM Corporation is taking steps toward halting the teacher shortage by helping its veteran employees launch new careers in teaching math and science. The corporation is paying the tuition costs up to $15,000 per employee.

The pilot program began in January of 2006 with 100 IBM employees in New York and North Carolina. Plans are being made by IBM to extend their teacher training program nationwide.

IBM says it is committed to helping the nation's schools recruit qualified people to teach math and science. IBM's research has revealed that there is a teacher shortage of more than a quarter-million math and science teachers. The corporation views this teacher shortage as a national crisis.

If education leaders do not prepare and develop new teachers, private businesses and industries in increased numbers may take over this important responsibility.

Source: J. Van, "IBM Wants to Stem Slide in Math, Science," *The Houston Chronicle*, September 15, 2005.

- *Key 7:* School systems must actively market and recruit new teachers and effective educational leaders. The plan should also include new teacher and educational leadership training programs, school–university leadership academies, internships, and other measures designed to recruit and retain new teachers and educational leaders with skills in attracting and supporting teachers.
- *Key 8:* Teacher preparation and professional development programs are critical for continuous teacher professional development. As information rapidly accelerates and discoveries on teaching and learning are made, teachers' professional growth (whether at universities, colleges, or other higher education institutions) is imperative for an ever-changing world if students are to be prepared for this new millennium.
- *Key 9:* Policymakers must give considerable attention to the training and preparation of new teachers and educational leaders in order to ensure that they conceptually understand current research on preferred practices so as not to delay educational reform. Plans for recruitment and retention of new teachers need to be clearly understood and demonstrated by all educational leaders. Increasing classroom visitations, in-depth conferencing, and open communications during goal-setting conferences are essential to the recruitment and retention of new teachers.
- *Key 10:* The presented recommendations represent a systematic approach to addressing twenty-first-century teacher recruiting and retention. There are no magical formulas. Anything less than a systematic reengineering will compound the shortages of quality teachers.

The recruiting and retaining of new teachers through effective leadership of all educational leaders is but one challenge school districts face (Murphy & Datnow, 2000; Peterson, 2002). Additional resources without new teacher and educational leader preparation, performance descriptions, and professional development will likely contribute to the ongoing cycle of shortcomings in student achievement. Educational leaders must achieve the respect and support of those they lead.

DILEMMAS THAT DEFINE FUTURE PRACTICES

Education during the twenty-first century will face dilemmas not known to prior generations of educational leaders. Mastery learning will return resoundingly, brain research will enable unprecedented discoveries, and parental involvement and ethics in instruction will escalate in need. Educational leaders will not only need to remain abreast of these discoveries and advancements but they will also need to engage in lifelong learning. Each of these educational imperatives is reviewed briefly.

Mastery Learning

The twenty-first-century pendulum of student achievement will swing to the opposite side, away from a highly scripted, scheduled, and this-way-or-the-highway mentality. Mastery learning will be based on research that asserts that all students will master content when they are given varying degrees of time and multiple efforts (Slavin, 1987). During the twenty-first century, learning will be eventually considered more important than performance on a single indicator such as a statewide test.

Mastery learning will be more developmentally appropriate to the needs of each learner and lifelike in terms of revising prior academic efforts to higher levels of mastery. In addition, students will not have to waste their learning time trying to figure out what they need to remember—the information will be clear, concise, and organized. Once students successfully complete each assessment, they will expand their learning adventure to include more complex information because they will have a basic foundation.

Students' mastery learning opportunities will demonstrate increases in both cognitive and affective domains (Block, Efthim, & Burns, 1989). Mastery learning will provide learning opportunities that will result in positive gains. These gains will include, but are not limited to, those presented in Key Box 14.2.

KEY BOX 14.2

Advantages of Mastery Learning for Students

- Positive attitudes toward subject matter
- Increase in self-concept
- Higher levels of motivation in students wanting to succeed in their coursework
- Fewer students dropping out of high schools or turning off to school in lower grades
- Higher student ratings of teachers using mastery learning techniques
- Increased time on task by students
- Higher levels of subject-matter comprehension
- Group-based mastery learning strategies for teaching life skills such as team building

Mastery learning will be considered increasingly important. Historically it was believed that boys and girls learn differently; twenty-first-century research will verify different learning methods by gender. Some generalities have been made regarding these gender differences. Males are more likely to outperform females on some spatial tasks. Also, boys are more adept at motor skills. Likewise, males will be better able to match lines with identical slopes and perform better on tests of mathematical reasoning. Female students are not inferior, however, as tests indicate that girls outpace boys in several tasks as well. For instance, when girls are read a story, paragraph, or a list of unrelated words, they demonstrate better recall. Likewise, girls are more accomplished at rapidly identifying matching items, mathematical calculation tests, and precise manual tasks involving fine-motor skills. The ramifications for educators will be obvious. All this points in the direction that twenty-first-century educators will need to implement mastery learning.

Brain Research

Amazing discoveries in brain research will benefit educators during the twenty-first century. Advanced research ahead will include understanding that brains come with a degree of prewiring for some functions, such as oral language and basic mathematics, and this wiring can be altered (Casey, Giedd, & Thomas, 2000; Kolb, 2000). The brain at birth is not a complete and unified tabula rasa, but an elaborate structure with many parts. The most effective educational experience that tunes this rough-and-ready apparatus into a skillful organ capable of doing the most precise job will drive instructional and learning enhancements (Wolfe, 2001).

The idea that children need enrichment in their lives at an early age to promote learning will come from continued brain research experiments. From such studies, educational leaders will discover that young children's brains will need to have enriched educational environments or they will suffer learning difficulties (Jensen, 1998). The rapid acceleration of what is known about brain growth development may significantly benefit successful twenty-first-century educators. Discoveries such as DNA intervention leading to healthier and longer life will elevate education to greater heights during the new millennium.

Just imagine researchers using brain research information to work with stroke patients. Through intense therapy, stroke victims who have lost the use of a limb may be able to regain movement, even if the loss was as much as 20 years ago. This therapy may also work for children with cerebral palsy and those who have lost the ability to speak (Wilson, 2001). Similar therapeutic programs will be used with children diagnosed as dyslexic to help them master basic reading skills. The assumption here is that their dyslexic tendencies are caused by faulty wiring problems in the brain, which can be corrected. This vein of brain research appears to have a very promising future in both the medical and educational fields.

Educational leaders should know that some of the current brain research will border on science fiction. One such set of experiments will be the noninvasive technique of transcranial magnetic stimulation. In this technique, tiny electric currents will be directly induced into the neural circuitry of a person's brain through strong, short magnetic pulses. The resulting currents literally will turn parts of the brain on and off. This stimulation will have the potential to greatly aid in the understanding of how the brain works, in correcting its dysfunctions, and in improving its abilities (Davis, 2001; Wolfe, 2001). Although there will be some side effects and the process is still experimental, some day one might be able to put on a cap equipped with transcranial magnetic stimulation, activate it, and be instantly and completely alert no matter how fatigued one might be.

Another aspect of brain research will be the chemical approach. Mind-altering chemicals have a long history; however, future research will use chemicals that are intended to improve cognition (Kwon & Lawson, 2000). Memory-enhancing drugs will be produced by several large drug firms during the twenty-first century (Sousa, 2001; Wilson, 2001). Until the advent of Viagra, there was little interest in enhancement drugs, but this interest will continue to pick up steam during the new millennium. Most of these chemicals will be under scrutiny for side effects. Most of the work will center on helping persons with life-changing events like Alzheimer's. Discoveries will be considered for multiple uses, such as power thinking before major memory challenges such as tests and the like.

Appropriate Parent Involvement

The most important role a parent will play will be to stay involved. Successful twenty-first-century educational leaders will encourage and promote parental involvement through communication, communication, and more communication. As presented in Key Box 14.3, communication networks will link school and home.

KEY BOX 14.3

Modes of Communication Used by Educational Leaders

- Letters/Notes/Memos
- PTA/PTO meetings
- School councils/Committees
- Drop-in visits to school
- E-mail and Internet websites
- Phone calls to teacher
- Parent/teacher conferences

There are a variety of ways that parents and guardians will reciprocate in communicating with educators, as well as provide general support for schools and teachers. Some great ways that parents will become a part of the education process are presented in Key Box 14.4.

KEY BOX 14.4

Parental Support and Participation in Children's Education

- Going to school and meeting with the teacher
- Actively supporting school goals for learning and appropriate behavior
- Participating in parenting skills training
- Noting their children's progress in school and complimenting them
- Getting children their own library cards and keeping magazines, newspapers, and books around the house
- Helping children break down large jobs—such as dressing themselves, homework, and chores—into small steps so that they can manage them successfully

- Developing a reasonable and consistent schedule for chores
- Setting and following through on rules about TV viewing during the week
- Playing games together
- Talking regularly about events happening at work, in the neighborhood, and around the world
- Making sure that children have adequate after-school supervision (if they are alone at home, introduce them to trusted neighbors)
- Getting to know the parents of children's friends.

Simply put, the best way parents can ensure the very best education for their child(ren) is to participate in school initiatives and related activities. Parents must get involved and stay involved!

Ethics

Mastery learning, learning based on brain research development, and parental programs are forecasted for lasting twenty-first-century educational reform; so too is the teaching of ethics. Recent corporate and governmental scandals have brought ethics back into the limelight. That is to say, given the current ethical climate as reflected by the plethora of new stories in the media, the teaching of ethics is becoming more and more important, for these students will soon graduate and contribute to the communities in which they will reside. Despite widespread disagreement that ethics should be an integral part of K–12 curriculum, the twenty-first century will not allow the inertia of resistance.

Educational leaders who are considering the implementation of the teaching of ethics will have an arduous challenge ahead in terms of ethics training. In a faster changing twenty-first-century world, students will no doubt be in need of ethics, beliefs, and identities. However, before setting voyage on the teaching of ethics, or *ethics education,* the educational leader will need to thoroughly think this one through in terms of the training of staff (Pojman, 2002).

RESEARCH KEYS

To enrich your understanding of **ethics education,** log on to www.researchnavigator.com and search Ebsco's ContentSelect.

Research Navigator.com

The foundation of change in the teaching of ethics in twenty-first-century schools will be the training of educators, students, parents, and community members. Many approaches to ethics training/education will require an external or trained facilitator working with small groups of people. Expertise in the facilitation of professional learning in small groups and knowledge of ethics will be essential. The distribution of this expertise and knowledge across all school sites will not be even (Palmer, 2000). Ethics training, conceived as a formal learning program delivered to teachers, will become difficult because of the unavailability of skilled facilitators.

Professional development of educators in ethics instruction will take on many shapes and forms. Because the depth and breadth of experience of supervisors and mentors will vary considerably across education systems, a workplace learning model of teacher professional development will need to be supplemented by additional training for educational leaders and mentors (Thiroux, 1998: Wekesser, 1998). Support will need to be provided for interschool networks. In short, a comprehensive approach to "ethics training" will be dependent on an open workplace culture of inquiry and professional learning.

A word of caution: the term *ethical conduct* will provoke debates about the distinctions between codes of conduct and their purposes and ethical principles and their place in the teaching profession. Some will argue that codes of conduct mandate specific behaviors in particular situations but do not promote individual adherence to ethical principles (Thomson, 2000). The gray areas in decision making that confront most teachers on a regular basis will arise in the face of competing interests and values. Codes of conduct may assist, but will not give clear definition to, teachers' decision making. In other words, the organization or system will mandate what not to do in particular situations but it will be impossible to list all possible situations that arise. This will become the territory of ethical decision making. The delivery of training related to codes of conduct will be possible. Training individuals to adhere to particular ethical principles when making decisions will not be possible.

A gaze into the crystal ball in search of what this century's ethics curriculum will include is exciting. Beyond the framework of definitions, discoveries, and practices will be found questions, debates, and additional discoveries. This vibrant exchange of ideas will include philosophical concepts encapsulating rights, freedoms, responsibility, duty, justice, and equity. Higher-level studies in ethics will include objectivism (all reality is objective and external to the mind), deontology (the study of moral obligation), relativism (where all truth is relative to the individual), teleology (natural processes or occurrences), and axiology (the study of the nature of values). The teaching of ethics in the twenty-first century may be a case of either get on board or get out of the way, because it is coming to a school or school district near you that you will be leading.

Lifelong Learning

Lifelong learning in the twenty-first century will discover its roots in rich history (Knowles, 1980; Smith & McCann, 2001). As lifelong learning has driven the development of human potential since the ancient Chinese, Greek, Hebrew, and Roman teachers extended their teaching to adults, so too should today's educational leaders continue to professionally and personally grow and develop to stay abreast in a fast-changing century. As early man philosophized about the goals—but apparently not the process—of adult learning, and used parables, Socratic dialogue, and techniques they invented to share information and wisdom, educational leadership of the twenty-first century will be a mixture of science, technology, and medicine. The philosophy of Thomas Jefferson that "lifelong learning is basic to the foundation of democracy—by creating an informed citizenry" will hold true as educational leaders continue to learn and encourage all others to do the same.

A true understanding of lifelong learning for the twenty-first century dates back to World War I, when educators started to understand that adults learn differently than children. As early education experts noted, adult education needs to be built around the adult student's needs and interests, not around subject matter. With the first surge of interest and theories about adult education beginning in the 1920s, lifelong education will be particularly needed to meet the ever-changing conditions of the twenty-first century (Pratt, 1998).

Adult learning, at least in higher education, received broader, more formal attention after World War II with the GI Bill. The government's rationale for this bill, with appropriate generalization for the twenty-first century, was to prepare veterans:

- to read: "In an ever-changing society, one must read widely to have a full knowledge of what has been done."
- to think: "For the Nation to grow, one must think on what you read, let the ideas roll around in one's mind, turn them over, look at them from all angles."
- to do: "Thinking alone will not help mankind nor advance civilization. . . . Put your thinking into action."

The motivation of the last two decades propelled the contexts of lifelong education for the twenty-first century. As recently as the 1980s, adult educators noted that education was still not universally approached as a lifelong process (Schapiro, 1999). Except to maintain certification, most educators and other professionals did not have a conscious attitude about being lifelong learners. Instead, lifelong learning was hidden. Many people worked in the same place during their entire careers. Careers were directed and controlled by employers who determined what new knowledge and skills employees needed for the next steps in a career path within their organizations.

In 1980, the noted educator Malcolm Knowles predicted a vision for the 1990s—that lifelong learning would finally become the organizing principle of all education (Knowles, 1980). Knowles warned that lifelong learning would be the only defense against a world of accelerating change. As children will need to develop skills of inquiry, adults will need resources and support for self-directed inquiry and learning.

Perhaps it was technology, downsizing, and reorganization in the 1990s that finally gave society the jolt it needed to see lifelong learning the way Knowles envisioned. Moreover, rapid changes in the education profession have made it imperative for educators to stay ahead of the times (Tisdell, 2001). Change will impact education in the twenty-first century more directly than ever before. What a time to be a lifelong learner!

INSTRUCTION AND TECHNOLOGY

With the 1957 launching of *Sputnik,* an unmanned Soviet satellite, a national interest in educational reform was stirred and the so-called golden age of education began. Among the national efforts to reform education was the emergence of educational technologies as a catalyst for rethinking education. With the advent of microcomputers in the 1970s, technology costs were reduced and school personnel found it affordable to purchase computers for the schools and classrooms (Cotton, 1991; Heinich, Molenda, Russell, & Smaldino, 1996).

Originally, computers were primarily used for reinforcing traditional instruction in the K–12 environment. But in more recent years, methods of teaching strategies have been based on engaging students in ways that allow them to develop and construct their own mental structure in a particular study (McNabb, Hawkes, & Rouk, 1999). Computers enhance children's self-concept and provide opportunities for children to share leadership roles more frequently and develop positive attitudes toward learning. How teachers integrate technology into the curriculum is critical to the teaching and learning environment. Today's successful educational leaders have an understanding of both the power and limitations of the computer and of what computers can and cannot do for the educational development of children (Murphy & Louis, 1999).

Teachers' access to personal computers at school and at home has increased to the point where, in 1998, 93 percent of teachers in grades 4 through 12 were using computers as a part of their professional lives. Although a majority of all public school teachers may have computers in their classrooms, a vast majority of all teachers feel they are not at all prepared or only somewhat prepared to use technology in their teaching. The twenty-first century will leave no exception; classroom teachers will provide technology-supported learning opportunities for their students.

Research specific to exemplary technology instruction reveals a diversity of methods and usages (Rocha, 2001; Cuban 1993). No two teachers are alike and most choose from a large repertoire of teaching strategies as particular situations warrant. Technology use actually prompts teachers to change their practices in the direction of more individualized approaches. Researchers warn that changing the beliefs of teachers is neither quickly nor easily accomplished.

Although the transformation to computer-assisted instruction has not been a rapid one, technology has provided new breadth and depth to instruction with the option of transforming the role of the classroom teacher. Teachers have been the first to recognize that using technology can increase students' self-esteem and confidence, enhance their content-area understanding, and make them informed about and emphatic to world events (Cordes & Miller, 1999). This new technology-using role for teachers underscores the need for high-quality professional development in determining what and how students learn best with what technology tools. This new role will necessitate professional development.

The need to prepare teachers to use technology efficiently to support teaching and learning has not gone unnoticed. However limited in scope, technology instruction for student and teacher use was related to teaching about technology rather than showing learners how to use it across the curriculum (Cuban, 1993; Rocha, 2001). Successful twenty-first-century educational leaders will provide effective leadership that encourages teachers to integrate technology into instruction. Such educational leadership will include making the technologies available seven days a week and twenty-four hours a day. The limited technology dollars must be used wisely for maintaining and upgrading equipment, training, and instructional and technical support.

Keys to Effective Technology Preparation

Educational leaders need to provide teachers with professional development programs to gain and apply new technical skills, stay abreast of trends, and maintain their professional edge as knowledge advances. Although many educators are aware of the need for professional development in the successful integration of technology into the curriculum, the education community has not reached consensus about reliable, generalizable, or conclusive training models. However, research and studies of effective technology staff development programs (Bowman, Newman, & Masterson, 2001) have produced the keys to technology training, as presented in Key Box 14.5.

KEY BOX 14.5

Effective Twenty-First-Century Technology Training

- Teachers are teamed for training with the team concept providing support.
- Training offers ongoing rather than "one-shot" professional development activities.
- Times to learn and access to equipment are provided both during and after school hours.
- Focus is on the integration of technology tools into instruction.
- A flexible schedule of targeted instruction is provided.
- Best practices are shared and encouraged with all participants.
- The use of particular technologies in schools is modeled.

After goals and visions of learning with technology are established, it is vital for educational leaders to provide teachers with continuous professional development in technology. Professional development opportunities must be focused, coherent, sustained, and create an ethic of collaboration (McKenzie, 1999). Ongoing professional development is necessary to help teachers learn not only how to use the technology but also how to use it to provide meaningful instruction and activities. Teachers must be offered training beyond the use of computers to implement technology assisted instruction.

Prevention Keys to Technology Implementation

IN THE NEWS

State Support Varies Widely

Technology spending is determined by budget surplus more than fiscal planning.

With many states tightening their fiscal belts because of revenue shortfalls, state funding for K–12 educational technology has been on the downturn. While some states devote considerable aid to school technology, many others rely more on federal money to pay for software, teacher training, and data management. Melinda D. George, the executive director of the State Educational Technology Directors Association based in Arlington, Virginia, asserts that many states have faced huge budget deficits resulting in a large scaling back on many education programs.

Successful educational leaders, knowing the importance of technology, will work diligently to attain these powerful learning tools and provide the necessary training.

Source: R. R. Borja, "State Support Varies Widely," *Education Week*, May 5, 2005.

If the implementation of technology is going to be successful, educational leaders will need to provide instructional technology leadership. In this role, the leaders will need to remove hurdles, overcome impediments to change, and rally the troops to teach lessons enriched by technology. There are several factors that prevent teachers' adoption of technology that educational leaders need to know. Based on governmental findings (Office of Technology Assessment, 1995), the impediments to wider spread technology usage are presented in Key Box 14.6.

Impediments to Overcome to Increase Technology Usage

- Teachers' inaccessibility to hardware, preventing expanded utilization
- Costs of training, equipment, and maintenance
- Complexity of applications for instruction
- Teachers' and administrators' apprehension about logistical and technical problems
- Few verifications of the benefits of technology
- Teacher accountability for implementation of computer-assisted instruction
- The fear that children will learn less effectively with little research to override these feelings
- Limited capabilities of machines, with perceptions often based on earlier experiences with outdated hardware and applications
- The fear that staff members will be replaced by machines
- Perceptions of the negative aspects of technology (copyright infringement, control of student access, and privacy issues)

It is imperative that educational leaders in both curriculum and technology work together to encourage and support classroom teachers' implementation of computer-assisted instruction. In addition, school leaders will need to keep abreast of, and communicate the findings of, the research. If technology is to have widespread use, educational leaders will need to discover more effective ways to encourage and support teachers using technology. In addition, they will need to provide resources for teachers to learn more about the use of technology as a tool for teaching and learning.

Improving Instruction

The use of computer-assisted instruction is not without a dark side. Today, not only have billions of dollars been allocated to public elementary and secondary schools to purchase educational technology, but elected officials have attempted to lead this bandwagon and take credit for the parade. Former President Clinton, Vice President Gore, and Secretary of Education Riley challenged all schools to be connected to the national information infrastructure. Federal legislation, such as Goals 2000 and No Child Left Behind, have moved educational technology to a prominent position.

Despite all these proclamations from our nation's leaders, examples of schoolwide use of computer-assisted instruction are comparatively rare and isolated. Use of computer-assisted instruction tends to be limited to individual teachers. Research is sparse, worse yet contradictory, in revealing the increase of student achievement through computer-assisted instruction.

Although it is clear that students will need to be proficient in data and word processing and other computer applications in order to be competitive in the labor and undergraduate markets, it is less clear to what degree, if any, computer-assisted instruction increases student achievement. In an ideal world, policymakers, practitioners, and parents who want to know whether technology is the boon to teachers and students that it claims to be would simply read the research findings and come to an easy answer.

Technology Assessment

Computers are reshaping children's lives at home and at school in profound and unexpected ways (Cordes & Miller, 1999). Although drill-and-practice programs appear to improve scores modestly on some standardized tests in narrow skills areas, there is no clear evidence that students' sustained use of multimedia machines, the Internet, or other popular applications has any impact on academic achievement. Adding confusion to the debate over whether or not computer-assisted instruction increases student achievement (Cuban, 2001b), the three keys listed in Key Box 14.7 demonstrate the difficulty in assessing computer efficacy in classrooms.

> ### KEY BOX 14.7
>
> **Difficulties in Assessing Computer Efficacy in Classrooms**
>
> - Research on the efficacy of technology in education is guilty, as is education at large, of not having a clear focus.
> - Researchers study different outcomes in many ways, such as student grade level, socioeconomic status, and aptitudes.
> - Studies of different types of computer use make different assumptions about teachers' roles in computer-using classrooms.

Furthermore, the research on instructional design has provided conflicting perceptions of the role of computers in current educational practices. Debates have been focused on whether educational media, such as computers, are more than a mere delivery system for instruction (Louis, Marks, & Kruse, 1996). The three keys generally emerging from this debate as presented in Key Box 14.8.

> ### KEY BOX 14.8
>
> **Three Questions to Guide Instructional Technology Expansion**
>
> - Does the presence of technology influence learning?
> - What is the learners' role in technology-based learning?
> - How important are teachers to the success of technology?

Research on the effectiveness of computers in the student learning environment reflects a variety of conclusions. Some evidence supported improvements in student achievement when technology was integrated and used in the core curricula (Mann, Shakeshaft, Becker, & Kottkamp, 1999). Students seem to enjoy classes more when computer help was provided and suggested learning as much or more from computer-based tutoring as from peer and cross-age tutoring.

The best use of technology is its capacity to support pedagogical approaches that encourage students to become active participants in their own learning and to acquire critical thinking skills and more complex understandings. With all this, the correlation between computer-assisted instruction and increased student achievement is relatively undocumented.

In 1994, $2.4 billion was spent on educational technology in kindergarten through twelfth grade and $6 billion in higher education (National Center for Education Statistics, 2000). Since 1994, billions of dollars continue to be spent by educational institutions on purchasing and upgrading of additional computers and accessories. These technology dollars have not been come by easily! Insufficient funding, the tightening of fiscal belts by schools, and budgetary shortages have prompted several to inquire why computer-assisted instruction is still a top fiscal priority. This perspective may be amplified in considering that less than 5 percent of published research in computer-assisted instruction is sufficiently empirical, quantitative, and valid to support conclusions with respect to the effectiveness of technology in educational learning outcomes (Jones & Paolucci, 1999).

With billions of dollars spent where too few empirical studies containing unclear conclusions exist, several red flags are raised. Fiscally today, educational leaders need to prioritize each dollar in terms of gains made in increased student achievement. In other words, whether purchases for computer-assisted instruction are educationally wise will be an important question for twenty-first-century educational leaders. Just what is the "bang for the buck" spent for computer purchases intended for increasing student achievement?

The billion-dollar question is: Do students learn more through computer-assisted instruction? Of hundreds of studies involving computers and students in grades K through 12, few have focused on learner outcomes. On the other hand, several problems have been reported, including dropped computers and broken monitors; misplaced accessories such as cards, disks, and batteries; technical problems such as freezing, crashing, and misaligned printing (requiring the addition of technicians); physical strains among laptop users (back and neck); and the lack of proper training (Rocha, 2001).

The bottom line may be found after wading through the hype about the potential of computers: The research suggests there is no academic improvement among most students who use computers (Bulkeley, 1997). This is not to say that a computer cannot make it easier for students to locate and download information, prepare and present reports, or even communicate with others all over the world. Studies are lacking at best, contradictory in general, that show that computers motivate students to learn or improve their learning.

Technology Leadership

Educational leaders in the twenty-first century may need to bite the technology bullet. Tough decisions need to be made that are educationally wise and fiscally prudent. School budgets are continually getting tighter while increased student achievement is not an option.

Research needs to remain as the basis for decision making, such as the effective schools research that has increased in importance the past several decades largely because of its impact on increasing student achievement (Edmonds, 1979; Purkey & Smith, 1983). Educational leaders need to be knowledgeable of educational research findings, as these research findings will drive the actions of administrators when considering technology initiatives.

In addition, educational leaders need to know the dark side of technological advances in schools. Each technological breakthrough in the past resulted in disappointment followed by disillusionment and eventually abandonment (Hannafin & Sevenye, 1993). Why is this so? Many teachers have been shy of integrating technology into their classes because of the additional time and effort needed to learn and implement the technology, lack of confidence in its efficacy, poor quality software (this excuse is wearing increasingly thin), and good old-fashioned fear of machines. An underlying change in teaching pedagogy must take place, as computers are too expensive to serve as dust collectors.

THE FUTURE IS NOW

From an ever-increasing teacher shortage to biting the technology bullet with brain research, mastery, and lifelong learning, the twenty-first century promises to be an exciting time for educational leaders. As for the keys presented in this chapter and throughout our book, it is our intent that you are informed and prepared. There is no question that education is in a state of flux, and leaders who are willing to take the bull by the horns and lead are to be commended and appreciated!

THE REFLECTIVE PRACTITIONER

Welcome to your fourteenth Reflective Practitioner, which is again based on all six ISLLC Standards and your reading of Chapter 14. It is intended to provoke your thoughtful reflection and to stimulate discussion among colleagues, classmates, and peers. The Reflective Practitioner provides opportunities to synthesize issues, make comparisons, and apply theory to practice. We hope it will motivate you to search for evidence, thus increasing your comprehension of the text and helping you examine your convictions and discover new and shared perspectives.

ISLLC Standard 1
A school administrator is an educational leader who promotes the success of all students by facilitating the development, articulation, implementation, and stewardship of a vision of learning that is shared and supported by the school community.

ISLLC Standard 2
A school administrator is an educational leader who promotes the success of all students by advocating, nurturing, and sustaining a school culture

and instructional program conducive to student learning and staff professional growth.

ISLLC Standard 3
A school administrator is an educational leader who promotes the success of all students by ensuring management of the organization, operations, and resources for a safe, efficient, and effective learning environment.

ISLLC Standard 4
A school administrator is an educational leader who promotes the success of all students by collaborating with families and community members, responding to diverse community interests and needs, and mobilizing community resources.

ISLLC Standard 5
A school administrator is an educational leader who promotes the success of all students by acting with integrity, fairness, and in an ethical manner.

ISLLC Standard 6
A school administrator is an educational leader who promotes the success of all students by understanding, responding to, and influencing

the larger political, social, economic, legal, and cultural context.

Scenario

Ms. Evelyn Page is the principal of Central Elementary School, where there are 734 students enrolled and thirty-seven teachers comprising the faculty. The teachers and their principal at Central Elementary School are not unified, with constant disagreement on a variety of issues. Ms. Page, in her third year, is viewed by many teachers as indecisive, lacking follow-through and seeming to care more about the maintenance and operation of the school rather than her own teachers. In addition, statewide test scores are far below all other schools in the Central School District, staff retention is below 60 percent, and attrition is at an alarming high rate at Central Elementary School.

For months, Ms. Page had been looking forward to the Principals' State Fall Conference. This year's conference was entitled "ISAIL or Improving Student Achievement through Instructional Leadership." She couldn't believe how fast time had flown by and that she was now sitting in the first general session of the conference. To commence the three days of professional development, a distinguished panel was assembled.

Dr. Glenda Moore, the first panelist and host principal for this year's conference, shared the findings established last year by the National Association of School Principals. "Historically, the principals' effectiveness emphasized the managerial responsibilities of maintaining facilities, ensuring student discipline, and meeting state reporting requirements. However, the educational reform movement of the past two decades has focused a great deal of new attention to the role of principals as instructional leaders. Increasingly, the principals' instructional leadership role has gained importance, while their managerial role has diminished in importance."

Dr. Paul Williams, the second panelist and state principal of the year, argued that the work of "school principals is under more pressure today than ever before to be accountable for student achievement. Principals today more than ever need to be instructional leaders. Supervising lunch rooms and troubleshooting bus issues will no longer suffice." Dr. Williams exemplified the research with testimony that his school did so well academically because all of his principals are capable instructional leaders.

Dr. James Brady, national principal of the year two years in a row, shared his thoughts as a panelist. "It is my responsibility as an instructional leader to pro-

mote effective pedagogies so that my teachers' teaching practices are effective and therefore increase student achievement. Teacher recruitment, teacher retention, and best instructional practices are my responsibility as the instructional leader of my teachers, and I make sure that their professional development is grounded in content-specific pedagogy sustained and linked to the curriculum. My instructional leadership as principal has unified our staff under one common vision, to increase student achievement."

Dr. Phyllis Ierga, final panelist, professor, and researcher, cautioned the assembly. "Although research is generally supportive of the instructional leadership role of a principal, not all principals are in agreement. It is critical, now more than ever, for principals to air their concerns, come to grips with their convictions, and stand and deliver with all their might."

Dr. JoAnn Germiter, the moderator and active member of the Interstate Licensure School Standard Council, summed up the panelists' contributions, thanked the panelists for their contributions, and wished each conference participant a wonderful conference. In closing, the moderator extended a challenge to all, asserting that everyone needs to "base future decisions on research, especially the six National Standards for School Leaders developed by the Interstate School Leaders Licensure Council."

If the panelist messages weren't sufficiently convincing, the rest of the day devoted to Improving Student Achievement through Instructional Leadership laid any doubts to rest. Yet, Ms. Page's ultimate realization of the importance of principals being instructional leaders came that evening. Although her colleagues invited Ms. Page to go out for dinner, she decided that an early evening return to her hotel room for quiet contemplation was best. Before going to sleep, Ms. Page checked her e-mail. There was one new message. It was from Mrs. Denise Eaaly, Central School District #1's National Teacher of the Year. Her words were: "I QUIT. I can no longer work for you. You care more about facilities than your staff, and cannot be depended on. Before leaving for the conference, you evidently thought it was more important to investigate a reported roof leak than keep your appointment with us eighth-grade teachers. Now I am sorry to be so direct, but I am so frustrated and I didn't want to go above you in reporting this to the superintendent. Respectfully, Denise."

Ms. Page quickly replied to Ms. Eaaly's e-mail without hesitation. She replied, "Please do not quit. I am attending a conference up north. The theme of the Conference is "Improving Student Achievement through

Instructional Leadership." I have learned much. I will contact you when I get back to the district. Sincerely, Ms. Page."

The remaining sessions of the conference reinforced the correlations between schools with higher student achievement and principals who are engaged as instructional leaders. Ms. Page thought long and hard about the restructuring of her principal's role from managerial to instructional leadership. She knew if transformation were to be successful and sustained over

time, she needed to maximize participation and ownership in this restructuring process. She was uncertain as to what this change might incur. The seven-hour drive home from the conference provided time for Ms. Page to reflect.

First thing Monday morning, Ms. Page sent a memo to Ms. Eaaly, requesting her presence at a meeting on Wednesday at 8:30 A.M. The five letters—ISAIL—were inscribed at the top of the memo. Wednesday could not come fast enough for both Ms. Page and Ms. Eaaly.

QUESTIONS FOR REFLECTIVE THINKING

1. Putting yourself in the shoes of Ms. Page, what would you honestly share with Ms. Eaaly at your Wednesday morning meeting? Please include the appropriate ISLLC standards as part of your rationale for your response.

2. What do you see as the educational leader's role—managerial, instructional, or both? According to the ISLLC Standards, should an educational leader be an instructional leader or a manager? Please present rationales for your replies.

3. Based on your reading of Chapter 14, what keys would you use to curb teacher departures in your school district? What ISLLC Standards are impacted by a shortage of teachers? Please describe the impact on each Standard you identified.

4. Is it likely that twenty-first-century teachers will implement mastery learning? What conditions would have to be in place for mastery learning to be fully implemented? How would mastery learning impact ISLLC Standards 1, 2, and 3?

5. How might ISLLC Standards 5 and 6 be very important principles for educational leaders in the Frederick County Schools engaging in the enhancing of collaborative partnerships? Please explain.

6. ISLLC Standard 4 underscores the importance of educational leaders collaborating with families. What keys to parental involvement presented in Chapter 14 would maximize your collaboration with families as an educational leader?

7. Based on your reading of Chapter 14, what is the best use of the limited technology funding for your school and school district? What ISLLC Standards are most impacted by the dollars spent on technology? Please explain your responses.

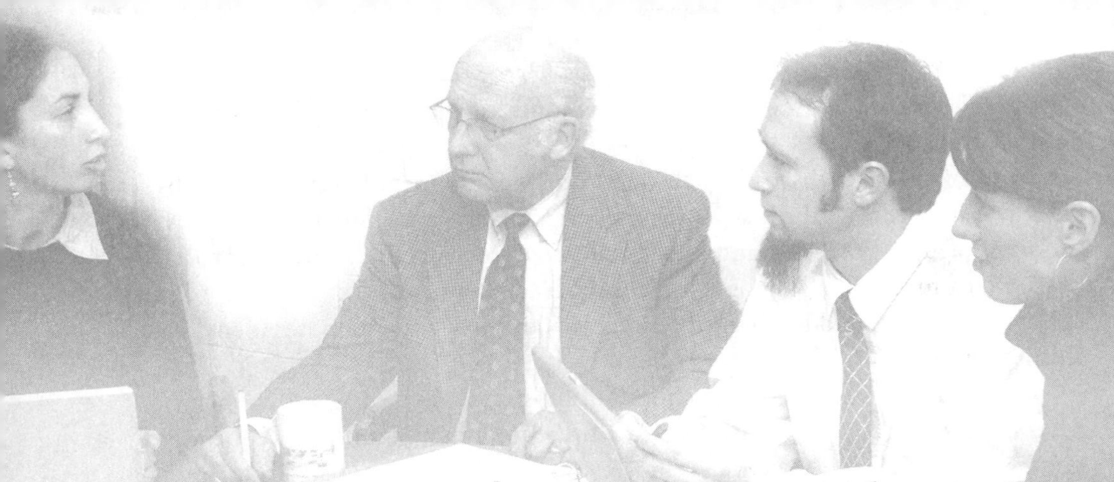

chapter **15**

ISLLC *Standards* 1–6

For Your Future and Beyond

A total commitment is paramount to reaching the ultimate in performance.
—Tom Flores, Former NFL Coach

Your last Action Focus takes you to a Superintendent of the Year ceremony in Boston.

"We are honored to bestow this prestigious honor of Superintendent of the Year on Superintendent Regina Gibbs," said Executive Director Wayne White. "Under her leadership, the Summit Public Schools has continued to move to the forefront in many areas, including student achievement; building a "professional family" comprised of students, faculty, parents, and community members; providing leadership for continuous improvements; empowering others; and maintaining fiscal management. Dr. Gibbs, a compassionate steward for education, is truly deserving of this award!"

"It's a real honor for our school system," Gibbs said. "It's a reflection that we have one of the best systems in the state." Gibbs added that she considered the honor more of an accomplishment for the system than personal.

"It's an emotional thing for me when I think about it," said a humbled Gibbs. "It's a good feeling to be selected by your peers as 'a coach of coaches' in front of all the other educational leaders."

"Dr. Gibbs's first priority is the students she serves, followed closely by the adults she works with and supervises," said Mark DuBois, superintendent of a neighboring school district. "While she has experienced much success over the years, she has remained very humble, always recognizing the contributions of others before self."

In supporting the recommendation for Superintendent of the Year, county superintendent Frank Roerts stated, "I consider Regina Gibbs to be one of the finest superintendents in our state. She exemplifies the traits of educational leadership mandated by our challenging times. She is a thinker, a planner, a designer, and a change agent. She runs a student-first school system and prizes academic excellence."

Gibbs has been superintendent in Summit Public Schools since 1999. Prior to that, she served as assistant superintendent, principal, guidance counselor, and teacher. Gibbs has taken an active role in community affairs, serving as president of both the Summit County Chamber of Commerce and the Summit County Rotary Club.

Summit County instructional supervisor Mark Jenny, who said that Gibbs's initiatives have moved the district forward in many ways, nominated Dr. Gibbs. "She has begun several new and innovative programs, including 'Professional Learning Communities.' Gibbs is a visioning leader with such extraordinary focus for lasting reforms and the skills to lead others to agree and attain her focus," said Jenny.

The Boston Association of School Administrators is the largest school administrators group in Massachusetts, representing more than 3,500 education leaders. Formed in 1959, the Massachusetts Association of School Administrators connects education leaders to policymakers, legislators, and other interest groups, and provides numerous benefits and services to Massachusetts' school administrators.

KEYS TO SUCCESSFUL TWENTY-FIRST-CENTURY EDUCATIONAL LEADERSHIP

As highlighted in your Chapter 15 Action Focus, successful twenty-first-century educational leaders will not fit the prior century's common notion of leader as hero. Rather, successful educational leaders of the new millennium, such as Superintendent Gibbs, will lead like a designer, change agent, coach, and steward while implementing the keys to educational leadership. In doing so, successful educational leaders will maintain an extraordinary ability to maintain focus. After all, obstacles to their success will only be those frightful things they see when they take their focus off their goals. Just as Gibbs was commended for her focus by her colleagues in handling difficult situations, so too will all successful twenty-first-century educational leaders need to work diligently and successfully in achieving the following focuses (Marks & Printy, 2002; Senge, Cambron-McCabe, Lucas, Smith, Dutton, & Kleiner, 2000).

- *Action Key 1: Educational facilitation focus.* This century's educational leadership will be based on informal or nonformal teaching, better described as *facilitation.* Educational leaders will be involved in facilitating the development of a cohesive learning group that values diversity and explores conflict constructively (Laurie, 2000). This process will be based on respect, encouragement, and community building. As the shortage of teachers escalates during this century and state teacher certification requirements are relaxed, it will be important for educational leaders to maintain an educational facilitation focus.
- *Action Key 2: Learner focus.* Educational leaders as learning facilitators will need to understand the context in which their leadership is situated: the learners' needs, desires, and strengths, and the issues being addressed. Successful twenty-first-century educational leadership will provide ample opportunity for those they lead to engage in the learning process through ongoing processes of visioning, planning, decision making, and reflecting

about their learning experiences (Kotter, 1999; Wilhelm, 1996). If education is to improve, it will take the commitment and conviction of *all* educators.

- *Action Key 3: Educational leadership focus.* Learner-focused educational leadership development will not mean leader focused. Leadership will exist as a set of relationships among group or organization members. Everyone in a school or school system will have leadership potential to play leadership roles at various times. This view will imply a group-centered approach to leadership development—one centered on organizational development and capacity building.
- *Action Key 4: Issue/action focus.* Out-of-context educational leadership development programs will have limited impact because the transfer of learning to real-life situations rarely happens. Therefore, educational leadership efforts that will aim for long-term impact will need to incorporate learning that is centered on real issues that individuals and groups will be facing (Kowalski, 2003a). Learning that is centered on real issues is learning in action, encouraging ongoing reflection or collective self-examination.
- *Action Key 5: Nonprescriptive educational leadership focus.* The content of twenty-first-century educational leadership efforts will not be prescribed; rather, the content will be determined with and by participants. The first meeting may very well consist of an overview of community action leadership, an outline of possible content areas, and an organizational diagnosis exercise (DenHartog & Verburg, 1997). The outline may be organized around the action values and then subdivided into many more specific topics from which to choose. Empowerment and ownership will be held at a premium.
- *Action Key 6: Process as content focus.* In many ways, the process or methodology of educational leadership efforts will be the content. By being part of an educational leadership group based on methodological principles,

IN THE NEWS

Extra Credit at O.C. School: Improved Scores Make a Principal One of the Five in the Nation to Win a Terrel H. Bell Award

Principal Linda Reed holds keys to successful twenty-first-century educational leadership.

One month after Hayden Elementary School had won a Blue Ribbon Award, its principal, Linda Reed, was recognized as one of the five best school leaders in the country as she was presented the Terrel H. Bell Award. Upon accepting this prestigious honor, Principal Reed commented that educational leaders must maintain their focus.

The first *action focus* she stated must be for all students to reach a high academic mark. Hayden Elementary School has done such an incredible job over time in improving test scores for all students despite some challenges at a campus where 65 percent of the students are still learning English and 66 percent are poor.

Principal Reed's commented that a *facilitation focus* is imperative where principals support their teachers by eliminating learning distractions. It is clearly understood at Hayden Elementary School that Principal Reed believes her teachers are the best at what they do and all students are capable of meeting high expectations.

Hayden Elementary School's principal stands tall when it comes to her *educational leadership focus* valuing the relationships between parents and educators. Reed believes that there is a strong correlation between parent involvement and high student achievement. From her sixteen years of teaching before entering administration, Reed knows that when parents value education and are willing to devote their time and energy to their child's education, their children will do better in school.

As Principal Reed is a successful visioning leader, so too will other educational leaders need to emulate her actions to promote the success of all students and faculty.

Source: F. Leal, "Extra Credit at O. C. School: Improved Scores Make a Principal One of Five in the Nation to Win a Terrel H. Bell Award," *Orange County Register* (Santa Ana, CA), December 6, 2005.

participants will learn facilitation, community building, teamwork, group planning and decision making, organizational development, conflict management, and group reflection (Awamleh & Gardner, 1999). These leadership qualities might just be the silver lining in cloudy past performances of many twentieth-century educational leaders.

Visioning Leadership

Successful twenty-first-century educational leaders will need to inspire those they lead by establishing, implementing, and assessing an attractive, worthwhile, achievable vision of the future. Visions of grand educational futures merge as powerful driving forces (Bennis, 1989; Marks & Printy, 2002; Nanus, 1992). Visioning leadership—that is, educational leaders who become the guardians and perpetuators of these visions—holds the keys to successful educational leadership. Visioning educational leadership will turn visions into action by overcoming resistance to change and achieving superlative results (Bell & Harrison, 1995; Holmes, 1993; Sergiovanni, 1990, 1996b).

The cornerstones of successful visioning educational leadership are communication, communication, and communication! The relationship between communication and vision is manifested in two different ways. First, vision will be resident in a leader and communication will be the medium by which vision will be carried to followers. Second, communication will be integral to the conception and cocreation of visioning leadership. Effective visioning leadership communication will have an empowering effect on shared vision. To further illustrate the powers of visioning educational leadership, the keys for aspiring and current educational leaders searching for twenty-first-century educational leadership are presented in Key Box 15.1 (Deal & Peterson, 2000; Donaldson, 2001; Koestenbaum, 2002).

KEY BOX 15.1

Keys to Twenty-First Century Visioning by Successful New Millennium Educational Leaders

- Seeing things differently
- Doing things differently
- Transcending diversity
- Answering a higher calling
- Ceasing opportunities
- Accepting reality
- Valuing the past, but knowing when to leave it
- Maximizing direction
- Building a brighter tomorrow

- *Key 1: Seeing things differently.* Effective educational leaders will have the visioning required to see things differently than others. Effective visioning educational leaders will collect and arrange the data in ways that allow them to conceive of new and unseen phenomena (Schein, 1999). A core characteristic of all effective visioning leadership will be the ability to create a vision of where they are trying to go. In addition, successful twenty-first-century visioning leaders will articulate their vision clearly to those they lead so that everyone will come to know their personal role in achieving that vision.

● *Key 2: Doing things differently.* Alternatively, visioning educational leadership comprises a synergistic process involving educational leaders and those they lead. This conception of visioning educational leadership engages educational leaders and their followers in coconstructing a vision (DenHartog & Verburg, 1997; Sergiovanni, 1990, 2000c). From the ownership of vision building and implementing, synergy flows. There is no greater power than an idea whose time has come. Such synergy flowing from shared visions have historically sent individuals to the moon, into uncharted water ways, and to break past barriers.

● *Key 3: Transcending diversity.* Visioning educational leadership will shatter the nontraditional roles of the past, once and for all. Visioning educational leadership will transcend across race, gender, and disabilities (Donaldson, 2001; Kirkpatrick & Locke, 1996). In this context, visioning educational leadership will derive its power and authority from all participating—that is, educational leaders and those they lead. Visioning educational leadership is vision driven, transcending color, creed, nationality, gender, or handicap. It will be coconstructed by the group with the group's culture, beliefs, and values of the school or school system in turn shaping the vision. Effective visioning educational leadership will empower, inspire, and motivate others to their highest calling.

● *Key 4: Answering a higher calling.* Successful visioning educational leaders will share a vision: an inspiring innovative future. This developing and promulgating of a vision will be the highest calling and truest purpose of leadership. History has revealed that humans instinctively follow the leader who follows his/her dream (Bennis, 1989; Donaldson, 2001; Education Trust, 2002). Likewise, visioning educational leaders who present a vision will be the individuals who are followed. These leaders will be the ones who are able to communicate visions that offer a goal, get a group to work together, and contribute their best toward the achievement of that vision. Clearly, the visioning educational leaders' ability to express an effective vision will achieve greater support from those who are led.

A point of distinction needs clarification here before proceeding to our next key. It has been held in the past that vision has been a leader's creation. We argue this point, asserting that leadership will come from a vision, not restricted to coming solely from a leader (Terry, 1993; Yukl, 1994). We agree that from either perspective, vision will give the perception of leadership. In either case, it will be the idea or vision that will generate the force that moves the group to its highest calling or level of achievement.

● *Key 5: Ceasing opportunities.* Do not fear unfortunate circumstances! The salience and force of a visioning educational leadership may be increased by crisis (Ackerman, 2003; Boal & Bryson, 1988). Numerous studies reveal that crisis and change are important to leadership in general and perhaps to visioning in particular. *Educational visions* of successful twenty-first-century leaders must view crisis as a resource for a group, organization, or leader. For example, crisis can affect the perceived need for change and/or perceptions of the level of ability necessary to effect change. During a period when the group perceives the existence of a crisis, a vision for changing the group's direction may become salient. The same vision probably would not have been salient prior to the onset of the perception of crisis. Indeed, without the force that manifests through perception of crisis, the group may lose its ability to affect any significantly different outcomes for the future.

Consequently, crises can become a resource for changing behaviors. Some educational leaders may use crises rhetorically to influence followers to unlearn old activities and to search for new behaviors that will influence the outcome of a crisis. Crises may even result in shifts in values and ideologies that would not be as achievable absent crises (Laurie, 2000). In a sense, crises can provide the educational leader greater latitude and freedom to act.

RESEARCH KEYS

To enrich your understanding of **educational vision,** log on to www.researchnavigator.com and search Ebsco's ContentSelect.

Research Navigator.com

- *Key 6: Accepting reality.* Successful visioning educational leaders will know that "the visioning" will be based in the current reality of those they lead (let's say faculty to illustrate this point). This "reality" will be at least partially a symbolic, social coconstruction held by the faculty. The reality of the faculty will include what is important to the faculty and how well or poorly the faculty is doing, whether it is an honor to be a member, and how necessary it is that decisions ought to be made in a particular way or favoring a particular value (Barth, 2001; Bell & Harrison, 1995; Sergiovanni, 1990). Successful educational leadership must understand the socially constructed reality of the staff (or other group) in order to understand how a particular visioning might affect others. Symbolic reality is not necessarily logical or objective. Lack of awareness or acknowledgment of this can frustrate the efforts of educational leaders and group members.
- *Key 7: Valuing the past, but knowing when to leave it.* Visioning educational leadership will be concerned with a future substantially different from the present. Educational leaders will provide direction during the twenty-first century for those they lead through changing times. Although visioning will be formed in the present, it is targeted at lifting those that are led out of the present and focusing them on a compelling future (Hargreaves, Earl, Moore, & Manning, 2001; Komives, Lucas, & McMahon, 1998). Visioning will be the bridge to the future, where tomorrow begins! The future as provided by the visioning will be based on improvements, enhancements, and a more desirable future. Visioning educational leaders may therefore be thought of as the conduits for an improved educational future.
- *Key 8: Maximizing direction.* In addition to the significant gains visioning educational leadership will bestow on all successful twenty-first-century educational leaders and those they lead, it will also enhance the meaning of group life and activities. Visioning educational leadership will make meaningful the activities undertaken to accomplish the future as outlined in the vision. By making activities meaningful, vision increases a group's synergy, which will help others place their concerns in the perspective of the agreed visioning. Consequently, visioning educational leadership brings reason for change to the work of the group or organization. Visioning educational leadership will take those that are led out of a mundane reality and move them to a state of opportunity and challenge (Awamleh & Gardner, 1999; DenHartog & Verburg, 1997; Earl, 2004).

Visioning educational leadership creates energy because when educators and all others are striving to achieve a shared vision, everyone works together as a team. The difference between an aggregate of individuals and a team is synergy focused on common goals or practices (Schein, 1999). Successful visioning educational leadership for the twenty-first century is dipped and dyed in the principle that **T**ogether **E**veryone **A**chieves **M**ore (TEAM).

- *Key 9: Building a brighter tomorrow.* Visioning educational leadership is about hopes, purposes, and where education needs to go. It moves a group forward in spite of challenges and opposition. Through visioning educational leadership, those who are led are inspired. Effective visioning educational leadership evokes a commitment to affecting the future. Energy among educational leaders and those who are led is generated by the desire to improve the future. This energy provides part of the motivational force associated with visioning, just as crisis provides force or impetus for a group to achieve a brighter tomorrow.

Successful twenty-first-century visioning educational leaders motivate those they lead to transcend temporal concerns (Snyder, Dowd, & Houghton, 1994). Visioning educational leadership is a vicarious experience lifting a group out of the present and transporting the group to where it hopes to be.

Visioning educational leadership inspires people by transcending current limitations, seeing things differently, applying synergy, transcending human conditions, and calling everyone to the highest level of commitment and performance (Nanus, 1992). Visioning educational leadership constitutes a commitment to influence the future by looking at a crisis as promising, becoming aware of symbolic realities, and not settling for past performance in an ever-changing world (Napolitano & Henderson, 1998). Visioning educator leadership offers opportunities for educational leaders and those they lead to exceed their own perceived limitations and work diligently and successfully for a brighter educational future.

SUCCESSFUL VISIONING

In the twenty-first century, leadership will be defined as a social interaction in which one person (the visioning educational leader) influences the activities of other people (the followers) within a given frame of circumstances toward achieving a shared vision (Marks & Printy, 2002; Snyder, Dowd, & Houghton, 1994). In essence, *visioning* is at the heart of leadership. Successful visioning educational leadership will be dependent on several facets of social interaction in which the followers will be motivated toward the achievement of a shared vision. Sounds simple enough? Think it through again in consideration of the ever-changing times, education under fire, and the tremendous pressures for superior performance.

Strategies for Conflict Resolution

Even with the most widely supported visioning, conflicts will arise. Each conflict to be resolved will comprise a different combination of impediments to favorable change, or will have different variations of similar impediments. Thus, the success in resolving a conflict by the visioning educational leaders will be determined by the strategy they select in resolving a conflict (Ackerman, 2003; Mandl & Sethi, 1996). In selecting which strategy to resolve a challenge or conflict, visioning educational leaders will need to consider numerous variables. Is the conflict to be resolved most successfully through a people-oriented or task-oriented strategy? Intelligence, knowledge relevant to the tasks to be performed, competence, and social skills needed for successful remedy constitute additional variables that need to be considered by the successful visioning educational leaders. Even partiality to a visioning leadership style—whether it be democratic, authoritative, laissez-faire, transformational, or transactional—will be part and parcel to the educational leaders' development of strategies (Barth, 2001; Burtis, 1995; Hart, 1998). In addition, the strategy for conflict resolution articulated by the leader will need to correspond to that leader's qualities, style, and capabilities, for if it does not, preferred accomplishments will be jeopardized.

Attributes of Followers

In promotion of a shared vision, visionary educational leaders will carefully assess and take into consideration the attributes of those they lead (DeCrane, 1996; Earl, 2004). Visioning educational leaders will consider the level of psychological maturity, such as their ability and willingness to confront obstacles and complexities, and the level of motivation of those they lead. Mature and experienced educators will have acquired more technical skills and cognitive abilities in coping with difficulties and challenges at work. In comparison with less mature followers, experienced followers will be better able to defer gratification, deal with long-term commitments, cope with multiple goals, and face ambiguous missions more effectively.

IN THE NEWS

Bringing New Vision to Education: Principal Lauded for Innovation Wins Leadership Award

Principal Helena Nobles-Jones is honored as a successful twenty-first-century visioning leader in changing environments.

The sharecropper's daughter rose quite far in the educational world of the nation's capital. Throughout her thirty years of experience as a teacher, administrative intern, assistant principal, principal, and then assistant superintendent, Helena Nobles-Jones has soared as a visioning leader. In fact, her visioning and love for children inspired her to leave the bureaucratic maze of central office and return to the principalship to open a new high school in Prince George's County.

A panel of administrators selected her this fall from among the leaders of 199 county schools to receive the Washington Post Distinguished Educational Leadership Award. Principal Nobles-Jones was selected among her peers for this honor because of her abilities and talents as a visioning leader and her commitment to the highest academic standards for all children. She continuously promotes the success of her students and faculty. Nobles-Jones does not tire when it comes to encouraging all others to do their best and never stop learning.

Leaders such as Helena Nobles-Jones use their visioning abilities to lead America's new millennium schools into the future.

Source: N. Anderson, "Bringing New Vision to Education: Principal Lauded for Innovation Wins Leadership Award," *The Washington Post*, November 17, 2005.

Leadership in Stable and Changing Environments

Another key that affects visioning is change or the lack thereof. The latter is sometimes termed *dynamic* or *turbulent*. These characteristics will impact the organization's functioning, the ability to plan ahead, and the feasibility of pursuing goals steadfastly. A high level of heterogeneity will lead to a high rate of change and will increase the uncertainty that is perceived by members of the organization with regard to its future. In either case, the leaders' ability in a changing environment to define long-range mission statements will be constrained, and their perceived risks will be greater. Thus, visioning educational leaders operating in a turbulent environment will need to define mission statements that delineate exactly what is to be done, how, and when (Bennis, 1989; Hargreaves, Earl, Moore, & Manning, 2001; Nanus, 1992;).

Visioning as a Tool

Visioning educational leadership may be contorted into a powerful twenty-first-century tool. Visioning educational leaders may occasionally be tempted to use visioning in manipulative ways, to achieve preferred outcomes such as better results, to gain greater involvement by followers, and to attain increased dedication from followers. That is, visionary educational leaders may be fully aware of their own qualities, of their followers' specific attributes, and of the nature of the organizational environment and nonetheless choose to articulate a visioning that intentionally disregards some of these characteristics. They may be tempted to do so under the assumption or conviction that their strategy will best serve the organization's purposes. This approach will exploit the discrepancy between the given circumstances and the vision as a strategy to induce followers to apply themselves to achieve the organizational goals (Kotter, 1999; Schein, 1999). This manipulative strategy of the visioning leader will create a discrepancy between the vision and the reality, with the visioning leader's credibility being held as questionable to say the least.

Fundamental Biases

Visioning educational leaders must be careful in being biased toward attending to the interests of the followers (Melendez, 1996). Such leaders will tend to deemphasize visioning, opting for close relationships with followers. To illustrate within a school context, the visioning educational leader (the principal) may put much emphasis on maintaining wholesome staff relationships and tend not to develop an encouraging atmosphere for the students. However, such a visioning educational leader might face difficulties when defining the organizational mission statement if the conditions of the environment do not correspond to the needs and the demands of the learners. Overlooking these conditions may produce a dysfunctional vision (Sergiovanni, 1990). Hence, such partiality may result in a school deferring the opportunities to implement new technologies and instruction methods because the principal may be overly attentive to the teachers who favor the known and familiar over the need to acquire updated technology and revise teaching methods. A school that surrenders to such teachers' resistance and that lags behind the changes of its environment fails to keep up with the times, and therefore may fall behind compared to other learning institutions.

Environments

The "outward" oriented visioning educational leader will tend to place more value on the characteristics of the environment and less emphasis on the followers. This type of leader tends to be concerned mainly with satisfying environmental needs rather than reacting to personnel and curricula deficiencies and demands (Kouzes

& Posner, 1995). Returning to the school setting, a principal who strives for litter-free hallways and beautiful grounds, but does so without taking into consideration the interests of the school staff, will profess a visioning of the school's mission statement that will likely fall short in conveying the need for substantial and significant changes in the school. Hear this clearly: Twenty-first-century visionary educational leadership will not tolerate this environment-only leadership. Such environmental concentration is better delegated, with more important student, faculty, parent, and community concerns attended to by visionary educational leaders.

Continuing Concerns

The successful twenty-first-century visioning educational leader is attentive to the needs of both the followers and the environment. This leader enhances the probability that there will be an alignment of the needs of the followers to the circumstances of the organizational environment (DenHartog & Verburg, 1997). The visioning educational leader who incorporates these important conditions will be providing optimal leadership for schools by successfully uniting vision and its mission statement and successfully serving the three elements of leadership: the leaders, the followers, and the environment.

Differing Priorities

Successful visioning educational leaders will be aware that operational performance goals of various levels (i.e., elementary, middle, and high school) may not always be congruent and, indeed, may come into conflict with other levels. Thus, the continuity issue arises as to how or whether a change in the performance of one work level affects changes in the performance of another work level. For example, some elementary schools may not want to emphasize the same goals as high schools in the same school district, such as career preparation or competition in sports, whereas high schools may wish to emphasize careers and winning teams. In brief, the goals and perspectives of various organizational levels may be incongruent, leading to the potential accomplishment of respective operational performance goals, although organizational performance at a higher level of analysis does not get maximized (Boal & Bryson, 1988; Kotter, 1999; Krzyzewski, 2000; Laurie, 2000).

Multilevel Performances

The performance of individuals and groups may need to be linked if higher-level organizational performance (i.e., districtwide) is to be achieved. Important influences on linkages or interconnectivities will be revealed in the nature of the relationships that exist among individuals and among work units. Cohesive intragroup and intergroup relationships are likely to be spawned by successful twenty-first-century visionary school district leaders and their cascading leadership impact, which, in turn, encourages the cooperative pursuit of school district goals (DeCrane, 1996). In short, intergroup cohesion will make it possible to achieve simultaneously the possibly divergent goals of organizational levels (i.e., elementary, middle, and high school) in such a manner that the ultimate performance of the organization has the potential to be maximized. For example, a school district may have an overall mission such as the proficiency of all students on statewide tests.

Managed Conflict

As a caveat, a managed level of intergroup conflict, or level at which conflict may be resolved or tolerated, generally will result in positive movement toward organizational goals, innovation and change, problem solutions, and creativity and quick adaptation to environmental changes (Boal & Deal, 1988; Donaldson, 2001; Schein, 1999). The key for twenty-first-century visioning educational leaders to hold is whether this conflict is life giving or life disabling. In other words, intergroup cohesion should not be so great as to stifle healthy or constructive disagreements among groups nor hinder accomplishments of high-level goals.

Organizational Cohesion

Successful educational leaders will realize their ultimate impact in terms of maximizing organizational outcomes such as student achievement. That is, when the cohesion-building effects of visioning educational leadership help to realize coordination or synergy with regard to the operational performance (such as academic gains), organizational performance will likely be maximized (Awamleh & Gardner, 1999). Stated another way, the overall performance of organizations is likely to be enhanced when visioning educational leaders coordinate the performance goals of groups in such a manner that one group is not accomplishing its goals at the expense of another or without concern for another.

Systemic Perspective

The primary cognitive skill of top-echelon twenty-first-century educational leaders will be to have a systemic perspective involving the ability to integrate and harmonize various organizational—or even societal—subsystems. This systemic perspective will be best accomplished when leaders simultaneously utilize visioning educational leadership as the ability to inspire individuals or groups to work for the betterment of the greater organization (Bass, 1997; Koestenbaum, 2002). For example, a president of a national principals' association uses his or her visioning leadership qualities not only to inspire individuals and groups to work for the betterment of the larger organization (public schools) but to have public schools seen as a force for social change.

Win–Win Teaming

Twenty-first-century educational leaders will demonstrate high degrees of intergroup cohesion, coupled with agreement regarding organizational goals. This cohesion and agreement of goals will result in performance that is oriented toward achievement of those goals and greater achievement by all involved (Sergiovanni, 1990, 2000a). To illustrate, two small neighboring rural school districts are facing fiscal hardships. Both decide to combine their purchasing power to enable each to purchase technology at lower costs. The fundamental change was a result of both school districts acting as a team and becoming more responsible for the group as a whole in a more cost-effective and efficient way.

In retrospect, successful twenty-first-century visioning educational leadership will influence performance at all levels (schools) throughout the organization (school district) and include numerous organizations (all school districts within a state or nation). The visioning educational leadership paradigm will be used in the future by visioning educational leaders who follow the keys presented in this chapter and other cutting-edge discoveries to gain increased student achievement by motivating and inspiring faculty, students, parents, and community members.

TAKING CARE OF BUSINESS

Even the most skillful and well-intentioned educational leader will need to be cognizant of the pitfalls, the detractors, and the disablers of educational leadership. It is most unfortunate that in the past, qualified educational leaders have left the profession upset, frustrated, or with ill health. Educational leadership is more challenging today than ever before (Grogan & Andews, 2002; Peterson, 2002).

RESEARCH KEYS

To enrich your understanding of **principal shortage**, log on to www.researchnavigator.com and search Ebsco's ContentSelect.

ResearchNavigator.com

A flurry of new millennium studies responding with reasons and resolutions for unprecedented shortages of qualified educational leaders has streamed forward (including but not limited to Aiken, 2002; Barth, 2001; Capasso & Daresh, 2001; Glassman, Cibulka, & Ashby, 2002; Grogan & Andrews, 2002; Kowalski, 2003b). Knowing the landmines of the trade is important to the health and well-being of twenty-first-century educational leaders. Hence, the stress keys to successful educational leadership follow:

- *Stress Key 1: Long hours.* We know from our experiences that it is not uncommon for educational leaders to work upward of 54 to 80 hours each week, including evenings and weekends. This is a taxing schedule for even the most energetic individual. No matter how involved a principal is, there seems to be the compelling feeling of needing to do more.
- *Stress Key 2: Too much on your plate.* Few duties fall outside the scope of an educational leader's description. When one task is complete, two more are added to the plate. Educators in general, educational leaders especially, for some reason are reluctant to selectively abandon the outdated or antiquated (Grogan & Andrews, 2002). Constantly putting out fires and mending fences keep the most energetic educational leaders pulled in several directions at the same time and often at wit's end.
- *Stress Key 3: Government mandates and accountability.* Nearly every lawmaker wants to be dubbed the education czar. New laws and requirements at the state and federal levels are being passed in record numbers—often with little foresight. Too often what federal and state legislatures mandate is inadequately funded (Daresh, 2002). High-stakes testing, standardized testing programs, school takeovers, teacher recruitment and retention, and legislation, such as the No

Child Left Behind Act appear from the outset to stack the odds against effective educational leadership.

- *Stress Key 4: Critical issues of society brought to school.* School safety, substance abuse, teen pregnancy, and teen suicide scratch the surface of what educational leaders must cope with on a daily basis (McCarthy, 2001). Students today are coming to schools at younger ages with increased learning difficulties. As parents abdicate their responsibilities, schools are being asked to provide day care and other health-related services, thus creating more programs for the educational leaders to fund and oversee.

- *Key 5: Surpassing achievement standards.* Increasingly during this century, educational leaders will be under more pressure for students to achieve at all-time highs. To achieve desired heights, cutting-edge curricula and best practices in instruction are critical components (Muth & Barnett, 2001). However, with the tightening of budgets leaving insufficient financial support for program and skills development, as well as a shortage of qualified curriculum directors and instructional specialists, soaring achievement gains seem antithetical to available resources.

- *Key 6: Special education requirements.* Ever-present and increasing demands for expanding services, continually changing Individuals with Disabilities Education Act (IDEA) requirements, Section 504 accommodations, and other legislative mandates leave diminishing opportunities for innovation and creativity. Lawyers and advocates are commonplace, with conflicts resolved in courtrooms instead of board rooms increasing in number during the twenty-first century (Glass, Bjork, & Brunner, 2000). The endless hours and stress on educational leaders counter productivity and adversely impact the workday.

- *Key 7: School funding issues.* Managing complex budgets, shouldering the losses in program and personnel caused by shrinking dollars, and being held accountable for fund raising by many groups all play heavily on educational leaders' performance (Aiken, 2002). Many educational leaders agree that as school budgets get tighter, things get ugly.

- *Key 8: Little financial incentive.* The compensation for educational leaders is more negligible than negotiable. Take, for example, the daily rate of pay for a new assistant principal. It is barely 5 percent more than that of an experienced teacher when one calculates this sum into a principal's eleven months of working several nights per week supervising extracurricular activities and on-call twenty-four hours a day, seven days a week for emergencies (Daresh, 2002). The under-funding of educational leaders is not just true of principals but all educational leaders. Compared with their counterparts in business and industry with similar education and experience, educational leaders are underpaid. It's true that educational leaders do not enter the profession to get rich; however, they should have equal opportunities to provide for their own families as individuals holding important status in a community.

- *Key 9: Inability to fire incompetent teachers.* The dismissal of a tenured teacher is a long, exhausting, and expensive process. It is not uncommon that legal proceedings take place over several years, taking educational leaders away from proactive and progressive initiatives. Often, the pursuit of dismissal is not a well-paved road, with aggressive challenges from opponents along the way (Cooper,

Fusarelli, & Carella, 2000). The process of teacher dismissal is so cumbersome that educational leaders tend to prolong dismissal proceedings.

• *Key 10: Contractual agreements.* Constraints in employee contracts often preclude educational leaders from making rapid change and school improvements more expeditiously. For example, the school improvement process, as stipulated in many collective bargaining agreements, requires hours of discussion with all stakeholders present to implement a single idea. With a high school faculty of ninety, it might take two to three years to implement a variation in the workday such as block scheduling (Kowalski, 2003a). Such initiatives often consume an educational leader's time and energy, leading to a reduction in other school improvements and personal exhaustion.

By defining realistically the conditions that discourage candidates from seeking educational leadership positions, identification of viable solutions to recruit and retain educational leaders may commence. Educational leaders should all join together to seek both short-term and long-term remedies (Jackson & Kelley, 2002). For example, although increasing the salaries of educational leaders may not be an option, reducing the number of required meetings they are mandated to attend is an important starting point. Adequate staffing instead of adding additional responsibilities to current educational leaders is a must. Finally, educational leaders joining together to brainstorm and prioritize responsibilities in which essential duties are acknowledged and other requirements abandoned provides an opportunity for educational leaders to address important needs. Too often, educational leaders focus on their own agendas, being remiss in changing the culture downtown that significantly may change the outcome uptown. Restructuring the educational leaders' roles and responsibilities with meaningful adjustments, often at little to no cost to the district, will help maintain quality educational leaders and attract new aspiring candidates.

LASTING EDUCATIONAL LEADERSHIP REFORMS

Twenty-first-century schools will not be similar to the schools of the prior century. For that matter, schools of the future will be different from any schools of the past. Schools of the new millennium will be value added, customer oriented, and market driven. Competition will be fierce among all schools: public, private, parochial, and for profit. Students will be the recipients of services that have been unavailable before. Public education will emerge as the champion for all students and the restored foundation of democracy.

Specifically, what will be the keys to twenty-first-century schools? There is no simple answer! However, some items have emerged from our sixty years of collective educational experience. It is our intent to shed important light on educational excellence for this new century as presented within the following keys.

• *Key 1:* Education in the new century will not be a delivery system for collections of fragmented information in the guise of curricula. Rather, education will be a process that encourages continual progress through the improvement of one's abilities, the expression of one's interests, and the growth of one's character (Jackson & Kelley, 2002).

● *Key 2:* Successful schools will be a place where students, teachers, administrators, and others take pride and joy in their work. The transformation of twenty-first-century schools will mean a systemically changed organization, not just patched-up versions of the original (Peterson, 2002).

● *Key 3:* Schools of the new century will focus on helping students maximize their own potentials through continuous improvement of teachers and students working together. Maximization of test scores and assessment symbols will be less important than the progress inherent in the continuous learning process of each student (DuFour & Eaker, 1998).

● *Key 4:* Educational leaders will adopt and fully support the new philosophy of continuous improvement through greater empowerment of teacher–student teams (Murphy & Forsyth, 1999). Cyclical application of the new philosophy, with the sole intent of improving districtwide test scores, will be avoided, as it destroys interpersonal trust that is essential to success.

IN THE NEWS

The Kalamazoo Promise: College Tuition for All Grades

Kalamazoo Public Schools is an example of a twenty-first-century school district that is value added, competitive, customer oriented, and market driven.

In an unprecedented move to transform Kalamazoo Public Schools (KPS) and its entire community into an exciting place to live, study, and work, KPS announced a program to provide four years of full tuition scholarships to its graduates to any public college or university in Michigan beginning with the class of 2006.

The KPS scholarship program, entitled the Kalamazoo Promise, will provide 100 percent of tuition and mandatory fees for KPS graduates who have been enrolled in the KPS School District since kindergarten and whose parents live in the school district's boundaries. A partial scholarship will be given to students who enter after kindergarten and before their sophomore year.

Kalamazoo Promise not only has significant incentives for graduates, it will benefit the entire community. First, a scholarship program of this magnitude will boost the community's tax base as families move into the district. Second, the Kalamazoo Promise will result in a better-educated workforce and provide incentives for businesses to locate within the KPS boundaries. It will present everyone with an opportunity to move ahead, to break cycles of poverty, and to stop the district's enrollment decline.

Speculation continues to circulate about who the donors might be. School district officials are sworn to secrecy, and school board members don't even know who the contributors are. Attorneys for the school district affirm that the donor base has the money to meet this commitment.

KPS graduates about 500 students a year and about 75 percent go on to college. The cost of the Kalamazoo Promise will be about $3 million in its first year of operation and then $12 million annually by the time four graduating classes are in college.

As exemplified by the Kalamazoo Public Schools, the keys to twenty-first-century school reform will be unique, diverse, and varied.

Source: J. Mack, "The Kalamazoo Promise: College Tuition for All Grades," *Kalamazoo Gazette* (MI), November 11, 2005.

● *Key 5:* Reliance on tests as the major means of assessment of student production will be inherently wasteful, nonreliable, and not authentic. It will be too late at the end of the unit to assess students' progress if the goal is to maximize student productivity. Tests and other indicators of student learning will be shown by students' performance, applying information, and employing skills to real-life challenges (McCarthy, 2001). Students in successful twenty-first-century schools will be taught how to assess their own work and progress if they are to take ownership of their own educational processes.

● *Key 6:* Relationships will be built in schools that are established on trust and collaboration between school and community. Everyone's roles in educating students will be recognized and honored (National Policy Board for Educational Administration, 2002). All educational leaders working together whenever possible will maximize the potential of students.

- *Key 7:* Educational leaders will create and maintain the context in which teachers will be empowered to make continuous progress in the quality of their learning and other aspects of personal development, while they learn valuable lessons from temporary failures.

- *Key 8:* Educational leaders will institute programs of training for new staff members unfamiliar with the specific culture and expectations of the school. Effective training programs will show new teachers how to set goals, how to teach effectively, and how to assess the quality of their work with students (Usdan, 2002b). Teachers will also institute programs in which students learn how to be more effective in their schoolwork and how to assess the quality of their work. Teachers will show students by attitude and actions what a good learner is all about.

- *Key 9:* Educational leaders will work with teachers, parents, students, and members of the community as coaches and mentors so that students' accomplishments will be maximized by all those who support the common effort (Normore, 2004). Educational leaders will be service oriented.

- *Key 10:* Fear will be eliminated, as it is counterproductive in successful schools. It will be perceived as destructive of school culture and everything good that is intended to take place (Starratt, 2004). Institutional changes will reflect shared power, shared responsibilities, and shared rewards.

- *Key 11:* Teacher and student productivity will be enhanced when teachers, grades, and school levels (i.e., elementary, middle, high schools) combine talents to create more integrated opportunities for learning and discovery. Cross-departmental and multilevel quality teams will break down role and status barriers as well as increase productivity.

- *Key 12:* Teachers, students, administrators, families, and community members will collectively arrive at slogans and school themes to improve their work together (Madsen & Hipp, 1999). Power, responsibility, and rewards will be equitably distributed. When educational goals are not met, the system will be fixed instead of placing blame on individuals.

- *Key 13:* Assignments and tests that focus attention on numerical or letter grades and production completion will not fully reflect the quality of student progress and performance. Grades will not become the bottom-line product of successful twenty-first-century schools. Short-term gains will not replace student investment in long-term learning, and this long-term focus will also prove productive in the short run.

- *Key 14:* Teachers and students will want to do their best and feel pride in it. Schools will dedicate themselves to removing the systemic causes of teacher and student failures through close collaborative efforts.

- *Key 15:* All stakeholders will benefit from the encouragement to enrich their education by exploring ideas and interests beyond the boundaries of their professional and personal worlds. Administrators, teachers, and students will require continuous learning programs to be on the leading edge to maximize student achievement (Barth, 2001).

Successful twenty-first-century educational leaders will put this new philosophy into action so it will become embedded into the culture of the school. Teachers and students alone will not be lassoed to carry out the changes alone.

Top-level encouragement from all educational leaders to the full implementation of this transformation will prevail (Normore, 2004; Quick & Normore, 2004; Shapiro, Poliner, & Stefkovich, 2001; Starratt, 2004). The building of the critical mass of school and community people to implement the plan is imperative to ensure the continuance of these educational leadership reforms.

DON'T GIVE UP THE SHIP, DRIVE IT!

Throughout this chapter and text as a whole, keys to successful twenty-first-century educational leadership have been presented. The task of pulling together these various ideas into a relevant and meaningful whole is like creating a key ring to hold one's most valuable keys. The holder of the keys considers many choices of key rings: Some will be small, others large; some can be fastened to belts, some will even be noise activated, and some will be expensive, whereas others will be inexpensive. All are sold for the same purpose: to hold your entry devices, your keys, that allow entryway into your most treasured places—your home, your car, and your office, to mention a few.

Similarly, you are your metaphoric key ring. You will decide what keys to hold, which keys are most important, which ones you may even color code in importance. Some keys you will decide not to hold, as perhaps they have lesser importance in your life. Regardless of the value you place on each key, each key performs an important function. Yet the decision is yours to carry that key wherever you go by placing it on your key chain or not. It is clear, however, that you will not be able to enter a passageway unless you have your key with you—at least without destruction, damage, or using someone else's key. Choose your keys wisely.

As *Keys to Successful 21st Century Educational Leadership* draws to a close, educational leaders are challenged to make their own decisions from the numerous keys presented in this book, to capture those ideas worthy of providing a legacy, and to achieve long-term images that can guide their efforts in improving twenty-first-century education, where educational leaders not only open entryways for themselves but also for those they lead and those they serve. Although it may be easier for educational leaders to rely on past practices, the future key holders of educational organizations will strive diligently and successfully in increasing achievement for all students by unlocking their potentials first and foremost (Deal & Peterson, 2000; Hoy & Hoy, 2003; Koestenbuam, 2002; Kouzes & Posner, 2002; Soder, 2001).

For two key makers, our collective years of experience have shaped our keys for twenty-first-century educational leaders as presented in this book. When all keys are joined together on the key ring of life, these keys provide opportunities to go where past educational barriers provided no entryway. Two key makers, determined to improve schools by increasing student achievement, begin a dialogue with other key makers that impact lives significantly. The two key makers may not have the only design, but it may make others begin the dialogue of how best to impact learning. And in the final analysis, if all else fails, if one key can be easily turned into an improvement for learners, then our shaping of keys has been rewarded. May the keys you select bring success to your twenty-first-century leadership and to the lives of those you serve.

THE REFLECTIVE PRACTITIONER

Welcome to your fifteenth Reflective Practitioner containing your Chapter 15 scenario, again based on all six ISLLC Standards and your reading of Chapter 15. It is intended to provoke your thoughtful reflection and to stimulate discussion among colleagues, classmates, and peers. The Reflective Practitioner provides opportunities to synthesize issues, make comparisons, and apply theory to practice. We hope it will motivate you to search for evidence, thus increasing your comprehension of the text and helping you examine your convictions and discover new and shared perspectives.

- **ISLLC Standard 1**
A school administrator is an educational leader who promotes the success of all students by facilitating the development, articulation, implementation, and stewardship of a vision of learning that is shared and supported by the school community.

- **ISLLC Standard 2**
A school administrator is an educational leader who promotes the success of all students by advocating, nurturing, and sustaining a school culture and instructional program conducive to student learning and staff professional growth.

- **ISLLC Standard 3**
A school administrator is an educational leader who promotes the success of all students by ensuring management of the organization, operations, and resources for a safe, efficient, and effective learning environment.

- **ISLLC Standard 4**
A school administrator is an educational leader who promotes the success of all students by collaborating with families and community members, responding to diverse community interests and needs, and mobilizing community resources.

- **ISSLC Standard 5**
A school administrator is an educational leader who promotes the success of all students by acting with integrity, fairness, and in an ethical manner.

- **ISLLC Standard 6**
A school administrator is an educational leader who promotes the success of all students by understanding, responding to, and influencing the larger political, social, economic, legal, and cultural context.

Scenario

The auditorium is full of educational leaders from across the nation. You are not certain why you have journeyed to Washington, D.C., but you do know that if it wasn't for a close professional friend of yours, you wouldn't be in attendance. The master of ceremonies welcomes the over 5,000 guests, presents a short overview of the purpose of the twenty-first-century educational summit to recognize outstanding lifetime accomplishments of exemplary educational leaders, and then introduces the President of the United States.

The president thanks the National Board of Educational Leaders (NBEL) for the opportunity to present the most prestigious award to the nation's most notable educational leader. (You are thinking just about now, "What's with all this political hoopla?"). The president reads a long list of lifetime educational accomplishments that sound faintly familiar. You are surprised that the descriptions of these accomplishments occurred in school districts in which you have served. The President of the United States then announces the award recipient's name proudly. It is you!

Regaining a state of consciousness was your first goal. Wiping the tears out of your eyes may have been your second response. You walk up to the podium to shake the hand of the President of the United States, while searching for words to accurately describe your past thirty-two years of educational leadership accomplishments.

QUESTIONS FOR REFLECTIVE THINKING

1. What would you like to be able to say in reference to your accomplishments thirty years from now? Please detail your response and give reasons why.
2. In achievement of the National ISLLC Standards, which ISLLC Standards would you feel most accomplished in mastering? Please select your words thoughtfully as to what you would say from the

podium in Washington before the educational leaders from across the nation.

3. What keys have you discovered in your reading of Chapter 15 that you feel would be most helpful to your successful educational leadership? Which of your selected keys are related to ISLLC Standards? Which ISLLC Standards? Please explain.

4. Describe your educational leadership vision for the twenty-first century. Base your response, where applicable, on the six ISLLC Standards and your reading of Chapter 15.

5. How important is visioning educational leadership to your success as a twenty-first-century educational leader? Which ISLLC Standards affirm your role as a visionary leader? Please explain.

APPENDIX

ISLLC Standards for School Leaders: Knowledge, Dispositions, and Performances

Standard 1: A school administrator is an educational leader who promotes the success of all students by **facilitating the development, articulation, implementation, and stewardship of a vision of learning that is shared and supported by the school community.**

Knowledge
The administrator has knowledge and understanding of:
- learning goals in a pluralistic society
- the principles of developing and implementing strategic plans
- systems theory
- information sources, data collection, and data analysis strategies
- effective communication
- effective consensus-building and negotiation skills

Dispositions
The administrator believes in, values, and is committed to:
- the educability of all
- a school vision of high standards of learning
- continuous school improvement
- the inclusion of all members of the school community
- ensuring that students have the knowledge, skills, and values needed to become successful adults
- a willingness to continuously examine one's own assumptions, beliefs, and practices
- doing the work required for high levels of personal and organization performance

Performances
The administrator facilitates processes and engages in activities ensuring that:
- the vision and mission of the school are effectively communicated to staff, parents, students, and community members
- the vision and mission are communicated through the use of symbols, ceremonies, stories, and similar activities
- the core beliefs of the school vision are modeled for all stakeholders
- the vision is developed with and among stakeholders
- the contributions of school community members to the realization of the vision are recognized and celebrated

- progress toward the vision and mission is communicated to all stakeholders
- the school community is involved in school improvement efforts
- the vision shapes the educational programs, plans, and actions
- an implementation plan is developed in which objectives and strategies to achieve the vision and goals are clearly articulated
- assessment data related to student learning are used to develop the school vision and goals
- relevant demographic data pertaining to students and their families are used in developing the school mission and goals
- barriers to achieving the vision are identified, clarified, and addressed
- needed resources are sought and obtained to support the implementation of the school mission and goals
- existing resources are used in support of the school vision and goals
- the vision, mission, and implementation plans are regularly monitored, evaluated, and revised

Standard 2: A school administrator is an educational leader who promotes the success of all students by **advocating, nurturing, and sustaining a school culture and instructional program conducive to student learning and staff professional growth.**

Knowledge
The administrator has knowledge and understanding of:
- student growth and development
- applied learning theories
- applied motivational theories
- curriculum design, implementation, evaluation, and refinement
- principles of effective instruction
- measurement, evaluation, and assessment strategies
- diversity and its meaning for educational programs
- adult learning and professional development models
- the change process for systems, organizations, and individuals
- the role of technology in promoting student learning and professional growth
- school cultures

Dispositions
The administrator believes in, values, and is committed to:
- student learning as the fundamental purpose of schooling
- the proposition that all students can learn
- the variety of ways in which students can learn
- lifelong learning for self and others
- professional development as an integral part of school improvement
- the benefits that diversity brings to the school community
- a safe and supportive learning environment
- preparing students to be contributing members of society

Performances

The administrator facilitates processes and engages in activities ensuring that:

- all individuals are treated with fairness, dignity, and respect
- professional development promotes a focus on student learning consistent with the school vision and goals
- students and staff feel valued and important
- the responsibilities and contributions of each individual are acknowledged
- barriers to student learning are identified, clarified, and addressed
- diversity is considered in developing learning experiences
- lifelong learning is encouraged and modeled
- there is a culture of high expectations for self, student, and staff performance
- technologies are used in teaching and learning
- student and staff accomplishments are recognized and celebrated
- multiple opportunities to learn are available to all students
- the school is organized and aligned for success
- curricular, co-curricular, and extra-curricular programs are designed, implemented, evaluated, and refined
- curriculum decisions are based on research, expertise of teachers, and the recommendations of learned societies
- the school culture and climate are assessed on a regular basis
- a variety of sources of information is used to make decisions
- student learning is assessed using a variety of techniques
- multiple sources of information regarding performance are used by staff and students
- a variety of supervisory and evaluation models is employed
- pupil personnel programs are developed to meet the needs of students and their families

Standard 3: A school administrator is an educational leader who promotes the success of all students by **ensuring management of the organization, operations, and resources for a safe, efficient, and effective learning environment.**

Knowledge

The administrator has knowledge and understanding of:

- theories and models of organizations and the principles of organizational development
- operational procedures at the school and district level
- principles and issues relating to school safety and security
- human resources management and development
- principles and issues relating to fiscal operations of school management
- principles and issues relating to school facilities and use of space
- legal issues impacting school operations
- current technologies that support management functions

Dispositions

The administrator believes in, values, and is committed to:

- making management decisions to enhance learning and teaching

- taking risks to improve schools
- trusting people and their judgments
- accepting responsibility
- high-quality standards, expectations, and performances
- involving stakeholders in management processes
- a safe environment

Performances

The administrator facilitates processes and engages in activities ensuring that:
- knowledge of learning, teaching, and student development is used to inform management decisions
- operational procedures are designed and managed to maximize opportunities for successful learning
- emerging trends are recognized, studied, and applied as appropriate
- operational plans and procedures to achieve the vision and goals of the school are in place
- collective bargaining and other contractual agreements related to the school are effectively managed
- the school plant, equipment, and support systems operate safely, efficiently, and effectively
- time is managed to maximize attainment of organizational goals
- potential problems and opportunities are identified
- problems are confronted and resolved in a timely manner
- financial, human, and material resources are aligned to the goals of schools
- the school acts entrepreneurially to support continuous improvement
- organizational systems are regularly monitored and modified as needed
- stakeholders are involved in decisions affecting schools
- responsibility is shared to maximize ownership and accountability
- effective problem-framing and problem-solving skills are used
- effective conflict resolution skills are used
- effective group-process and consensus-building skills are used
- effective communication skills are used
- a safe, clean, and aesthetically pleasing school environment is created and maintained
- human resource functions support the attainment of school goals
- confidentiality and privacy of school records are maintained

Standard 4: A school administrator is an educational leader who promotes the success of all students by **collaborating with families and community members, responding to diverse community interests and needs, and mobilizing community resources.**

Knowledge

The administrator has knowledge and understanding of:
- emerging issues and trends that potentially impact the school community
- the conditions and dynamics of the diverse school community

- community resources
- community relations and marketing strategies and processes
- successful models of school, family, business, community, government, and higher education partnerships

Dispositions

The administrator believes in, values, and is committed to:

- schools operating as an integral part of the larger community
- collaboration and communication with families
- involvement of families and other stakeholders in school decision-making processes
- the proposition that diversity enriches the school
- families as partners in the education of their children
- the proposition that families have the best interests of their children in mind
- resources of the family and community needing to be brought to bear on the education of students
- an informed public

Performances

The administrator facilitates processes and engages in activities ensuring that:

- high visibility, active involvement, and communication with the larger community is a priority
- relationships with community leaders are identified and nurtured
- information about family and community concerns, expectations, and needs is used regularly
- there is outreach to different business, religious, political, and service agencies and organizations
- credence is given to individuals and groups whose values and opinions may conflict
- the school and community serve one another as resources
- available community resources are secured to help the school solve problems and achieve goals
- partnerships are established with area businesses, institutions of higher education, and community groups to strengthen programs and support school goals
- community youth family services are integrated with school programs
- community stakeholders are treated equitably
- diversity is recognized and valued
- effective media relations are developed and maintained
- a comprehensive program of community relations is established
- public resources and funds are used appropriately and wisely
- community collaboration is modeled for staff
- opportunities for staff to develop collaborative skills are provided

Standard 5: A school administrator is an educational leader who promotes the success of all students by **acting with integrity, fairness, and in an ethical manner.**

Knowledge
The administrator has knowledge and understanding of:
- the purpose of education and the role of leadership in modern society
- various ethical frameworks and perspectives on ethics
- the values of the diverse school community
- professional codes of ethics
- the philosophy and history of education

Dispositions
The administrator believes in, values, and is committed to:
- the ideal of the common good
- the principles in the Bill of Rights
- the right of every student to a free, quality education
- bringing ethical principles to the decision-making process
- subordinating one's own interest to the good of the school community
- accepting the consequences for upholding one's principles and actions
- using the influence of one's office constructively and productively in the service of all students and their families
- development of a caring school community

Performances
The administrator:
- examines personal and professional values
- demonstrates a personal and professional code of ethics
- demonstrates values, beliefs, and attitudes that inspire others to higher levels of performance
- serves as a role model
- accepts responsibility for school operations
- considers the impact of one's administrative practices on others
- uses the influence of the office to enhance the educational program rather than for personal gain
- treats people fairly, equitably, and with dignity and respect
- protects the rights and confidentiality of students and staff
- demonstrates appreciation for and sensitivity to the diversity in the school community
- recognizes and respects the legitimate authority of others
- examines and considers the prevailing values of the diverse school community
- expects that others in the school community will demonstrate integrity and exercise ethical behavior
- opens the school to public scrutiny
- fulfills legal and contractual obligations
- applies laws and procedures fairly, wisely, and considerately

Standard 6: A school administrator is an educational leader who promotes the success of all students by **understanding, responding to, and influencing the larger political, social, economic, legal, and cultural context.**

Knowledge
The administrator has knowledge and understanding of:
- principles of representative governance that undergird the system of American schools
- the role of public education in developing and renewing a democratic society and an economically productive nation
- the law as related to education and schooling
- the political, social, cultural, and economic systems and processes that impact schools
- models and strategies of change and conflict resolution as applied to the larger political, social, cultural, and economic contexts of schooling
- global issues and forces affecting teaching and learning
- the dynamics of policy development and advocacy under our democratic political system
- the importance of diversity and equity in a democratic society

Dispositions
The administrator believes in, values, and is committed to:
- education as a key to opportunity and social mobility
- recognizing a variety of ideas, values, and cultures
- importance of a continuing dialogue with other decision makers affecting education
- actively participating in the political and policy-making context in the service of education
- using legal systems to protect student rights and improve student opportunities

Performances
The administrator facilitates processes and engages in activities ensuring that:
- the environment in which schools operate is influenced on behalf of students and their families
- communication occurs among the school community concerning trends, issues, and potential changes in the environment in which schools operate
- there is ongoing dialogue with representatives of diverse community groups
- the school community works within the framework of policies, laws, and regulations enacted by local, state, and federal authorities
- public policy is shaped to provide quality education for students
- lines of communication are developed with decision makers outside the school community

Source: Council of Chief State School Officials (1996). *Interstate School Leaders Licensure Consortium (ISLLC) standards for school leaders.* Washington, DC: Author. Used with permission.

REFERENCES

"IN THE NEWS" REFERENCES

Anderson, N. (2005, November 17). Bringing new vision to education: Principal lauded for innovation wins leadership award. *Washington Post.*

Anderson, N. (2005, November 24). Filling new schools: An intricate question. *Washington Post.*

Archer, J. (2004, September 15). Districts across the country are struggling with how to focus efforts of instructional leaders. *Education Week.*

Archer, J. (2005, September 8). What do good leaders do right? *Education Week.*

Archer, J. (2005, September 14). Lessons for leaders. *Education Week.*

Bassett, P. F. (2002, February 6). Why good students are counter-culture. *Education Week.*

Borja, R. R. (2005, May 5). State support varies widely. *Education Week.*

DePriest, J. (2005, December 16). Schools chief suits up for his seasonal job—Working as part-time Santa fills Jim Watson's schedule—and heart. *Charlotte Observer.*

de Vise, D. (2005, September 29). Viers Mill School wins Blue Ribbon. *Washington Post.*

Diamond, L. (2005, December 1). The end of an era: Principal says farewell. *Atlanta Journal-Constitution.*

Donsky, P. (2005, October 3). High-tech boards at head of the class. *Atlanta-Journal Constitution.*

Duncan, A. (2005, March 23). Proponents of community schools argue for wider view of education. *Education Week.*

Forti, V. (2005, November 16). Where does all the money go? *Education Week.*

Garrett, R. T., & Stutz, T. (2005, August 4). Legislative logjam blocking textbooks: With funding in limbo, schools scramble to find some subject materials. *Dallas Morning Star.*

Gehring, J. (2005, February 16). More boards mulling policy governance. *Education Week.*

Helms, D. A. (2005, December 6). N.C., S.C. teachers earn national accreditation. *Charlotte Observer.*

Hernandez, L. A. (2005, December 8). Principals receive Post Leadership Award. *Washington Post.*

Hess, F. M., & Kelly, A. P. (2005, May 18). Content matters in preparing educational leaders. *Education Week.*

Lane, C. (2005, June 28). Court splits over commandments. *Washington Post.*

Leal, F. (2005, December 6). Extra credit at O. C. school: Improved scores make a principal one of five in the nation to win a Terrel H. Bell Award. *Orange County Register* (Santa Ana, CA).

Mack, J. (2005, November 11). The Kalamazoo Promise: College tuition for all grads. *Kalamazoo Gazette* (Kalamazoo, MI).

Martinez, A. (2005, October 29). A community effort. *Miami Herald.*

Matter of principals. (2005, October 6). *Arizona Republic.*

May, R. P. (2005, August 12). The dropout problem: Not students, but teachers. *Austin Chronicle.*

MiMassa, C. M., & Rubin, J. (2005, January 10). Teachers unions blast governor's merit pay plan. Some educators call proposal untenable, costly. Others say it may help attract instructors. *Los Angeles Times.*

Olson, L. (1997, June 25). Annenberg challenge. *Education Week.*

Protecting mediocre teachers. (2005, December 9). *Chicago Times.*

Puriefoy, W. D. (2005, June 8). Why the public is losing faith in the No Child Law. *Education Week.*

Reinold, C. (2004, October 28). Candidates sound off—Where they stand on overcrowding, the gifted. *Atlanta-Journal Constitution.*

Robelen, E. W. (2005, May 18). News in brief: A Washington roundup. Wide school role urged. *Education Week.*

Rosen, D. S. P. (2005, March 17). School districts expand career curriculum to prepare youths. *Houston Chronicle.*

Rubin, J. (2005, September 21). Grove Schools win $500,000 Eli Broad Prize in national contest. *Los Angeles Times.*

Salzman, A. (2005, November 20). Special education and minorities. *New York Times.*

Samuels, C. A. (2005, September 7). Legal fight over special education in Baltimore enters new phase. *Education Week.*

Saulny, S. (2005, November 11). Science chief says schools in New York are failing. *New York Times.*

Staples, B. (2005, November 21). Why the United States should look to Japan for better schools. *New York Times.*

Sugameli, J. (2005, May 16). Students shadow area doctors—Troy High advance placement teenagers see medical career from physician's view. *Detroit News.*

Thamel, P., & Wilson, D. (2005, November 27). Poor grades aside, athletes get into college on a $399 diploma. *New York Times.*

Togif, D. (2004, February 8). Superintendent finds one word can spell trouble. *Atlanta Journal-Constitution.*

Trouth, S. (2004, May 21). Three area school districts struggle to reach new pacts. *Lansing State Journal* (MI).

Van, J. (2005, September 15). IBM wants to stem slide in math, science. *Houston Chronicle.*

Wisby, G. (1997, November 30). The notion of intelligent emotion. *Chicago Sun-Times.*

Wiseman, M. (2004, November 18). 2 area principals win Post Leadership Awards. *Washington Post.*

Zorn, E. (2005, February 13). State set to start hacking at school rules. *Chicago Times.*

LEGAL REFERENCES

Abington School District v. Schempp, 374 U.S. 203 (1963).

Bethel School District No. 403 v. Fraser, 478 U.S. 675 (1986).

Board of Education of Independent School District v. Earls, 536 U.S. 822 (2002).

Chandler v. McMinnville School District, 978 F.2d 524 (1992).

Davis v. Monroe County Board of Education, 562 U.S. 629, 119S. Ct. 1661 (1999).

Hazelwood School District v. Kuhlmeier, 484 U.S. 260, 108 S. Ct. 562 (1988).

Lee v. Weisman, 505 U.S. 577, 112 S. Ct. 2649 (1992).

No Child Left Behind Act of 2001. www.ed.gov/offices/oese.esca.

Peter W. v. San Francisco Unified School District, 60 Cal. App.3d814, 131Cal.; Rptr. 854 (1976).

Rowinsky v. Bryan Independent School District, 117 S. Ct. 165 (1996).

Santa Fe Independent School District v. Jane Doe, 120 S. Ct. 2266; 147 L. Ed. 2d 295 (2000).

Tinker v. Des Moines Independent Community School District, 393 U.S. 503, 89 S. Ct. 733 (1969).

Widmar v. Vincent, 454 U.S. 263, 102 S. Ct. 269 (1981).

REFERENCES

Achilles, C., Harman, P., & Egelson, P. (1995). Using research results on class size to improve pupil achievement outcomes. *Research in the Schools, 2*(2), 23–30.

Ackerman, D. (2003). Taproots for a new century: Tapping the best of traditional and progressive education. *Phi Delta Kappan, 85*(5), 344–349.

Adelman, H. S., & Taylor, L. (2004). Advancing mental health in schools: Guiding frameworks and strategic approaches. In K. Robinson (Ed.), *Advances in school-based mental health.* Kingston, NJ: Civic Research Institute.

Adler, R. P. (1999). *Information literacy: Advancing opportunities for learning in the digital age.* Washington, DC: The Aspen Institute Forum on Communications and Society.

Aiken, J. A. (2002). The socialization of new principals: Another perspective on principal retention. *Education Leadership Review, 3*(1), 32–40.

Allen, M., & Palaich, R. (2000). *In pursuit of quality teaching: Five key strategies for policymakers.* Denver, CO: Education Commission of the States.

Alnoor, E. (2005, March). Accountability myopia: Losing sight of organizational learning. *Nonprofit and Voluntary Sector Quarterly, 34,* 56–87.

American Academy of Pediatrics. (2004). School-based mental health services: Committee on school health. *Pediatrics, 113*(6), 1839–1845.

Anft, M., & Williams, G. (2004, August). Redefining good governance. *Chronicle of Philanthropy, 16,* 6–10.

Angulo, M. (2001, March). Leveraging learning for generation I. *School Administrator, 53*(3), 28–31.

Antonucci, M. (2001). *Measure for measure: A magnified look at standardized tests.* Sacramento, CA: Educational Intelligence Agency.

Apple, M., & King, J. (1983). *Humanistic education.* Berkeley, CA: McCutcheon.

Archer, J. (2000, May 17). Ohio court again overturns finance system. *Education Week, 19*(36), 1, 25.

Arthur, W. B. (1996, July–August). Increasing returns and the new world of business. *Harvard Business Review, 74*(4), 100–109.

Ash, R. C., & Persall, M. (2000). The principal as chief learning officer: Developing teacher leaders. *NASSP Bulletin, 84,* 15–22.

Ashkanasy, N. M. (2003). Emotions in organizations: A multilevel perspective. In F. Dansereau & F. J. Yammarino (Eds.), *Research in multilevel issues (Vol. 2): Multi-level issues in organizational behavior and strategy* (pp. 9–54). Oxford, UK: Elsevier Science.

Ashkanasy, N. M., Hartel, C. E. J., & Daus, C. S. (2002). Advances in organizational behavior: Diversity and emotions. *Journal of Management, 28,* 307–338.

Association for Supervision and Curriculum Development. (2002, October). The world in the classroom. *Educational Leadership, 60*(2), 15–26.

Atwater, D., & Bass, B. M. (1994). Transformational leadership in teams. In B. M. Bass & B. Avolio (Eds.), *Improving organizational effectiveness through transformational leadership.* Thousand Oaks, CA: Sage.

Awamleh, R., & Gardner, W. L. (1999). Perceptions of leader charisma and effectiveness: The effects of vision, content, delivery, and organizational performance. *Leadership Quarterly, 10,* 345–373.

Baard, P. P., Deci, E. L., & Ryan, R. M. (2004). The relation of intrinsic need satisfaction to performance and well being in two work settings. *Journal of Applied Social Psychology, 34,* 2045–2068.

Bacon, D. (2001, May). The classroom had rats. *Progressive, 65*(5), 28–29.

Balla, V. (2002, October 25). End creative teaching officials says. *Stockton Record,* p. 21.

Baltzell, E. D. (1979). *Puritan Boston and Quaker Philadelphia: Protestant ethics and the spirit of class authority and leadership.* New York: Macmillan.

Bandura, A., Pastorelli, C., Barbaranelli, C., & Caprara, G. V. (1999). Self-efficacy childhood depression. *Journal of Personality and Social Psychology, 76,* 258–269.

Barchfeld-Venet, P. (2005). Formative assessment: The basics. *Alliance Access, 9*(1), 2–3.

Barnard, P. (1996). *Acquiring inter-personal skills* (2nd ed.). London: Chapman & Hall.

Barnett, B. G., Basom, M. R., Yerkes, D. M., & Norris, C. I. (2000, April). Cohorts in educational leadership programs: Benefits, difficulties, and the potential for developing school leaders. *Educational Administration Quarterly, 36,* 255–282.

Baron, J. (2000). *Thinking and deciding* (3rd ed.). Cambridge: Cambridge University Press.

Bar-On, R., & Parker, J. D. A. (Eds.). (2000). *The handbook of emotional intelligence: Theory, development, assessment, and application at home, school, and in the workplace.* San Francisco: Jossey-Bass.

Barrett, P. M., & Olendick, T. H. (2004). *Handbook of interventions that work with children and adolescents: Prevention and treatment.* West Sussex, England: Wiley.

Barrow, L., & Rouse, C. E. (2004). Using market valuation to assess the importance and efficiency of public school spending. *Journal of Public Economics, 88,* 1747–1769.

Barth, R. S. (2001). *Learning by heart.* San Francisco: Jossey-Bass.

Barton P. E. (2002). *Meeting the need for scientists, engineers, and an educated citizenry in a technology society.* Princeton, NJ: Educational Testing Service.

Bass, B. M. (1997). Concepts of leadership. In R. P. Vecchio (Ed.), *Leadership: Understanding the dynamics of power and influence in organizations* (pp. 3–23). Notre Dame, IN: University of Notre Dame.

Bass, R. (1990, Winter). From transactional to transformational leadership: Learning to share the vision. *Organizational Dynamics, 18*(3), 19–31.

Bazerman, M. H. (2002). *Judgment in managerial decision making* (4th ed.). New York: Wiley & Sons.

Beckner, W. (2004). *Ethics for educational leaders.* Boston: Allyn & Bacon.

Bell, J., & Harrison, B. T. (Eds.). (1995). *Vision and values in managing education: Successful leadership principles and practice.* London: David Fulton.

Benham, B. T., & O'Brien, L. (2002, September). Why are experienced teachers leaving the profession? *Phi Delta Kappan,* 24–32.

Bennett, W. (2004). *A nation still at risk.* ERIC Clearinghouse on Assessment and Evaluation. Eric Document Reproduction Service. (ED 429988).

Bennis, W., & Nanus, B. (1985). *Leaders: The Strategies for taking charge.* New York: Harper & Row.

Bennis, W. G. (1989). *On becoming a leader.* Reading, PA: Addison Wesley.

Berger, L. (2002). Business intelligence: Insights from the data pile. *New York Times.*

Berman, L. M. (1987). The teacher as decision maker. *Teacher renewal: Professional issues, personal choices.* New York: Columbia University.

Birr, D. (2000, December). Meeting the challenge: Providing high-quality school environments through energy performance contracting. *School Business Affairs, 66*(12), 34–36.

Black, L. D., & Hartel, C. E. J. (2002). The relationship between corporate social responsibility and public relations: Evidence from a scale development study. In D. Windsor & S. A. Welcomer (Eds.), *Proceedings of the Thirteenth Annual Meeting of the International Association for Business and Society* (pp. 100–104). Pittsburgh, PA: International Association for Business and Society.

Blackorby, J., Newman, L., & Finnegan, K. (1997, April). *School-linked services for students with disabilities and their families: A case study of 20 families.* Menlo Park, CA: SRI International.

Blackorby, J., Newman, L., & Finnegan, K. (1998, July). *Integrated services, high need communities, and special education: Lessons and paradoxes.* Menlo Park, CA: SRI International.

Block, J. H., Efthim, H. E., & Burns, R. B. (1989). *Building effective mastery learning schools.* New York: Longman.

Boal, K. B., & Bryson, J. M. (1988). Charismatic leadership: A phenomenological and structural approach. In J. G. Hunt et al. (Eds.), *Emerging leadership vistas* (pp. 11–28). Lexington, MA: Lexington Books.

Boice, J. P. (2004, March–April). The accountability factor. *Advancing Philanthropy, 11,* 18–22.

Bolman, L., & Deal, T. (1991). *Reframing organizations.* San Francisco: Jossey-Bass.

Bolman, L., & Deal, T. (1995). *Leading with soul: An uncommon journey of spirit.* San Francisco: Jossey-Bass.

Bolton, D. G. (2000, September). Critical issues in school governance. *School Business Affairs, 66*(9), 4–6.

Bond, M., & Keys, C. (1993). Empowerment, diversity, and collaboration: Promoting synergy on community boards. *American Journal of Community Psychology, 21*(1), 37–38.

Bong, M. (2002). Predictive utility of subject, task, and problem-specific self-efficacy judgments for immediate and delayed academic performances. *J. Exp. Educ. 70,* 133–162.

Bono, J. E., & Judge, T. A. (2003). Self-confidence at work: Understanding the motivational effects of transformational leaders. *Academy of Management Journal, 46,* 554–571.

Boston Excels Full Service Schools. (March 31, 2000). Briefing Paper. Boston Children's Institute.

Bowman, J., Newman, D., & Masterson, J. (2001). Adopting educational technology: Implications for designing interventions. *Journal of Educational Computing Research, 25,* 81–94.

Boykin, A. W., & Cunningham, R. T. (2001). The effects of movement expressiveness in story content and learning context on the analogical reasoning performance in African American children. *Journal of Negro Education, 70*(1–2), 72–83.

Bracey, G. W. (2001, January). Class size: an addendum. *Phi Delta Kappan, 82*(5), 14.

Bracey, G. W. (2002). *Put to the test: An educator's and consumer's guide to standardized testing,* rev. ed. Bloomington, IN: Phi Delta Kappa International.

Bradberry, T., & Greaves, J. (2005). *The emotional intelligence quick book: How to put your EQ to work.* New York: Simon & Schuster.

Bradshaw, L. K. (2000). The changing role of principals in school partnerships. *NASSP Bulletin, 84,* 86–96.

Bransford, J., Brown, A., & Cocking, R. (Eds.). (2000). *How people learn: Mind, brain, experience, and schools.* Washington, DC: National Academy Press.

Brookover, W. B., and Lezotte, L. W. (1979). *Changes in school characteristics coincident with changes in student achievement.* East Lansing, MI: Institute for Research on Teaching.

Brown, C., Smith, M., & Stein, M. (1995). *Linking teacher support to enhanced classroom instruction.* Paper presented at the annual meeting at the American Educational Research Association, New York.

Brown, E. J., & Bobrow, A. L. (2004). School entry after a community-wide trauma: challenges and lessons learned from September 11th, 2001. *Chin Child Fam Psychol Rev, 7*(4), 211–221.

Bruner, C., Bell, K., Brindis, C., Chang, H., & Scarbrough, W. (1993). *Charting a course: Assessing a community's strengths and needs.* New York: Columbia University, National Center for Service Integration.

Bruns, E. J., Walrath, C., Glass-Siegel, M., & Weist, M. D. (2004). School-based mental health services in Baltimore: Association with school climate and special education referrals. *Behavior Modification, 28*(4), 430–439.

Buckner, K. G., & McDowelle, J. O. (2000). Developing teacher leaders: Providing encouragement, opportunities, and support. *NASSP Bulletin, 84,* 35–41.

Bulach, C. R. (2001, October 18). *A comparison of character traits for rural, suburban, and urban students.* Presentation at the Character Education Partnership Conference, Denver, CO.

Bulach, C. R., Lunenburg, F. C., & McCallon, R. (1995). The influence of the principal's leadership style on school climate and student achievement. *People in Education, 3,* 333–350.

Bulkeley, W. M. (1997, November 17). Hard lessons. *Wall Street Journal, Technology Section,* pp. 1–6.

Burnard, P. (1996). *Acquiring interpersonal skills: A handbook of experimental learning for health officials.* London: Chapman & Hall.

Burris, V. (2001). The two faces of capital: Corporations and individual capitalists as political actors. *American Sociological Review, 66,* 497–505.

Burtis, J. O. (1995). Grouping and leading as citizen action. *Journal of Leadership Studies, 2*(2), 50–63.

Button, H. K., & Provenzo, E. F., Jr. (1989). *History of education and culture in America.* Englewood Cliffs, NJ: Prentice-Hall.

Bybee, R. W., & Kennedy, D. (2005). Math and science achievement. *Science, 307*(28), 481.

Calonius, E. (1991, March 25). The big payoff from lotteries. *Fortune,* p. 109.

Cambron-McCabe, N. H. (1993). Leadership for democratic authority. In J. Murphy (Ed.), *Preparing tomorrow's school leaders: Alternative designs.* University Park, PA: University Council for Educational Administration.

Capasso, R. L., & Daresh, J. C. (2001). *The school administration handbook: Leading, mentoring, and participating in the internship program.* Thousand Oaks, CA: Corwin.

Carnegie Corporation of New York. (2001, October 11). Seven school districts and their communities awarded grants in the schools for a new society initiative. Press release.

Carroll, T., & Fulton, K. (2004). The true cost of teacher turnover. *Threshold,* 16–17.

Casey, B. J., Giedd, J. N., & Thomas, K. M. (2000). Structural and functional brain development and its relation to cognitive development. *Biological Psychology, 54,* 241–257.

Castetter, W. B. (1996). *The human resource function in educational administration* (6th ed.). Englewood Cliffs, NJ: Prentice-Hall.

Certo, S. C. (2002). *Modern Management.* Englewood Cliffs, NJ: Prentice-Hall.

Cervero, R., Wilson, A. L., & Associates (Eds.). (2001). *Power in practice: Adult education and the struggle for knowledge and power in society.* San Francisco: Jossey-Bass.

Chandler, A.D., Jr., McCraw, T. K., & Tedlow, R. S. (1996). *Management past and present.* Cincinnati, OH: South-Western Publishing.

Chang, J. (2003, December). Want to improve productivity? Stop micromanaging your employees. *Sales and Marketing Management, 155*(12), 55.

Charles A. Dana Center, University of Texas at Austin. (1999). *Hope for urban education: A study of nine high-performing, high-poverty urban elementary schools.* Washington, DC: U.S. Department of Education, Planning and Evaluation Service.

Chaskin, R. J., & Rauner, D. M. (1995). Youth and caring. *Phi Delta Kappan,* 667–674.

Chatterji, P., Caffray, C. M., Crowe, M., Freeman, L., & Jensen, P. (2004). Cost assessment of a school-based mental health screening and treatment program in New York City. *Men Health Serv Res, 6*(3), 155–166.

Chen, M., & Armstrong, S. (2002). *Edutopia: Success stories for learning in the digital age.* San Francisco: Jossey-Bass.

Cherniss, C., & Adler, M. (2000). *Promoting emotional intelligence organizations: Making training in emotional intelligence effective.* Alexander, VA: American Society for Training and Development.

Chirkov, V., Ryan, R. M., Kim, Y., & Kaplan, U. (2003). Differentiating autonomy from individualism and independence: A self-determination theory perspective on internationalization of cultural orientations and well being. *Journal of Personality and Social Psychology, 84,* 97–109.

Chynoweth, J. (1994). *A guide to community-based, collaborative strategic planning.* Washington, DC: Council of Governors' Policy Board.

Ciruli Associates. (2002). *Survey of DPS teachers concerning recruitment and retention of new teachers.* Denver, CO: Author.

Clemen, R. T. (1996). *Making hard decisions: An introduction to decision analysis* (2nd ed.). Belmont, CA: Duxbury.

Clinchy, E. (2001, March). Needed: A new educational civil rights movement. *Phi Delta Kappan, 82*(7), 493–498.

Cohen, D., & Hill, H. (1997). *Instructional policy and classroom performance: The mathematics reform in California.* Paper presented at the Annual Meeting of the American Educational Research Association, Chicago, IL.

Cohen, M. D., March, J. G., & Olsen, J. P. (1972). A garbage can model of organization choice. *Administrative Science Quarterly, 17*(1), 1–25.

Columbo, M. G., & Delmastro, M. (2002). The determinant of organizational change and structural inertia: Technological and organizational factors. *Journal of Economics and Management Strategy, 11*(4), 595–635.

Conger, J. A., Kanungo, R. N., & Associates. (1989). *Charismatic leadership: The elusive factor in organizational effectiveness.* San Francisco: Jossey-Bass.

Cooper, B. S., Fusarelli, L. D., & Carella, V. A. (2000). *Career crisis in the superintendency? The results of a national survey.* Arlington, VA: American Association of School Administrators.

Cordes, C., & Miller, E. (1999). *Fool's gold: A critical look at computers in childhood.* Spring Valley, NY: Alliance for Childhood.

Cotton, K. (1991). *Computer-assisted instruction.* Portland, OR: Northwest Regional Educational Laboratory.

Council of Chief State School Officers. (1996). *Interstate school leaders licensure consortium: Standards for school leaders.* Washington, DC: CCSC Publications.

Covey, S. (1989). *The seven habits of highly effective people.* New York: Fireside Simon & Schuster.

Cox, W., Stewart, M., & Burybile, S. (2000, September). Linking student results with school spending. *School Business Affairs,* 42–44.

Creighton, T. (1998). Rethinking school leadership: Is the principal really needed? In R. Muth (Ed.), *Toward the year 2000: Leadership for quality schools,* Sixth Yearbook of the National Council of Professors of Educational Administration (pp. 14–19). Lancaster, PA: Technomic Press.

Cuban, L. (1984). *How teachers taught: Constancy and change in American classrooms, 1890–1980.* New York: Longman.

Cuban, L. (1993). Computers meet classroom: Classroom wins. *Teachers College Record, 95,* 185–210.

Cuban, L. (2001a). *How can I fix it?* New York: Teachers College Press.

Cuban, L. (2001b). *Oversold and underused: Computers in the classroom.* Cambridge, MA: Harvard University Press.

Cullen, R. B. (1997). *Workskills and national competitiveness: External benchmarks. Report No. 2: Benchmarking Australian Qualification Profiles.* A project conducted by Performance Management Solutions for ANTA. Hawthorn, Victoria: Performance Management Solutions Pty Ltd.

References

Cumming, J. J., & Maxwell, G. S. (1999). Contextualising authentic assessment. *Assessment in Education, Principles, Policy and Practice, 6*(2), 177–194.

Cunningham, W. G., & Cordiero, P. A. (2003). *Educational leadership: A problem-based approach* (2nd ed.). Boston: Allyn & Bacon.

Cunningham, W. G., & Gresso, D. W. (1993). *Cultural leadership: The culture of excellence in education.* Boston: Allyn & Bacon.

Czaja, M., & Lowe, J. (2001). Preparing leaders for ethical decisions. *The AASA Professor, 24*(1), 7–12.

D'Amico, J. (1982). Using effective school studies to create effective schools: No recipes yet. *Educational Leadership, 40*(3), 60–63.

Daresh, J. C. (1997). Improving principal preparation: A review of common strategies. *NASSP Bulletin, 81,* 3–8.

Daresh, J. C. (2002). *What it means to be a principal: Your guide to leadership.* Thousand Oaks, CA: Corwin.

Darling-Hammond, L. (1994). *Performance-based assessment and educational equity.* In L. S. Behar Horenstein & A. C. Ornstein (Eds.), *Contemporary issues in curriculum* (pp. 382–403). Boston: Allyn & Bacon.

Darling-Hammond, L. (1997). *Doing what matters most: Investing in quality teaching.* New York: National Commission on Teaching and America's Future.

Darling-Hammond, L. (1999). *Solving the dilemmas of teacher supply, demand, and standards: How we can ensure a competent, caring, and qualified teacher for every child.* New York: National Commission on Teaching and America's Future.

Darling-Hammond, L. (2000). *Solving the dilemmas of teacher supply, demand, and standards: How we can ensure a competent, caring, and qualified teacher for every child.* New York: National Commission on Teaching and America's Future.

Darling-Hammond, L. (2003). Keeping good teachers. *Educational Leadership, 60*(8), 6–13.

Darling-Hammond, L., & Youngs, P. (2002). Defining highly qualified teachers: What does scientifically-based research tell us? *Education Researcher, 31*(9), 13–25.

David, J. L., Purkey, S., & White, P. (1989). *Restructuring in progress: Lessons from pioneering districts.* Washington, DC: Center for Policy Research, National Governors Association.

Davis, E. B., & Ashton, R. H. (2002). Threshold adjustment in response to asymmetric loss functions: The case of auditors' substantial doubt thresholds. *Organizational Behavioral and Human Decision Processes, 89*(2), 1082–1099.

Davis, G. (2001). There is no four-object limit on attention. *Behavioral and Brain Sciences, 24*(1), 120.

Deal, T., & Peterson, K. D. (1998). *Shaping school culture: The heart of leadership.* San Francisco: Jossey-Bass.

Deal, T. E., & Peterson, K. D. (2000). *The leadership paradox: Balancing logic and artistry in schools.* San Francisco: Jossey-Bass.

Deci, E. L., Koestner, R., & Ryan, R. M. (1999). A meta-analytic review of experiments examining the effects of extrinsic rewards on intrinsic motivation. *Psychological Bulletin, 125,* 627–668.

Deci, E. L., & Ryan, R. M. (2000). The what and why of goal pursuits: Human needs and the self-determination of behavior. *Psychological Inquiry, 11,* 227–268.

DeCrane, A. C., Jr. (1996). A constitutional model of leadership. In F. Hesselbein, M. Goldsmith, & R. Beckhard (Eds.), *The leader of the future* (pp. 249–256). San Francisco: Jossey Bass.

DeGroot, M. (2004). *Optimal statistical decisions.* New York: Wiley Classics Library.

DenHartog, D. N., & Verburg, R. M. (1997). Charisma and rhetoric: Communication techniques of international business leaders. *Leadership Quarterly, 8,* 355–391.

Designs for Change. (1998). Practices of schools with substantially improved reading achievement. Available online: www.dfc1.org/summary/report.htm. Chicago: Chicago Public Schools.

Dewey, J. (1938). *Experience and education.* New York: Macmillan.

Digest of Educational Statistics, 2004. (2005). Washington, DC: U.S. Government Printing Office.

Dill, E. M., & Boykin, A. W. (2000). The comparative influence of individual, peer tutoring, and communal learning contexts on the text recall of African American children. *Journal of Black Psychology, 26*(1), 65–78.

Donahoe, T. (1993). Finding the way: Structure, time, and culture in school improvement. *Phi Delta Kappan, 75,* 298–305.

Donaldson, G. A. (2001). *Cultivating leadership in schools: Connecting people, purpose and practice.* New York: Teachers College Press.

Donaldson, L. (2001). *The contingency theory of organizations.* London: Sage.

Doyle, D. P., & Pimentel, S. (1999). *Raising the standard: An eight-step action guide for schools and communities.* Thousand Oaks, CA: Corwin Press.

Drucker, P. F. (2002). *The effective executive* (2nd ed.). New York: HarperCollins.

Dryfoos, J. (1994). *Full-service schools: A revolution in health and social services for children, youth, and families.* San Francisco: Jossey-Bass.

Dryfoos, J. (2002, January). Full-service community schools: Creating new institutions. *Phi Delta Kappan, 83*(5), 393–399.

Dubrin, A. J. (1996). *Reengineering survival guide.* Cincinnati, OH: Thompson Executive Press.

DuFour, R., & Eaker, R. (1998). *Professional learning communities at work: Best practices for enhancing student achievement.* Bloomington, IN: National Educational Service.

Dunn, L., & Kontos, S. (1997). *Developmentally appropriate practice: What does the research say.* Research Digest. Champaign, IL: ERIC Clearinghouse of Elementary and Early Childhood Education. (ERIC Document).

Earl, L. (2004). *Assessment as learning: Using classroom assessment to maximize student learning.* Thousand Oaks, CA: Corwin.

Edmonds, R. (1979). Some schools work and more can. *Social Policy, 17*(5), 17–18.

Educational Testing Service. (2002). *Pathwise Series.* Princeton, NJ: Author.

Education Trust. (2002, May). *Dispelling the myth . . . over time.* Washington, DC: Author.

Education Trust. (2002). *Education Week: The 2001 Education Trust State and National Data Book.* Washington DC: Author.

Education Week. (2004). Count me in: Quality counts, 112.

Edyburn, D., Higgins, K., & Boone, R. (Eds.). (2005). *Handbook of special education technology research practice.* Whitefish Bay, WI: Knowledge by Design.

Eisenhardt, K. M., Kahwajy, J. L., & Bourgeois, L. J. (1997). Conflict and strategic choice: How top management teams disagree. *California Management Review, 39*(2), 42–62.

Ellenberg, F. C. (1972). Factors affecting teacher morale. *National Association of Secondary School Principal Bulletin.*

Ellis, D., & Hughes, K. (2002). *Partnerships by design: Cultivating effective and meaningful school-family-community partnerships*. Portland, OR: Northeast Regional Educational Laboratory.

Elmore, R. F. (2000, Winter). *Building a new structure for school leadership*. Washington, DC: The Albert Shanker Institute.

English, F. W. (1994). *Theory in educational administration*. New York: HarperCollins.

Epstein, A. S. (1996). *Models of early childhood education*. Ypsilanti, MI: High/Scope Educational Research Foundation.

Ericson, D. P., & Ellet, F. S., Jr. (2002). The question of the student in education reform. *Education Policy Analysis Archives, 10*(31), 53–67.

Etzioni, A. (1961). *Modern organizations*. Reading, MA: Addison-Wesley.

Etzioni, A. (1967). Mixed scanning: A third approach to decision-making. In A. Faludi (Ed.), *A reader in planning theory*. New York: Pergamon.

Etzioni, A. (1990). *The moral dimension*. New York: Macmillan.

Evans, M. (2001). Creating knowledge management skills in primary care residents: A description of a new pathway to evidence-based practice in the community. *Evidence Based Medicine, 5*(6), 134.

Evans, S. W., Axelrod, J., & Langberg, J. M. (2004). Efficacy of a school-based treatment program for middle school youth with ADHD: Pilot data. *Bahav Modif, 28*(4), 528–547.

Evans, S. W., & Weist, M. D. (2004). Implementing empirically supported treatments in the schools: What are we asking? *Clin Child Fam Psychol Rev, 7*(4), 263–267.

Farkas, S., Johnson, J., & Foleno, T. (2000). *A sense of calling: Who teaches and why*. New York: Public Agenda.

Fayol, H. (1949). *General and industrial administration*. New York: Pitman. Originally published in French in 1916 with the title *Adminstration Industrielle et Generale*.

Fish, J. M. (2001). *Race and intelligence: Separating science from myth*. Mahwah, NJ: Erlbaum.

Fisher, A. (2004, August 23). In praise of micromanaging. *Fortune, 150*(4), 54–59.

Fisher, C., Dwyer, D., & Yocam, K. (1996). *Education and technology: Reflections on computing in classrooms*. San Francisco: Jossey-Bass.

Fox, E. (2005). Tracking U.S. trends. *Education Week, 24*(35), 40–42.

Fox, N., Leone, P., Rubin, K., Oppenheim, J., Miller, M., & Friedman, K. (1999). *Final report on the linkages to learning program and evaluation at Broad Acres Elementary School*. College Park: University of Maryland, Department of Special Education.

Fredericks, J. G. (2001). Why teachers leave. *The Education Digest, 66*(8), 46–48.

Freeman, R., & Lewis, R. (1998). *Planning and implementing assessment*. London: Kogan Page.

Freiberg, J. H. (1998). *Universal teaching strategies*. Boston: Allyn & Bacon.

Frunzi, G. L., & Savini, P. (1997). *Supervision: The art of management*. Upper Saddle River, NJ: Prentice-Hall.

Fullan, M. (2000a). *Change forces: The sequel*. London: Falmer.

Fullan, M. (2000b). The three stories of education reform. *Phi Delta Kappan, 81*, 581–584.

Fullan, M. (2001). *Leading in a culture of change*. San Francisco: Jossey-Bass.

Fullan, M. (2003). *The moral imperative of school leadership*. Thousand Oaks, CA: Corwin Press.

Fullan, M., & Hargreaves, A. (1996). *What's worth fighting for in your school*. New York: Teachers College Press.

Fullan, M. G. (1996). Turning systemic thinking on its head. In L. S. Behar Horensten & A. C. Ornstein (Eds.), *Contemporary issues in curriculum* (pp. 416–422). Boston: Allyn & Bacon.

Fulton, K. (1999). *Closing the gap: Delivering quality educational content in the digital divide*. University of Maryland, National Coalition for Technology in Education and Training.

Gagne, M., Ryan, R. M., & Bargmann, K. (2003). Autonomy support and need satisfaction in the motivation and well being of gymnasts. *Journal of Applied Sport Psychology, 15*, 372–390.

Gailbraith, J. (1973). *Designing complex organizations*. Reading, MA: Addison Wesley.

Gallimore, R., & Goldberg, C. (2001). Analyzing cultural models and settings to connect minority achievement and school improvement research. *Educational Psychologist, 36*, 45–56.

Garrett, T. A. (2001, Winter). Earmarked lottery revenues for education: A new test of fungibility. *Journal of Education Finance, 26*(3), 219–238.

Gaustello, S. J. (2002). *Managing emergent phenomena: Nonlinear dynamics in work organizations*. Mahwah, NJ: Erlbaum.

Gewertz, C. (2002, June 12). Qualifications of teachers falling short. *Education Week*, 1.

Gewertz, C. (2002, September 11). City districts seek teachers with licenses. *Education Week*, 1.

Ghahramani, S. (1996). *Fundamentals of probability*. Upper Saddle River, NJ: Prentice-Hall.

Glass, T. E., Bjork, L., & Brunner, C. C. (2000). *The study of the American school superintendency. A look at the superintendent of education in the new millennium*. Arlington, VA: American Association of School Administrators.

Glassman, N., Cibulka, J., & Ashby, D. (2002). Program self-evaluation for continuous improvement. *Educational Administration Quarterly, 38*, 257–288.

GOAL/QPC. (2002). *The TQM wheel*. Retrieved October 06, 2002, from the World Wide Web: www.goalqpc.com/what-weteach/tqmwheel.asp.

Goddard, R. D., Hoy, W. K., & Hoy, A. (2000). Academic emphasis of urban elementary schools and student achievement: A multi-level analysis. *Educational Administration Quarterly, 36*, 683–702.

Goddard, R. D., Sweetland, S. R., & Hoy, W. K. (2000). Academic emphasis of urban elementary schools and student achievement in middle schools: A multilevel analysis. *Educational Quarterly, 26*, 683–702.

Goleman, D. (1995). *Emotional intelligence: Why it matters more than IQ*. New York: Bantam.

Goleman, D. (2000). Leadership that get results. *Harvard Business Review, 78*, 78–90.

Goleman, D., Boyzatzis, R., & McKee, A. (2002). *Primal leadership: Realizing the power of emotional intelligence*. Cambridge, MA: Harvard University Press.

Gollwitzer, P. M. (1990). Action phases and mind-sets. In E. T. Higgins & R. M. Sorrentino (Eds.), *Handbook of motivation and cognition* (Vol. 2, pp. 53–92). New York: Guilford.

Gonder, P., & Hymes, D. (1994). *Improving school climate and culture*. Alexandria, VA: American Association of School Administrators, 1994.

Goodman, P., & Wright, G. (2004). *Decision analysis for management judgment* (3rd ed.). Chichester, England: Wiley.

Goodman, R. H., & Zimmerman, W. G., Jr. (2000). *Thinking differently: Recommendations for 21st century school board/superintendent leadership, governance, and teamwork for high student achievement*. Arlington, VA: Educational Research Service and New England School Development Council.

Gould, M. C. (2002). *Developing literacy and workplace skills: Teaching for 21st century employment.* Bloomington, IN: National Educational Service.

Grant, F. D. (2001, January). Fast-track teacher recruitment. *The School Administrator, 58,* 18–24.

Greenleaf, R. K. (1991). *Servant leadership: A journey into the nature of legitimate power and greatness.* New York: Paulist Press.

Greenleaf, R. K. (1998). *Power of servant leadership.* San Francisco: Berrett-Koehler.

Gregorc, A. F. (1984). Style as a symptom: A phenomenological perspective. *Theory into Practice, 23*(1), 14.

Grogan, M., & Andrews, R. (2002). Defining preparation and professional development for the future. *Educational Administration Quarterly, 38,* 233–256.

Gross, M. (1998). The imposed query. Implications for library service evaluation. *Reference and User Service Quarterly, 37,* 290–299.

Haertel, G., & Means, B. (2000). *Stronger designs for research on educational uses of technology: Conclusions and implications.* Arlington, VA: SRI International.

Haller, M. L. (2001). The preschool dilemma—It's not whether they go, but what they do when they get there. Developmentally appropriate practice. *Journal of Early Education and Family Review, 8*(3), 7–12.

Hallinger, P., & Heck, R. H. (1996, February). Reassessing the principal's role in school effectiveness: A review of empirical research, 1980–1995. *Educational Administration Quarterly, 32,* 5–44.

Hammel, G. (2002). *Leading the revolution: How to thrive in turbulent times by making innovation a way of life.* New York: Plume.

Hammond, D. (2000). Learning makes a quality school. *Education Policy Analysis Archives, 8*(1), 1–49.

Hank, R. (2000). *Collaborative leadership: Developing effective partnerships in communities and schools.* Thousand Oaks, CA: Corwin.

Hannafin, R. D., & Savenye, W. C. (1993). Technology in the classroom: The teacher's new role and resistance to it. *Educational Technology, 33*(6), 26–31.

Hansen, W. L., & Mitchell, N. J. (2000). Disaggregating and explaining corporate political activity: Domestic and foreign corporations in national politics. *American Political Science Review, 94,* 891–903.

Hanson, E. M. (2002). *Educational administration and organizational behavior* (5th ed.). Boston: Allyn & Bacon.

Hanson, T., & Austin, G. (2003). *Are student health risks and low resilience assets an impediment to the academic progress of schools?* California Healthy Kids Survey Factsheet 3. San Francisco: WestEd.

Hargreaves, A., Earl, L., Moore, S., & Manning, S. (2001). *Learning to change: Teaching beyond subjects and standards.* San Francisco: Jossey-Bass.

Harris, P. (2002). *Survey of California teachers.* Reading, England: Peter Harris Research Group.

Harrison, F. (1999). *The managerial decision-making process.* Boston: Houghton Mifflin.

Hart, T. E. (1998). *Vision as emerging leadership phenomenon.* Unpublished master's thesis, Kansas State University, Manhattan.

Heckscher, C. (2003). *Working changes: The new dynamics of organizational intervention.* New York: Oxford University Press.

Heinich, R., Molenda, M., Russell, J., & Smaldino, S. (1996). *Instructional media and technologies for learning.* Englewood Cliffs, NJ: Merrill.

Heller, R. (1998). *Communicate clearly.* New York: DK Publishing.

Helm, J. H., & Gronlund, G. (2000). Linking standards and engaged learning in the early years. *Early Childhood Research & Practice, 2,* 33–45.

Hersey, K. H., Blanchard, D. E., & Johnson, D. E. (1996). *Management of organizational behavior: Utilizing human resources* (7th ed.), Upper Saddle River, NJ: Prentice-Hall.

Hersey, P., & Blanchard, K. (1982). *Management and organization behavior: Utilizing human resources.* Englewood Cliffs, NJ: Prentice-Hall.

Herzberg, B., Mausner, B., & Snyderman, B. B. (1993). *The motivation to work.* Somerset, NJ: Transaction Publishers.

Herzberg, F. (1968). One more time: How do you motivate employees? *Harvard Business Review, 46,* 53–62.

Hiatt-Michael, D. B. (2001). *Promising practices to connect schools with the community.* Greenwich, CT: Information Age Publishing.

Hirsch, E. (1987). *Cultural literacy.* Boston: Houghton Muffin.

Hirsch, E., Koppich, J., & Knapp, M. (2001). *Revisiting what states are doing to improve the quality of teaching: An update on patterns and trends.* Seattle: Center for the Study of Teaching and Policy, University of Washington.

Hodgkinson, C. (1991). *Educational leadership.* Buffalo, NY: SUNY Press.

Holloway, J. (2001). The benefits of mentoring. *Educational Leadership, 58*(8), 85–86.

Holmes, G. (1993). *Essential school leadership: Developing vision and purpose in management.* London: Kogan Page.

Homans, G. C. (1961). *Social behavior.* New York: Harcourt, Brace and World.

Hope, W. C. (1999). Principal's orientation and induction activities as factors in teacher retention. *Clearing House, 73*(1), 54–56.

Hoy, A. W., & Hoy, W. K. (2003). *Instructional leadership: A learning centered guide.* Boston: Allyn & Bacon.

Hoy, W. K., & Sabo, D. J. (1998). *Quality middle schools: Open and healthy.* Thousand Oaks, CA: Corwin.

Hoyt, L. (2000). Partners at last: Head Start and elementary schools working together. *Young Children, 55*(4), 71–73.

Hull, J. (2004). Filing the gaps. *Threshold,* 8–11, 15.

Hunt, J. G., Osborn, R. N., & Schermerhorn, Jr. (2000). *Organizational behavior.* New York: Wiley.

Hunter, B. (2000, April). The unpopular issues of poverty and isolation. *School Administrator, 57*(4), 54.

Hunter, L., Hoagwood, K., Evans, S., Weist, M., Smith, C., Paternite, C., Horner, R., Osher, D., Jensen, P., & The School Mental Health Alliance. (2005). *Working together to promote academic performance, social and emotional learning, and mental health for all children.* New York: Center for the Advancement of Children's Mental Health at Columbia University.

Hussar, W. J. (1999). *Predicting the need for newly hired teachers in the United States to 2008–09* (NCES 1999-026). Washington, DC: National Center for Education Statistics.

Huxham, C. (1996). Group decision support for collaboration. In C. Huxham (Ed.), *Collaborative advantage* (pp. 141–151). London: Sage.

Ingersoll, R. (2002). The teacher shortage: A case of wrong diagnosis and wrong prescription. *NASSP Bulletin, 86*(631), 16–31.

Ingersoll, R. M. (2001a). Teacher turnover and teacher shortages: An organizational analysis. *American Educational Research Journal, 38*, 499–534.

Ingersoll, R. M. (2001b). *Teacher turnover, teacher shortages and the organization of schools.* Seattle: Center for the Study of Teaching and Policy, University of Washington.

Institute of Medicine. (June 17, 2003). *Hidden costs, value lost. Consequences of uninsured in America.* No. 5. Washington, DC: National Academics Press.

Jackson, B. L., & Kelley, C. (2002). Exceptional and innovative programs in educational leadership. *Educational Administration Quarterly, 38*, 192–212.

Jackson, P. M., & Fogarty, T. E. (2005). *Sarbanes-Oxley for nonprofits: A guide to gaining competitive advantage.* Hoboken, NJ: Wiley.

Jacobson, L. (1996). Guidelines seek to define role of academics in children's play. *Education Week, 12*(2), 28–47.

Jazzar, M. (2005, August). Tales of micromanagement. *American School Board Journal, 192*(8), 31, 47.

Jazzar, M., & Algozzine, B. (2006). *Critical issues in educational leadership.* Boston: Allyn & Bacon.

Jenkins, J., & Veal, M. (2002). Preservice teachers' PCK development during peer coaching. *Journal of Teaching in Physical Education, 22*(1), 49–68.

Jensen, E. (1998). *Teaching with the brain in mind.* Alexandria, VA: Association for Supervision and Curriculum Development.

Johnson, B. (1998). The relationships between elementary school teachers' perceptions of school climate, student achievement, teacher characteristics, and community and school context. *Dissertation Abstracts International, 59*(11), 4055. (Publication Number AAT 9911757).

Jones, I., & Gullo, D. F. (1999). Differential social and academic effects of developmentally appropriate practices and beliefs. *Journal of Research in Childhood Education, 14*, 26–35.

Jones, J. (2004, June). Accountability issues: Everyone is looking at NPO's. *Non Profit Times, 1*, 15–22.

Jones, T., & Paolucci, R. (1999). Research framework and dimensions for evaluating the effectiveness of educational technology systems on learning outcomes. *Journal of Research on Computing in Education, 32*, 17–28.

Joravsky, B. (2000). *From dream to reality: Three Chicago small schools.* Chicago: Small Schools Coalition.

Kaplan, L. S., & Owings, W. A. (2002). *Enhancing teacher quality.* Bloomington, IN: Phi Delta Kappa.

Kapstein, E. B. (2001). The corporate ethics crusade. *Foreign Affairs, 80*(5), 105–119.

Karoly, J. (1996). Using portfolios to assess students' academic strengths: A case study. *Social Work in Education, 18*, 179–186.

Katz, L. G. (1999). *Another look at what young children should be learning.* ERIC Digest. Champaign Clearinghouse on Elementary and Early Childhood Education. (ERIC Document No. ED430735).

Kehr, H. M. (2004). Integrating implicit motives, explicit motives, and perceived abilities: The compensatory model of work motivation and violation. *Academy of Management Review, 29*, 479–499.

Kelleher, P. (2001, March). Implementing high standards. *Education Week, 20*(25), 38–42.

Kelley, L. (2004). Why induction matters. *Journal of Teacher Education, 555*, 438–449.

Kingdon, J. (2003). *Agendas, alternatives, and public policies.* New York: Longman.

Kirkpatrick, S. A., & Locke, E. A. (1996). Direct and indirect effects of three core charismatic leadership components in performance and attitudes. *Journal of Applied Psychology, 81*, 36–51.

Knowles, M. (1980). *The modern practice of adult education: From pedagogy to andragogy* (2nd ed.). New York: Cambridge Books.

Knowles, M. et al. (1984). *Andragogy in action: Applying modern principles of adult education.* San Francisco: Jossey-Bass.

Knowles, M. S. (1986). *Using learning contracts.* San Francisco: Jossey-Bass.

Koestenbaum, P. (2002). *Leadership: The inner side of greatness, a philosophy for leaders.* San Francisco: Jossey-Bass.

Koestner, R., & Losier, G. F. (2002). Distinguishing three ways of being internally motivated: A closer look at introjection, identification, and intrinsic motivation. In E. L. Deci, R. M. Deci, & R. M. Ryan (Eds.), *Handbook of self-determination research* (pp. 101–121). Rochester, NY: University of Rochester Press.

Kohn, A. (2000). *The case against standardized tests.* Portsmouth, NH: Heinemann.

Kohn, A. (2001). Fighting the tests: A practical guide to rescuing our schools. *Phi Delta Kappan, 82*, 348–357.

Kolb, B. (2000). Experience and the developing brain. *Education Canada, 39*, 24–26.

Komives, S. R., Lucas, N., & McMahon, T. R. (1998). *Exploring leadership: For college students who want to make a difference.* San Francisco: Jossey-Bass.

Kotter, J. P. (1999). *John P. Kotter on what leaders really do.* Boston: Harvard Business Review Books.

Kouzes, J. M., & Posner, B. Z. (2002). *The five practices of exemplary leadership: When leaders are at their best.* San Francisco: Jossey-Bass.

Kouzes, J. M., & Posner, B. Z. (1995). *The leadership challenge.* San Francisco: Jossey-Bass.

Kowalski, T. J. (2003a). *Public relations in schools* (3rd ed.). Englewood Cliffs, NJ: Prentice-Hall.

Kowalski, T. J. (2003b). *Contemporary school administration: An introduction* (2nd ed.). Boston: Allyn & Bacon.

Kozol, J. (1991). *Savage inequalities: Children in America's schools.* New York: Harper Perennial.

Krzyzewski, M. (2000). *Leading with the heart: Coach K's successful strategies for basketball, business and life.* New York: Warner Books.

Kwon, Y., & Lawson, A. E. (2000). Linking brain growth with the development of scientific reasoning ability and conceptual change during adolescence. *Journal of Research in Science Teaching, 37*, 44–62.

Lally, J. R., Lerner, C., & Lurie-Hurvitz, E. (2001). National survey reveals gaps in the public's and parent's knowledge about early childhood development. *Young Children, 56*(2), 49–53.

Lane, B. A. (1992, February). Cultural leaders in effective schools: The builders and borders of excellence. *NASSP Bulletin.*

Laurie, D. L. (2000). *The real work of leaders.* Cambridge, MA: Perseus.

Lawson, M. B. (2001). In praise of slack: Time is of essence. *Academy of Management Executive, 18*(3), 125–135.

Lazear, D. (1999). *Multiple intelligence approaches to assessment: Solving the assessment conundrum.* Chicago: Zephyr.

Lee, V., & Smith, J. (1997). High school size: Which works best and for whom? *Educational Evaluation and Policy Analysis, 19*(3), 205–227.

References

Lein, L., Johnson, J. F., & Ragland, M. (1997). *Successful Texas schoolwide programs: Research study results*. Austin, TX: Charles A. Dana Center, University of Texas at Austin.

Leithwood, K., & Riehl, C. (2003). *What we know about successful leadership*. Chicago: American Educational Research Association.

Leithwood, K., Seashore-Louis, K., Anderson, S., & Wahlstrom, K. (2004). *How leadership influences student learning*. New York: Center for Applied Research and Educational Improvement and Ontario Institute for Studies in Education.

Levine, D. U., & LeZotte, L. W. (1995). Effective schools research. Information Analysis. (ERIC Document Reproduction No. ED 382724).

Lewin, I. (1948). Resolving social conflicts; selected papers on group dynamics. G. W. Lewin (Ed.), *Theory in social science*. New York: Harper & Row.

Lewin, K. (1935). *A dynamic theory of personality*. New York: McGraw-Hill.

Lezotte, L. (1989, August). Base school improvement on what we know about effective schools. *American School Board Journal, 174*, 18–20.

Lezotte, L. W., & Pepperl, J. C. (1999). *The effective school process: A proven path to learning for all*. Okemos, MI: Effective School Products.

Lieberman, A., & Miller, L. (1981). Synthesis of research on improving schools. *Educational Leadership, 39*, 583–586.

Lindblom, C. E. (1993). *The science of muddling through*. New York: Irvington.

Linn, R. L., & Haug, C. (2002, Spring). Stability of school-building accountability scores and gains. *Educational Evaluation and Policy Analysis*, 29–36.

Locke, E. A., & Latham, G. P. (1990). *A theory of goal setting and task performance*. Englewood Cliffs, NJ: Prentice-Hall.

Loucks-Horsley, S., Hewson, P. W., Love, N., & Stiles, K. E. (1998). *Designing professional development for teachers in science and mathematics*. Thousand Oaks, CA: Corwin.

Louis, K. S., & Kruse, S. (1995). *Professionalism and community in schools*. Thousand Oaks, CA: Corwin.

Louis, K. S., Marks, H. M., & Kruse, S. D. (1996). Teachers' professional community in restructuring schools. *American Journal of Education, 33*, 757–798.

Luehrman, T. A. (1998). Strategy as a portfolio of real options. *Harvard Business Review, 76*(5), 89–99.

Lumsden, L. (1998). Teacher morale. *ERIC Digest*, p. 120.

Madsen, J., & Hipp, K. A. (1999). The impact of leadership style on creating community in public and private schools. *International Journal of Education Reform, 8*(3), 260–273.

Mandl, A., & Sethi, D. (1996). Either/or yields to the theory of both. In F. Hesselbein, M. Goldsmith, & R. Bechhard (Eds.), *The leader of the future* (pp. 257–264). San Francisco: Jossey-Bass.

Mann, D., Shakeshaft, C., Becker, J., & Kottkamp, R. (1999). *West Virginia story: Achievement gains from a statewide comprehensive instructional technology program*. Charleston, WV: State Department of Education.

Mantle-Bromley, C., Gould, L. M., McWhorter, B. A., & Whaley, D.C. (2000, Spring). The effect of program structure on new teachers' employment and program satisfaction patterns. *Action in Teacher Education, 22*, 1–14.

Manzo, K. K. (2001, April 4). N.C. ordered to meet at-risk students' needs. *Education Week, 21*, 25.

Marburger, C. L. (1985). *One school at a time. School based management: A process for change*. Columbia, MD: The National Committee for Citizens in Education.

Marcon, R. A. (1995). Fourth-grade slump: The cause and cure. *Principal, 74*(5), 17–20.

Marengo, L., Dosi, G., Legrenzi, P., & Pasquali, C. (2000). The structure of problem-solving knowledge and the structure of organizations. *Industrial and Corporate Change, 9*(4), 757–788.

Marks, H. M., & Printy, S. M. (2002). Organizational learning in a high-stakes accountability environment: Lessons from an urban school district. *Research and Theory in Educational Administration, 1*(1), 1–35.

Marshall, S. (1997). Creating sustainable learning communities for the twenty-first century. In F. Hesselbein, M. Goldsmith, & R. Beckhard (Eds.), *The organization of the future*. New York: The Peter Drucker Foundation.

Marzano, R. J., Pickering, D. J., & McTighe, J. (1993). *Assessing student outcomes, performance assessment using the dimensions of learning model*. Alexandria, VA: Association for Supervision and Curriculum Development.

Mash, C. J., & Willis, G. (2003). *Curriculum: Alternative approaches* (3rd ed.). Columbia, OH: Merrill.

Mattocks, T. C., & Drake, D. D. (2001). The preparation of visionary leaders for practitioner roles: A challenge for graduate programs in educational administration and school organization. *The AASA Professor, 24*(2), 14–23.

Mayer, J. D., & Salovey, P. (1993). The intelligence of emotional intelligence. *Intelligence, 17*, 433–442.

Mayer, S. E., & Peterson, P. E. (1999). *Earning and learning: How schools matter*. Washington, DC: Brookings Institution.

Mayo, E. (1933). *The human problems of an industrial civilization*. New York: Macmillan.

McCarthy, M. (2001). Challenges facing educational leadership programs: Our future is now. *Teaching in Educational Administration Newsletter, 8*, 1, 4.

McCowin, C., Miles, D., & Hargodine, K. (2000). Why principals succeed: Comparing principal performance to national professional standards. *ERS Spectrum, 18*(2), 14–19.

McDowelle, J. O. (2000). Developing teacher leaders: Providing encouragement, opportunities and support. *NASSP Bulletin, 84*(616), 35–41.

McGregor, D. (1960). *The human side of enterprise*. New York: McGraw-Hill.

McKenzie, J. (1999). *How teachers learn technology best*. Bellingham, WA: FNO Press.

McLaughlin, M., & Yocom, D. J. (2005). Japanese method gets a Wyoming accent: Lab school in Laramie adapts lesson study concept to its own needs. *Journal of Staff Development, 26*(1), 53–56.

McNabb, M., Hawkes, M., & Rouk, U. (1999). *Critical issues in evaluating the effectiveness of technology*. Washington, DC: The Secretary's Conference on Educational Technology.

Means, B., Penuel, B., & Quellmalz, E. (2000). *Developing assessments for tomorrow's classrooms*. Washington, DC: Secretary's Conference on Educational Technology.

Melendez, S. E. (1996). An outsiders view of leadership. In F. Hesselbein, M. Goldsmith, & R. Beckhard, (Eds.), *The leader of the future* (pp. 295–302). San Francisco: Jossey-Bass.

Merlevede, P., & Bridoux, D. (2001). *7 steps to emotional intelligence*. United Kingdom: Crown House.

Meyer, T. (2002). Novice teacher learning communities. *American Secondary Education, 31*(1), 27–42.

Milakovich, M., & Gordon, G. (2001). *Public administration in America* (7th ed.). Belmont, CA: Wadworth Group/Thomson Learning.

Murnane, R. J., & Levy, F. (1996). *Teaching the new basic skills, principles for educating children to thrive in a changing economy.* New York: The Free Press.

Murnighan, J. K., & Mowen, J. C. (2002). *The art of high-stakes decision-making.* New York: Wiley.

Murphy, J. (1992*). The landscape of leadership preparation: Reframing the education of school administration.* Newbury Park, CA: Corwin.

Murphy, J. (2002). Reculturing the profession of educational leadership: New blueprints. In J. Murphy (Ed.), *The educational leadership challenge: Redefining leadership for the 21st century* (pp. 65–82). Chicago: National Society of Education.

Murphy, J. (2003, September). *Recruiting educational leadership: The ISLLC standards ten years out.* Paper prepared for the National Policy Board for Educational Administration.

Murphy, J., & Datnow, A. (2002). *Building a new structure for school leadership.* New York: The Albert Shanker Institute.

Murphy, J., & Forsyth, P. B. (Eds.). (1999). *Educational administration: A decade of reform.* Thousand Oaks, CA: Corwin.

Murphy, J., & Louis, K. S. (1999). *Handbook of research on educational administration.* San Francisco: Jossey-Bass.

Murphy, J., & Shipman, N. (1999). The interstate school leaders licensure consortium: Standards-based approach to strengthening educational leadership. *Journal of Personnel Evaluation in Education, 13,* 205–224.

Muth, R., & Barnett, B. (2001). Making the case for professional preparation: Using research for program improvement and political support. *Educational Leadership and Administration: Teaching and Program Development, 13,* 109–120.

Nabors, L. A., Leff, S. S., & Power, T. J. (2004, July). Quality improvement activities and expanded school mental health services. *Behav Modif, 28*(4), 596–616.

Nanus, B. (1992). *Visionary leadership.* San Francisco: Jossey-Bass.

Napolitano, C. S., & Henderson, L. J. (1998). *The leadership odyssey: A self development guide to new skills for new times.* San Francisco: Jossey-Bass.

National Association of Early Childhood Specialists in State Departments of Education. (2000). *Still! Unacceptable trends in kindergarten entry placement.* A Position Statement. Chicago: National Association of Early Childhood in State Departments of Education.

National Association of State Boards of Education. (1998). *The numbers game: Ensuring quantity and quality in the teaching work force.* Alexandria, VA: Author.

National Center for Educational Statistics. (1997). *Projections of educational statistics to 2007.* Washington, DC: U.S. Department of Education.

National Center for Educational Statistics. (2000). *Public school teachers' use of computers and Internet.* Washington, DC: U.S. Department of Education.

National Center for Educational Statistics. (2000–2001). *Characteristics of the 100 largest public elementary and secondary school districts in the United States.* Washington DC: Author.

National Center for Educational Statistics. (2004). *1.1 million home schooled students in the United States.* Washington, DC: U.S. Department of Education.

National Commission on Service Learning. (2002). Learning in deed: The power of service learning for American schools. *Educational Evaluation and Policy Analysis, 20,* 9–29.

National Commission on Teaching and America's Future. (2002). *Unraveling the teacher shortage problem: Teacher retention is key.* Washington, DC: National Commission on Teaching and America's Future.

National Commission on Teaching and America's Future. (2003). *No dream denied: A pledge to America's children* (p. 24). Washington, DC: Author.

National Education Association. (2001). *Testing plus real accountability with real results.* Washington, DC: Author.

National Education Goals Panel. (1999). *The national education goals report: Building a nation of learners, 1999.* Washington, DC: U.S. Government Printing Office.

National Institute for Literacy. (2002). *Characteristics of the workforce. Workforce education.* Available at www.nifl.gov.

National Policy Board for Educational Administration. (2002). Standards for advanced programs in educational leadership for principals, superintendents, curriculum directors, and supervisors. Retrieved September 16, 2005, from www.npbea.org/ELCC.

National Schools Network. (1997). *The authentic assessment kit.* Canberra: Commonwealth of Australia.

Neale, M., Bailey, M., & Ross, A. (1981). *Analysis of reading ability.* Boston: NFER-Nelson.

Nel, E. M. (2000). Academics, literacy, and young children: A plea for a middle ground. *Childhood Education, 76,* 136–141.

Nelson, F. H., Drown, R., & Gould, J. C. (2000). *Survey and analysis of teacher salary trends.* Washington, DC: American Federation of Teachers.

Neuharth-Pritchett, S. (2001, April 10–14). *Recommendations for kindergarten retention: Assessing children practices and their relationships.* Paper was presented at the Annual Meeting of the American Educational Research Association, Seattle, WA.

Newmann, F. M., Marks, H. M., & Gamoran, A. (1996). Authentic pedagogy and student performance. *American Journal of Education, 104,* 280–312.

Nicholson, H. J., Collins, C., & Holmer, H. (2004). Youth as people: The protective aspects of youth development in after school settings. *The Annals of the American Academic of Political and Social Science, 591,* 55–71.

Noonan, S. I. (2003). *The elements of leadership.* Metuchen, NJ: Scarecrow.

Normore, A. H. (2004). Ethics and values in leadership preparation programs: Finding the north star in the dust storm. *Journal of Values and Ethics in Educational Administration, 2*(2), 1–7.

Northouse, P. G. (1999). *Leadership: theory and practice.* Thousand Oaks, CA: Sage.

Norton, M. (2000). 25 years of company giving. In J. Smyth (Ed.), *The guide to UK company giving* (3rd ed., pp. 9–12). London: Directory of Social Change.

NSW Department of Education and Training. (1999). *Assessment and reporting issues 7–12, Bulletin 5: Portfolios.* Sydney: DET.

Odden, A. (2000, January). New and better forms of teacher compensation are possible. *Phi Delta Kappan, 81,* 361–366.

Office of Technology Assessment, U.S. Congress. (1995). *Teachers & technology: Making the connection.* Washington, DC: U.S. Government Printing Office.

O'Neill, L. (2004). Support systems. *Threshold, 12*–15.

Ornstein, A. C., Pajak, E., & Bohar-Horenstein, L. (2003). *Contemporary issues in curriculum* (3rd ed.). Boston: Allyn & Bacon.

Osher, B., & Ward, J. (1996). *Learning for the 21st century.* Dubuque, IA: Kendall Hunt.

Osterman, K. F., & Kottkamp, R. B. (1993). *Reflective practice for educators: Improving schooling through professional development.* Newbury Park, CA: Corwin Press.

Owens, R. G. (2004). *Organizational behavior in education: Adaptive leadership and school reform* (8th ed.). Boston: Allyn & Bacon.

Pajares, E., & Graham, L. (1999). Self-efficacy, motivation constructs, and mathematics performance of entering middle school students. *Contemporary Educational Psychology, 24,* 124–139.

Palmer, J. (2000). *Let your life speak.* San Francisco: Jossey-Bass.

Pearce, K. (2004, May). Original purpose: Completing the triad of accountability. *Philanthropist/Le Philanthrope, 18,* 225–237.

Pelled, L., Eisenhardt, K., & Xin, K. (1999). Exploring the black box: An analysis of work group diversity, conflict and performance. *Administrative Science Quarterly, 44,* 1–28.

Perkins, D. (1995). *Outsmarting I. Q.: The emerging science of learnable intelligence.* New York: The Free Press.

Peske, H. G., Liu, E., Johnson, S. M., Kauffman, D., & Kardos, S. M. (2001). The next generation of teachers: Changing conceptions of a career in teaching. *Phi Delta Kappan, 83,* 304–311.

Peterson, K. (2002). The professional development of principals: Innovations and opportunities. *Educational Administration Quarterly, 38,* 213–232.

Peterson, K. D., & Deal, T. E. (1998). How leaders influence culture of schools. *Educational Leadership, 56,* 28–30.

Phillips, G. (1993). *The school–classroom culture audit.* Vancouver, BC, Canada: Educserv, British Columbia School Trustees Publishing.

Pinar, W. E. (1999). *Contemporary curriculum discoveries.* New York: Peter Lang.

Pojman, L. (2002). *Ethics: Discovering right and wrong* (4th ed.). Belmont, CA: Wadsworth.

Porter, M. E., & Kramer, M. R. (2002). The competitive advantage of corporate philanthropy. *Harvard Business Review, 80*(12), 56–68.

Portner, H. (2001). *Training mentors is not enough: Everything else schools and districts need to do.* Thousand Oaks, CA: Corwin.

Prasch, J. (1990). *How to organize for school-based management.* Alexandria, VA: Association for Supervision and Curriculum Development.

Pratt, D. (1998). Andragogy as a relational construct. *Adult Education Quarterly, 38,* 160–172.

Projections of Education Statistics 2011. (2001). Washington, DC: U.S. Government Printing Office, Table 34, 89.

Puma, M. J., Karweit, N., Price, C., Ricciuti, A., Thompson, W., & Vaden-Kiernan, M. (1997). *Prospects: Final report on student outcomes.* Washington, DC: U.S. Department of Education, Planning and Evaluation Services.

Purkey, S. C., & Smith, M. S. (1982). Synthesis of research on effective schools. *Educational Leadership, 40*(3), 64–69.

Purkey, S. C., & Smith, M. S. (1983). Too soon to cheer? Synthesis of research on effective schools. *Educational Leadership, 40,* 64–69.

Quick, P., & Normore, A. H. (2004). Moral leadership in the 21st century: Everyone is watching—Especially the students. *Kappa Delta Pi, The Educational Forum, 68*(4), 336–447.

Raiffa, H. (1997). *Decision analysis: Introductory readings on choices under uncertainty.* New York: McGraw Hill.

Rainey, H. (2003). *Understanding and managing public organizations.* San Francisco: Jossey-Bass.

Rathbun, A. H., Walston, J. T., & Hausken, E. G. (2000). *Kindergarten teachers' use of developmentally appropriate practices: Results from the early childhood study, kindergarten class of 1998–1999.* Paper presented at the Annual Meeting of the American Educational Association, New Orleans.

Rayner, S. G., & Devi, U. (2001). Self-esteem and self-perceptions in the classroom: Valuing circle time? In R. J. Riding & S. G. Rayner (Eds.), *International perspectives on individual differences. Vol. 2: Self-perception* (pp. 171–208). Westport, CO: Ablex.

Rebore, R. W. (2001). *The ethics of educational leadership.* Upper Saddle River, NJ: Merrill/Prentice Hall.

Restine, N. (1997). Learning and development in the context(s) of leadership preparation. *Peabody Journal of Education, 72,* 117–130.

Reynolds, A. J., Temple, J. A., Robertson, D. L., & Mann, E. (2002). Prevention and cost-effectiveness in the Chicago Child-Parent Centers. Paper presented at the Biennial Meeting of Society for Research in Child Development, Tampa, Florida.

Reynolds, C. R. (2000). *Encyclopedia of special education* (2nd ed.). Boston: Watson Reference.

Reynolds, M. (1994). Democracy in higher education: Participatory action research in physics. Cornell University, Thesis, Cornell University Library.

Richard, A., & Sack, J. L. (2003, January 18). States brace for tough new year. *Education Week, 1,* 16–19.

Richardson, J. (2001, May). *Shared culture: A consensus of individual values. Results.* Oxford, OH: National Staff Development Council.

Rising to the challenge: Developing Excellent Professionals. (2004). College of Education, University of North Carolina at Charlotte.

Roberts, J. (1993). Leadership for school culture: Knowing the norms, behaviors, and issues. *NASSP Bulletin, 77,* 64–70.

Rocha, D. J. (2001, September 27). The emperor's new laptop. *Education Week,* 42–47.

Romano, M. T. (2002). Proposing new strategies for old challenges. In *Teachers, learners, and technology: A fifty-year perspective.* Grass Valley, CA: Performance Learning Systems.

Rothstein, R. (1998). What does education cost? *American School Board Journal, 185,* 30–33.

Rothstein, R. (2002a). *Defining failed schools is harder than it sounds.* New York Times Online. Available at www.nytimes.com.

Rothstein, R. (2002b, September 25). Teacher shortages vanish when the price is right. *New York Times,* p. B8.

Russo, J. E., & Schoemaker, P. J. H. (2002). *Winning decisions.* New York: Doubleday.

Ryan, K. (1987). *Character development in the schools and beyond.* New York: Praeger.

Ryan, R. M., & Deci, E. L. (2000). Self-determination theory and the facilitation of intrinsic motivation, social development, and well-being. *American Psychologist, 55,* 68–78.

Sahi, J. (2000). *Education and peace.* Pune: Akshar Mudra.

Sapre, P. M. (2000). Realizing the potential of management and leadership: Toward a synthesis of Western and indigenous perspectives in the modernization of non-Western societies. *International Journal of Leadership in Education, 3,* 293–305.

Sarason, S. B. (1982). *The culture of the school and the problem of change.* Boston: Allyn & Bacon.

Sasiia, D. H. (2001, Summer). Philanthropy and corporate citizenship: Strategic philanthropy is good corporate citizenship. *Journal of Corporate Citizenship,* (2), 57–54.

Schapiro, S. (1999). *Higher education for democracy: Experiments in progressive pedagogy at Goddard College.* New York: Peter Lang.

Schein, E. H. (1999). *The corporate culture survival guide: Sense and nonsense about cultural change.* San Francisco: Jossey-Bass.

Schein, E. M. (1996). Leadership and organizational culture. In F. Hesselbein, M. Goldsmith, & R. Beckhard (Eds.), *The leader of the future.* San Francisco: Jossey-Bass.

Schuerman, M. (2004). Sarbanes-oxymoron. *Robb Report Worth, 13,* 33.

Schweinhart, L. J., & Weikart, D. P. (1997a). The High/Scope preschool curriculum comparison to 23. *Early Childhood Research Quarterly, 12,* 117–143.

Schweinhart, L. J., & Weikart, D. P. (1997b). *Lasting differences: The High/Scope preschool co-comparison study through age 23.* High/Scope Educational Research Foundation Monograph No. 12. Ypsalini, MI: High Scope Press.

Schweitzer, C. (2004, January). The board balancing act: Achieving board accountability without micromanaging. *Association Management, 56,* 34–40.

Senge, P. (1990a). *The fifth dimension.* New York: Doubleday/Currency.

Senge, P. M. (1990b). *The fifth discipline: The art and practice of learning organization.* New York: Doubleday.

Senge, P. M. (2001). *Schools that learn.* New York: Doubleday.

Senge, P., Cambron-McCabe, N., Lucas, T., Smith, B., Dutton, J., & Kleiner, A. (2000). *Schools that learn: A fifth discipline fieldbook for educators, parents, and everyone who cares about education.* New York: Doubleday/Currency.

Sergiovanni, T. J. (1990). *Value-added leadership: How to get extraordinary performance in schools.* San Diego, CA: Harcourt Brace Jovanovich.

Sergiovanni, T. J. (1992). *Moral leadership: Getting to the heart of school improvement.* San Francisco: Jossey-Bass.

Sergiovanni, T. J. (1995). *The principalship: A reflective practice perspective.* Boston: Allyn & Bacon.

Sergiovanni, T. J. (1996a). *Leadership for the schoolhouse: How is it different? Why is it important?* San Francisco: Jossey-Bass.

Sergiovanni, T. J. (1996b). *Moral leadership: Getting to the heart of school improvement.* San Francisco: Jossey-Bass.

Sergiovanni, T. J. (1997). *Value-added leadership: How to get extraordinary performance in schools* (2nd ed.). New York: Harcourt Brace.

Sergiovanni, T. J. (2000a). *Getting to the heart of school improvement.* San Francisco: Jossey-Bass.

Sergiovanni, T. J. (2000b). *The lifeworld of leadership.* San Francisco: Jossey-Bass.

Sergiovanni, T. J. (2000c). *The principalship: A reflective practice perspective* (4th ed.). Boston: Allyn & Bacon.

Sergiovanni, T. J. (2001). *The principalship: A reflective practice perspective.* Boston. Allyn & Bacon.

Shapira, Z. (2002). *Organizational decision making.* New York: Cambridge University Press.

Shapiro, J. P., Poliner, J., & Stefkovich, A. J. (2001). *Ethical leadership and decision making in education: Applying theoretical perspectives to complex dilemmas.* Mahwah, NJ: Erlbaum.

Sheldon, K. M., Ryan, R. M., Deci, E. L., & Kasser, T. (2004). The independent effects of goal contents and motives on well-being: It's both what you pursue and why you pursue it. *Personality and Social Psychology Bulletin, 30,* 475–486.

Sherman, C. W., & Mueller, D. P. (1996). *Developmentally appropriate practice and student inner-city elementary schools.* Paper presented at Head Start's Third National Research Conference, Washington, DC. Document No. ED401354.

Siegrist, G. (1999). Educational leadership must move beyond management training to visionary and moral transformational leaders. *Education, 120,* 297–303.

Sinclair, M. (2004). Nonprofit whistleblowers need protection. *Non Profit Times, 18,* 1, 4, 7.

Sizer, T. R. (1988). A visit to an "Essential" school. *School Administrator, 45*(10), 18–19.

Skaalvik, E. M., & Skaalvik, S. (2002). Internal and external frames of reference for academic self-concept. *Educational Psychology, 37,* 233–244.

Slavin, R. E. (1987). Mastery learning reconsidered. *Review of Educational Research, 57,* 175–214.

Sloan, M. (1996). Assessment at work: I love this piece because . . . *Instructor, 105*(7), 30–32.

Smith, B. L., & McCann, J. (Eds.). (2001). *Reinventing ourselves: Interdisciplinary education collaborative learning, and experimentation in higher education.* Bolton, MA: Anker.

Smith, M., & Lindsay, L. (2001). *Leading change in your world.* Marion, IN: Triangle.

Smith, S. C., and Stolp, S. (1995). Transforming a school's culture through shared vision. *Oregon School Study Council, 35*(3), 1–6.

Snow, C. E., Burns, M. S., & Griffin, P. (1998). *Preventing reading difficulties in young children.* Washington, DC: National Academy.

Snyder, N. H., Dowd, J. J., Jr., & Houghton, D. M. (1994). *Vision, values, and courage.* New York: The Free Press.

Soder, R. (2001). *The language of leadership.* San Francisco: Jossey-Bass.

Sousa, D. (2001). *How the brain learns: A classroom teacher's guide.* Thousand Oaks, CA: Corwin.

Sparks, D. (2002). High-performing cultures increase teacher retention. Retrieved October 23, 2003, from the National Staff Development website: www.nsdc.org/library/results/res12-02spr.html.

Spillane, J. P., & Halverson, R., et al. (1999). *Distributed leadership: Toward a theory of school leadership practice.* Paper presented at the annual meeting of the American Educational Research Association, Montreal.

Spring, J. (2005). *Conflict of interests: The politics of American education* (5th ed.). New York: McGraw Hill.

Stacey, R. D. (1996). *Complexity and creativity in organizations.* San Francissco: Berrett-Keohler.

Stanovich, P. J., & Stanovich, K. E. (2003). *Using research and reason in education: How teachers can use scientifically based research to make curricular instructional decisions.* Jessup, MD: National Institute for Literacy.

Stansbury, K. (2001). What new teachers need. *Leadership, 30*(3), 18–21.

Starrat, R. J. (2004). *Ethical leadership.* San Francisco: Jossey-Bass.

Stefonek, T. (1991). *Alternative assessment: A national perspective.* Policy Briefs No. 15 & 16. Oak Brook, IL: North Central Regional Educational Laboratory.

Stivers, C. (2001). *Democracy, bureaucracy, and the study of administration.* Boulder CO: Westview.

Stone, C. (1995). School-community collaboration: Comparing three initiatives. *Phi Delta Kappan, 76,* 794–800.

Stone, D. (2002). *Policy paradox and political reason.* New York: Norton.

Sweeney, J. (1992). School climate: The key to excellence. *NASSP Bulletin.*

Taylor, B. M., Pearson, P. D., Clark, K., & Walpole, S. (2000). Effective schools and accomplished teachers: Lessons about primary grade reading instruction in low-income schools. *Elementary School Journal, 101*, 121–166.

Taylor, B. M., Pressley, M. P., & Pearson, P. D. (2002). Research-supported characteristics of teachers and schools that promote reading achievement. In B. M. Taylor & P. D. Pearson (Eds.), *Teaching reading: Effective schools, accomplished teachers* (pp. 361–374). Mahwah, NJ: Erlbaum.

Taylor, F. W. (1911). *Principles of scientific management*. New York: Harper.

The Teaching Commission. (2004). *Teaching at risk: A call to action* (pp. 48–59). New York: Author.

Terry, R. W. (1993). *Authentic leadership: Courage in action*. San Francisco: Jossey-Bass.

Thiroux, J. (1998). *Ethics: Theory and practice* (6th ed.). Upper Saddle River, NJ: Prentice-Hall.

Thomson, G. (2000). *On Kant*. Belmont, CA: Wadsworth Thomson.

Thomson, S. (1993). *Principals for our changing schools: Knowledge and skill base*. Boston: Rowan & Littlefield.

Thurlow, M. J., Ysseldyke, J., Gutman, S., & Geenen, K. (1998). *An analysis of inclusion of students with disabilities in state standards documents*. Technical Report No. 19. Minneapolis: University of Minnesota, National Center on Educational Outcomes.

Tirozzi, G. N. (2001). The artistry of leadership: The evolving role of the secondary school principal. *Phi Delta Kappan, 82*, 434–439.

Tisdell, E. (2001). *Feminist perspectives on adult education*. In A. L. Wilson & E. R. Hayes (Eds.), *Handbook of adult and continuing education*. San Francisco: Jossey-Bass.

Tugel, J. (2004). Time for science. *Alliance Access, 8*(2), 1–3.

U.S. Census Bureau. (2003, September). *Health insurance coverage in the United States: 2002*. Washington, DC: U.S. Department of Commerce.

U.S. Department of Education. (2000). *A talented dedicated, and well prepared teacher in every classroom: Information kit*. Washington, DC: Author.

U.S. Department of Education. (2002). *Meeting the highly qualified teachers challenge*. Washington, DC: Author.

U.S. Department of Education Initiative on Teaching. (2000). *Eliminating barriers to improving teaching*. Washington, DC: U.S. Department of Education.

Usdan, M. D. (2002a). Reactions to articles commissioned by the National Commission for the Advancement of Educational Leadership Preparation. *Educational Administration Quarterly, 38*(2), 300–307.

Usdan, M. D. (2002b). The new state politics of education. *The State Education Standard, 3*(2), 14–18.

Vallance, E. (1973). Hiding the hidden curriculum. *Curriculum Theory Network, 4*, 5–21.

VanMeter, E., & Murphy, J. (1997, July). *Using ISLLC standards to strengthen preparation programs in school administration*. Washington, DC: Council of Chief State School Officers.

Vecchio, R. R. (2002). *Organizational behavior: Core concepts*. Belmont, CA: South-Western Thomson Learning.

Wagner, C. R., & Hall-O'Phalen, M. (1998, November 3–6). *Improving schools through the administration and analysis of school culture audits*. Paper presented at the Mid-South Educational Research Association.

Walsh, K. (2001). *Teacher certification reconsidered: Stumbling for quality*. Baltimore, MD: The Abell Foundation.

Walster, E., Walster, G. W., & Berscheid, E. (1978). *Equity: Theory and research*. Boston: Allyn & Bacon.

Wasik, B. A. (2001). Teaching the alphabet to young children. *Young Children, 56*, 34–40.

Webb, L. (1990). Thoughts from a VC enthusiast. *Read 25*(1), 41–42.

Weiss, E. M., & Weiss, S. G. (1999). *Beginning teacher induction*. Washington, DC: ERIC Clearinghouse on Teaching and Teacher Education. (ERIC No. ED436487).

Weiss, I. R., Knapp, M. S., Hollweg, K. S., & Burrill, G. (Eds.). (2001). *Investigating the influence of standards: A framework for research in mathematics, science, and technology education*. Washington, DC: National Academy Press.

Weist, M. D., & Albus, K. E. (2004). Expanded school mental health: Exploring program details and developing the research base. *Behavior Modification, 28*(4), 463–471.

Wekesser, C. (1998). *Ethics*. San Diego, CA: Greenhaven.

Welcomer, S. A., Cochran, P. L., Rands, G., & Haggerty, M. (2003). Constructing a web: Effects of power and social responsiveness on firm-stakeholder relationships. *Business & Society, 42*(1), 43–82.

Welton, M. R. (Ed.). (1995). *In defense of the lifeworld: Critical perspectives on adult learning*. Albany: State University of New York Press.

Wilhelm, W. (1996). Learning from past leaders. In F. Hesselbein, M Goldsmith, & R. Beckhard (Eds.), *The leader of the future* (pp. 221–226). San Francisco: Jossey-Bass.

Wilson, M. (2001). The case for sensorimotor in working memory. *Psychonomic Bulletin & Review, 8*(1), 57.

Wolfe, P. (2001). *Brain matters: Translating research into classroom practice*. Alexandria, VA: Association for Supervision and Curriculum Development.

Wolverton, B. (2005, April 14). Taking aim at charity. *Chronicle of Philanthropy, 17*, 9.

Wong, C., & Law, K. (2002). The effects of leader and follower emotional intelligence on performance and attitude: An exploratory study. *Leadership Quarterly, 13*, 243–274.

Woods, J. M. (2001). The barefoot teacher. *College Teaching, 49*(2), 51–55.

Yoels, W. C., & Clair, J. M. (1995). Laughter in the clinic: Humor in social organizations. *Symbolic Interaction, 18*, 39–58.

Yoon, K. P., & Hwang, C. (1995). *Multiple attribute decision making: An introduction*. Thousand Oaks, CA: Sage.

Young, M. D., Petersen, G. T., & Short, P. M. (2002). The complexity of substantive reform: A call for interdependence among key stakeholders. *Educational Administration Quarterly, 38*, 137–175.

Ysseldyke, J., & Christensen, S. (1993–96). *TIES: The instructional environment system—II*. Longmont, CO: Sopris West.

Yukl, G. A. (1994). *Leadership in organizations* (3rd ed.). Englewood Cliffs, NJ: Prentice-Hall.

Zaccaro, S. J. (2001). *The nature of effective leadership: A conceptual and empirical analysis of success*. Washington: DC: American Psychological Association.

Zuckerman, J. (2001). Veteran teacher transformation in a collaborative mentoring relationship. *American Secondary Education, 29*(4), 18–29.

INDEX